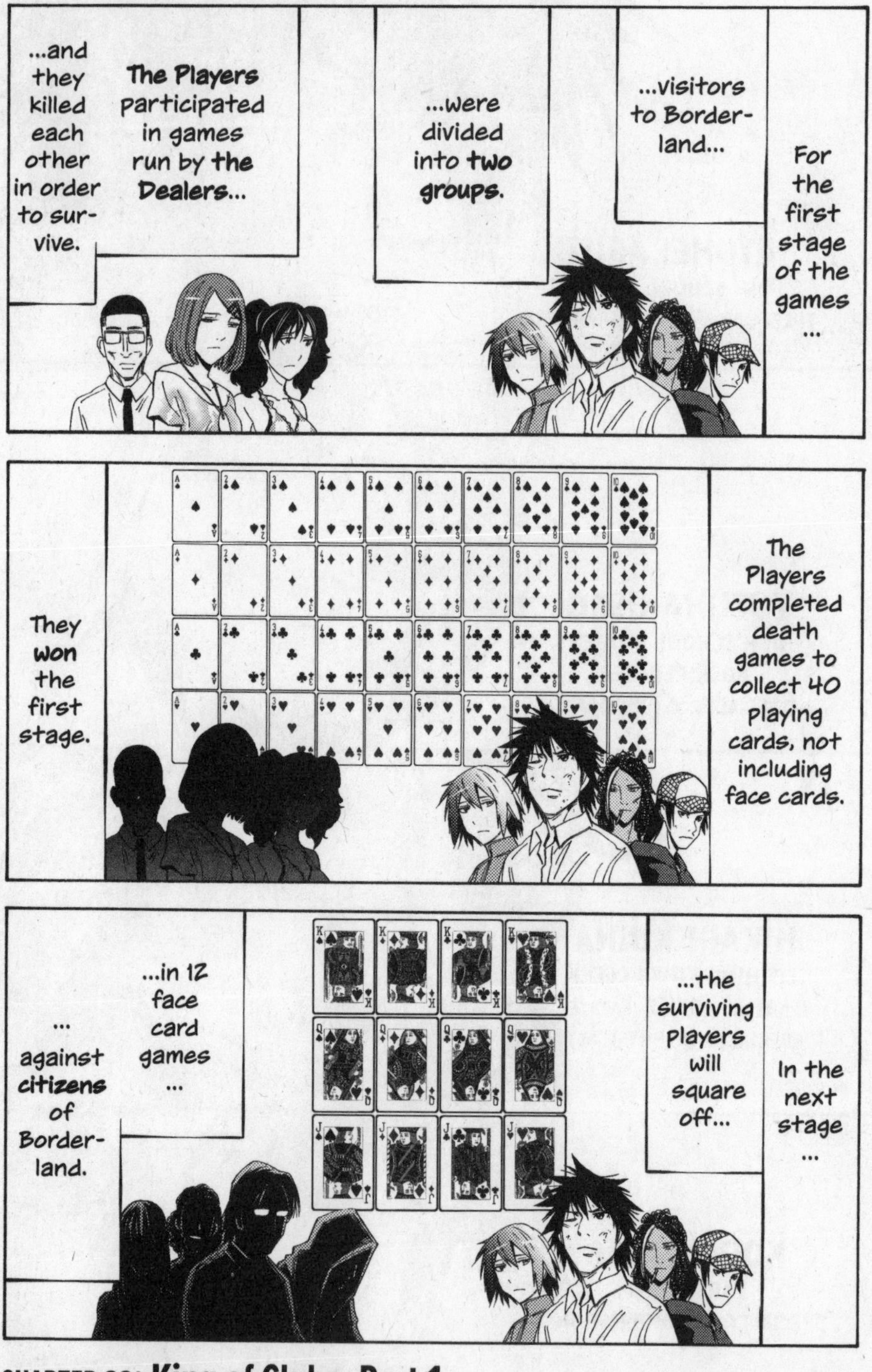
For the first stage of the games ...
...visitors to Borderland...
...were divided into two groups.
The Players participated in games run by the Dealers...
...and they killed each other in order to survive.
The Players completed death games to collect 40 playing cards, not including face cards.
They won the first stage.
In the next stage ...
...the surviving players will square off...
...in 12 face card games ...
... against citizens of Borderland.

CHAPTER 33: King of Clubs, Part 1

CHAPTER 33: King of Clubs, Part 1

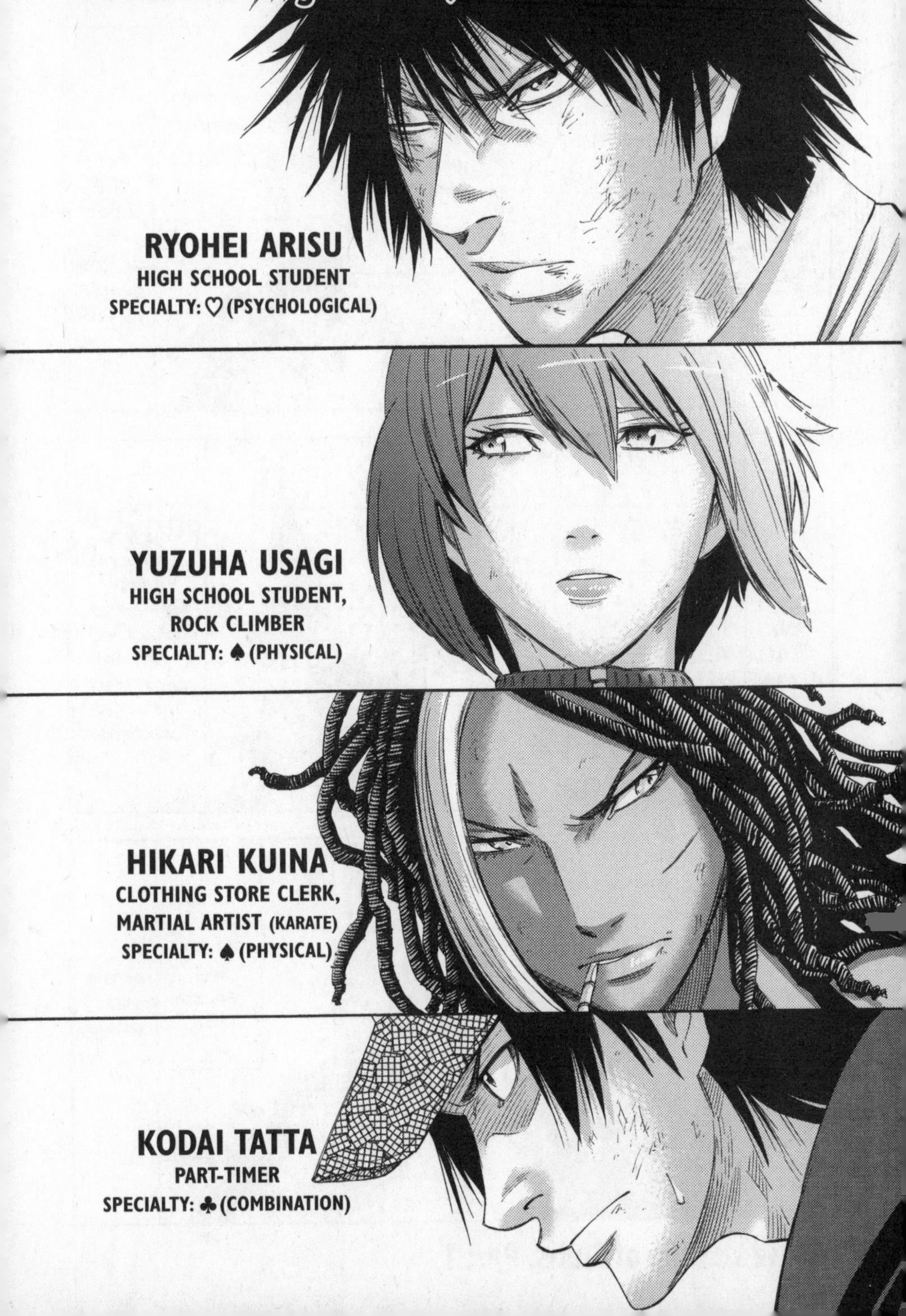
RYOHEI ARISU
HIGH SCHOOL STUDENT
SPECIALTY: ♡ (PSYCHOLOGICAL)
YUZUHA USAGI
HIGH SCHOOL STUDENT, ROCK CLIMBER
SPECIALTY: ♠ (PHYSICAL)
HIKARI KUINA
CLOTHING STORE CLERK, MARTIAL ARTIST (KARATE)
SPECIALTY: ♠ (PHYSICAL)
KODAI TATTA
PART-TIMER
SPECIALTY: ♣ (COMBINATION)

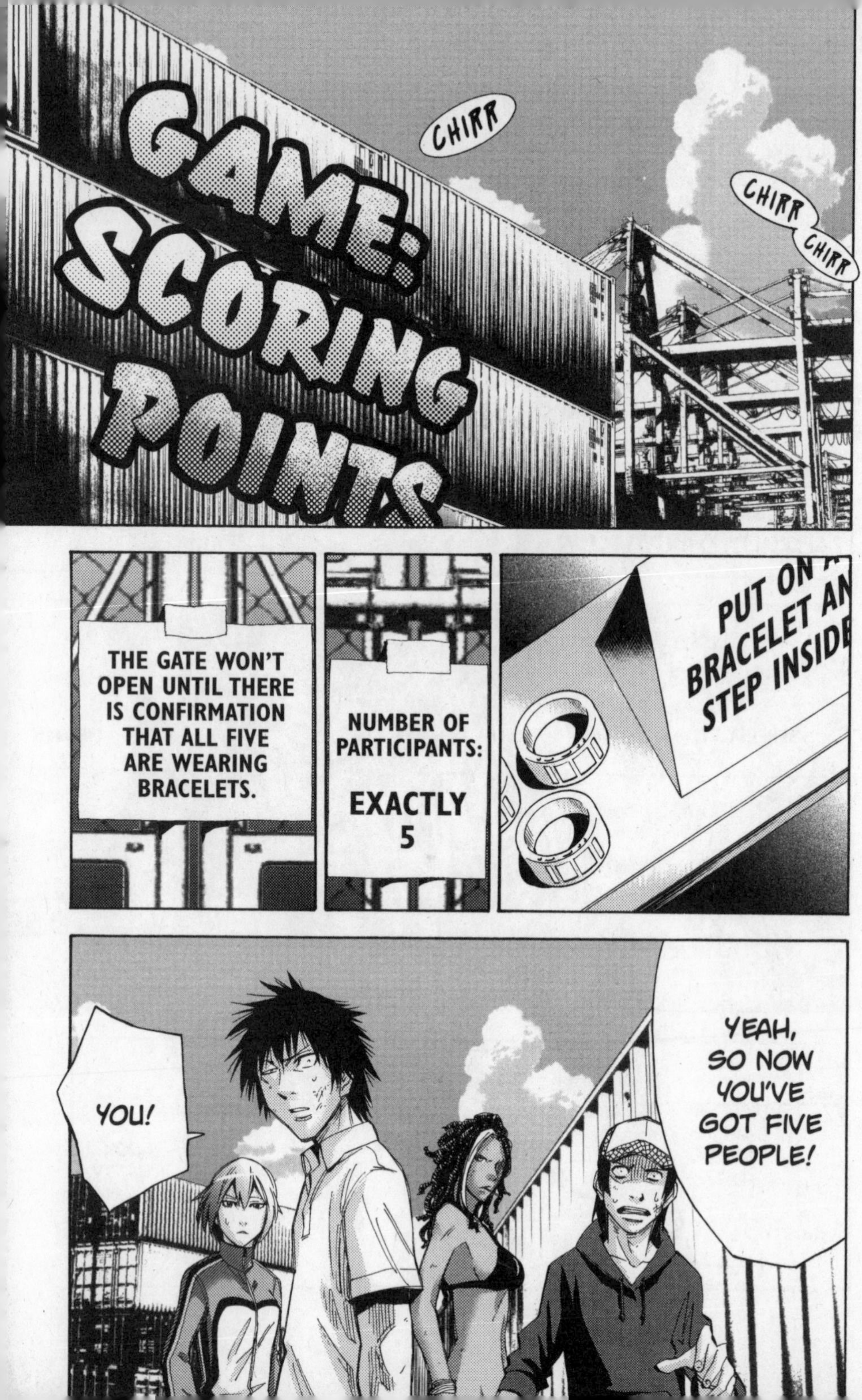
CHIRR
CHIRR
CHIRR
GAME: SCORING POINTS
PUT ON A BRACELET AN STEP INSIDE
NUMBER OF PARTICIPANTS: EXACTLY 5
THE GATE WON'T OPEN UNTIL THERE IS CONFIRMATION THAT ALL FIVE ARE WEARING BRACELETS.
YEAH, SO NOW YOU'VE GOT FIVE PEOPLE!
YOU!

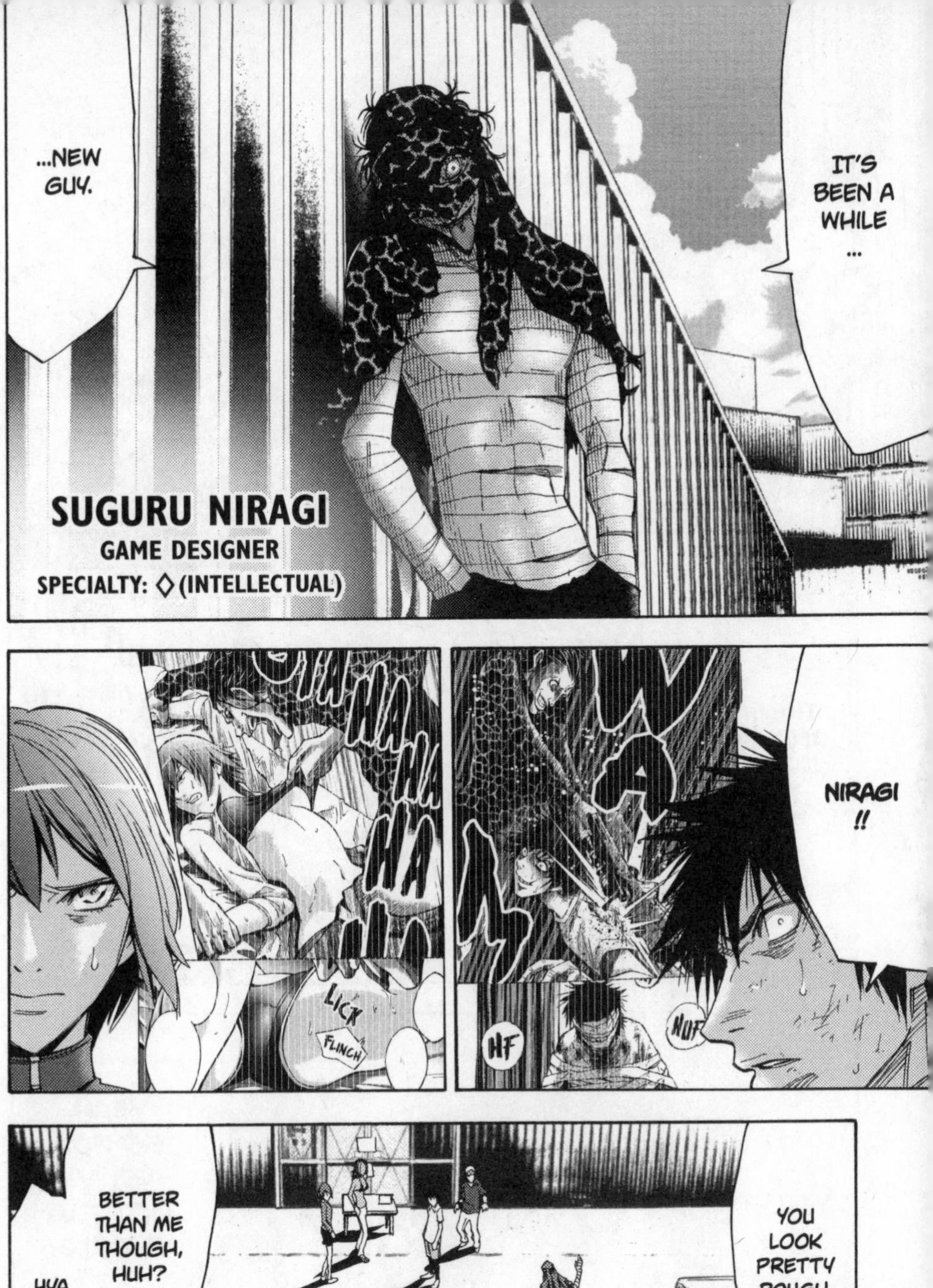
IT'S BEEN A WHILE ...
...NEW GUY.
SUGURU NIRAGI
GAME DESIGNER
SPECIALTY: ◊ (INTELLECTUAL)
NIRAGI !!
NUF
HF
HA
HA
HA
LICK
FLINCH
YOU LOOK PRETTY ROUGH.
BETTER THAN ME THOUGH, HUH?
HYA HA HA!

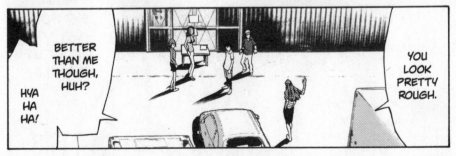

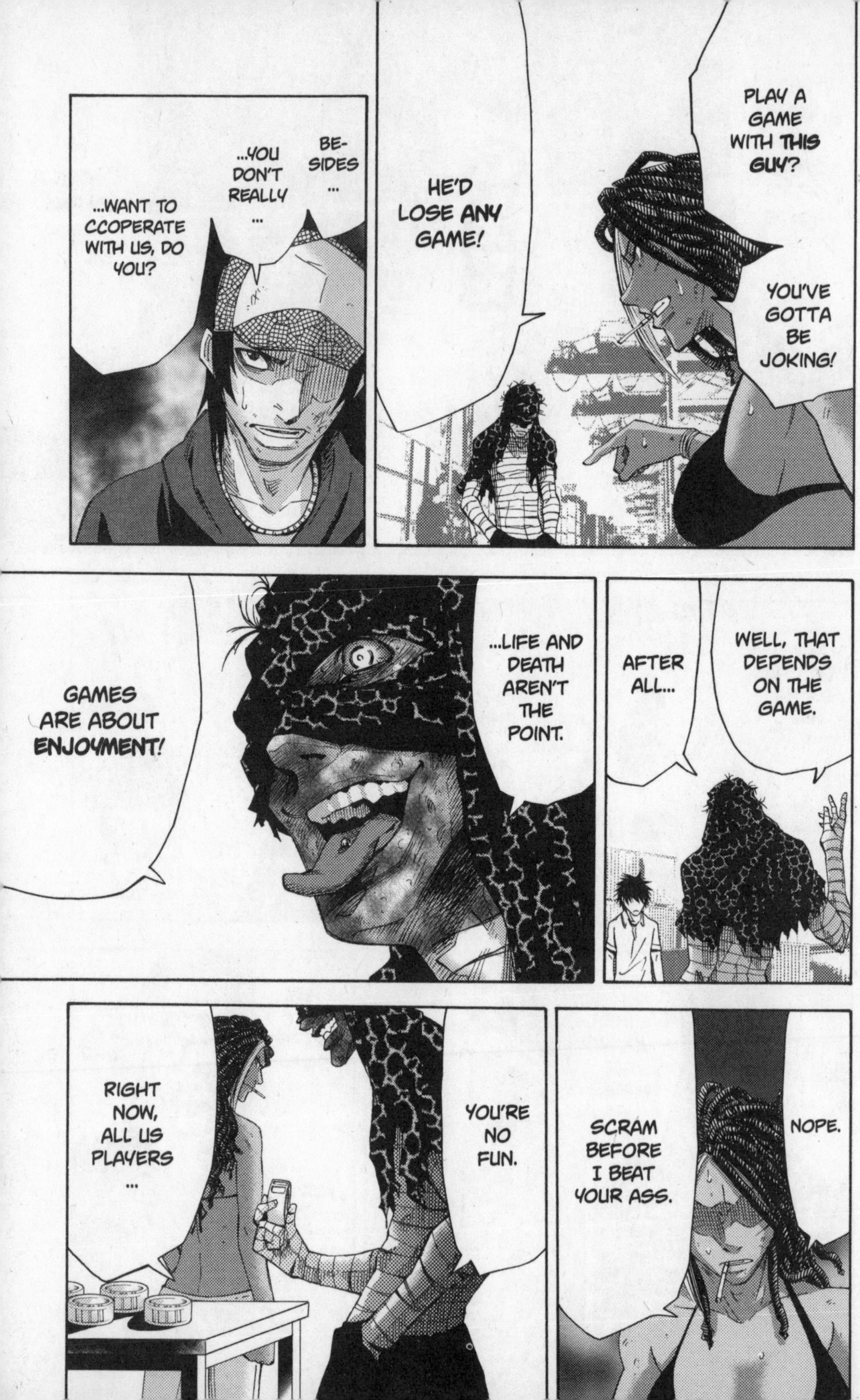
PLAY A GAME WITH THIS GUY?
YOU'VE GOTTA BE JOKING!
HE'D LOSE ANY GAME!
BE-SIDES ...
...YOU DON'T REALLY ...
...WANT TO CCOPERATE WITH US, DO YOU?
WELL, THAT DEPENDS ON THE GAME.
AFTER ALL...
...LIFE AND DEATH AREN'T THE POINT.
GAMES ARE ABOUT ENJOYMENT!
NOPE.
SCRAM BEFORE I BEAT YOUR ASS.
YOU'RE NO FUN.
RIGHT NOW, ALL US PLAYERS ...

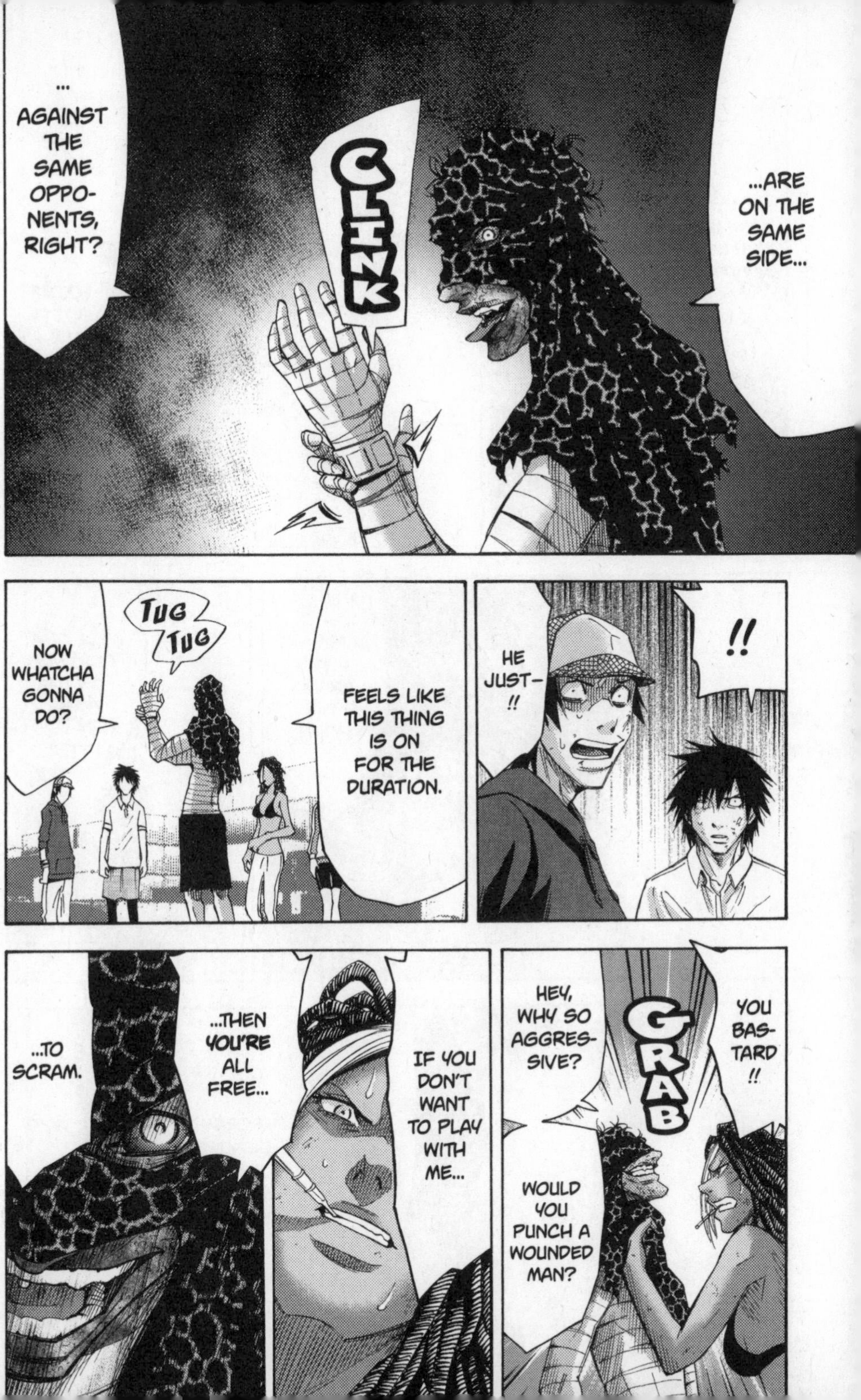

...ARE ON THE SAME SIDE...
CLINK
... AGAINST THE SAME OPPONENTS, RIGHT?
!!
HE JUST— !!
FEELS LIKE THIS THING IS ON FOR THE DURATION.
TUG TUG
NOW WHATCHA GONNA DO?
YOU BASTARD !!
GRAB
HEY, WHY SO AGGRESSIVE?
WOULD YOU PUNCH A WOUNDED MAN?
IF YOU DON'T WANT TO PLAY WITH ME...
...THEN YOU'RE ALL FREE...
...TO SCRAM.

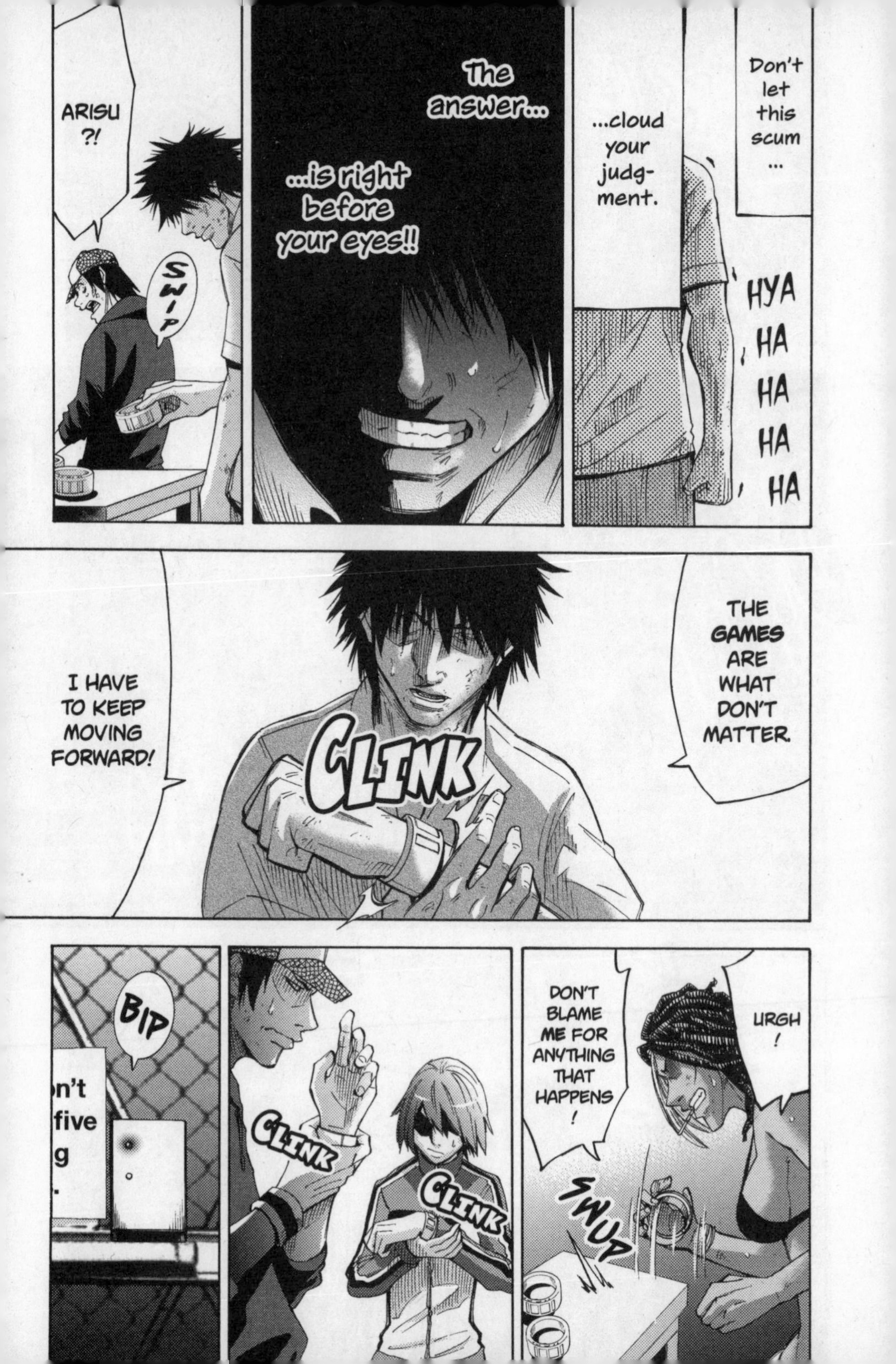

Don't let this scum...
...cloud your judgment.
HYA HA HA HA HA
The answer...
...is right before your eyes!!
ARISU?!
SWIP
THE GAMES ARE WHAT DON'T MATTER.
CLINK
I HAVE TO KEEP MOVING FORWARD!
URGH!
DON'T BLAME ME FOR ANYTHING THAT HAPPENS!
SWUP
CLINK
CLINK
BIP

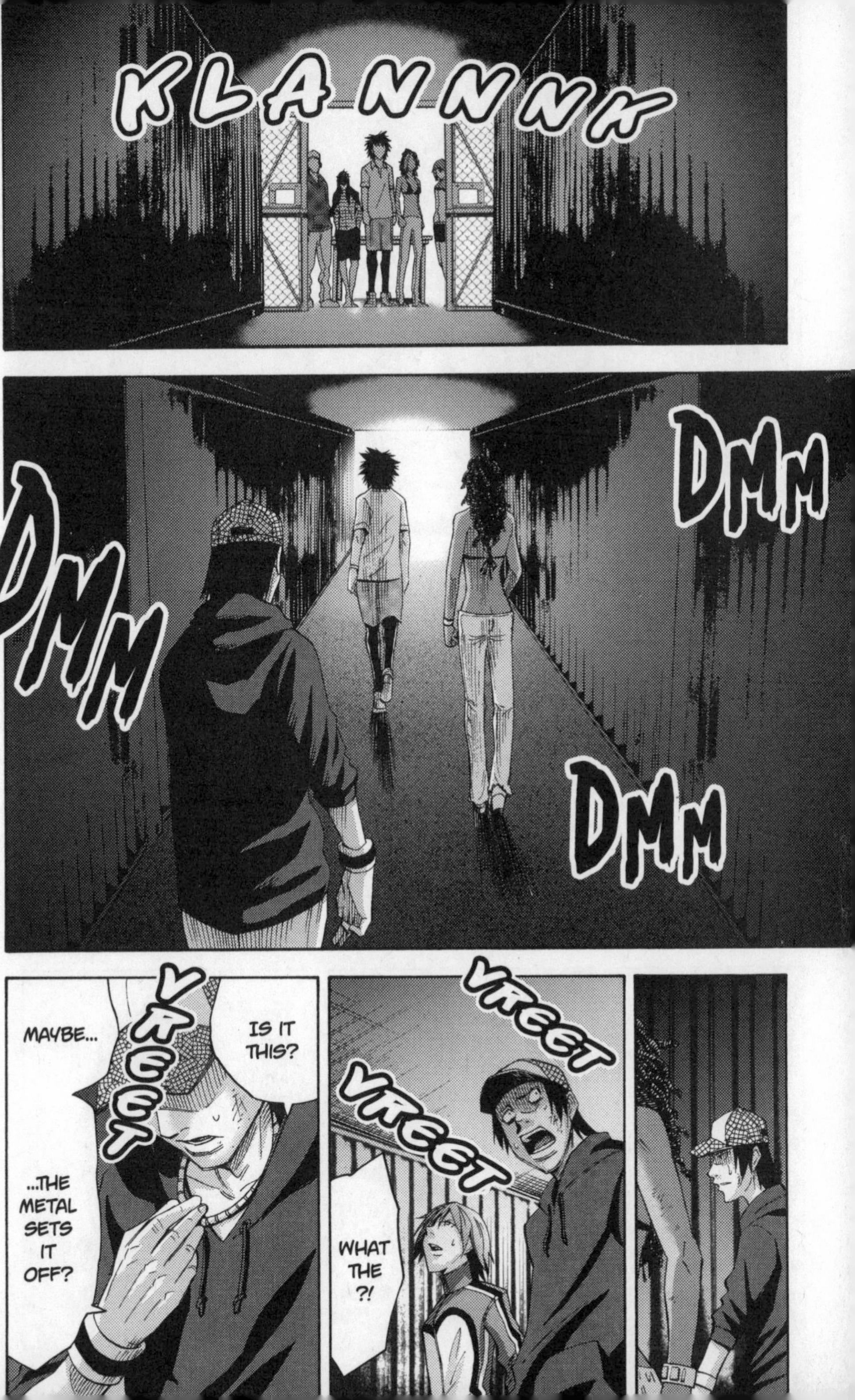
KLANNNK
DMM
DMM
DMM
VREET
VREET
WHAT THE ?!
VREET
IS IT THIS?
MAYBE...
...THE METAL SETS IT OFF?

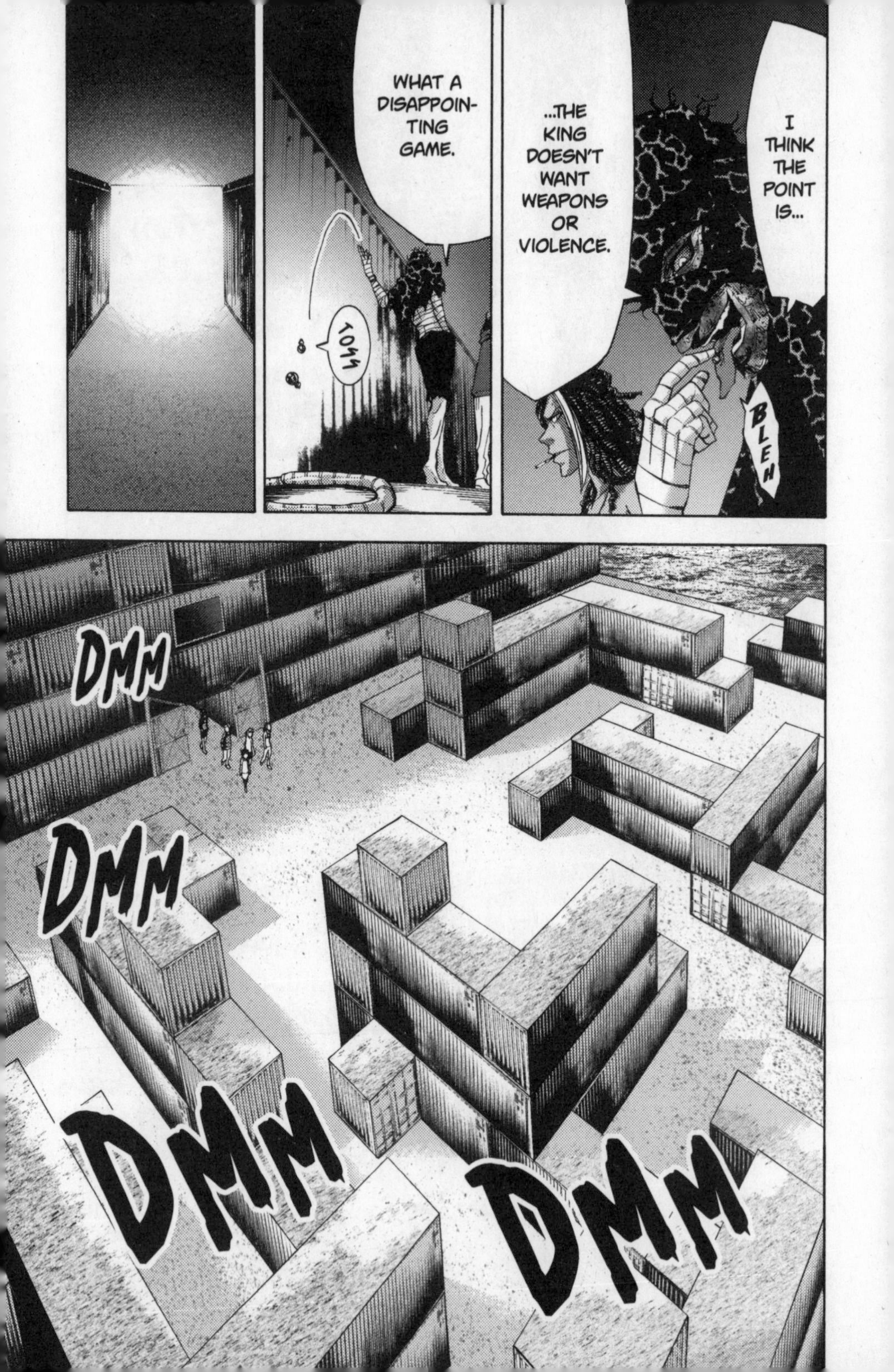

I THINK THE POINT IS...
...THE KING DOESN'T WANT WEAPONS OR VIOLENCE.
BLEH
WHAT A DISAPPOIN-TING GAME.
TOSS
DMM
DMM
DMM
DMM

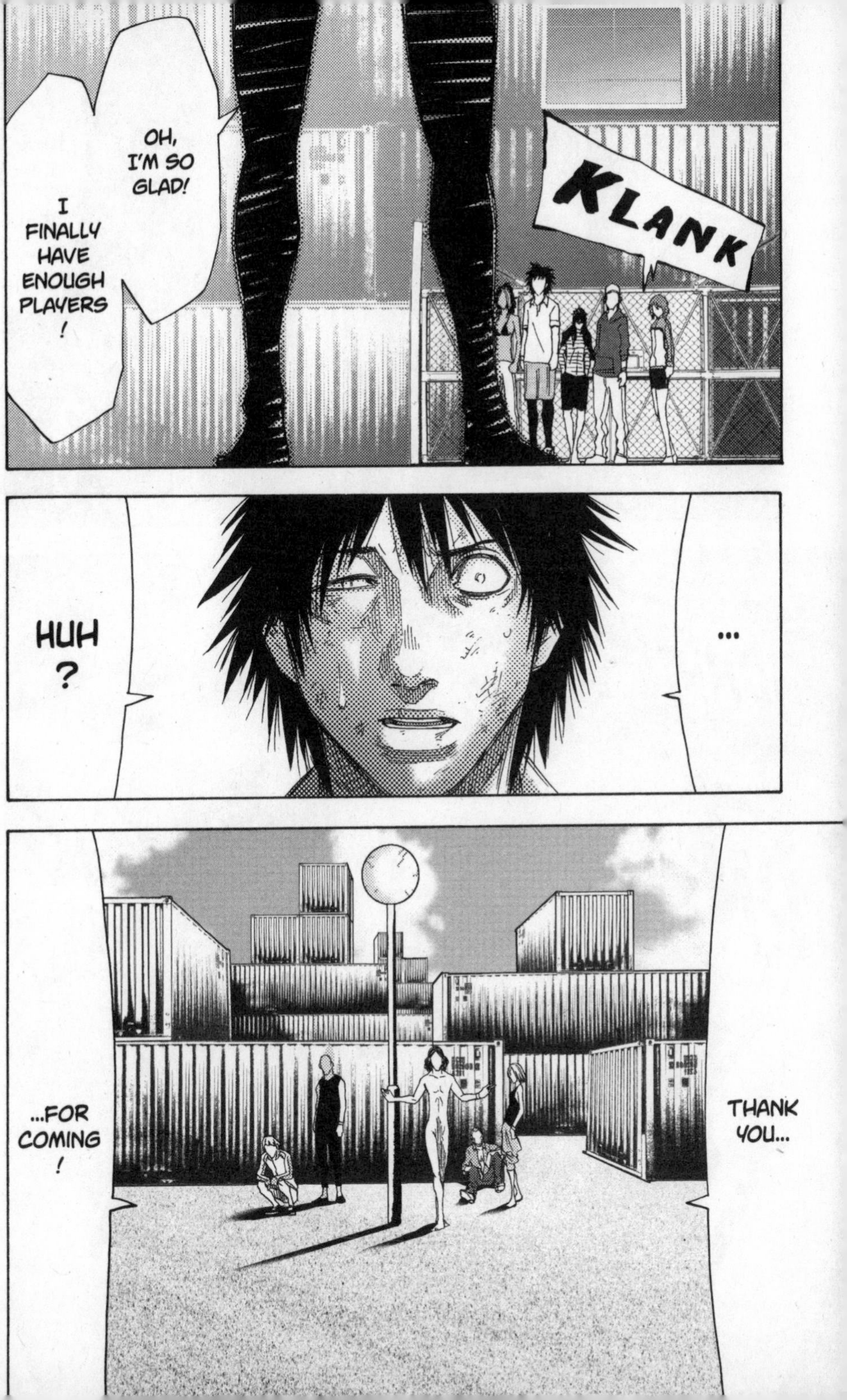
KLANK
OH, I'M SO GLAD! I FINALLY HAVE ENOUGH PLAYERS!
...
HUH?
THANK YOU...
...FOR COMING!

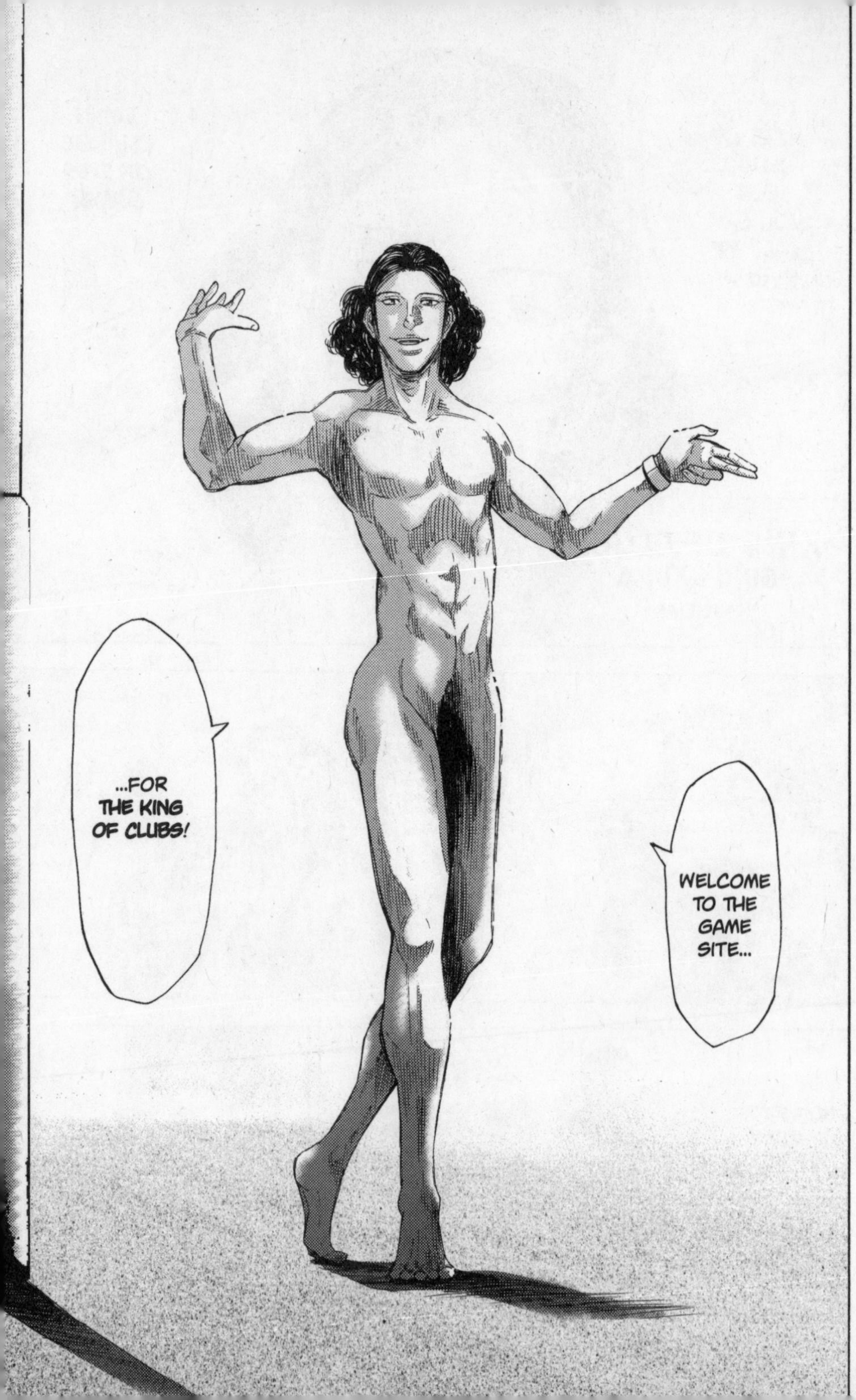
WELCOME TO THE GAME SITE...
...FOR THE KING OF CLUBS!

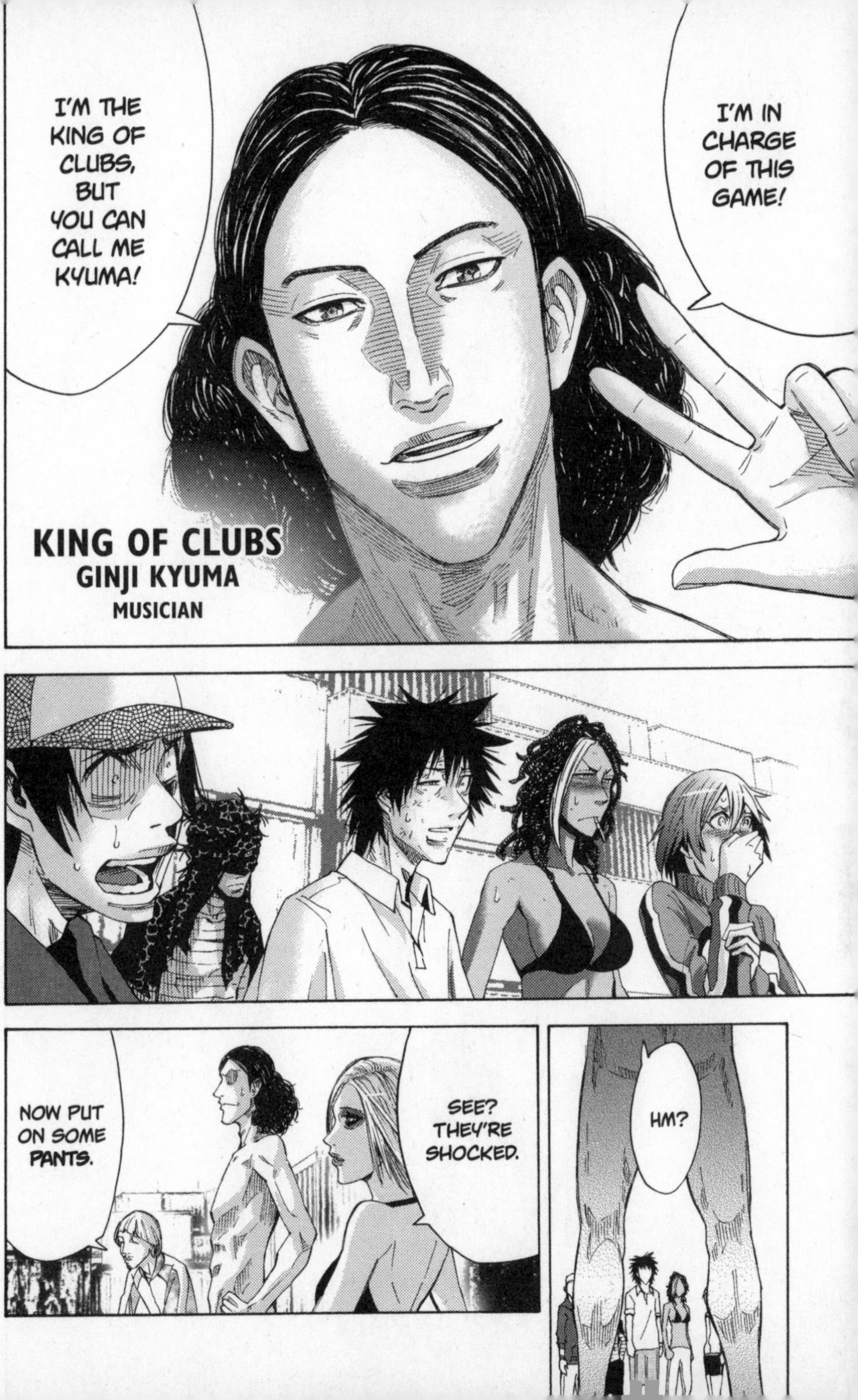
I'M IN CHARGE OF THIS GAME!
I'M THE KING OF CLUBS, BUT YOU CAN CALL ME KYUMA!
KING OF CLUBS
GINJI KYUMA
MUSICIAN
HM?
SEE? THEY'RE SHOCKED.
NOW PUT ON SOME PANTS.

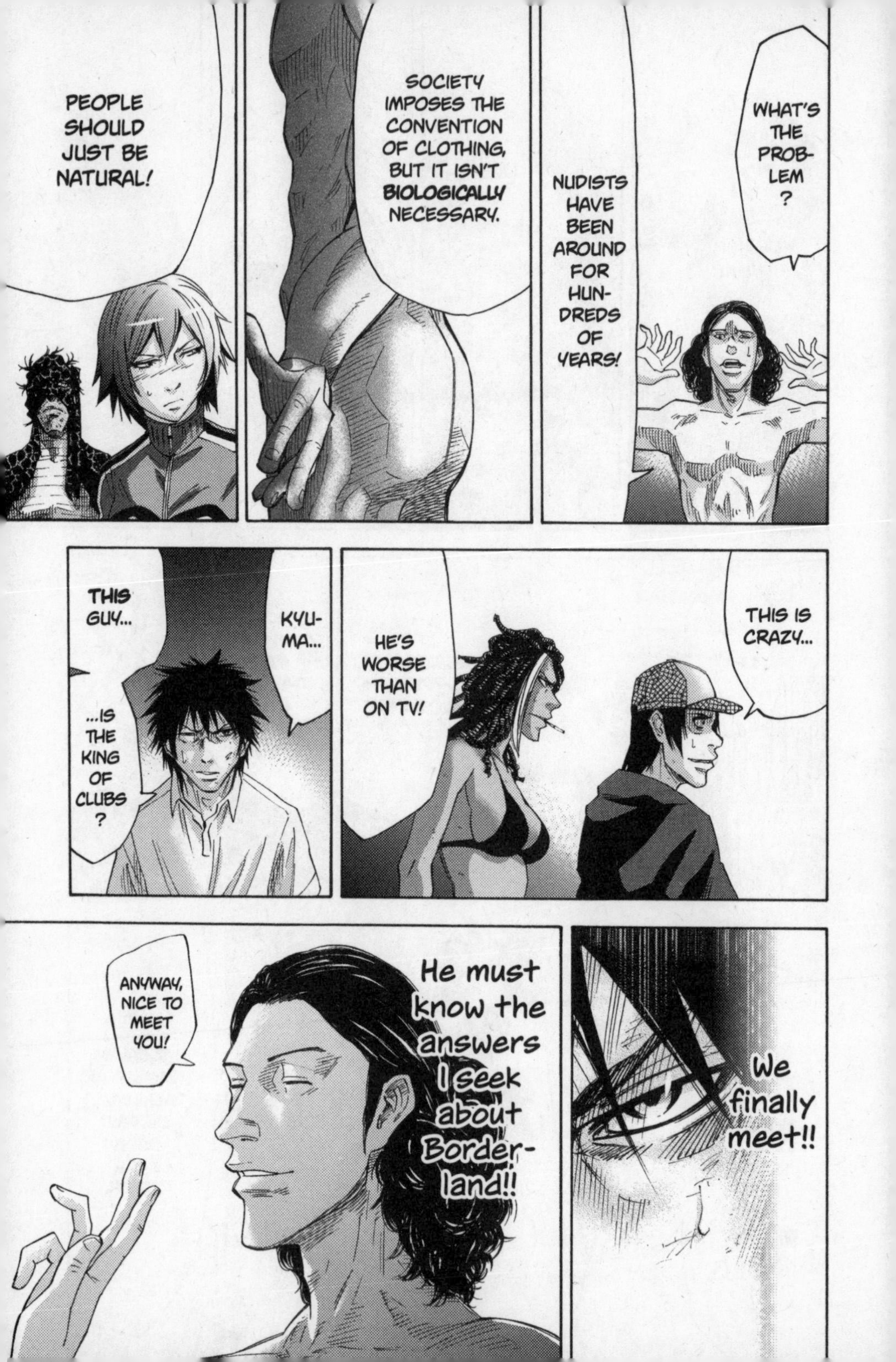
WHAT'S THE PROBLEM?
NUDISTS HAVE BEEN AROUND FOR HUNDREDS OF YEARS!
SOCIETY IMPOSES THE CONVENTION OF CLOTHING, BUT IT ISN'T **BIOLOGICALLY** NECESSARY.
PEOPLE SHOULD JUST BE NATURAL!
THIS IS CRAZY...
HE'S WORSE THAN ON TV!
KYUMA...
THIS GUY...
...IS THE KING OF CLUBS?
We finally meet!!
He must know the answers I seek about Borderland!!
ANYWAY, NICE TO MEET YOU!

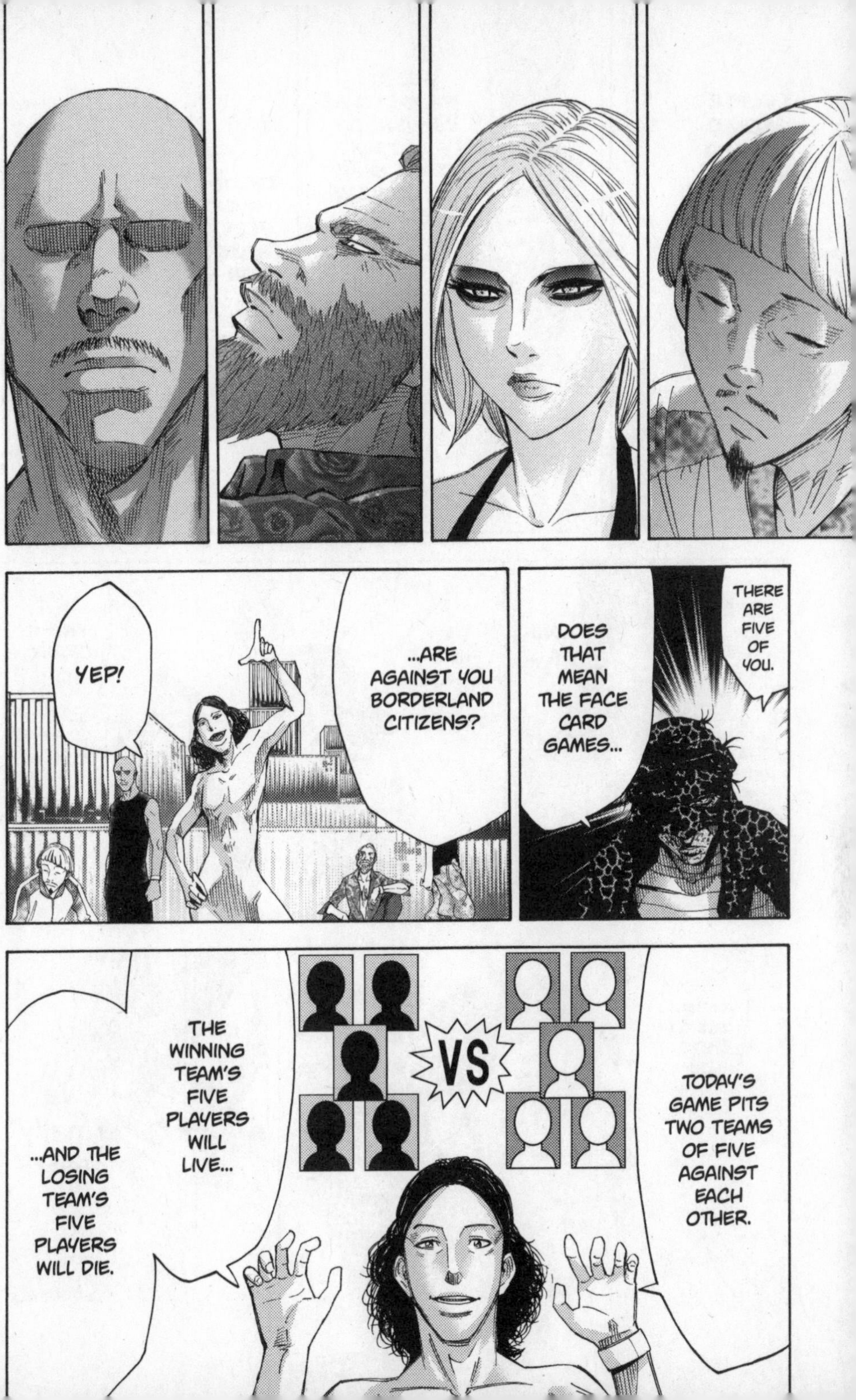
THERE ARE FIVE OF YOU.
DOES THAT MEAN THE FACE CARD GAMES...
...ARE AGAINST YOU BORDERLAND CITIZENS?
YEP!
TODAY'S GAME PITS TWO TEAMS OF FIVE AGAINST EACH OTHER.
VS
THE WINNING TEAM'S FIVE PLAYERS WILL LIVE...
...AND THE LOSING TEAM'S FIVE PLAYERS WILL DIE.

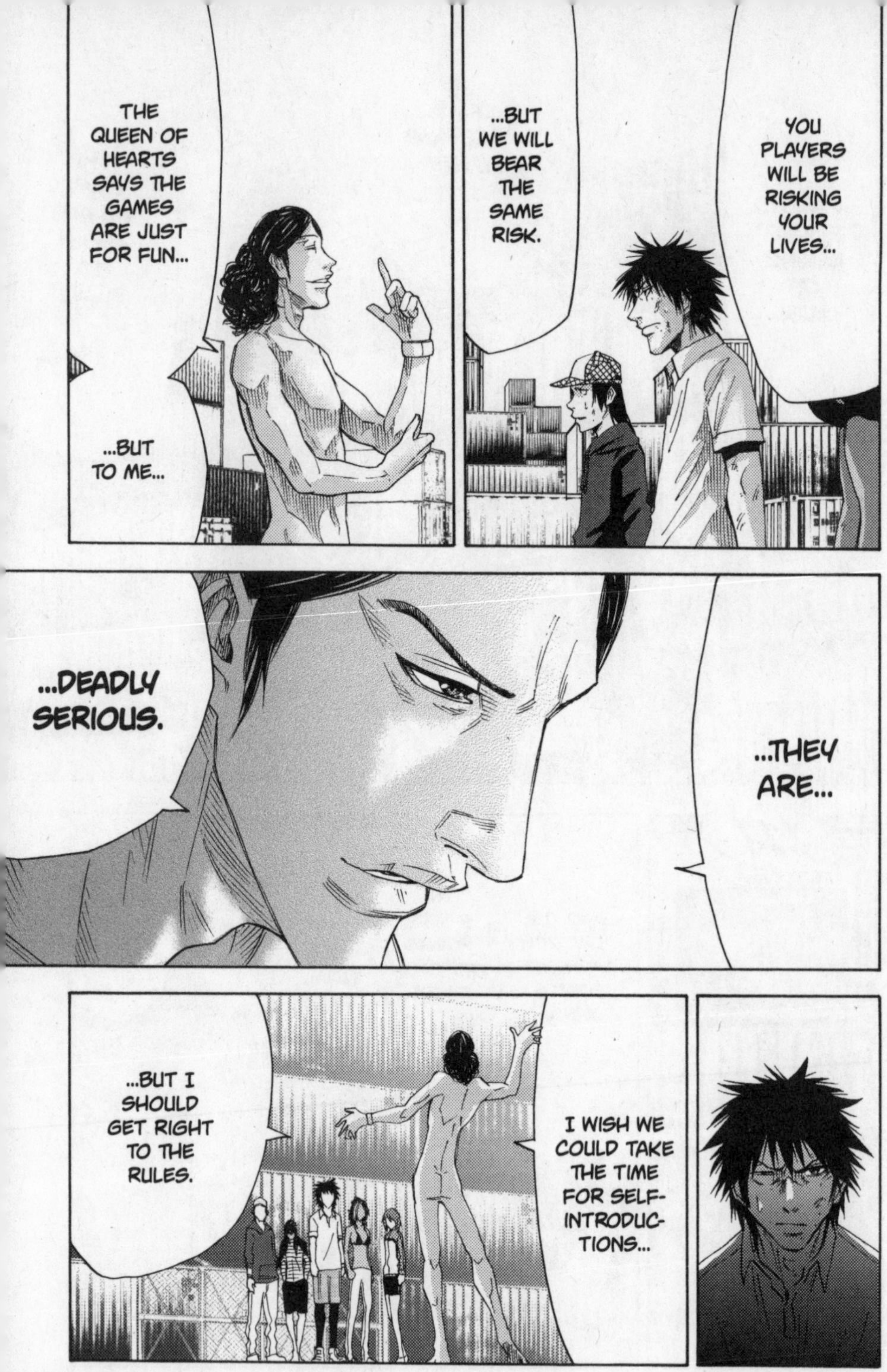
YOU PLAYERS WILL BE RISKING YOUR LIVES...
...BUT WE WILL BEAR THE SAME RISK.
THE QUEEN OF HEARTS SAYS THE GAMES ARE JUST FOR FUN...
...BUT TO ME...
...THEY ARE...
...DEADLY SERIOUS.
I WISH WE COULD TAKE THE TIME FOR SELF-INTRODUCTIONS...
...BUT I SHOULD GET RIGHT TO THE RULES.

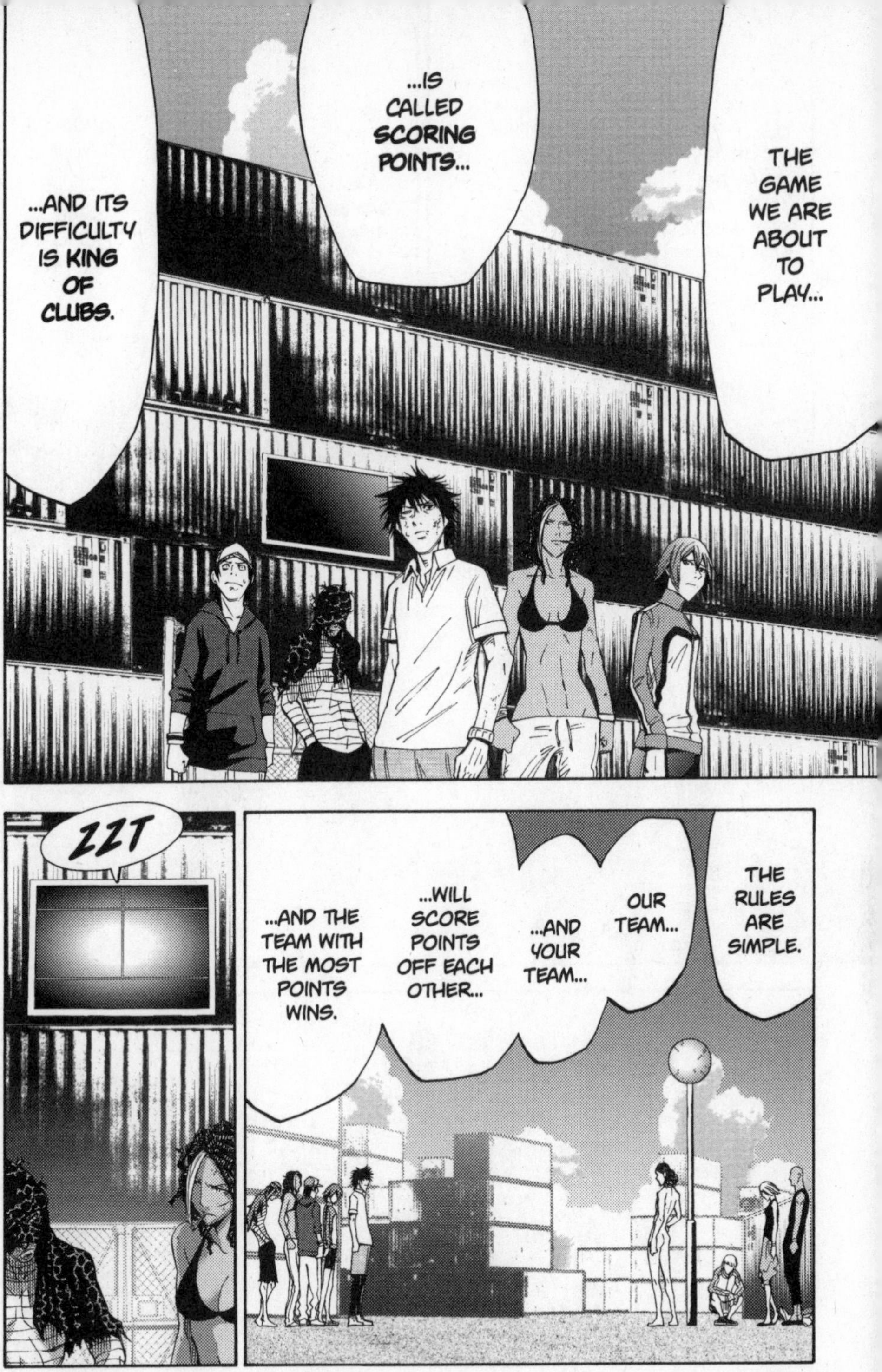
THE GAME WE ARE ABOUT TO PLAY...
...IS CALLED SCORING POINTS...
...AND ITS DIFFICULTY IS KING OF CLUBS.
THE RULES ARE SIMPLE.
OUR TEAM...
...AND YOUR TEAM...
...WILL SCORE POINTS OFF EACH OTHER...
...AND THE TEAM WITH THE MOST POINTS WINS.
ZZT

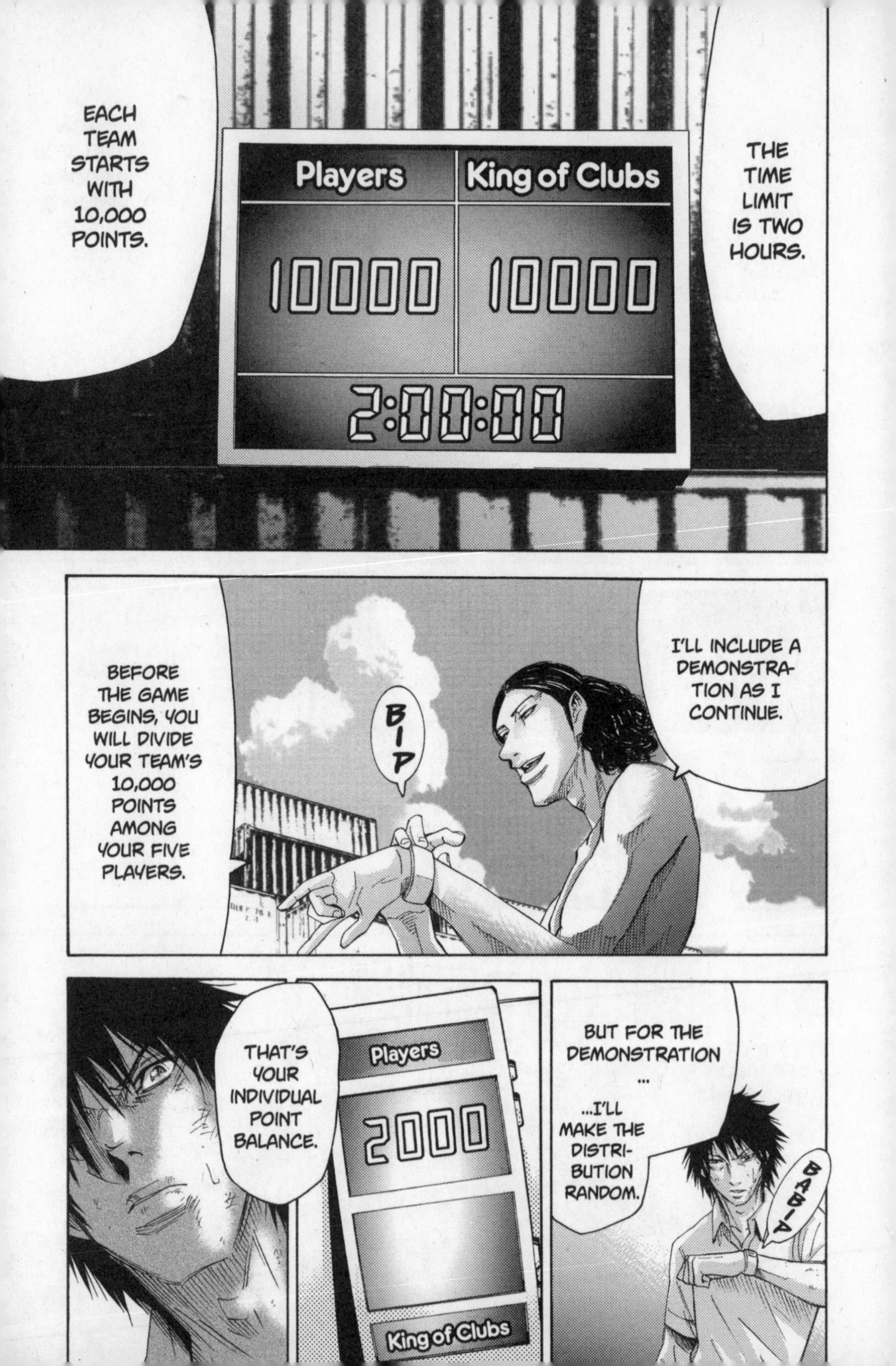
THE TIME LIMIT IS TWO HOURS.
Players
King of Clubs
10000
10000
2:00:00
EACH TEAM STARTS WITH 10,000 POINTS.
I'LL INCLUDE A DEMONSTRATION AS I CONTINUE.
BIP
BEFORE THE GAME BEGINS, YOU WILL DIVIDE YOUR TEAM'S 10,000 POINTS AMONG YOUR FIVE PLAYERS.
BUT FOR THE DEMONSTRATION ...
...I'LL MAKE THE DISTRIBUTION RANDOM.
BABIA
THAT'S YOUR INDIVIDUAL POINT BALANCE.
Players
2000
King of Clubs

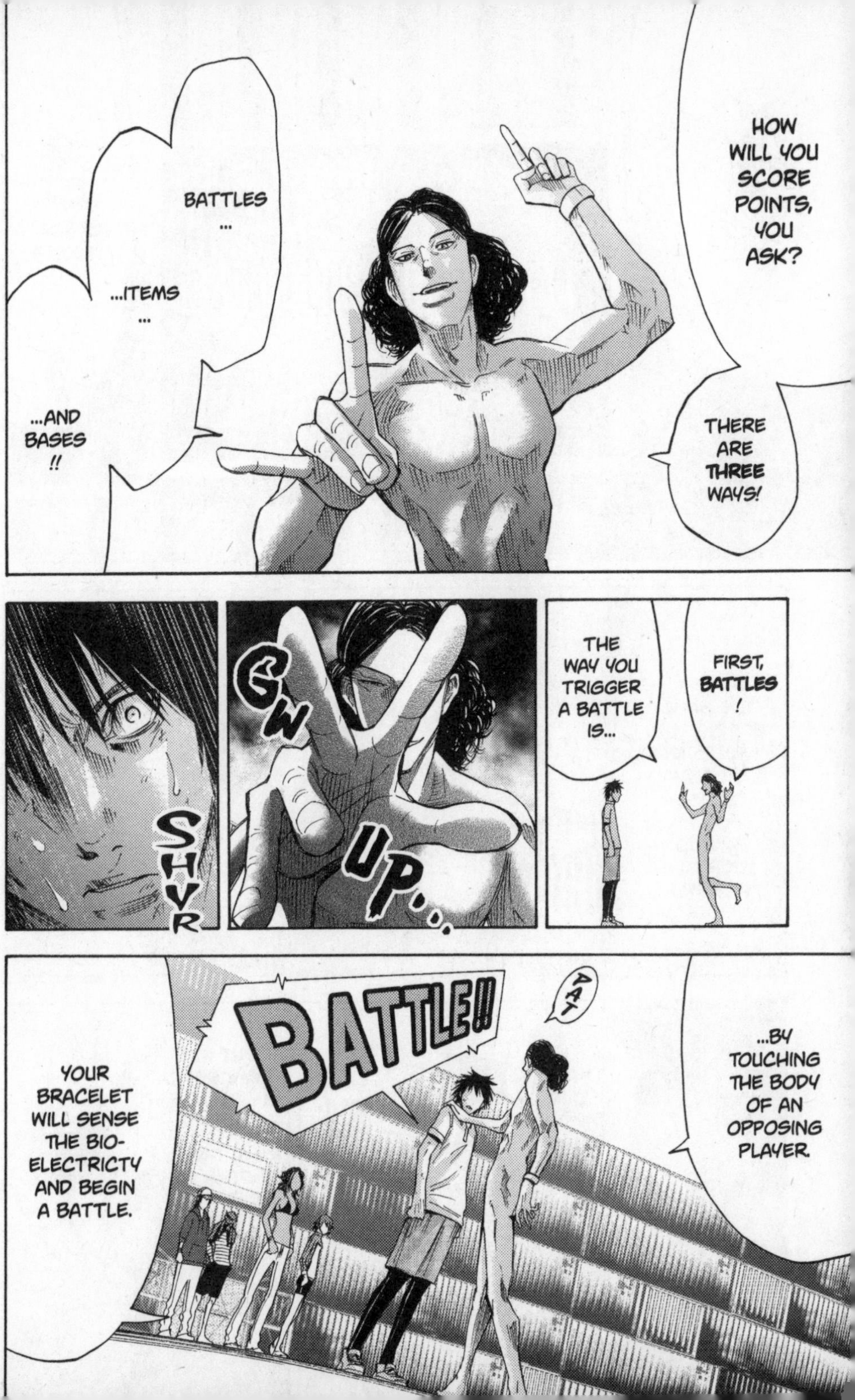
HOW WILL YOU SCORE POINTS, YOU ASK?
THERE ARE THREE WAYS!
BATTLES ...
...ITEMS ...
...AND BASES !!
FIRST, BATTLES !
THE WAY YOU TRIGGER A BATTLE IS...
GW UP...
SHVR
...BY TOUCHING THE BODY OF AN OPPOSING PLAYER.
PAT
BATTLE!!
YOUR BRACELET WILL SENSE THE BIO-ELECTRICTY AND BEGIN A BATTLE.

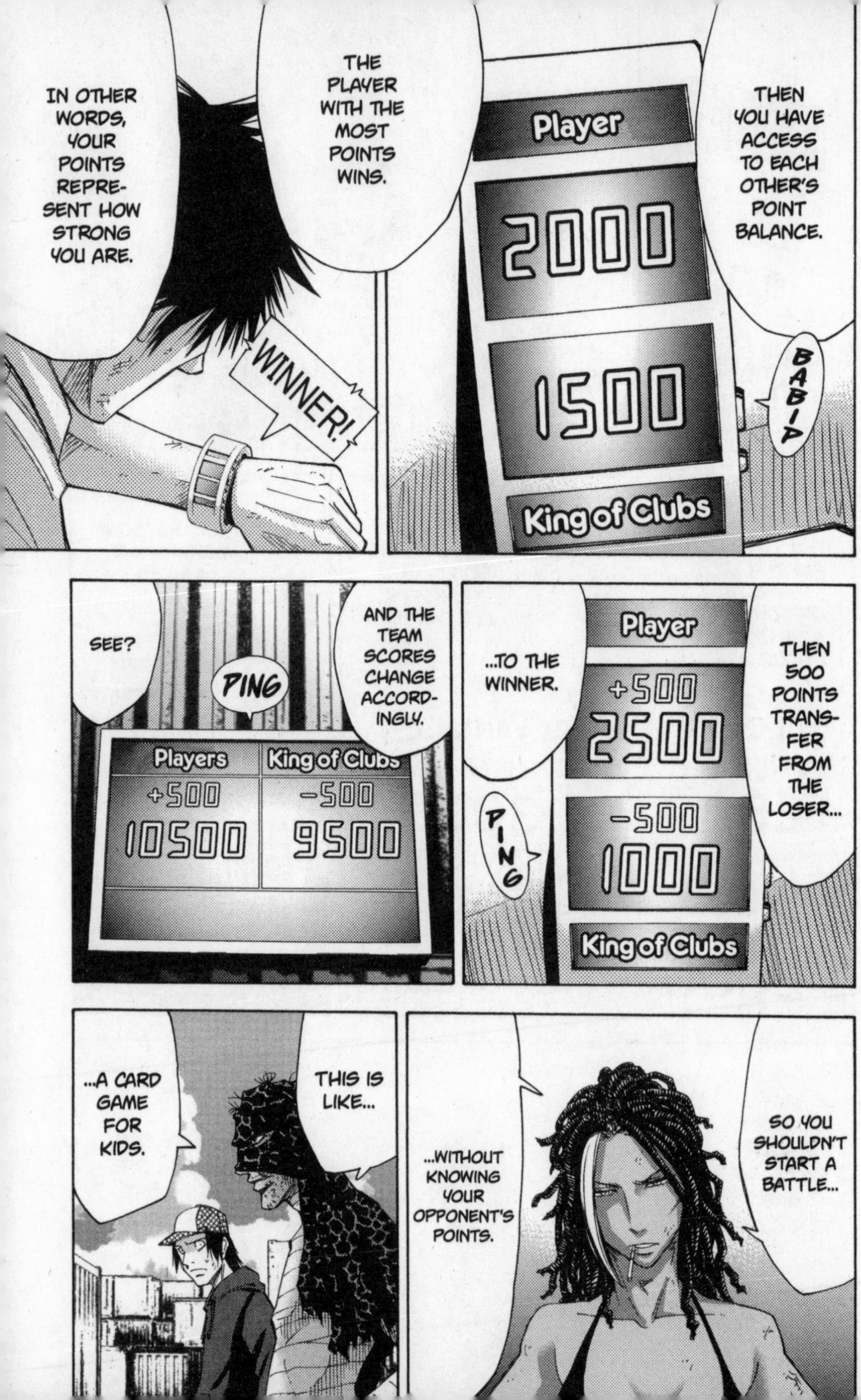
THEN YOU HAVE ACCESS TO EACH OTHER'S POINT BALANCE.
Player
2000
1500
King of Clubs
BABIP
THE PLAYER WITH THE MOST POINTS WINS.
IN OTHER WORDS, YOUR POINTS REPRE-SENT HOW STRONG YOU ARE.
WINNER!
THEN 500 POINTS TRANS-FER FROM THE LOSER...
...TO THE WINNER.
Player
+500
2500
-500
1000
King of Clubs
PING
AND THE TEAM SCORES CHANGE ACCORD-INGLY.
PING
SEE?
Players
+500
10500
King of Clubs
-500
9500
SO YOU SHOULDN'T START A BATTLE...
...WITHOUT KNOWING YOUR OPPONENT'S POINTS.
THIS IS LIKE...
...A CARD GAME FOR KIDS.

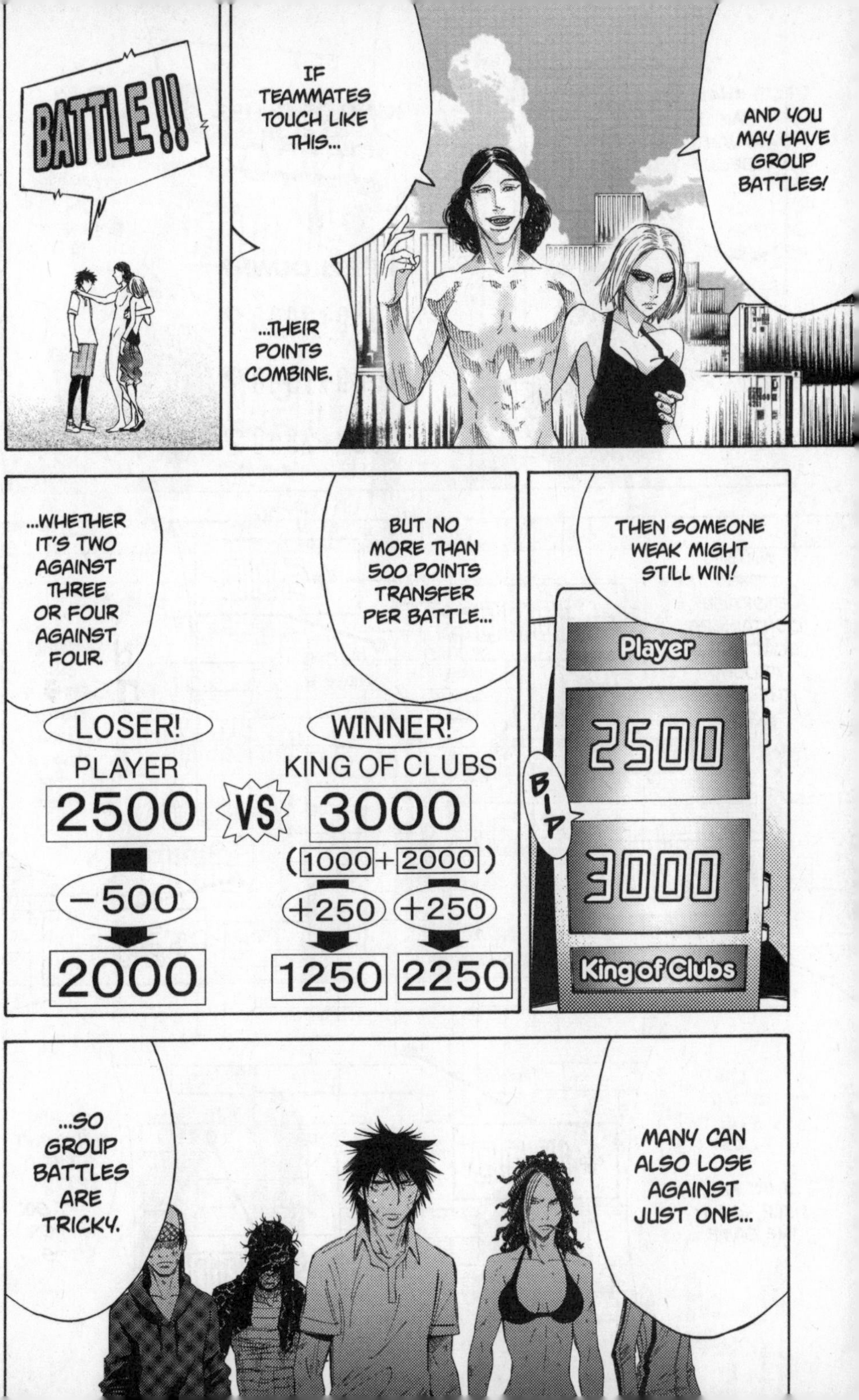
IF TEAMMATES TOUCH LIKE THIS...
...THEIR POINTS COMBINE.
AND YOU MAY HAVE GROUP BATTLES!
BATTLE!!
THEN SOMEONE WEAK MIGHT STILL WIN!
Player
2500
BIP
3000
King of Clubs
BUT NO MORE THAN 500 POINTS TRANSFER PER BATTLE...
...WHETHER IT'S TWO AGAINST THREE OR FOUR AGAINST FOUR.
LOSER!
PLAYER
2500
−500
2000
VS
WINNER!
KING OF CLUBS
3000
(1000+2000)
+250
+250
1250
2250
MANY CAN ALSO LOSE AGAINST JUST ONE...
...SO GROUP BATTLES ARE TRICKY.

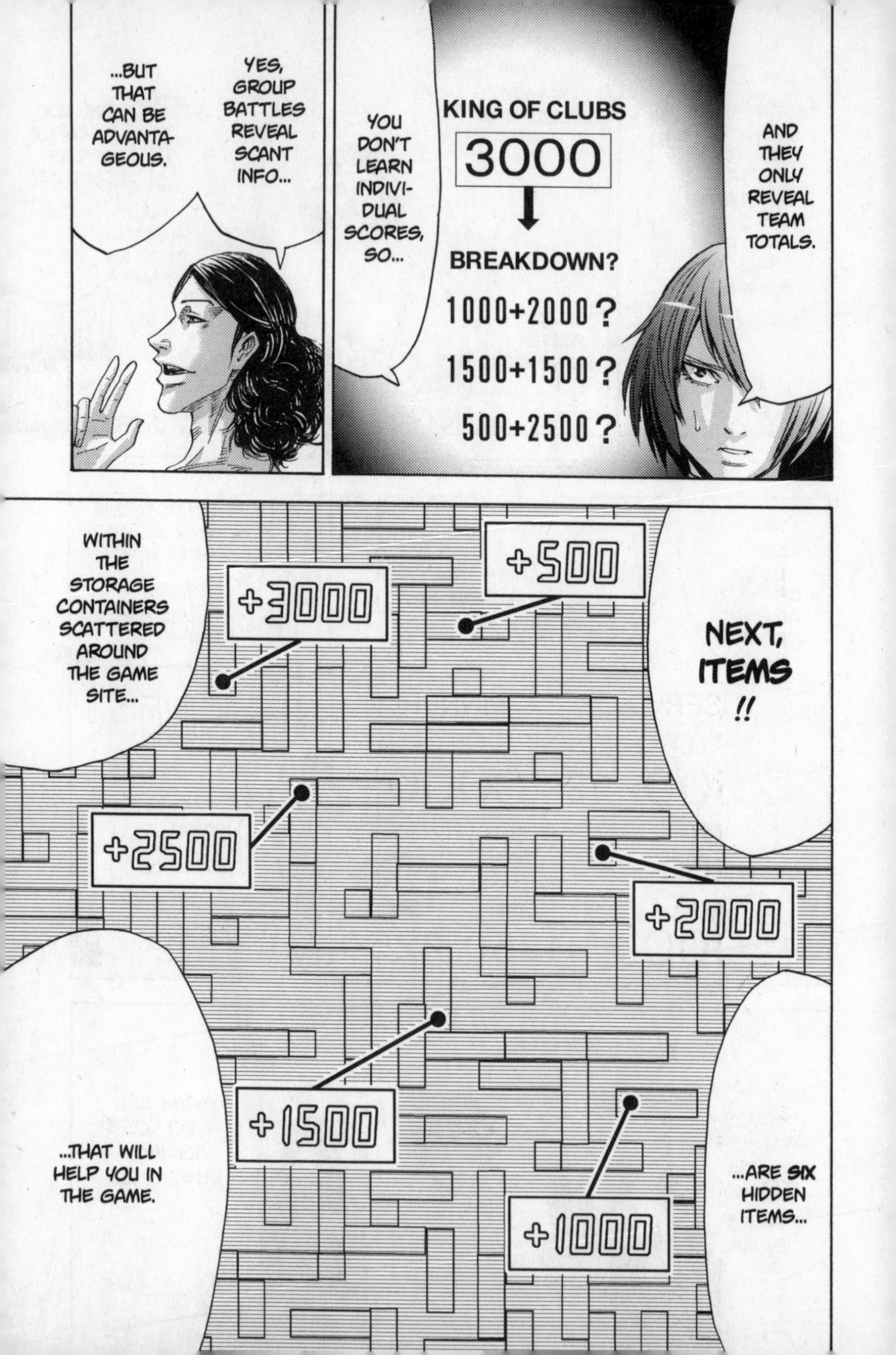
AND THEY ONLY REVEAL TEAM TOTALS.
KING OF CLUBS
3000
BREAKDOWN?
1000+2000?
1500+1500?
500+2500?
YOU DON'T LEARN INDIVIDUAL SCORES, SO...
YES, GROUP BATTLES REVEAL SCANT INFO...
...BUT THAT CAN BE ADVANTAGEOUS.
NEXT, ITEMS!!
WITHIN THE STORAGE CONTAINERS SCATTERED AROUND THE GAME SITE...
+500
+3000
+2000
+2500
...ARE SIX HIDDEN ITEMS...
+1000
+1500
...THAT WILL HELP YOU IN THE GAME.

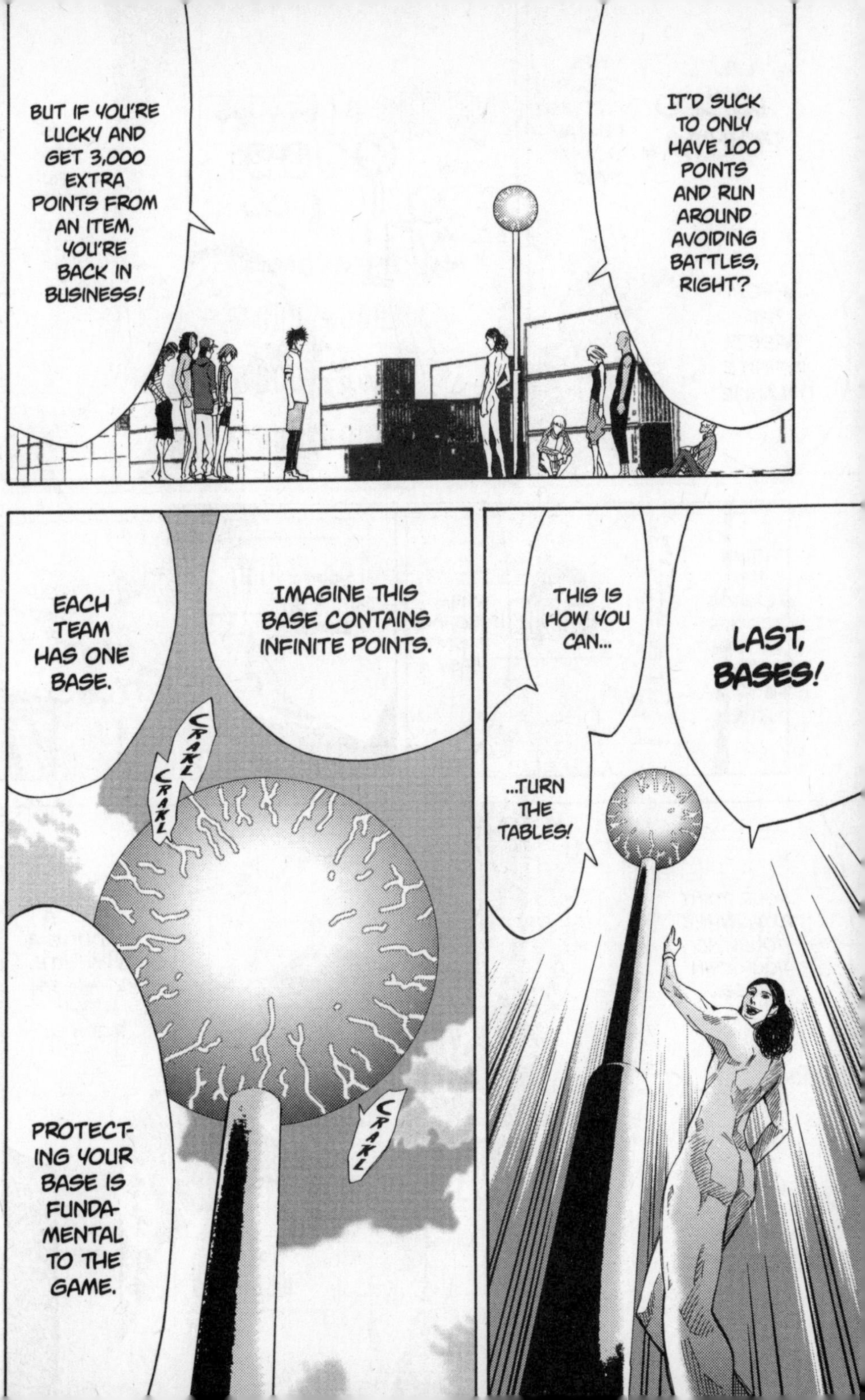
IT'D SUCK TO ONLY HAVE 100 POINTS AND RUN AROUND AVOIDING BATTLES, RIGHT?
BUT IF YOU'RE LUCKY AND GET 3,000 EXTRA POINTS FROM AN ITEM, YOU'RE BACK IN BUSINESS!
LAST, BASES!
THIS IS HOW YOU CAN...
...TURN THE TABLES!
IMAGINE THIS BASE CONTAINS INFINITE POINTS.
EACH TEAM HAS ONE BASE.
CRAKL CRAKL
CRAKL
PROTECTING YOUR BASE IS FUNDAMENTAL TO THE GAME.

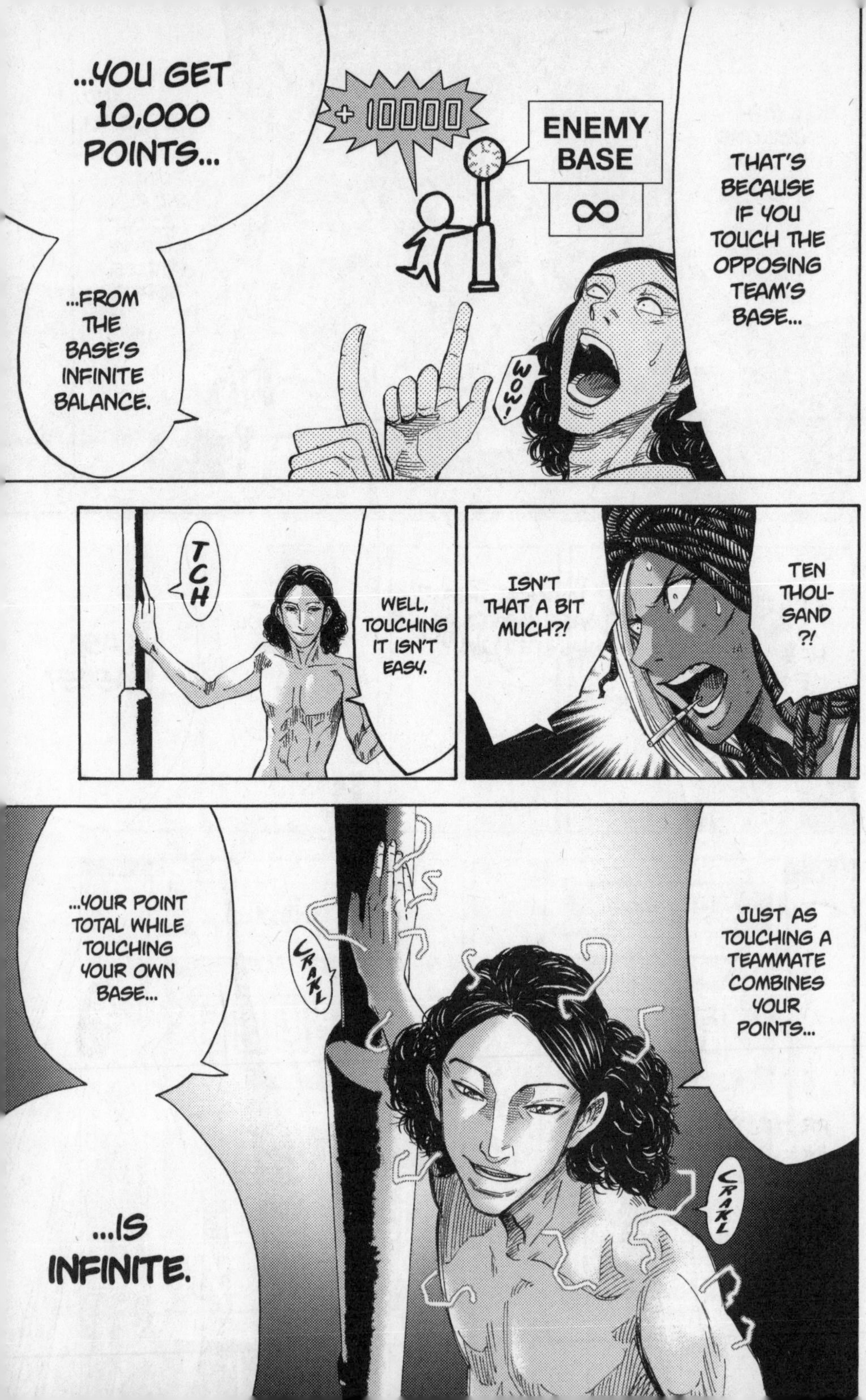
THAT'S BECAUSE IF YOU TOUCH THE OPPOSING TEAM'S BASE...
ENEMY BASE
∞
+10000
WOW!
...YOU GET 10,000 POINTS...
...FROM THE BASE'S INFINITE BALANCE.
TEN THOUSAND?!
ISN'T THAT A BIT MUCH?!
WELL, TOUCHING IT ISN'T EASY.
TCH
JUST AS TOUCHING A TEAMMATE COMBINES YOUR POINTS...
CRAK!
CRAK!
...YOUR POINT TOTAL WHILE TOUCHING YOUR OWN BASE...
...IS INFINITE.

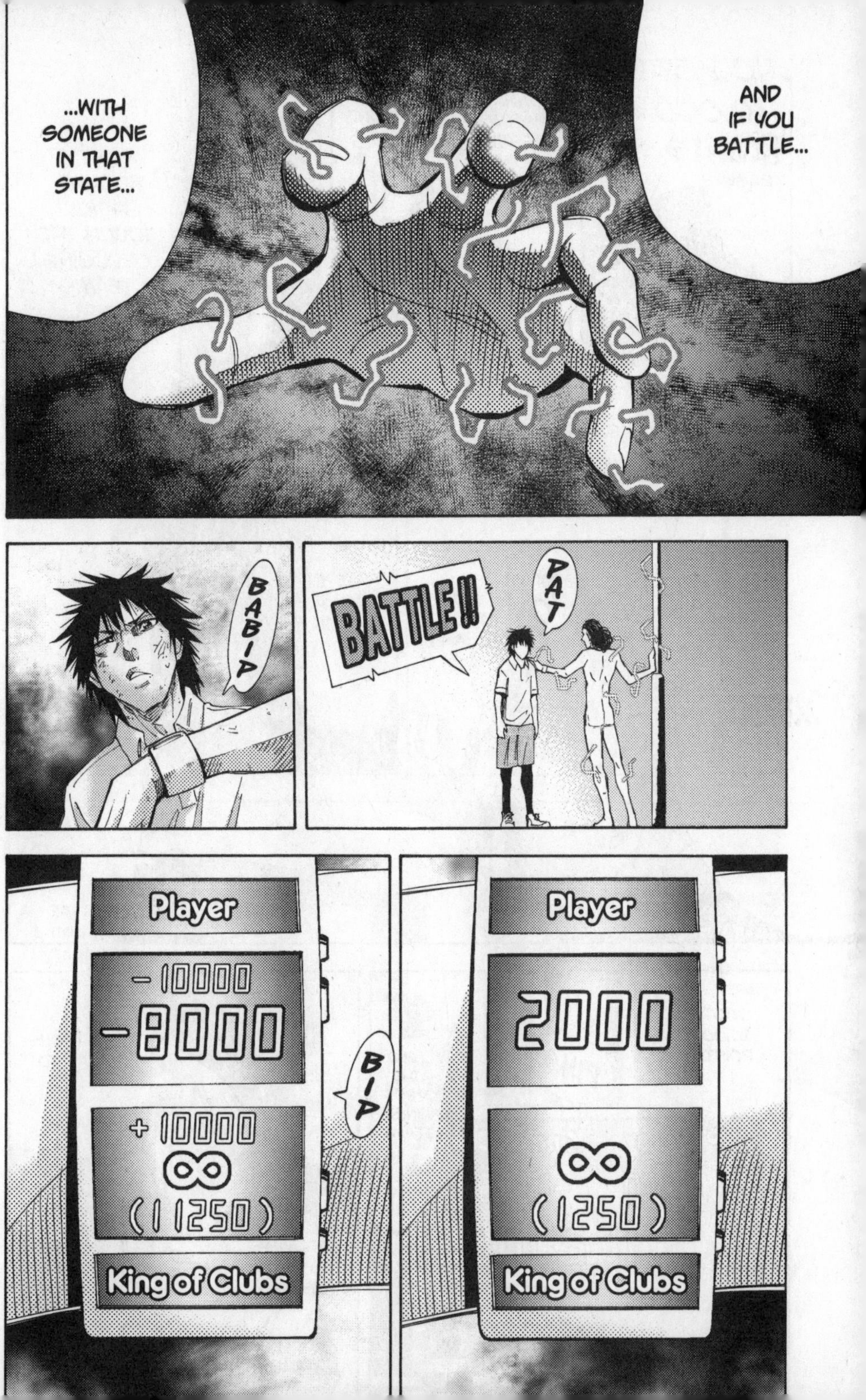
AND IF YOU BATTLE...
...WITH SOMEONE IN THAT STATE...
PAT
BATTLE!!
BABIP
Player
2000
∞
(1250)
King of Clubs
BIP
Player
-10000
-8000
+10000
∞
(11250)
King of Clubs

...THE MIDDLE OF THE GAME...

RIGHT IN...

WHAT HAPPENS IF YOUR POINTS GO BELOW ZERO?

WAIT A SECOND.

...IS 10,000!

THE POINT TRANSFER...

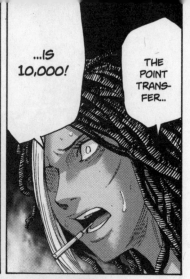

...DIE.

POOF!

...YOU UP AND...

...GETS 10,000 POINTS.

PING

...AND THE OPPOSING TEAM...

...YOU DIE...

IF YOU FAIL TO TOUCH THE ENEMY BASE...

Players	King of Club
-10000	+10000
0	20000

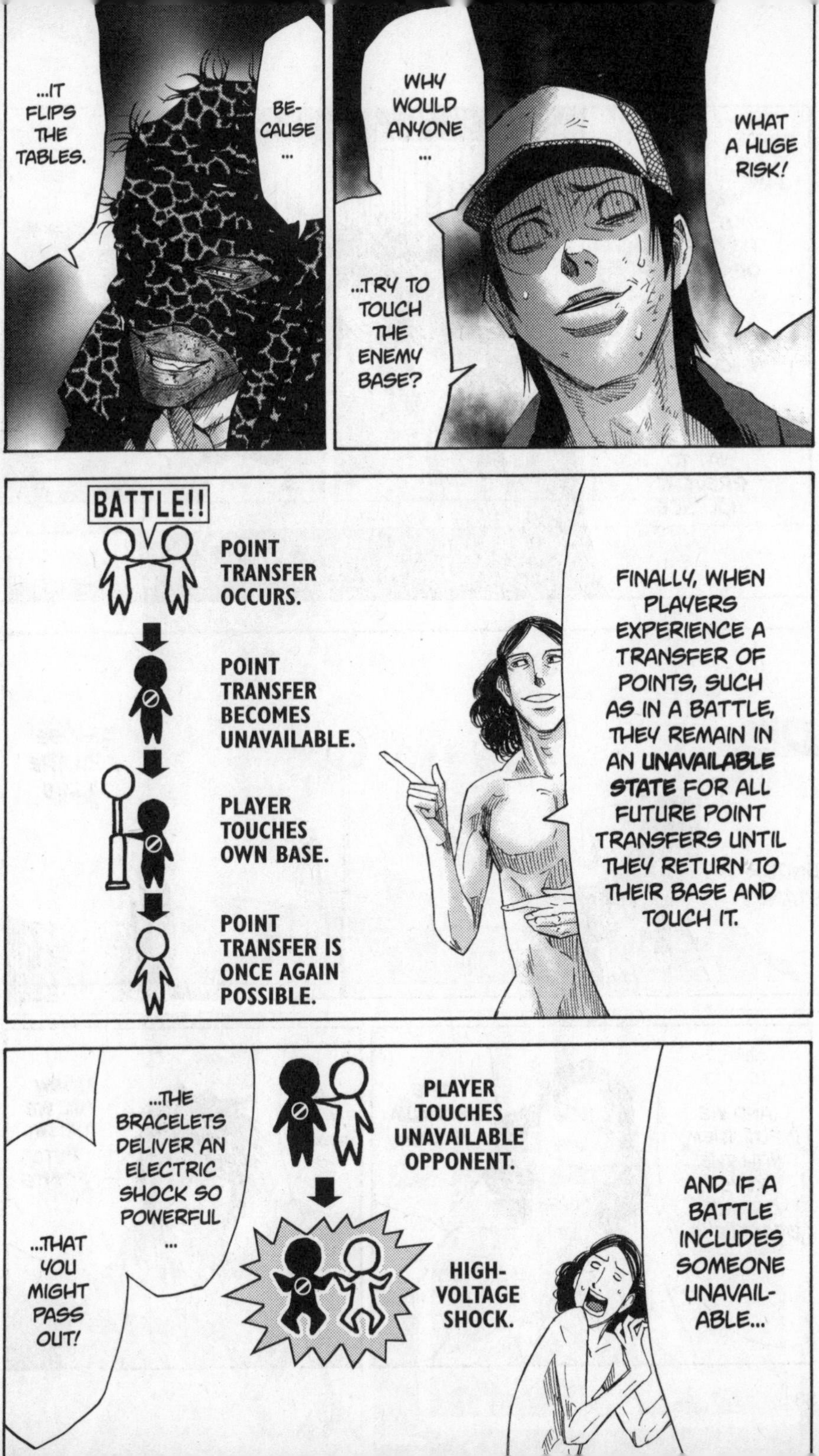
WHAT A HUGE RISK!
WHY WOULD ANYONE ...
...TRY TO TOUCH THE ENEMY BASE?
BE-CAUSE ...
...IT FLIPS THE TABLES.
FINALLY, WHEN PLAYERS EXPERIENCE A TRANSFER OF POINTS, SUCH AS IN A BATTLE, THEY REMAIN IN AN **UNAVAILABLE STATE** FOR ALL FUTURE POINT TRANSFERS UNTIL THEY RETURN TO THEIR BASE AND TOUCH IT.
BATTLE!!
POINT TRANSFER OCCURS.
POINT TRANSFER BECOMES UNAVAILABLE.
PLAYER TOUCHES OWN BASE.
POINT TRANSFER IS ONCE AGAIN POSSIBLE.
AND IF A BATTLE INCLUDES SOMEONE UNAVAIL-ABLE...
PLAYER TOUCHES UNAVAILABLE OPPONENT.
HIGH-VOLTAGE SHOCK.
...THE BRACELETS DELIVER AN ELECTRIC SHOCK SO POWERFUL ...
...THAT YOU MIGHT PASS OUT!

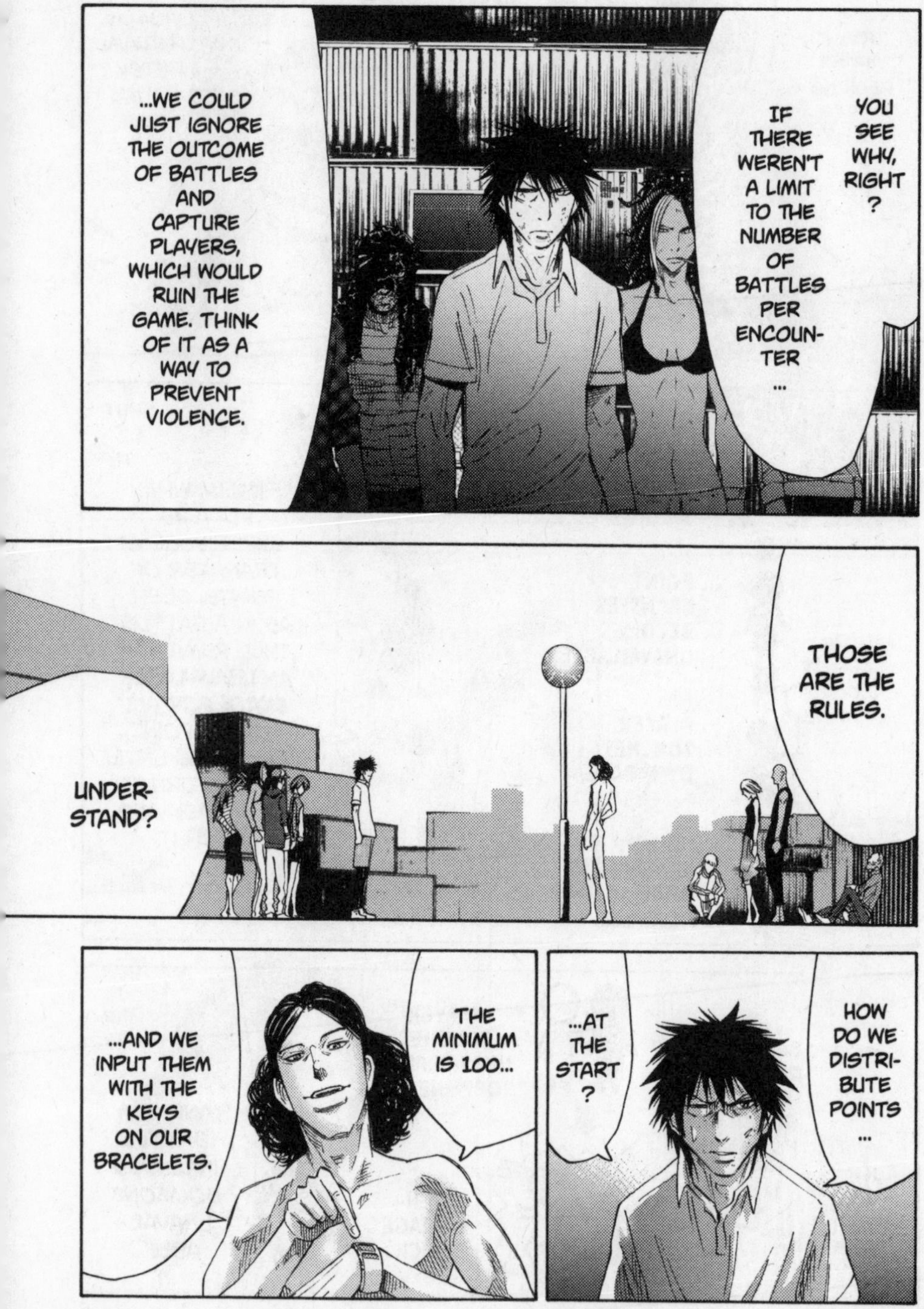
YOU SEE WHY, RIGHT?
IF THERE WEREN'T A LIMIT TO THE NUMBER OF BATTLES PER ENCOUNTER...
...WE COULD JUST IGNORE THE OUTCOME OF BATTLES AND CAPTURE PLAYERS, WHICH WOULD RUIN THE GAME. THINK OF IT AS A WAY TO PREVENT VIOLENCE.
THOSE ARE THE RULES.
UNDER-STAND?
HOW DO WE DISTRI-BUTE POINTS...
...AT THE START?
THE MINIMUM IS 100...
...AND WE INPUT THEM WITH THE KEYS ON OUR BRACELETS.

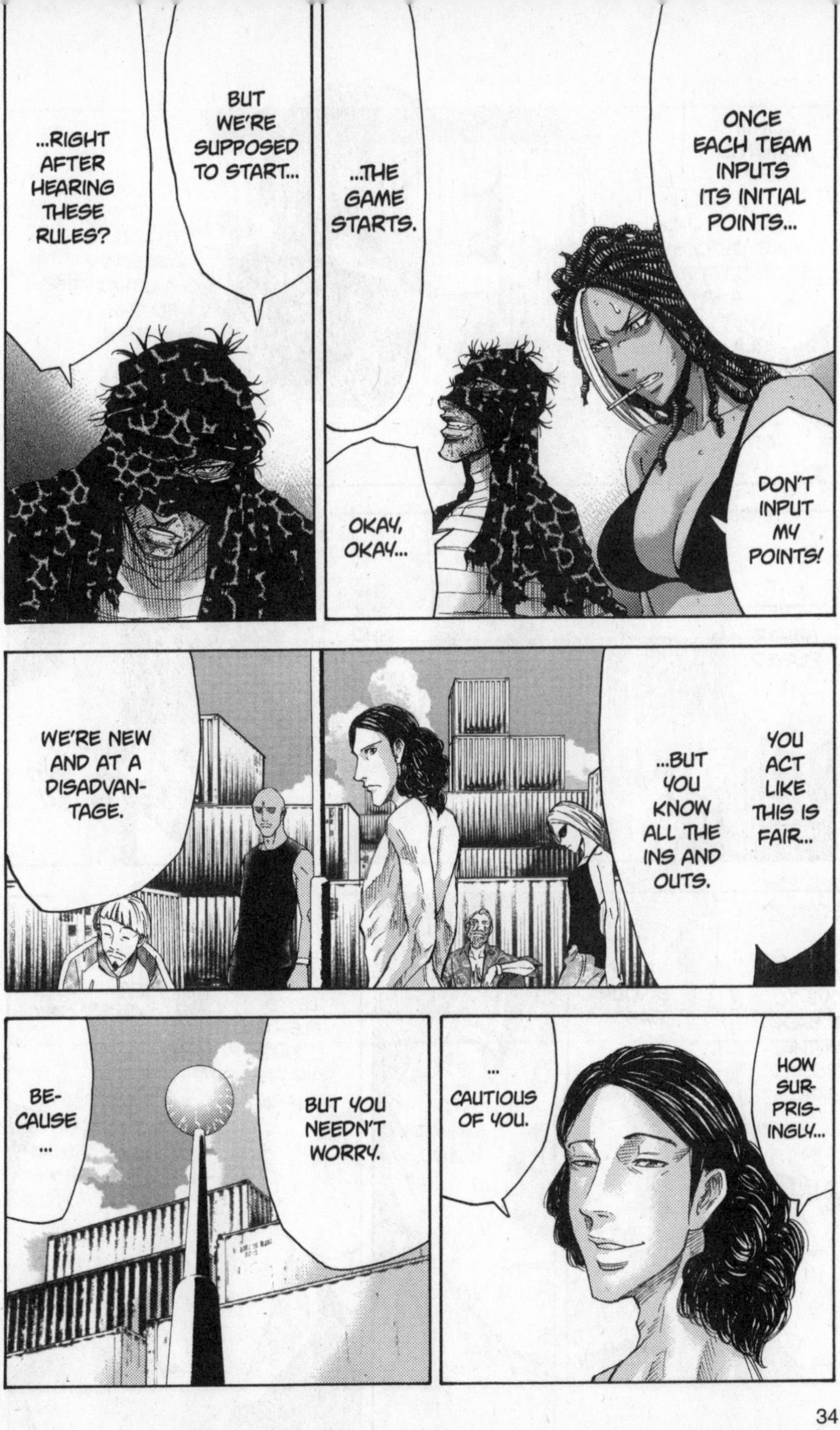
ONCE EACH TEAM INPUTS ITS INITIAL POINTS...
...THE GAME STARTS.
DON'T INPUT MY POINTS!
OKAY, OKAY...
BUT WE'RE SUPPOSED TO START...
...RIGHT AFTER HEARING THESE RULES?
YOU ACT LIKE THIS IS FAIR...
...BUT YOU KNOW ALL THE INS AND OUTS.
WE'RE NEW AND AT A DISADVAN-TAGE.
HOW SUR-PRIS-INGLY...
...CAUTIOUS OF YOU.
BUT YOU NEEDN'T WORRY.
BE-CAUSE ...

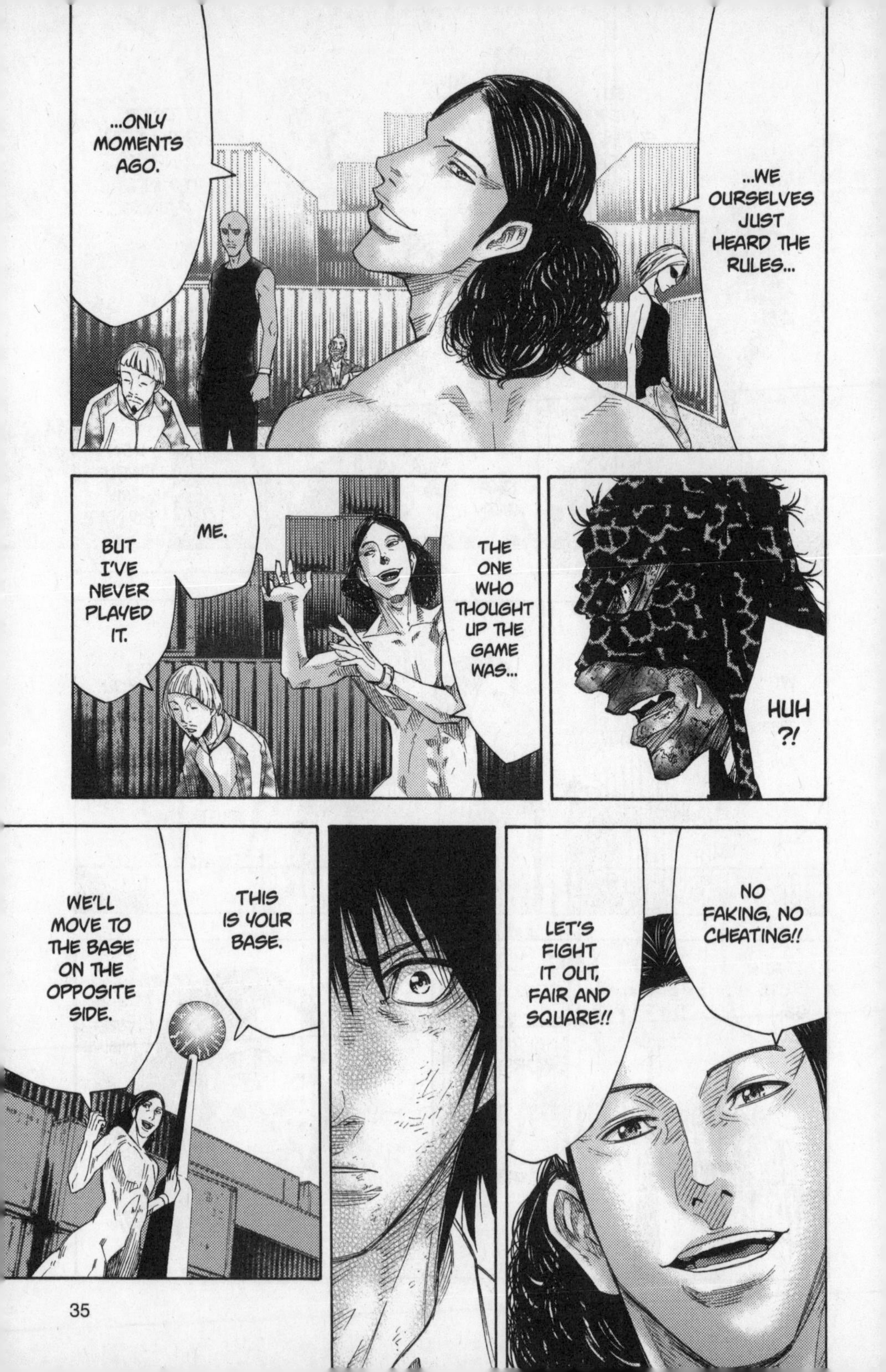
...WE OURSELVES JUST HEARD THE RULES...
...ONLY MOMENTS AGO.
HUH ?!
THE ONE WHO THOUGHT UP THE GAME WAS...
ME.
BUT I'VE NEVER PLAYED IT.
NO FAKING, NO CHEATING!!
LET'S FIGHT IT OUT, FAIR AND SQUARE!!
THIS IS YOUR BASE.
WE'LL MOVE TO THE BASE ON THE OPPOSITE SIDE.

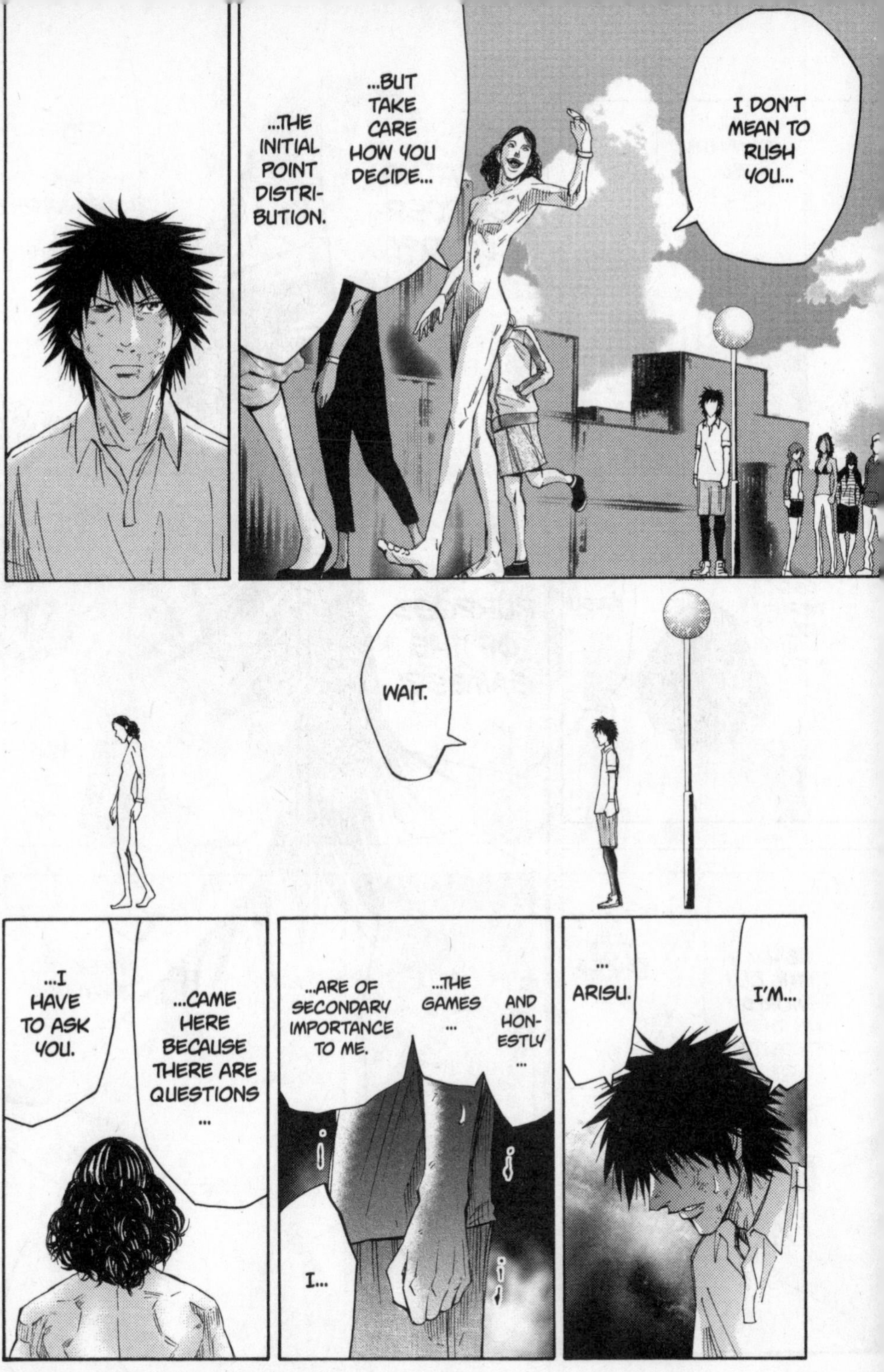
I DON'T MEAN TO RUSH YOU...
...BUT TAKE CARE HOW YOU DECIDE...
...THE INITIAL POINT DISTRIBUTION.
WAIT.
I'M...
...ARISU.
AND HONESTLY...
...THE GAMES...
...ARE OF SECONDARY IMPORTANCE TO ME.
I...
...CAME HERE BECAUSE THERE ARE QUESTIONS...
...I HAVE TO ASK YOU.

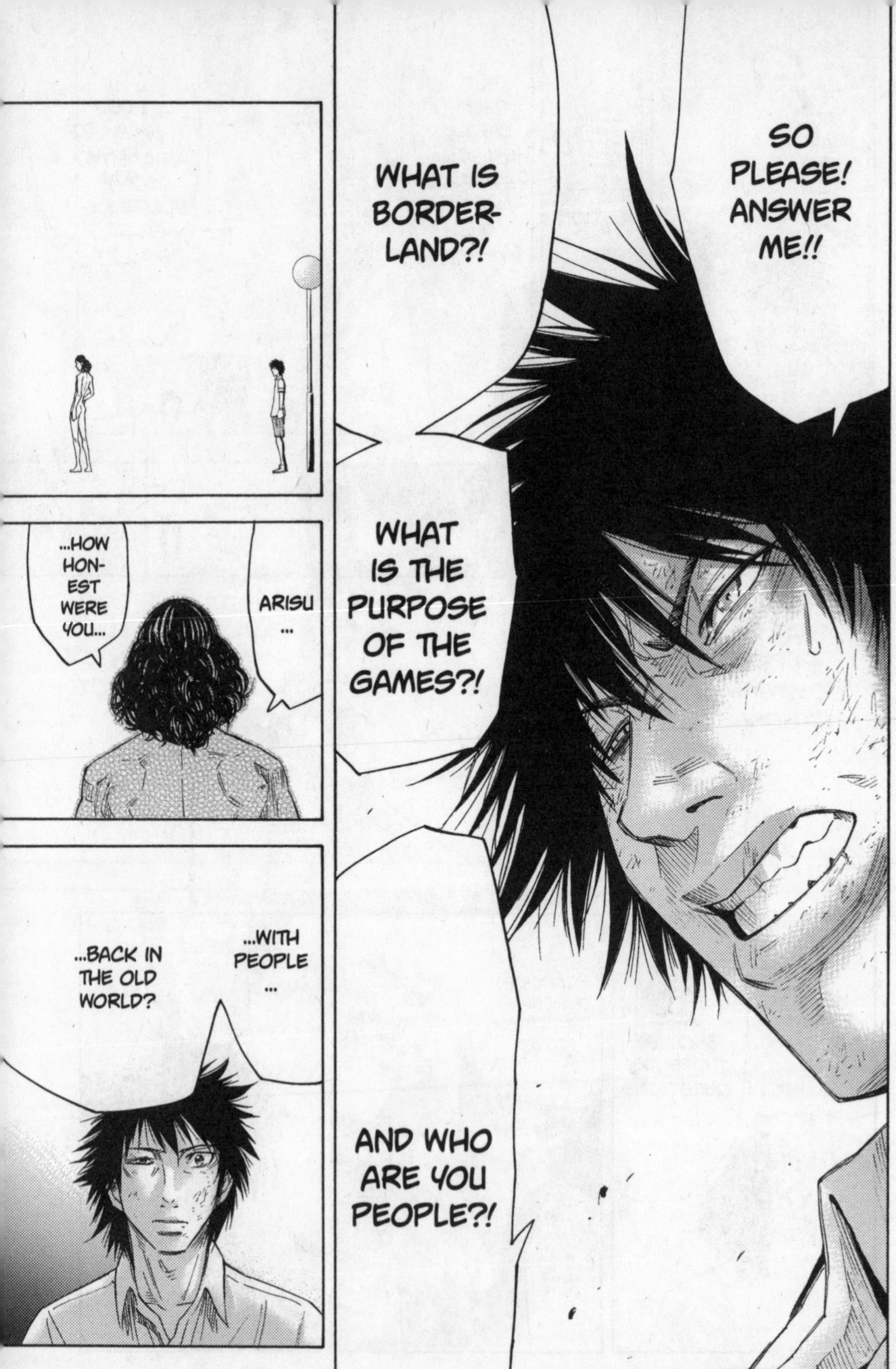
SO PLEASE! ANSWER ME!!
WHAT IS BORDER-LAND?!
WHAT IS THE PURPOSE OF THE GAMES?!
AND WHO ARE YOU PEOPLE?!
ARISU ...
...HOW HON-EST WERE YOU...
...WITH PEOPLE ...
...BACK IN THE OLD WORLD?

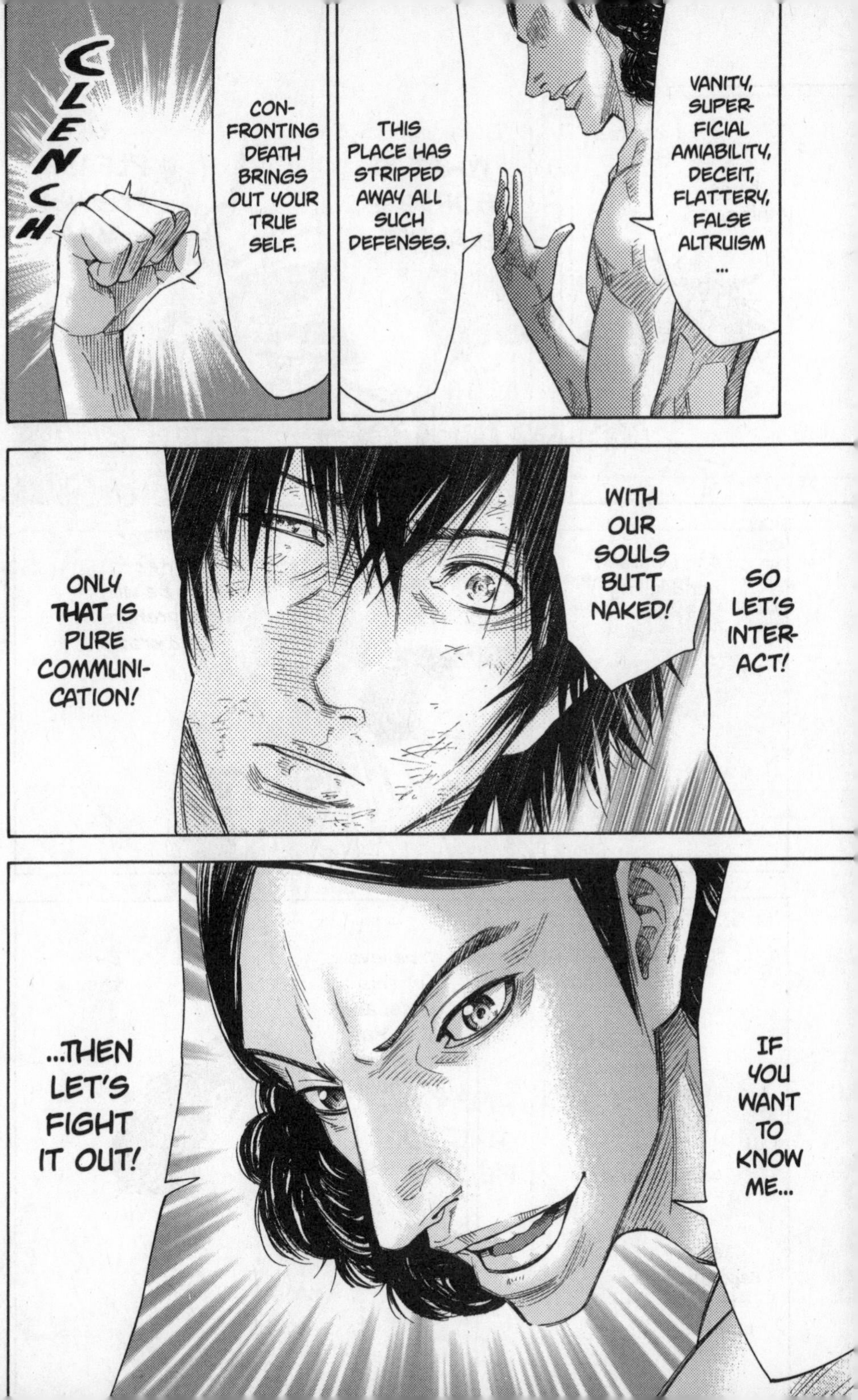
VANITY, SUPERFICIAL AMIABILITY, DECEIT, FLATTERY, FALSE ALTRUISM ...
THIS PLACE HAS STRIPPED AWAY ALL SUCH DEFENSES.
CONFRONTING DEATH BRINGS OUT YOUR TRUE SELF.
CLENCH
SO LET'S INTERACT!
WITH OUR SOULS BUTT NAKED!
ONLY THAT IS PURE COMMUNICATION!
IF YOU WANT TO KNOW ME...
...THEN LET'S FIGHT IT OUT!

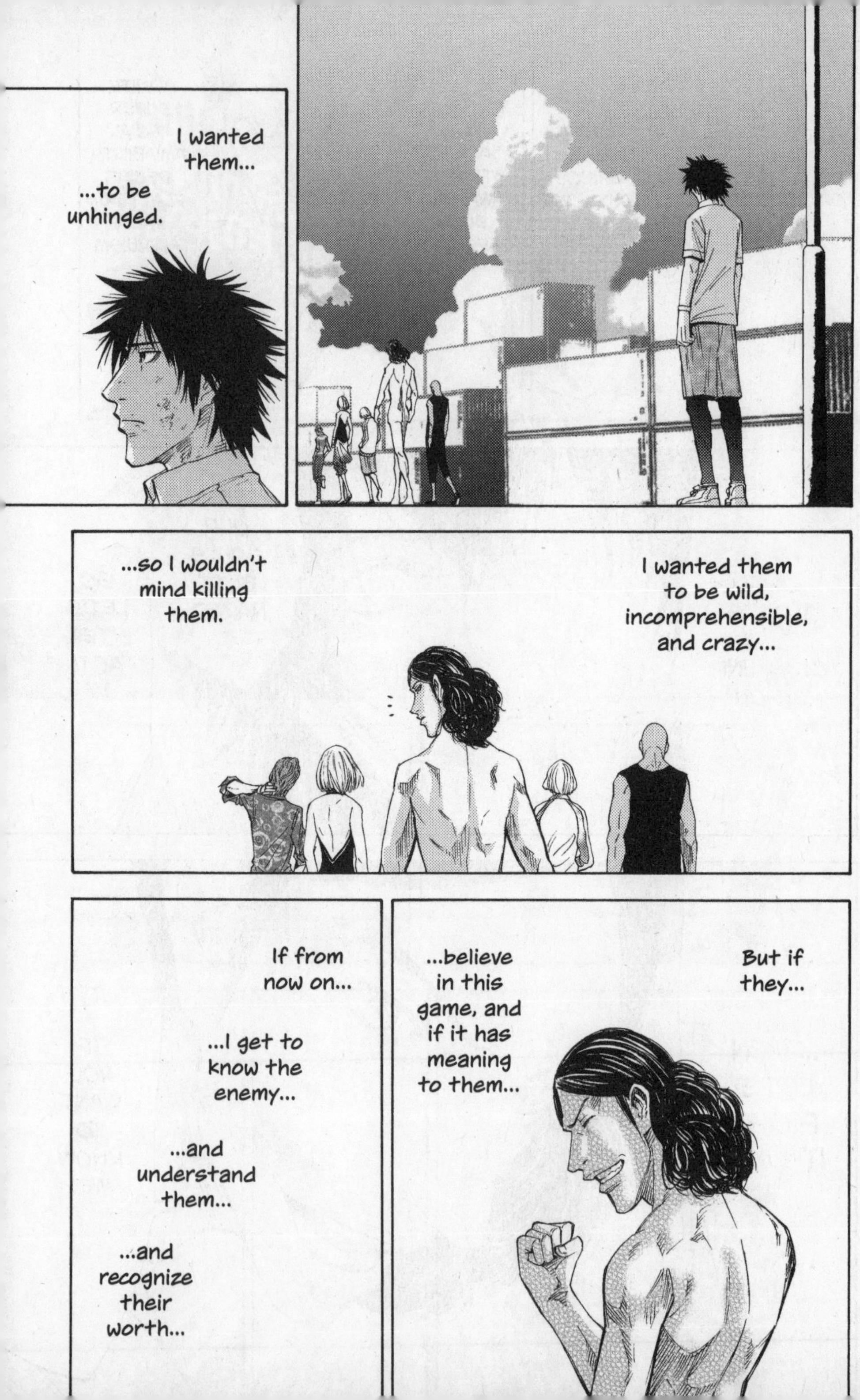
I wanted them...
...to be unhinged.
I wanted them to be wild, incomprehensible, and crazy...
...so I wouldn't mind killing them.
But if they...
...believe in this game, and if it has meaning to them...
If from now on...
...I get to know the enemy...
...and understand them...
...and recognize their worth...

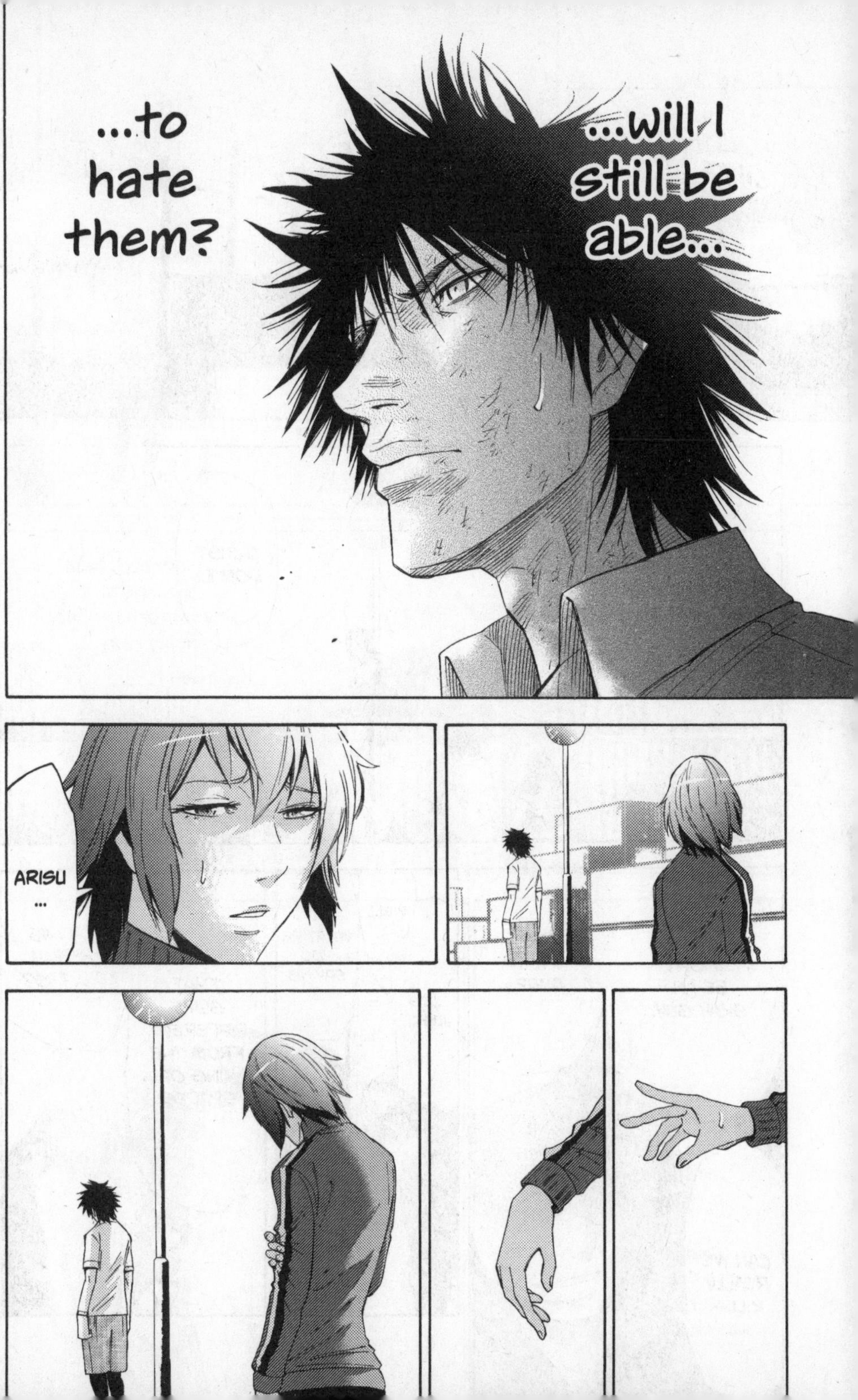
...will I still be able...
...to hate them?
ARISU ...

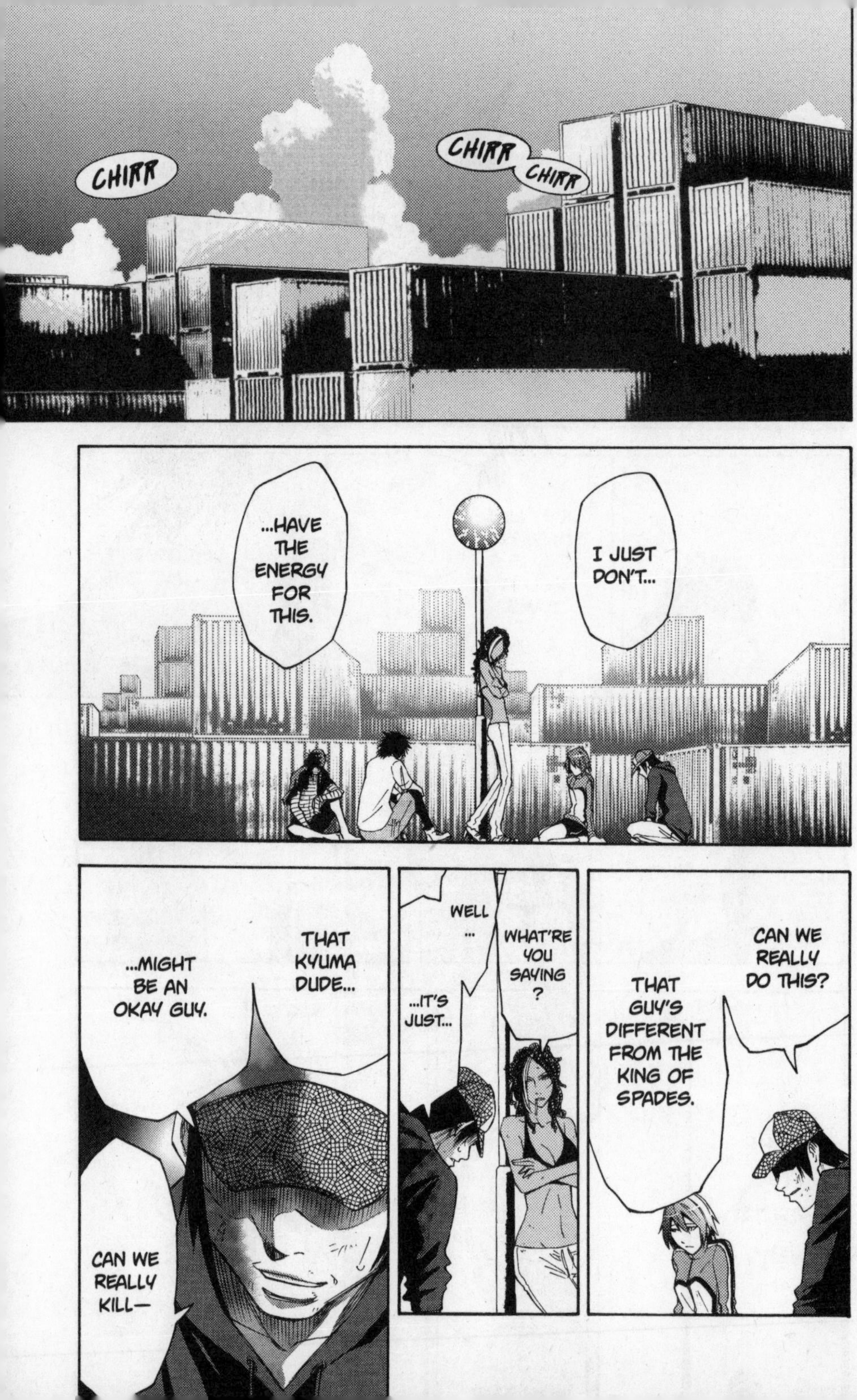
CHIRR
CHIRR
CHIRR
I JUST DON'T...
...HAVE THE ENERGY FOR THIS.
CAN WE REALLY DO THIS?
THAT GUY'S DIFFERENT FROM THE KING OF SPADES.
WHAT'RE YOU SAYING?
WELL...
...IT'S JUST...
THAT KYUMA DUDE...
...MIGHT BE AN OKAY GUY.
CAN WE REALLY KILL—

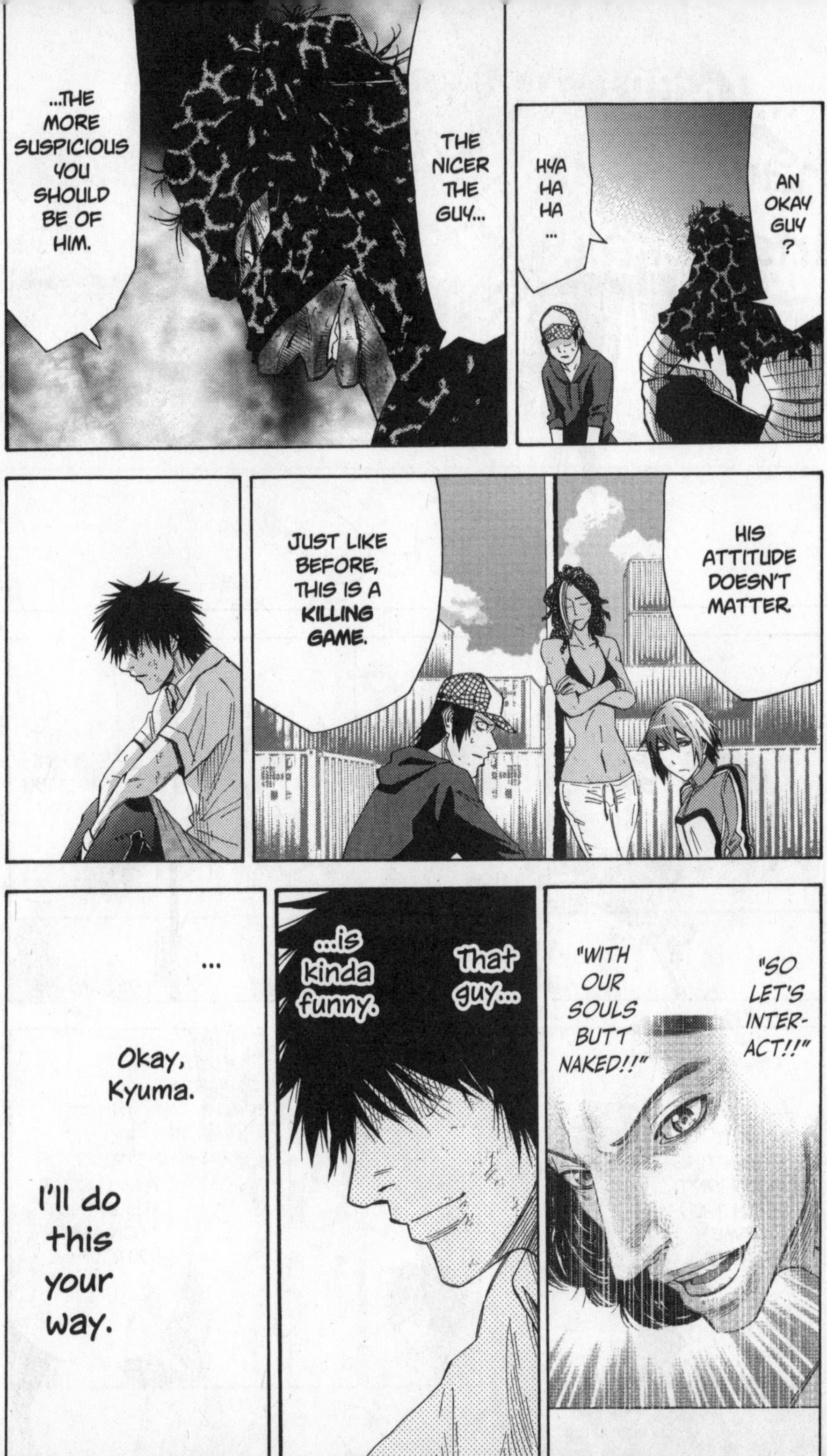
AN OKAY GUY?
HYA HA HA ...
THE NICER THE GUY...
...THE MORE SUSPICIOUS YOU SHOULD BE OF HIM.
HIS ATTITUDE DOESN'T MATTER.
JUST LIKE BEFORE, THIS IS A KILLING GAME.
"SO LET'S INTER-ACT!!"
"WITH OUR SOULS BUTT NAKED!!"
That guy...
...is kinda funny.
...
Okay, Kyuma.
I'll do this your way.

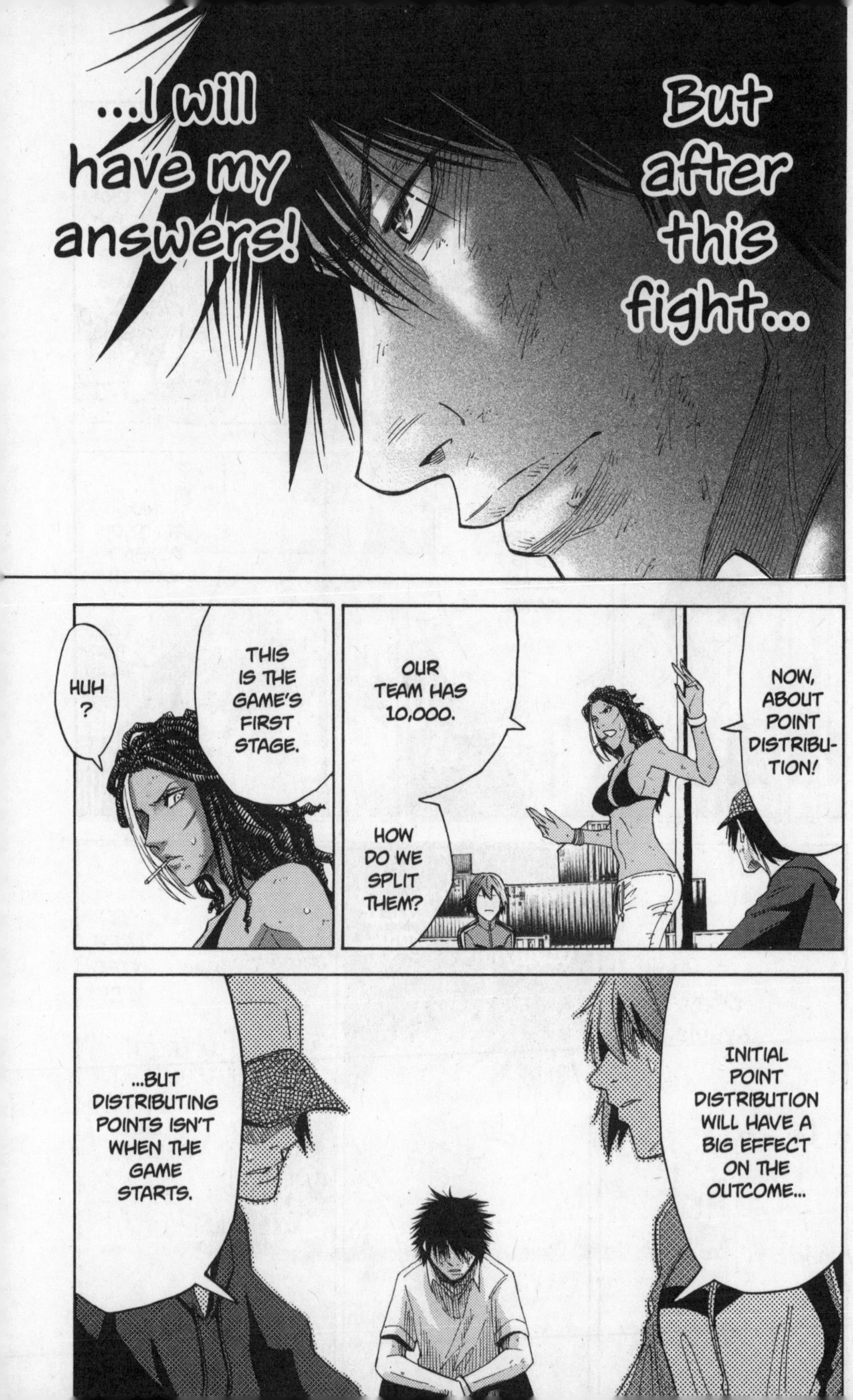
But after this fight...
...I will have my answers!
NOW, ABOUT POINT DISTRIBUTION!
OUR TEAM HAS 10,000.
HOW DO WE SPLIT THEM?
THIS IS THE GAME'S FIRST STAGE.
HUH?
INITIAL POINT DISTRIBUTION WILL HAVE A BIG EFFECT ON THE OUTCOME...
...BUT DISTRIBUTING POINTS ISN'T WHEN THE GAME STARTS.

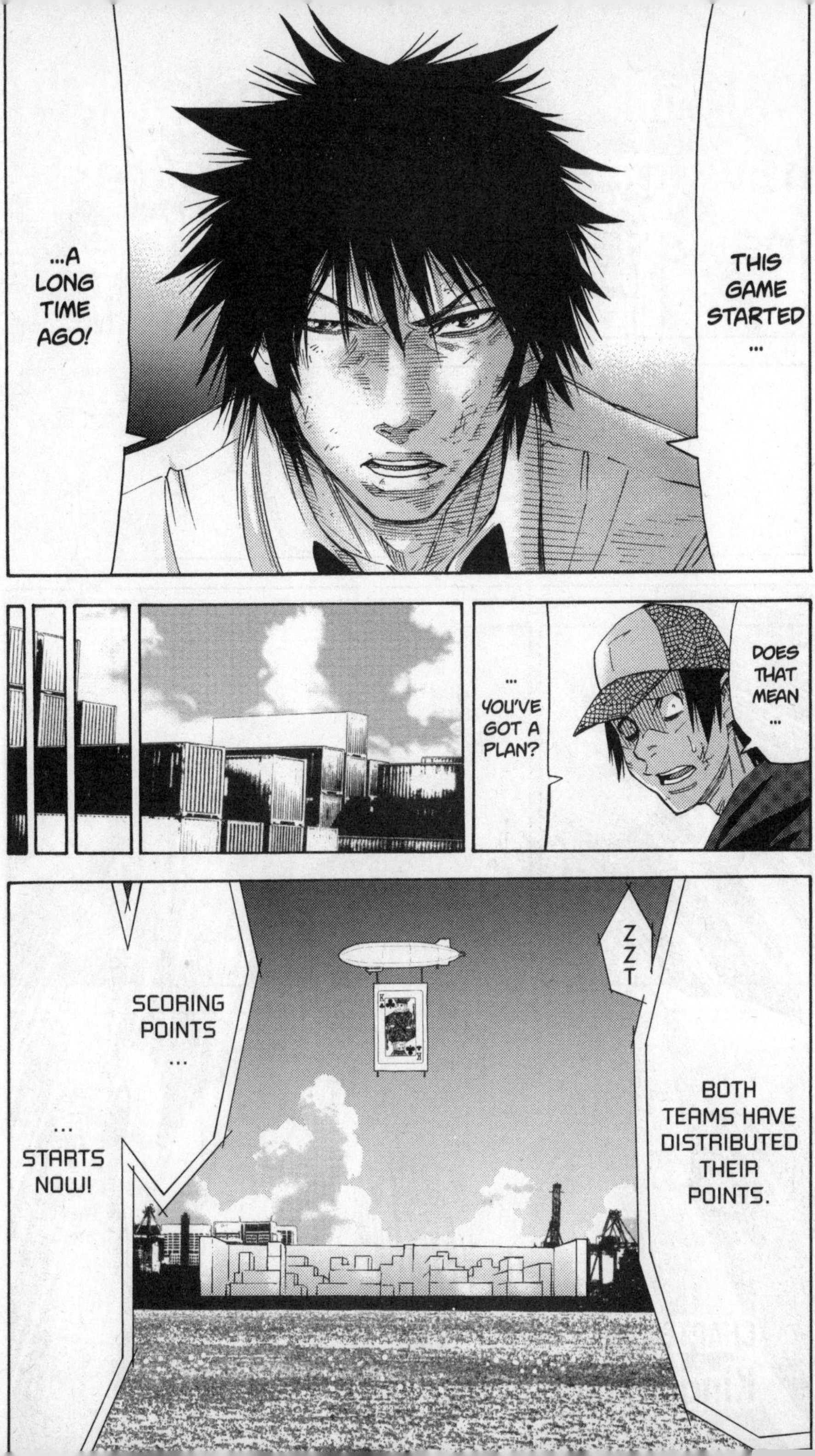
THIS GAME STARTED ...
...A LONG TIME AGO!
DOES THAT MEAN ...
... YOU'VE GOT A PLAN?
ZZT
BOTH TEAMS HAVE DISTRIBUTED THEIR POINTS.
SCORING POINTS ...
... STARTS NOW!

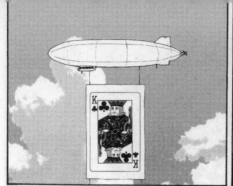

GAME: SCORING POINTS

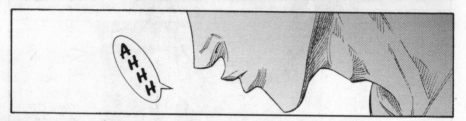

AHHH

CHAPTER 34:
King of Clubs, Part 2

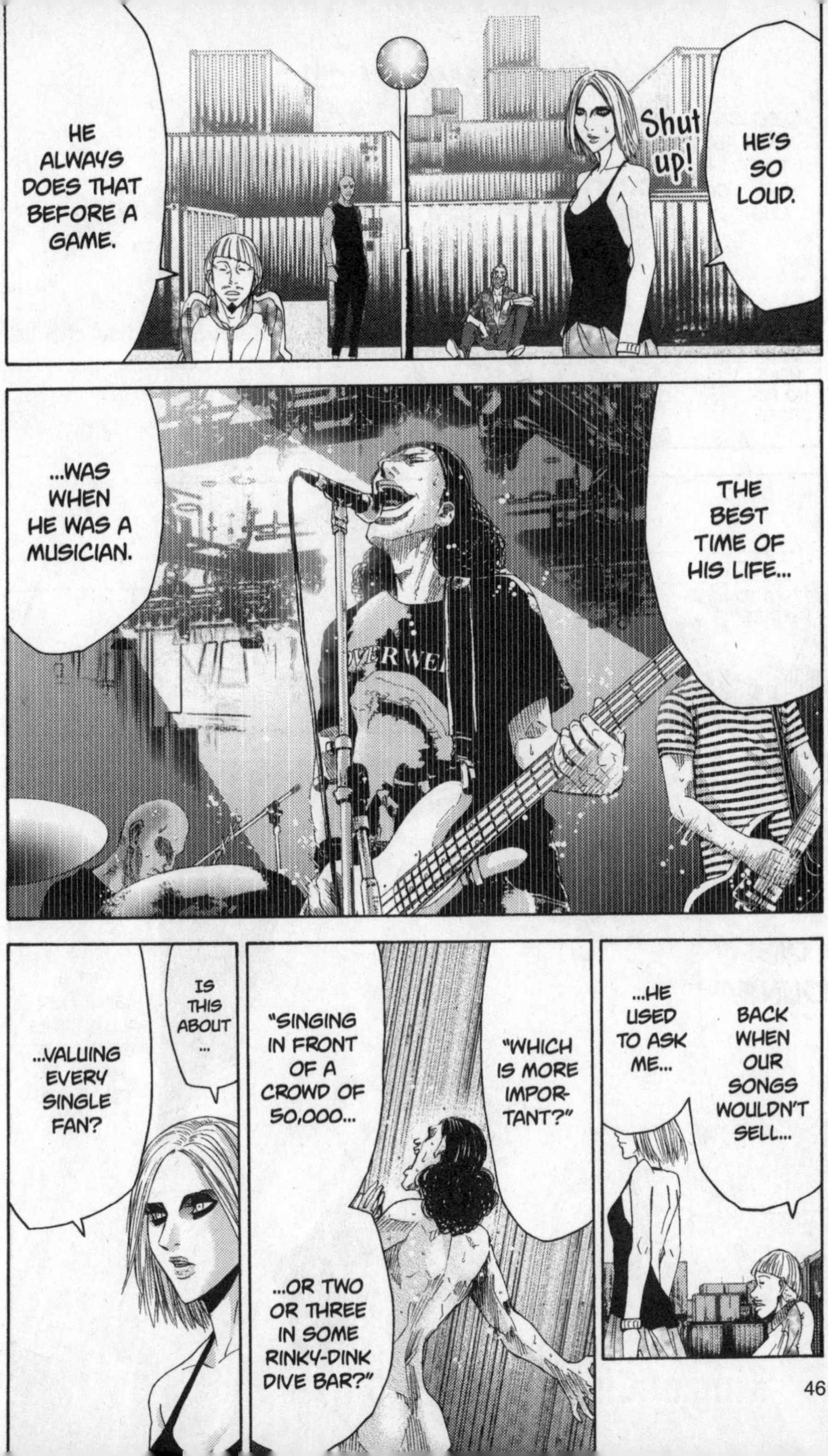
HE'S SO LOUD.
Shut up!
HE ALWAYS DOES THAT BEFORE A GAME.
THE BEST TIME OF HIS LIFE...
...WAS WHEN HE WAS A MUSICIAN.
BACK WHEN OUR SONGS WOULDN'T SELL...
...HE USED TO ASK ME...
"WHICH IS MORE IMPOR-TANT?"
"SINGING IN FRONT OF A CROWD OF 50,000...
...OR TWO OR THREE IN SOME RINKY-DINK DIVE BAR?"
IS THIS ABOUT ...
...VALUING EVERY SINGLE FAN?

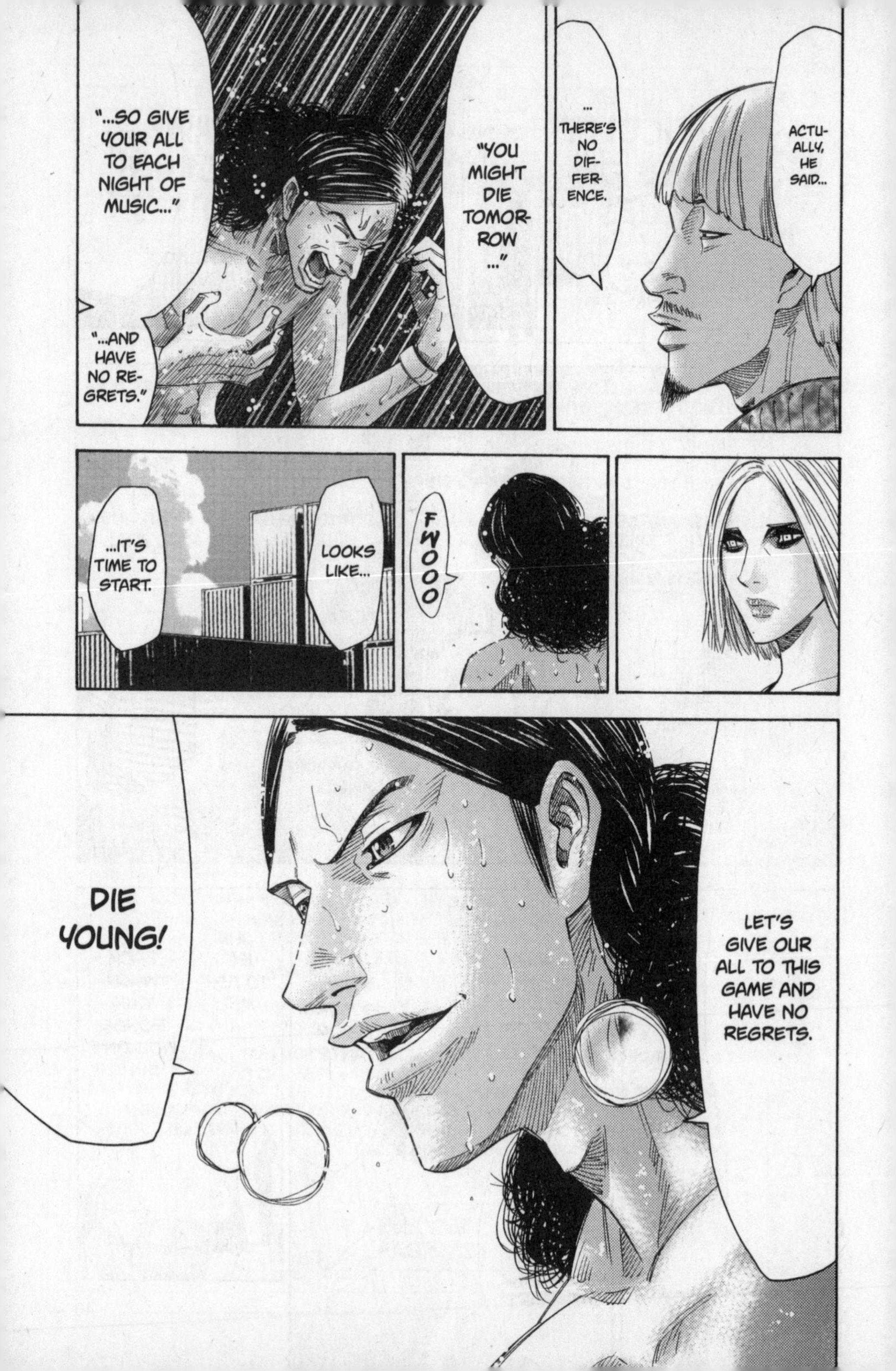
ACTU-ALLY, HE SAID...
... THERE'S NO DIF-FER-ENCE.
"YOU MIGHT DIE TOMOR-ROW ..."
"...SO GIVE YOUR ALL TO EACH NIGHT OF MUSIC..."
"...AND HAVE NO RE-GRETS."
FWOOO
LOOKS LIKE...
...IT'S TIME TO START.
LET'S GIVE OUR ALL TO THIS GAME AND HAVE NO REGRETS.
DIE YOUNG!

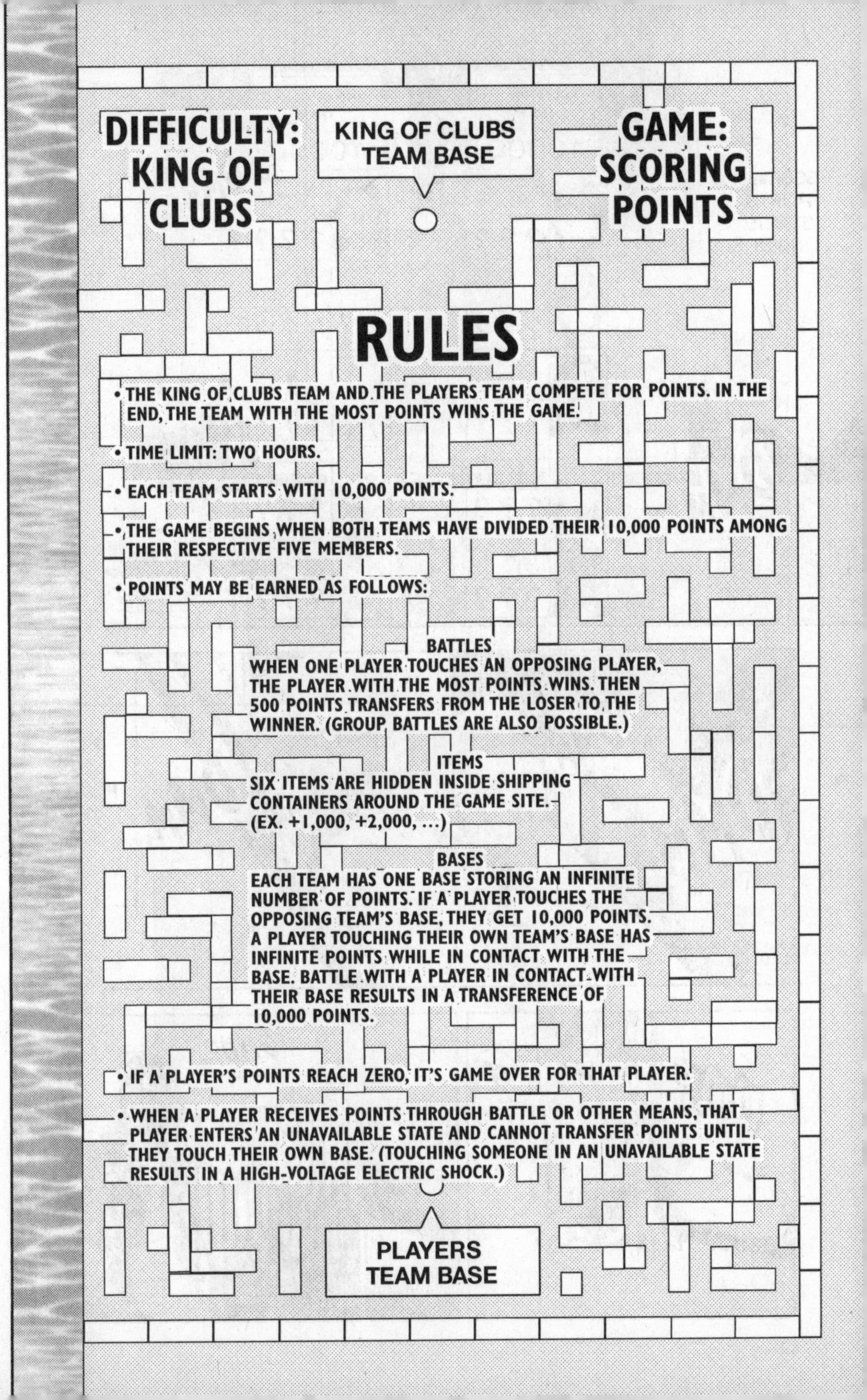
DIFFICULTY: KING OF CLUBS
KING OF CLUBS TEAM BASE
GAME: SCORING POINTS
RULES
• THE KING OF CLUBS TEAM AND THE PLAYERS TEAM COMPETE FOR POINTS. IN THE END, THE TEAM WITH THE MOST POINTS WINS THE GAME.
• TIME LIMIT: TWO HOURS.
• EACH TEAM STARTS WITH 10,000 POINTS.
• THE GAME BEGINS WHEN BOTH TEAMS HAVE DIVIDED THEIR 10,000 POINTS AMONG THEIR RESPECTIVE FIVE MEMBERS.
• POINTS MAY BE EARNED AS FOLLOWS:
BATTLES
WHEN ONE PLAYER TOUCHES AN OPPOSING PLAYER, THE PLAYER WITH THE MOST POINTS WINS. THEN 500 POINTS TRANSFERS FROM THE LOSER TO THE WINNER. (GROUP BATTLES ARE ALSO POSSIBLE.)
ITEMS
SIX ITEMS ARE HIDDEN INSIDE SHIPPING CONTAINERS AROUND THE GAME SITE. (EX. +1,000, +2,000, ...)
BASES
EACH TEAM HAS ONE BASE STORING AN INFINITE NUMBER OF POINTS. IF A PLAYER TOUCHES THE OPPOSING TEAM'S BASE, THEY GET 10,000 POINTS. A PLAYER TOUCHING THEIR OWN TEAM'S BASE HAS INFINITE POINTS WHILE IN CONTACT WITH THE BASE. BATTLE WITH A PLAYER IN CONTACT WITH THEIR BASE RESULTS IN A TRANSFERENCE OF 10,000 POINTS.
• IF A PLAYER'S POINTS REACH ZERO, IT'S GAME OVER FOR THAT PLAYER.
• WHEN A PLAYER RECEIVES POINTS THROUGH BATTLE OR OTHER MEANS, THAT PLAYER ENTERS AN UNAVAILABLE STATE AND CANNOT TRANSFER POINTS UNTIL THEY TOUCH THEIR OWN BASE. (TOUCHING SOMEONE IN AN UNAVAILABLE STATE RESULTS IN A HIGH-VOLTAGE ELECTRIC SHOCK.)
PLAYERS TEAM BASE

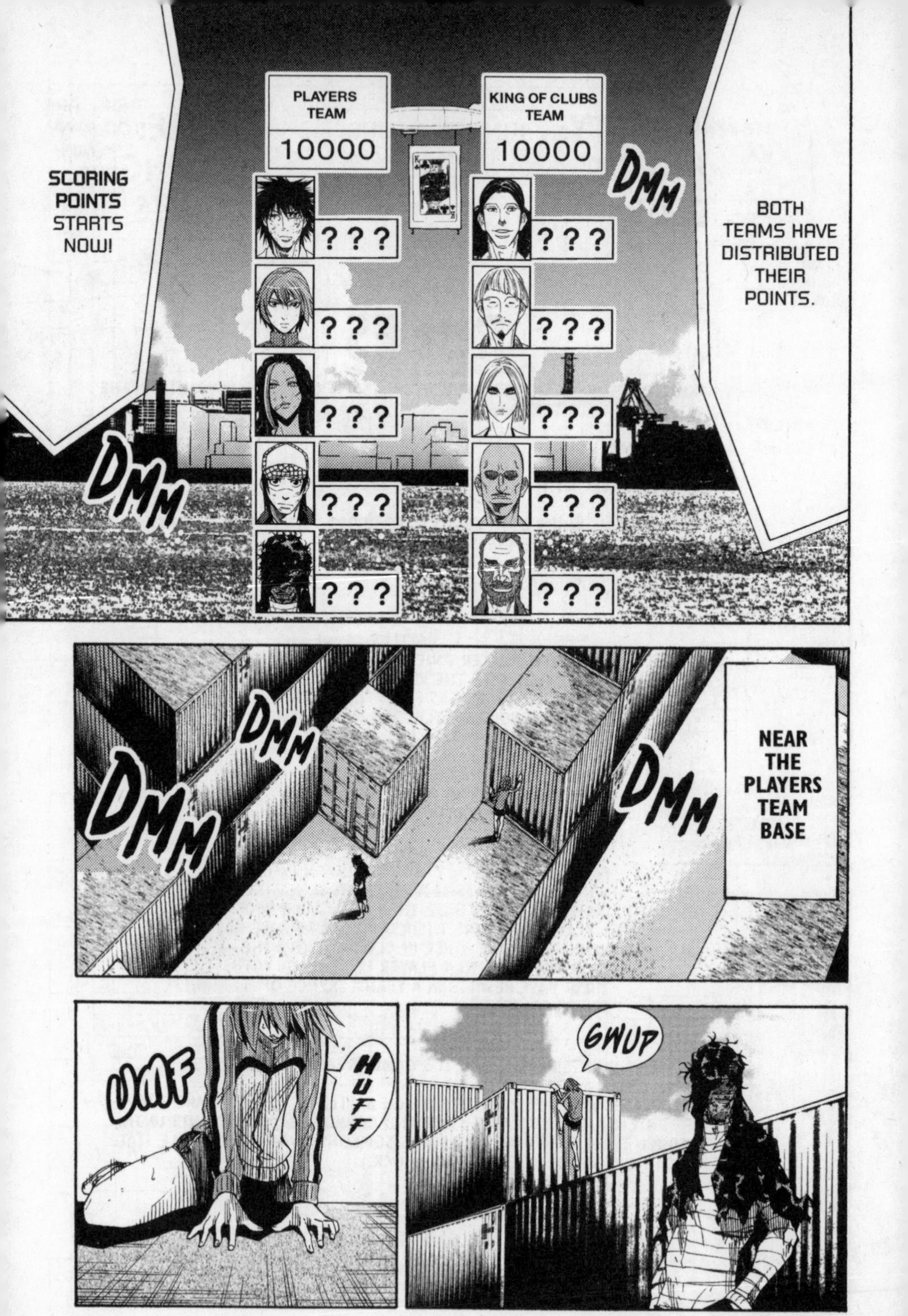
BOTH TEAMS HAVE DISTRIBUTED THEIR POINTS.
DMM
PLAYERS TEAM
10000
KING OF CLUBS TEAM
10000
???
???
???
???
???
???
???
???
???
???
SCORING POINTS STARTS NOW!
DMM
NEAR THE PLAYERS TEAM BASE
DMM
DMM
DMM
GWUP
HUFF HUFF
UMF

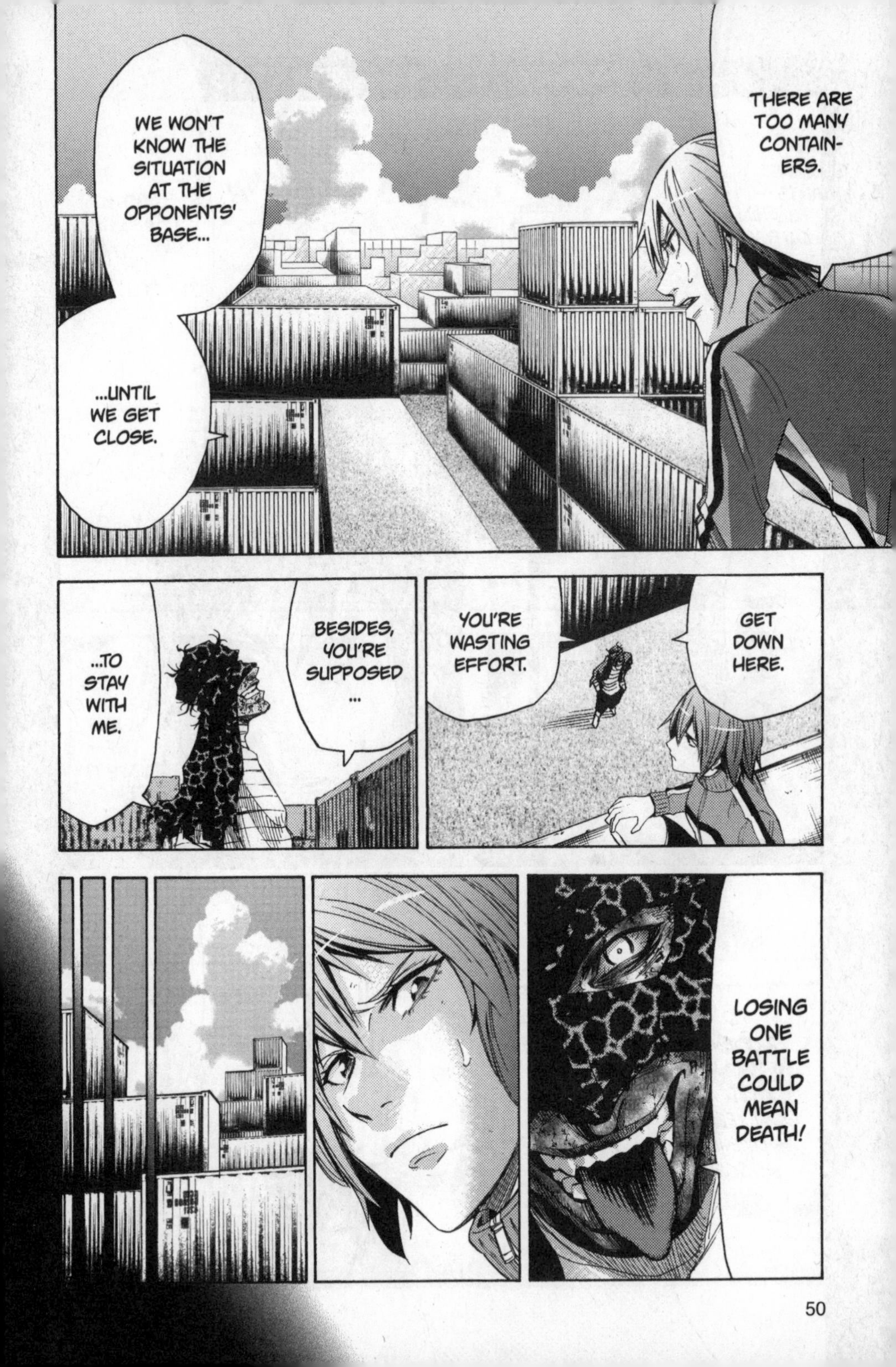
THERE ARE TOO MANY CONTAIN-ERS.
WE WON'T KNOW THE SITUATION AT THE OPPONENTS' BASE...
...UNTIL WE GET CLOSE.
GET DOWN HERE.
YOU'RE WASTING EFFORT.
BESIDES, YOU'RE SUPPOSED ...
...TO STAY WITH ME.
LOSING ONE BATTLE COULD MEAN DEATH!

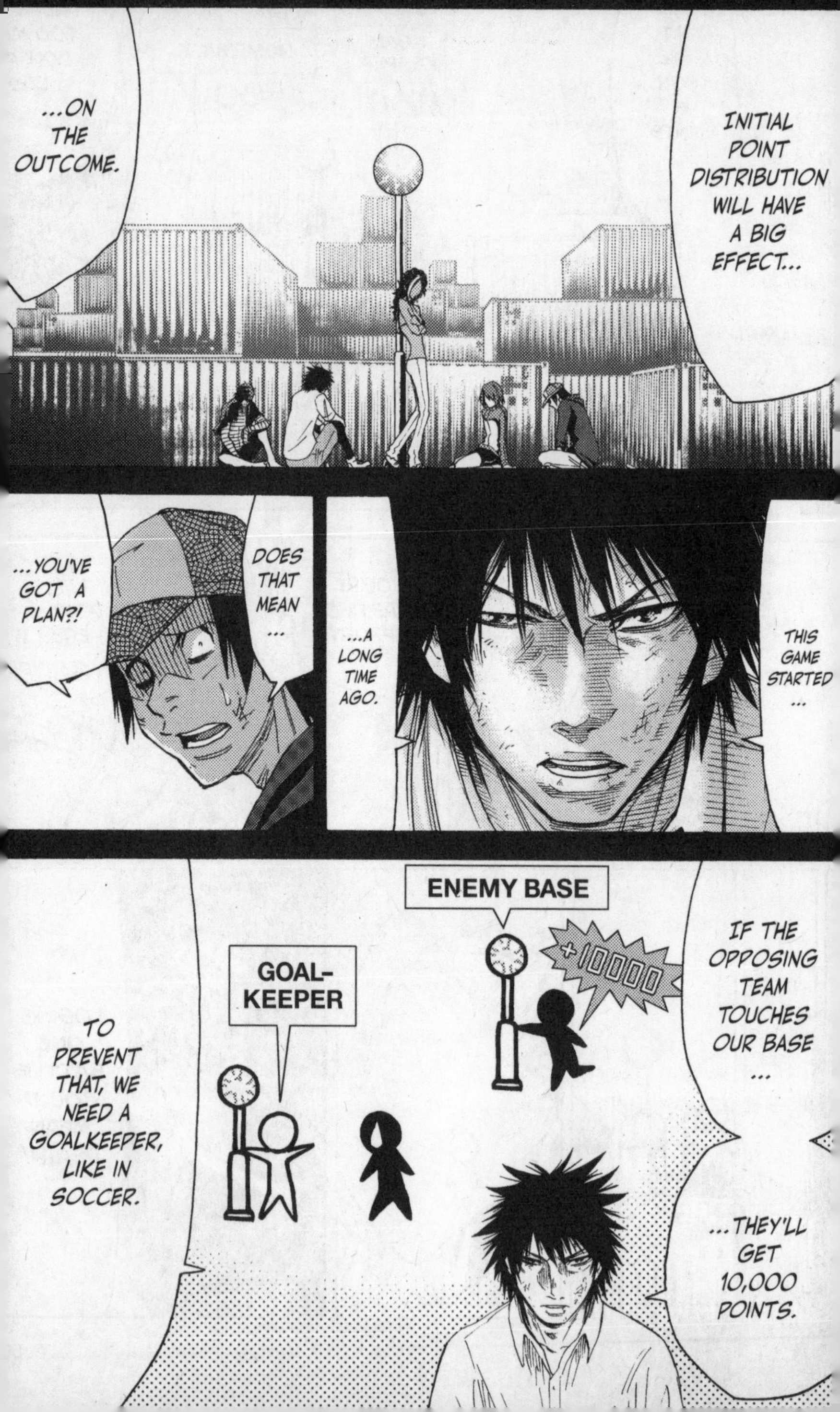

INITIAL POINT DISTRIBUTION WILL HAVE A BIG EFFECT...
...ON THE OUTCOME.
THIS GAME STARTED ...
...A LONG TIME AGO.
DOES THAT MEAN ...
...YOU'VE GOT A PLAN?!
IF THE OPPOSING TEAM TOUCHES OUR BASE ...
ENEMY BASE
+10000
...THEY'LL GET 10,000 POINTS.
GOAL-KEEPER
TO PREVENT THAT, WE NEED A GOALKEEPER, LIKE IN SOCCER.

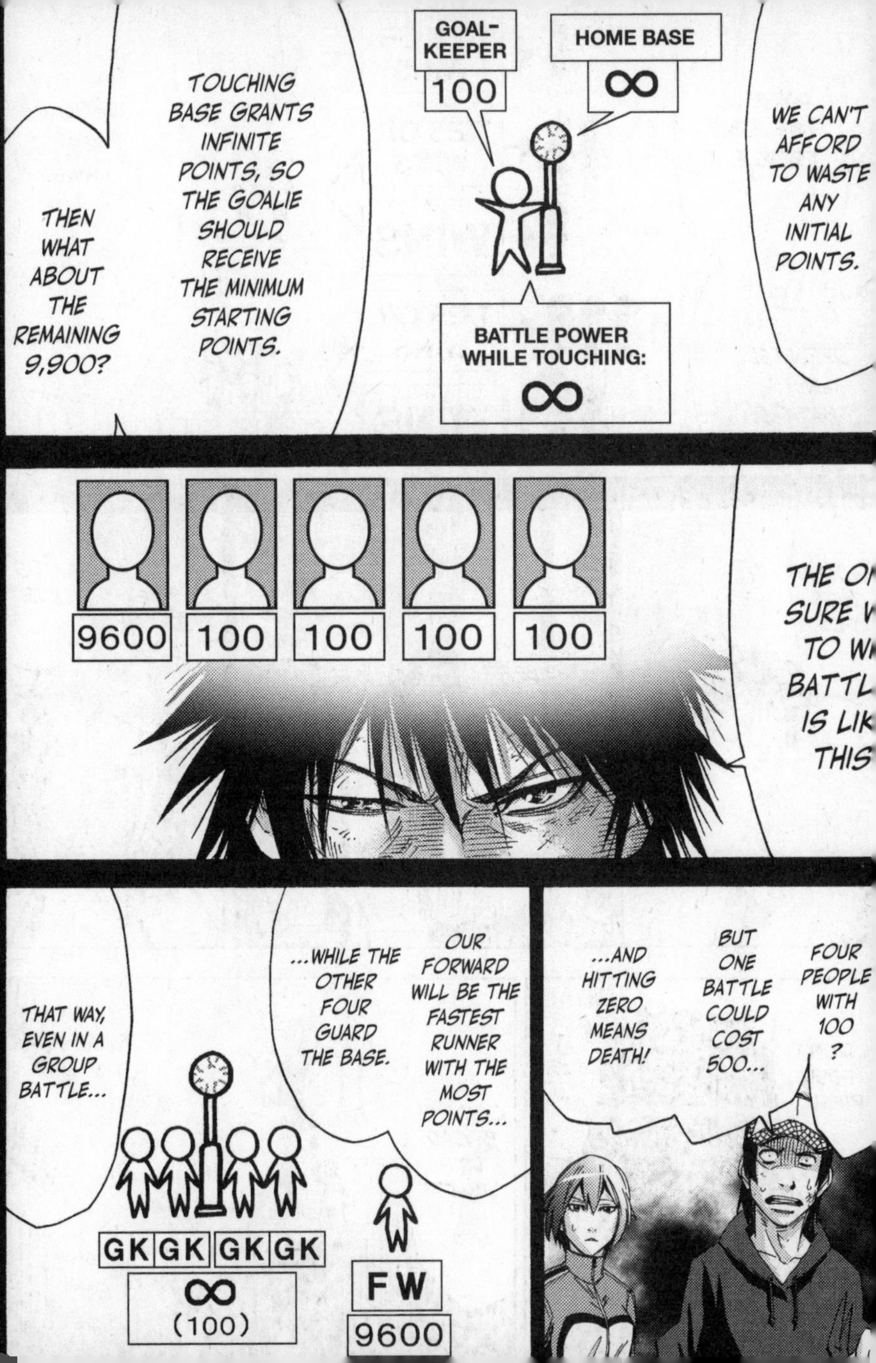
WE CAN'T AFFORD TO WASTE ANY INITIAL POINTS.
HOME BASE
∞
GOAL-KEEPER
100
BATTLE POWER WHILE TOUCHING:
∞
TOUCHING BASE GRANTS INFINITE POINTS, SO THE GOALIE SHOULD RECEIVE THE MINIMUM STARTING POINTS.
THEN WHAT ABOUT THE REMAINING 9,900?
THE O SURE W TO W BATTL IS LIK THIS
9600
100
100
100
100
FOUR PEOPLE WITH 100?
BUT ONE BATTLE COULD COST 500...
...AND HITTING ZERO MEANS DEATH!
OUR FORWARD WILL BE THE FASTEST RUNNER WITH THE MOST POINTS...
...WHILE THE OTHER FOUR GUARD THE BASE.
THAT WAY, EVEN IN A GROUP BATTLE...
GK GK GK GK
∞
(100)
FW
9600

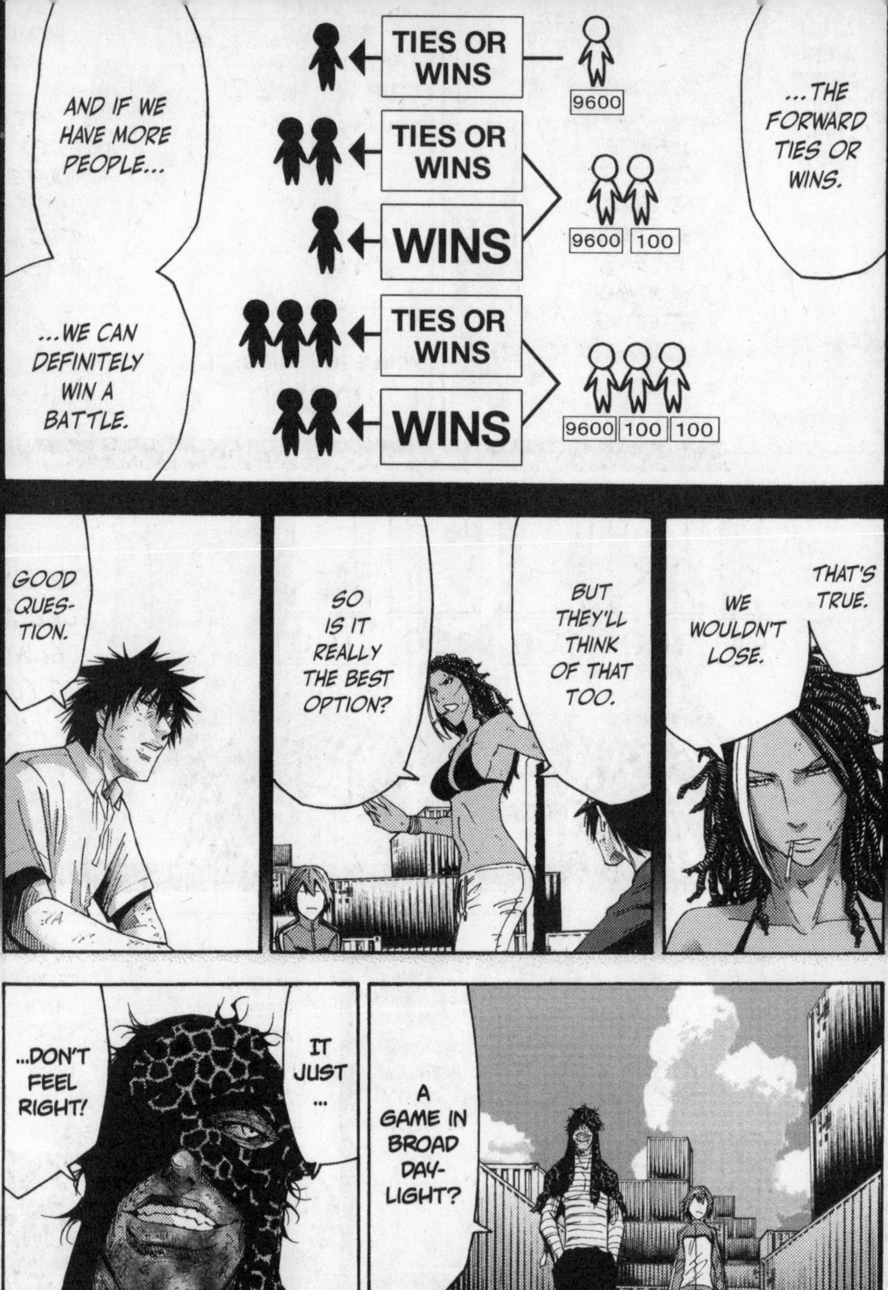
...THE FORWARD TIES OR WINS.
TIES OR WINS
9600
TIES OR WINS
WINS
9600
100
TIES OR WINS
WINS
9600
100
100
AND IF WE HAVE MORE PEOPLE...
...WE CAN DEFINITELY WIN A BATTLE.
THAT'S TRUE.
WE WOULDN'T LOSE.
BUT THEY'LL THINK OF THAT TOO.
SO IS IT REALLY THE BEST OPTION?
GOOD QUES-TION.
A GAME IN BROAD DAY-LIGHT?
IT JUST...
...DON'T FEEL RIGHT!

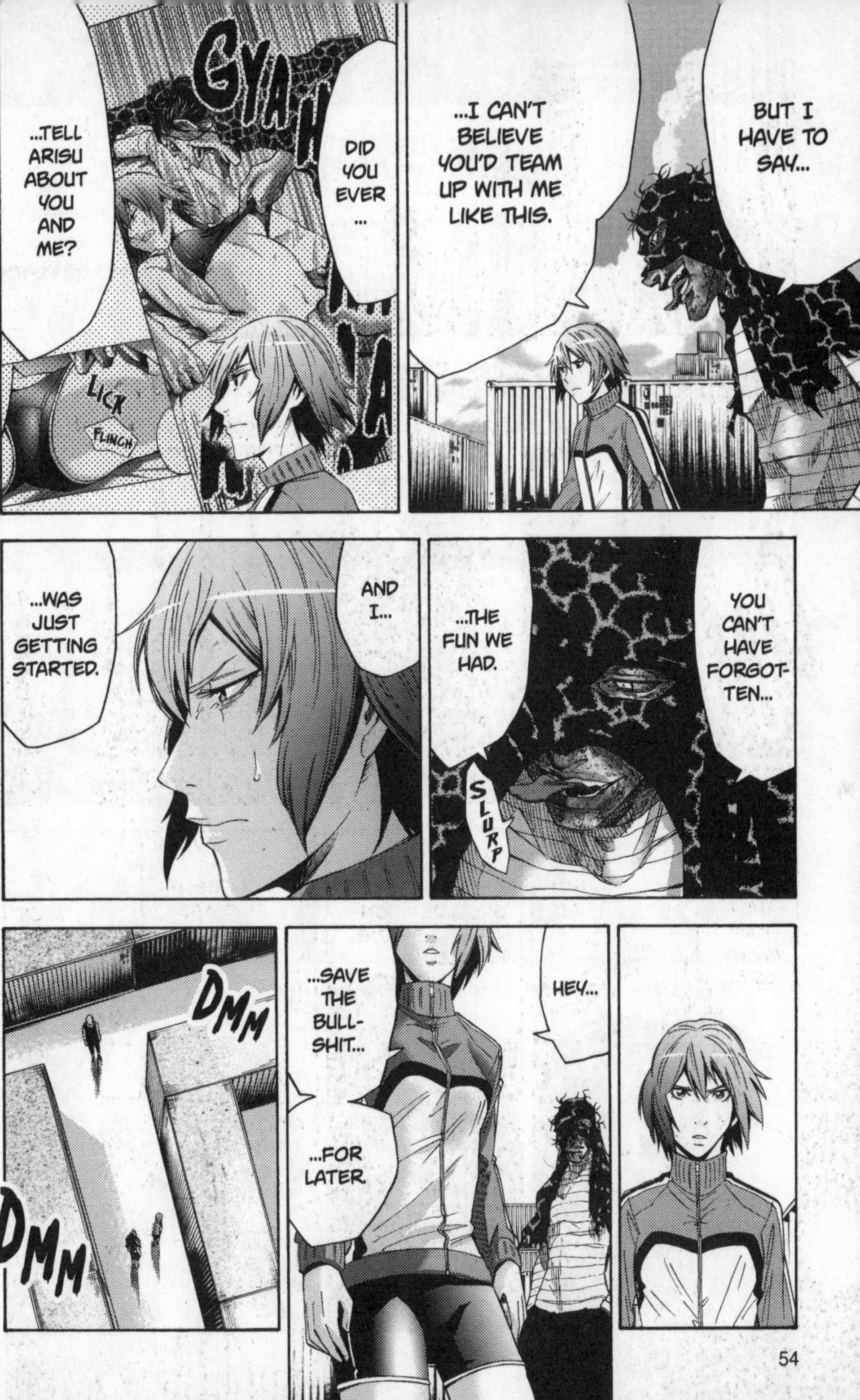

BUT I HAVE TO SAY...
...I CAN'T BELIEVE YOU'D TEAM UP WITH ME LIKE THIS.
DID YOU EVER ...
...TELL ARISU ABOUT YOU AND ME?
GYAH
LICK
FLINCH
YOU CAN'T HAVE FORGOT-TEN...
...THE FUN WE HAD.
SLURP
AND I...
...WAS JUST GETTING STARTED.
HEY...
...SAVE THE BULL-SHIT...
...FOR LATER.
DMM
DMM

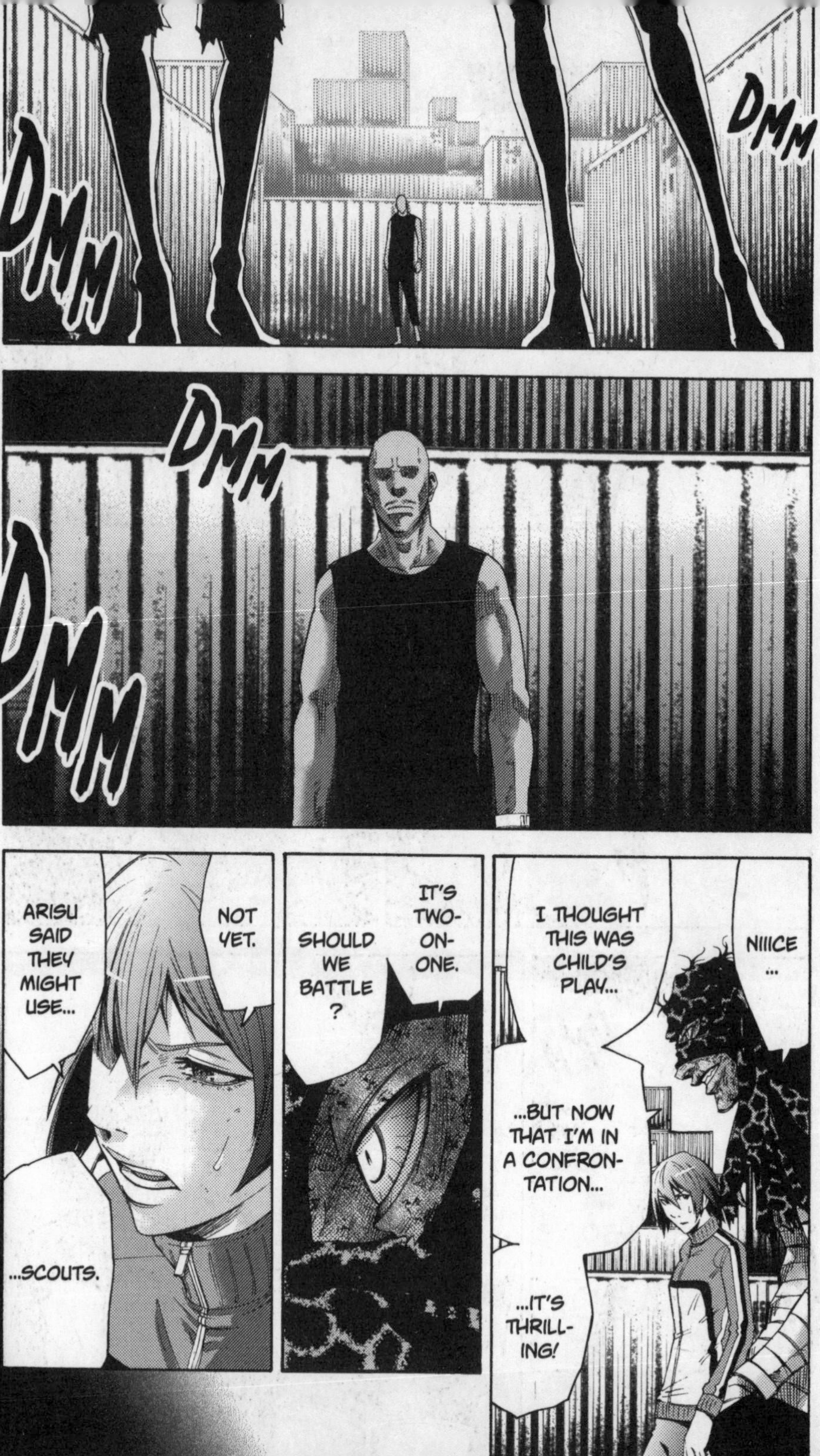
DMM
DMM
DMM
DMM
NIIICE...
I THOUGHT THIS WAS CHILD'S PLAY...
...BUT NOW THAT I'M IN A CONFRONTATION...
...IT'S THRILLING!
IT'S TWO-ON-ONE.
SHOULD WE BATTLE?
NOT YET.
ARISU SAID THEY MIGHT USE...
...SCOUTS.

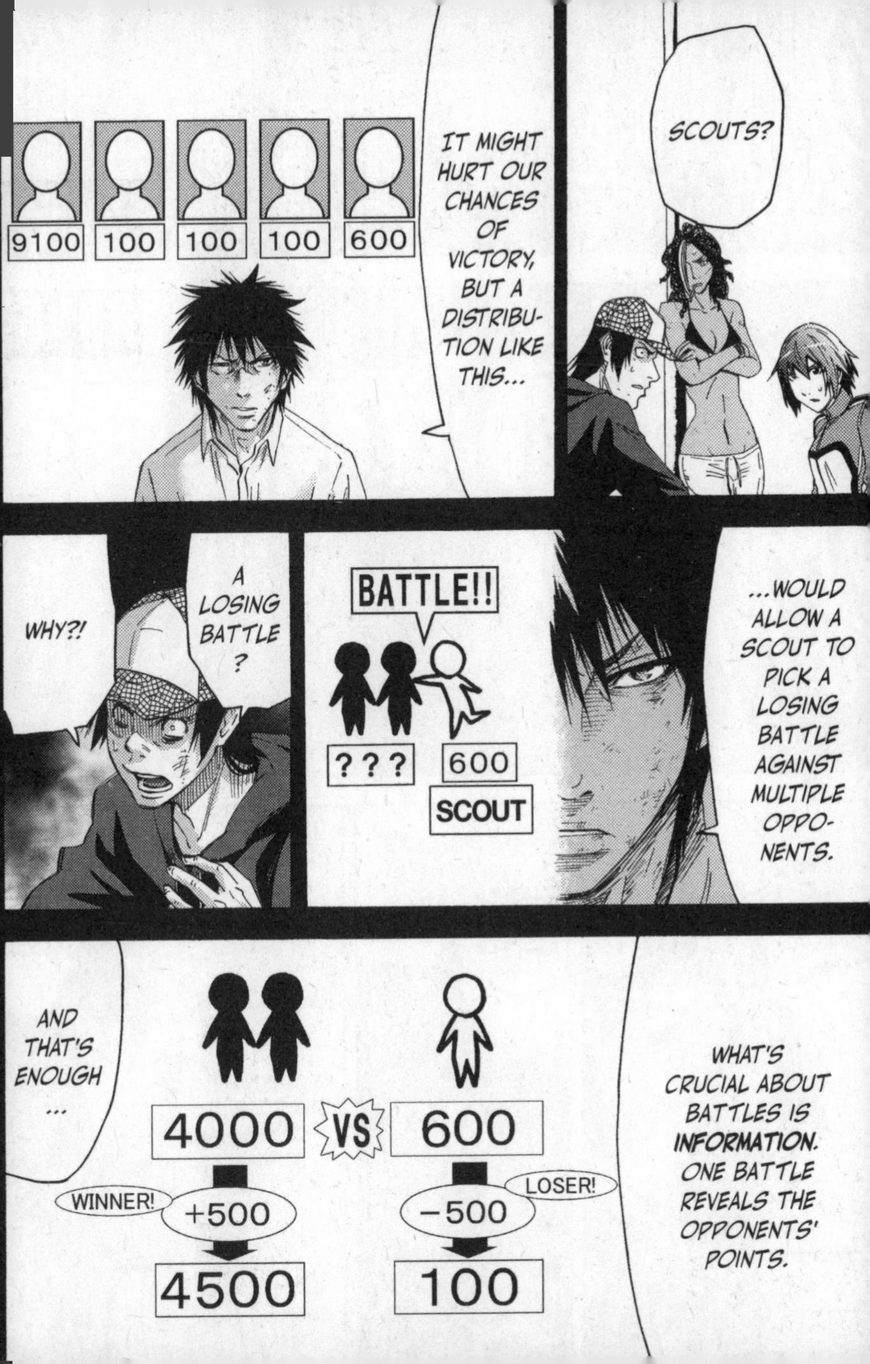
SCOUTS?
IT MIGHT HURT OUR CHANCES OF VICTORY, BUT A DISTRIBUTION LIKE THIS...
9100
100
100
100
600
...WOULD ALLOW A SCOUT TO PICK A LOSING BATTLE AGAINST MULTIPLE OPPONENTS.
BATTLE!!
???
600
SCOUT
A LOSING BATTLE?
WHY?!
WHAT'S CRUCIAL ABOUT BATTLES IS INFORMATION. ONE BATTLE REVEALS THE OPPONENTS' POINTS.
4000
VS
600
WINNER!
+500
LOSER!
−500
4500
100
AND THAT'S ENOUGH...

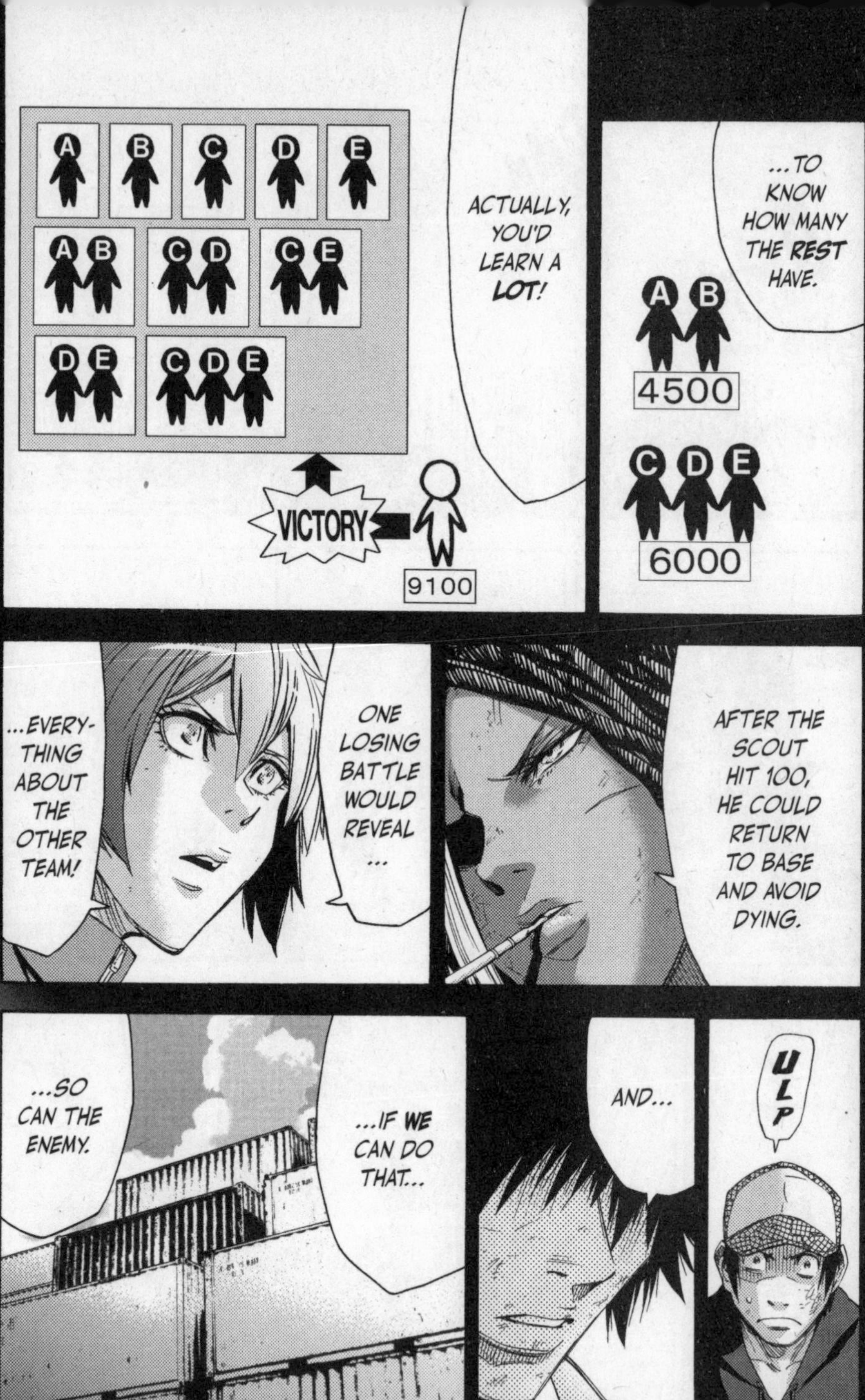
...TO KNOW HOW MANY THE REST HAVE.
A B
4500
C D E
6000
ACTUALLY, YOU'D LEARN A LOT!
A B C D E
A B
C D
C E
D E
C D E
VICTORY
9100
AFTER THE SCOUT HIT 100, HE COULD RETURN TO BASE AND AVOID DYING.
ONE LOSING BATTLE WOULD REVEAL...
...EVERYTHING ABOUT THE OTHER TEAM!
ULP
AND...
...IF WE CAN DO THAT...
...SO CAN THE ENEMY.

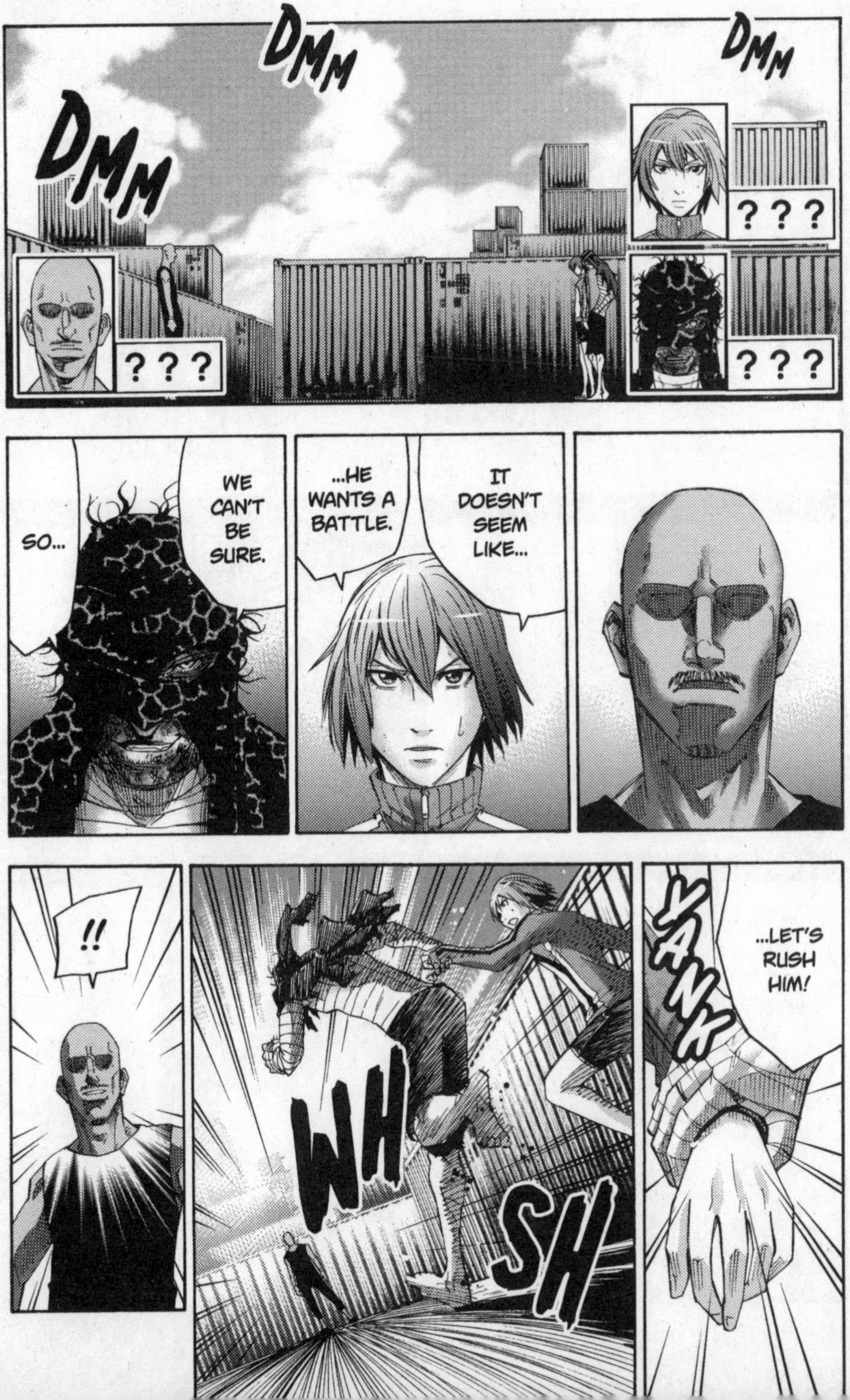
DMM
???
DMM
???
DMM
???
IT DOESN'T SEEM LIKE...
...HE WANTS A BATTLE.
WE CAN'T BE SURE.
SO...
...LET'S RUSH HIM!
YANK
WHSH
!!

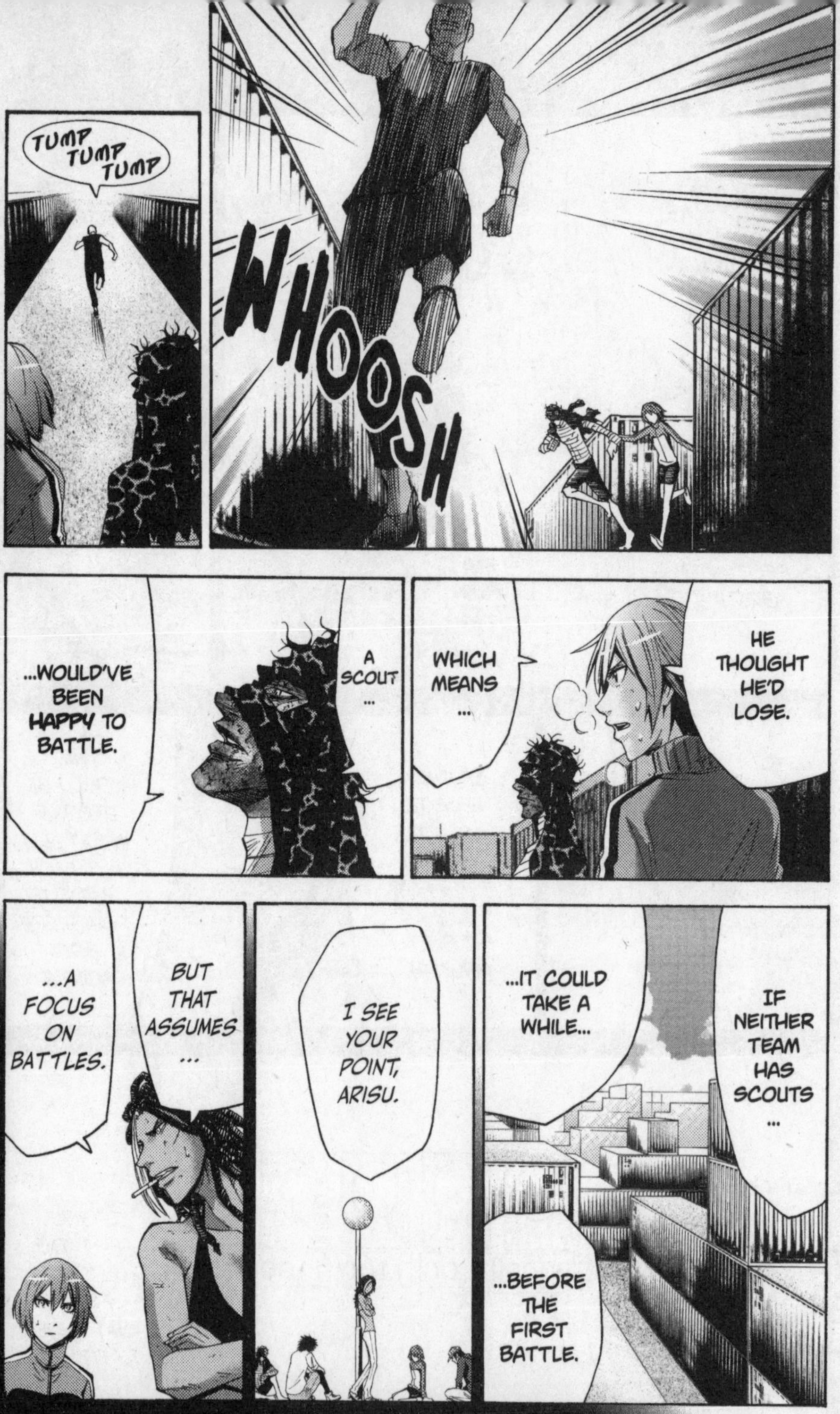
WHOOSH
TUMP TUMP TUMP
HE THOUGHT HE'D LOSE.
WHICH MEANS ...
A SCOUT ...
...WOULD'VE BEEN HAPPY TO BATTLE.
IF NEITHER TEAM HAS SCOUTS ...
...IT COULD TAKE A WHILE...
...BEFORE THE FIRST BATTLE.
I SEE YOUR POINT, ARISU.
BUT THAT ASSUMES ...
...A FOCUS ON BATTLES.

...SO THEY WOULD MOVE AROUND THE VAST GAME SITE IN A GROUP.

BUT THEIR OPPONENTS COULD SPLIT INTO GROUPS TOO.

FW
9100

100 100

ACCORDING TO THAT PLAN, ANYONE BUT THE FORWARD WOULD DIE IN A LOSING BATTLE...

...THE ITEMS.

YES. THE PROBLEM IS...

...SO LOOK AT IT LIKE THIS.

YEAH...

IF THEY WERE TO START SNAGGING ITEMS FOR 1,000 OR 2,000 POINTS...

THAT WOULD BE STRONG IN BATTLE, BUT EACH BATTLE TRANSFERS 500 POINTS.

IF ONE OF THE THREE WITH 1,100 POINTS LOSES A BATTLE...

...THEN FOUR MIGHT SEARCH ALONE FOR ITEMS.

6600	1100	1100	1100	100
FW				**GK**

IF YOU SHIFT THE FOCUS FROM BATTLES TO ITEMS...

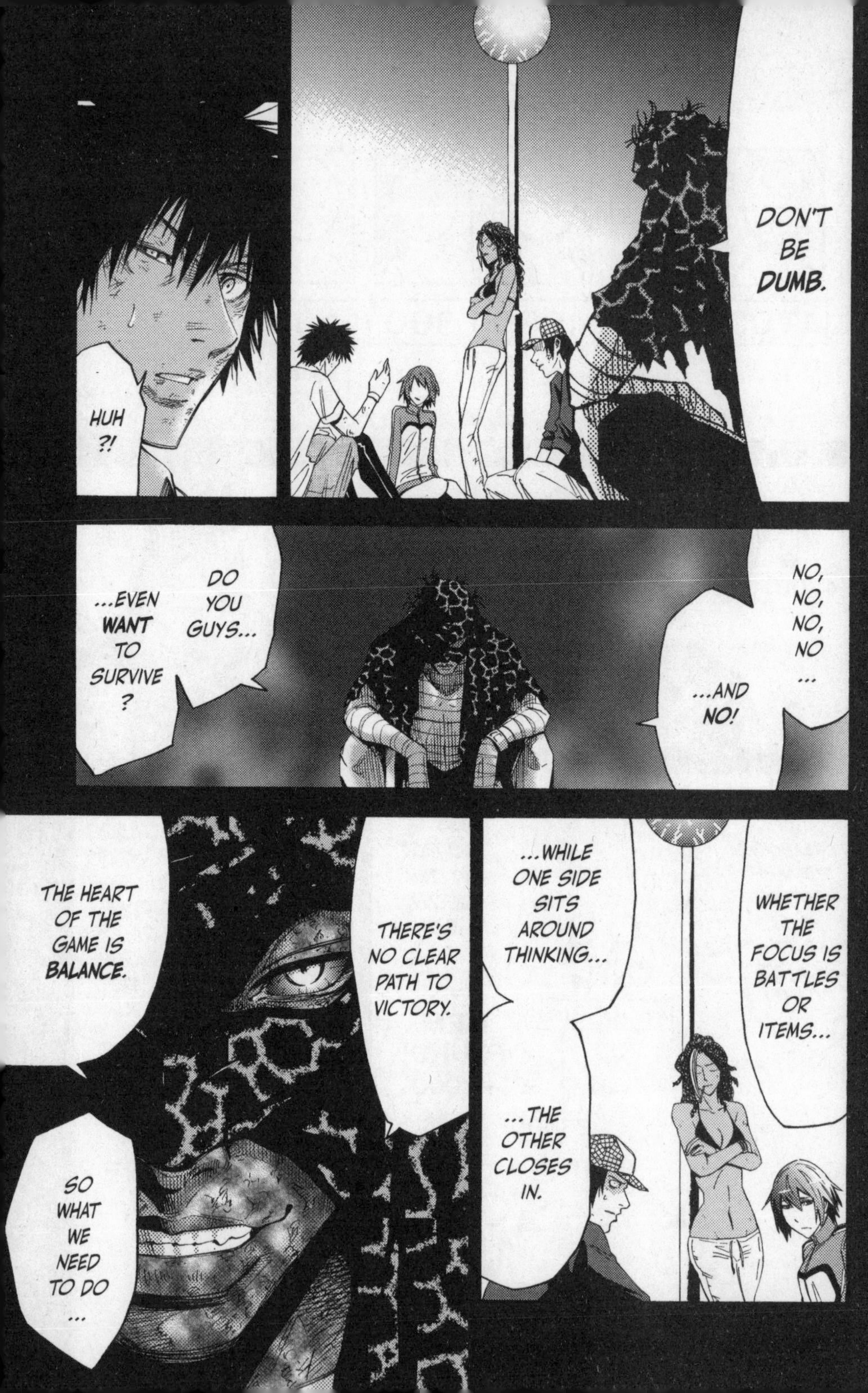
DON'T BE **DUMB.**
HUH ?!
NO, NO, NO, NO ...
...AND **NO!**
DO YOU GUYS...
...EVEN **WANT** TO SURVIVE ?
WHETHER THE FOCUS IS BATTLES OR ITEMS...
...WHILE ONE SIDE SITS AROUND THINKING...
...THE OTHER CLOSES IN.
THERE'S NO CLEAR PATH TO VICTORY.
THE HEART OF THE GAME IS **BALANCE.**
SO WHAT WE NEED TO DO ...

4700	300	4600	300	100
				GK

...COMES DOWN TO ONE THING

4700	300	4600	300

WE SHOULD PAIR UP TO FIND THE ITEMS.

...THIS ARRANGEMENT?!

WHY...

...IN-CREASING THE NUMBER OF PLAYERS SEARCHING FOR ITEMS!

...MORE PEOPLE COULD OPERATE ALONE...

BUT IF YOU GOT AN ITEM BEFOREHAND...

4600	300

↓

ITEM FOUND!
+2000

2300

SPLIT UP

4600		2300

...AND PROTECT THE BASE WITH YOUR REMAINING 50 POINTS.

WITH 300 POINTS, YOU COULD SURVIVE A LOSING GROUP BATTLE...

4600	300

−500

LOSER!

(−250)(−250)

4350	50

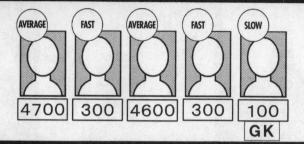

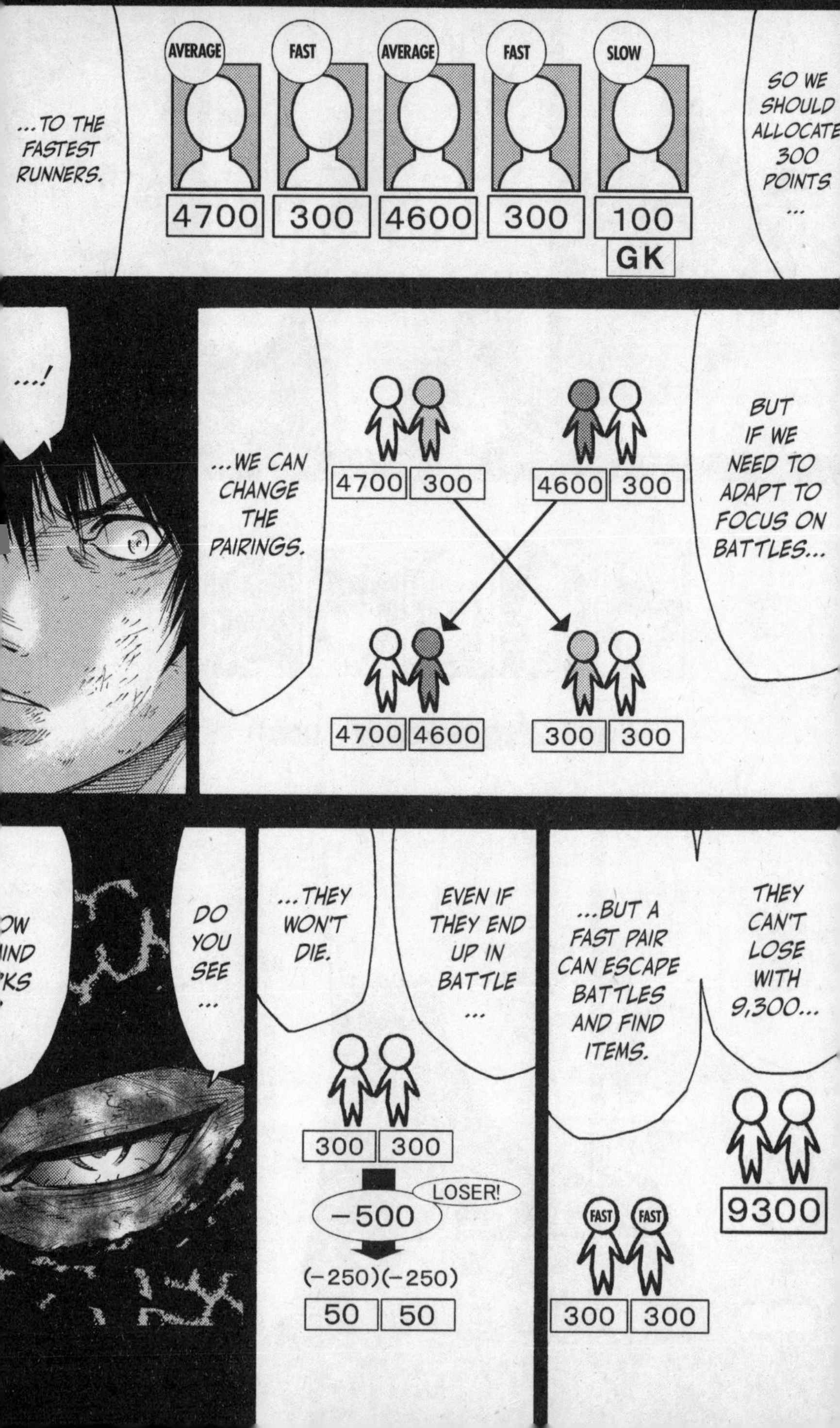

...TO THE FASTEST RUNNERS.

AVERAGE	FAST	AVERAGE	FAST	SLOW
4700	300	4600	300	100 GK

SO WE SHOULD ALLOCATE 300 POINTS...

...!

...WE CAN CHANGE THE PAIRINGS.

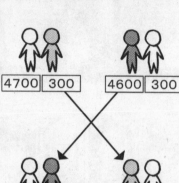

4700 300   4600 300

4700 4600   300 300

BUT IF WE NEED TO ADAPT TO FOCUS ON BATTLES...

...OW ...IND ...KS

DO YOU SEE ...

...THEY WON'T DIE.

EVEN IF THEY END UP IN BATTLE...

300 300

−500   LOSER!

(−250)(−250)

50 50

...BUT A FAST PAIR CAN ESCAPE BATTLES AND FIND ITEMS.

THEY CAN'T LOSE WITH 9,300...

9300

FAST FAST

300 300

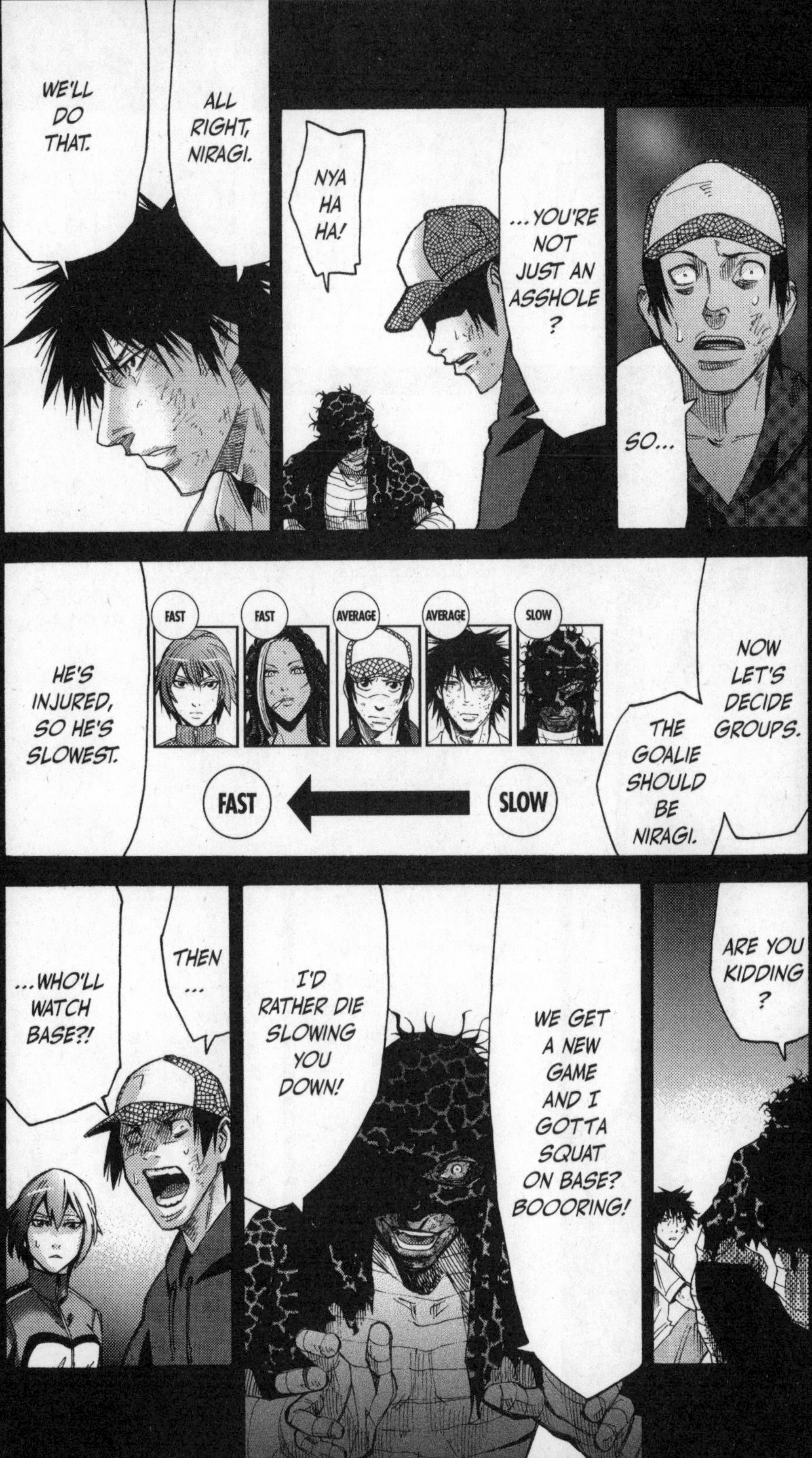
SO...
...YOU'RE NOT JUST AN ASSHOLE?
NYA HA HA!
ALL RIGHT, NIRAGI.
WE'LL DO THAT.
NOW LET'S DECIDE GROUPS.
THE GOALIE SHOULD BE NIRAGI.
FAST
FAST
AVERAGE
AVERAGE
SLOW
FAST
SLOW
HE'S INJURED, SO HE'S SLOWEST.
ARE YOU KIDDING?
WE GET A NEW GAME AND I GOTTA SQUAT ON BASE? BOOORING!
I'D RATHER DIE SLOWING YOU DOWN!
THEN...
...WHO'LL WATCH BASE?!

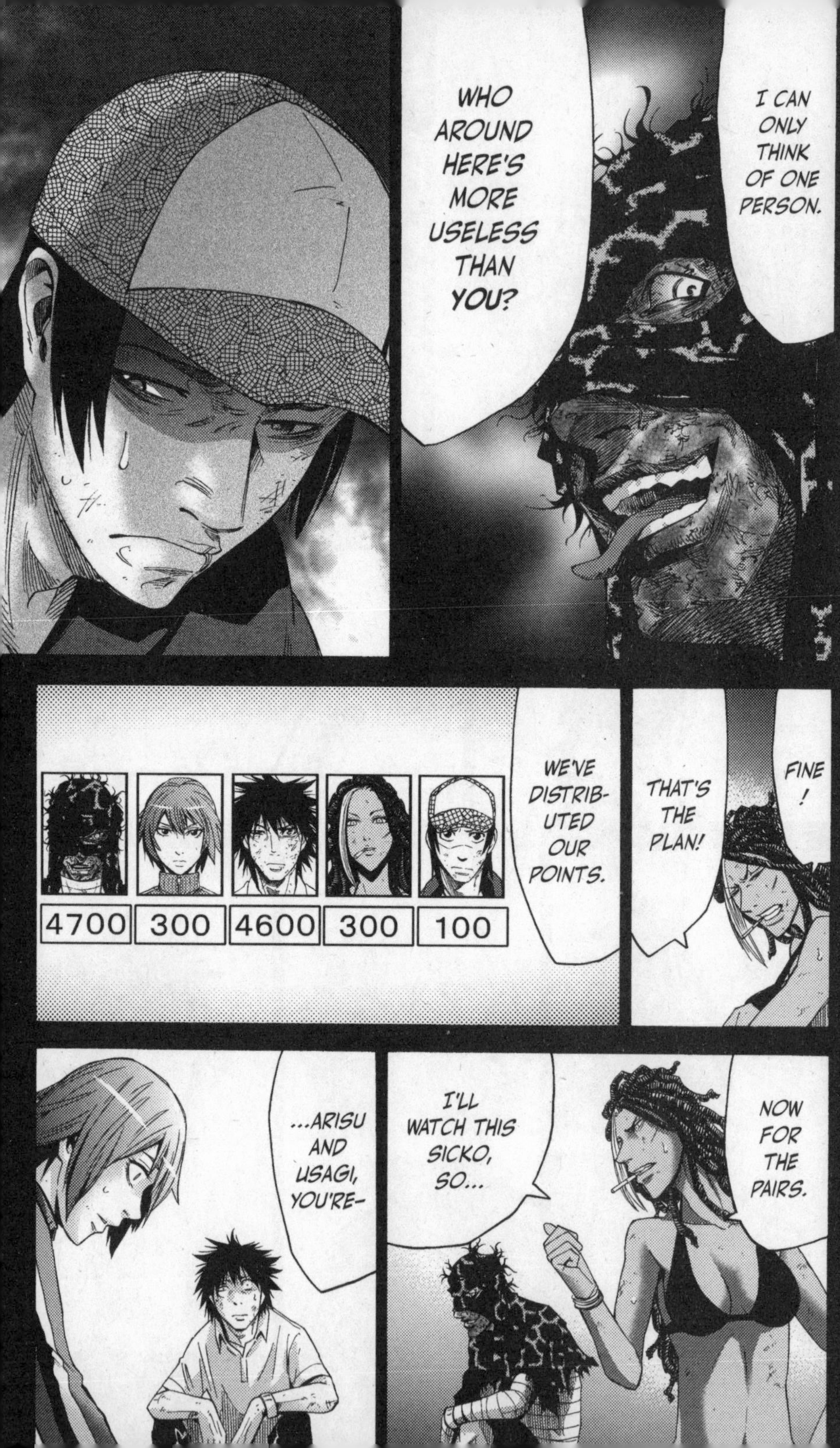
I CAN ONLY THINK OF ONE PERSON.
WHO AROUND HERE'S MORE USELESS THAN YOU?
FINE!
THAT'S THE PLAN!
WE'VE DISTRIB-UTED OUR POINTS.
4700
300
4600
300
100
NOW FOR THE PAIRS.
I'LL WATCH THIS SICKO, SO...
...ARISU AND USAGI, YOU'RE-

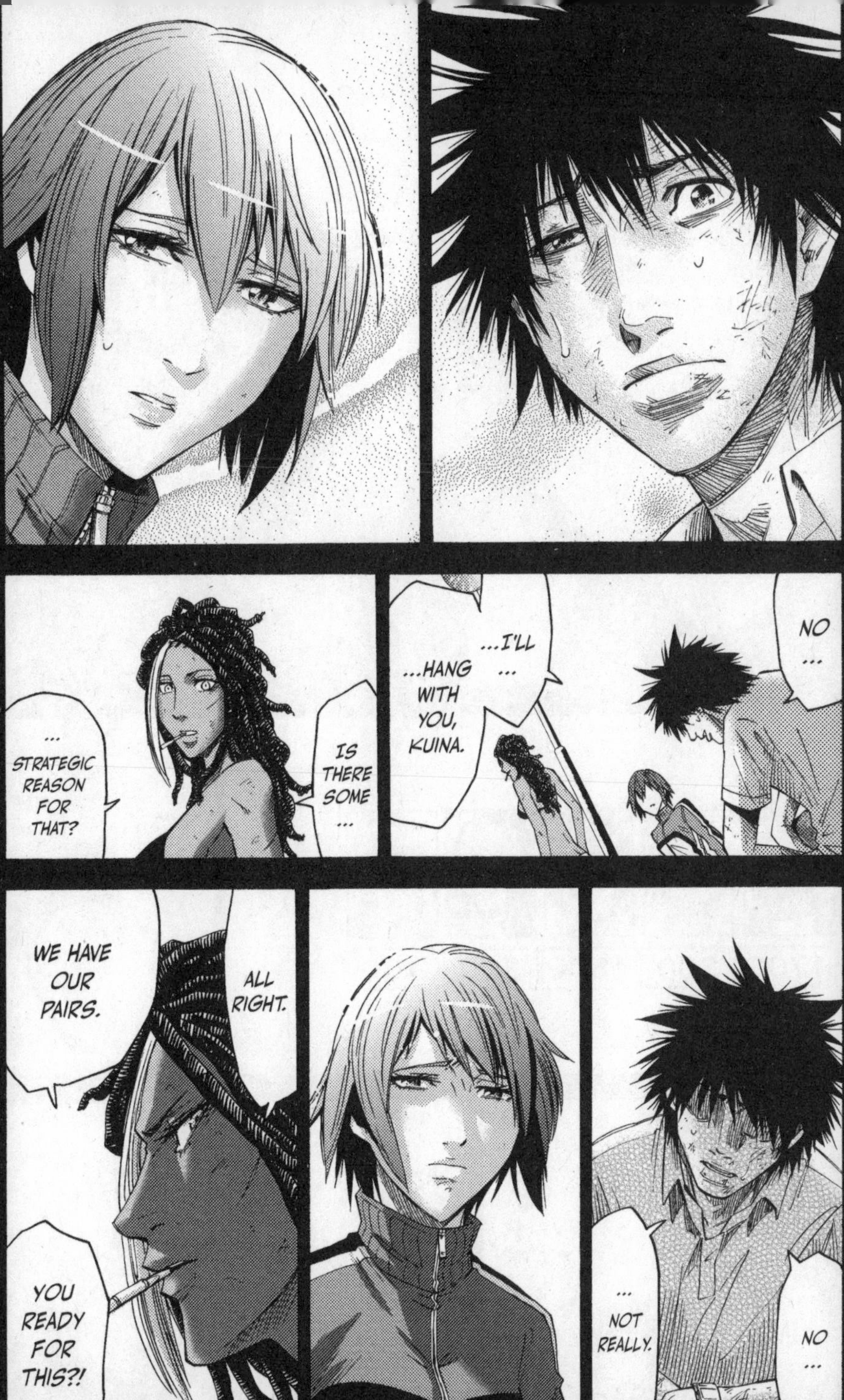
NO ...
...I'LL ...
...HANG WITH YOU, KUINA.
IS THERE SOME ...
... STRATEGIC REASON FOR THAT?
NO ...
... NOT REALLY.
ALL RIGHT.
WE HAVE OUR PAIRS.
YOU READY FOR THIS?!

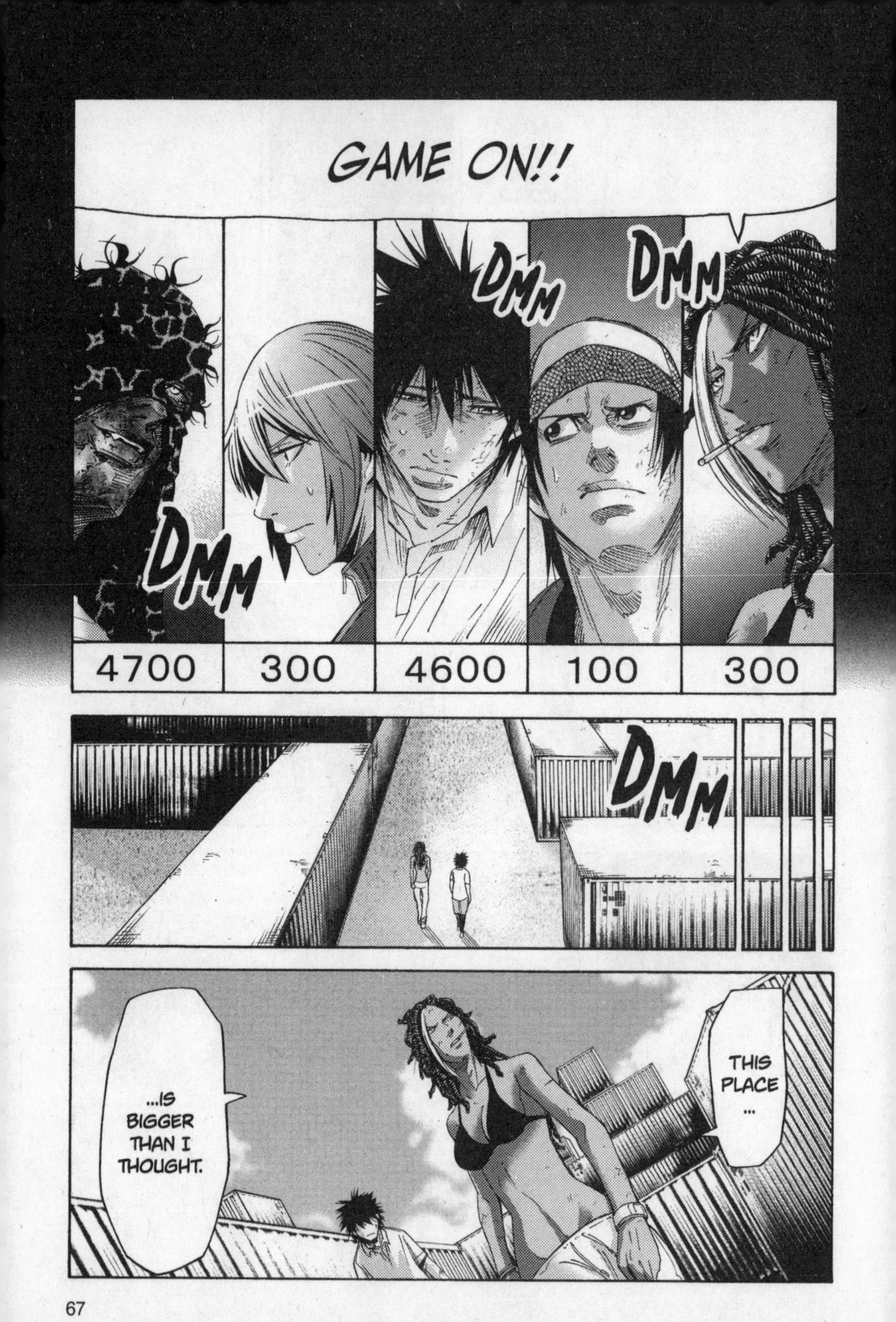
GAME ON!!
DMM
DMM
DMM
DMM
300
100
4600
300
4700
DMM
THIS PLACE ...
...IS BIGGER THAN I THOUGHT.

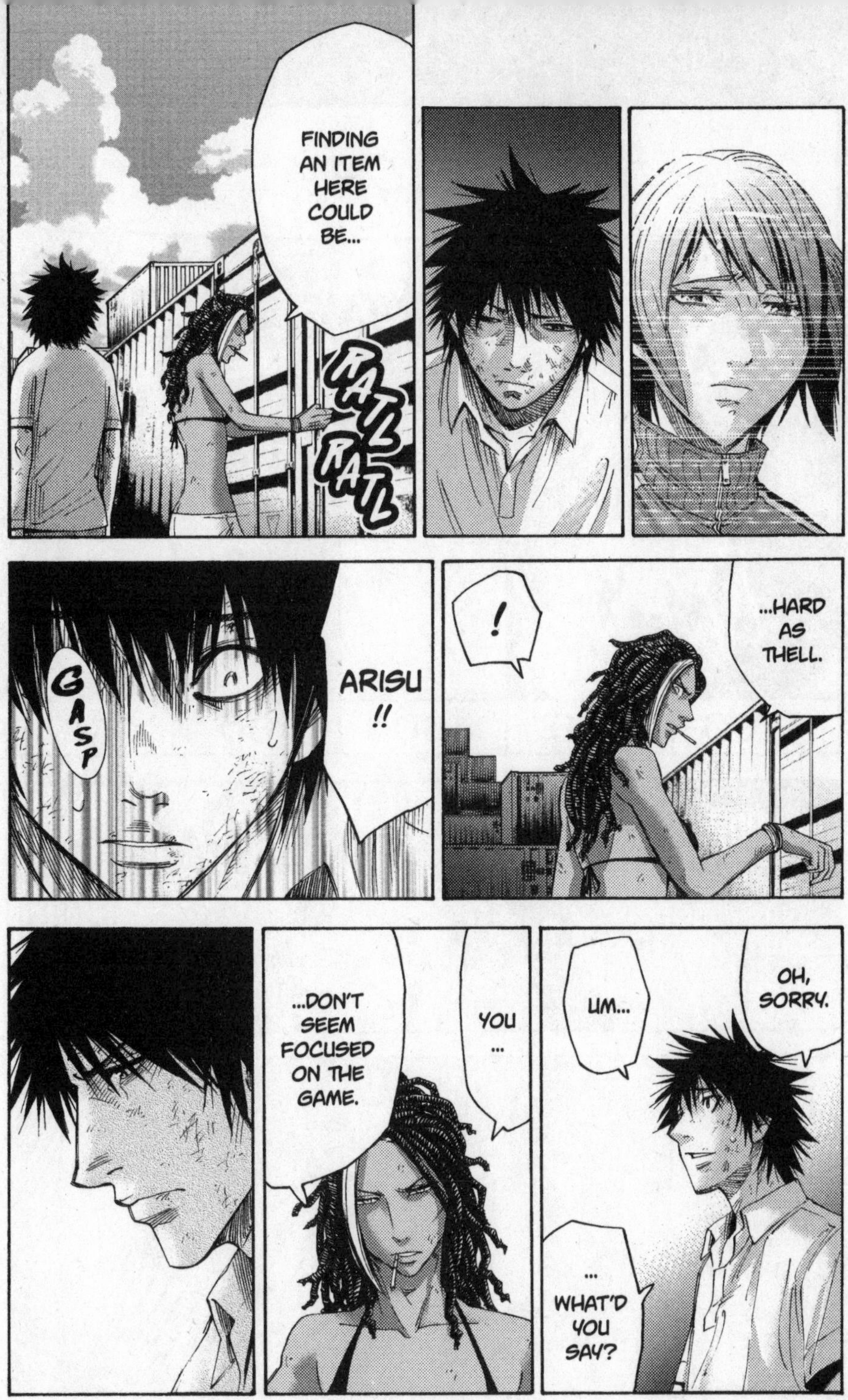
FINDING AN ITEM HERE COULD BE...
RATL RATL
...HARD AS THELL.
!
ARISU!!
GASP
OH, SORRY.
UM...
... WHAT'D YOU SAY?
YOU ...
...DON'T SEEM FOCUSED ON THE GAME.

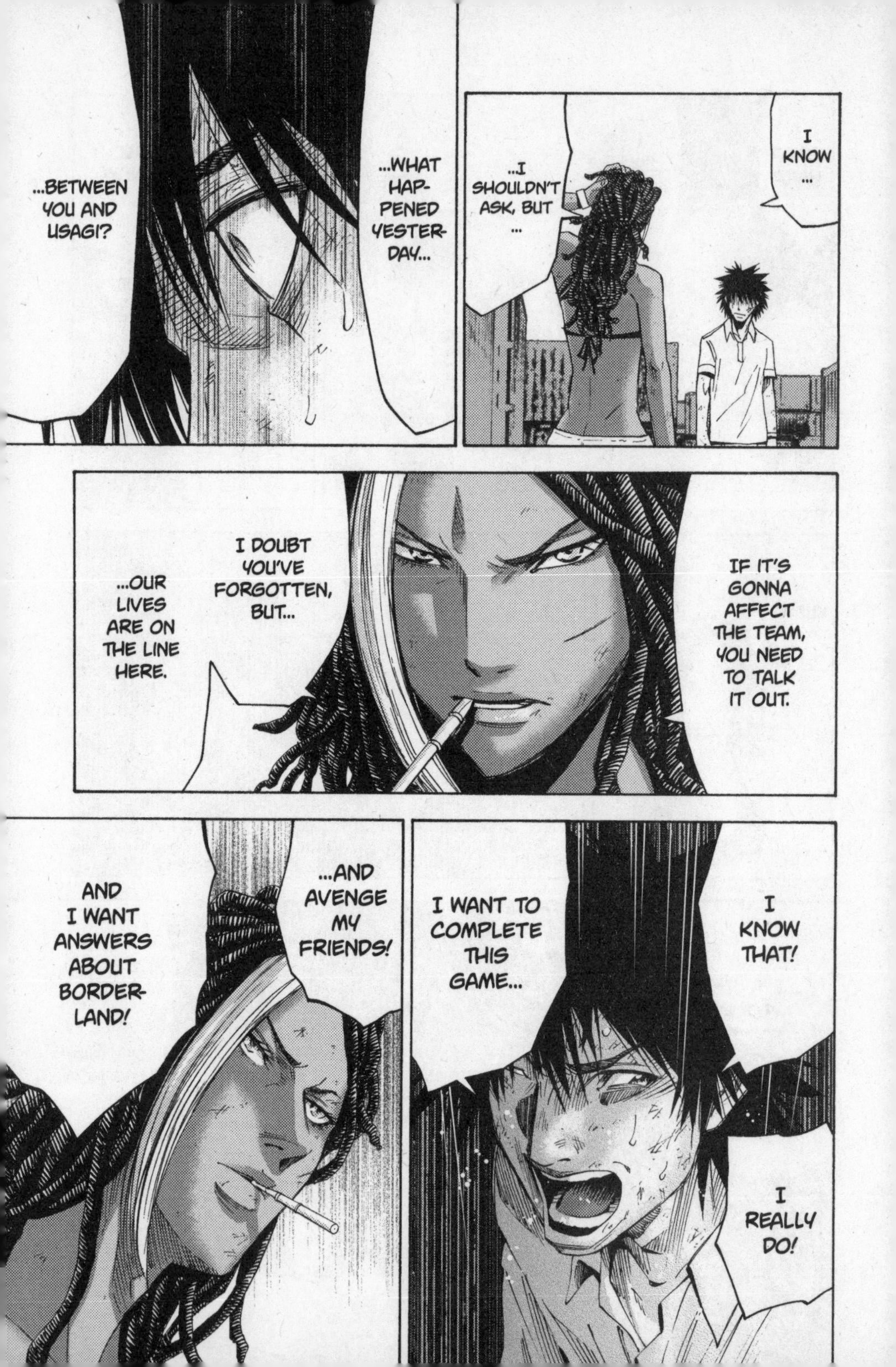
I KNOW ...
...I SHOULDN'T ASK, BUT ...
...WHAT HAPPENED YESTERDAY...
...BETWEEN YOU AND USAGI?
IF IT'S GONNA AFFECT THE TEAM, YOU NEED TO TALK IT OUT.
I DOUBT YOU'VE FORGOTTEN, BUT...
...OUR LIVES ARE ON THE LINE HERE.
I KNOW THAT!
I WANT TO COMPLETE THIS GAME...
I REALLY DO!
...AND AVENGE MY FRIENDS!
AND I WANT ANSWERS ABOUT BORDERLAND!

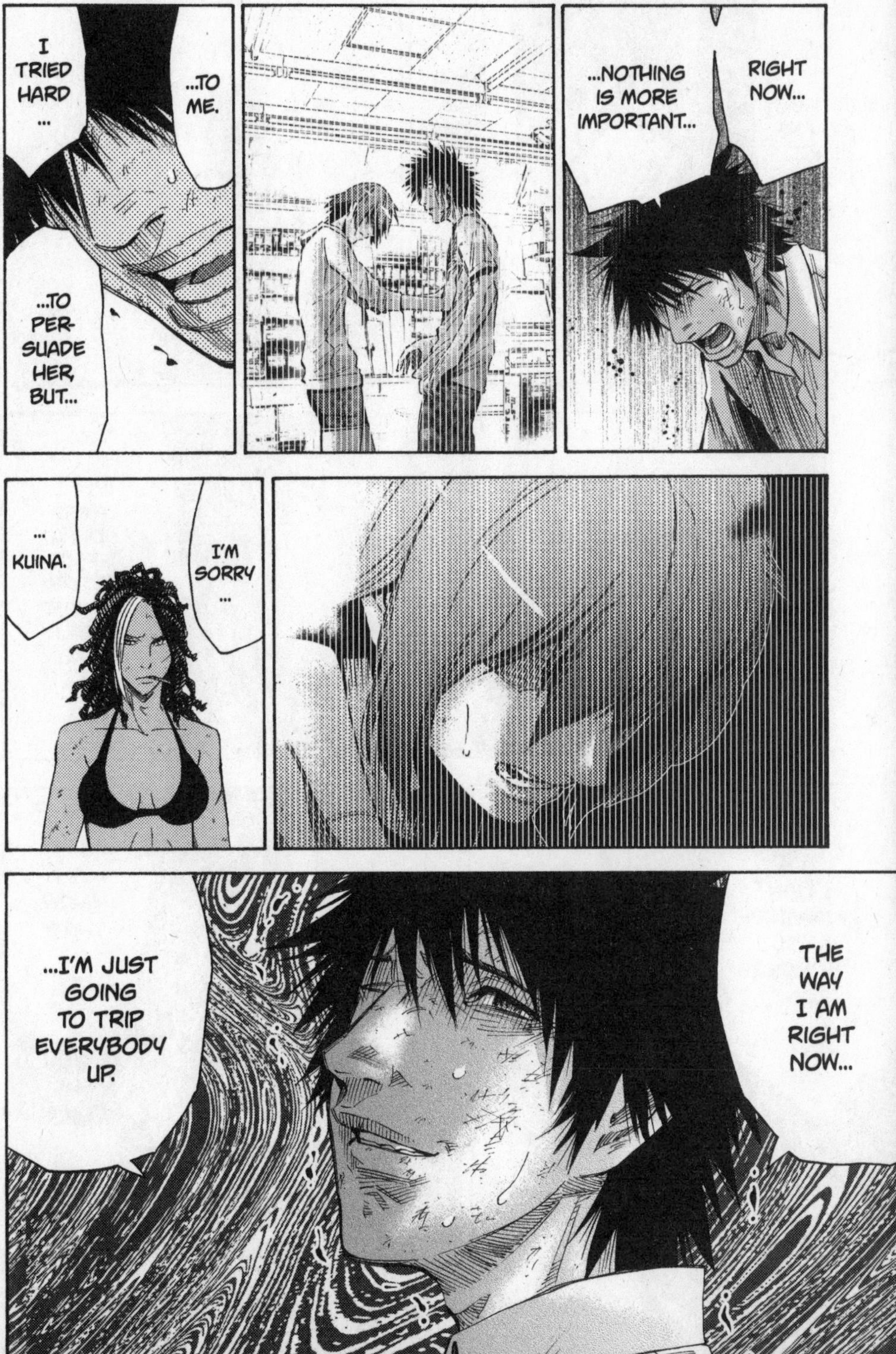
RIGHT NOW...
...NOTHING IS MORE IMPORTANT...
...TO ME.
I TRIED HARD ...
...TO PERSUADE HER, BUT...
I'M SORRY ...
... KUINA.
THE WAY I AM RIGHT NOW...
...I'M JUST GOING TO TRIP EVERYBODY UP.

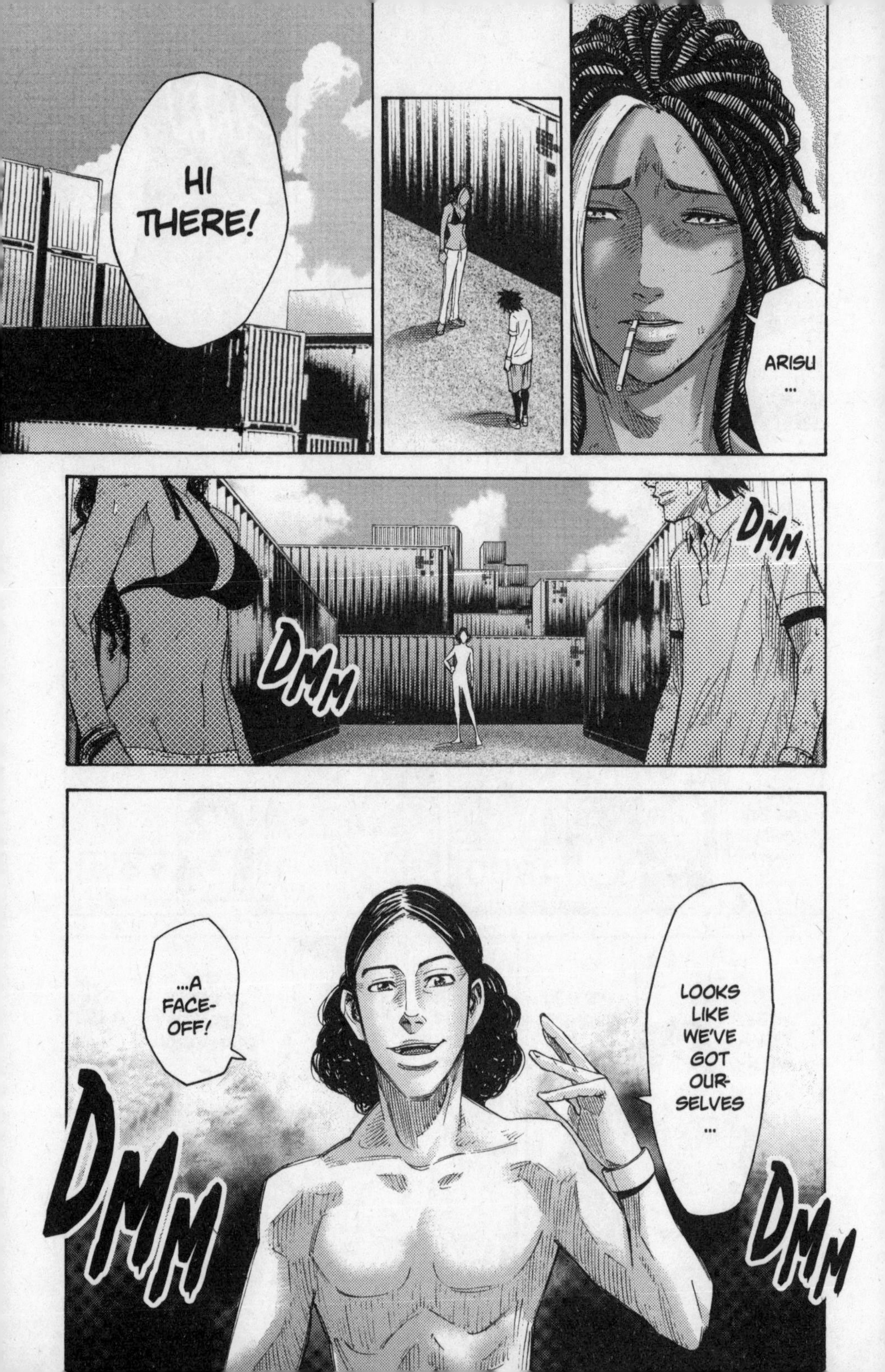
ARISU ...
HI THERE!
DMM
DMM
LOOKS LIKE WE'VE GOT OUR-SELVES ...
...A FACE-OFF!
DMM
DMM

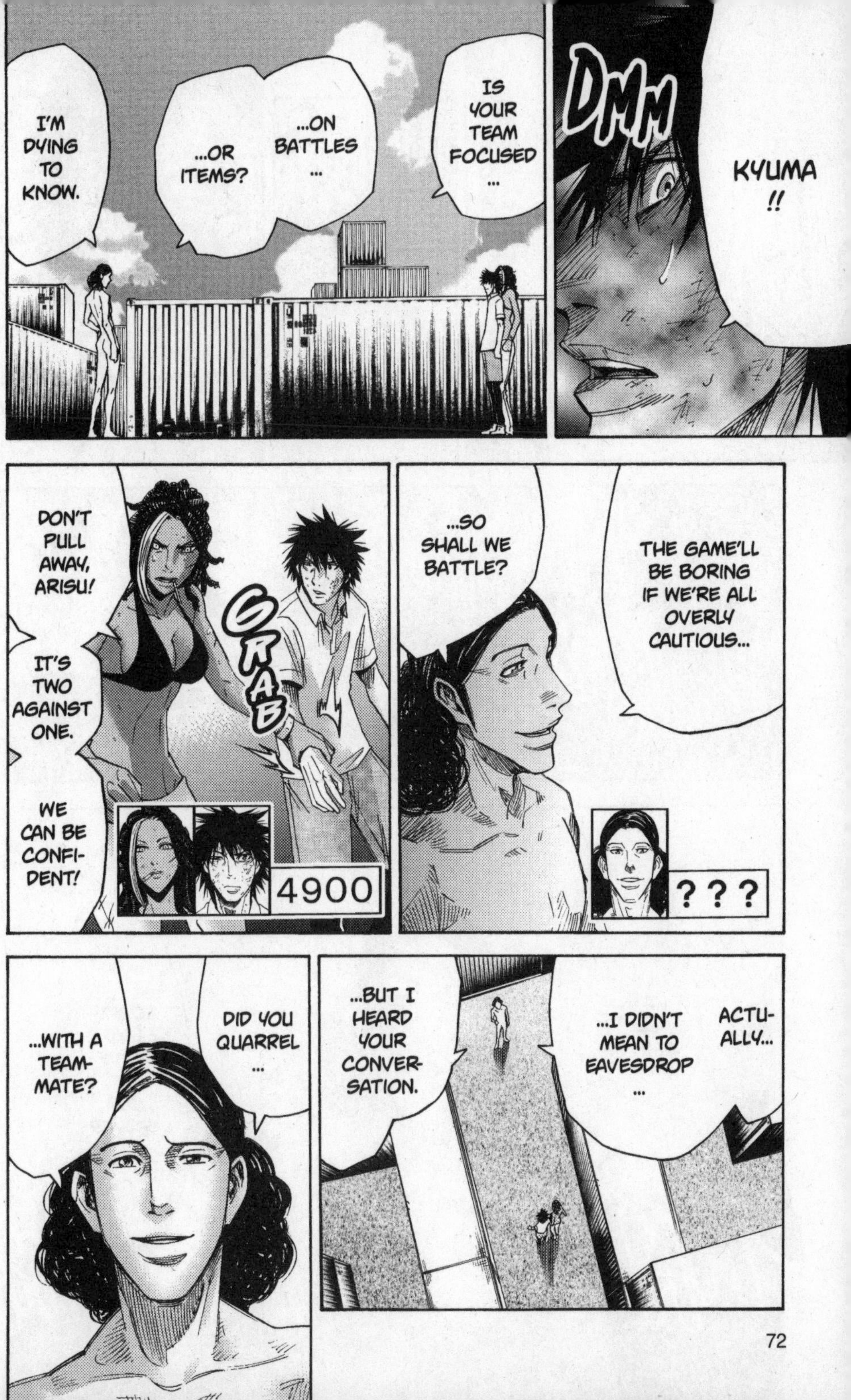
DMM
KYUMA!!
IS YOUR TEAM FOCUSED...
...ON BATTLES...
...OR ITEMS?
I'M DYING TO KNOW.
THE GAME'LL BE BORING IF WE'RE ALL OVERLY CAUTIOUS...
...SO SHALL WE BATTLE?
???
GRAB
DON'T PULL AWAY, ARISU!
IT'S TWO AGAINST ONE.
WE CAN BE CONFI-DENT!
4900
ACTU-ALLY...
...I DIDN'T MEAN TO EAVESDROP...
...BUT I HEARD YOUR CONVER-SATION.
DID YOU QUARREL...
...WITH A TEAM-MATE?

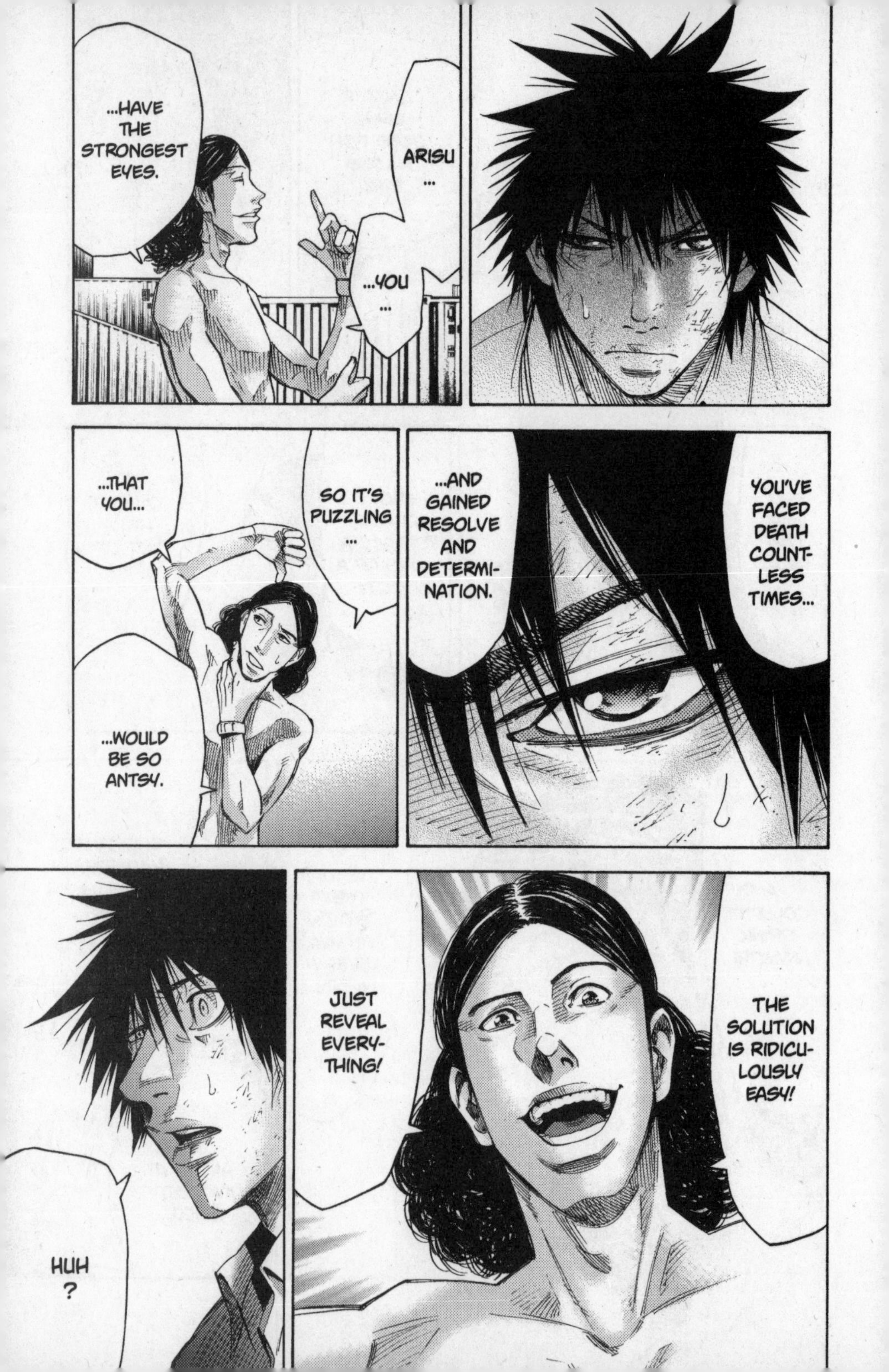
ARISU ...
...YOU ...
...HAVE THE STRONGEST EYES.
YOU'VE FACED DEATH COUNT-LESS TIMES...
...AND GAINED RESOLVE AND DETERMI-NATION.
SO IT'S PUZZLING ...
...THAT YOU...
...WOULD BE SO ANTSY.
THE SOLUTION IS RIDICU-LOUSLY EASY!
JUST REVEAL EVERY-THING!
HUH ?

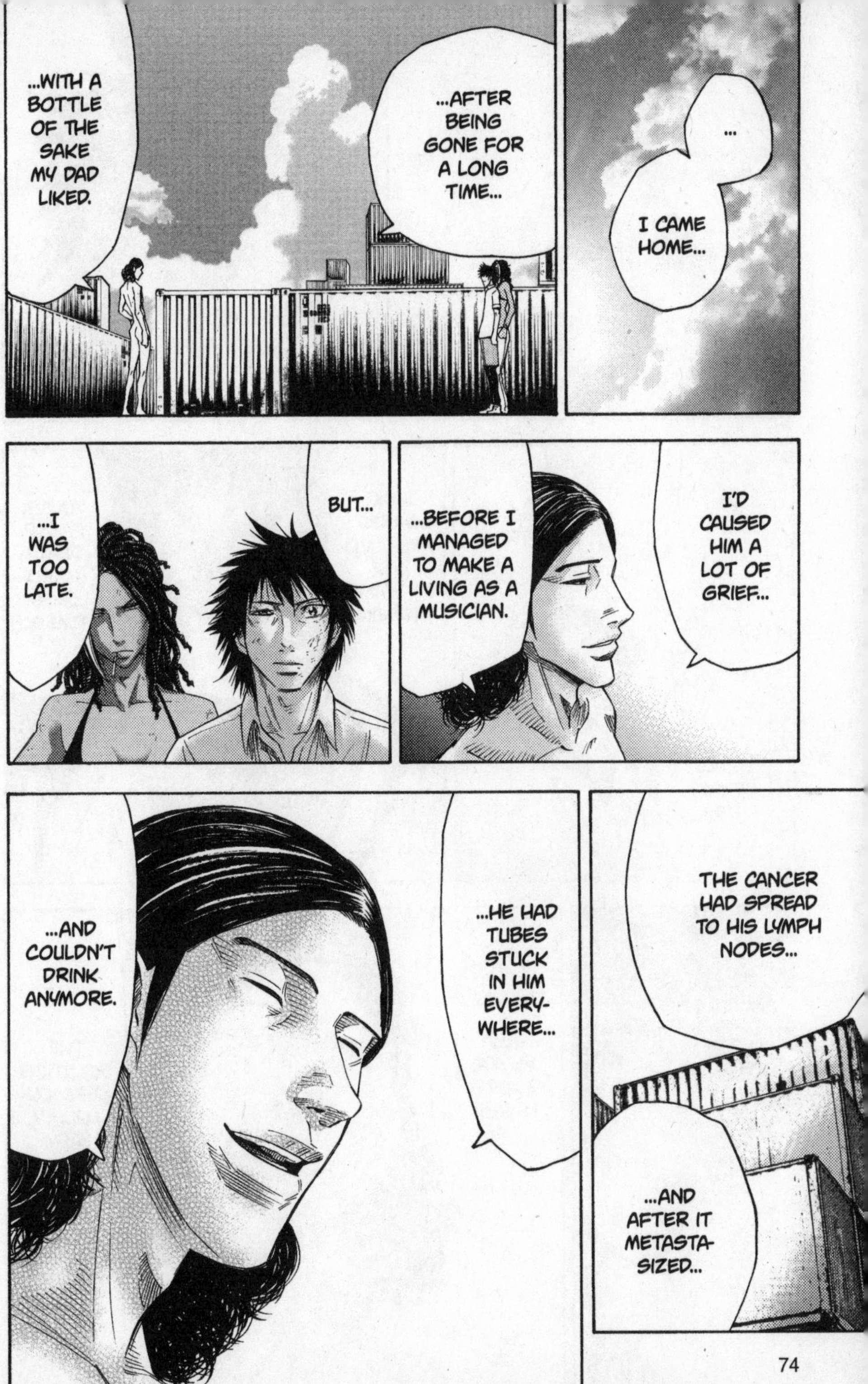
...
I CAME HOME...
...AFTER BEING GONE FOR A LONG TIME...
...WITH A BOTTLE OF THE SAKE MY DAD LIKED.
I'D CAUSED HIM A LOT OF GRIEF...
...BEFORE I MANAGED TO MAKE A LIVING AS A MUSICIAN.
BUT...
...I WAS TOO LATE.
THE CANCER HAD SPREAD TO HIS LYMPH NODES...
...AND AFTER IT METASTA-SIZED...
...HE HAD TUBES STUCK IN HIM EVERY-WHERE...
...AND COULDN'T DRINK ANYMORE.

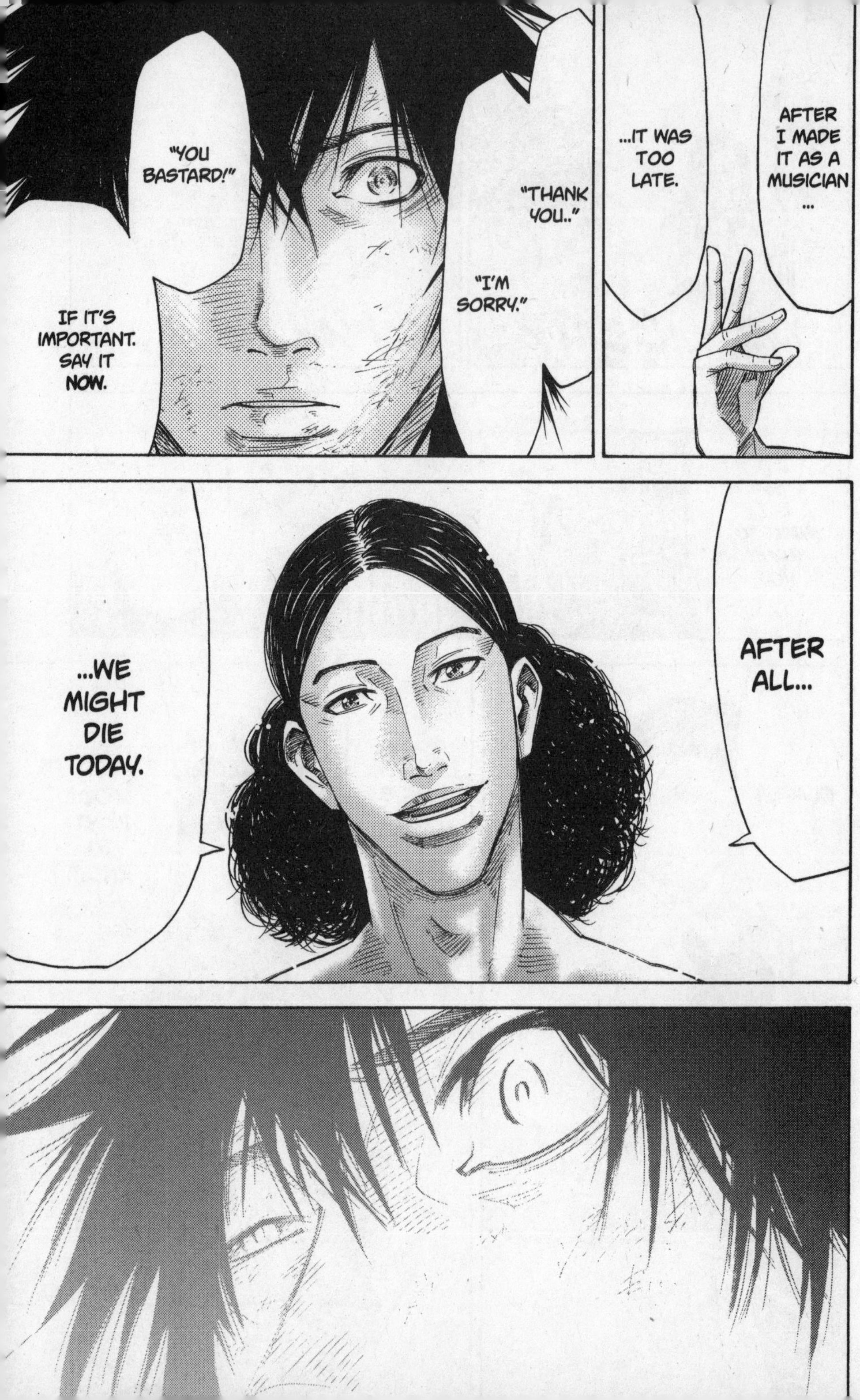
AFTER I MADE IT AS A MUSICIAN ...
...IT WAS TOO LATE.
"THANK YOU.."
"I'M SORRY."
"YOU BASTARD!"
IF IT'S IMPORTANT. SAY IT NOW.
AFTER ALL...
...WE MIGHT DIE TODAY.

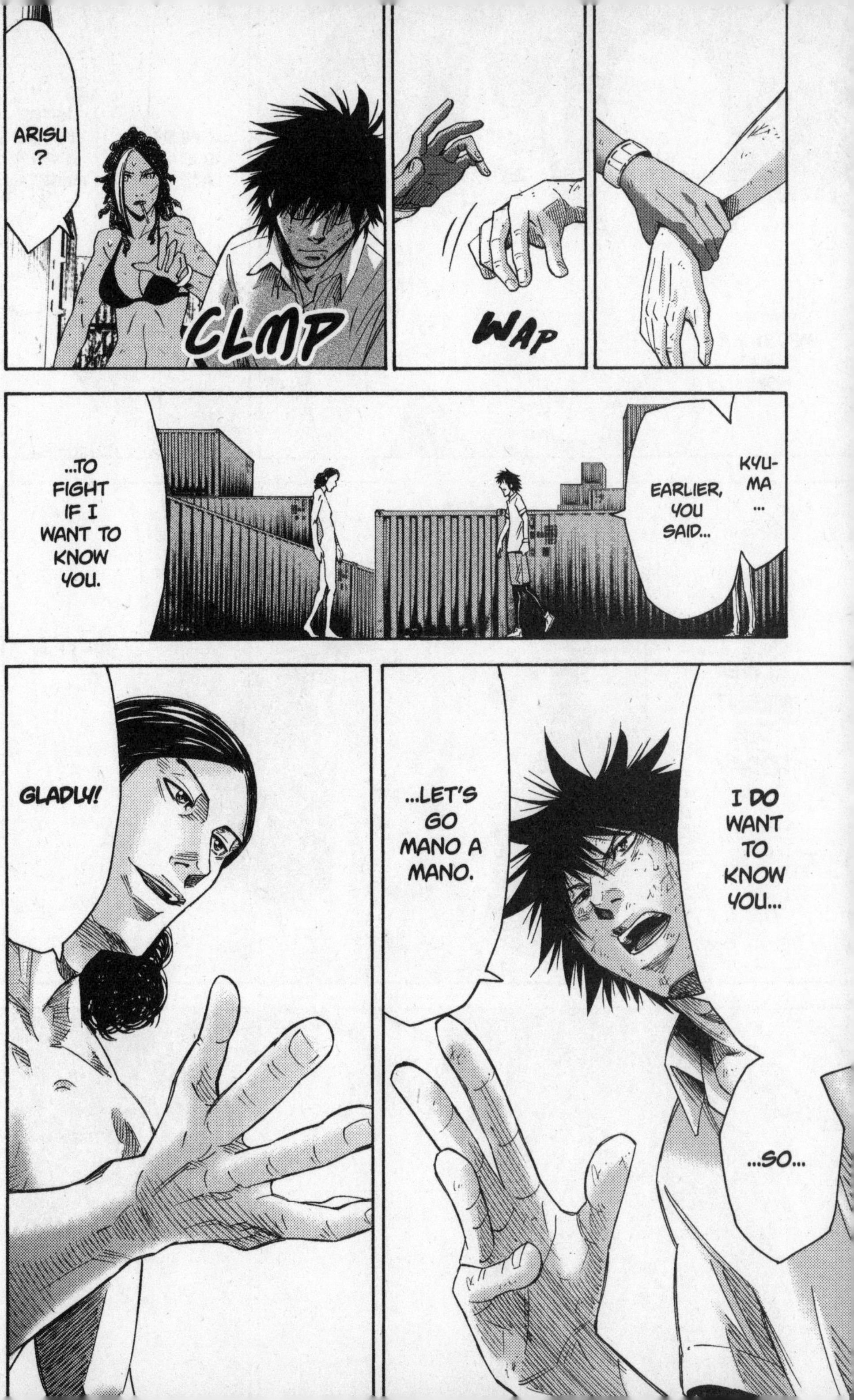
WAP
ARISU ?
CLMP
KYU-MA ...
EARLIER, YOU SAID...
...TO FIGHT IF I WANT TO KNOW YOU.
I DO WANT TO KNOW YOU...
...SO...
...LET'S GO MANO A MANO.
GLADLY!

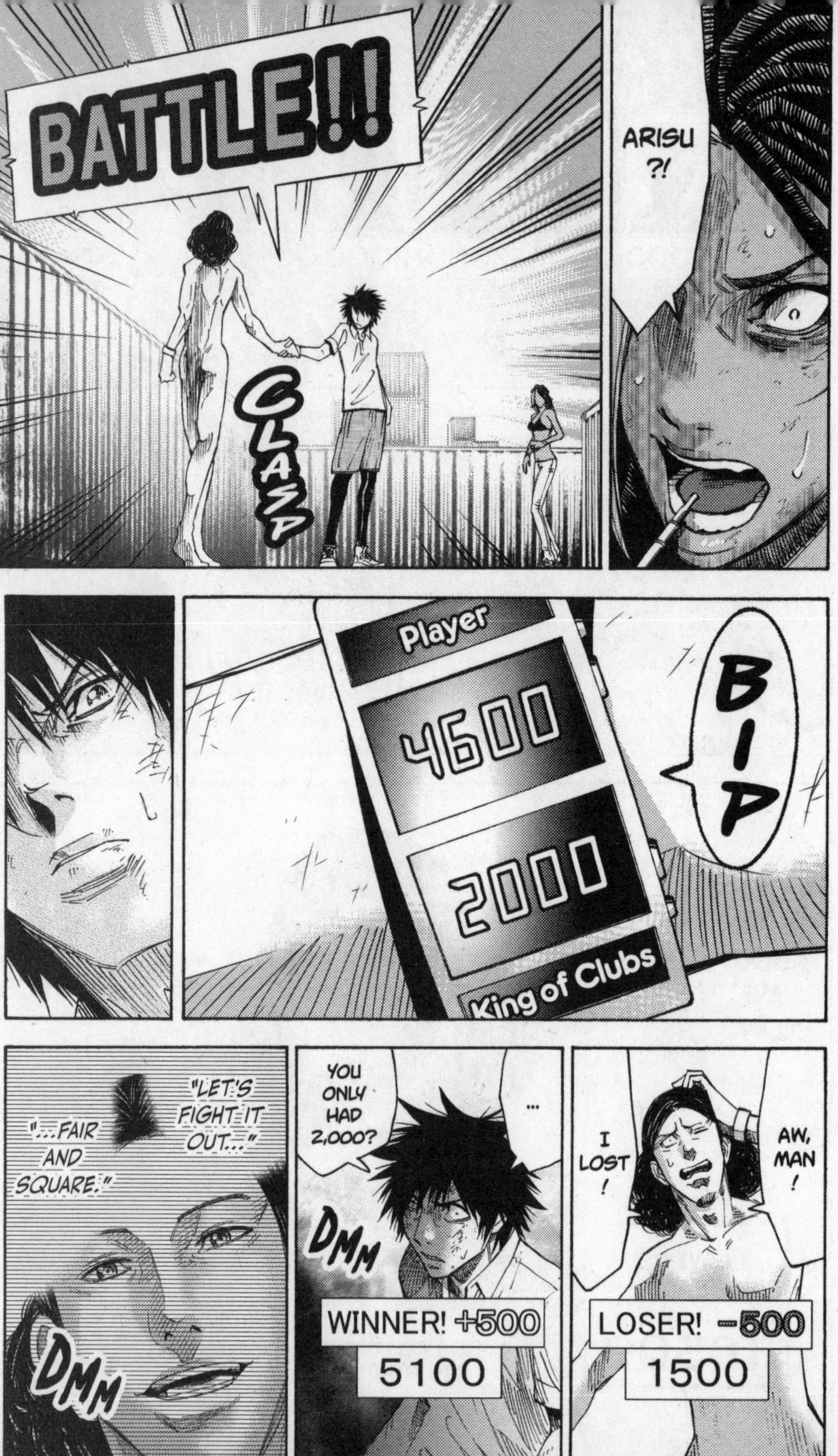
ARISU ?!
BATTLE!!
CLASP
BIP
Player
4600
2000
King of Clubs
AW, MAN!
I LOST!
LOSER! -500
1500
...
YOU ONLY HAD 2,000?
DMM
WINNER! +500
5100
"LET'S FIGHT IT OUT..."
"...FAIR AND SQUARE."
DMM

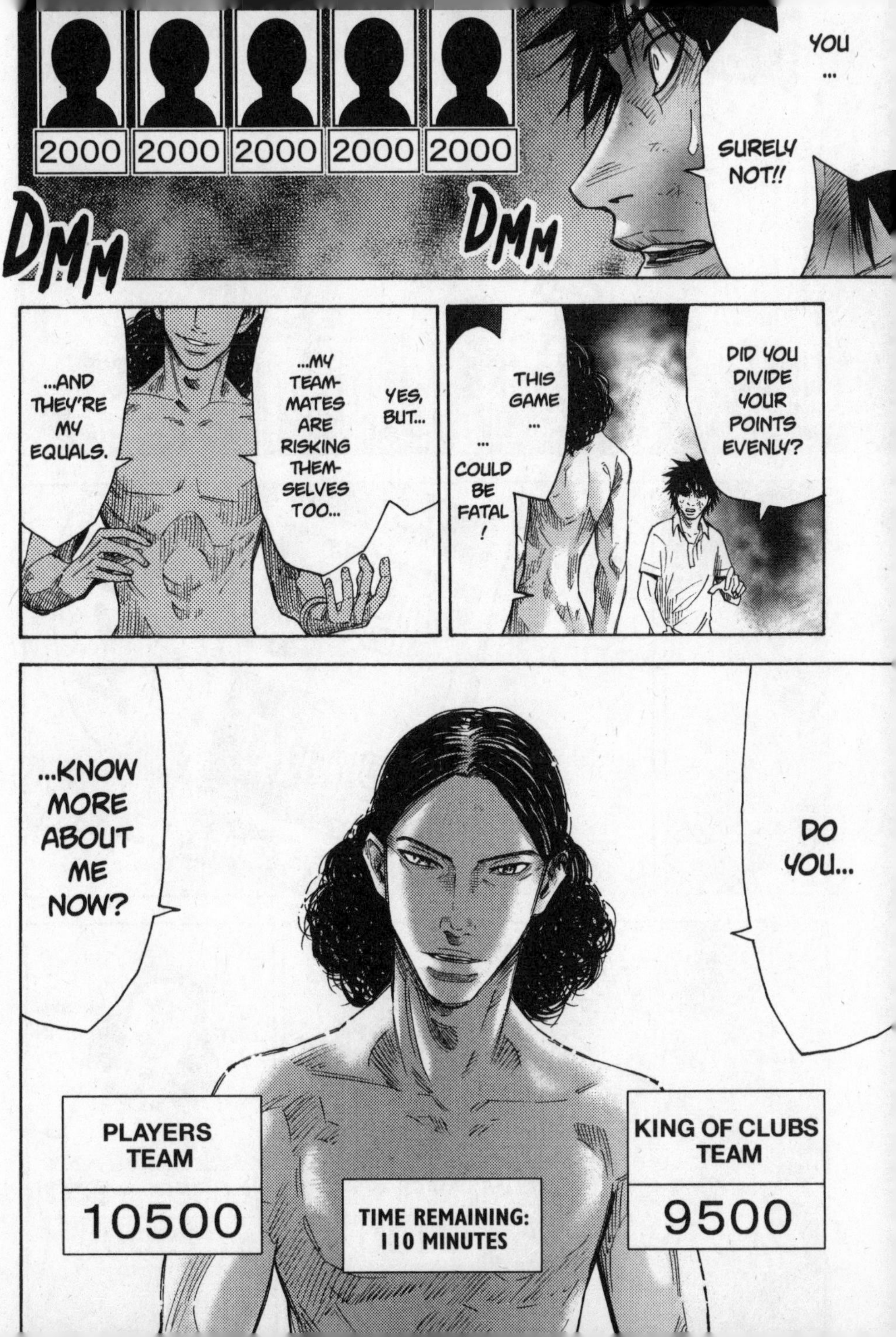
YOU ...
SURELY NOT!!
2000
2000
2000
2000
2000
DMM
DMM
DID YOU DIVIDE YOUR POINTS EVENLY?
THIS GAME ...
... COULD BE FATAL!
YES, BUT...
...MY TEAM-MATES ARE RISKING THEM-SELVES TOO...
...AND THEY'RE MY EQUALS.
DO YOU...
...KNOW MORE ABOUT ME NOW?
KING OF CLUBS TEAM
9500
TIME REMAINING: 110 MINUTES
PLAYERS TEAM
10500

Arisu and Kyuma were the first to battle.

...began to lean in one side's favor.

After that, the struggle...

CHAPTER 35: King of Clubs, Part 3

GYA HA HA!

URGH...

WINNER			LOSER	
4700 +250	300 +250		2000 -250	2000 -250
4950	550		1750	1750

EACH OF YOU STARTED WITH 2,000 POINTS.

ARISU WAS RIGHT.

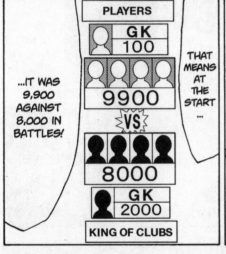

...IT WAS 9,900 AGAINST 8,000 IN BATTLES!

THAT MEANS AT THE START...

PLAYERS

| GK |
| 100 |

9900

VS

8000

| GK |
| 2000 |

KING OF CLUBS

...BUT YOU GAVE THEM 2,000.

WHAT A BIG WASTE.

YOUR GOALIE HAS INFINTE POINTS WHILE TOUCHING BASE...

PING

PING

Players	King of Clubs
+500	-500
11000	9000

1:37:55

BOTH TEAMS' POINTS HAVE CHANGED.

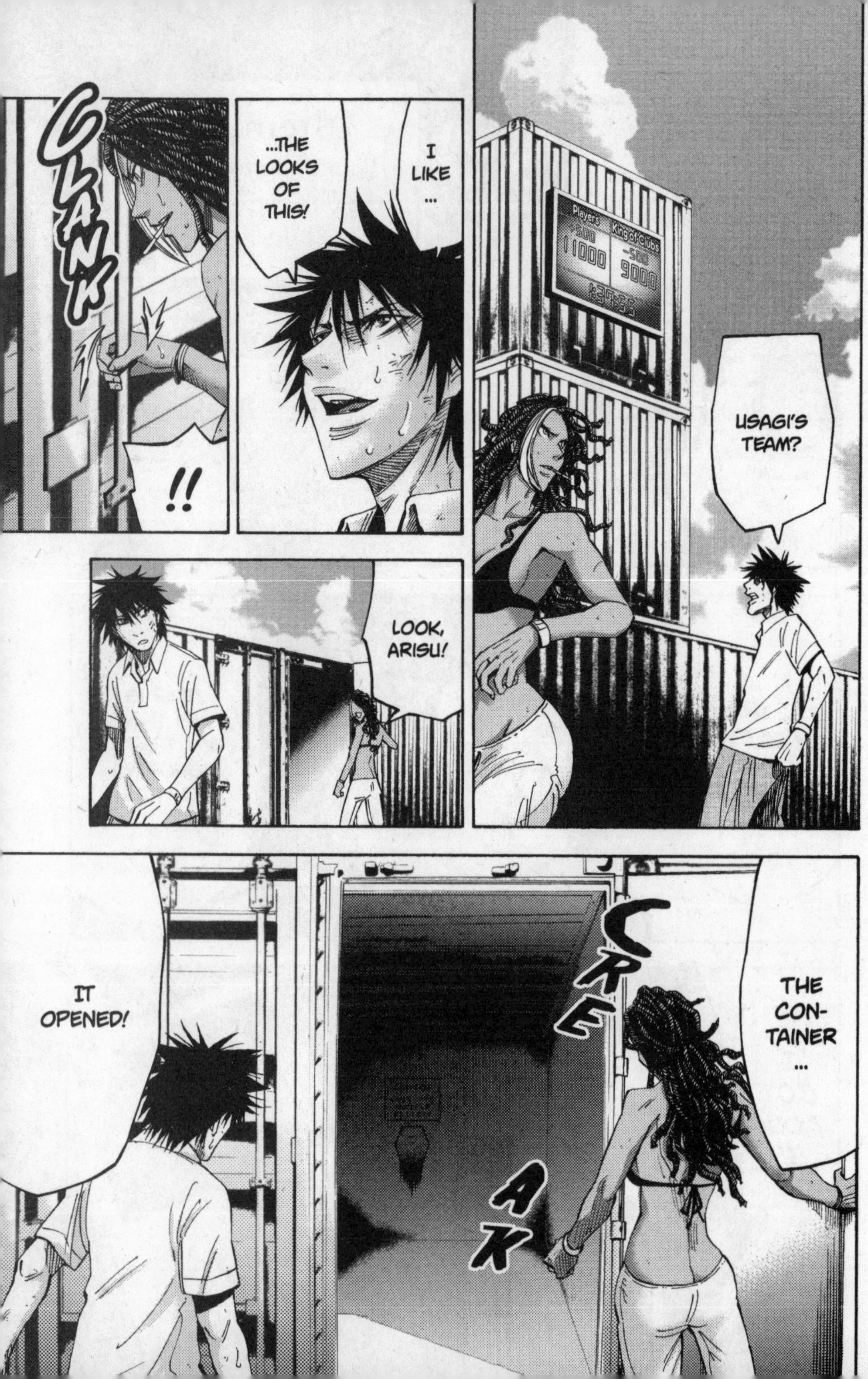
Players
+500
11000
King of Clubs
-500
9000
USAGI'S TEAM?
I LIKE ...
...THE LOOKS OF THIS!
CLANK
!!
LOOK, ARISU!
THE CON- TAINER ...
CREAK
IT OPENED!

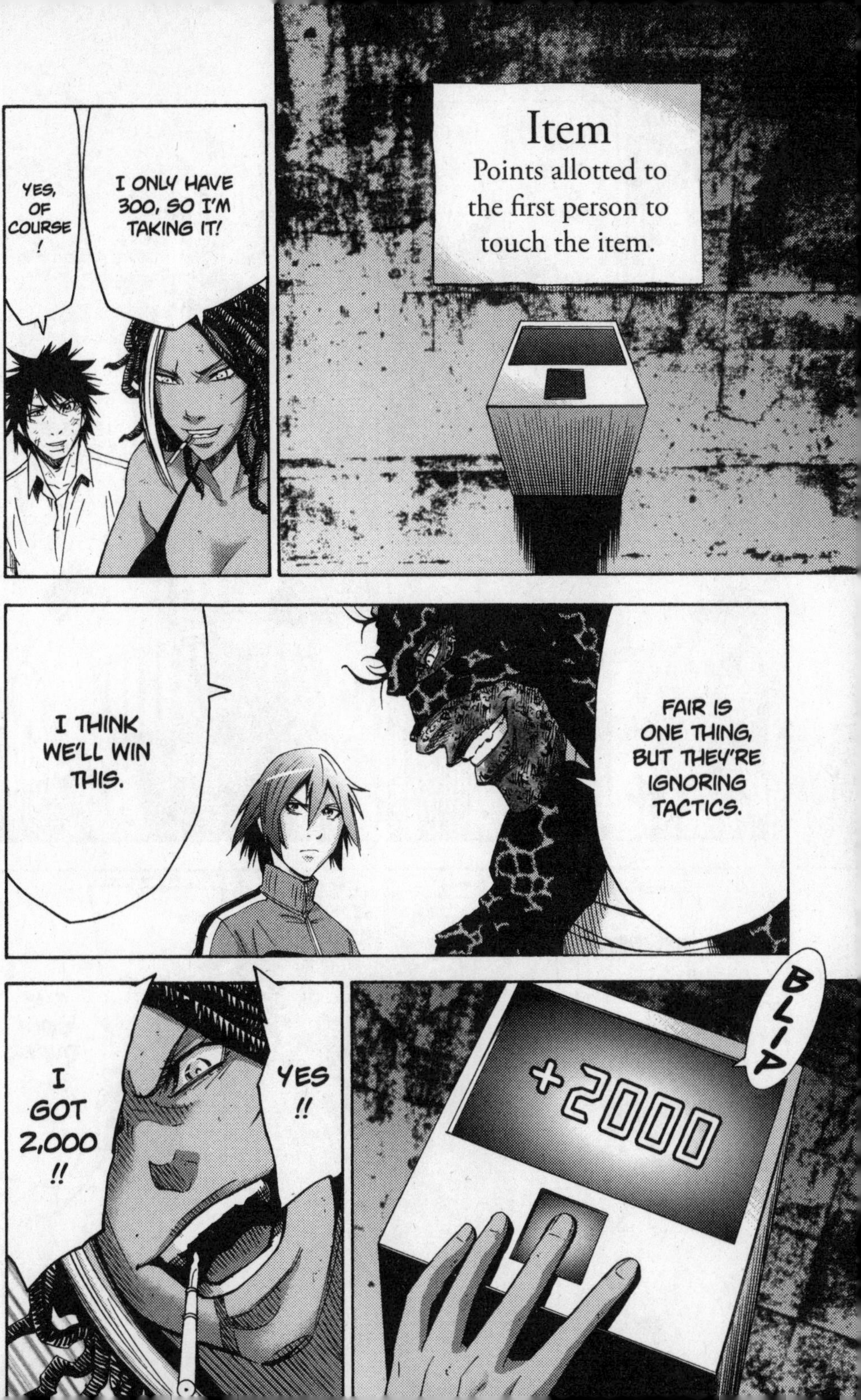
Item
Points allotted to the first person to touch the item.
I ONLY HAVE 300, SO I'M TAKING IT!
YES, OF COURSE!
FAIR IS ONE THING, BUT THEY'RE IGNORING TACTICS.
I THINK WE'LL WIN THIS.
BLIP
+2000
YES!!
I GOT 2,000!!

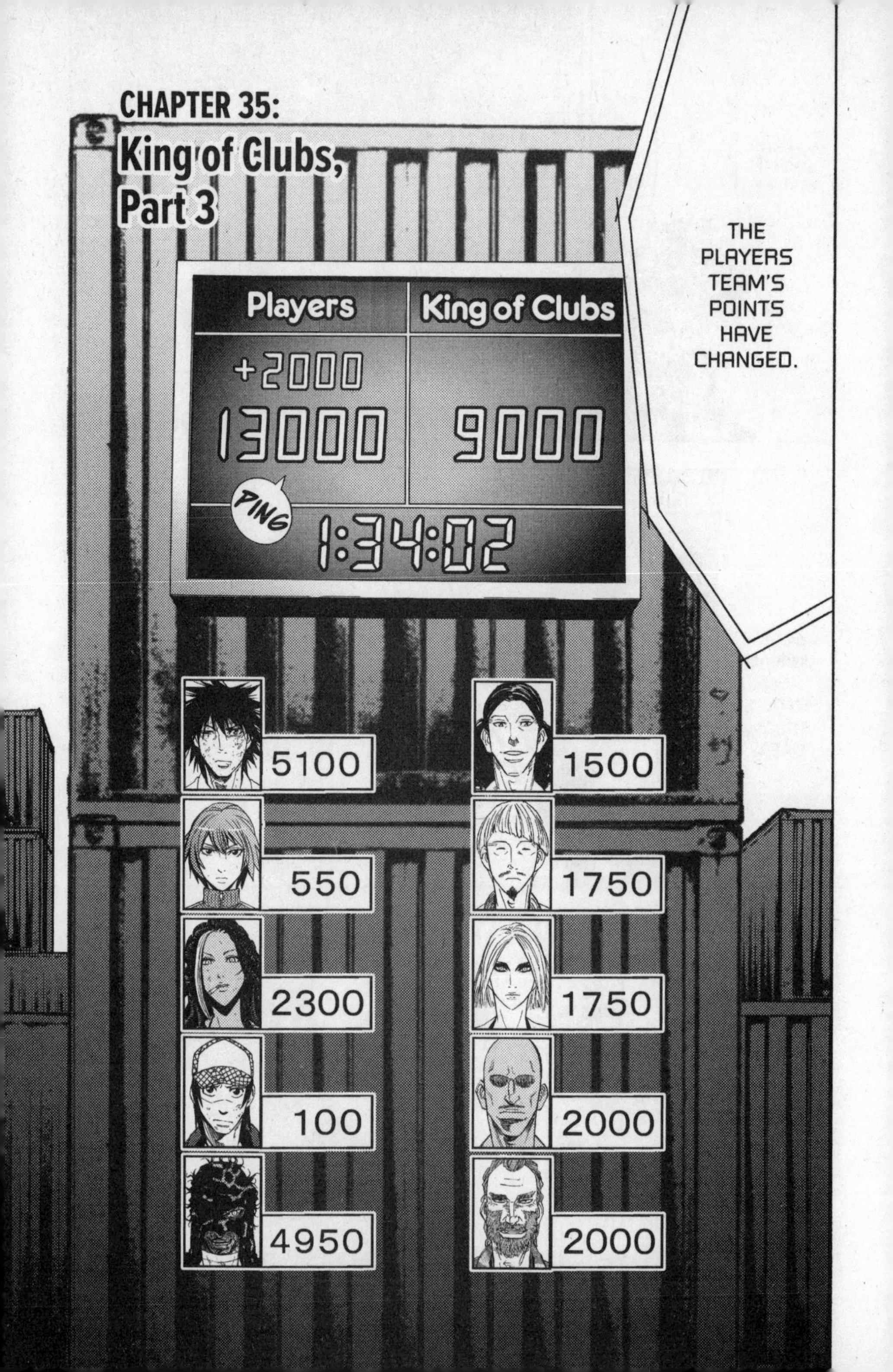
CHAPTER 35:
King of Clubs,
Part 3
Players
King of Clubs
+2000
13000
9000
PING
1:34:02
5100
1500
550
1750
2300
1750
100
2000
4950
2000
THE PLAYERS TEAM'S POINTS HAVE CHANGED.

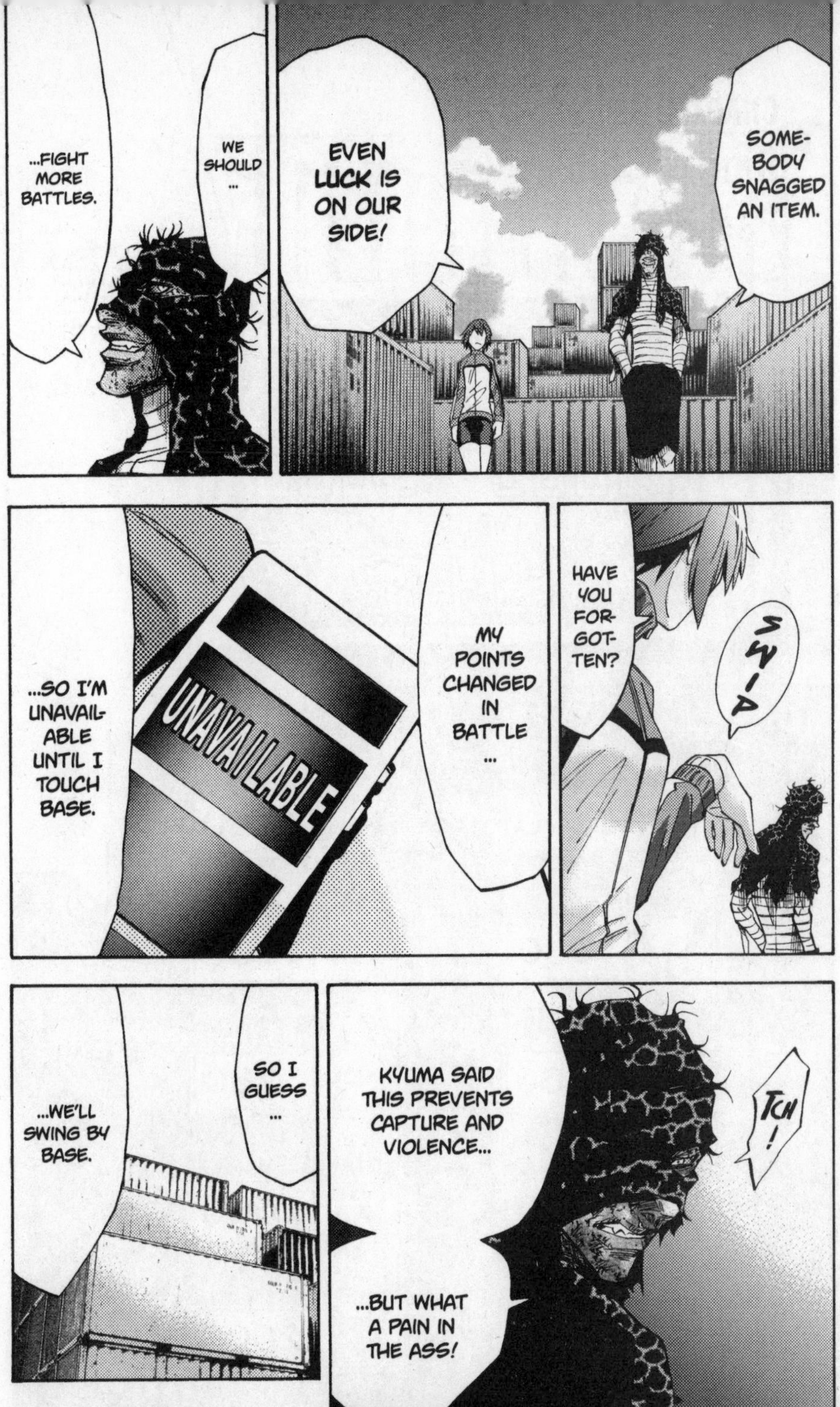
SOMEBODY SNAGGED AN ITEM.
EVEN LUCK IS ON OUR SIDE!
WE SHOULD ...
...FIGHT MORE BATTLES.
HAVE YOU FORGOTTEN?
SWIP
MY POINTS CHANGED IN BATTLE ...
UNAVAILABLE
...SO I'M UNAVAILABLE UNTIL I TOUCH BASE.
TCH!
KYUMA SAID THIS PREVENTS CAPTURE AND VIOLENCE...
...BUT WHAT A PAIN IN THE ASS!
SO I GUESS ...
...WE'LL SWING BY BASE.

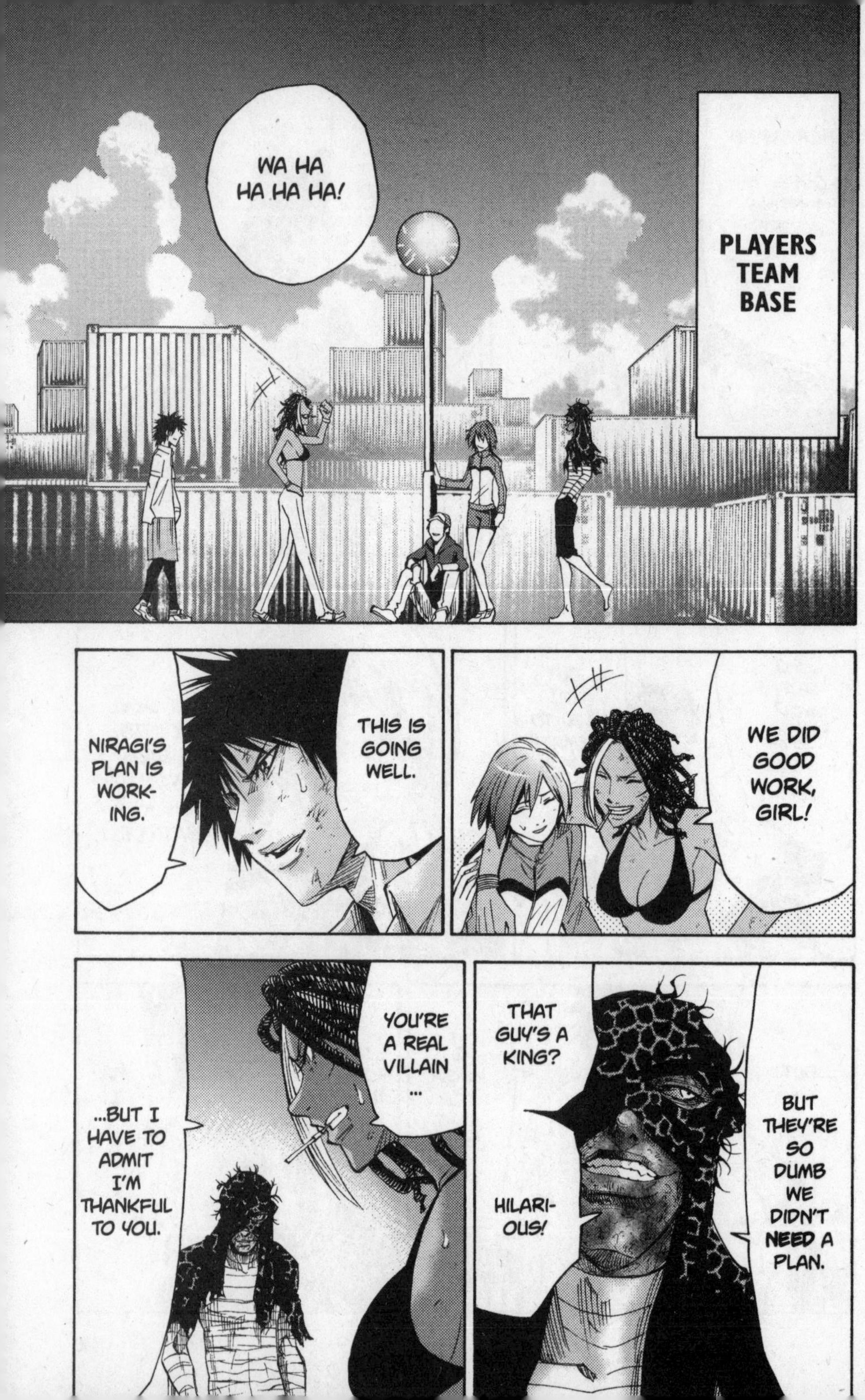
PLAYERS TEAM BASE
WA HA HA HA HA!
WE DID GOOD WORK, GIRL!
THIS IS GOING WELL.
NIRAGI'S PLAN IS WORK-ING.
THAT GUY'S A KING?
HILARI-OUS!
BUT THEY'RE SO DUMB WE DIDN'T NEED A PLAN.
YOU'RE A REAL VILLAIN ...
...BUT I HAVE TO ADMIT I'M THANKFUL TO YOU.

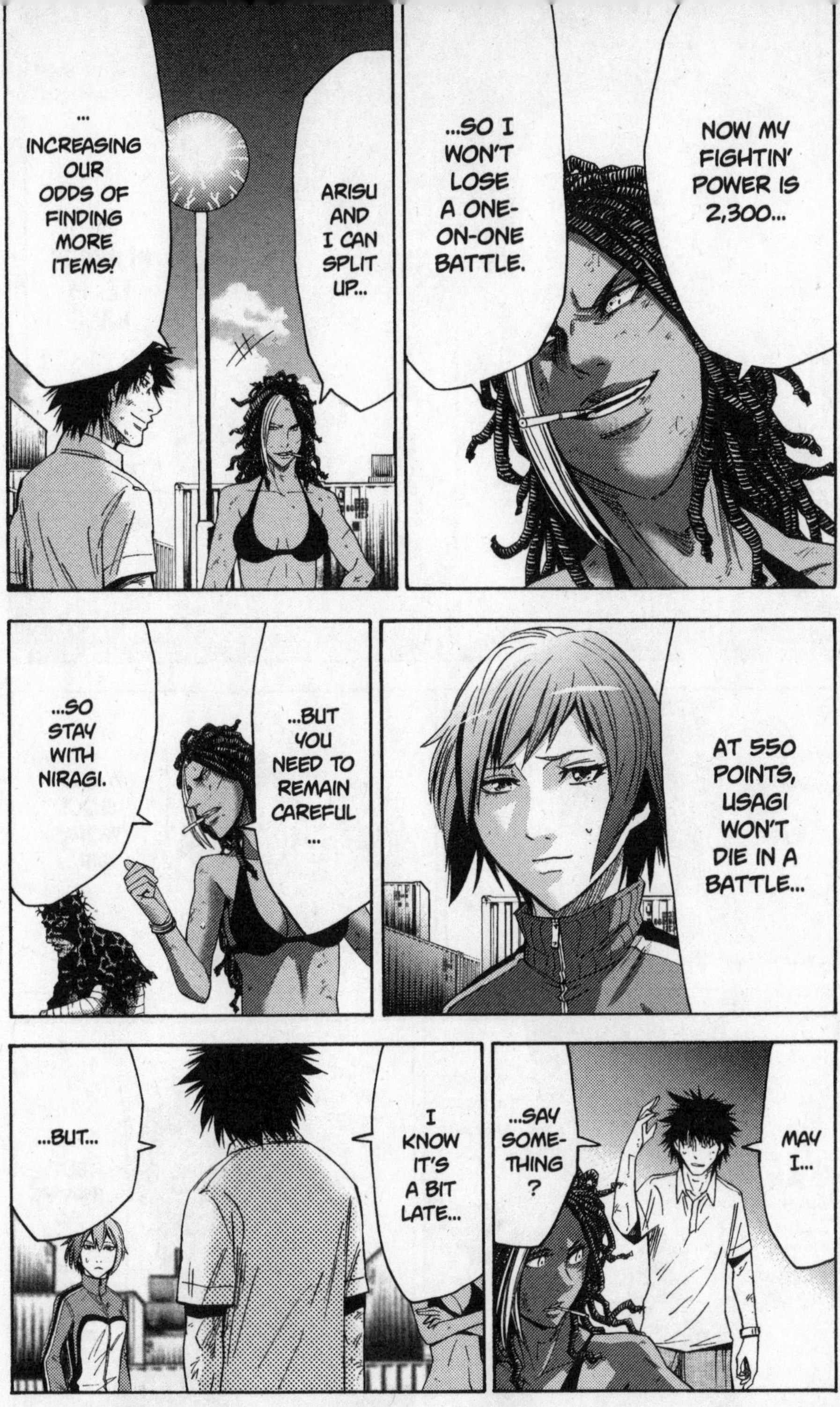

NOW MY FIGHTIN' POWER IS 2,300...
...SO I WON'T LOSE A ONE-ON-ONE BATTLE.
ARISU AND I CAN SPLIT UP...
... INCREASING OUR ODDS OF FINDING MORE ITEMS!
AT 550 POINTS, USAGI WON'T DIE IN A BATTLE...
...BUT YOU NEED TO REMAIN CAREFUL ...
...SO STAY WITH NIRAGI.
MAY I...
...SAY SOME-THING ?
I KNOW IT'S A BIT LATE...
...BUT...

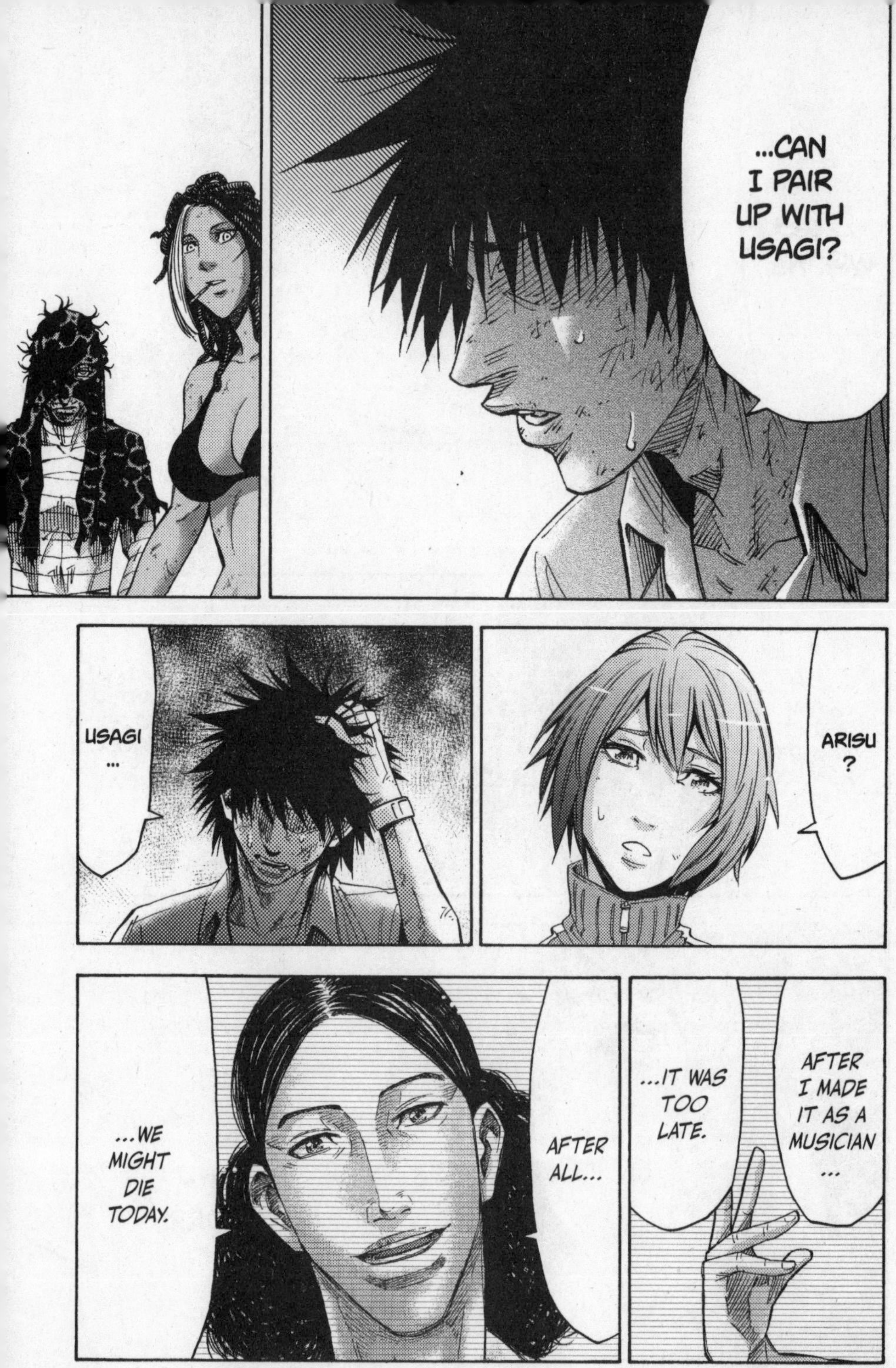
...CAN I PAIR UP WITH USAGI?
ARISU?
USAGI...
AFTER I MADE IT AS A MUSICIAN...
...IT WAS TOO LATE.
AFTER ALL...
...WE MIGHT DIE TODAY.

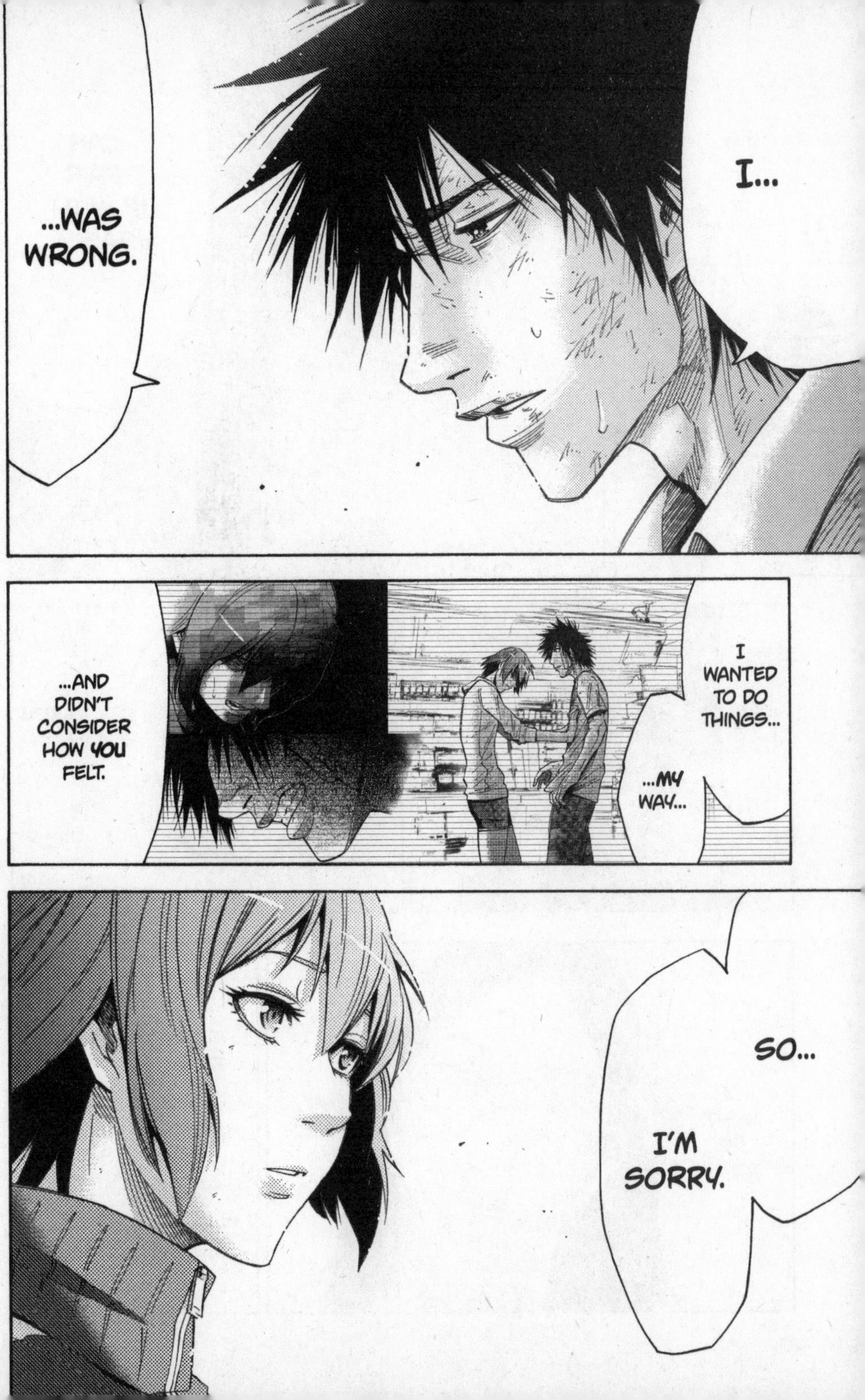
I...
...WAS WRONG.
I WANTED TO DO THINGS...
...MY WAY...
...AND DIDN'T CONSIDER HOW YOU FELT.
SO...
I'M SORRY.

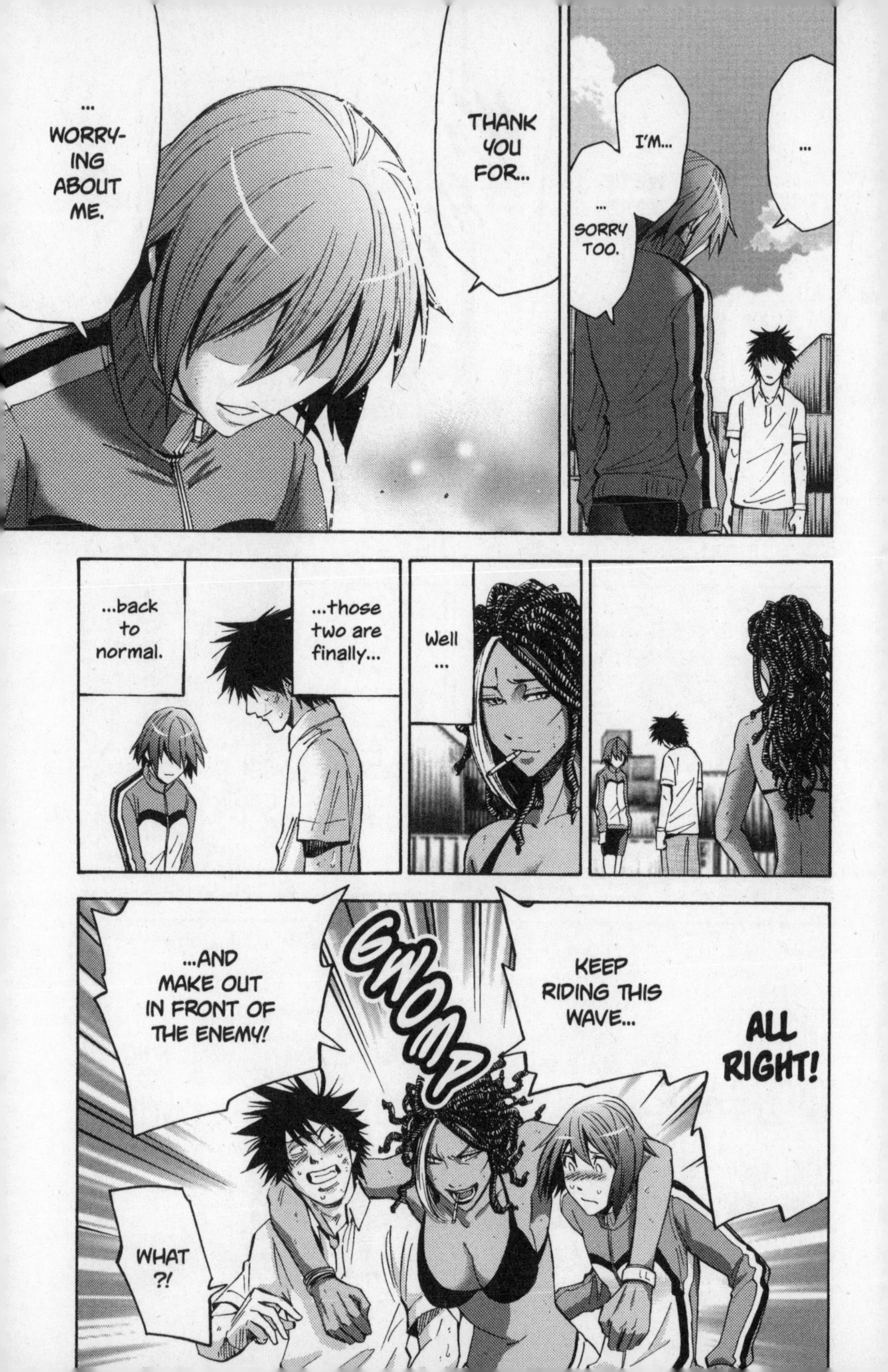
...
I'M...
... SORRY TOO.
THANK YOU FOR...
... WORRYING ABOUT ME.
Well ...
...those two are finally...
...back to normal.
ALL RIGHT!
KEEP RIDING THIS WAVE...
GWOMP
...AND MAKE OUT IN FRONT OF THE ENEMY!
WHAT ?!

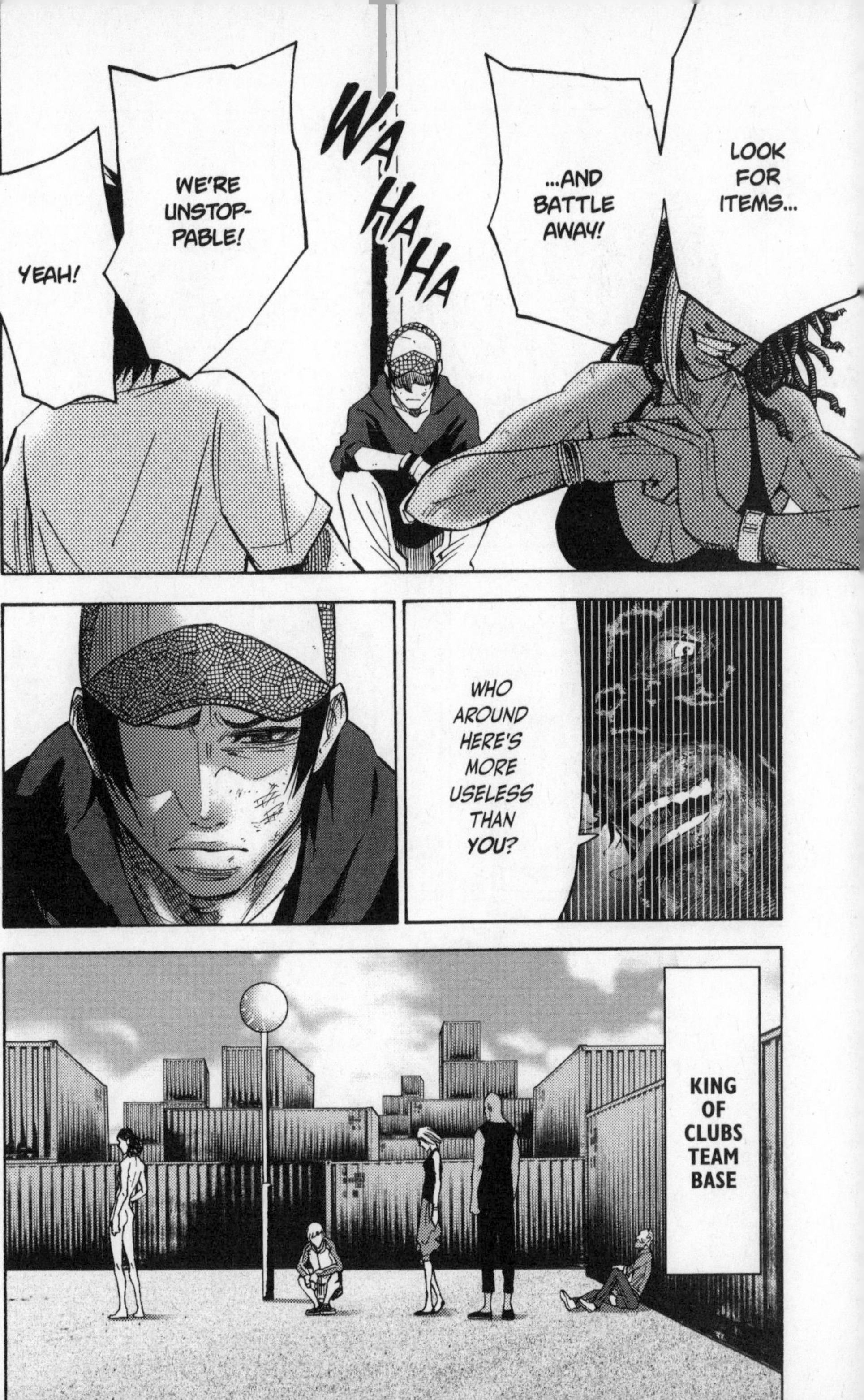
LOOK FOR ITEMS...
...AND BATTLE AWAY!
WAHAHAHA
WE'RE UNSTOP-PABLE!
YEAH!
WHO AROUND HERE'S MORE USELESS THAN YOU?
KING OF CLUBS TEAM BASE

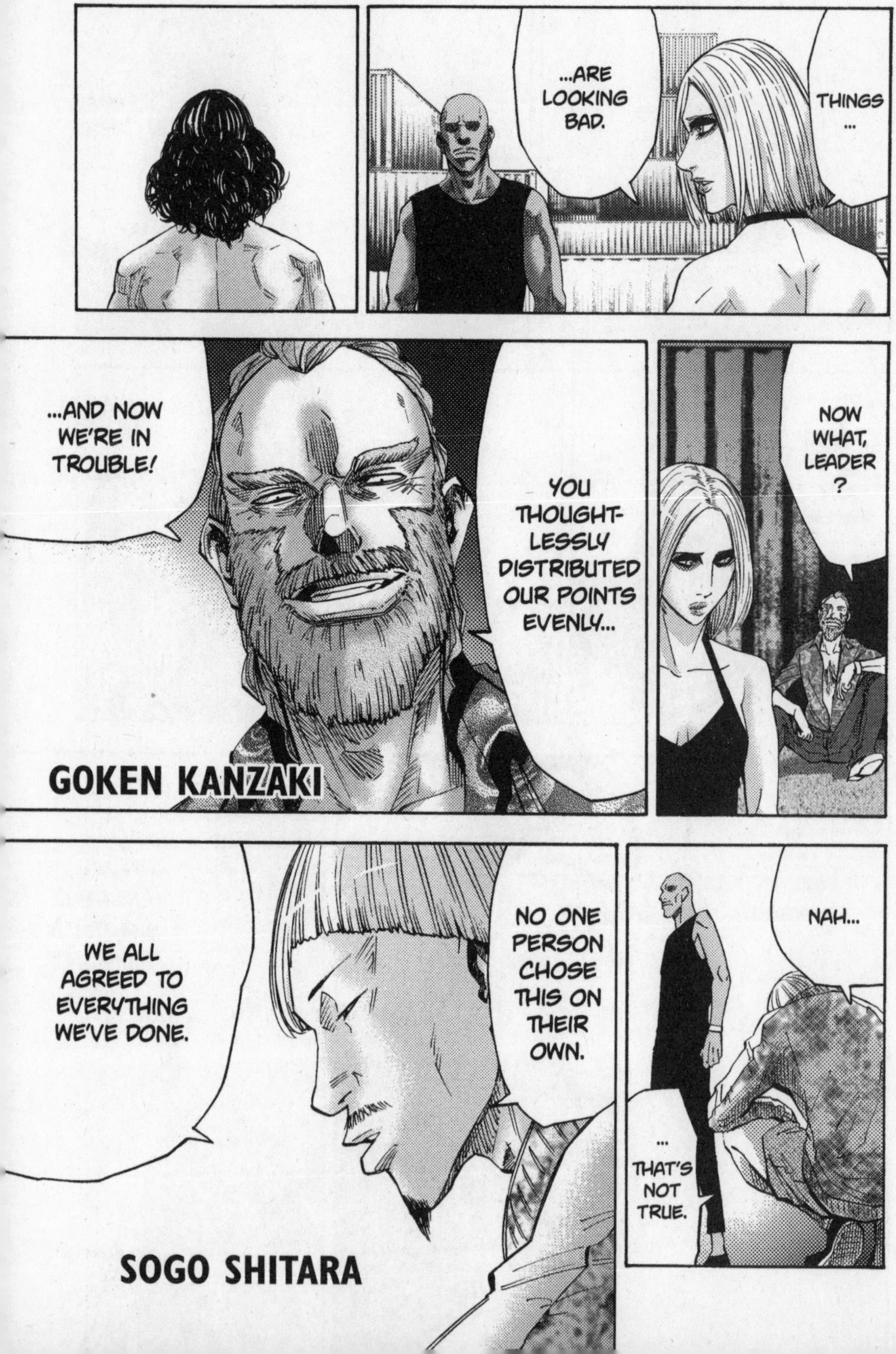
THINGS ...
...ARE LOOKING BAD.
NOW WHAT, LEADER?
YOU THOUGHT-LESSLY DISTRIBUTED OUR POINTS EVENLY...
...AND NOW WE'RE IN TROUBLE!
GOKEN KANZAKI
NAH...
... THAT'S NOT TRUE.
NO ONE PERSON CHOSE THIS ON THEIR OWN.
WE ALL AGREED TO EVERYTHING WE'VE DONE.
SOGO SHITARA

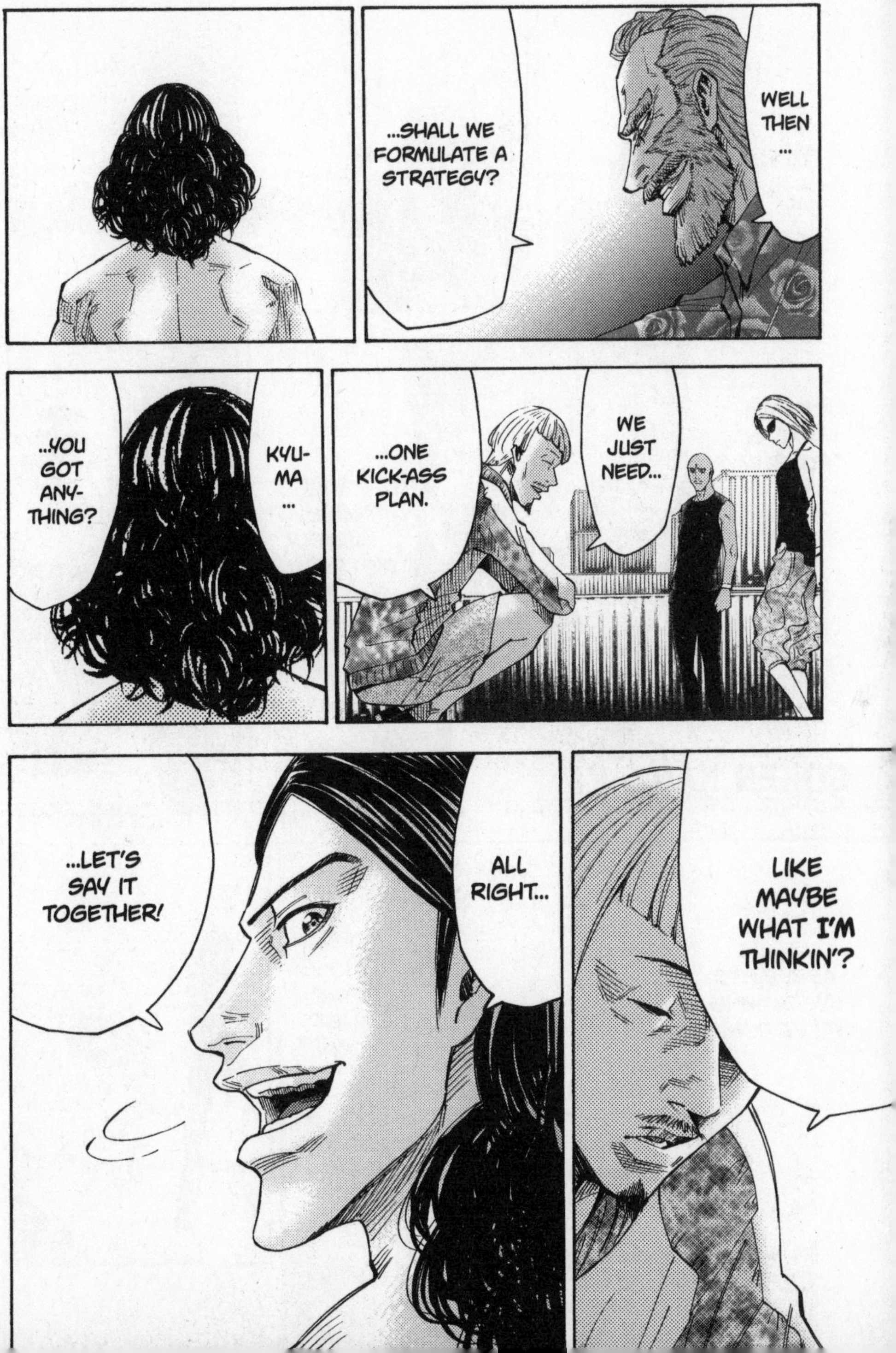
WELL THEN ...
...SHALL WE FORMULATE A STRATEGY?
WE JUST NEED...
...ONE KICK-ASS PLAN.
KYU-MA ...
...YOU GOT ANY-THING?
LIKE MAYBE WHAT I'M THINKIN'?
ALL RIGHT...
...LET'S SAY IT TOGETHER!

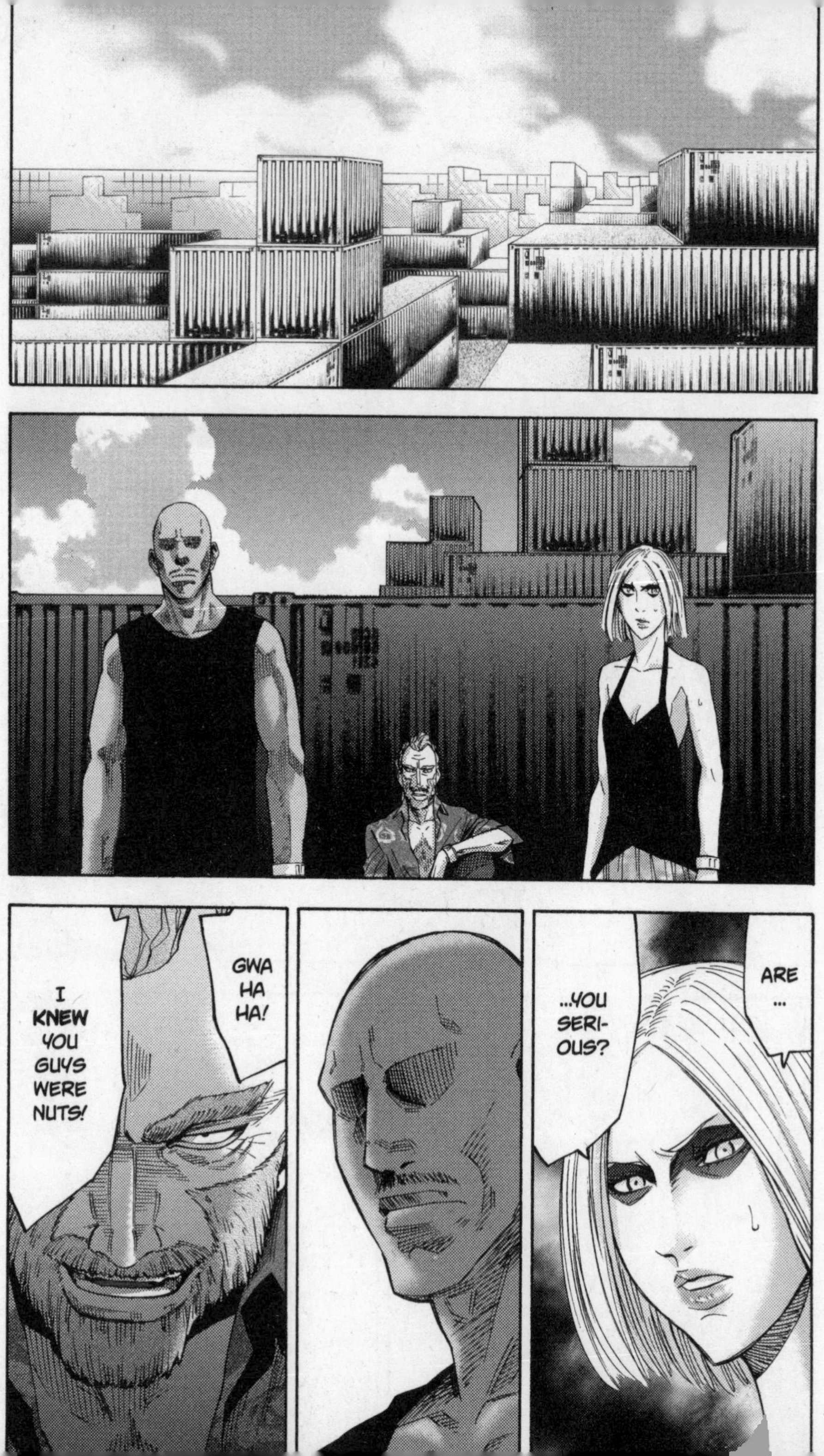
ARE...
...YOU SERIOUS?
GWA HA HA!
I KNEW YOU GUYS WERE NUTS!

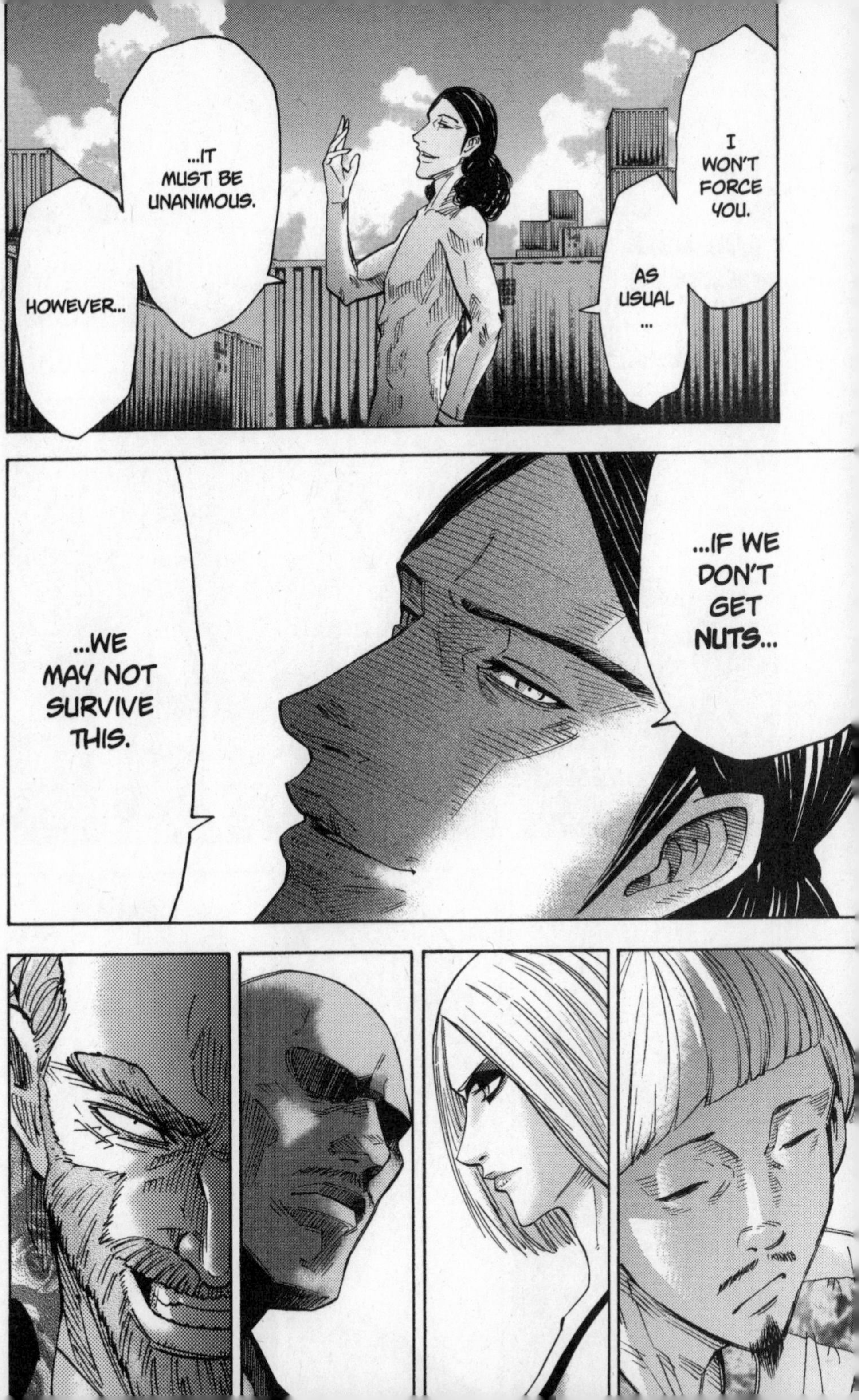

I WON'T FORCE YOU.
AS USUAL...
...IT MUST BE UNANIMOUS.
HOWEVER...
...IF WE DON'T GET NUTS...
...WE MAY NOT SURVIVE THIS.

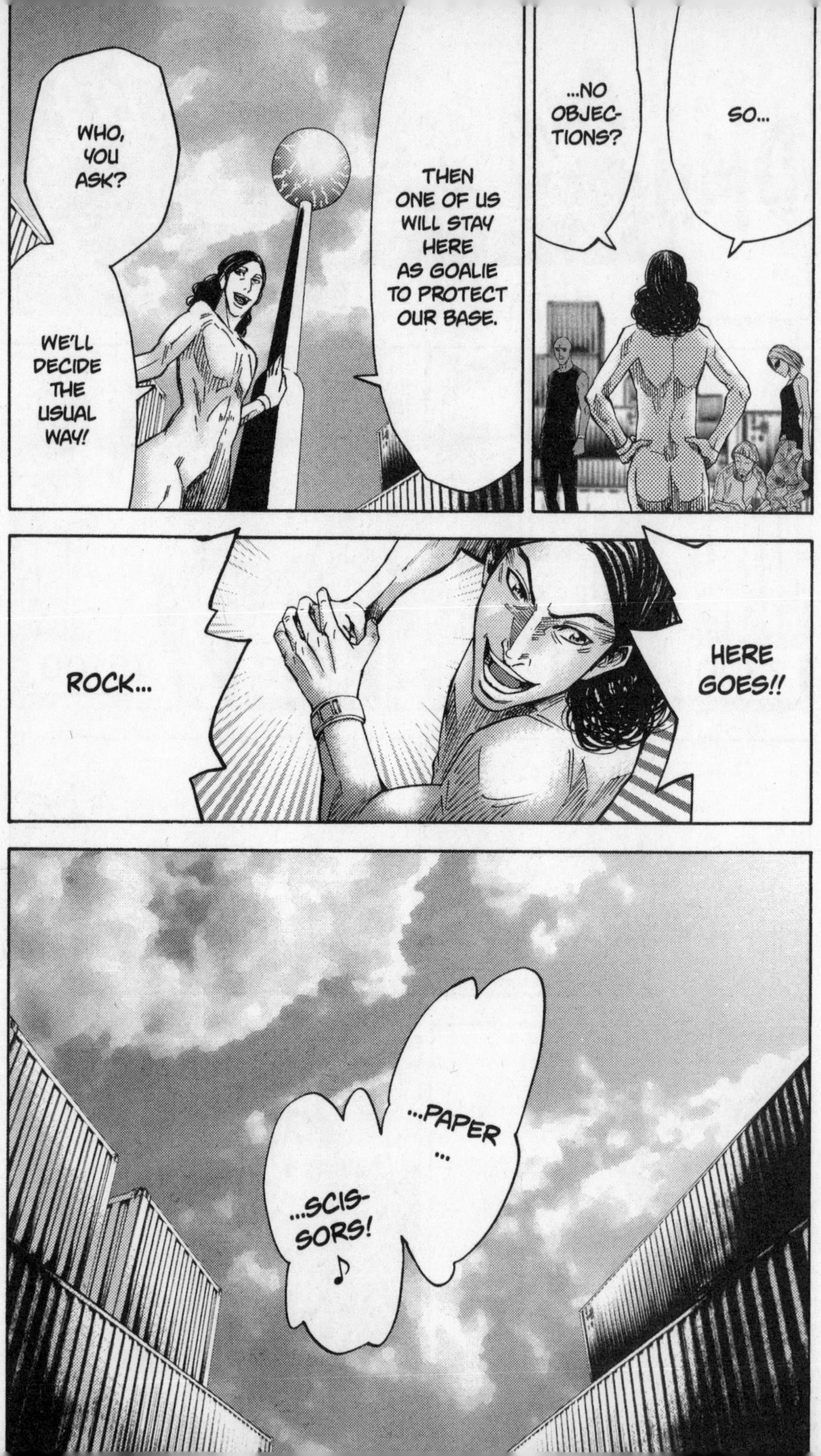
SO...
...NO OBJEC-TIONS?
THEN ONE OF US WILL STAY HERE AS GOALIE TO PROTECT OUR BASE.
WHO, YOU ASK?
WE'LL DECIDE THE USUAL WAY!
HERE GOES!!
ROCK...
...PAPER ...
...SCIS-SORS! ♪

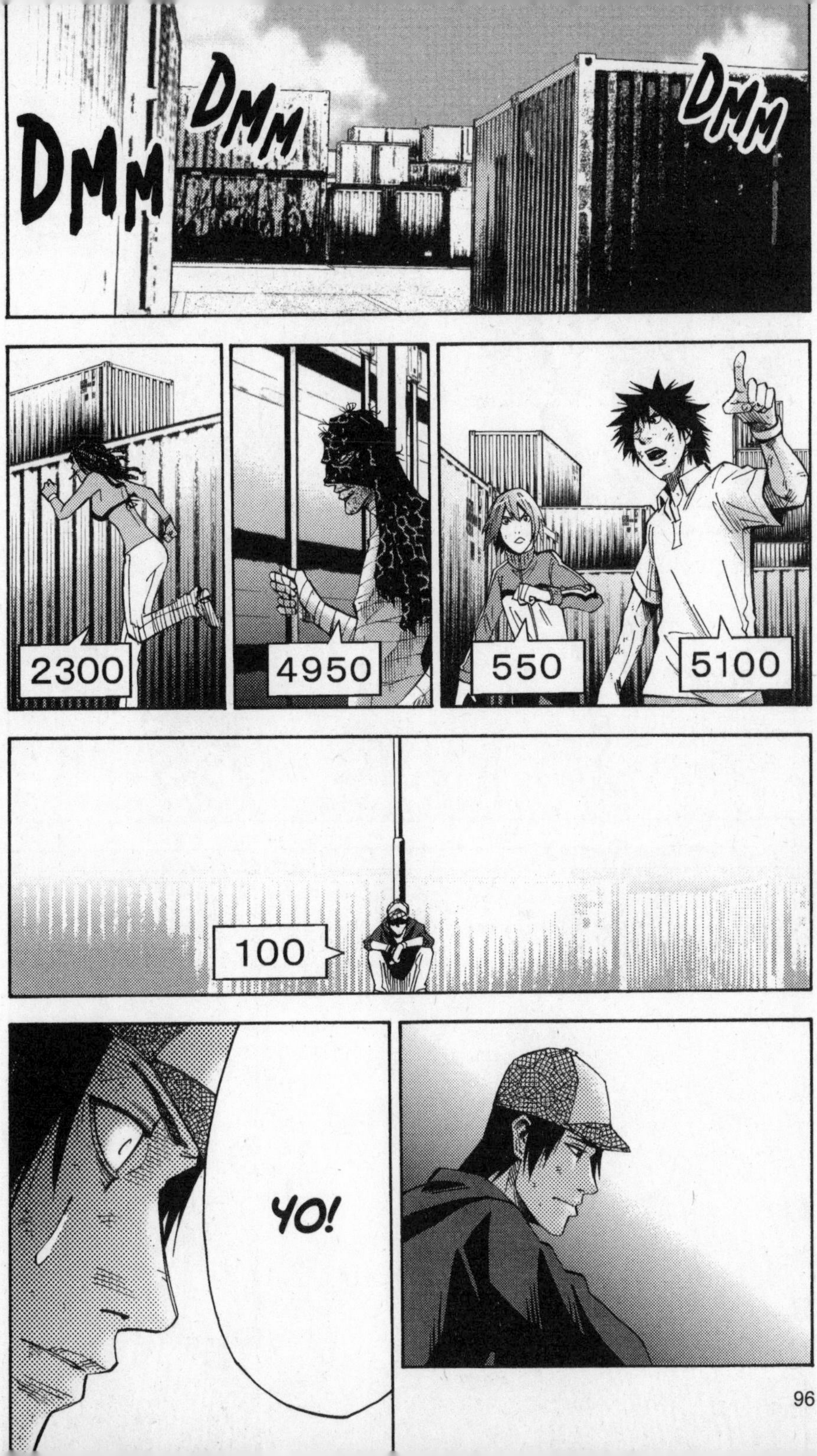
DMM
DMM
DMM
5100
550
4950
2300
100
YO!

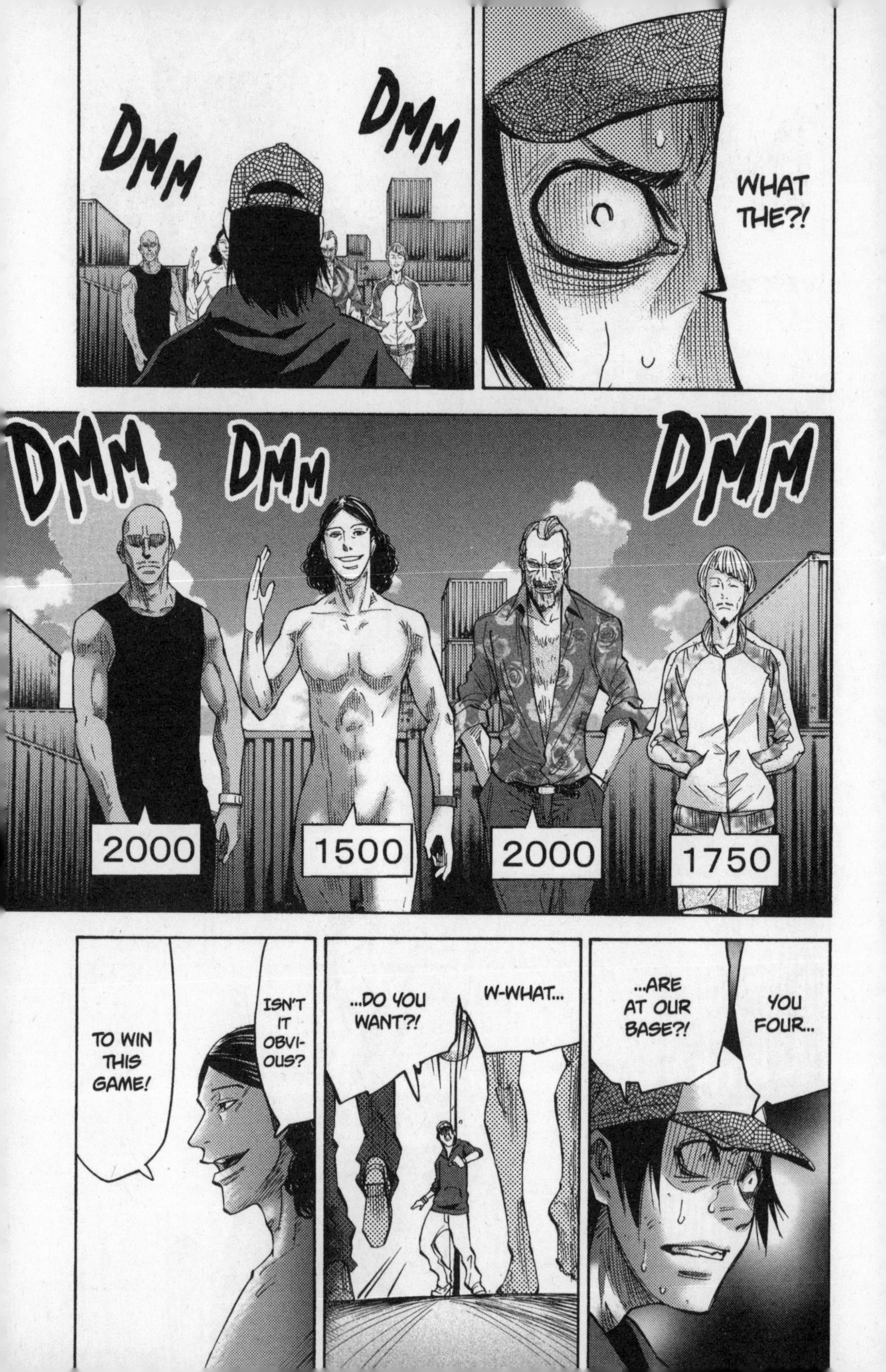
WHAT THE?!
DMM
DMM
DMM
DMM
DMM
1750
2000
1500
2000
YOU FOUR...
...ARE AT OUR BASE?!
W-WHAT...
...DO YOU WANT?!
ISN'T IT OBVIOUS?
TO WIN THIS GAME!

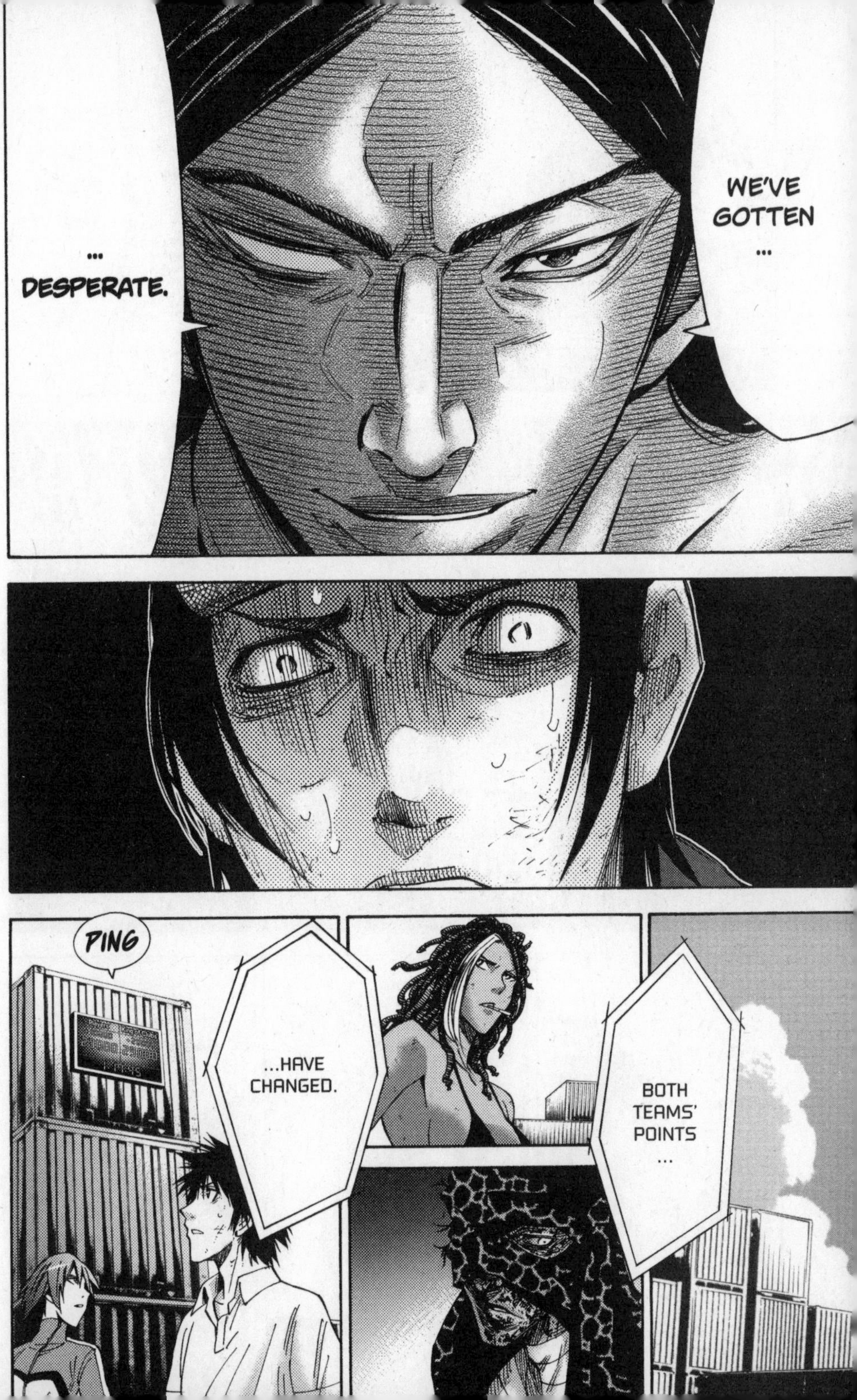
WE'VE GOTTEN ...
... DESPERATE.
BOTH TEAMS' POINTS ...
...HAVE CHANGED.
PING

WHAT ?!

...

DMM

DMM

DMM

DMM

Players	King of Clubs
+10000	+20000
23000	29000

1:17:45

THAT'S...

...A BIG CHANGE IN POINTS!

...THE FUCK JUST HAP- PENED ?!

WHAT ...

THE HELL, MAN!!

THEY GOT 20,000?!

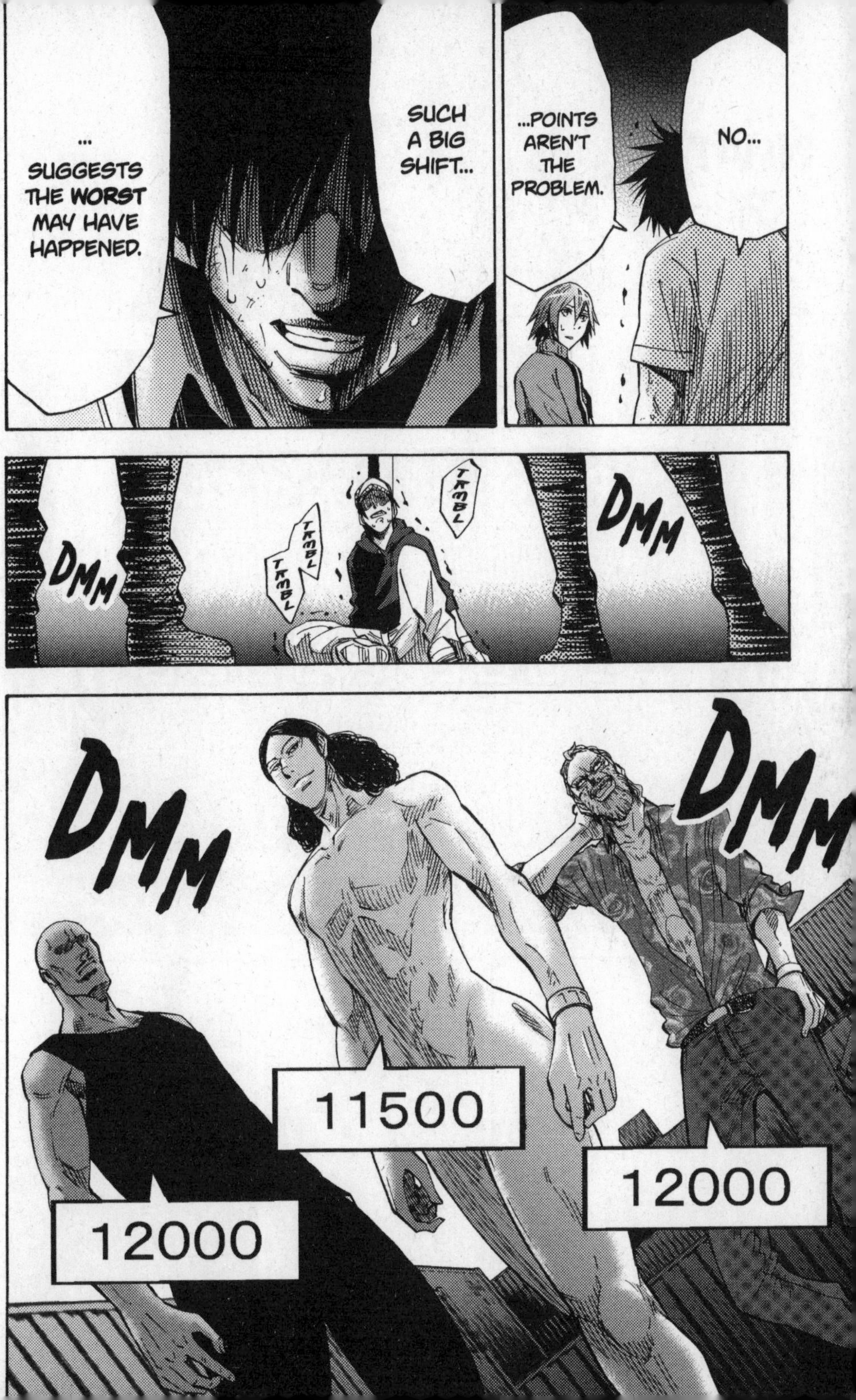
NO...
...POINTS AREN'T THE PROBLEM.
SUCH A BIG SHIFT...
... SUGGESTS THE WORST MAY HAVE HAPPENED.
DMM
TRMBL
TRMBL
TRMBL
DMM
DMM
DMM
12000
11500
12000

THE MAIN STORY WILL RESUME ON PAGE 175

THIS IS A SIDE STORY

SIDE STORY 3: Six of Diamonds, Part 1

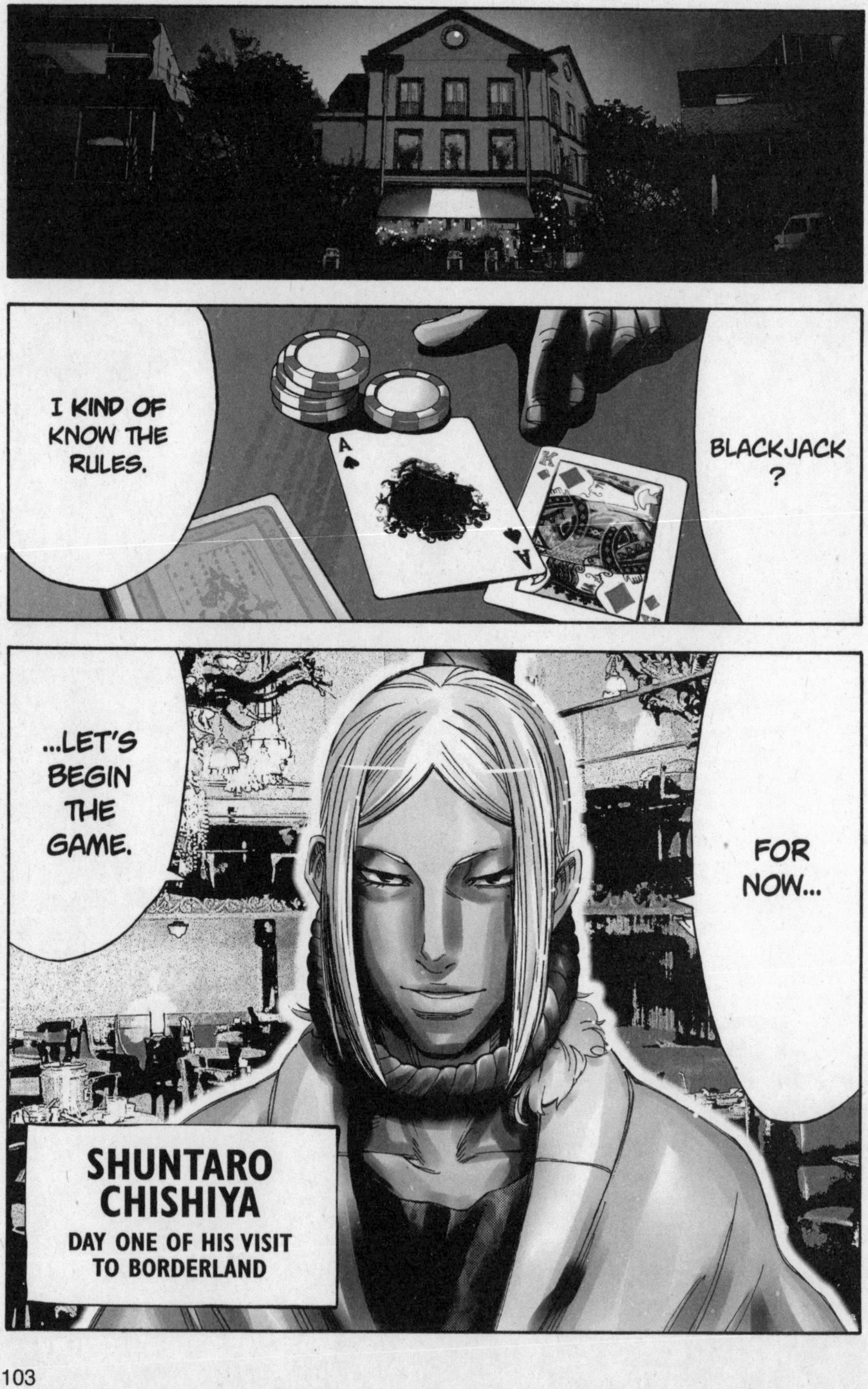
BLACKJACK?
I KIND OF KNOW THE RULES.
FOR NOW...
...LET'S BEGIN THE GAME.
SHUNTARO CHISHIYA
DAY ONE OF HIS VISIT TO BORDERLAND

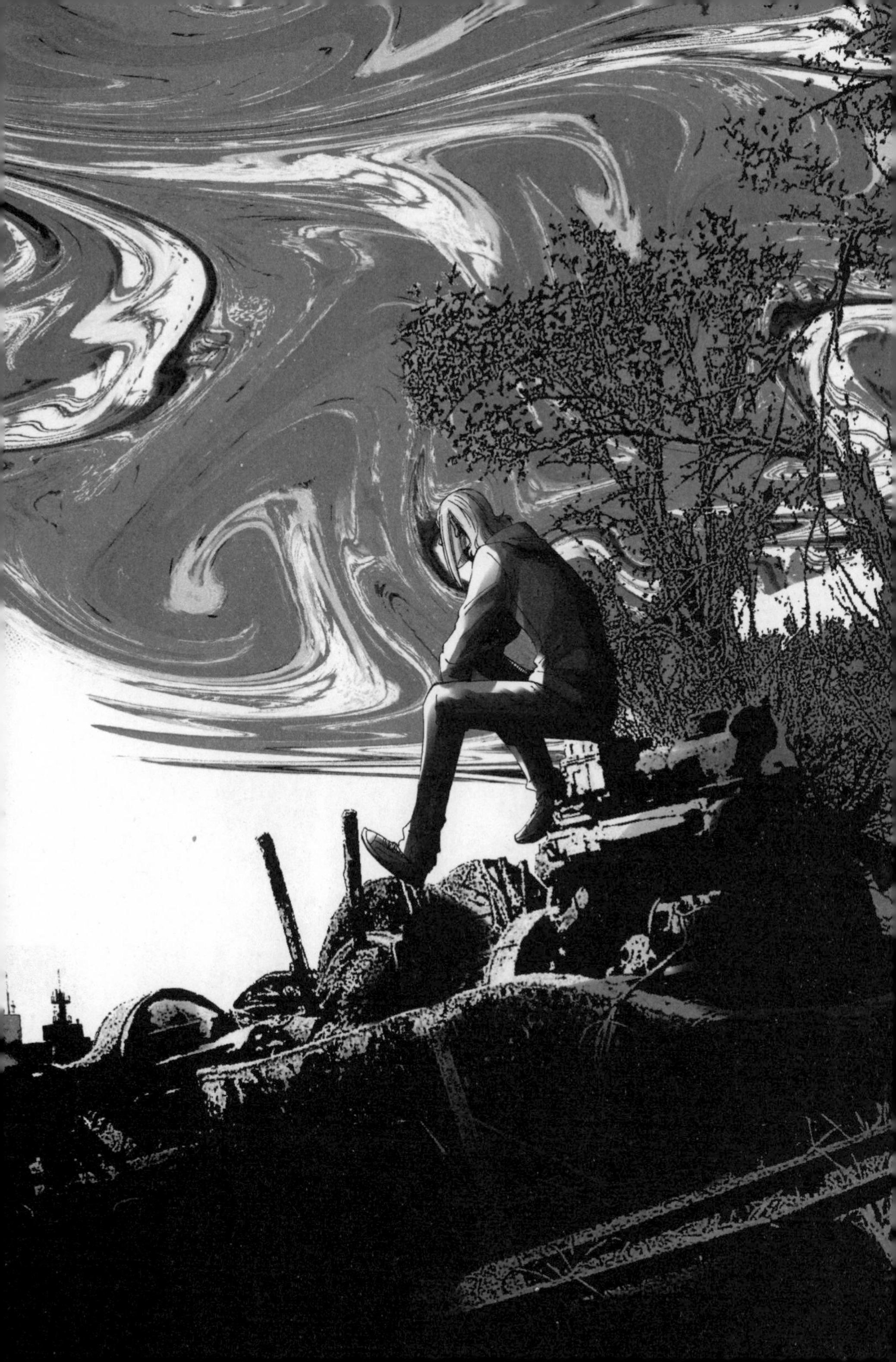

SIDE STORY 3: Six of Diamonds, Part 1

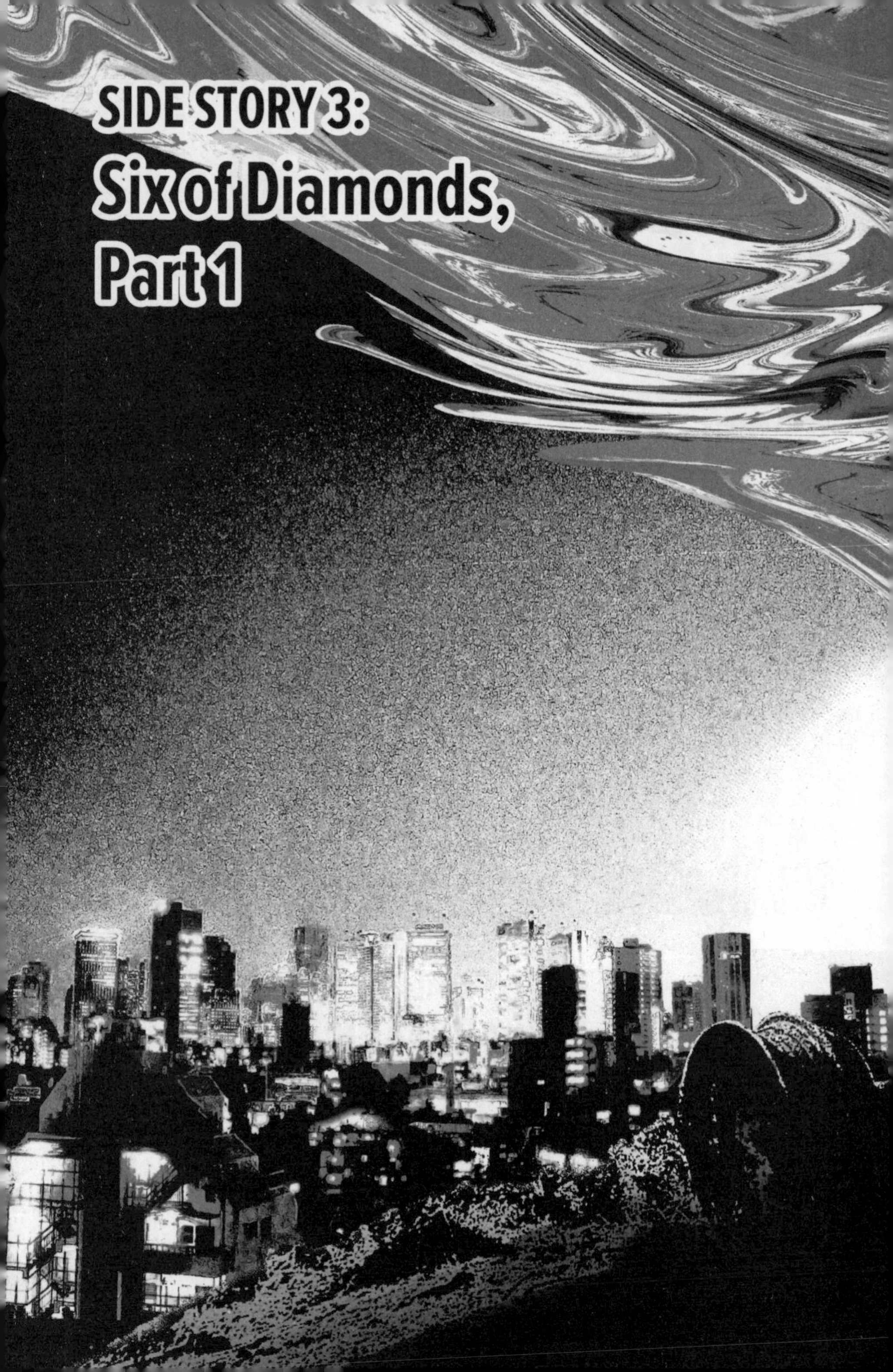

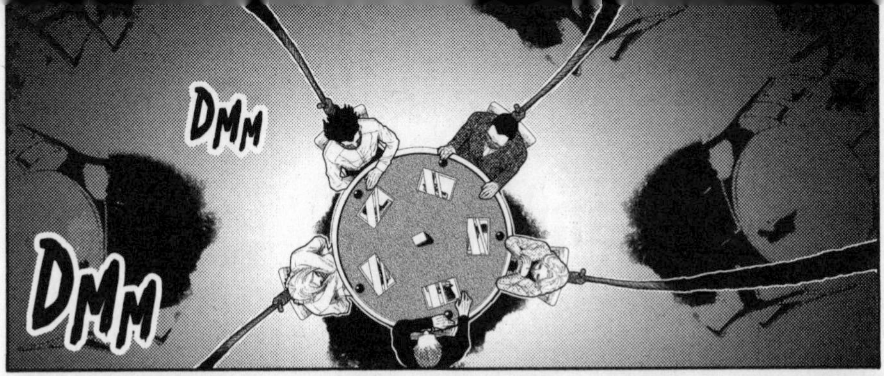
DMM
DMM

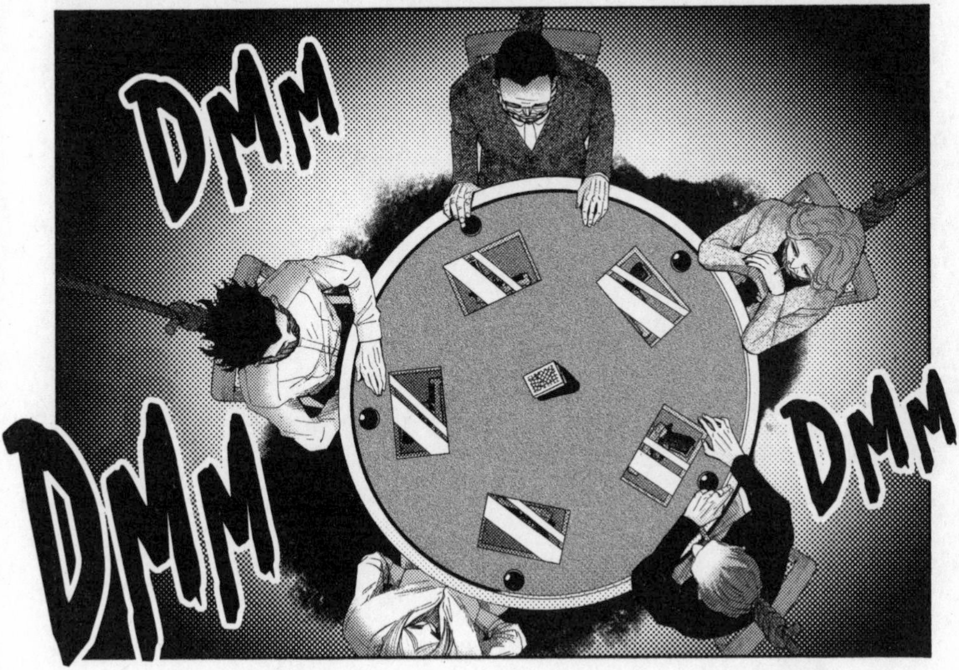
DMM
DMM
DMM

GAME:

BLACKJACK

DIFFICULTY:

SIX OF DIAMONDS

NUMBER OF PLAYERS: 5

PRIZE: AMMO CLIP

THE GAME WILL BEGIN WHEN EVERY PLAYER IS FITTED WITH A NOOSE.

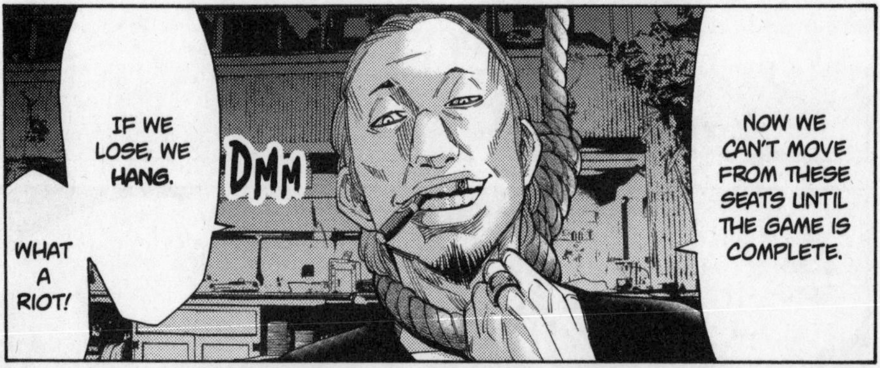
NOW WE CAN'T MOVE FROM THESE SEATS UNTIL THE GAME IS COMPLETE.
DMM
IF WE LOSE, WE HANG.
WHAT A RIOT!

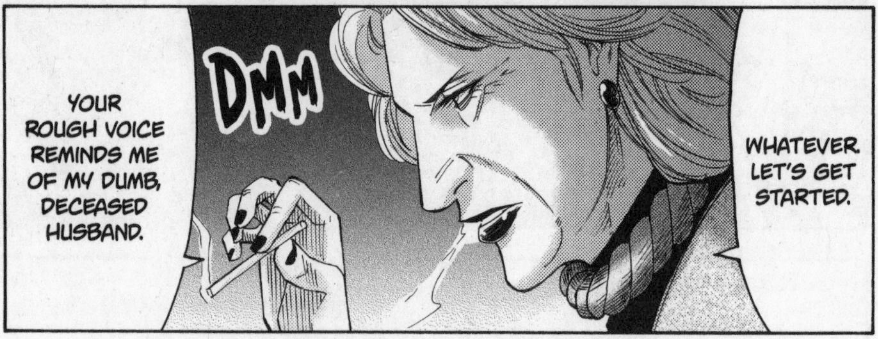
WHATEVER. LET'S GET STARTED.
DMM
YOUR ROUGH VOICE REMINDS ME OF MY DUMB, DECEASED HUSBAND.

TIME LIMIT: 1 HOUR

A GAME OVER IS CALLED IF:

- TIME RUNS OUT
- A PLAYER LOSES ALL THEIR CHIPS DURING THE GAME
- THERE IS AN INVALID CHIP EXCHANGE
- THERE IS AN INVALID PUNISHMENT

THE GAME IS COMPLETE IF:

- ONLY ONE PLAYER REMAINS WHEN TIME RUNS OUT

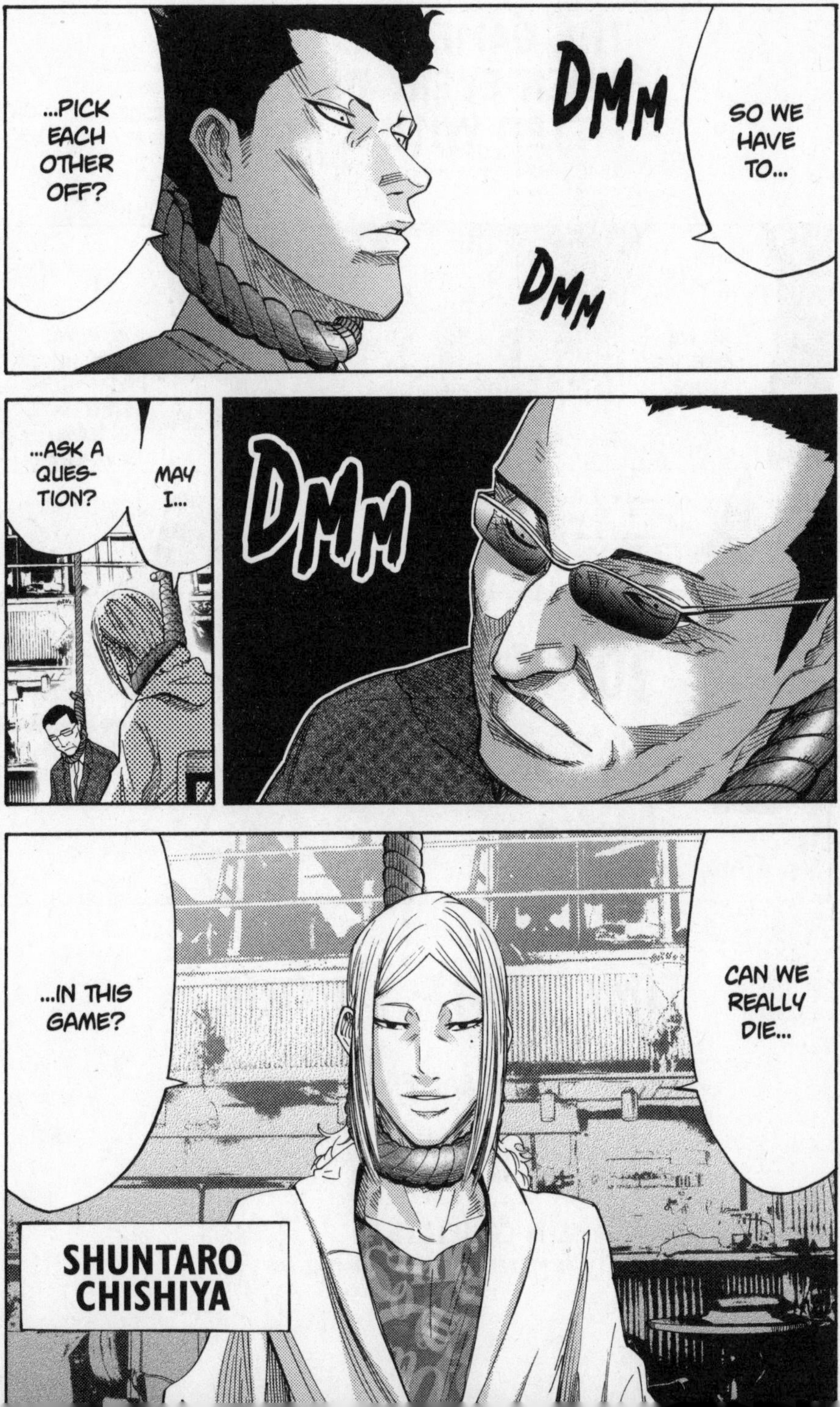
SO WE HAVE TO...
DMM
DMM
...PICK EACH OTHER OFF?
DMM
MAY I...
...ASK A QUES-TION?
CAN WE REALLY DIE...
...IN THIS GAME?
SHUNTARO CHISHIYA

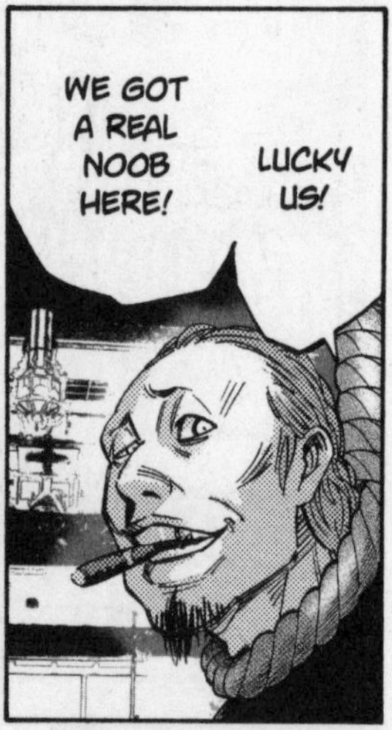
WE GOT A REAL NOOB HERE!
LUCKY US!
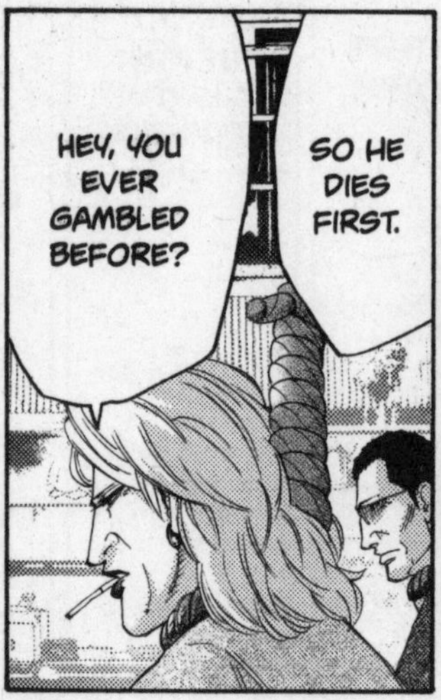
HEY, YOU EVER GAMBLED BEFORE?
SO HE DIES FIRST.
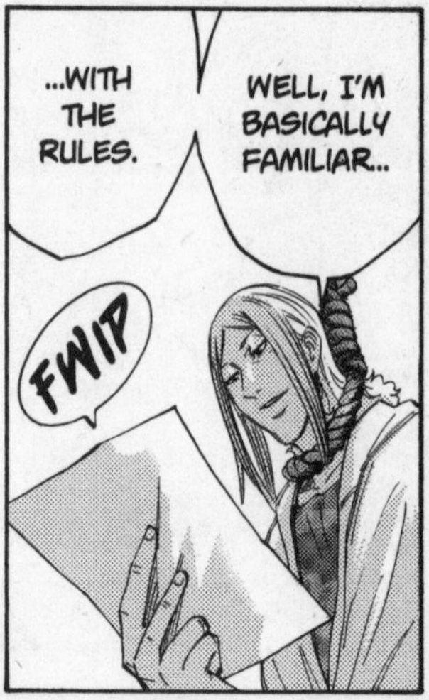
WELL, I'M BASICALLY FAMILIAR...
...WITH THE RULES.
FWIP
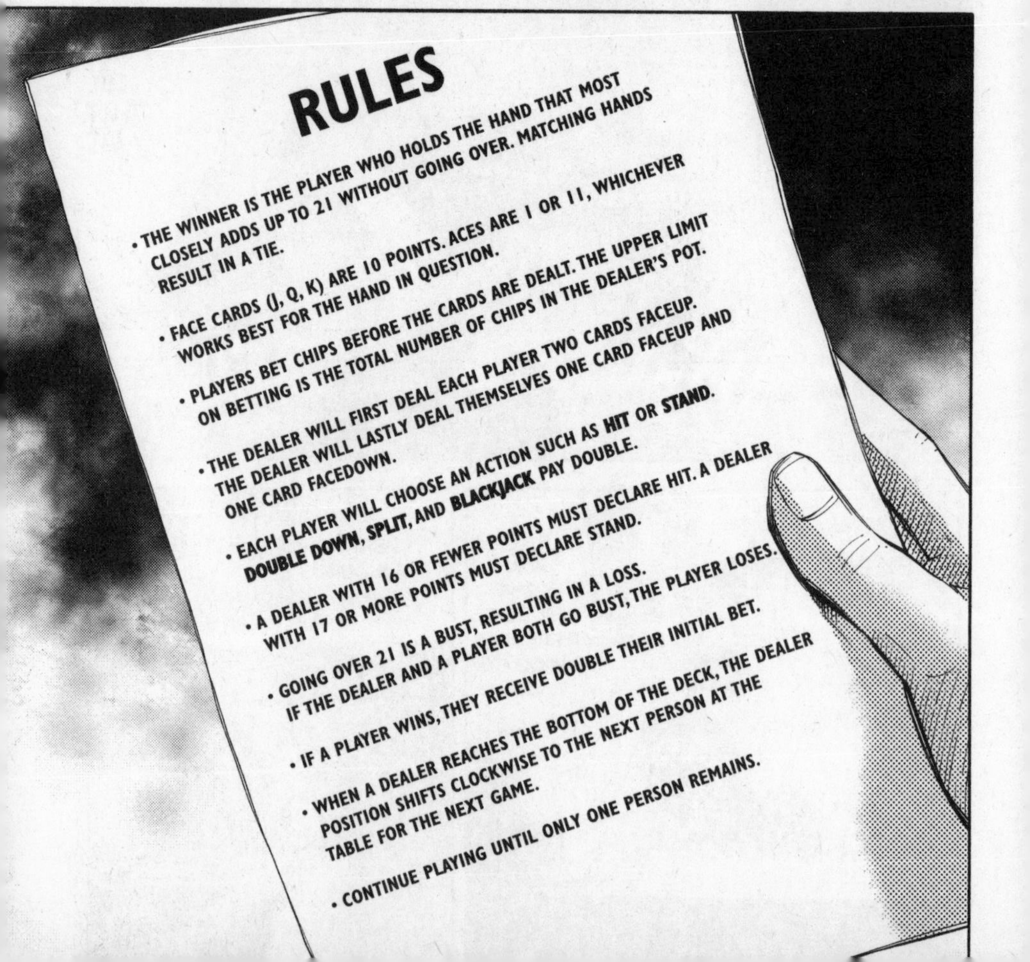

RULES

- THE WINNER IS THE PLAYER WHO HOLDS THE HAND THAT MOST CLOSELY ADDS UP TO 21 WITHOUT GOING OVER. MATCHING HANDS RESULT IN A TIE.
- FACE CARDS (J, Q, K) ARE 10 POINTS. ACES ARE 1 OR 11, WHICHEVER WORKS BEST FOR THE HAND IN QUESTION.
- PLAYERS BET CHIPS BEFORE THE CARDS ARE DEALT. THE UPPER LIMIT ON BETTING IS THE TOTAL NUMBER OF CHIPS IN THE DEALER'S POT.
- THE DEALER WILL FIRST DEAL EACH PLAYER TWO CARDS FACEUP. THE DEALER WILL LASTLY DEAL THEMSELVES ONE CARD FACEUP AND ONE CARD FACEDOWN.
- EACH PLAYER WILL CHOOSE AN ACTION SUCH AS **HIT** OR **STAND**. **DOUBLE DOWN**, **SPLIT**, AND **BLACKJACK** PAY DOUBLE.
- A DEALER WITH 16 OR FEWER POINTS MUST DECLARE HIT. A DEALER WITH 17 OR MORE POINTS MUST DECLARE STAND.
- GOING OVER 21 IS A BUST, RESULTING IN A LOSS. IF THE DEALER AND A PLAYER BOTH GO BUST, THE PLAYER LOSES.
- IF A PLAYER WINS, THEY RECEIVE DOUBLE THEIR INITIAL BET.
- WHEN A DEALER REACHES THE BOTTOM OF THE DECK, THE DEALER POSITION SHIFTS CLOCKWISE TO THE NEXT PERSON AT THE TABLE FOR THE NEXT GAME.
- CONTINUE PLAYING UNTIL ONLY ONE PERSON REMAINS.

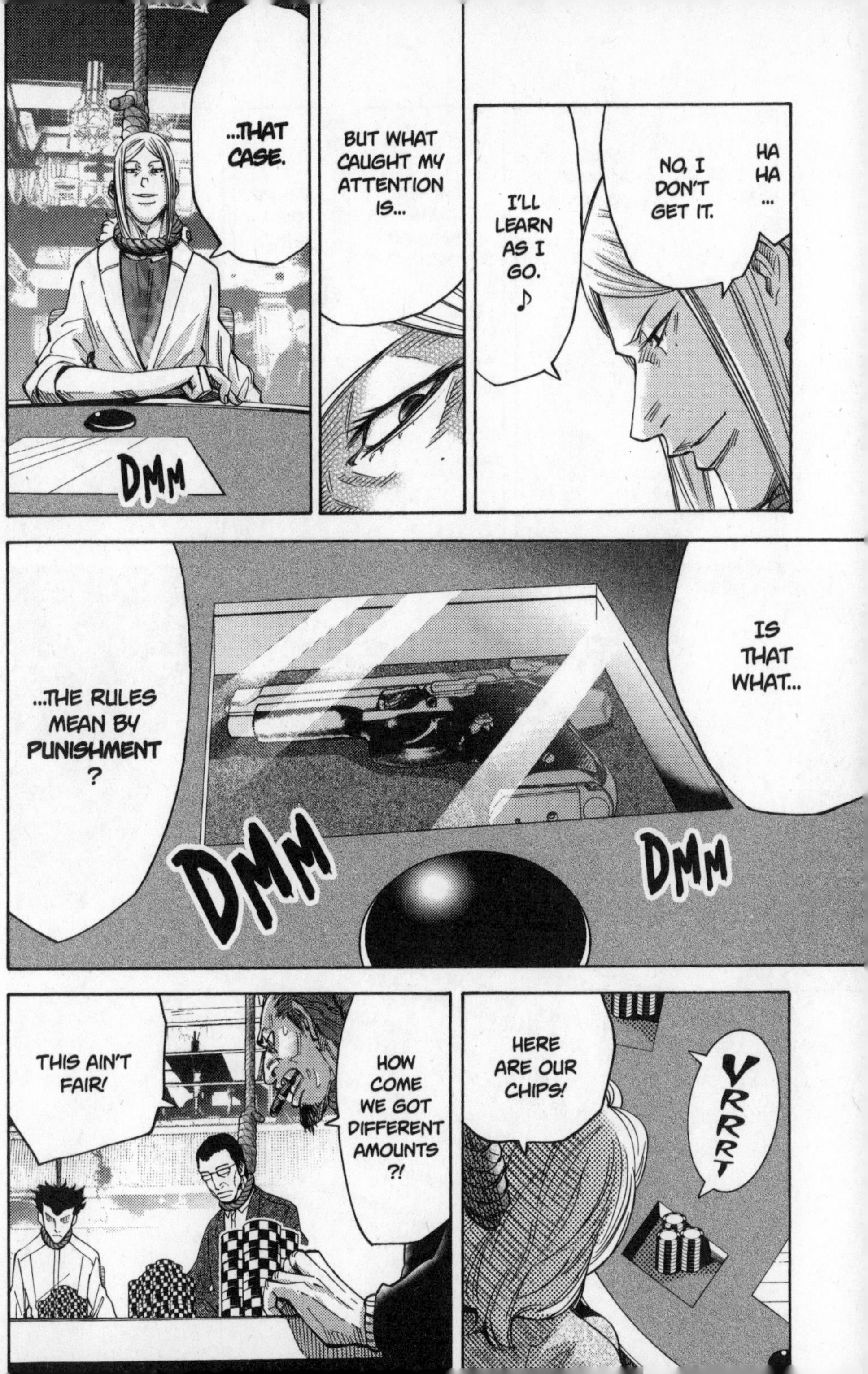
HA HA ...
NO, I DON'T GET IT.
I'LL LEARN AS I GO. ♪
BUT WHAT CAUGHT MY ATTENTION IS...
...THAT CASE.
DMM
IS THAT WHAT...
DMM
DMM
...THE RULES MEAN BY PUNISHMENT ?
VRRRT
HERE ARE OUR CHIPS!
HOW COME WE GOT DIFFERENT AMOUNTS ?!
THIS AIN'T FAIR!

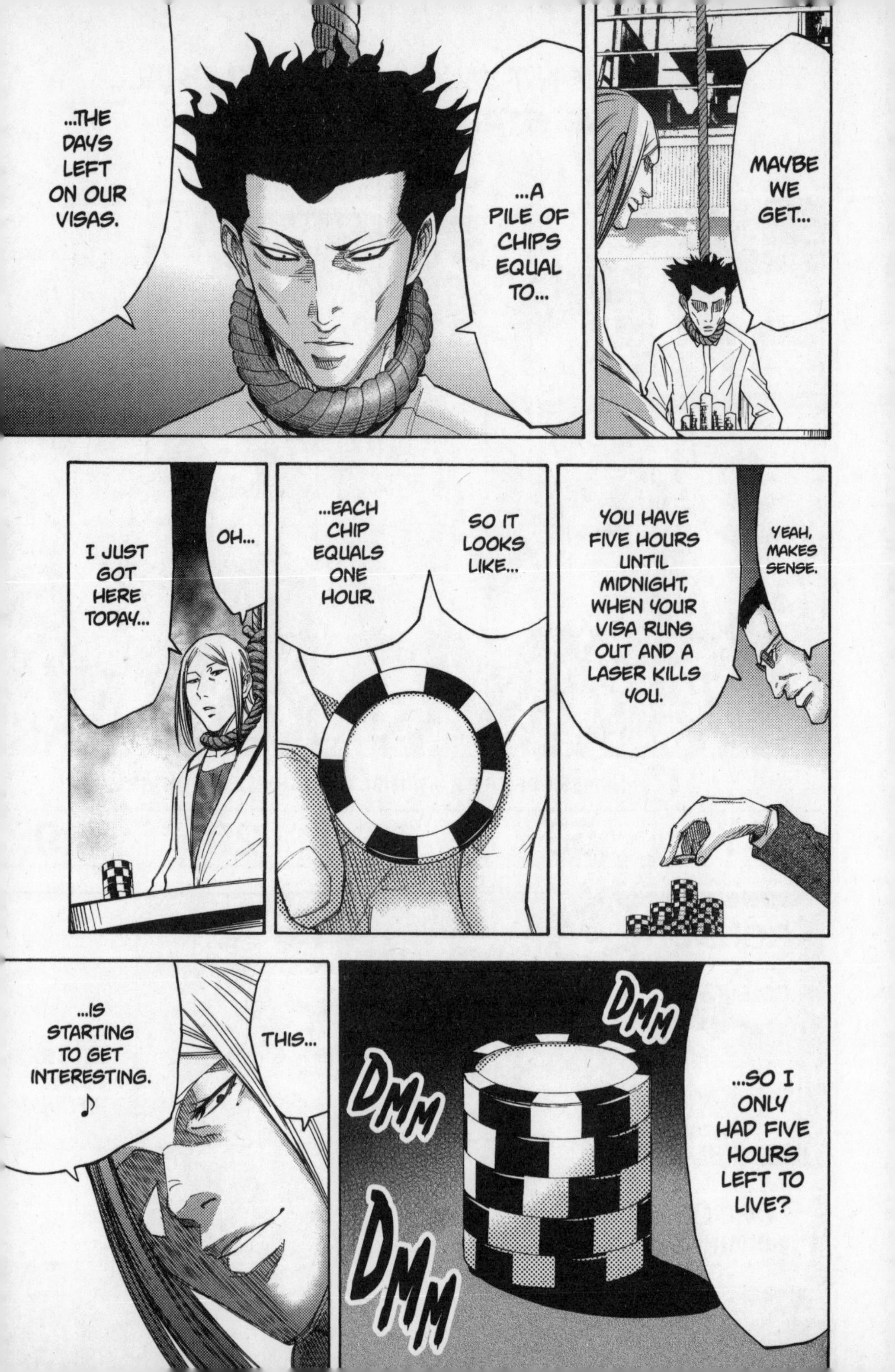
MAYBE WE GET...
...A PILE OF CHIPS EQUAL TO...
...THE DAYS LEFT ON OUR VISAS.
YEAH, MAKES SENSE.
YOU HAVE FIVE HOURS UNTIL MIDNIGHT, WHEN YOUR VISA RUNS OUT AND A LASER KILLS YOU.
SO IT LOOKS LIKE...
...EACH CHIP EQUALS ONE HOUR.
OH...
I JUST GOT HERE TODAY...
...SO I ONLY HAD FIVE HOURS LEFT TO LIVE?
DMM
DMM
DMM
THIS...
...IS STARTING TO GET INTERESTING. ♪

THERE ISN'T MUCH TIME, SO SHALL WE START THE GAME? ♪

🔘 NUMBER OF CHIPS = NUMBER OF HOURS LEFT ON VISA

77	53	5	29	29

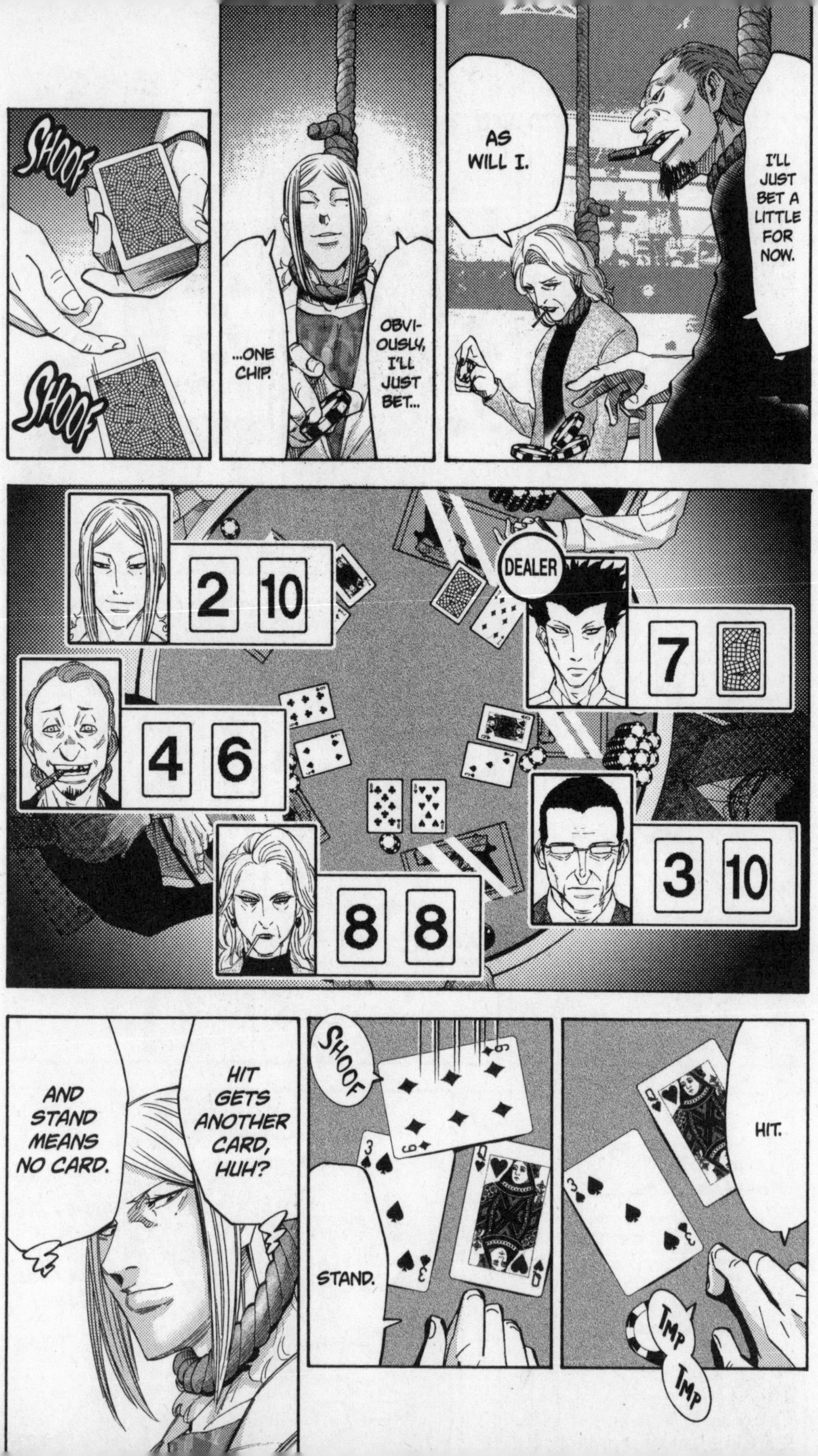
I'LL JUST BET A LITTLE FOR NOW.
AS WILL I.
OBVIOUSLY, I'LL JUST BET...
...ONE CHIP.
SHOOF
SHOOF
DEALER
7
2 10
3 10
4 6
8 8
HIT.
TMP
TMP
SHOOF
STAND.
HIT GETS ANOTHER CARD, HUH?
AND STAND MEANS NO CARD.

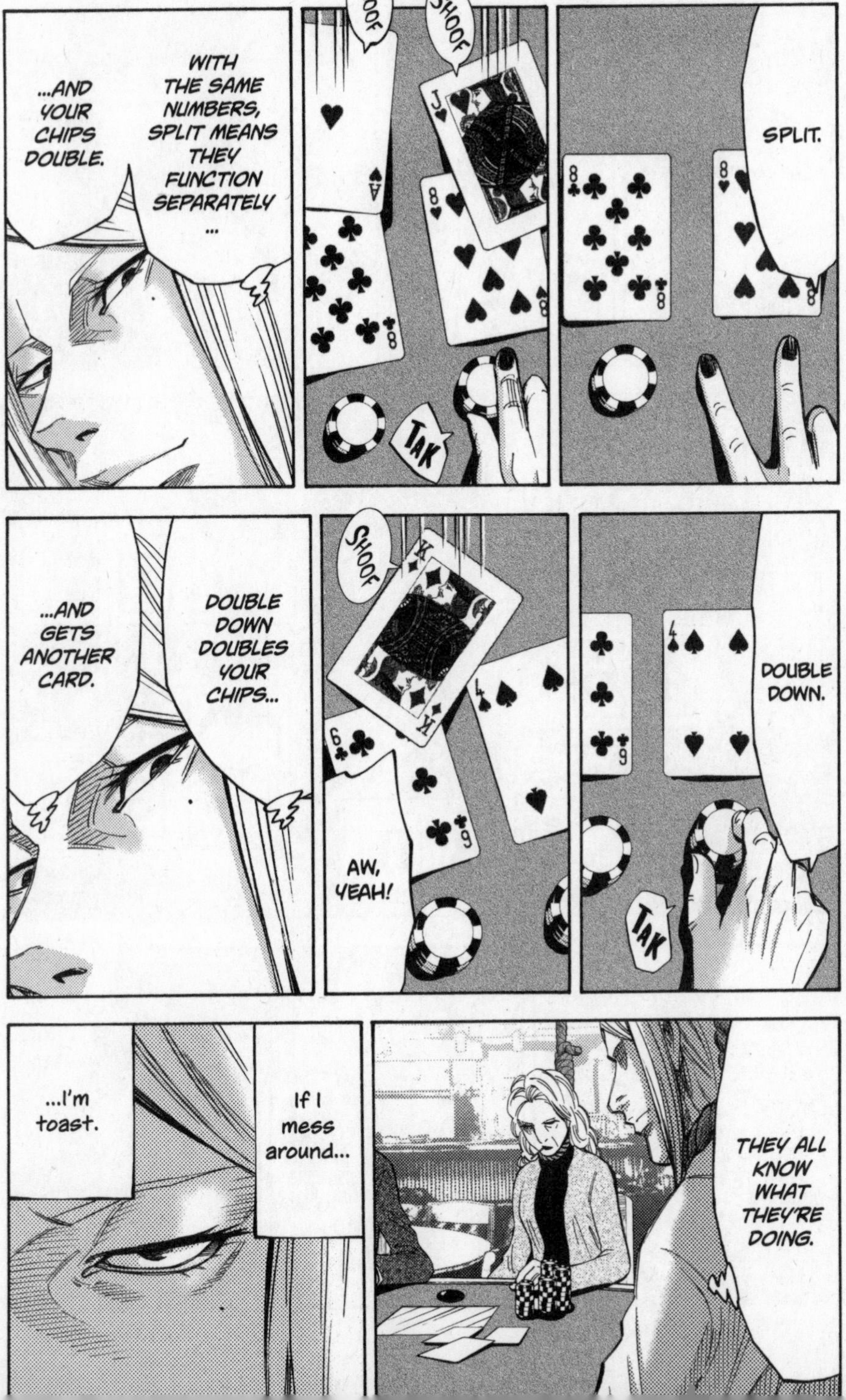
SPLIT.
SHOOF
SHOOF
TAK
WITH THE SAME NUMBERS, SPLIT MEANS THEY FUNCTION SEPARATELY ...
...AND YOUR CHIPS DOUBLE.
DOUBLE DOWN.
TAK
SHOOF
AW, YEAH!
DOUBLE DOWN DOUBLES YOUR CHIPS...
...AND GETS ANOTHER CARD.
THEY ALL KNOW WHAT THEY'RE DOING.
If I mess around...
...I'm toast.

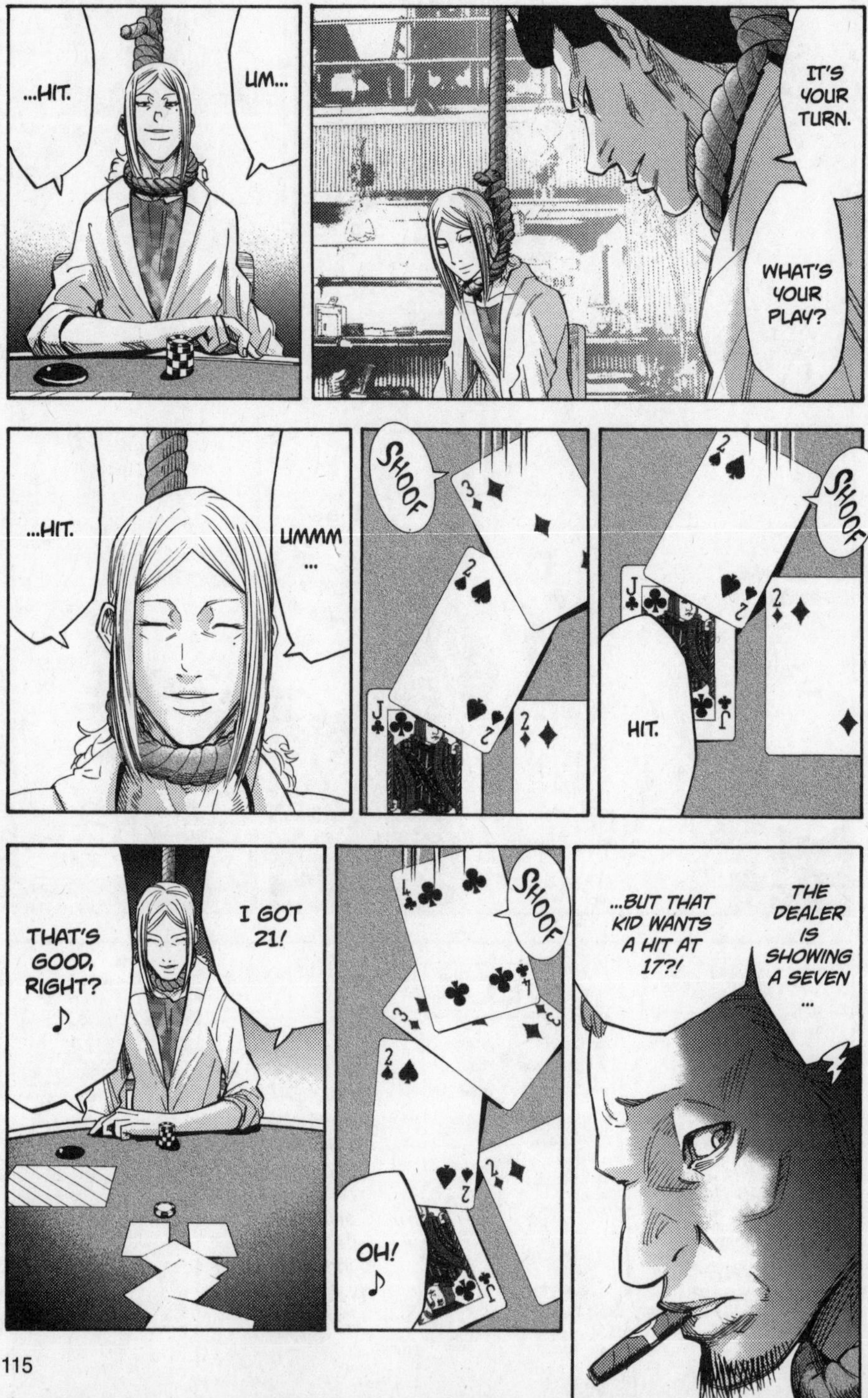

IT'S YOUR TURN.
WHAT'S YOUR PLAY?
UM...
...HIT.
SHOOF
HIT.
SHOOF
UMMM ...
...HIT.
THE DEALER IS SHOWING A SEVEN ...
...BUT THAT KID WANTS A HIT AT 17?!
SHOOF
OH! ♪
I GOT 21!
THAT'S GOOD, RIGHT? ♪

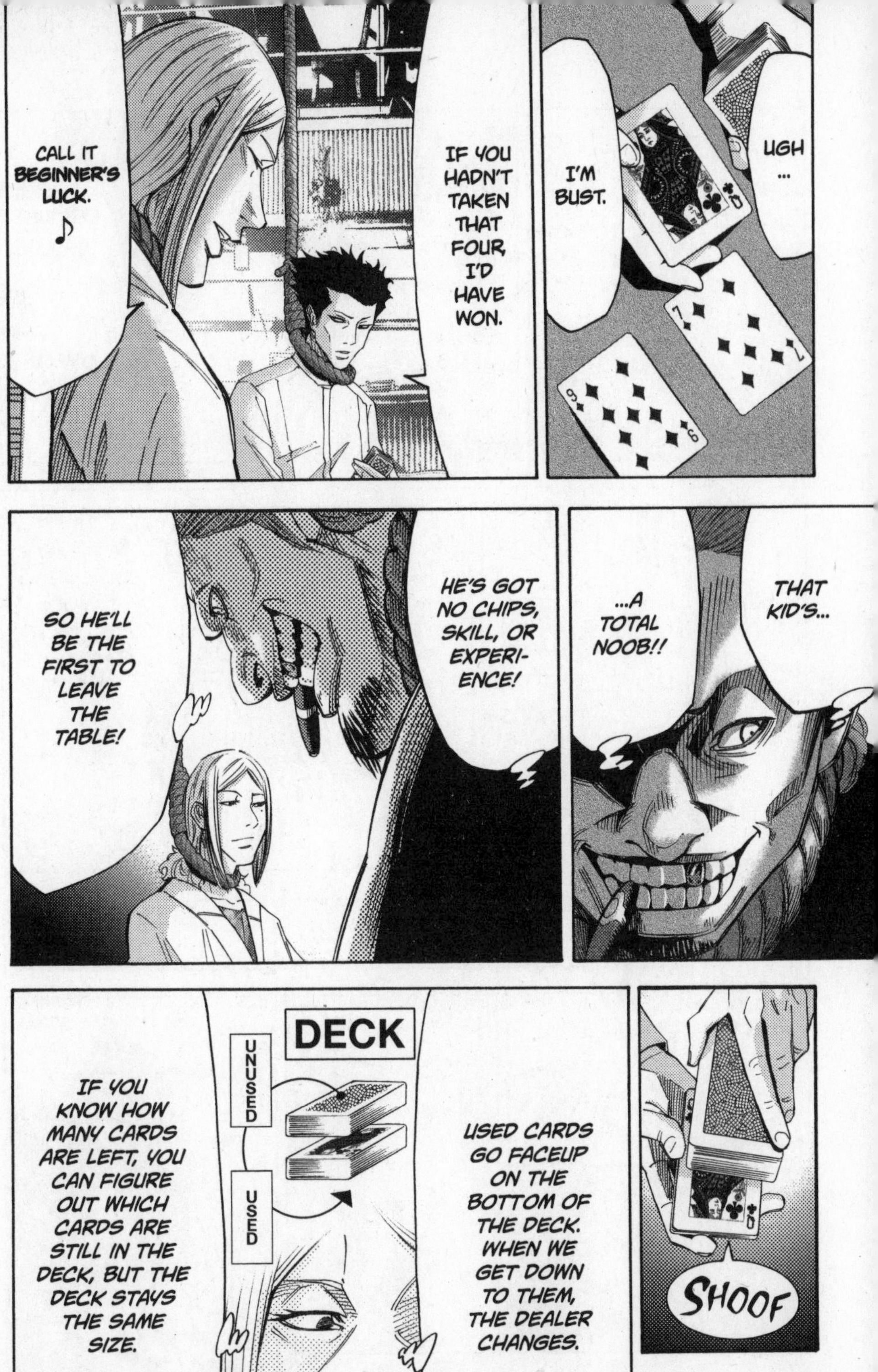
UGH ...
I'M BUST.
IF YOU HADN'T TAKEN THAT FOUR, I'D HAVE WON.
CALL IT BEGINNER'S LUCK. ♪
THAT KID'S...
...A TOTAL NOOB!!
HE'S GOT NO CHIPS, SKILL, OR EXPERIENCE!
SO HE'LL BE THE FIRST TO LEAVE THE TABLE!
SHOOF
USED CARDS GO FACEUP ON THE BOTTOM OF THE DECK. WHEN WE GET DOWN TO THEM, THE DEALER CHANGES.
DECK
UNUSED
USED
IF YOU KNOW HOW MANY CARDS ARE LEFT, YOU CAN FIGURE OUT WHICH CARDS ARE STILL IN THE DECK, BUT THE DECK STAYS THE SAME SIZE.

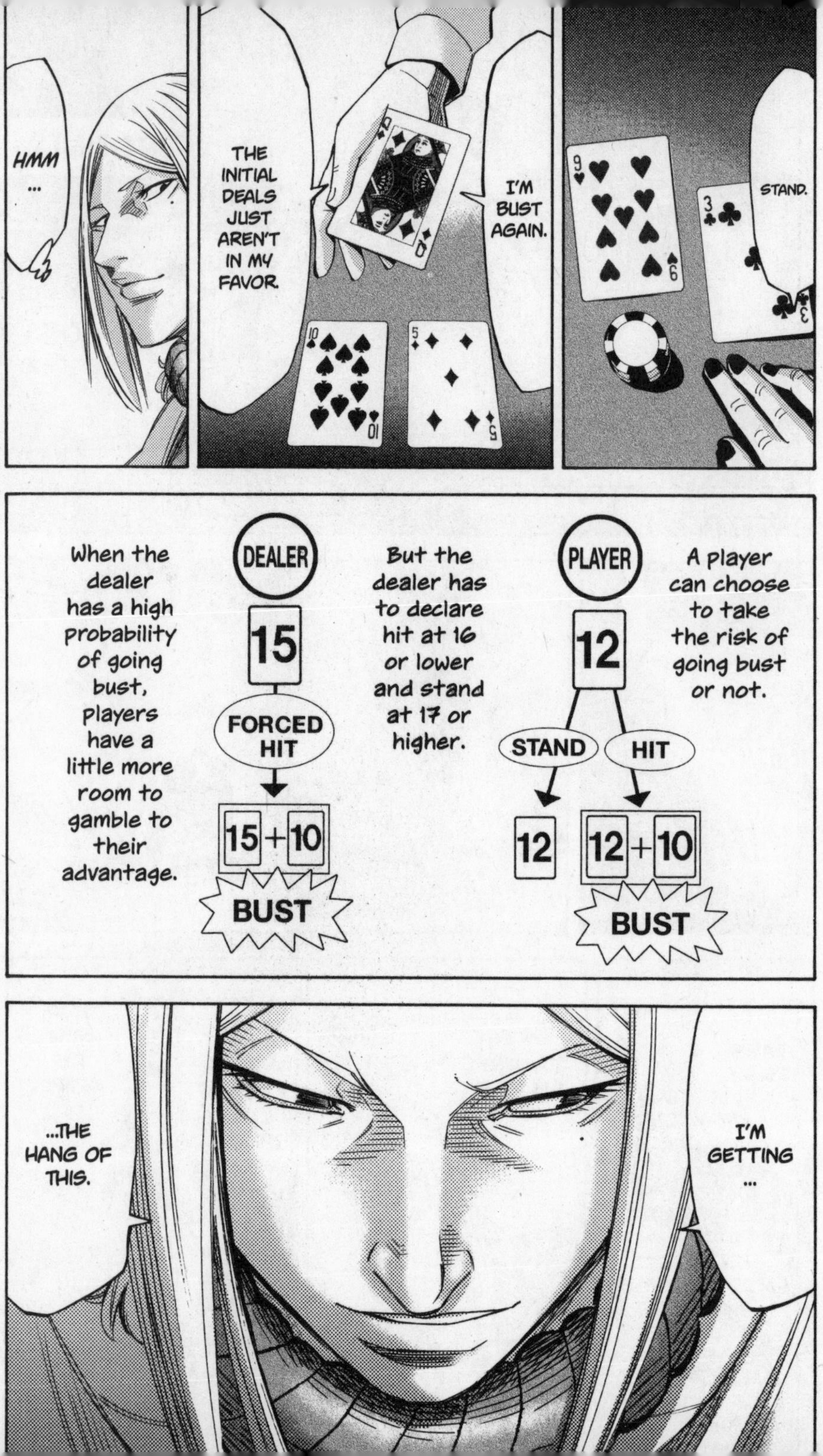
STAND.
I'M BUST AGAIN.
THE INITIAL DEALS JUST AREN'T IN MY FAVOR
HMM ...
A player can choose to take the risk of going bust or not.
PLAYER
12
STAND
HIT
12
12 + 10
BUST
But the dealer has to declare hit at 16 or lower and stand at 17 or higher.
DEALER
15
FORCED HIT
15 + 10
BUST
When the dealer has a high probability of going bust, players have a little more room to gamble to their advantage.
I'M GETTING ...
...THE HANG OF THIS.

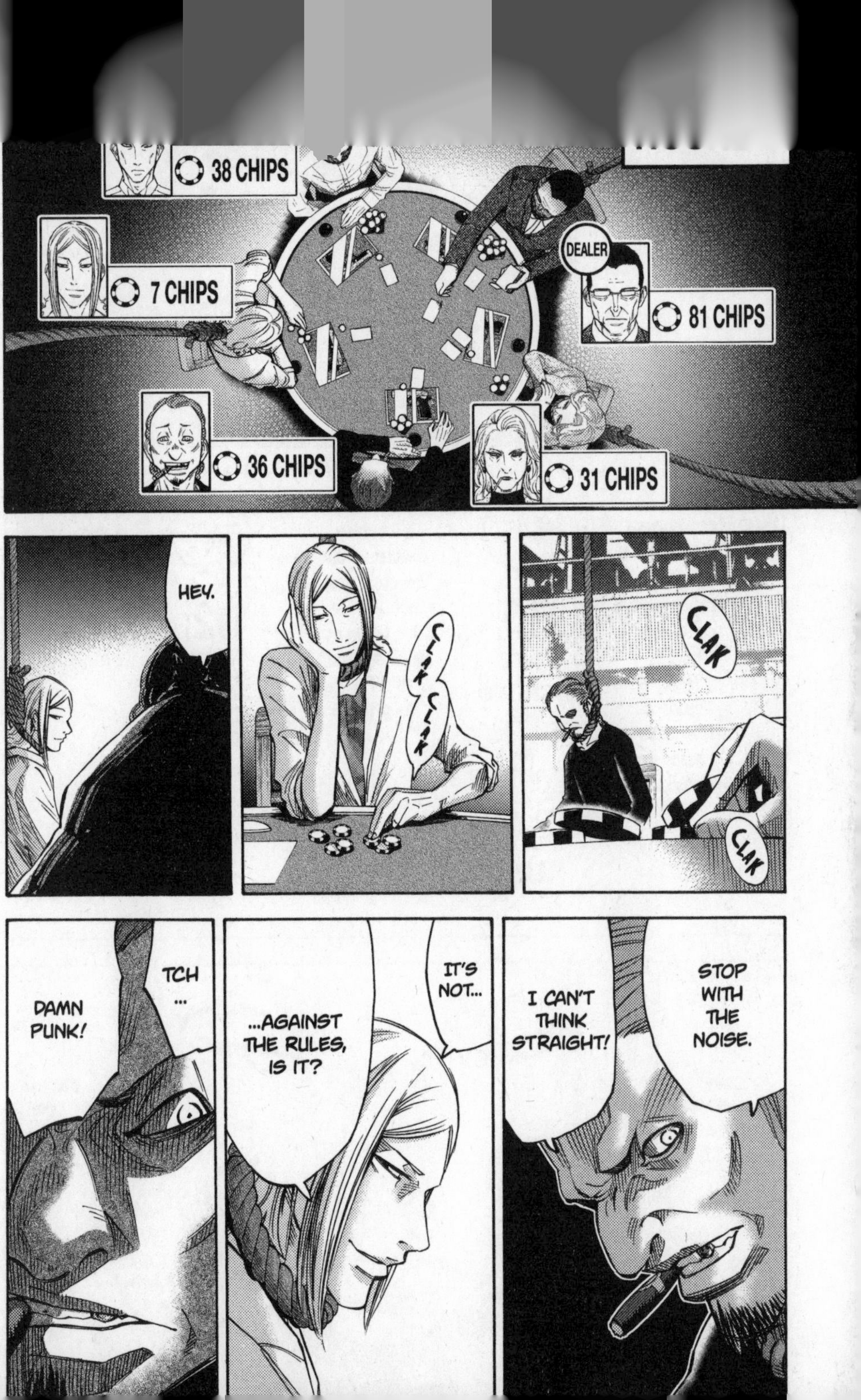
DEALER
81 CHIPS
38 CHIPS
7 CHIPS
31 CHIPS
36 CHIPS
CLAK
CLAK
CLAK CLAK CLAK
HEY.
STOP WITH THE NOISE.
I CAN'T THINK STRAIGHT!
IT'S NOT...
...AGAINST THE RULES, IS IT?
TCH ...
DAMN PUNK!

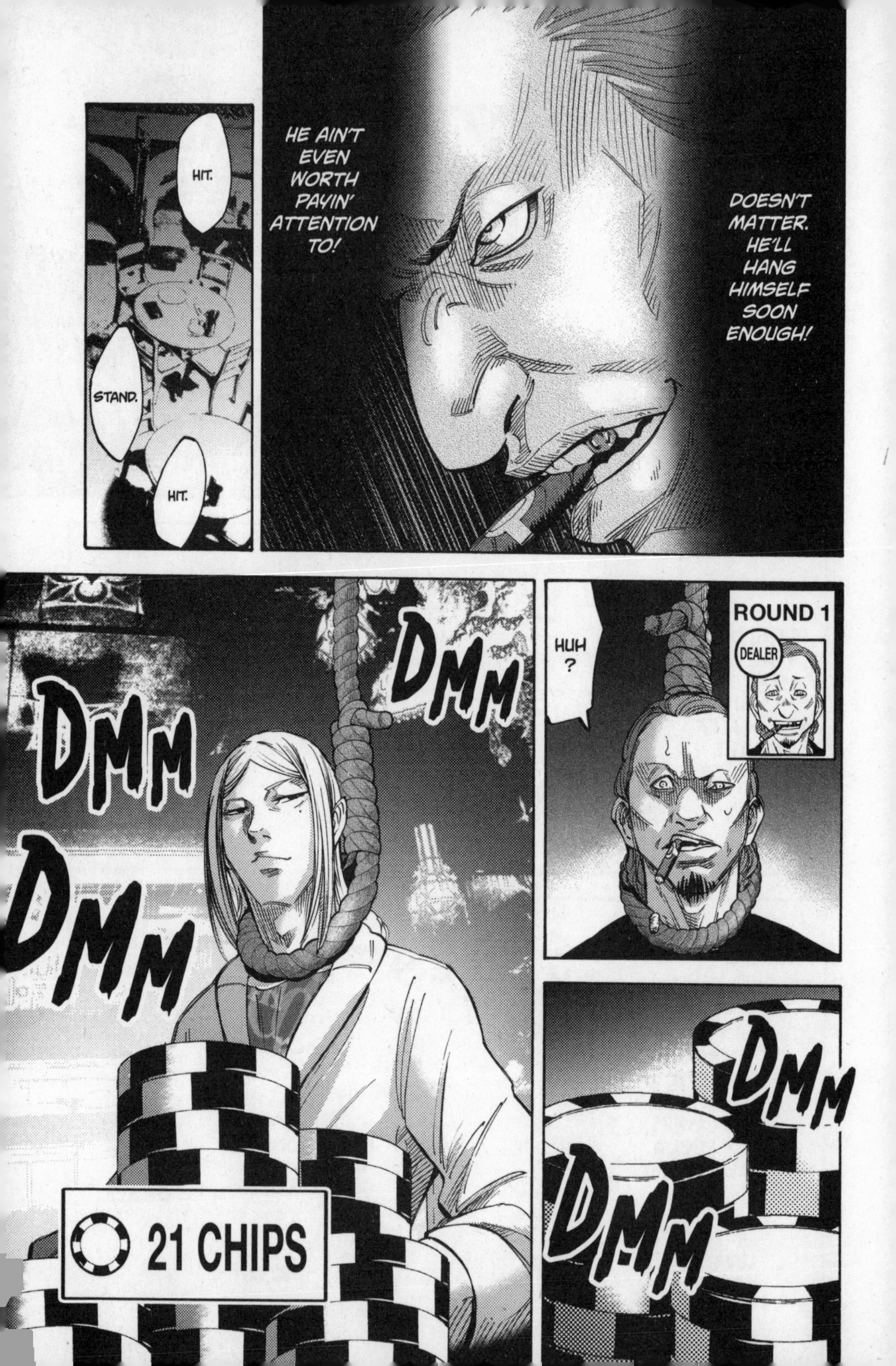
DOESN'T MATTER. HE'LL HANG HIMSELF SOON ENOUGH!
HE AIN'T EVEN WORTH PAYIN' ATTENTION TO!
HIT.
STAND.
HIT.
ROUND 1
DEALER
HUH?
DMM
DMM
DMM
DMM
DMM
21 CHIPS

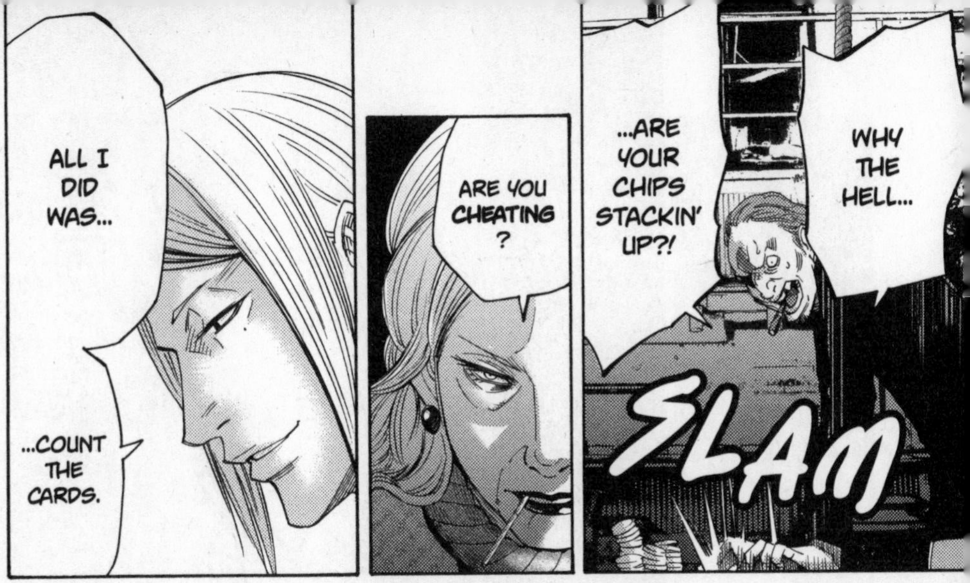
WHY THE HELL...
...ARE YOUR CHIPS STACKIN' UP?!
SLAM
ARE YOU CHEATING?
ALL I DID WAS...
...COUNT THE CARDS.

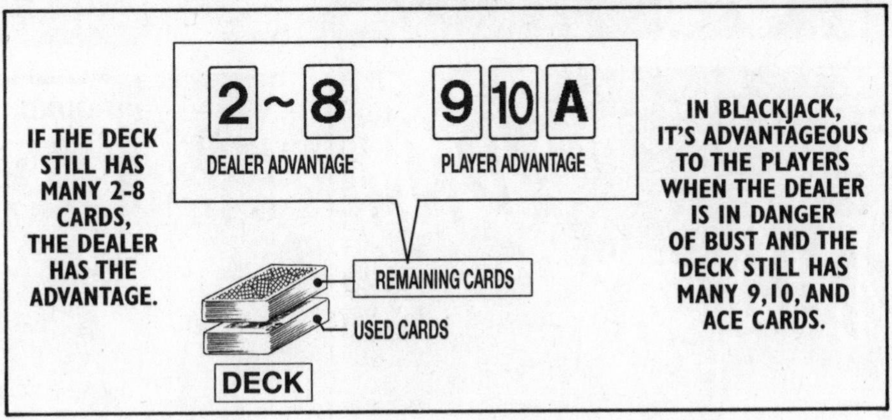
IN BLACKJACK, IT'S ADVANTAGEOUS TO THE PLAYERS WHEN THE DEALER IS IN DANGER OF BUST AND THE DECK STILL HAS MANY 9,10, AND ACE CARDS.
2 ~ 8
DEALER ADVANTAGE
9 10 A
PLAYER ADVANTAGE
REMAINING CARDS
USED CARDS
DECK
IF THE DECK STILL HAS MANY 2-8 CARDS, THE DEALER HAS THE ADVANTAGE.

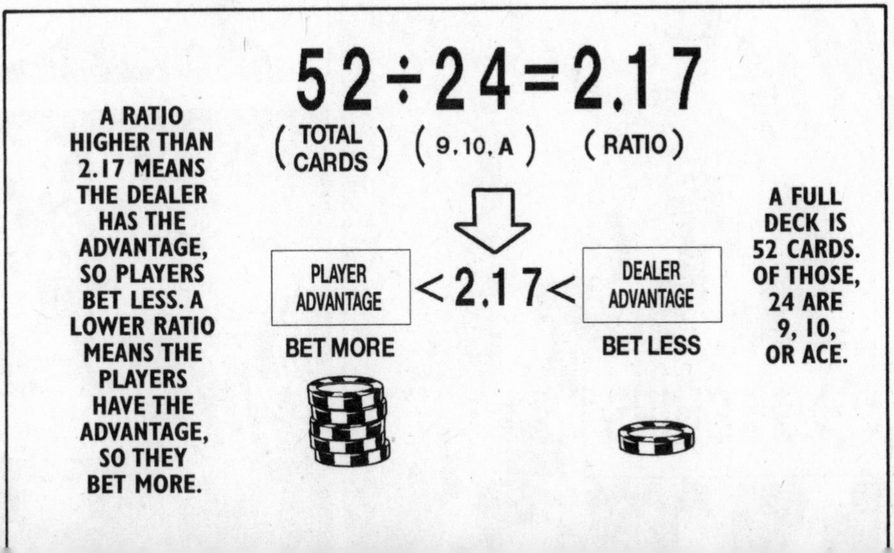
A FULL DECK IS 52 CARDS. OF THOSE, 24 ARE 9, 10, OR ACE.
52÷24=2.17
(TOTAL CARDS) (9, 10, A) (RATIO)
PLAYER ADVANTAGE <2.17< DEALER ADVANTAGE
BET MORE
BET LESS
A RATIO HIGHER THAN 2.17 MEANS THE DEALER HAS THE ADVANTAGE, SO PLAYERS BET LESS. A LOWER RATIO MEANS THE PLAYERS HAVE THE ADVANTAGE, SO THEY BET MORE.

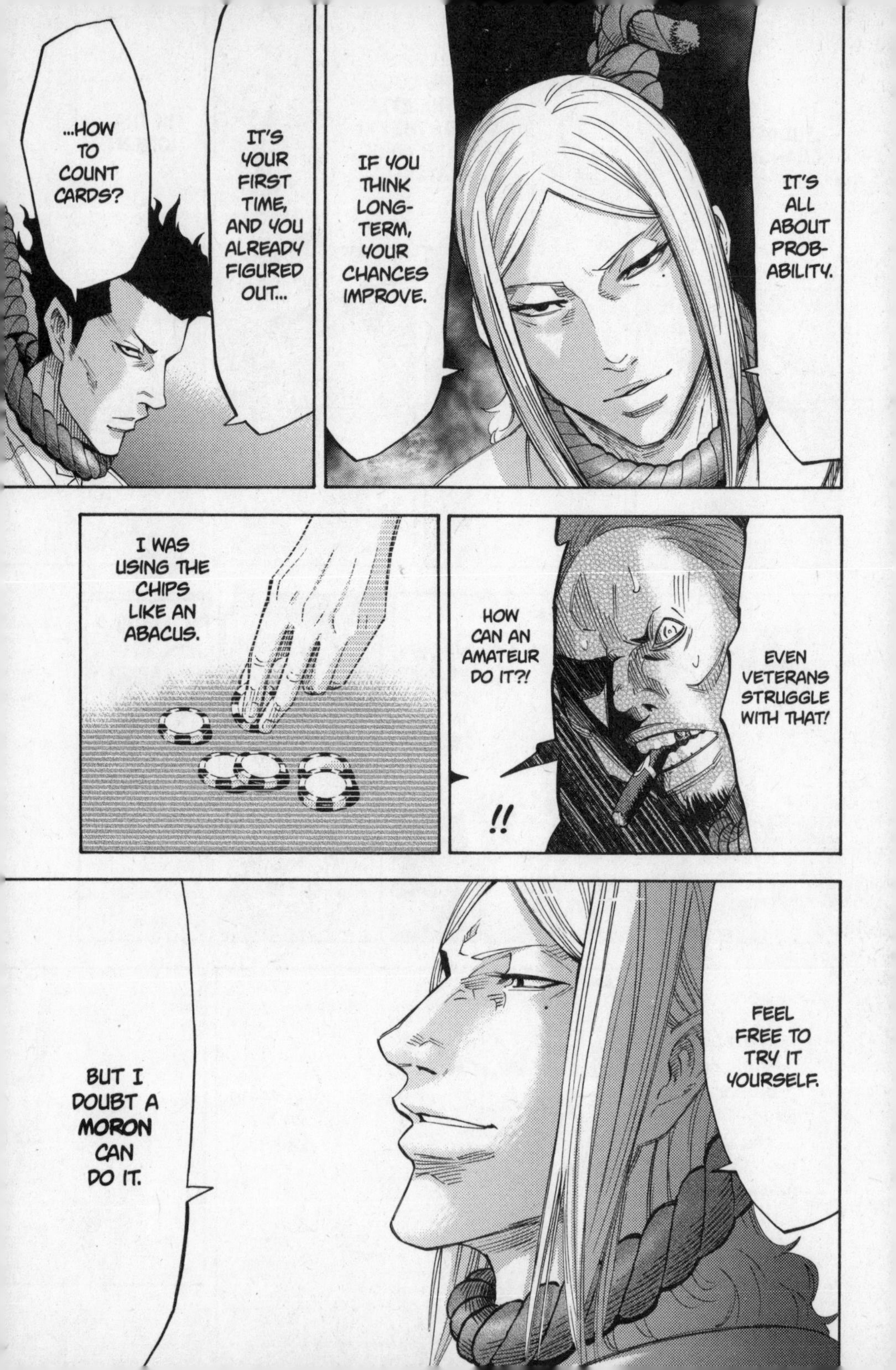
IT'S ALL ABOUT PROB-ABILITY.
IF YOU THINK LONG-TERM, YOUR CHANCES IMPROVE.
IT'S YOUR FIRST TIME, AND YOU ALREADY FIGURED OUT...
...HOW TO COUNT CARDS?
EVEN VETERANS STRUGGLE WITH THAT!
HOW CAN AN AMATEUR DO IT?!
!!
I WAS USING THE CHIPS LIKE AN ABACUS.
FEEL FREE TO TRY IT YOURSELF.
BUT I DOUBT A MORON CAN DO IT.

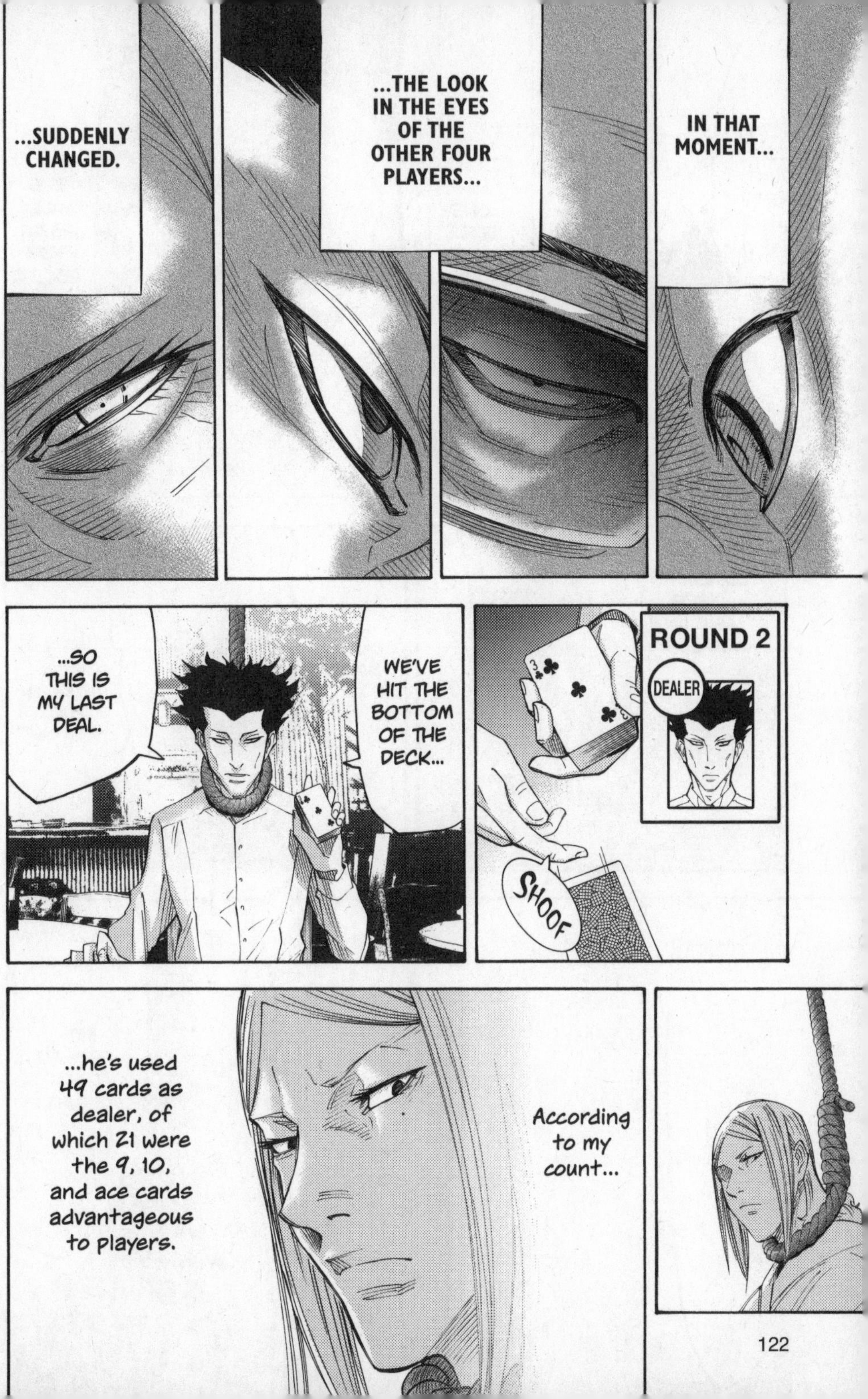
IN THAT MOMENT...
...THE LOOK IN THE EYES OF THE OTHER FOUR PLAYERS...
...SUDDENLY CHANGED.
ROUND 2
DEALER
SHOOF
WE'VE HIT THE BOTTOM OF THE DECK...
...SO THIS IS MY LAST DEAL.
According to my count...
...he's used 49 cards as dealer, of which 21 were the 9, 10, and ace cards advantageous to players.

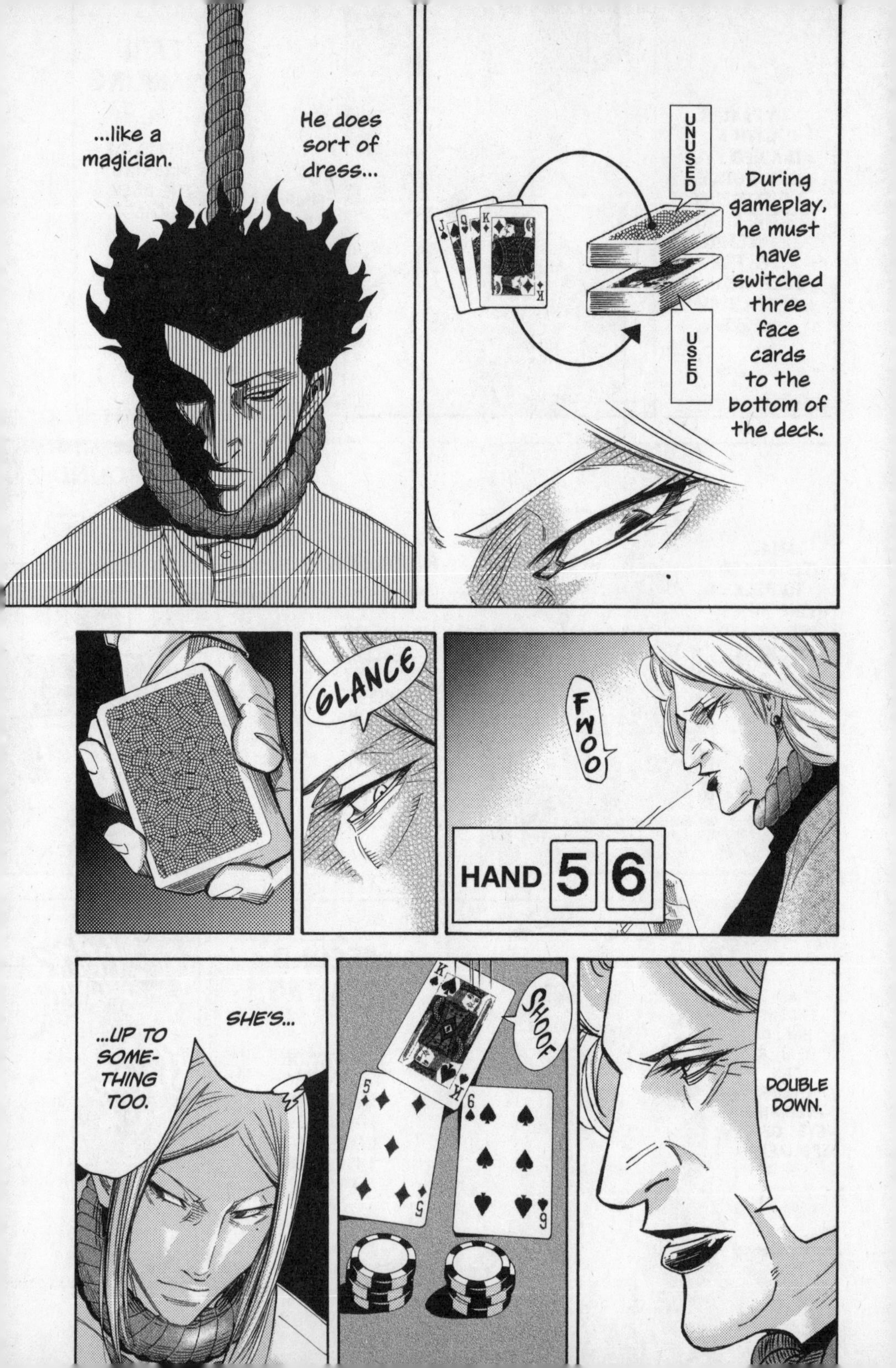
UNUSED
USED
During gameplay, he must have switched three face cards to the bottom of the deck.
He does sort of dress...
...like a magician.
FWOO
HAND 56
GLANCE
DOUBLE DOWN.
SHOOF
SHE'S...
...UP TO SOMETHING TOO.

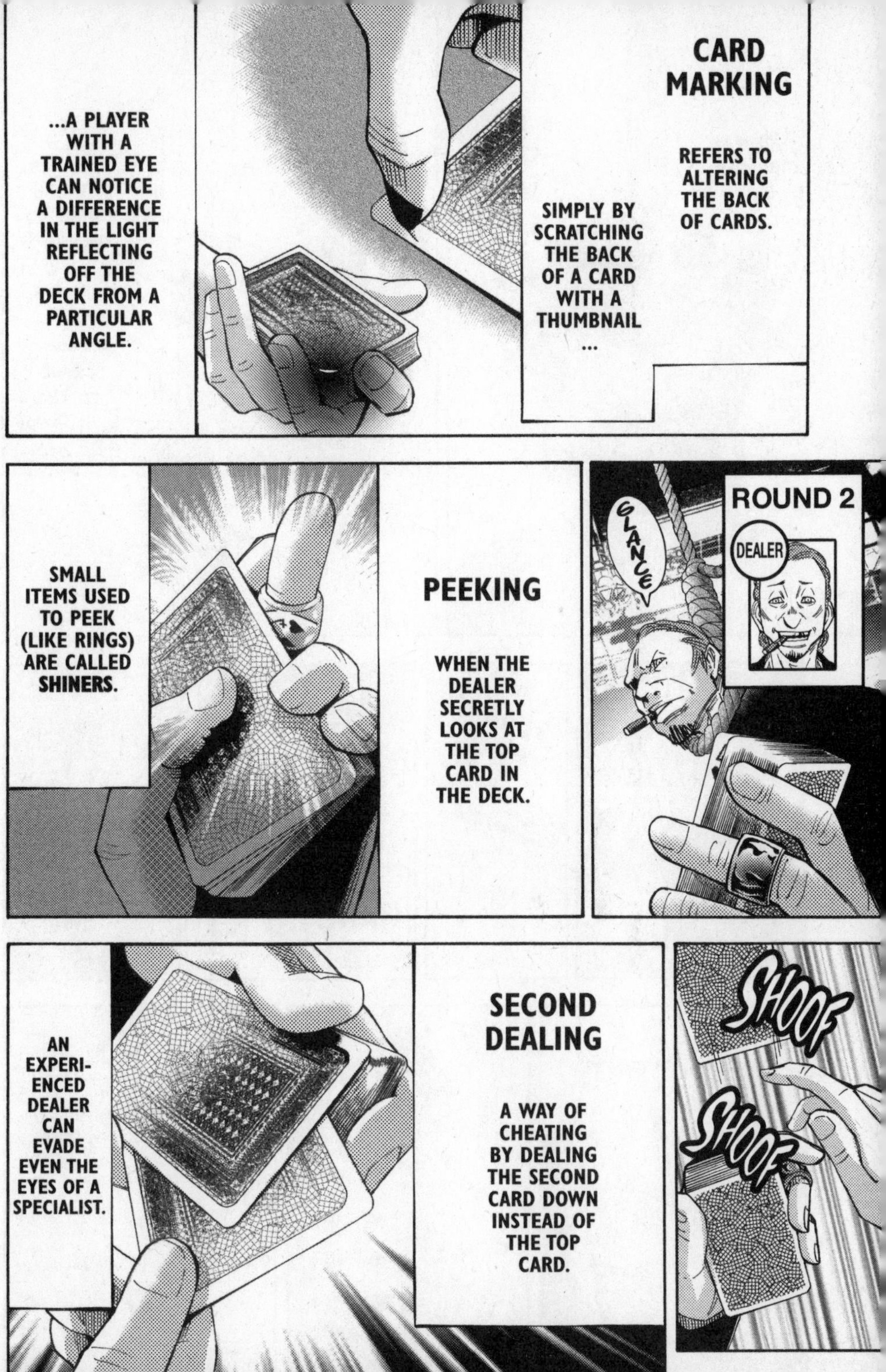
CARD MARKING
REFERS TO ALTERING THE BACK OF CARDS.
SIMPLY BY SCRATCHING THE BACK OF A CARD WITH A THUMBNAIL ...
...A PLAYER WITH A TRAINED EYE CAN NOTICE A DIFFERENCE IN THE LIGHT REFLECTING OFF THE DECK FROM A PARTICULAR ANGLE.
ROUND 2
DEALER
GLANCE
PEEKING
WHEN THE DEALER SECRETLY LOOKS AT THE TOP CARD IN THE DECK.
SMALL ITEMS USED TO PEEK (LIKE RINGS) ARE CALLED SHINERS.
SHOOF
SHOOF
SECOND DEALING
A WAY OF CHEATING BY DEALING THE SECOND CARD DOWN INSTEAD OF THE TOP CARD.
AN EXPERI-ENCED DEALER CAN EVADE EVEN THE EYES OF A SPECIALIST.

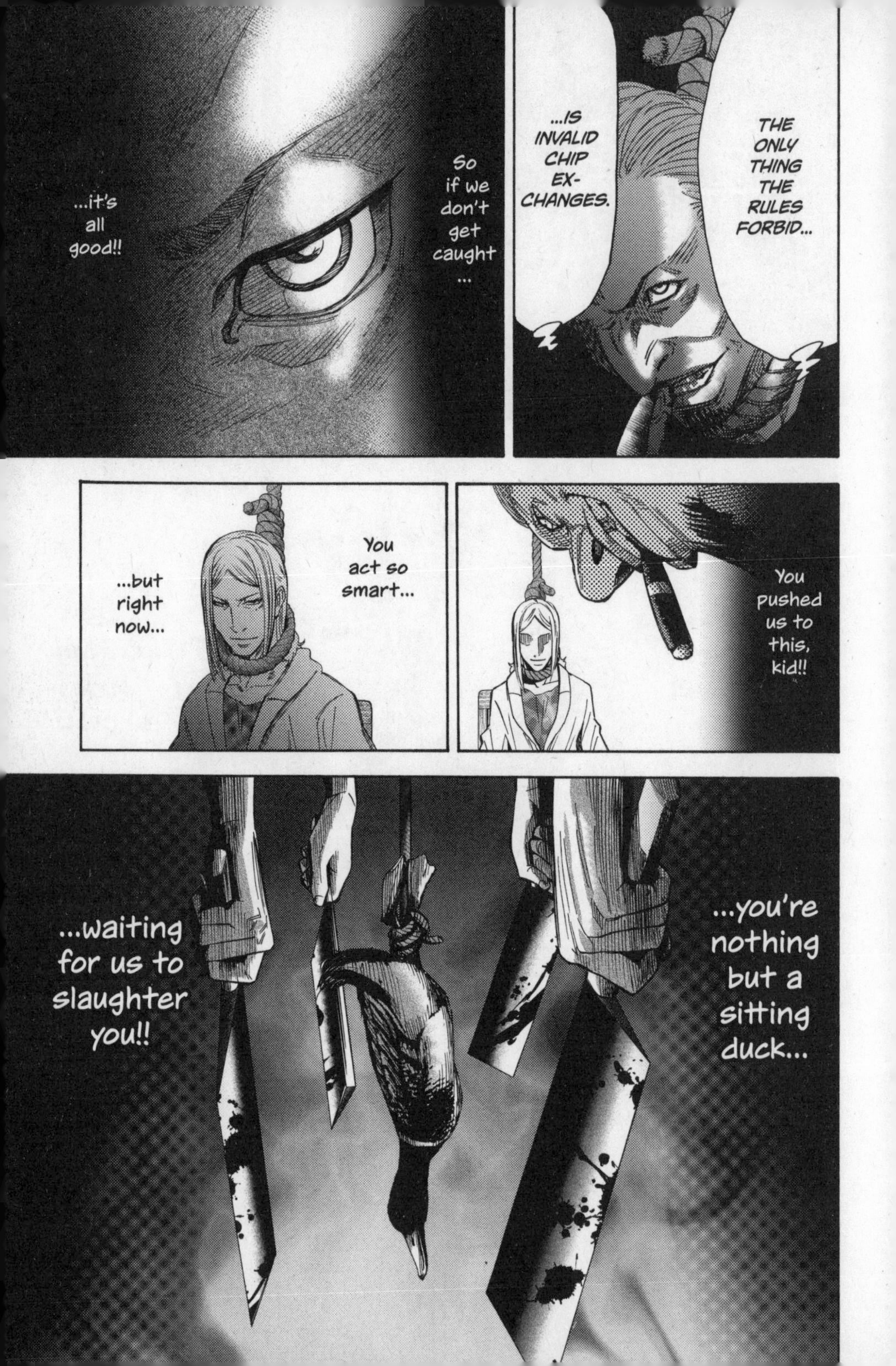
THE ONLY THING THE RULES FORBID...
...IS INVALID CHIP EX-CHANGES.
So if we don't get caught...
...it's all good!!
You pushed us to this, kid!!
You act so smart...
...but right now...
...you're nothing but a sitting duck...
...waiting for us to slaughter you!!

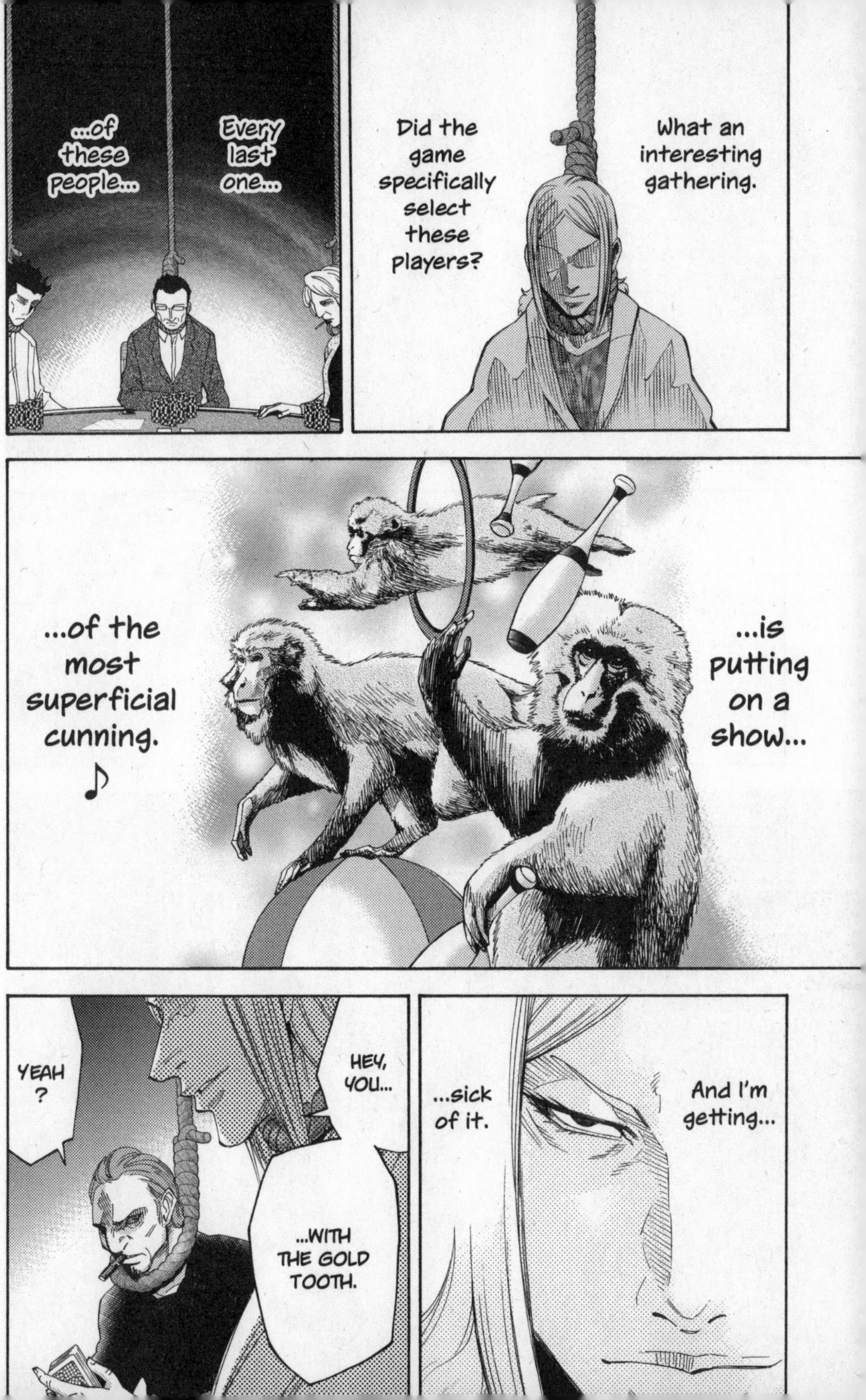

What an interesting gathering.
Did the game specifically select these players?
Every last one...
...of these people...
...is putting on a show...
...of the most superficial cunning. ♪
And I'm getting...
...sick of it.
HEY, YOU...
...WITH THE GOLD TOOTH.
YEAH?

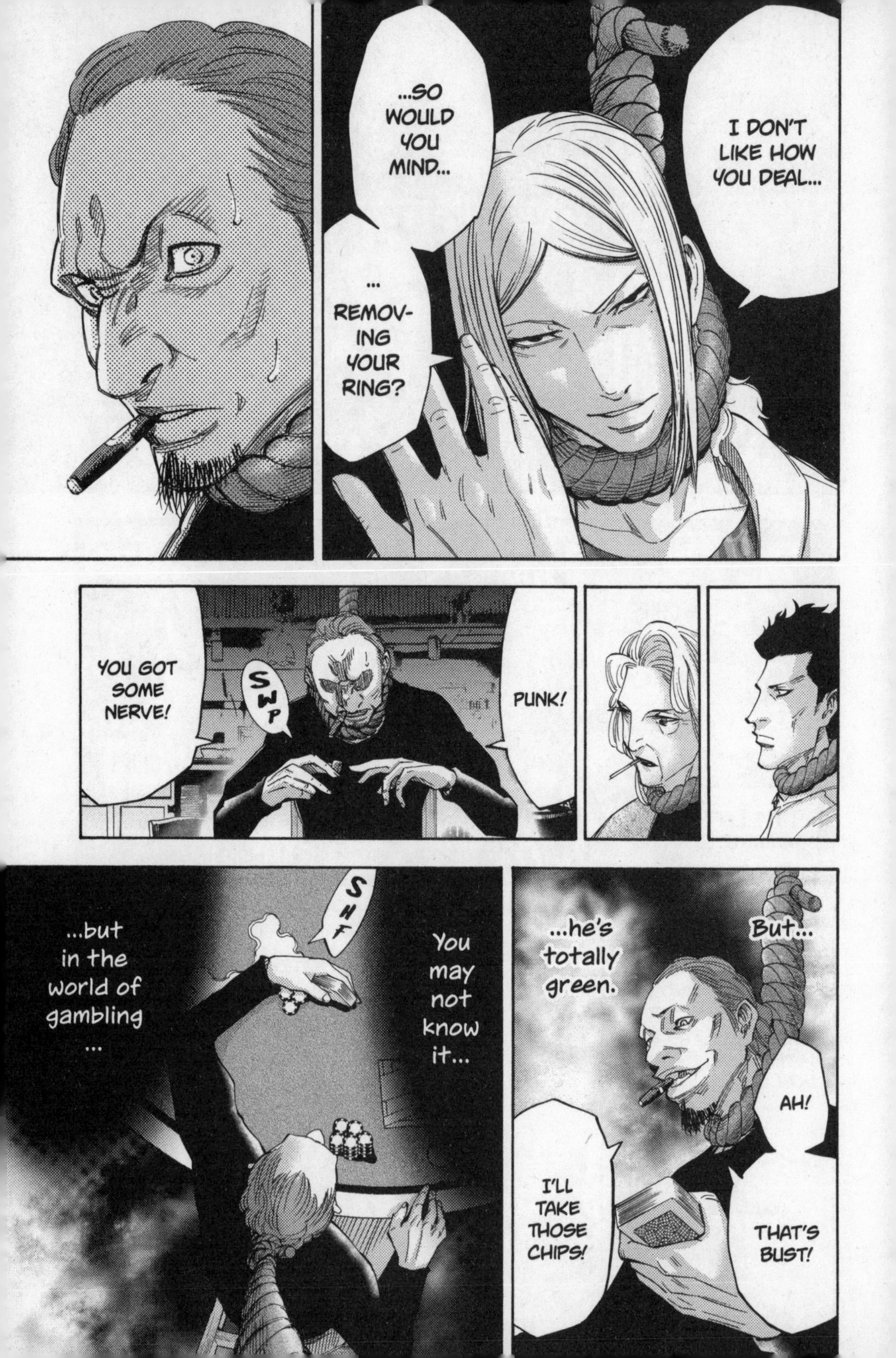
I DON'T LIKE HOW YOU DEAL...
...SO WOULD YOU MIND...
... REMOVING YOUR RING?
PUNK!
SWP
YOU GOT SOME NERVE!
But...
...he's totally green.
AH!
THAT'S BUST!
I'LL TAKE THOSE CHIPS!
You may not know it...
SNF
...but in the world of gambling ...

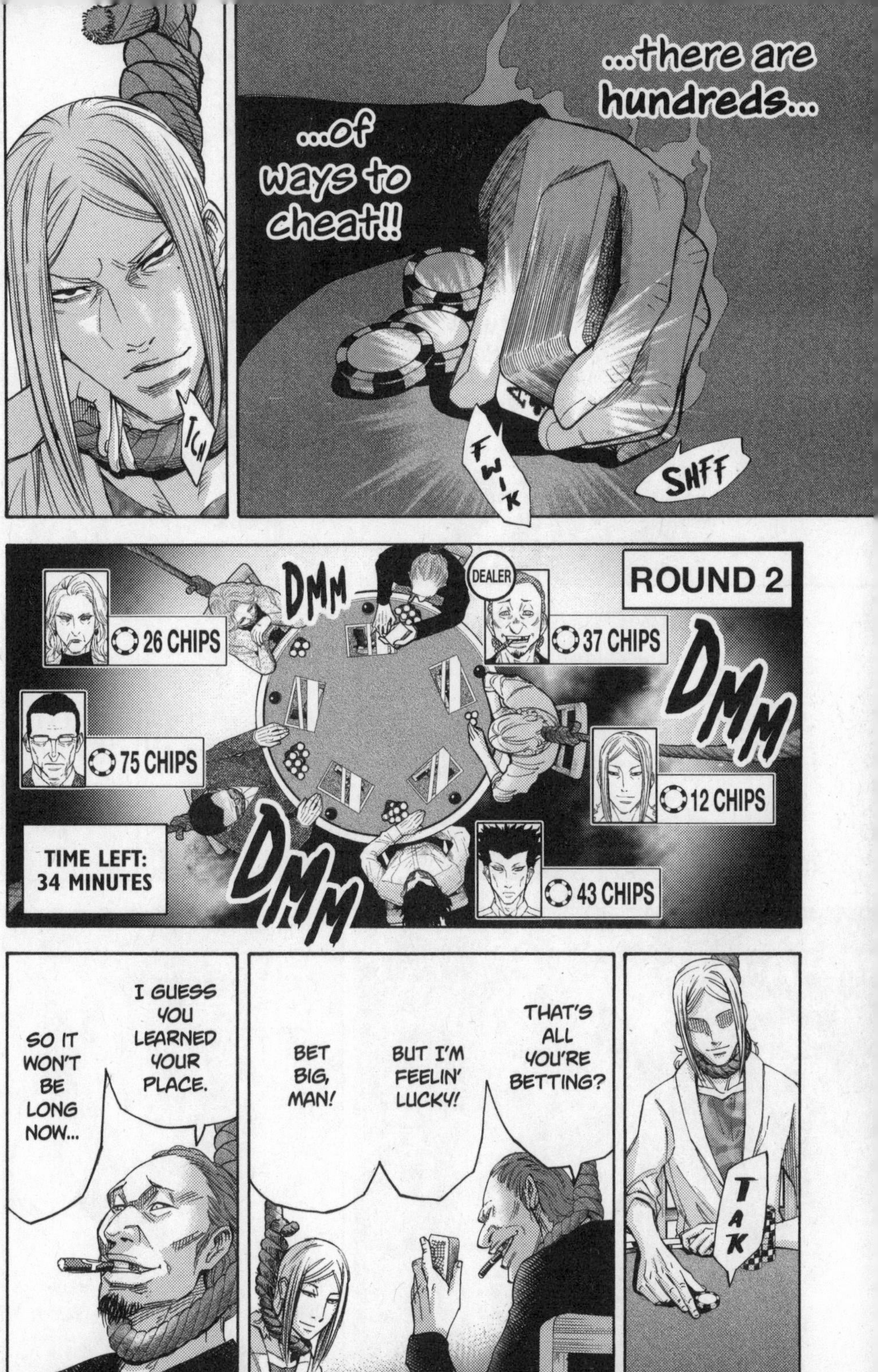
...there are hundreds...
...of ways to cheat!!
SHFF
FWIK
TCH
ROUND 2
DEALER
DMM
37 CHIPS
DMM
26 CHIPS
75 CHIPS
12 CHIPS
DMM
43 CHIPS
TIME LEFT: 34 MINUTES
TAK
THAT'S ALL YOU'RE BETTING?
BUT I'M FEELIN' LUCKY!
BET BIG, MAN!
I GUESS YOU LEARNED YOUR PLACE.
SO IT WON'T BE LONG NOW...

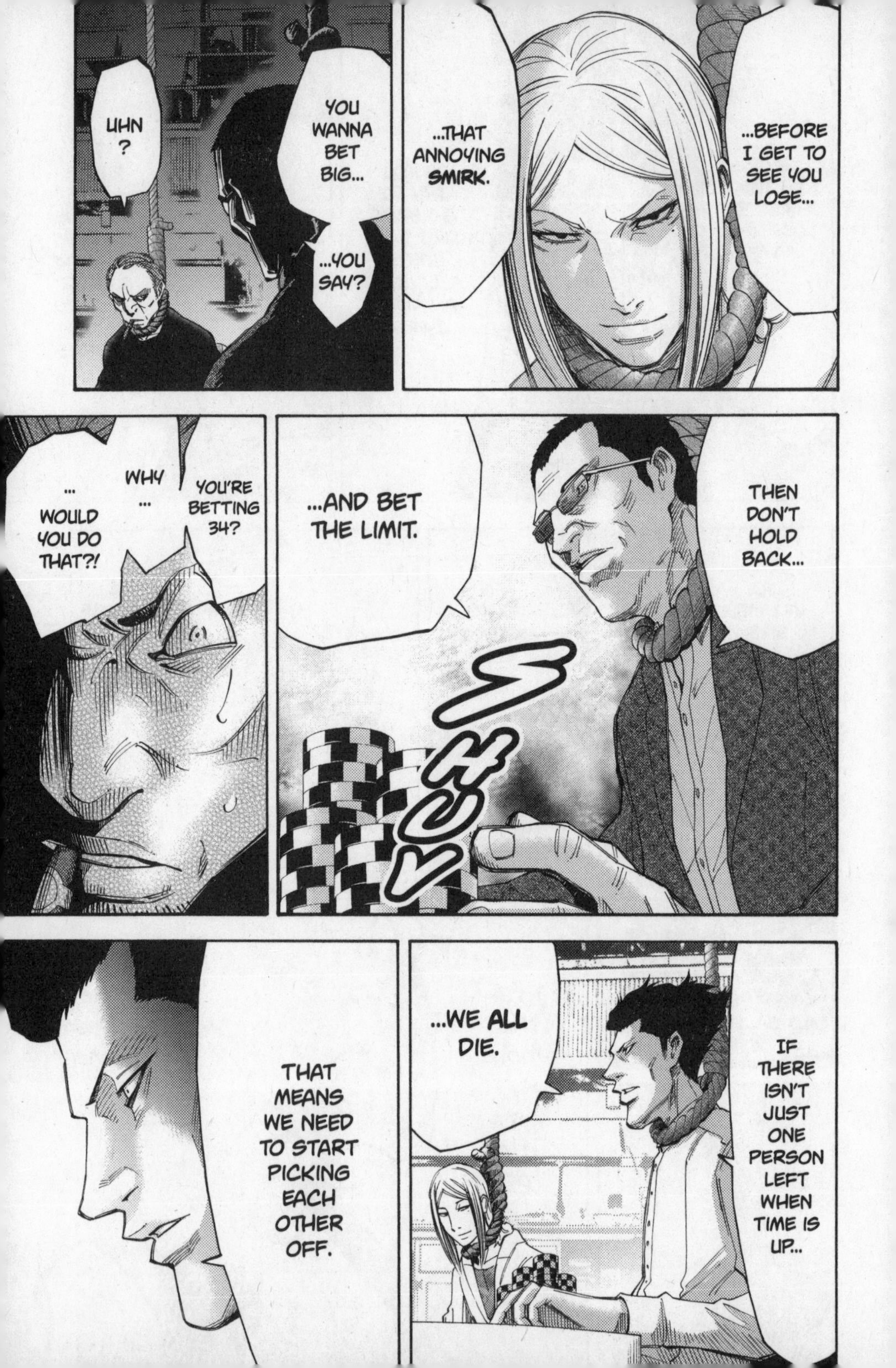
...BEFORE I GET TO SEE YOU LOSE...
...THAT ANNOYING SMIRK.
YOU WANNA BET BIG...
...YOU SAY?
UHN ?
THEN DON'T HOLD BACK...
...AND BET THE LIMIT.
SHUV
YOU'RE BETTING 34?
WHY ...
... WOULD YOU DO THAT?!
IF THERE ISN'T JUST ONE PERSON LEFT WHEN TIME IS UP...
...WE ALL DIE.
THAT MEANS WE NEED TO START PICKING EACH OTHER OFF.

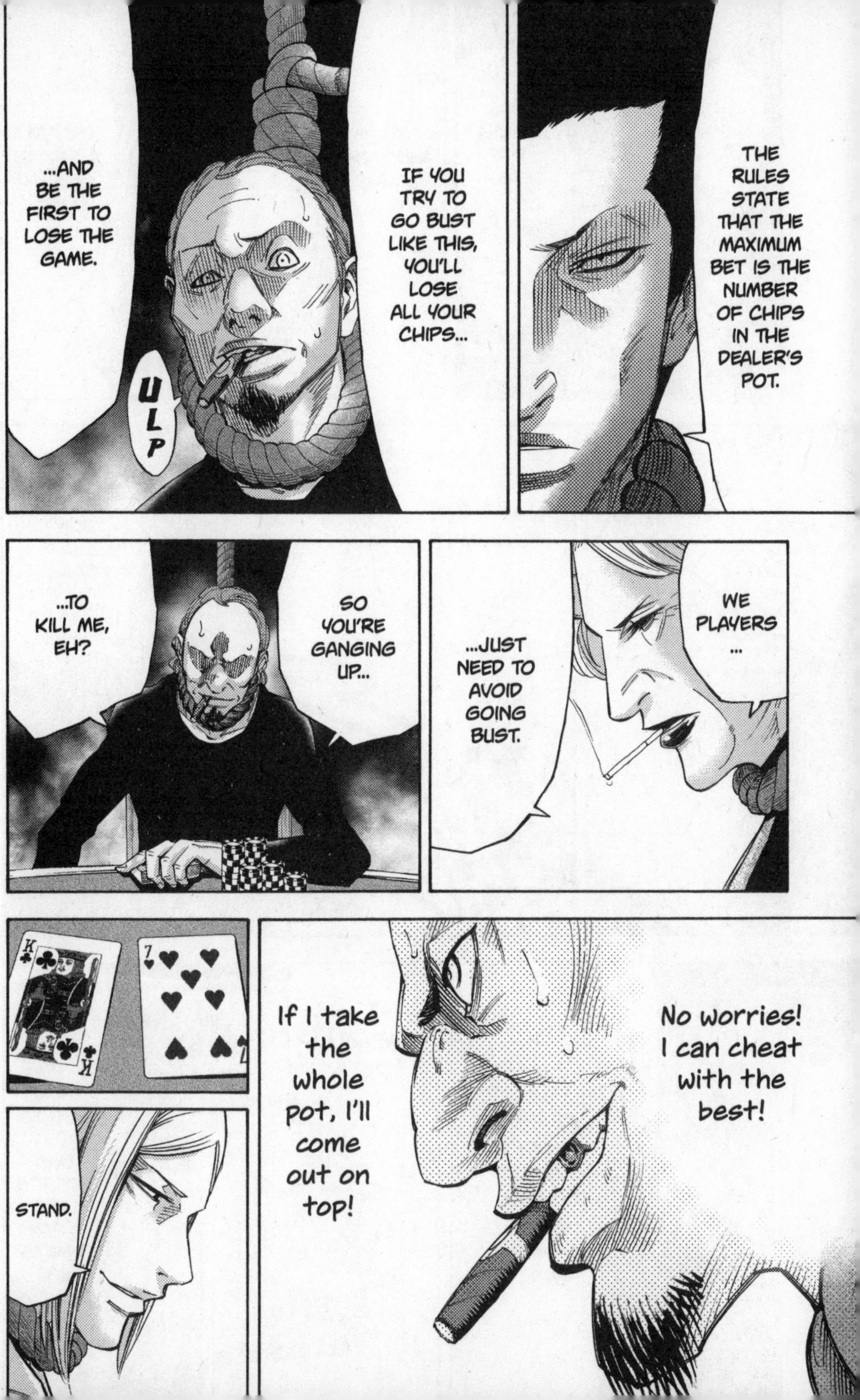
THE RULES STATE THAT THE MAXIMUM BET IS THE NUMBER OF CHIPS IN THE DEALER'S POT.
IF YOU TRY TO GO BUST LIKE THIS, YOU'LL LOSE ALL YOUR CHIPS...
...AND BE THE FIRST TO LOSE THE GAME.
ULP
WE PLAYERS ...
...JUST NEED TO AVOID GOING BUST.
SO YOU'RE GANGING UP...
...TO KILL ME, EH?
No worries! I can cheat with the best!
If I take the whole pot, I'll come out on top!
STAND.

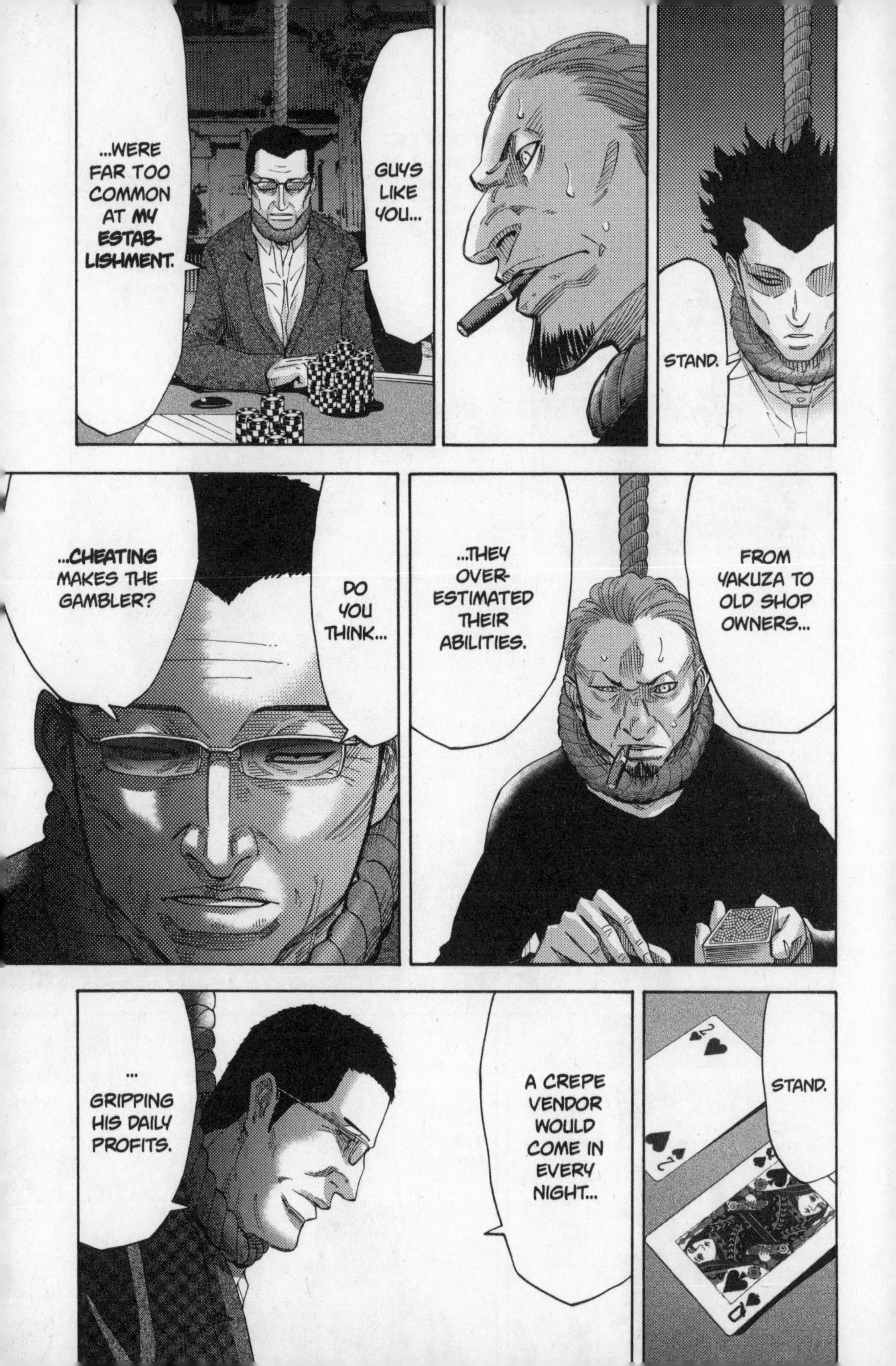
STAND.
GUYS LIKE YOU...
...WERE FAR TOO COMMON AT MY ESTAB-LISHMENT.
FROM YAKUZA TO OLD SHOP OWNERS...
...THEY OVER-ESTIMATED THEIR ABILITIES.
DO YOU THINK...
...CHEATING MAKES THE GAMBLER?
STAND.
A CREPE VENDOR WOULD COME IN EVERY NIGHT...
...GRIPPING HIS DAILY PROFITS.

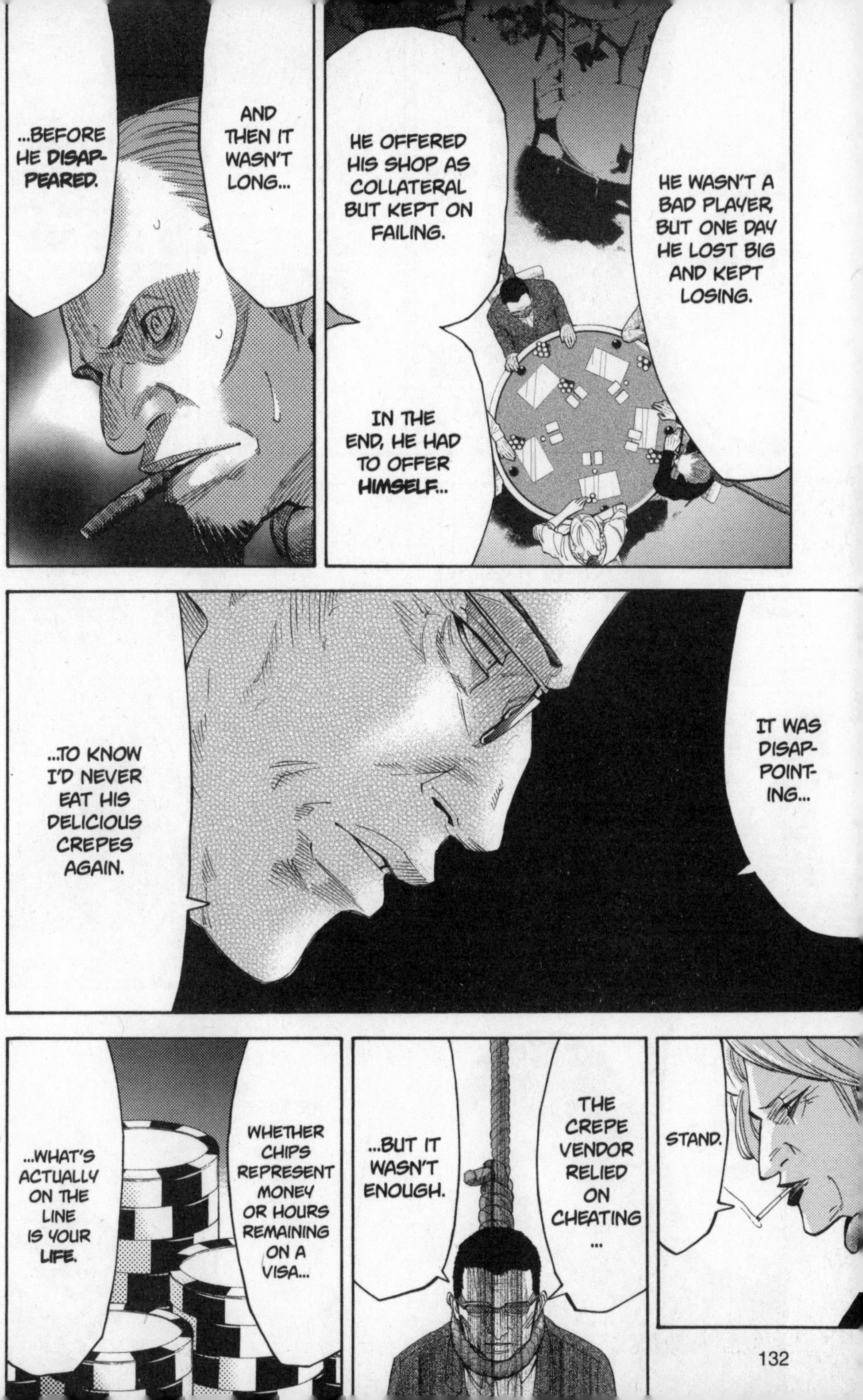
HE WASN'T A BAD PLAYER, BUT ONE DAY HE LOST BIG AND KEPT LOSING.
HE OFFERED HIS SHOP AS COLLATERAL BUT KEPT ON FAILING.
IN THE END, HE HAD TO OFFER **HIMSELF**...
AND THEN IT WASN'T LONG...
...BEFORE HE **DISAPPEARED.**
IT WAS DISAPPOINTING...
...TO KNOW I'D NEVER EAT HIS DELICIOUS CREPES AGAIN.
STAND.
THE CREPE VENDOR RELIED ON CHEATING...
...BUT IT WASN'T ENOUGH.
WHETHER CHIPS REPRESENT MONEY OR HOURS REMAINING ON A VISA...
...WHAT'S ACTUALLY ON THE LINE IS YOUR **LIFE.**

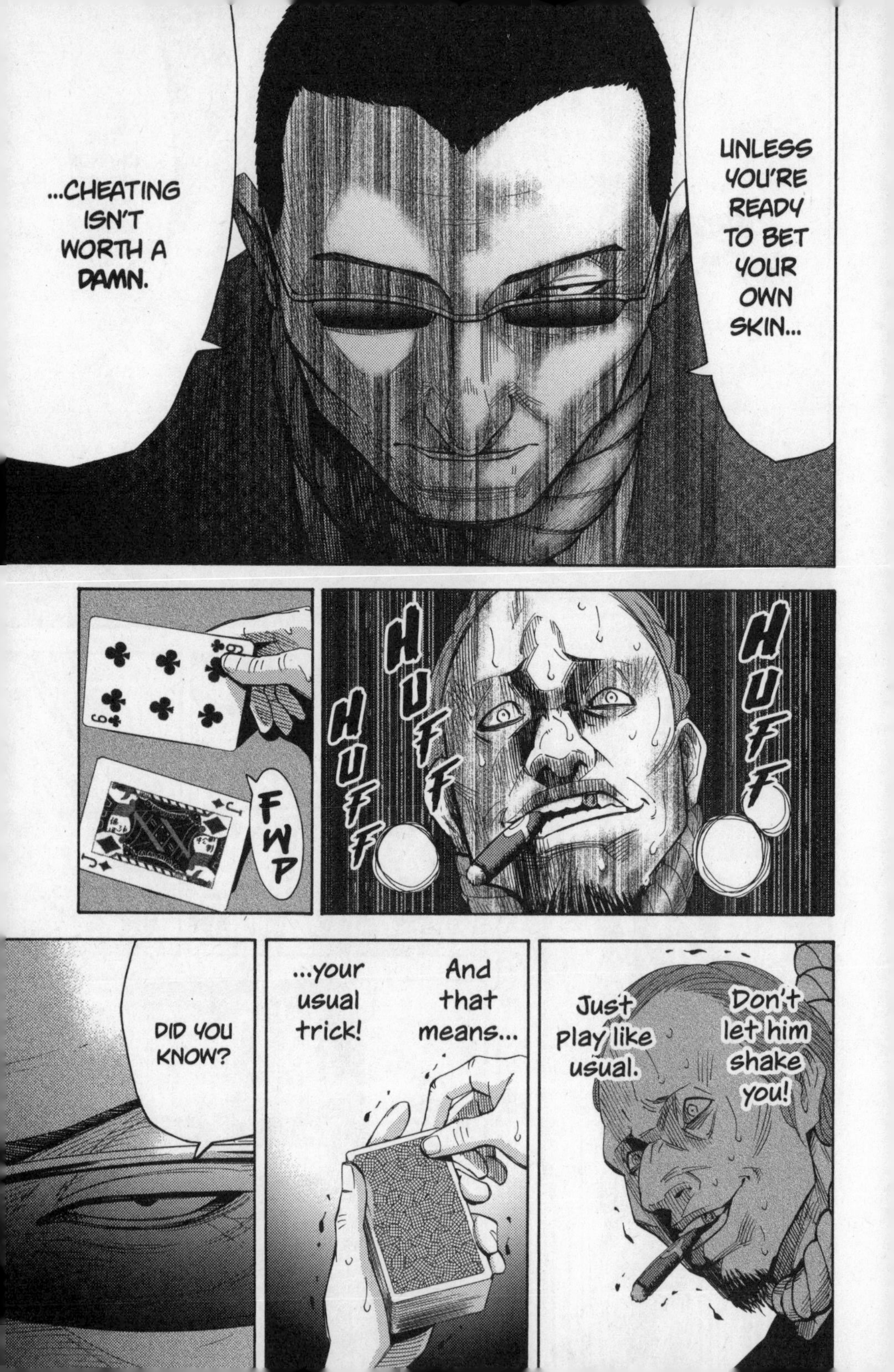
UNLESS YOU'RE READY TO BET YOUR OWN SKIN...
...CHEATING ISN'T WORTH A DAMN.
HUFF
HUFF
HUFF
HUFF
FWP
Don't let him shake you!
Just play like usual.
And that means...
...your usual trick!
DID YOU KNOW?

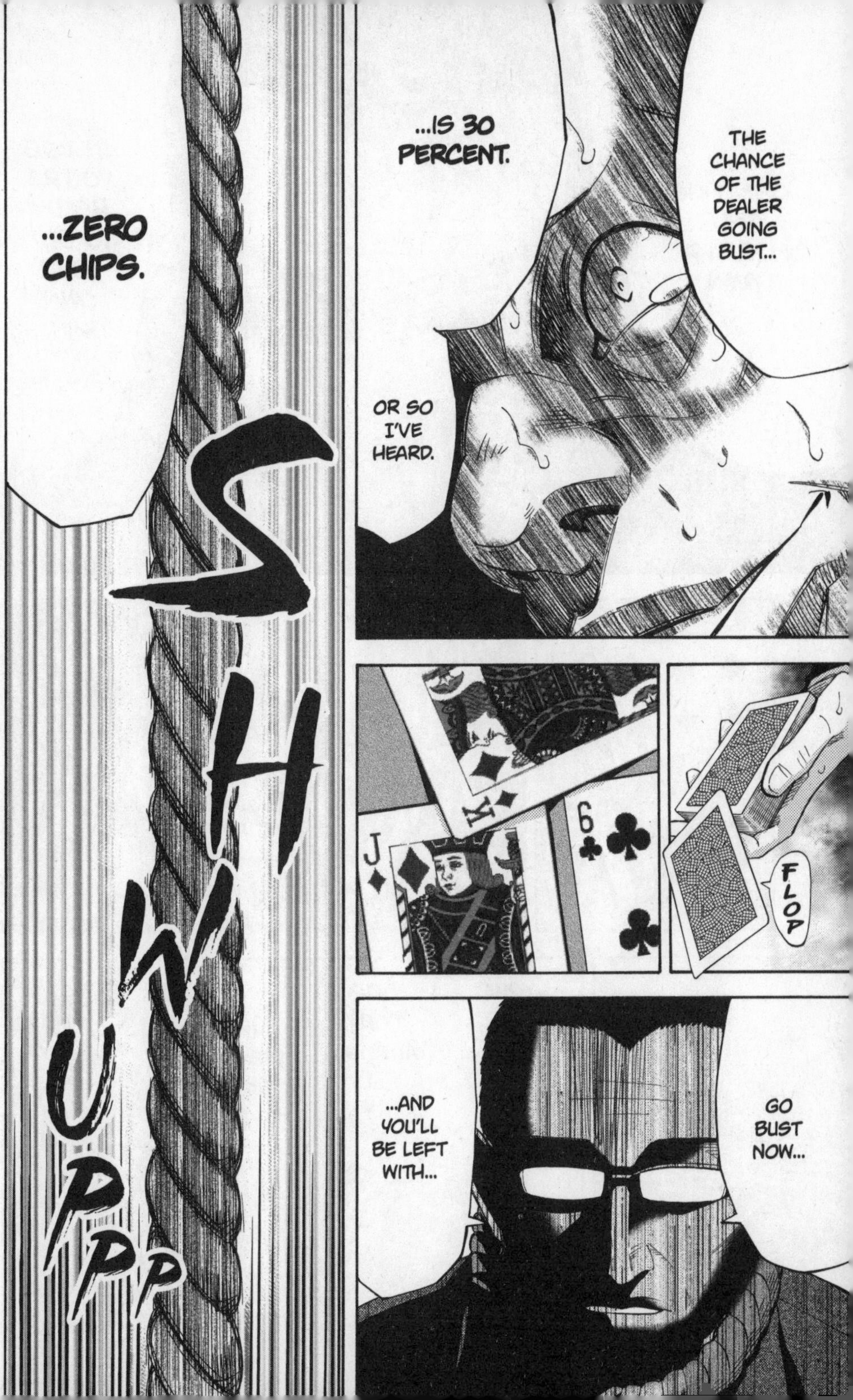
THE CHANCE OF THE DEALER GOING BUST...
...IS 30 PERCENT.
OR SO I'VE HEARD.
FLOP
GO BUST NOW...
...AND YOU'LL BE LEFT WITH...
...ZERO CHIPS.
SHWUPPP

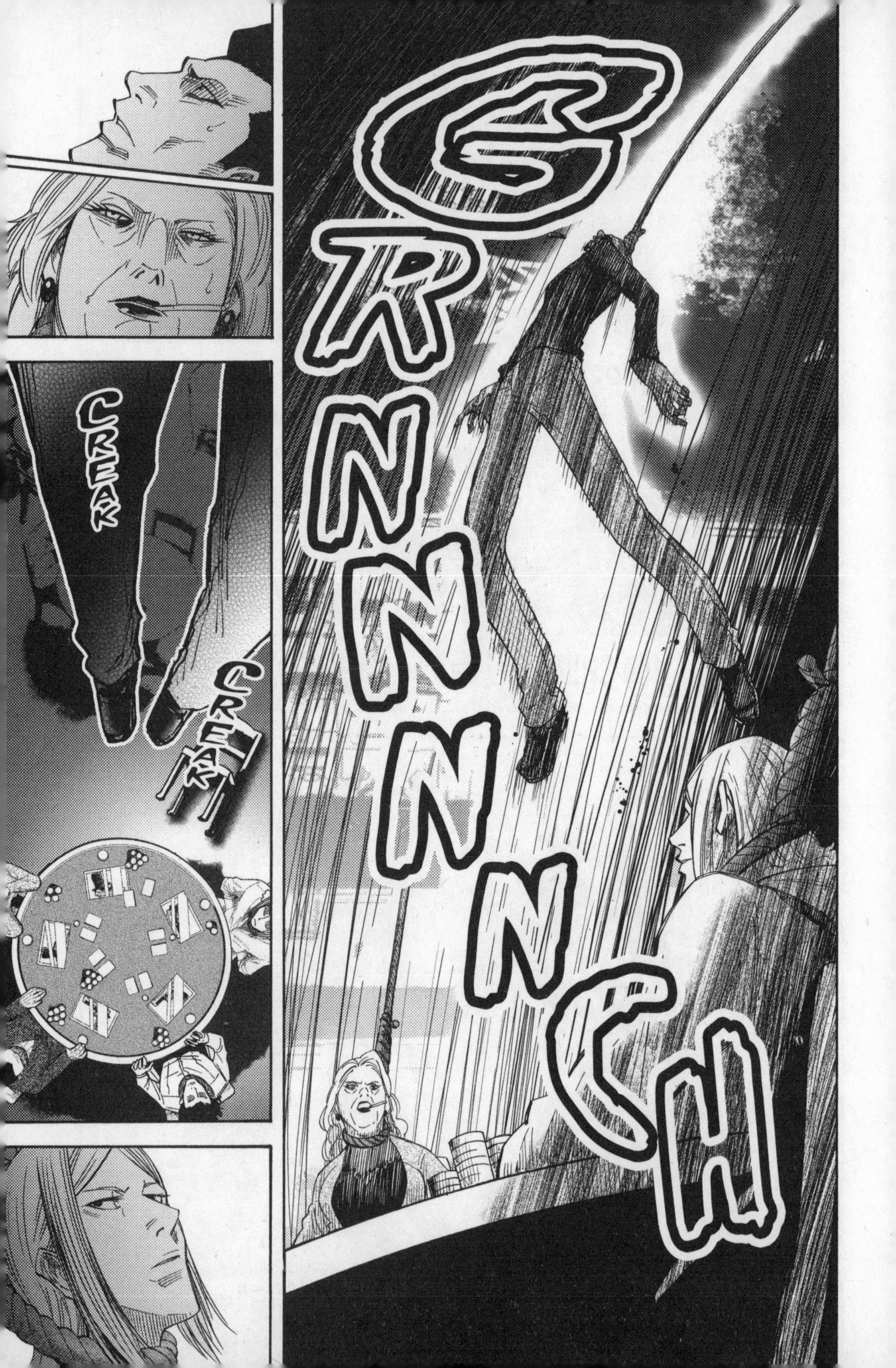
GRRNNNNNCH
CREAK
CREAK

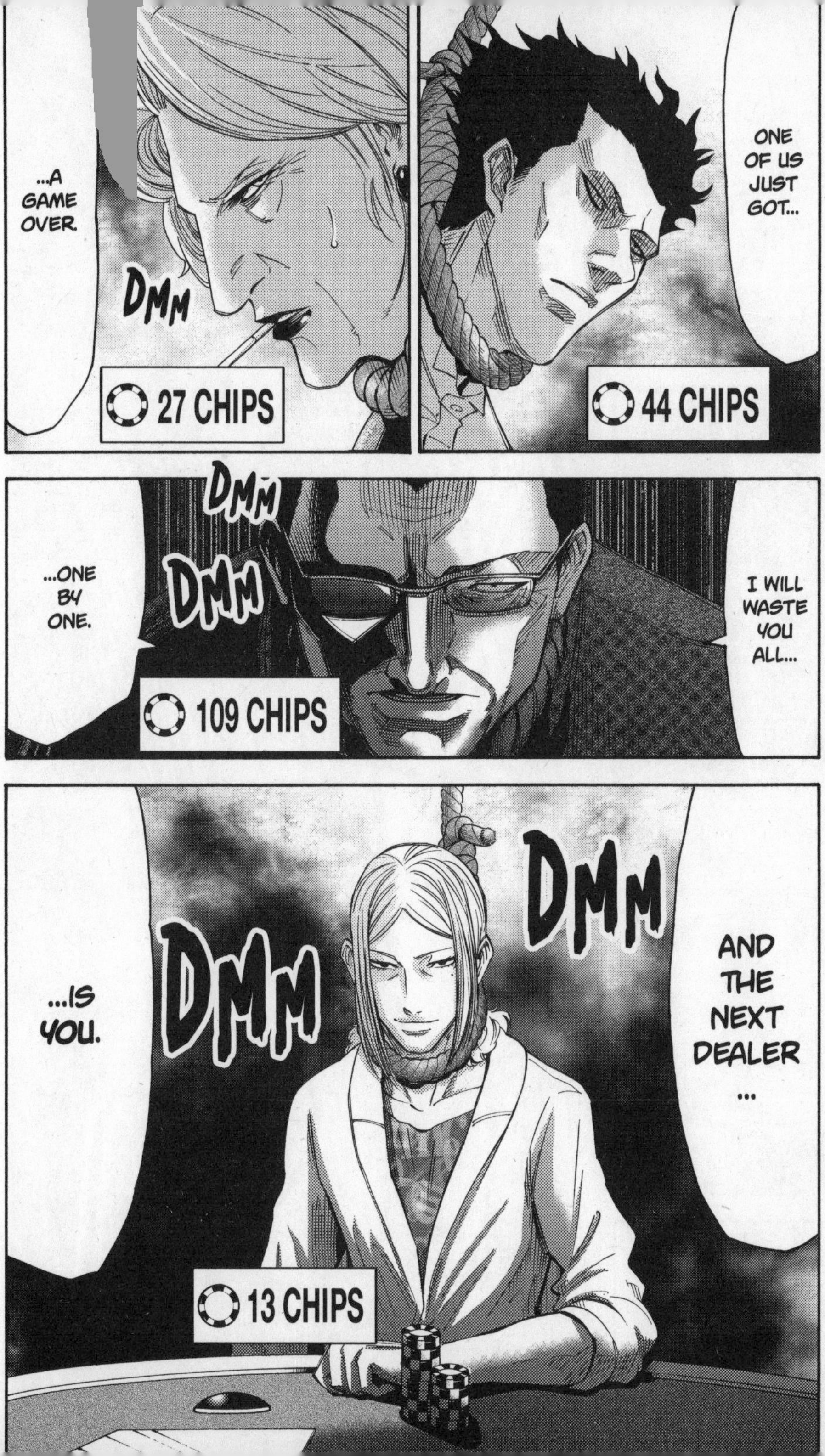
ONE OF US JUST GOT...
44 CHIPS
...A GAME OVER.
DMM
27 CHIPS
I WILL WASTE YOU ALL...
DMM
DMM
...ONE BY ONE.
109 CHIPS
AND THE NEXT DEALER ...
DMM
DMM
...IS YOU.
13 CHIPS

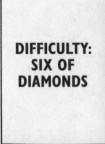

GAME: BLACKJACK
DIFFICULTY: SIX OF DIAMONDS
TIME LIMIT: 1 HOUR
THE LAST SURVIVING PLAYER WINS THE GAME.
BUT IF TIME RUNS OUT, A PLAYER RUNS OUT OF CHIPS, THERE'S AN INVALID EXCHANGE OF CHIPS, OR AN INVALID PUNISHMENT...
...IT'S GAME OVER.

SIDE STORY 3: Six of Diamonds, Part 2

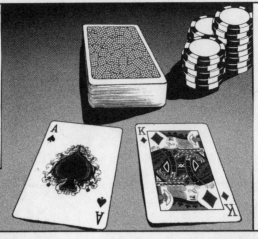

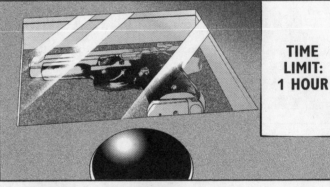

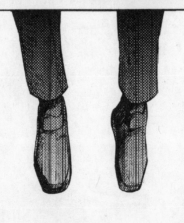

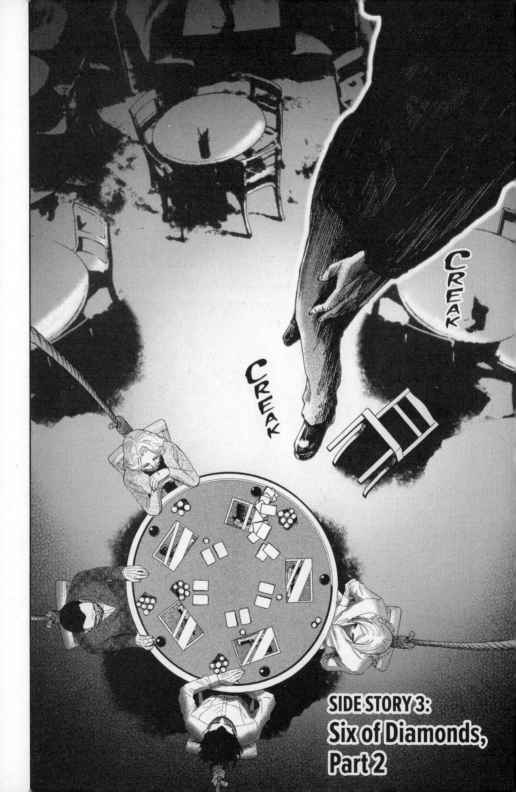

SIDE STORY 3:
Six of Diamonds,
Part 2

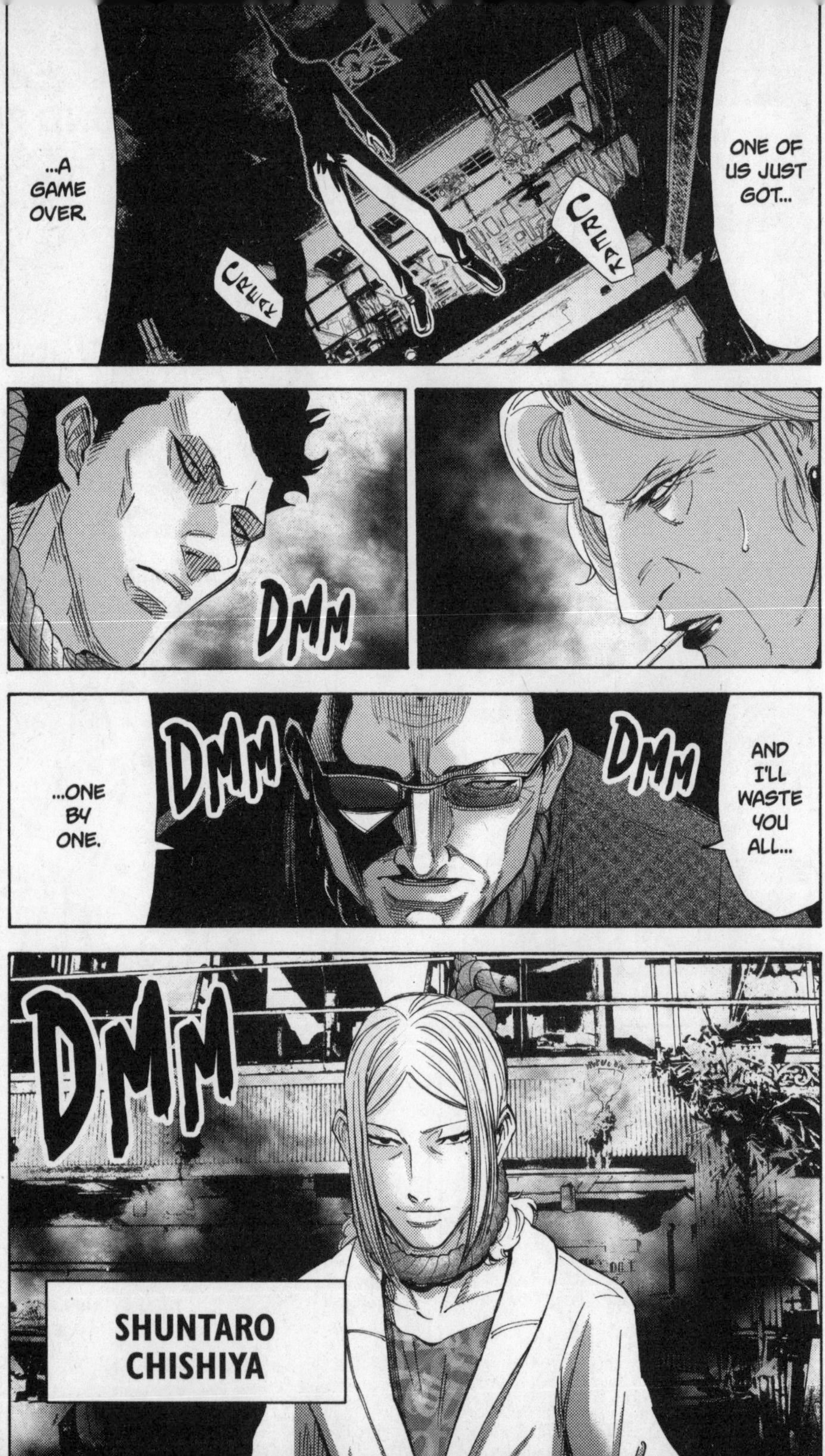
ONE OF US JUST GOT...
CREAK
CREAK
...A GAME OVER.
DMM
AND I'LL WASTE YOU ALL...
DMM
DMM
...ONE BY ONE.
DMM
SHUNTARO CHISHIYA

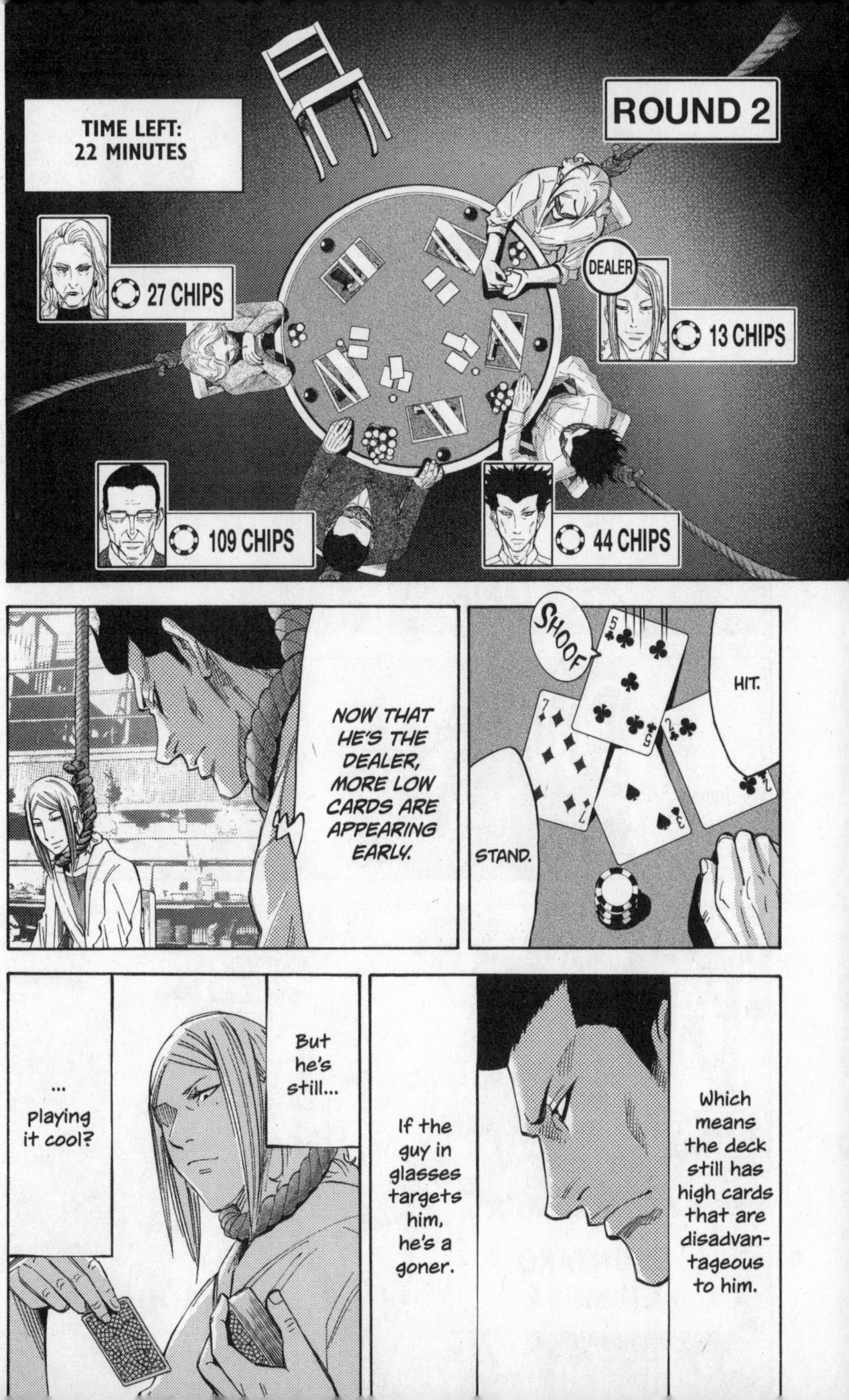
ROUND 2
DEALER
13 CHIPS
TIME LEFT:
22 MINUTES
27 CHIPS
44 CHIPS
109 CHIPS
SHOOF
HIT.
STAND.
NOW THAT HE'S THE DEALER, MORE LOW CARDS ARE APPEARING EARLY.
Which means the deck still has high cards that are disadvan-tageous to him.
If the guy in glasses targets him, he's a goner.
But he's still...
... playing it cool?

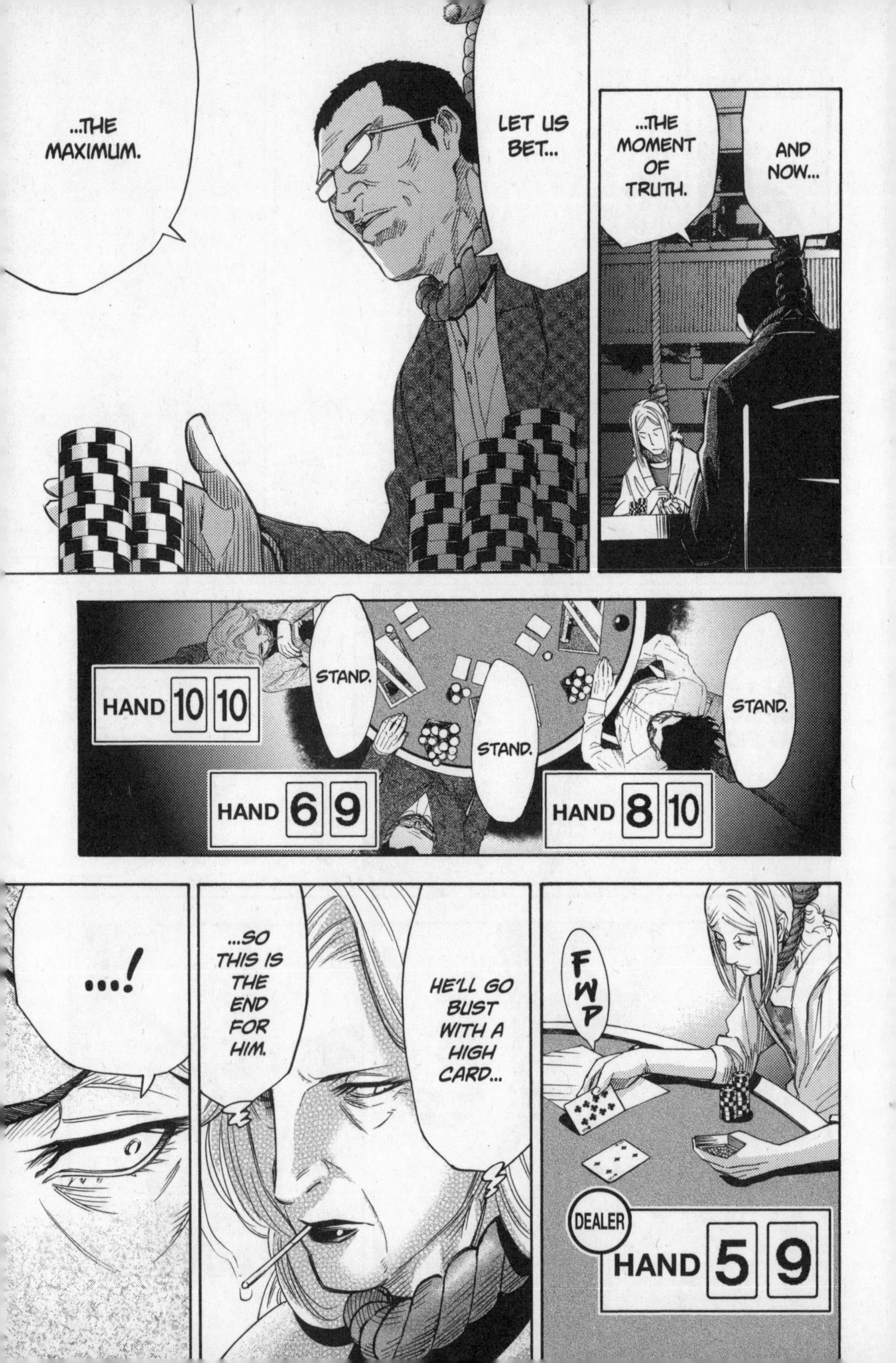
AND NOW...
...THE MOMENT OF TRUTH.
LET US BET...
...THE MAXIMUM.
STAND.
HAND 8 10
STAND.
HAND 6 9
STAND.
HAND 10 10
FWP
DEALER
HAND 5 9
HE'LL GO BUST WITH A HIGH CARD...
...SO THIS IS THE END FOR HIM.
...!

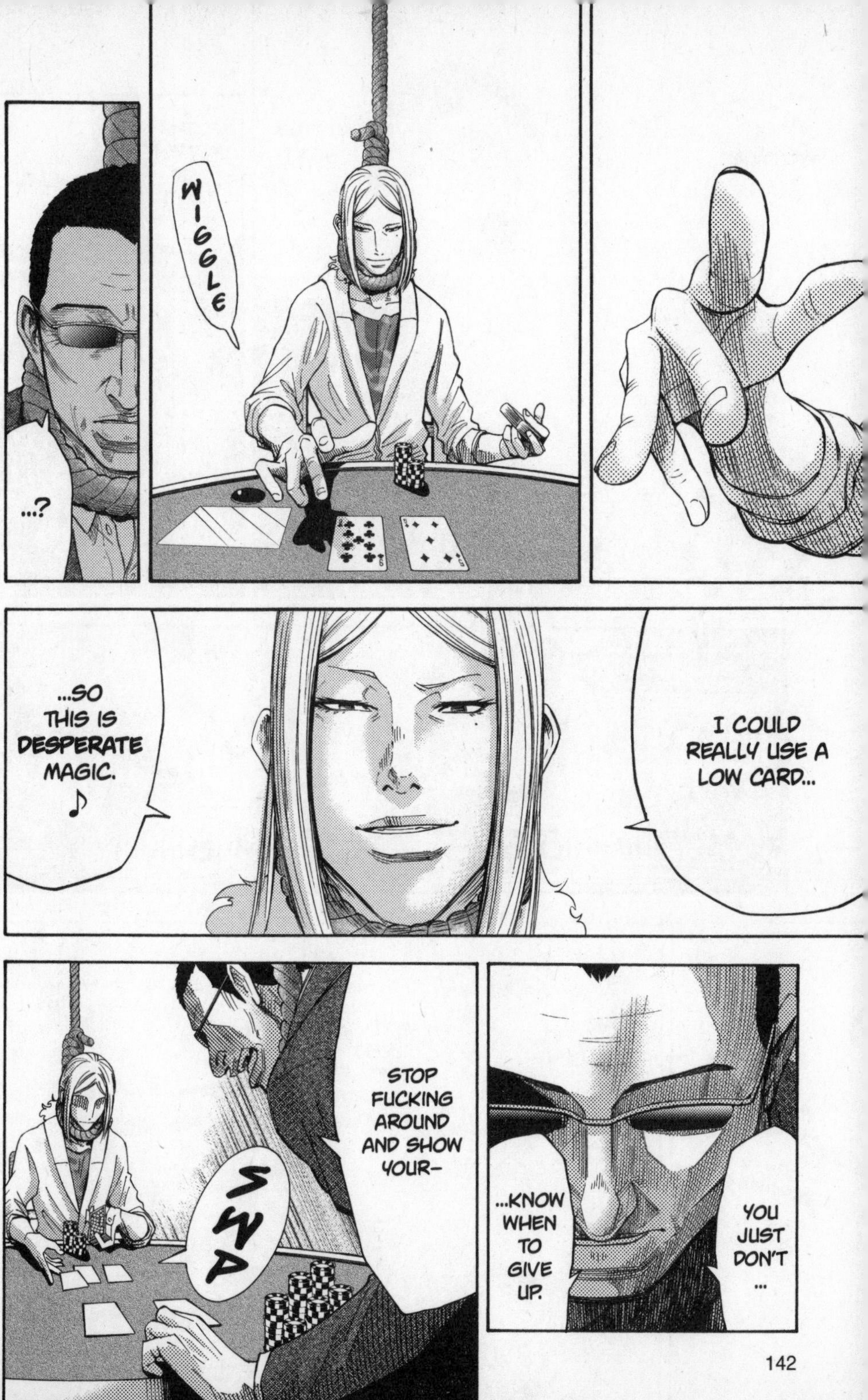
WIGGLE
...?
I COULD REALLY USE A LOW CARD...
...SO THIS IS DESPERATE MAGIC. ♪
YOU JUST DON'T ...
...KNOW WHEN TO GIVE UP.
STOP FUCKING AROUND AND SHOW YOUR–
SWP

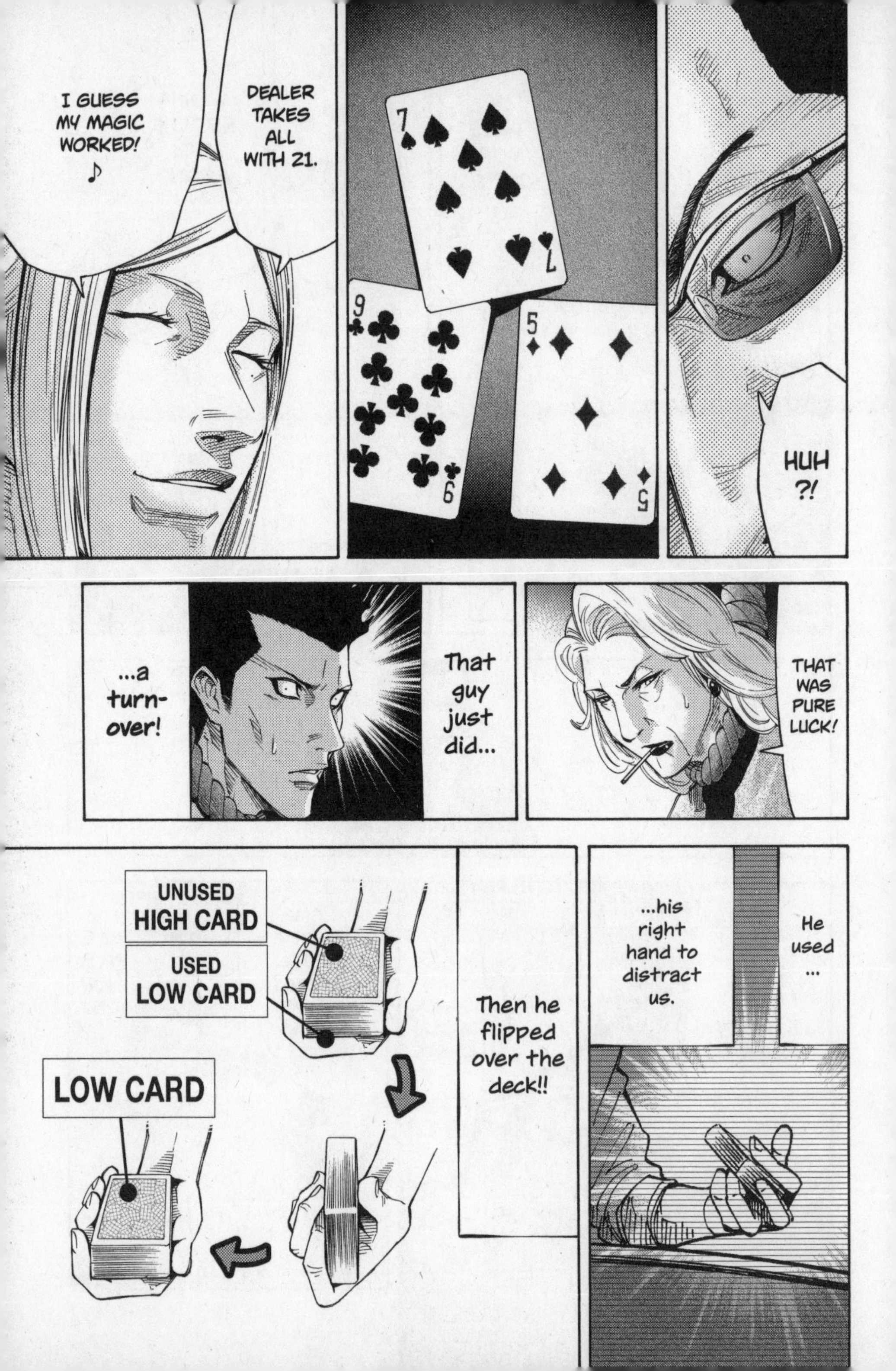
HUH ?!
DEALER TAKES ALL WITH 21.
I GUESS MY MAGIC WORKED! ♪
THAT WAS PURE LUCK!
That guy just did...
...a turn-over!
He used ...
...his right hand to distract us.
Then he flipped over the deck!!
UNUSED HIGH CARD
USED LOW CARD
LOW CARD

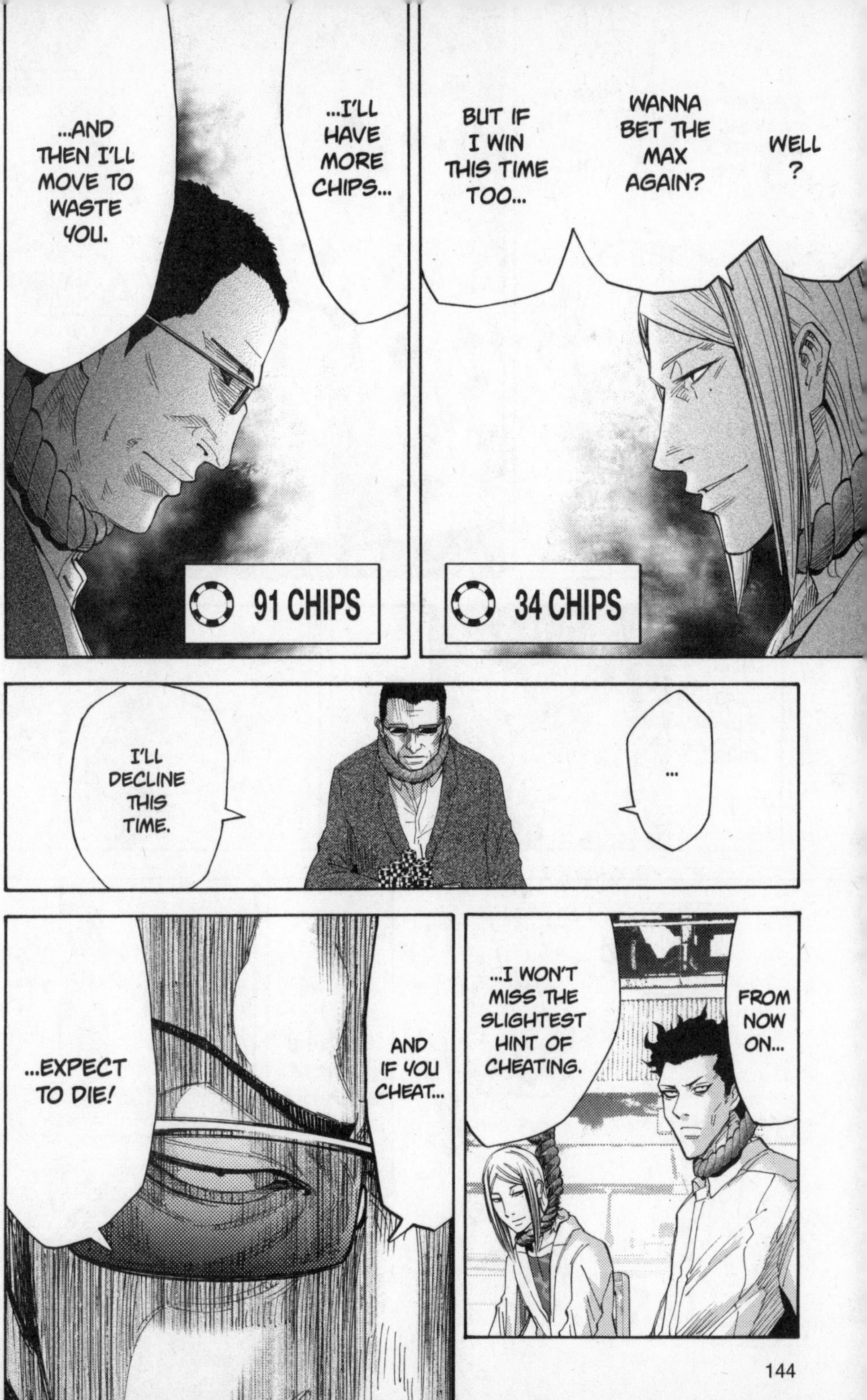
WELL ?
WANNA BET THE MAX AGAIN?
BUT IF I WIN THIS TIME TOO...
34 CHIPS
...I'LL HAVE MORE CHIPS...
...AND THEN I'LL MOVE TO WASTE YOU.
91 CHIPS
...
I'LL DECLINE THIS TIME.
FROM NOW ON...
...I WON'T MISS THE SLIGHTEST HINT OF CHEATING.
AND IF YOU CHEAT...
...EXPECT TO DIE!

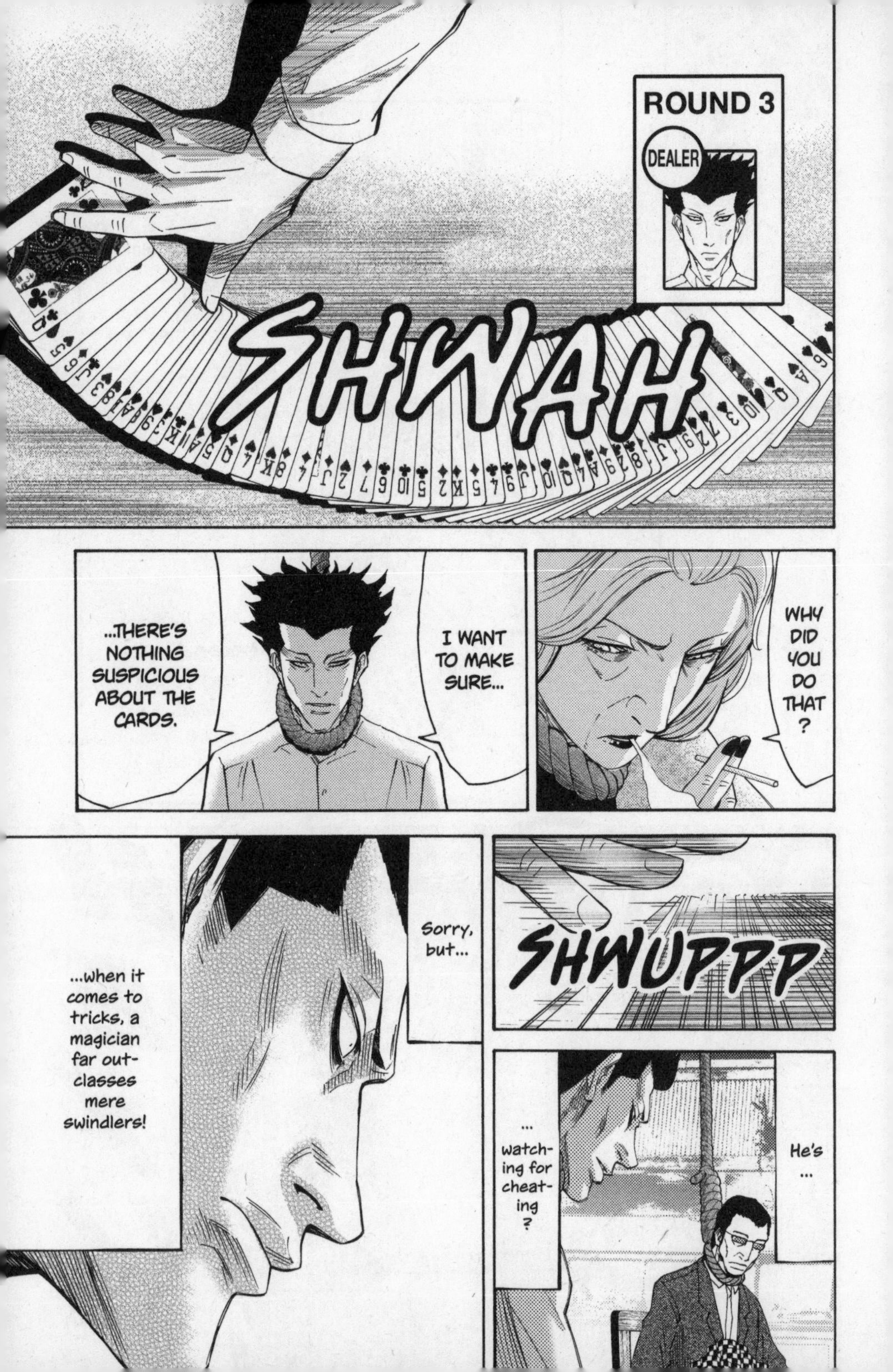
ROUND 3
DEALER
SHWAH
WHY DID YOU DO THAT?
I WANT TO MAKE SURE...
...THERE'S NOTHING SUSPICIOUS ABOUT THE CARDS.
SHWUPPP
He's...
...watching for cheating?
Sorry, but...
...when it comes to tricks, a magician far outclasses mere swindlers!

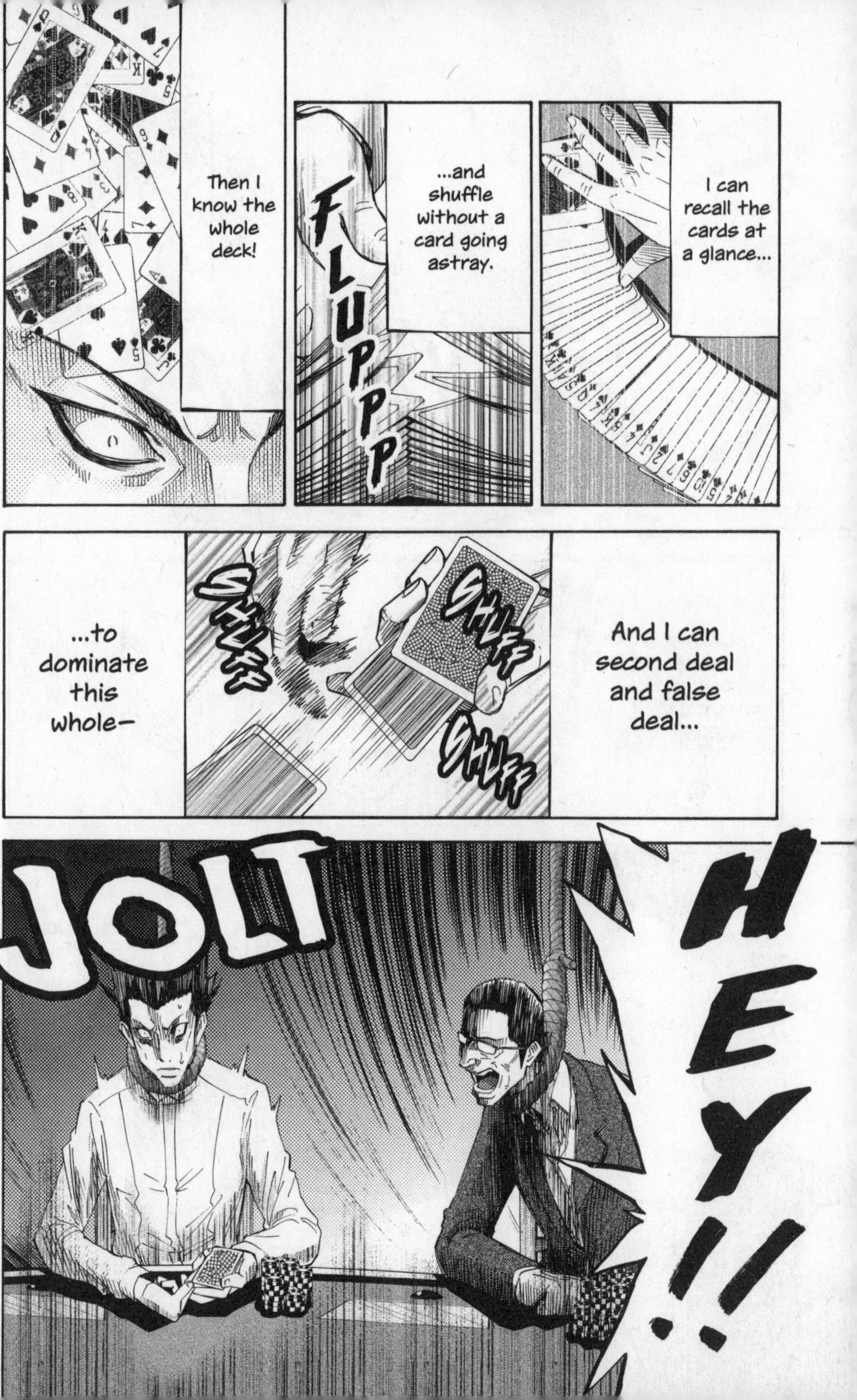
I can recall the cards at a glance...
...and shuffle without a card going astray.
FLUPPP
Then I know the whole deck!
And I can second deal and false deal...
SHUFF
SHUFF
SHUFF
...to dominate this whole—
HEY!!
JOLT

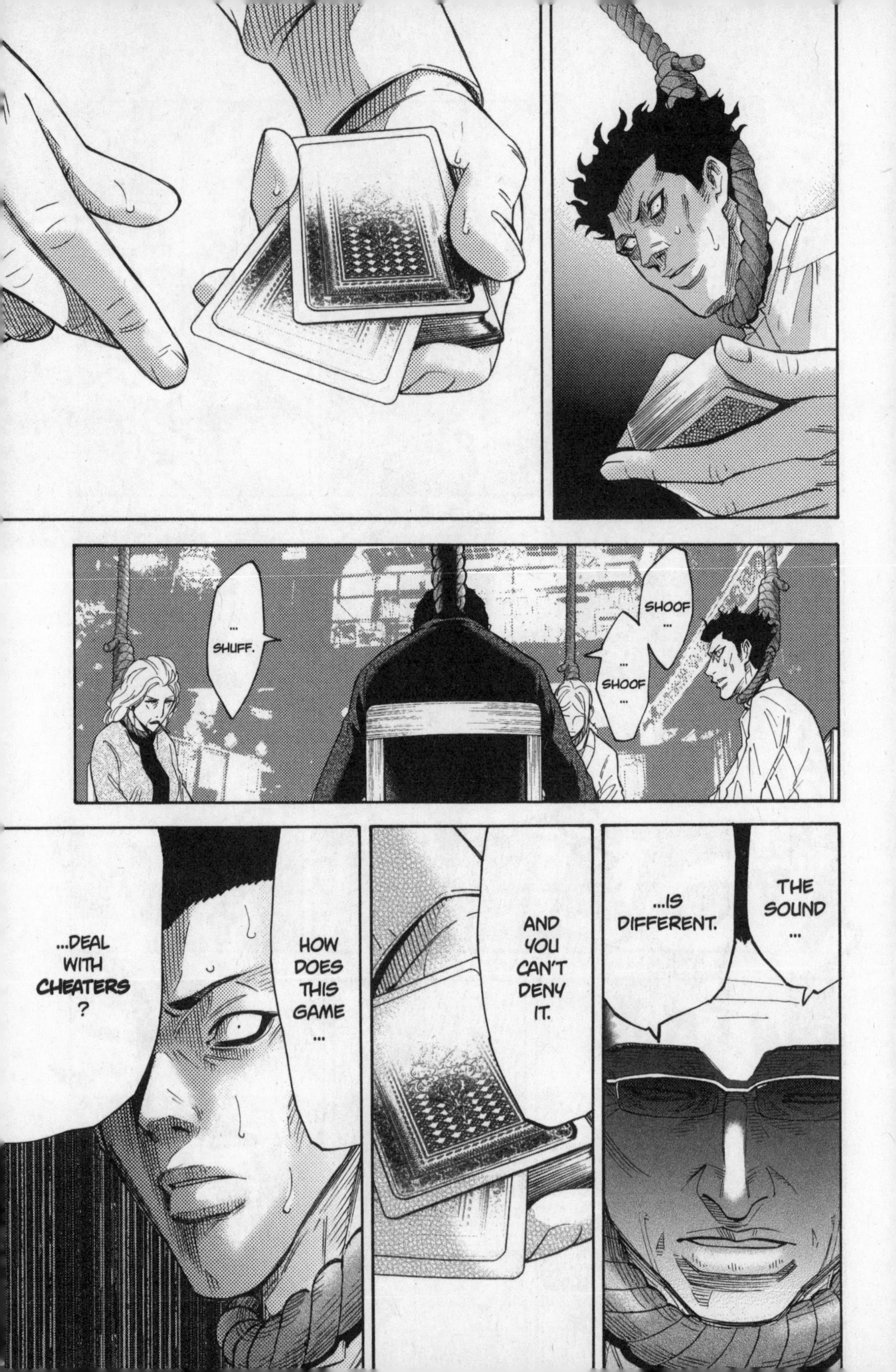
SHOOF ...
... SHOOF ...
... SHUFF.
THE SOUND ...
...IS DIFFERENT.
AND YOU CAN'T DENY IT.
HOW DOES THIS GAME ...
...DEAL WITH CHEATERS ?

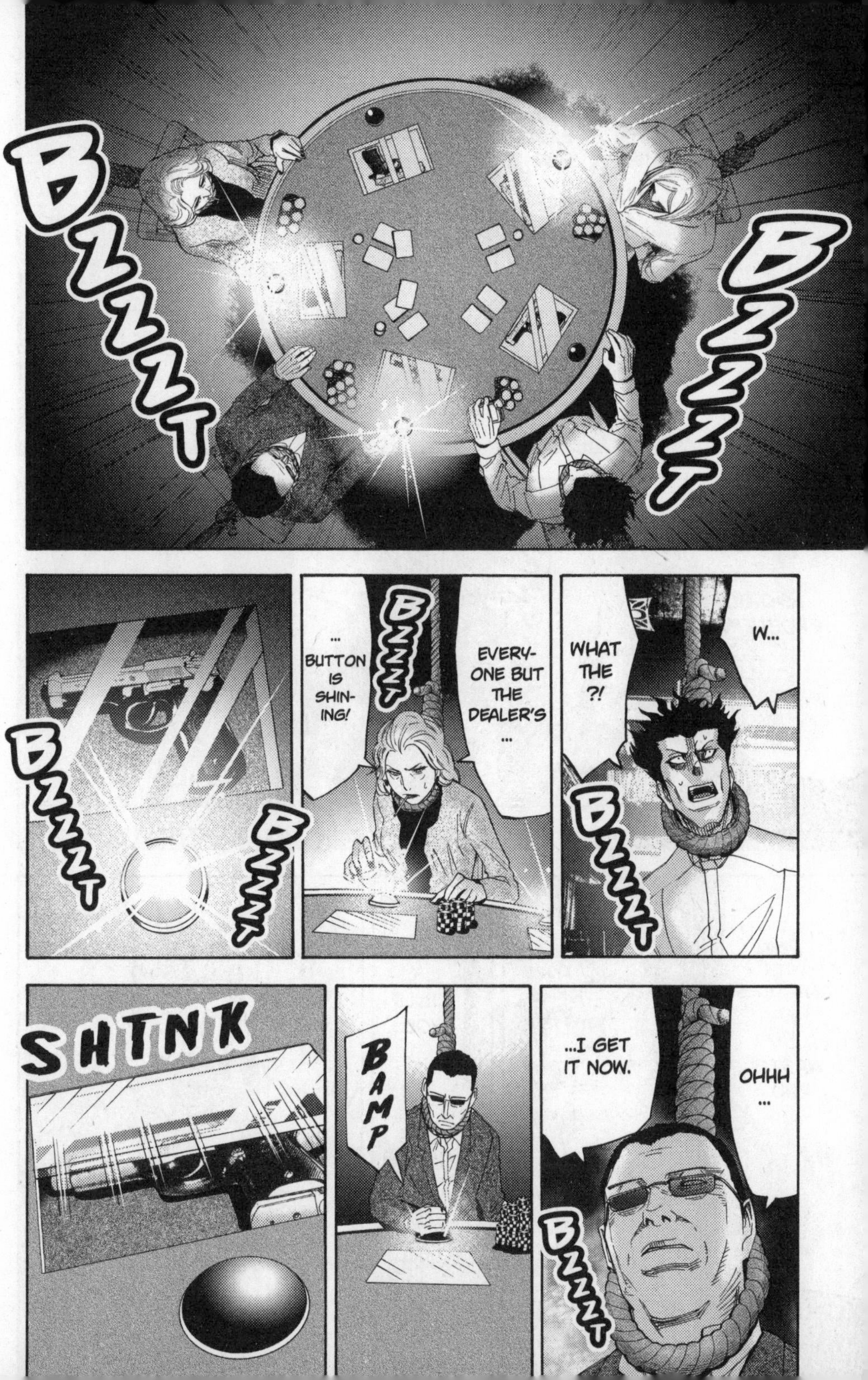
BZZZZT
BZZZZT
W...
WHAT THE ?!
BZZZT
EVERY-ONE BUT THE DEALER'S ...
... BUTTON IS SHINING!
BZZZT
BZZZT
BZZZT
OHHH ...
...I GET IT NOW.
BZZZT
BAMP
SHTNK

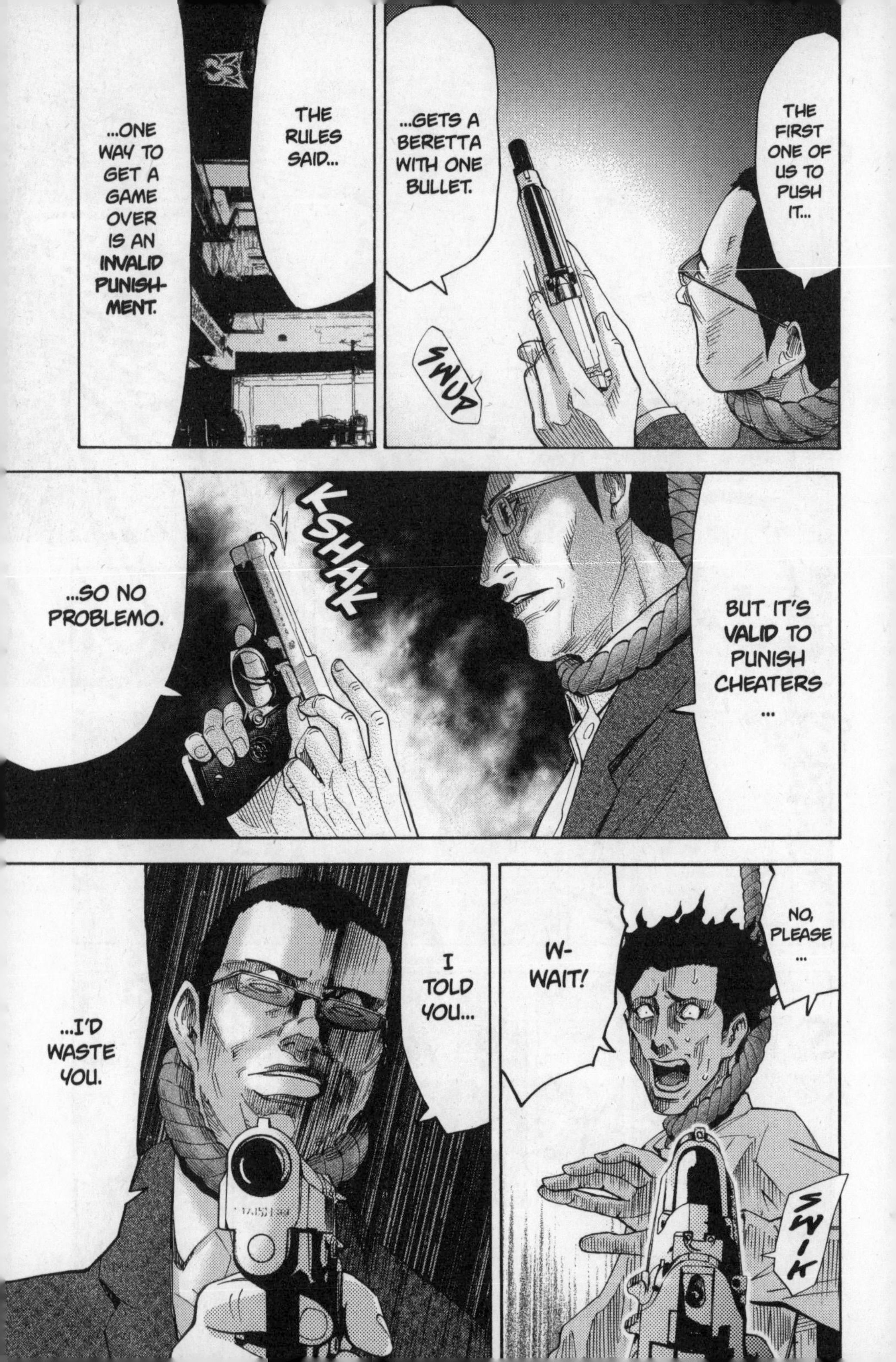
THE FIRST ONE OF US TO PUSH IT...
...GETS A BERETTA WITH ONE BULLET.
SWUP
THE RULES SAID...
...ONE WAY TO GET A GAME OVER IS AN INVALID PUNISHMENT.
BUT IT'S VALID TO PUNISH CHEATERS...
KSHAK
...SO NO PROBLEMO.
NO, PLEASE...
W-WAIT!
SWIK
I TOLD YOU...
...I'D WASTE YOU.

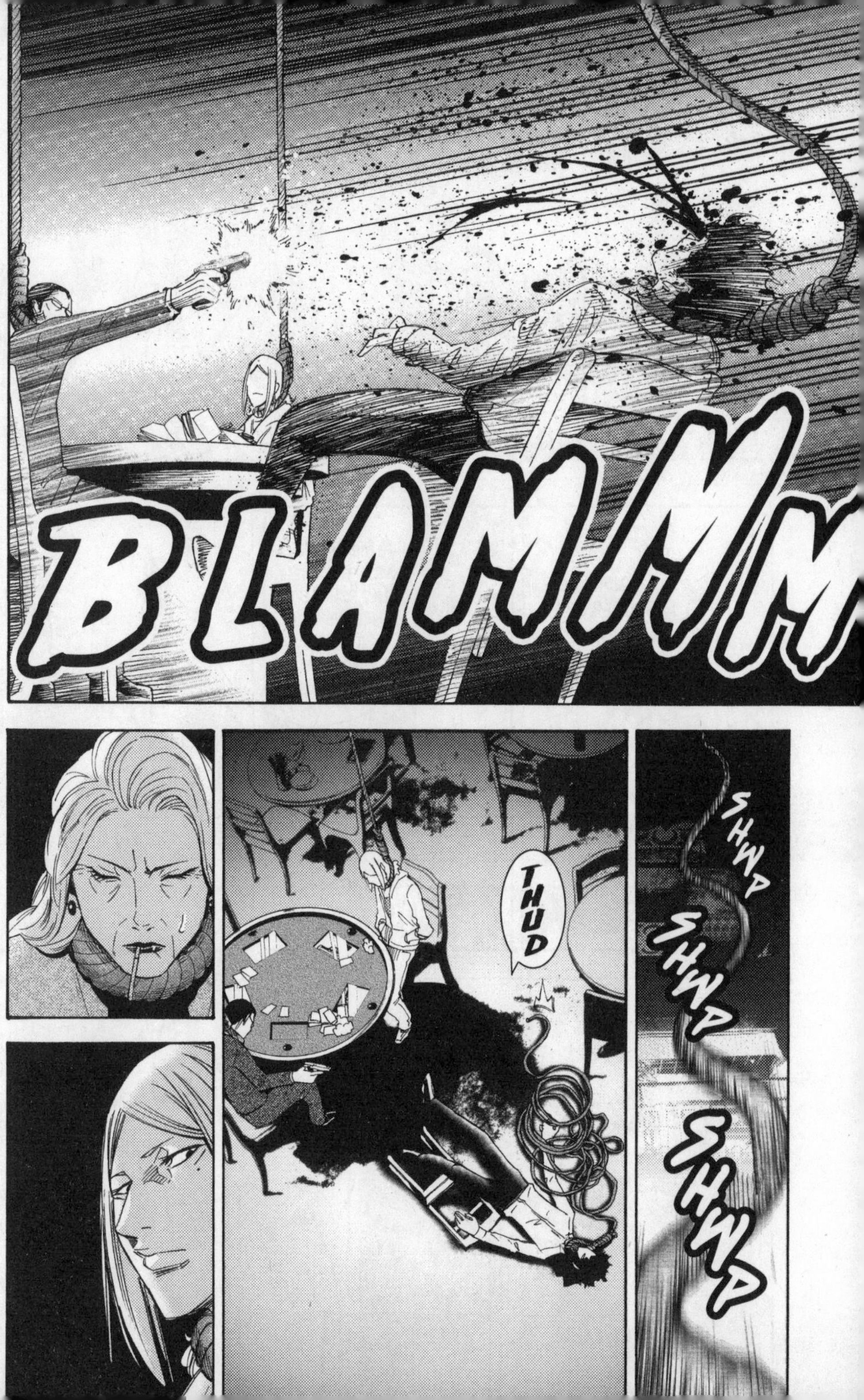
BLAMMM
SHWP
SHWP
SHWP
SHWP
SHWP
THUD

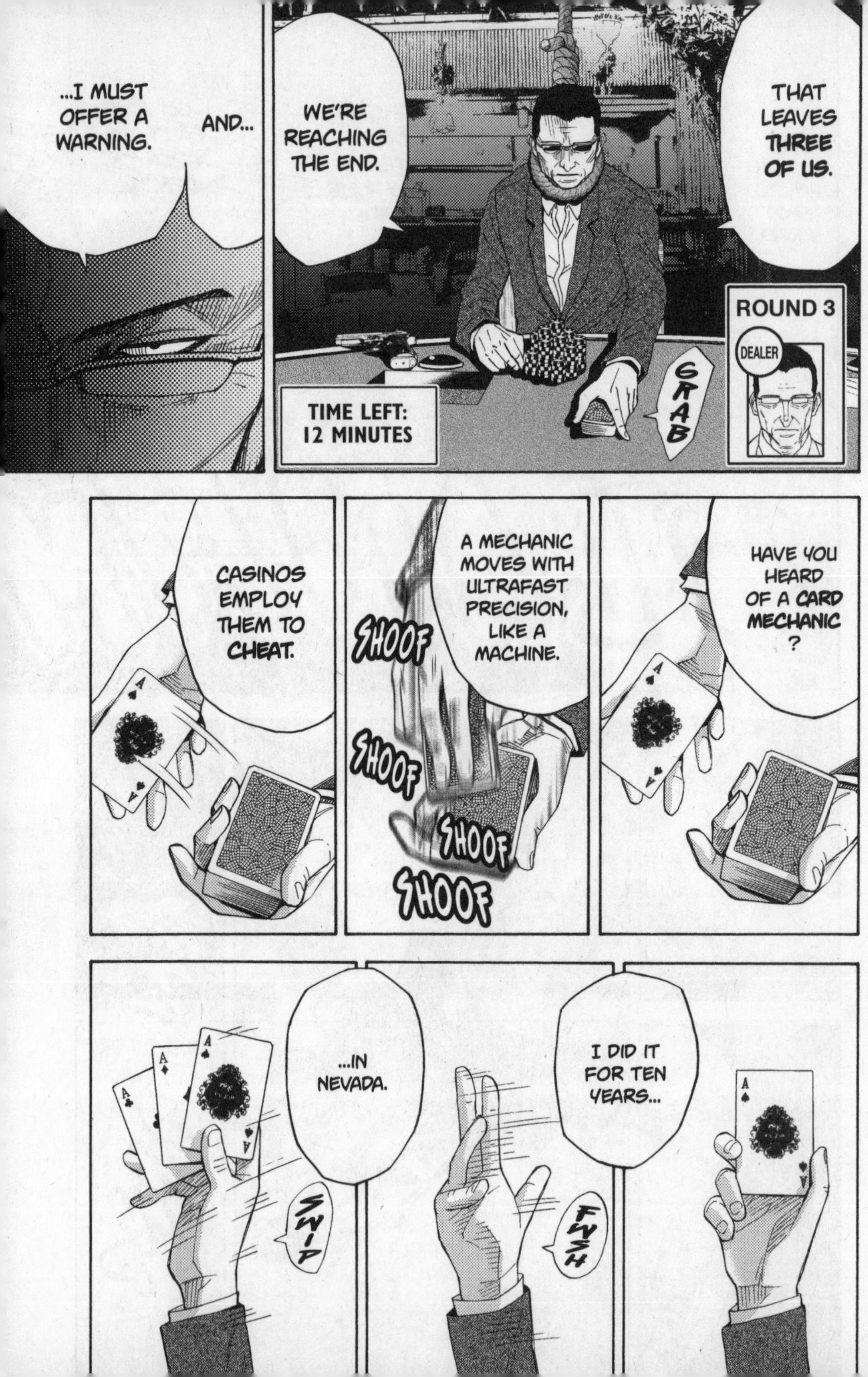
THAT LEAVES THREE OF US.
ROUND 3
DEALER
GRAB
TIME LEFT: 12 MINUTES
WE'RE REACHING THE END.
AND...
...I MUST OFFER A WARNING.
HAVE YOU HEARD OF A CARD MECHANIC?
A MECHANIC MOVES WITH ULTRAFAST PRECISION, LIKE A MACHINE.
SHOOF
SHOOF
SHOOF
SHOOF
CASINOS EMPLOY THEM TO CHEAT.
I DID IT FOR TEN YEARS...
FWSH
...IN NEVADA.
SWIP

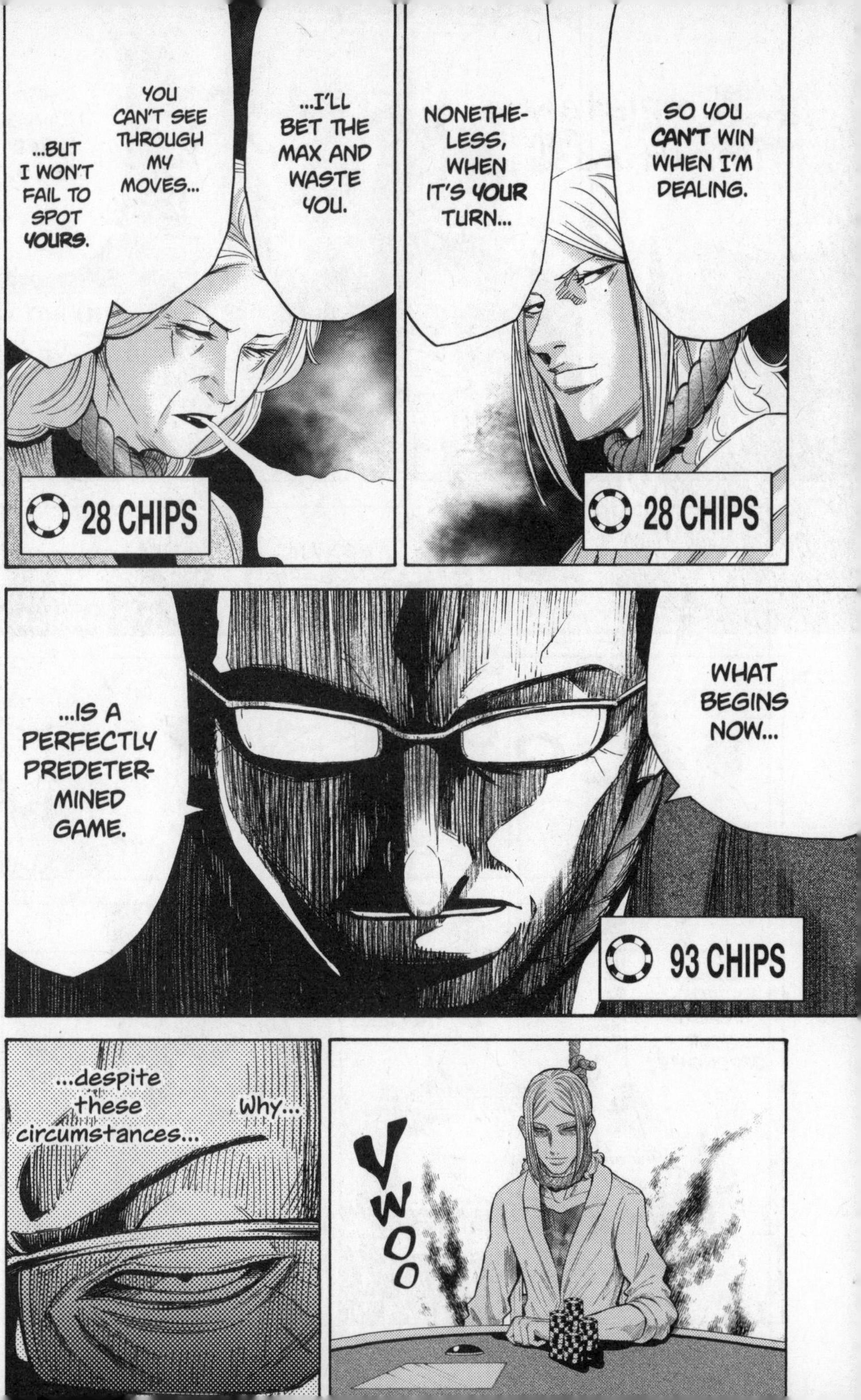
SO YOU CAN'T WIN WHEN I'M DEALING.
NONETHE-LESS, WHEN IT'S YOUR TURN...
28 CHIPS
...I'LL BET THE MAX AND WASTE YOU.
YOU CAN'T SEE THROUGH MY MOVES...
...BUT I WON'T FAIL TO SPOT YOURS.
28 CHIPS
WHAT BEGINS NOW...
...IS A PERFECTLY PREDETER-MINED GAME.
93 CHIPS
VWOO
Why...
...despite these circumstances...

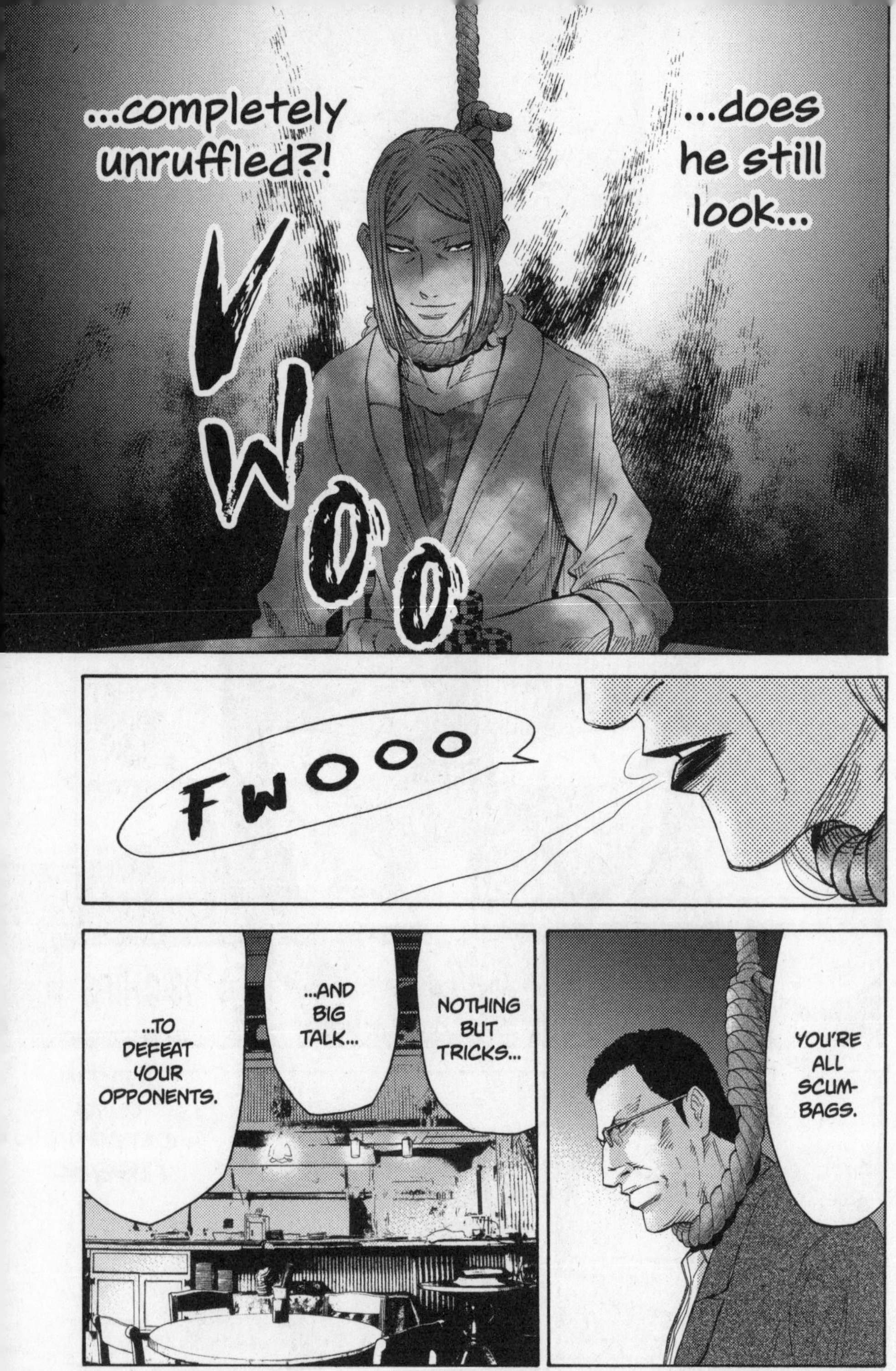
...does he still look...
...completely unruffled?!
WOO
FWOOO
YOU'RE ALL SCUM-BAGS.
NOTHING BUT TRICKS...
...AND BIG TALK...
...TO DEFEAT YOUR OPPONENTS.

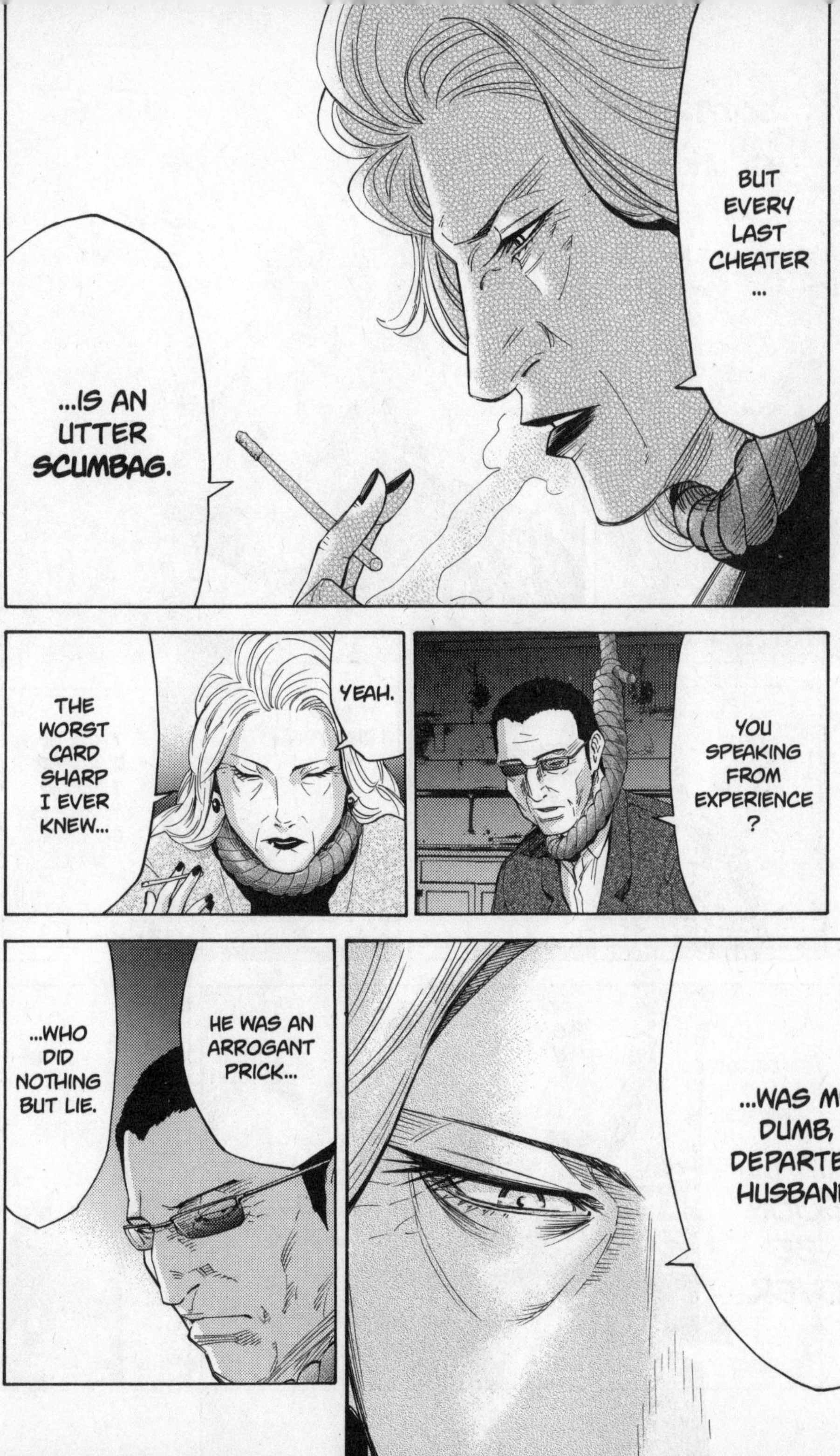
BUT EVERY LAST CHEATER ...
...IS AN UTTER SCUMBAG.
YOU SPEAKING FROM EXPERIENCE ?
YEAH.
THE WORST CARD SHARP I EVER KNEW...
...WAS MY DUMB, DEPARTED HUSBAND.
HE WAS AN ARROGANT PRICK...
...WHO DID NOTHING BUT LIE.

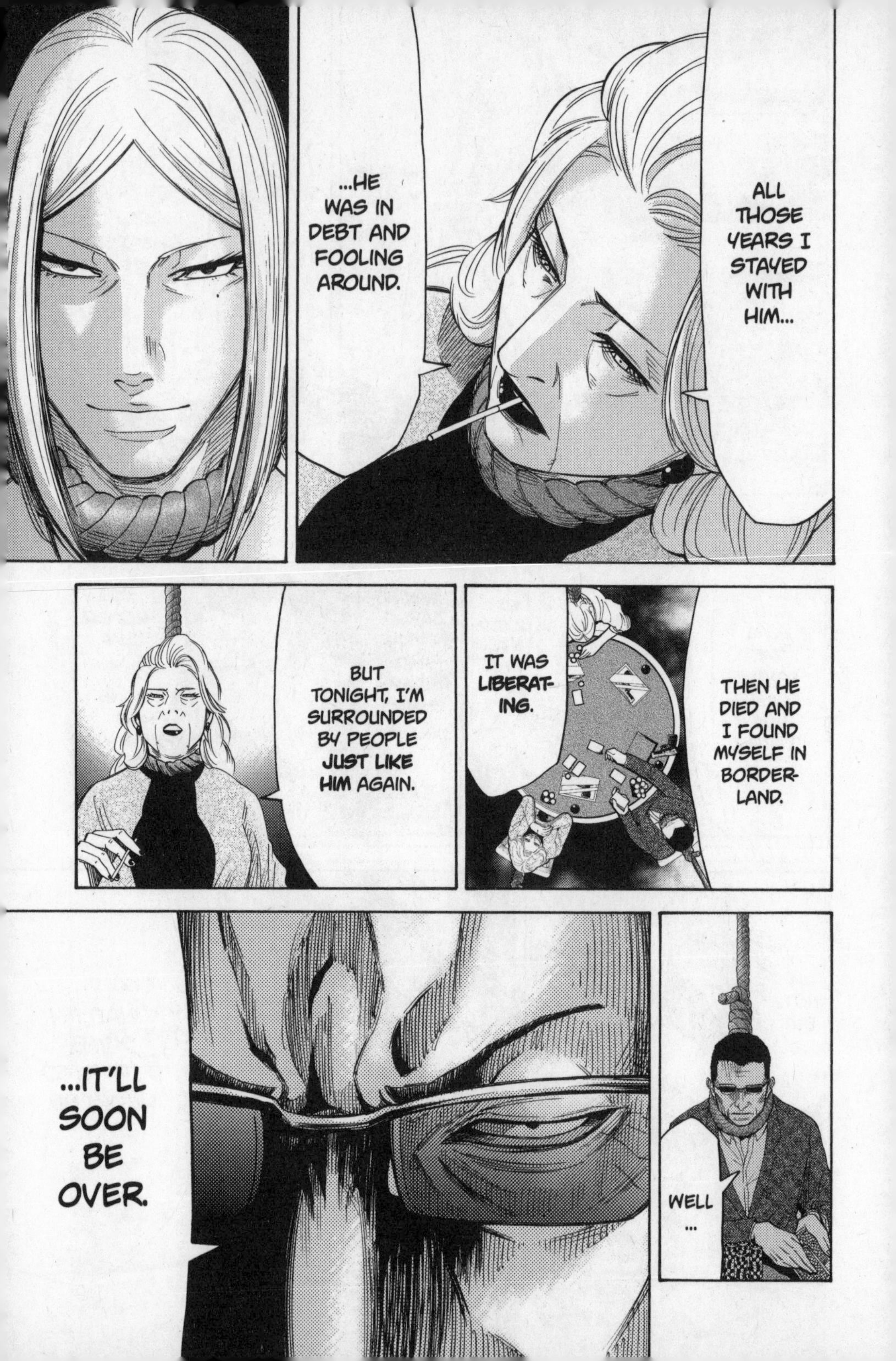
ALL THOSE YEARS I STAYED WITH HIM...
...HE WAS IN DEBT AND FOOLING AROUND.
THEN HE DIED AND I FOUND MYSELF IN BORDERLAND.
IT WAS LIBERAT-ING.
BUT TONIGHT, I'M SURROUNDED BY PEOPLE JUST LIKE HIM AGAIN.
WELL ...
...IT'LL SOON BE OVER.

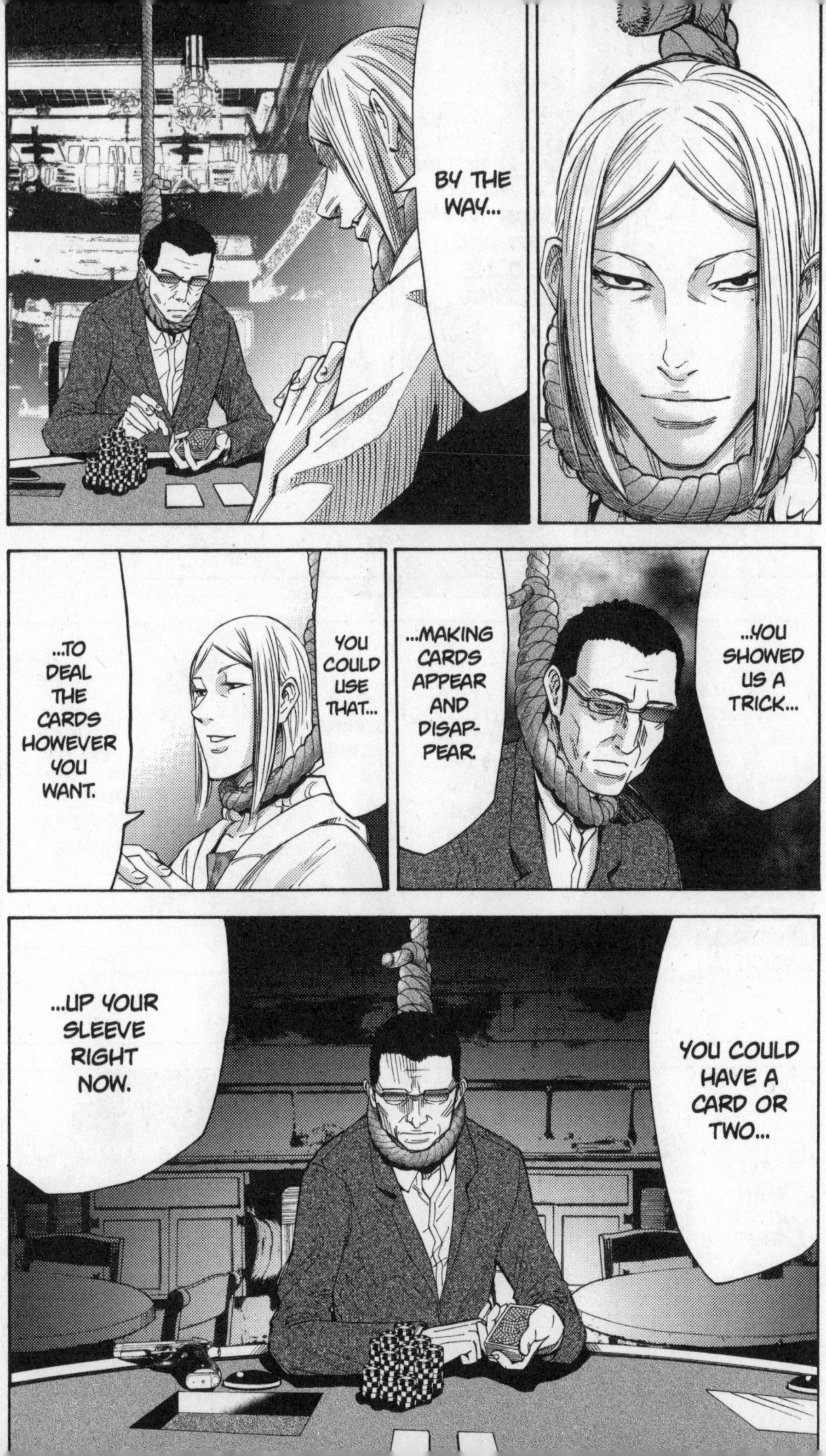
BY THE WAY...
...YOU SHOWED US A TRICK...
...MAKING CARDS APPEAR AND DISAP-PEAR.
YOU COULD USE THAT...
...TO DEAL THE CARDS HOWEVER YOU WANT.
YOU COULD HAVE A CARD OR TWO...
...UP YOUR SLEEVE RIGHT NOW.

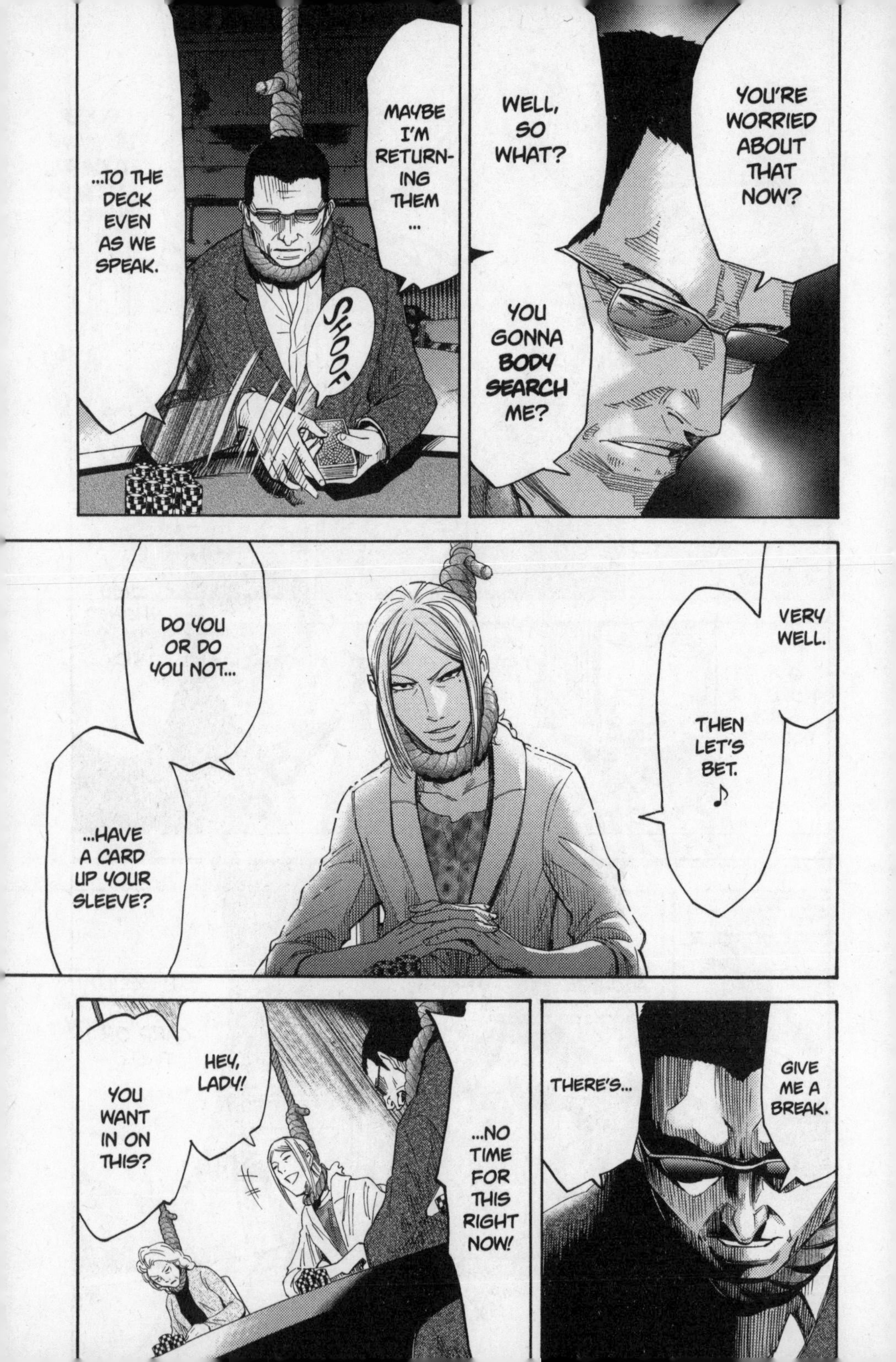

YOU'RE WORRIED ABOUT THAT NOW?
WELL, SO WHAT?
YOU GONNA **BODY SEARCH** ME?
MAYBE I'M RETURNING THEM ...
...TO THE DECK EVEN AS WE SPEAK.
SHOOF
VERY WELL.
THEN LET'S BET. ♪
DO YOU OR DO YOU NOT...
...HAVE A CARD UP YOUR SLEEVE?
GIVE ME A BREAK.
THERE'S...
...NO TIME FOR THIS RIGHT NOW!
HEY, LADY!
YOU WANT IN ON THIS?

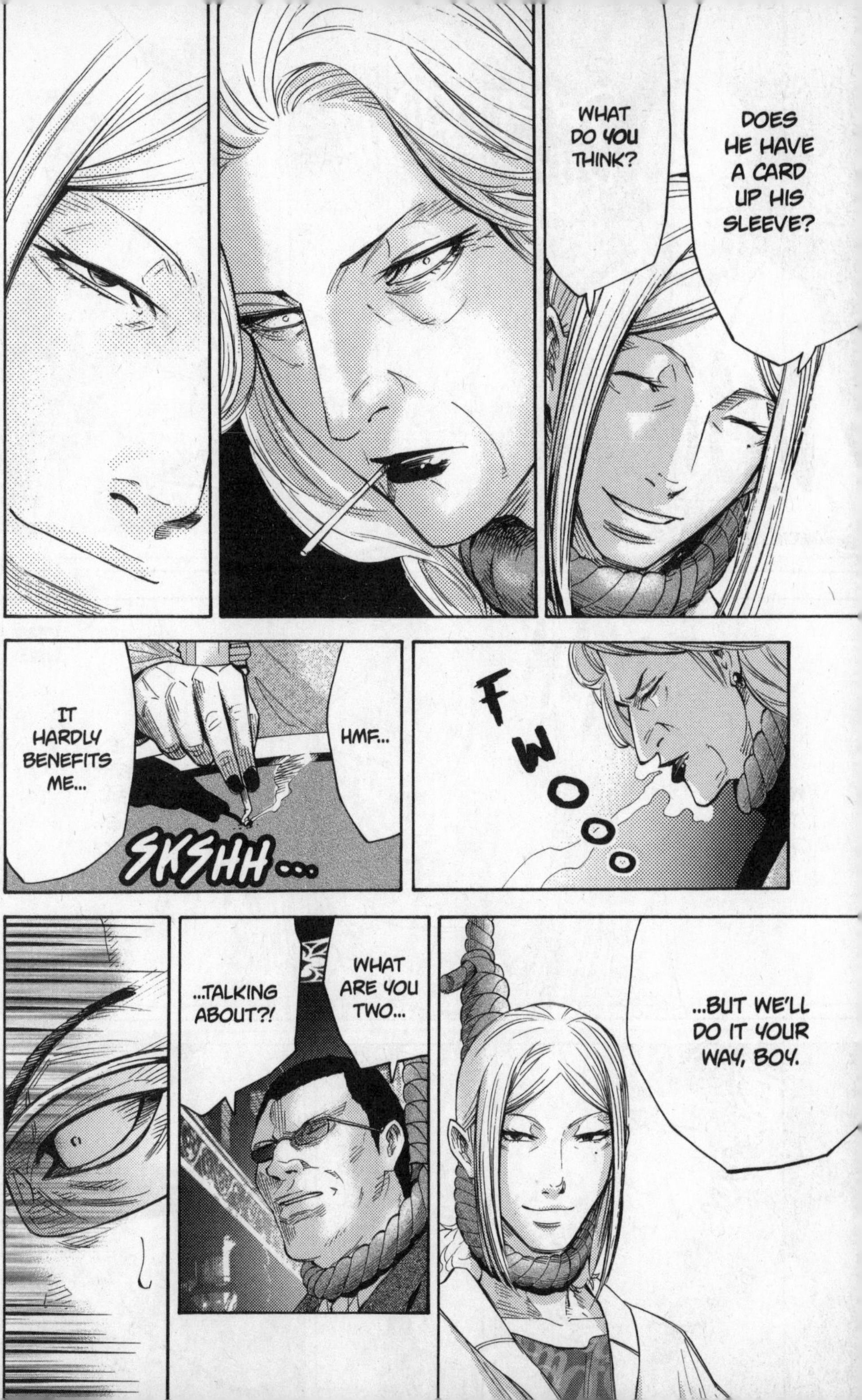
DOES HE HAVE A CARD UP HIS SLEEVE?
WHAT DO YOU THINK?
FWOOO
HMF...
IT HARDLY BENEFITS ME...
SKSHH...
...BUT WE'LL DO IT YOUR WAY, BOY.
WHAT ARE YOU TWO...
...TALKING ABOUT?!

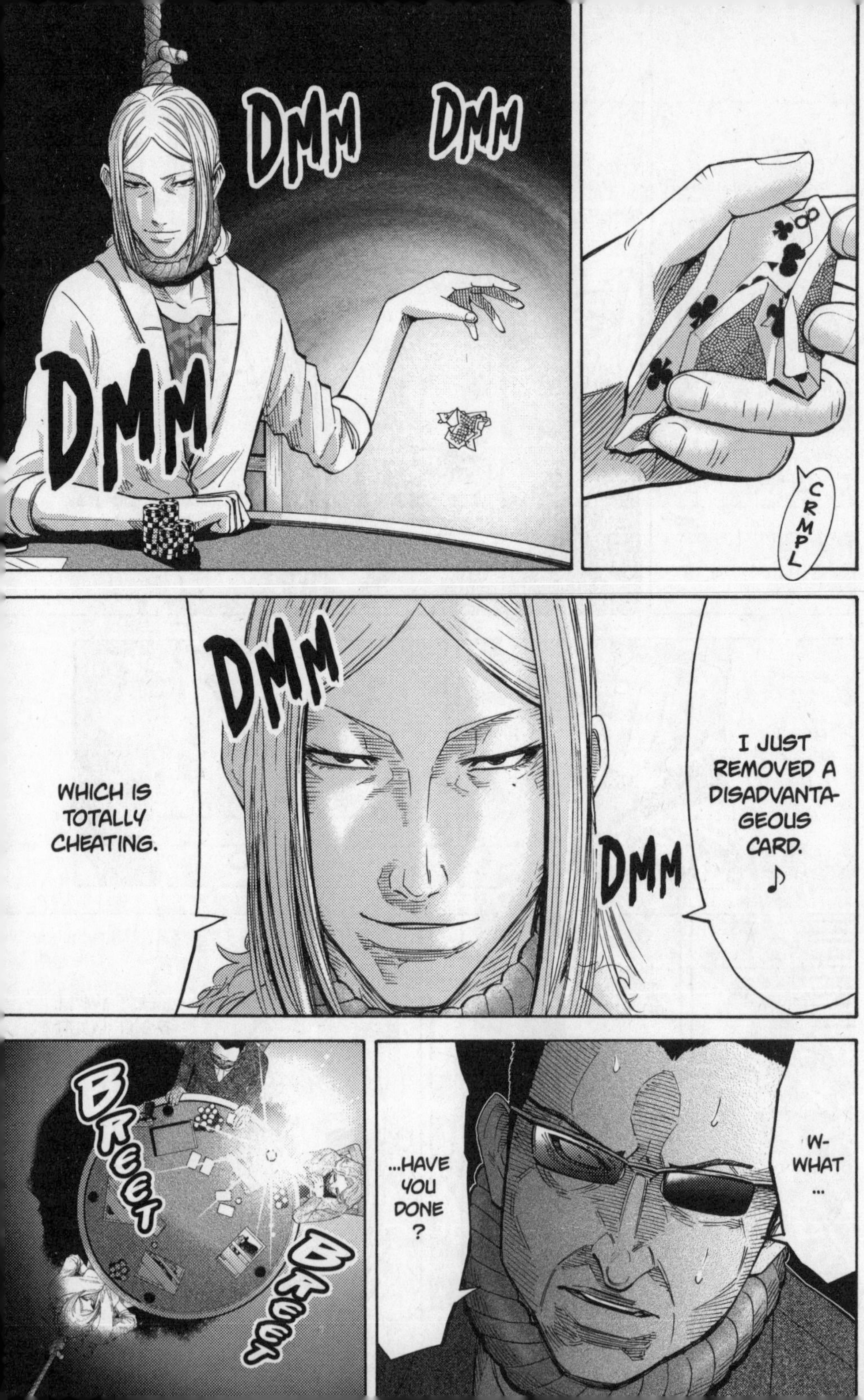
CRMPL
DMM
DMM
DMM
I JUST REMOVED A DISADVANTAGEOUS CARD. ♪
DMM
DMM
WHICH IS TOTALLY CHEATING.
W-WHAT ...
...HAVE YOU DONE ?
BREET
BREET

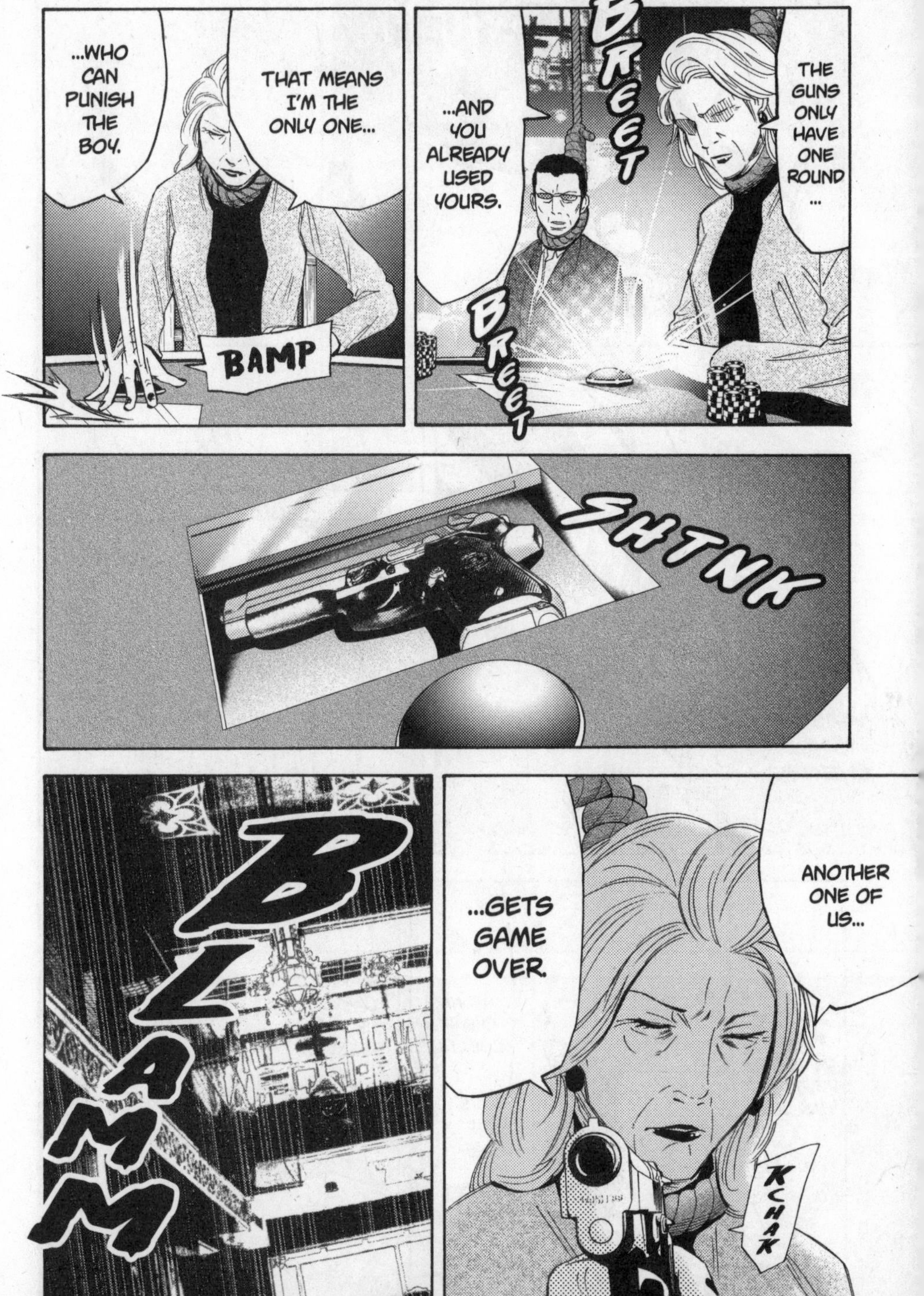
THE GUNS ONLY HAVE ONE ROUND ...
...AND YOU ALREADY USED YOURS.
BREET
BREET
THAT MEANS I'M THE ONLY ONE...
...WHO CAN PUNISH THE BOY.
BAMP
SHTNK
ANOTHER ONE OF US...
...GETS GAME OVER.
KCHAK
BLAMM

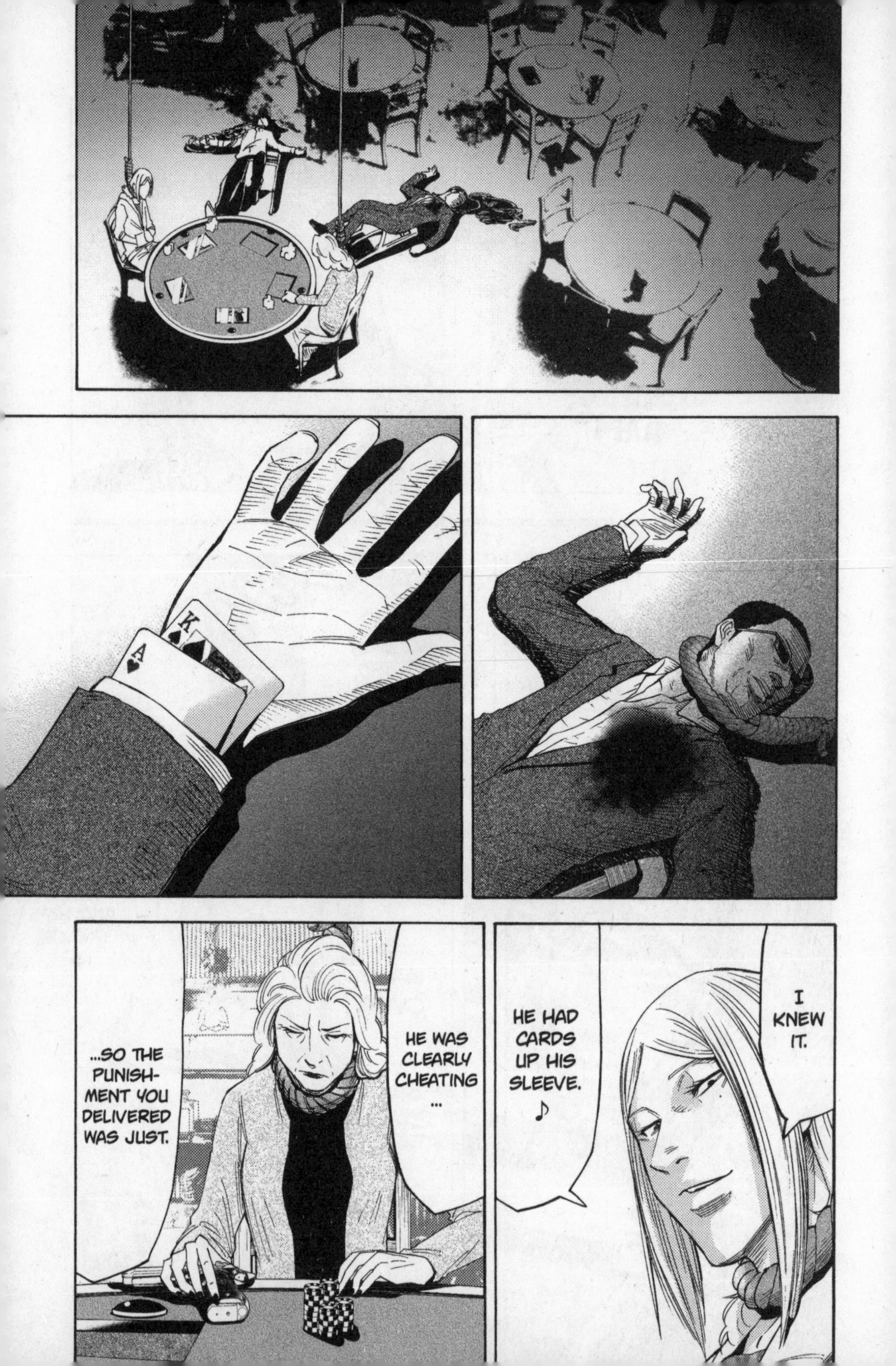
I KNEW IT.
HE HAD CARDS UP HIS SLEEVE. ♪
HE WAS CLEARLY CHEATING...
...SO THE PUNISHMENT YOU DELIVERED WAS JUST.

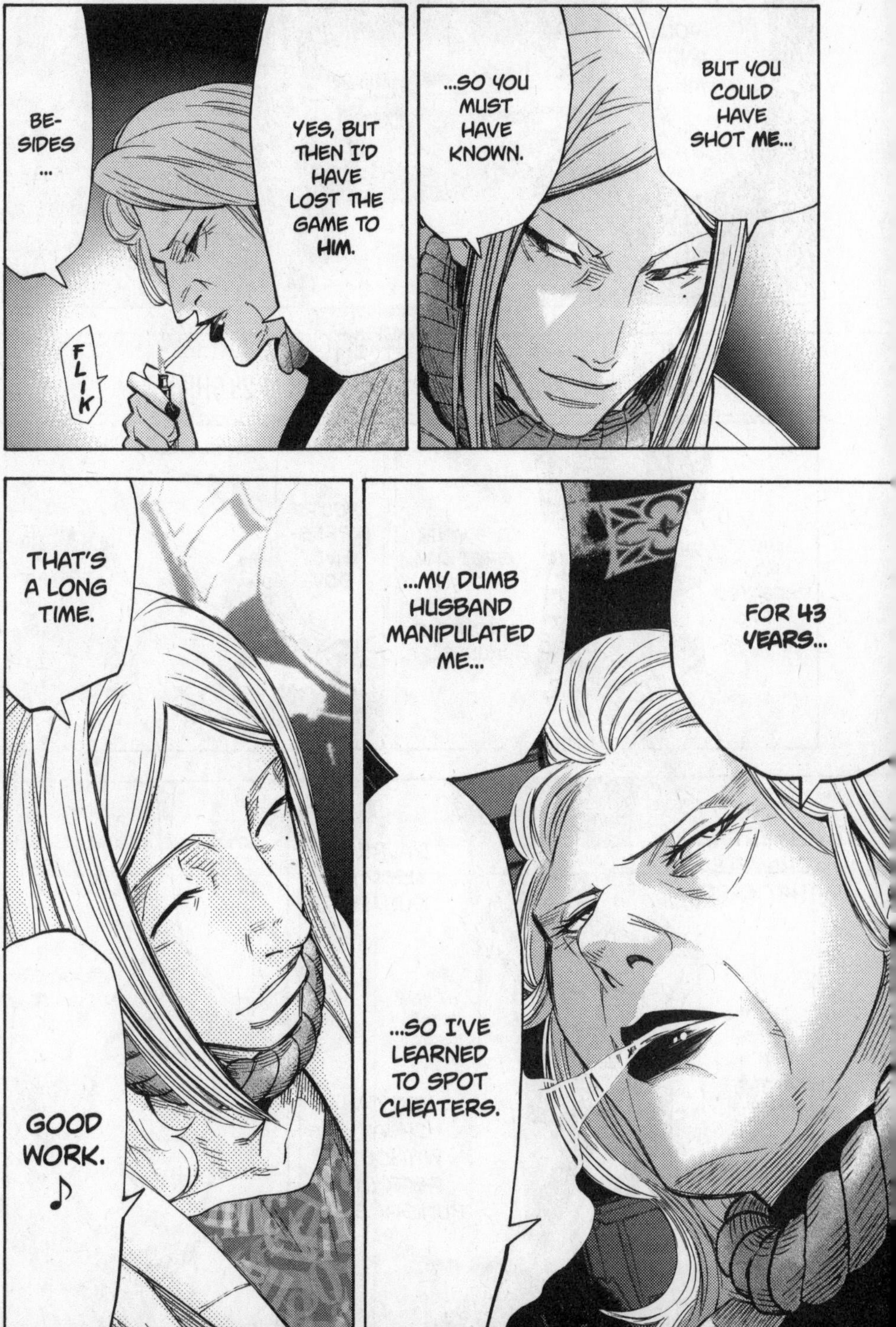
BUT YOU COULD HAVE SHOT ME...
...SO YOU MUST HAVE KNOWN.
YES, BUT THEN I'D HAVE LOST THE GAME TO HIM.
BE-SIDES ...
FLIK
FOR 43 YEARS...
...MY DUMB HUSBAND MANIPULATED ME...
...SO I'VE LEARNED TO SPOT CHEATERS.
THAT'S A LONG TIME.
GOOD WORK. ♪

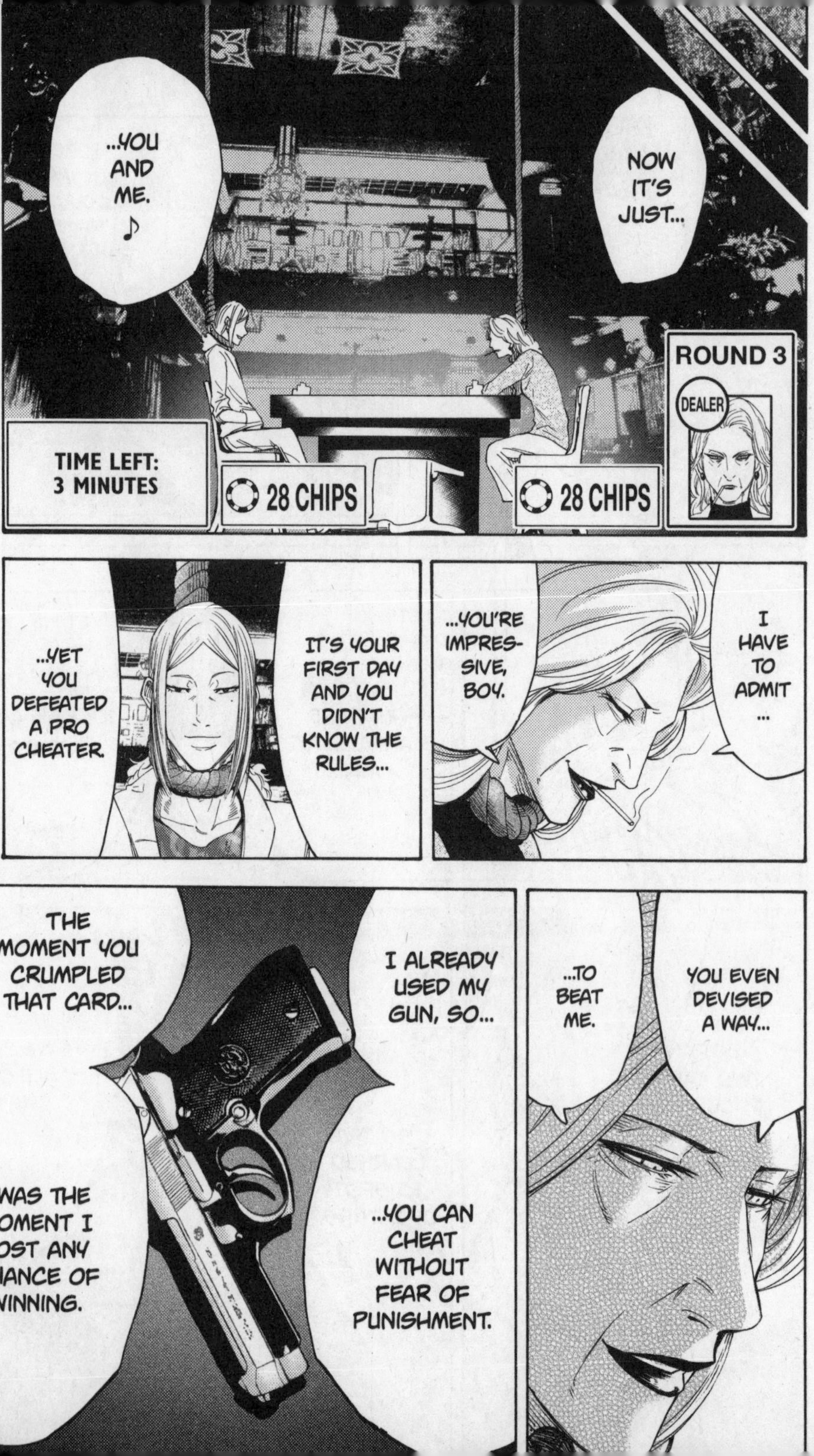
NOW IT'S JUST...
...YOU AND ME. ♪
ROUND 3
DEALER
28 CHIPS
28 CHIPS
TIME LEFT: 3 MINUTES
I HAVE TO ADMIT...
...YOU'RE IMPRESSIVE, BOY.
IT'S YOUR FIRST DAY AND YOU DIDN'T KNOW THE RULES...
...YET YOU DEFEATED A PRO CHEATER.
YOU EVEN DEVISED A WAY...
...TO BEAT ME.
I ALREADY USED MY GUN, SO...
...YOU CAN CHEAT WITHOUT FEAR OF PUNISHMENT.
THE MOMENT YOU CRUMPLED THAT CARD...
...WAS THE MOMENT I LOST ANY CHANCE OF WINNING.

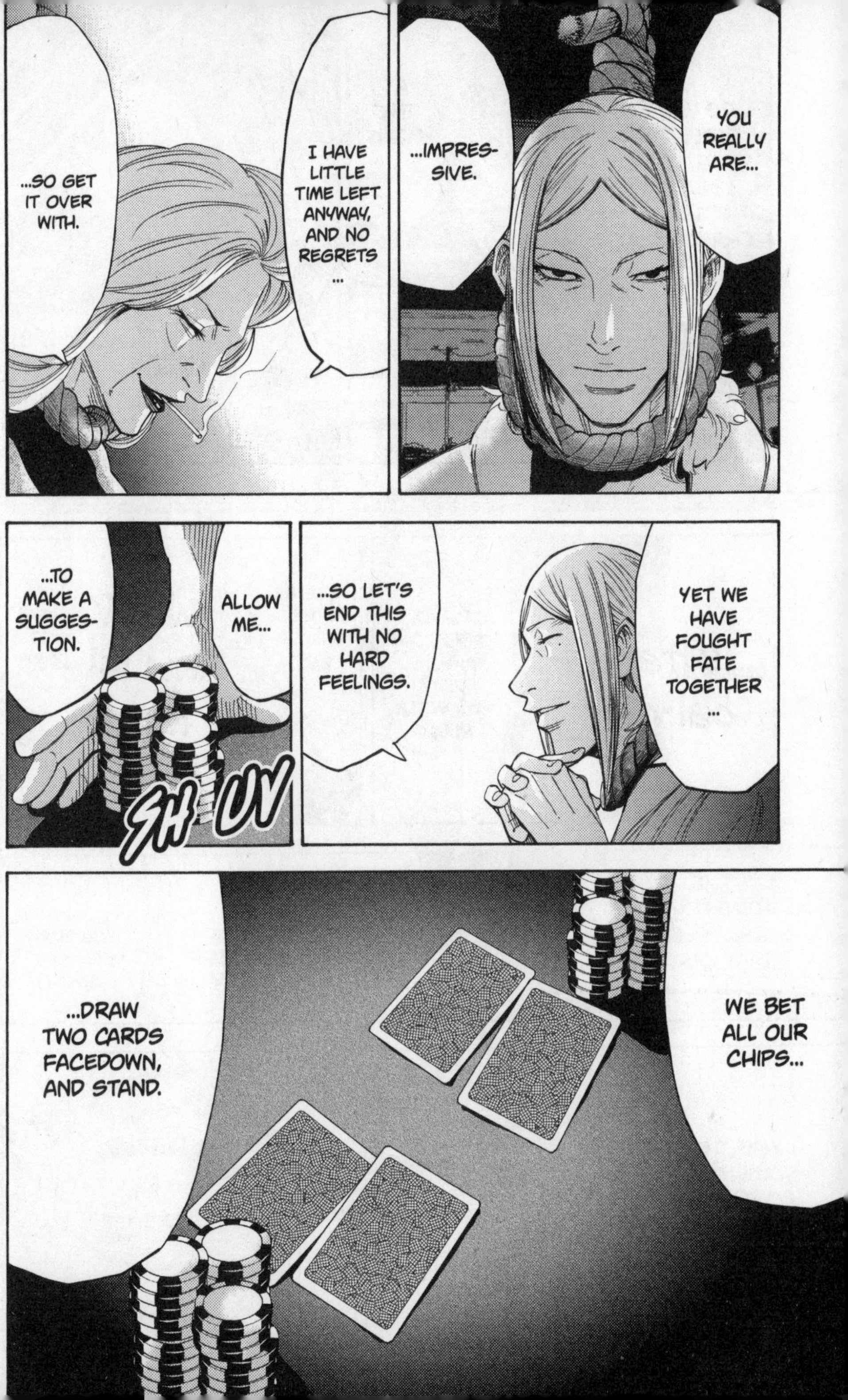
YOU REALLY ARE...
...IMPRES- SIVE.
I HAVE LITTLE TIME LEFT ANYWAY, AND NO REGRETS ...
...SO GET IT OVER WITH.
YET WE HAVE FOUGHT FATE TOGETHER ...
...SO LET'S END THIS WITH NO HARD FEELINGS.
ALLOW ME...
...TO MAKE A SUGGES- TION.
SHUV
WE BET ALL OUR CHIPS...
...DRAW TWO CARDS FACEDOWN, AND STAND.

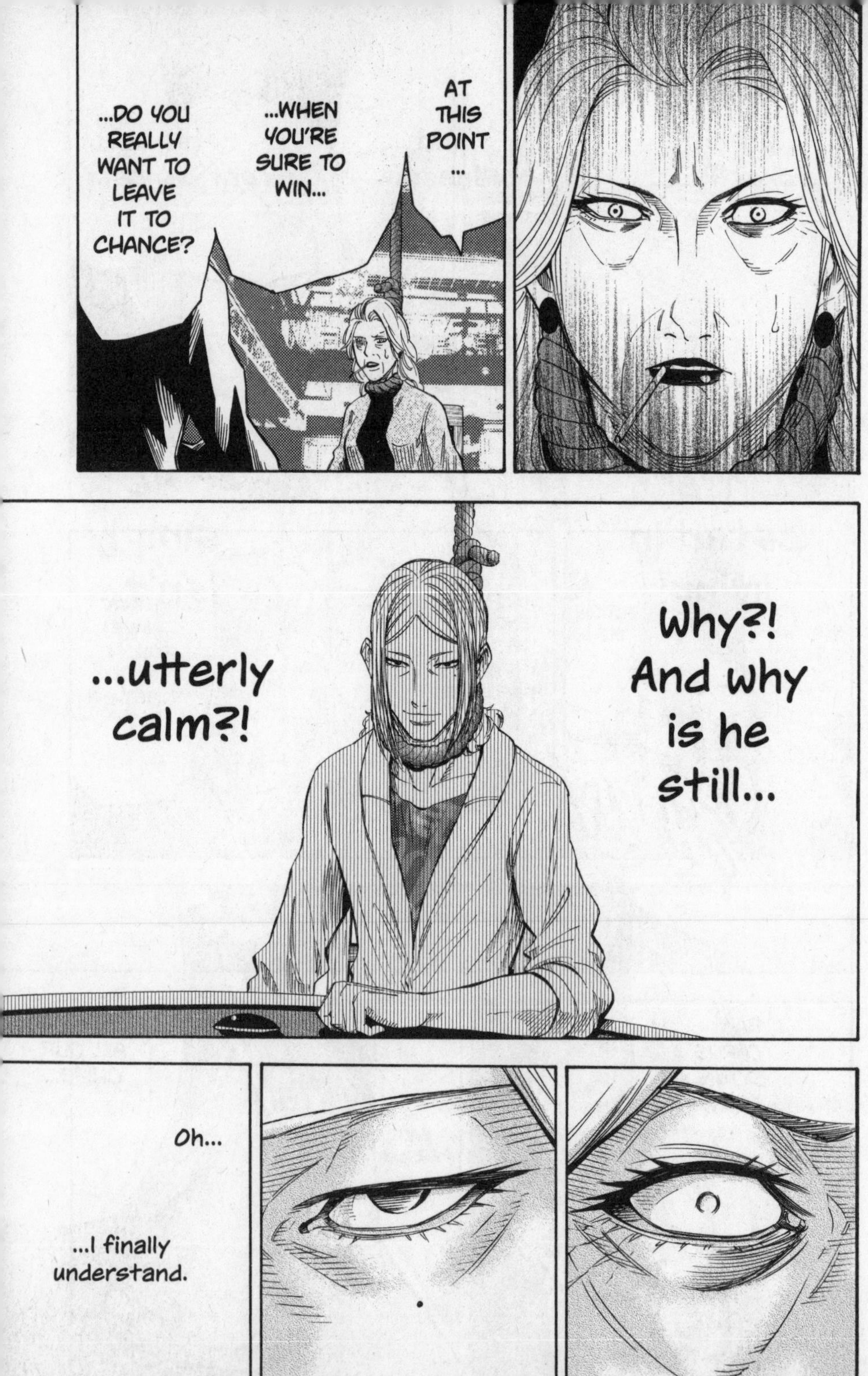
AT THIS POINT...
...WHEN YOU'RE SURE TO WIN...
...DO YOU REALLY WANT TO LEAVE IT TO CHANCE?
Why?! And why is he still...
...utterly calm?!
Oh...
...I finally understand.

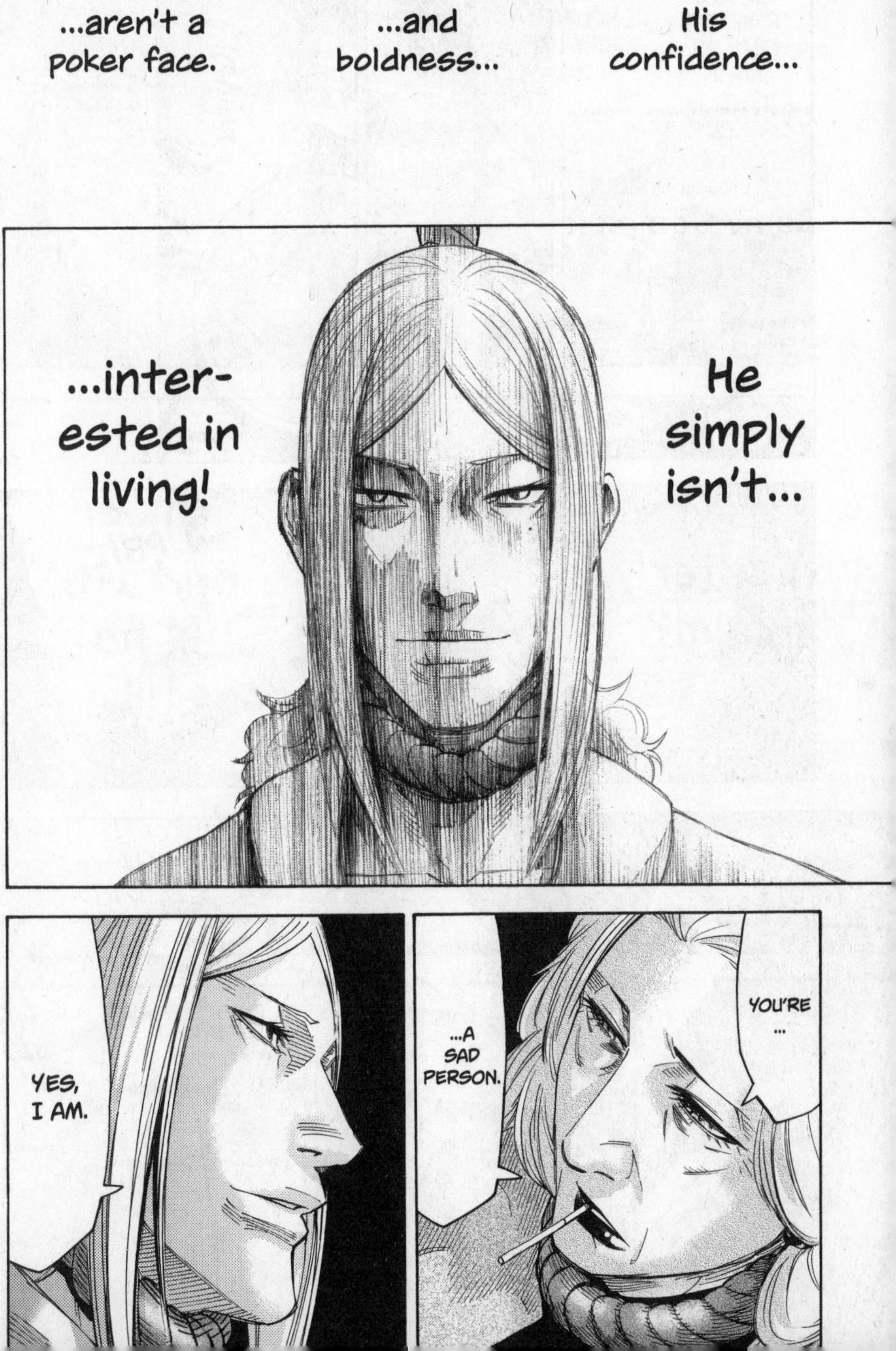
His confidence...
...and boldness...
...aren't a poker face.
He simply isn't...
...interested in living!
YOU'RE ...
...A SAD PERSON.
YES, I AM.

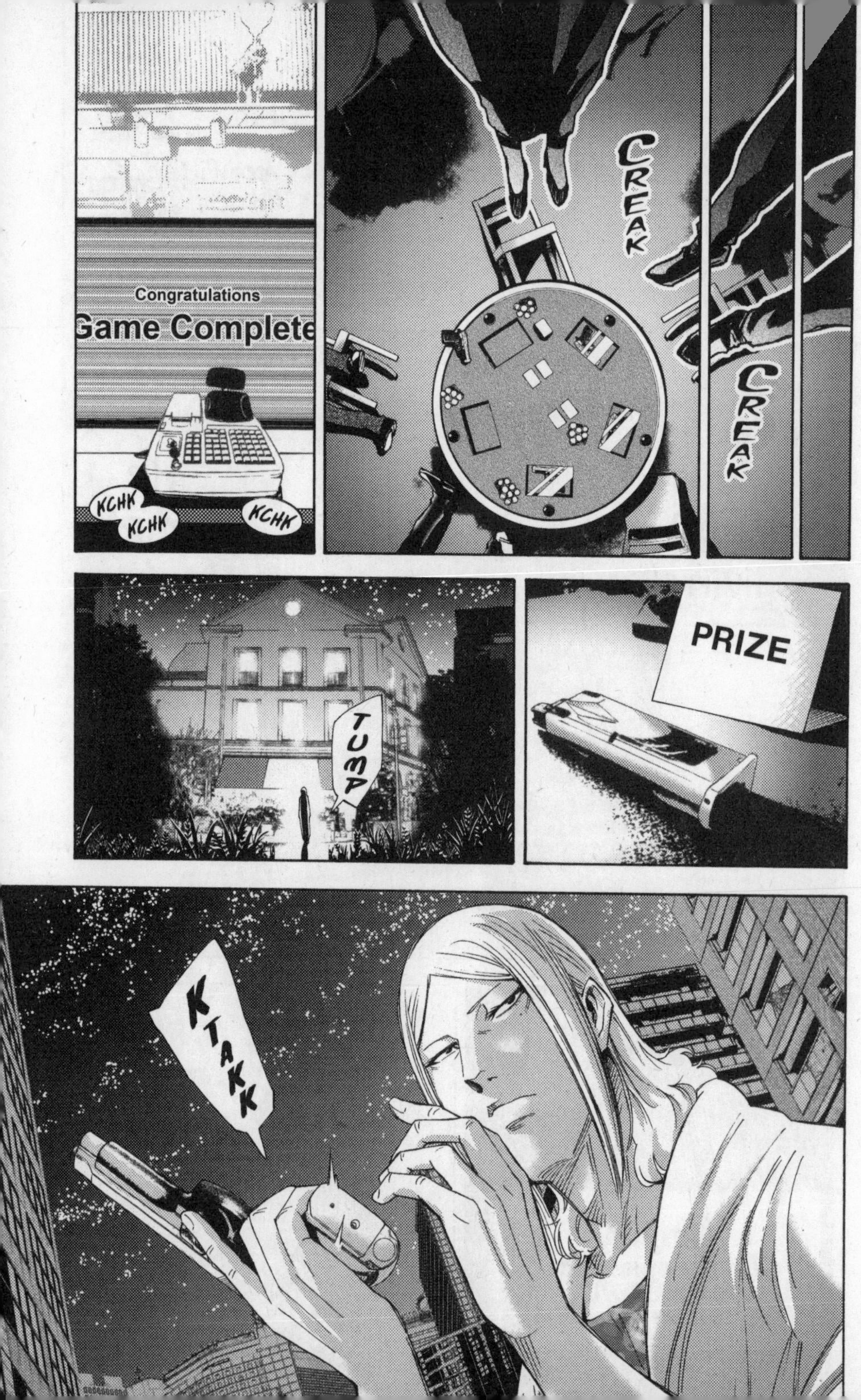
CREAK
CREAK
Congratulations
Game Complete
KCHK
KCHK
KCHK
PRIZE
TUMP
KTAKK

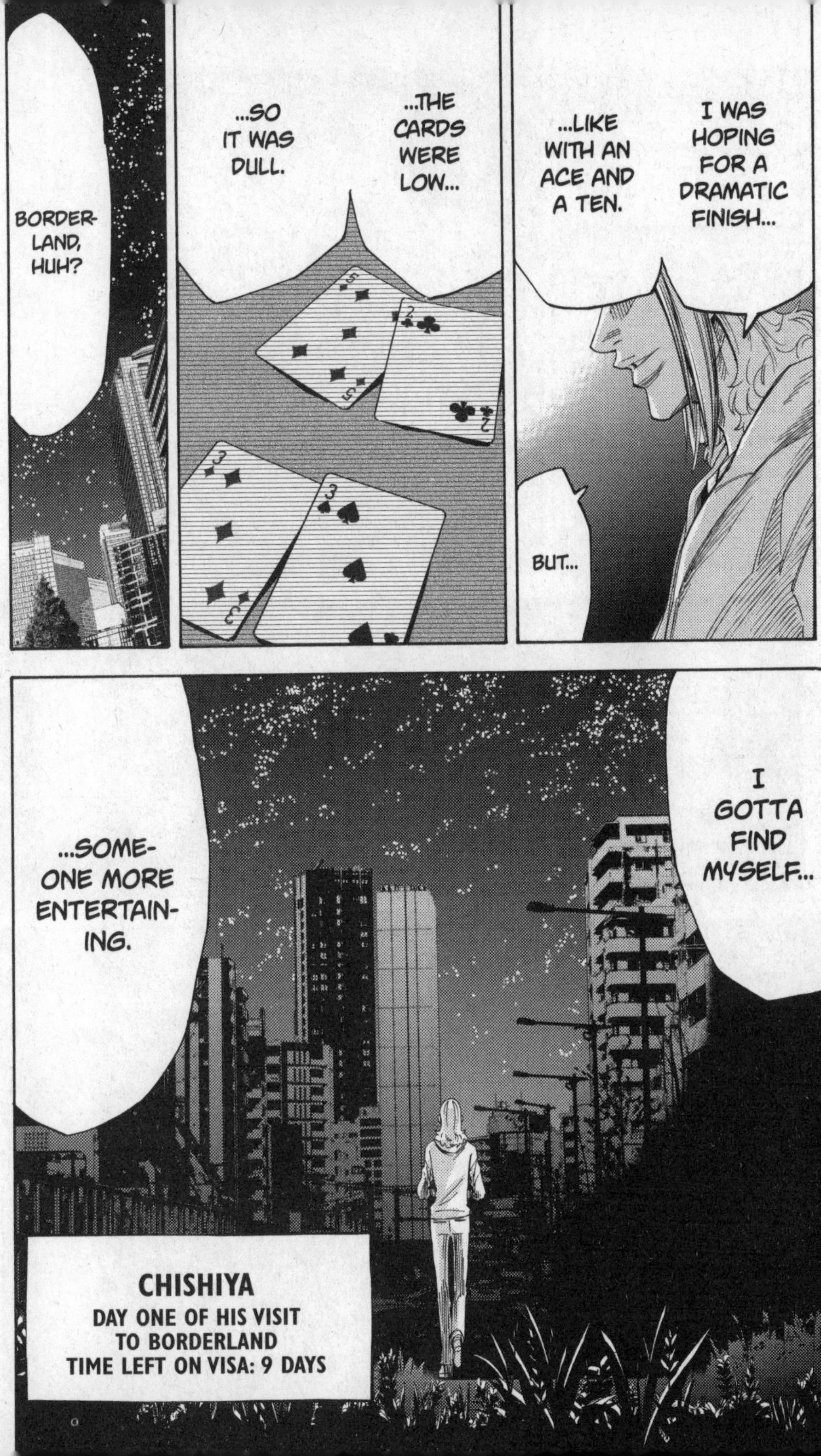
I WAS HOPING FOR A DRAMATIC FINISH...
...LIKE WITH AN ACE AND A TEN.
BUT...
...THE CARDS WERE LOW...
...SO IT WAS DULL.
BORDER-LAND, HUH?
I GOTTA FIND MYSELF...
...SOME-ONE MORE ENTERTAIN-ING.
CHISHIYA
DAY ONE OF HIS VISIT TO BORDERLAND
TIME LEFT ON VISA: 9 DAYS

Close your eyes and imagine that you might actually die today.

Yes...at this moment I don't have any regrets.

Let's live today so we don't have anything to regret.

— HARO ASO

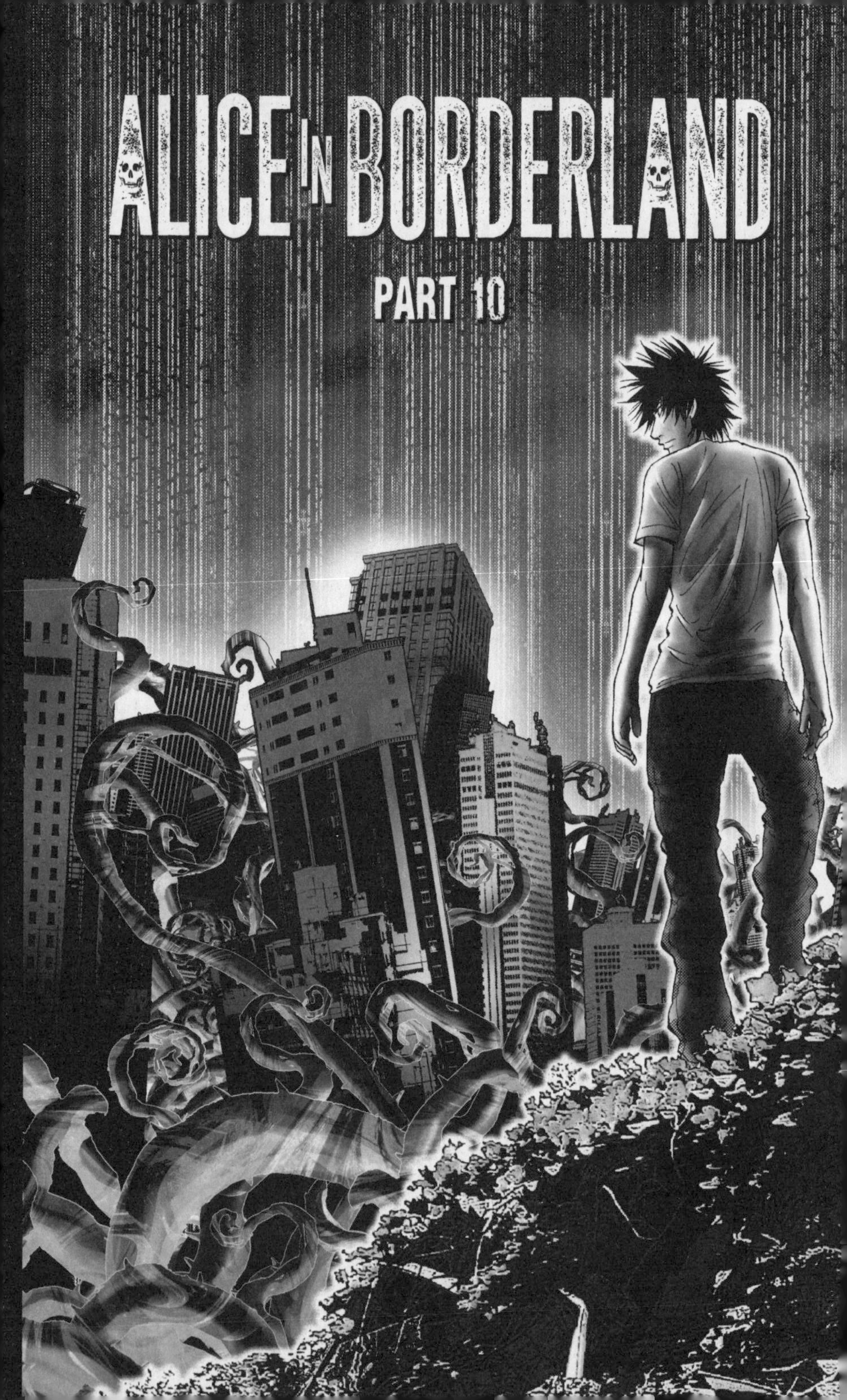
ALICE IN BORDERLAND
PART 10

ALICE IN BORDERLAND

PART 10

CHAPTER 36: King of Clubs, Part 4

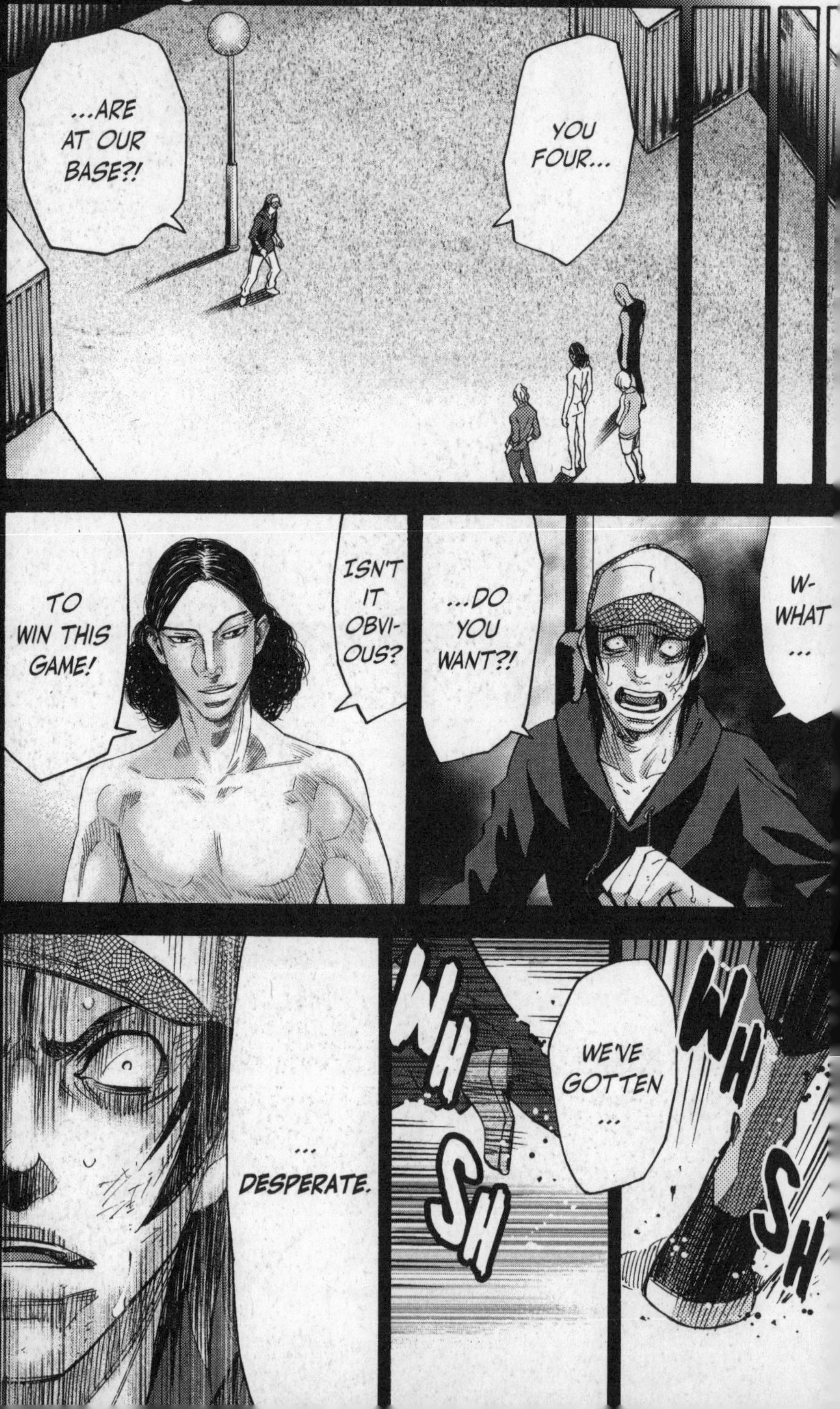
YOU FOUR...
...ARE AT OUR BASE?!
W-WHAT...
...DO YOU WANT?!
ISN'T IT OBVI-OUS?
TO WIN THIS GAME!
WHSH
WE'VE GOTTEN...
WHSH
...DESPERATE.

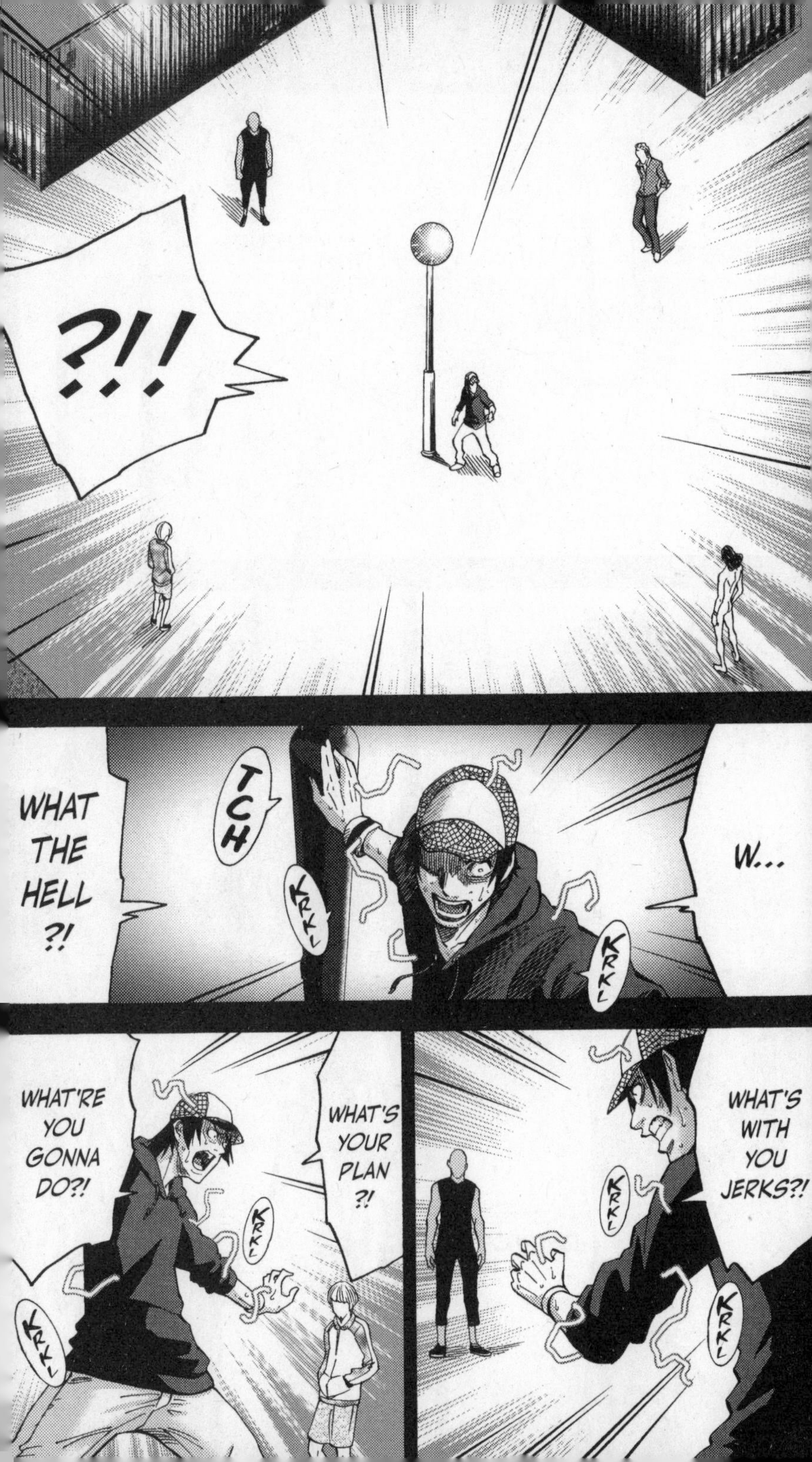
?!!
W...
TCH
KRKL
KRKL
WHAT THE HELL ?!
WHAT'S WITH YOU JERKS?!
KRKL
KRKL
WHAT'S YOUR PLAN ?!
WHAT'RE YOU GONNA DO?!
KRKL
KRKL

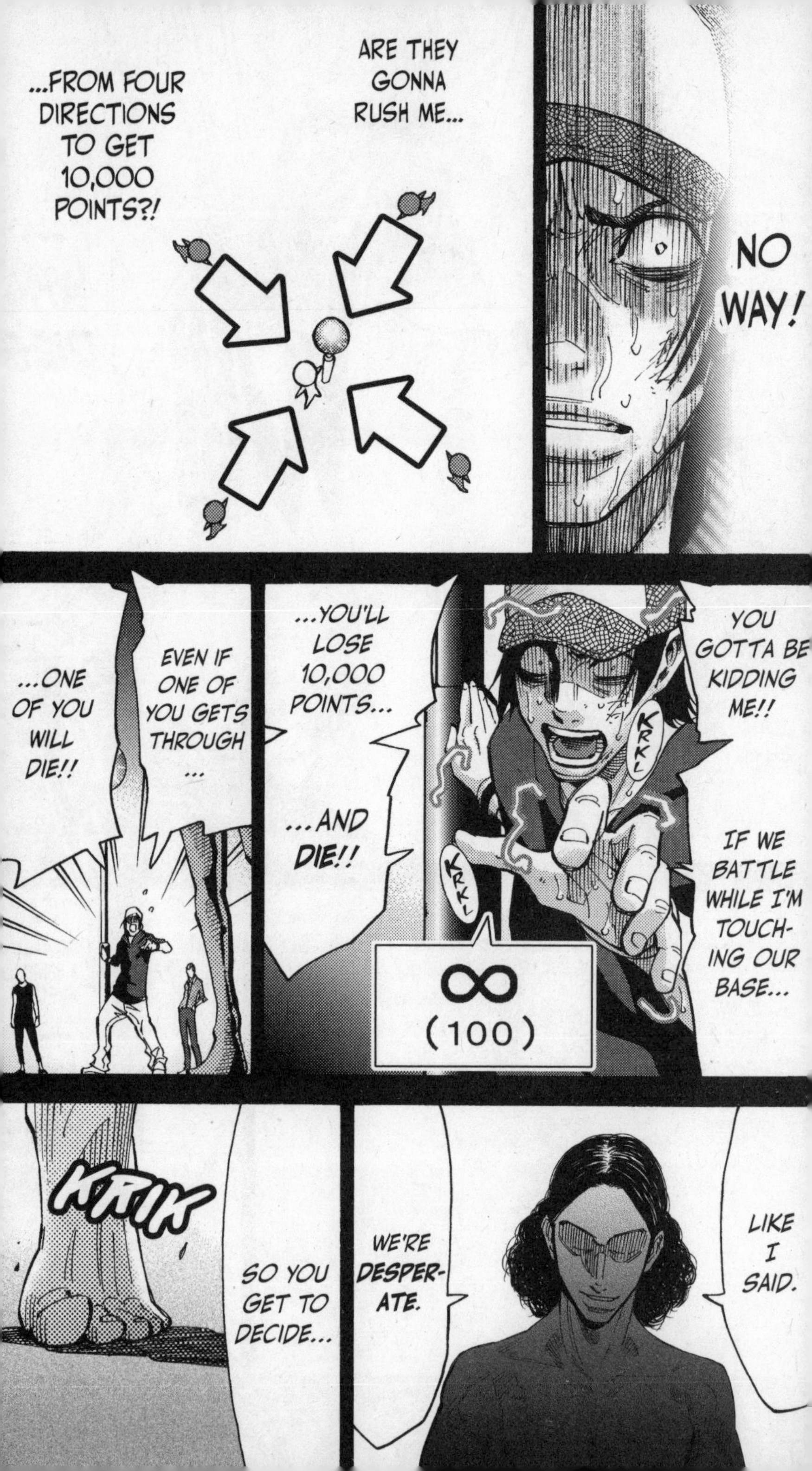
NO WAY!
ARE THEY GONNA RUSH ME...
...FROM FOUR DIRECTIONS TO GET 10,000 POINTS?!
YOU GOTTA BE KIDDING ME!!
KRKL
KRKL
IF WE BATTLE WHILE I'M TOUCH-ING OUR BASE...
∞ (100)
...YOU'LL LOSE 10,000 POINTS...
...AND DIE!!
EVEN IF ONE OF YOU GETS THROUGH ...
...ONE OF YOU WILL DIE!!
LIKE I SAID.
WE'RE DESPER-ATE.
SO YOU GET TO DECIDE...
KRIK

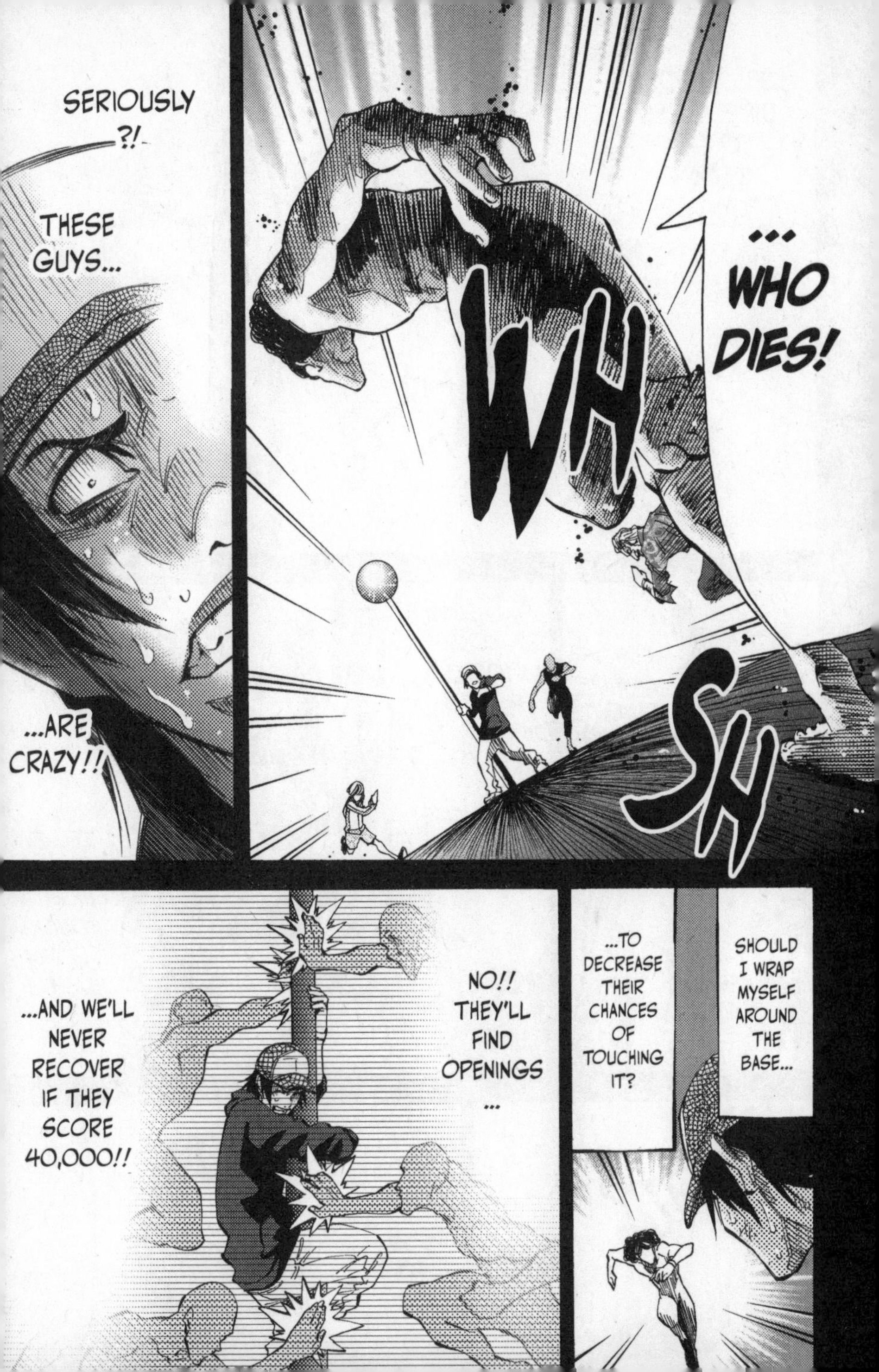
...WHO DIES!
WH
SH
SERIOUSLY?!
THESE GUYS...
...ARE CRAZY!!
SHOULD I WRAP MYSELF AROUND THE BASE...
...TO DECREASE THEIR CHANCES OF TOUCHING IT?
NO!! THEY'LL FIND OPENINGS...
...AND WE'LL NEVER RECOVER IF THEY SCORE 40,000!!

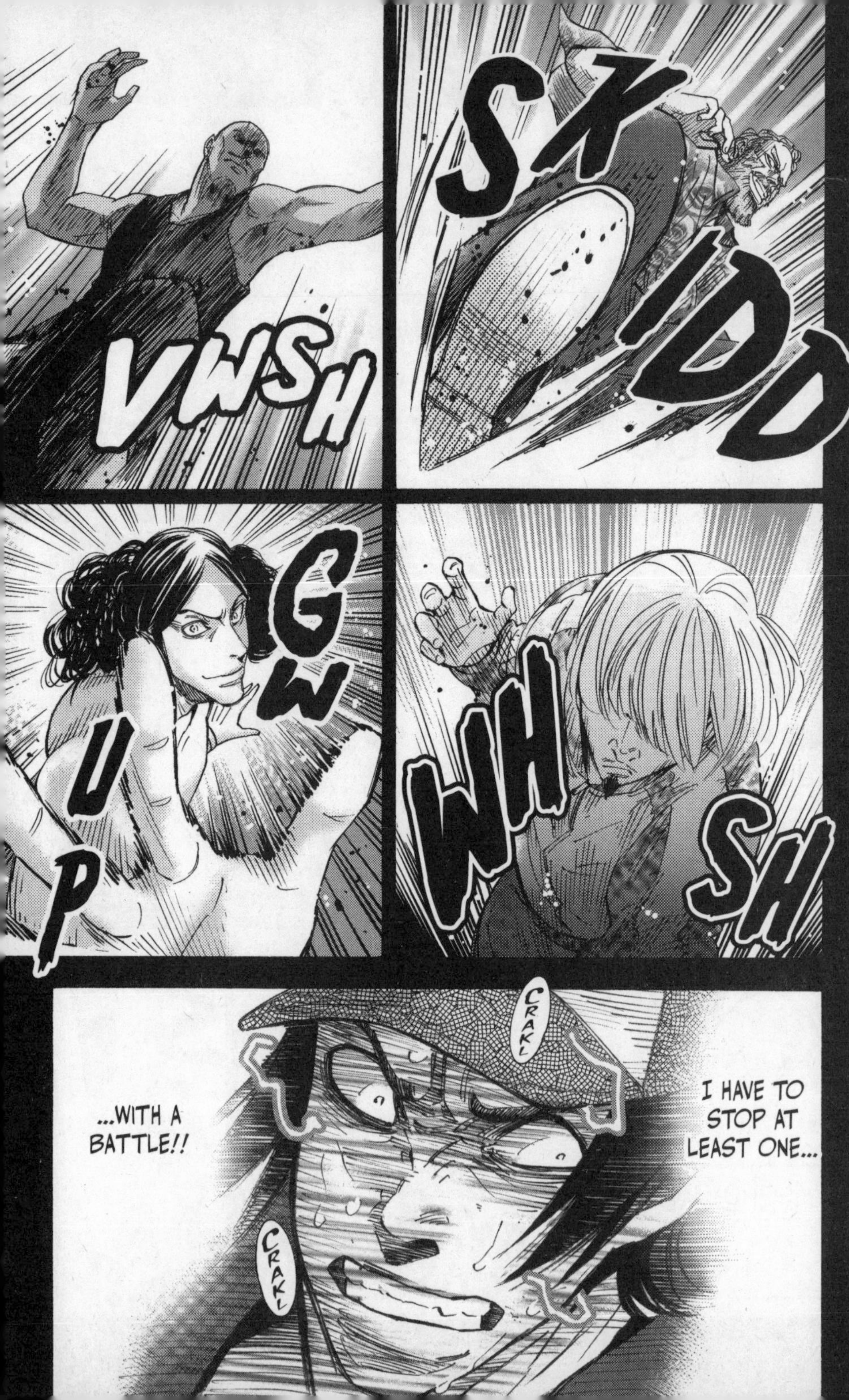
SKIDD
VWSH
WH SH
GWUP
I HAVE TO STOP AT LEAST ONE...
CRAK!
...WITH A BATTLE!!
CRAK!

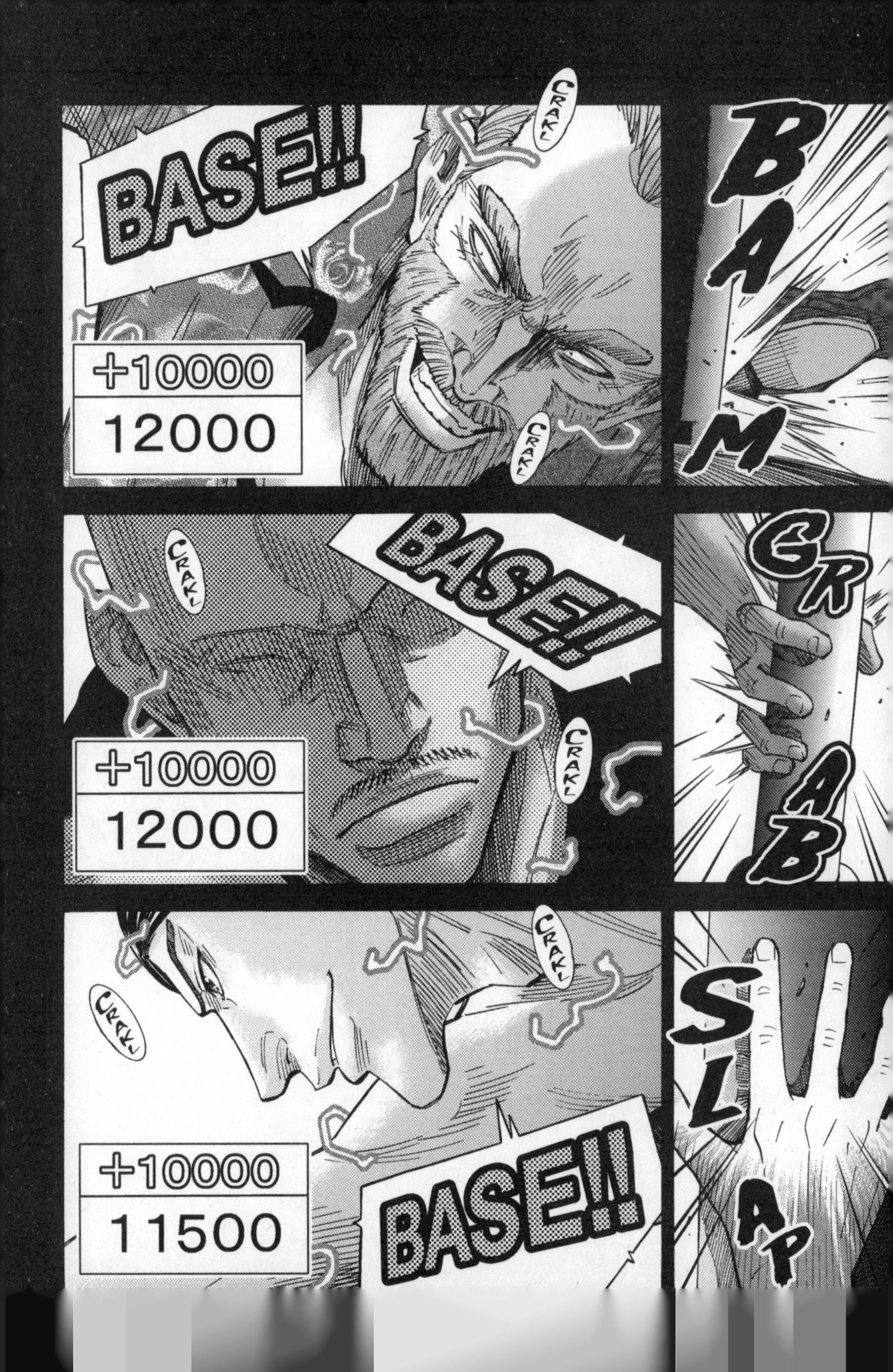
BAM
CRAKL
BASE!!
CRAKL
+10000
12000
GRAB
BASE!!
CRAKL
CRAKL
+10000
12000
SLAP
CRAKL
CRAKL
BASE!!
+10000
11500

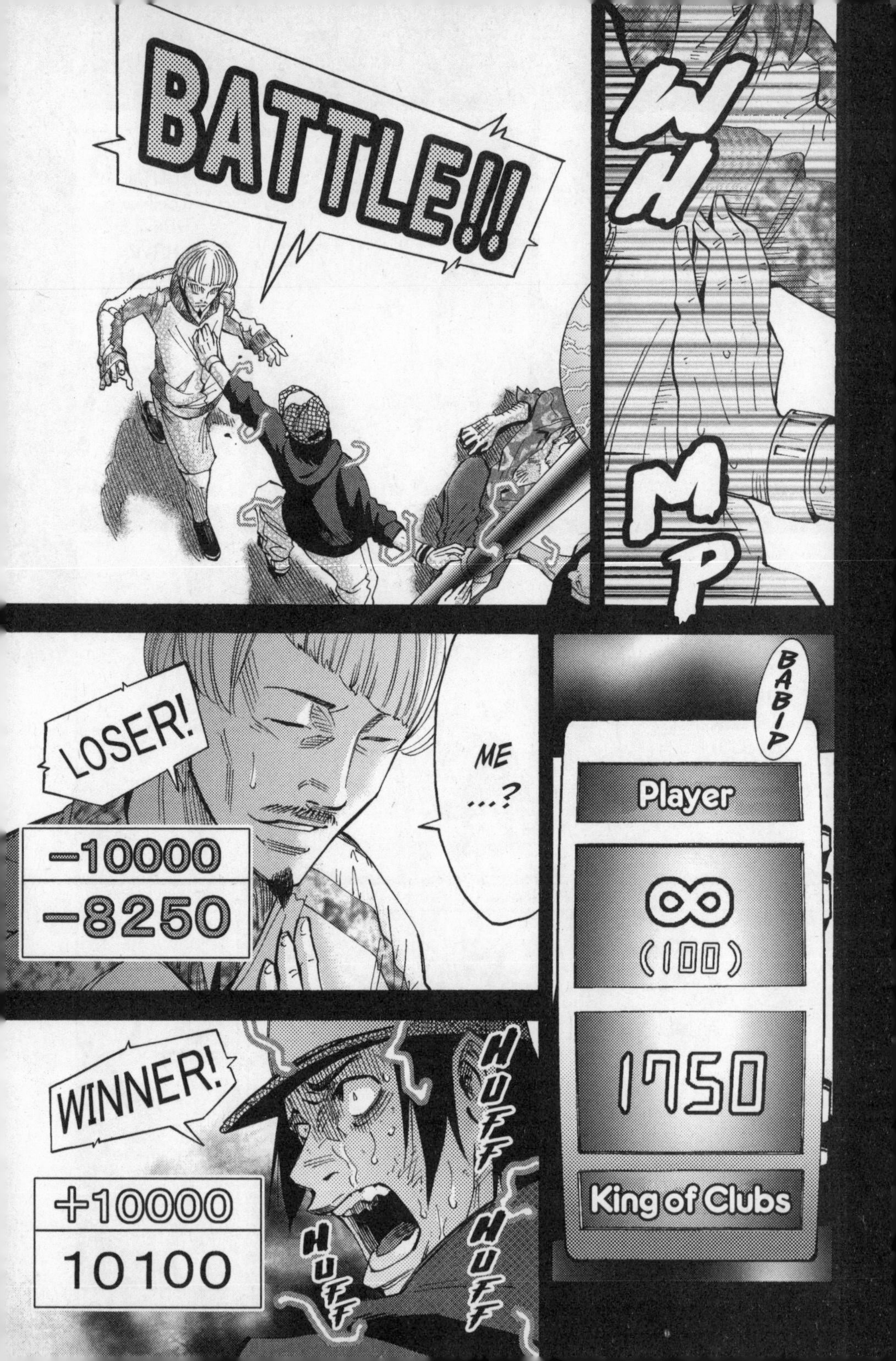
WHMP
BATTLE!!
BABIP
Player
∞
(100)
1750
King of Clubs
ME ...?
LOSER!
−10000
−8250
HUFF HUFF
HUFF
WINNER!
+10000
10100
HUFF

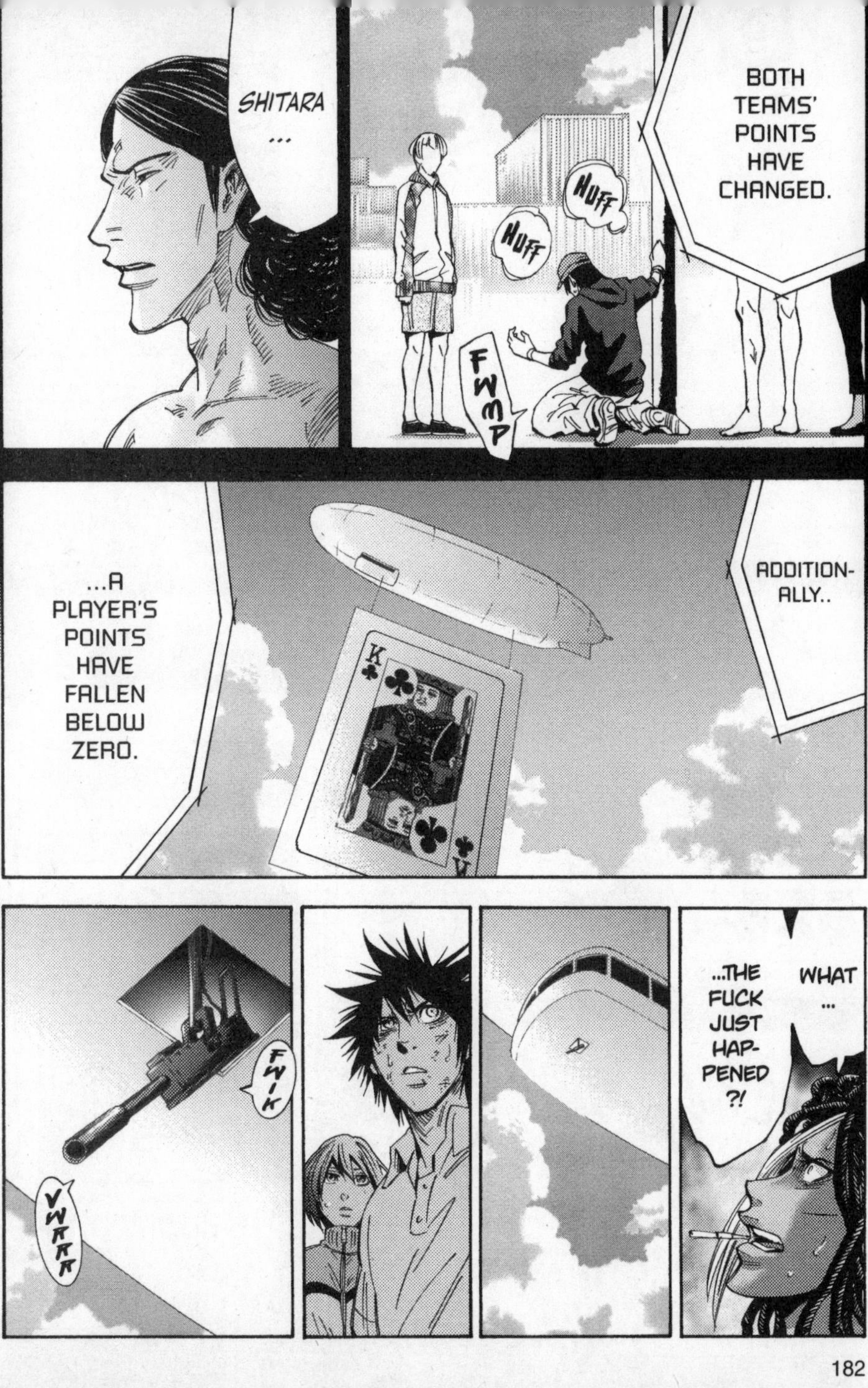
BOTH TEAMS' POINTS HAVE CHANGED.
HUFF
HUFF
FWMP
SHITARA ...
ADDITIONALLY..
...A PLAYER'S POINTS HAVE FALLEN BELOW ZERO.
WHAT ...
...THE FUCK JUST HAPPENED?!
FWIK
VWRRR

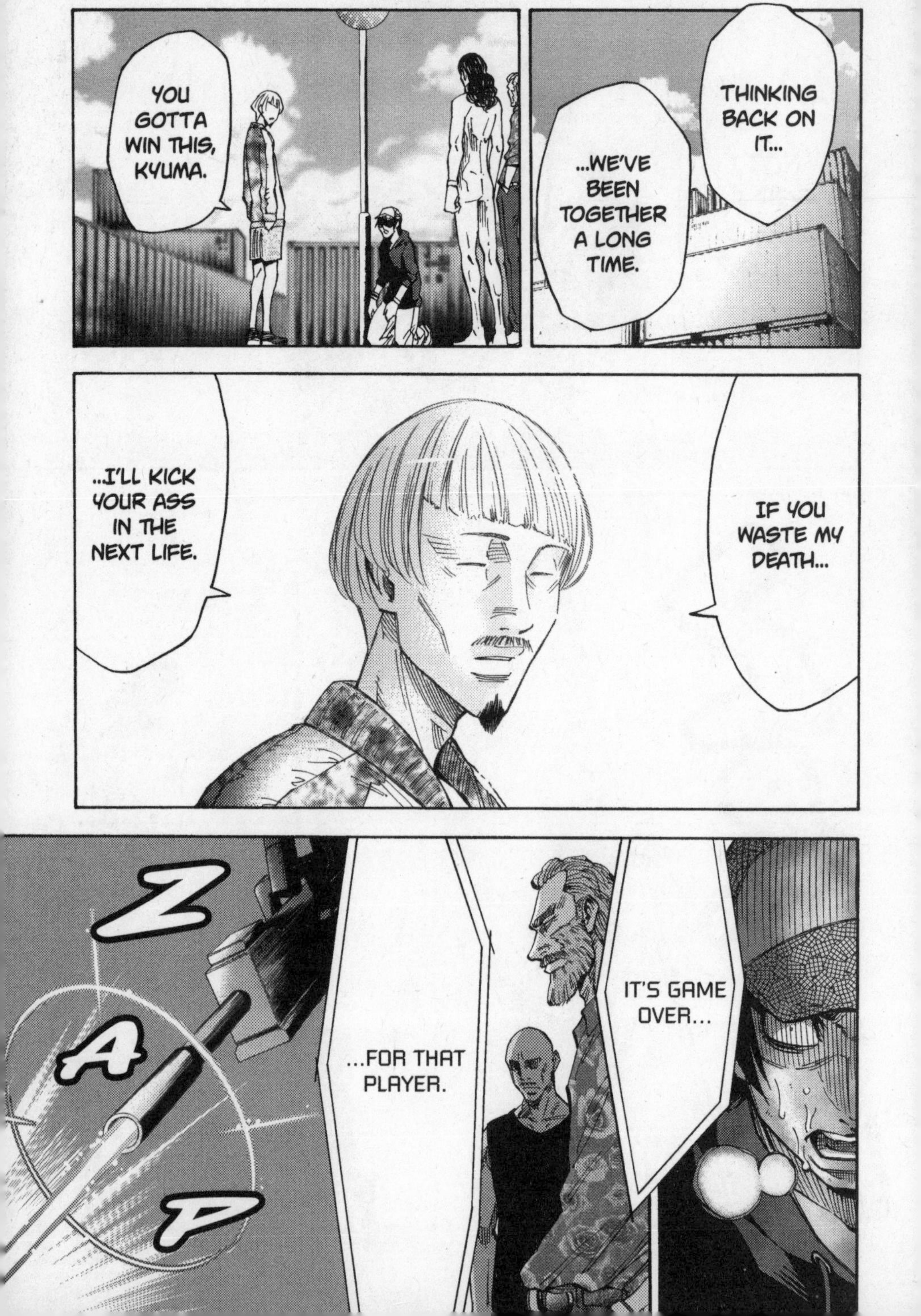
THINKING BACK ON IT...
...WE'VE BEEN TOGETHER A LONG TIME.
YOU GOTTA WIN THIS, KYUMA.
IF YOU WASTE MY DEATH...
...I'LL KICK YOUR ASS IN THE NEXT LIFE.
IT'S GAME OVER...
...FOR THAT PLAYER.
ZAP

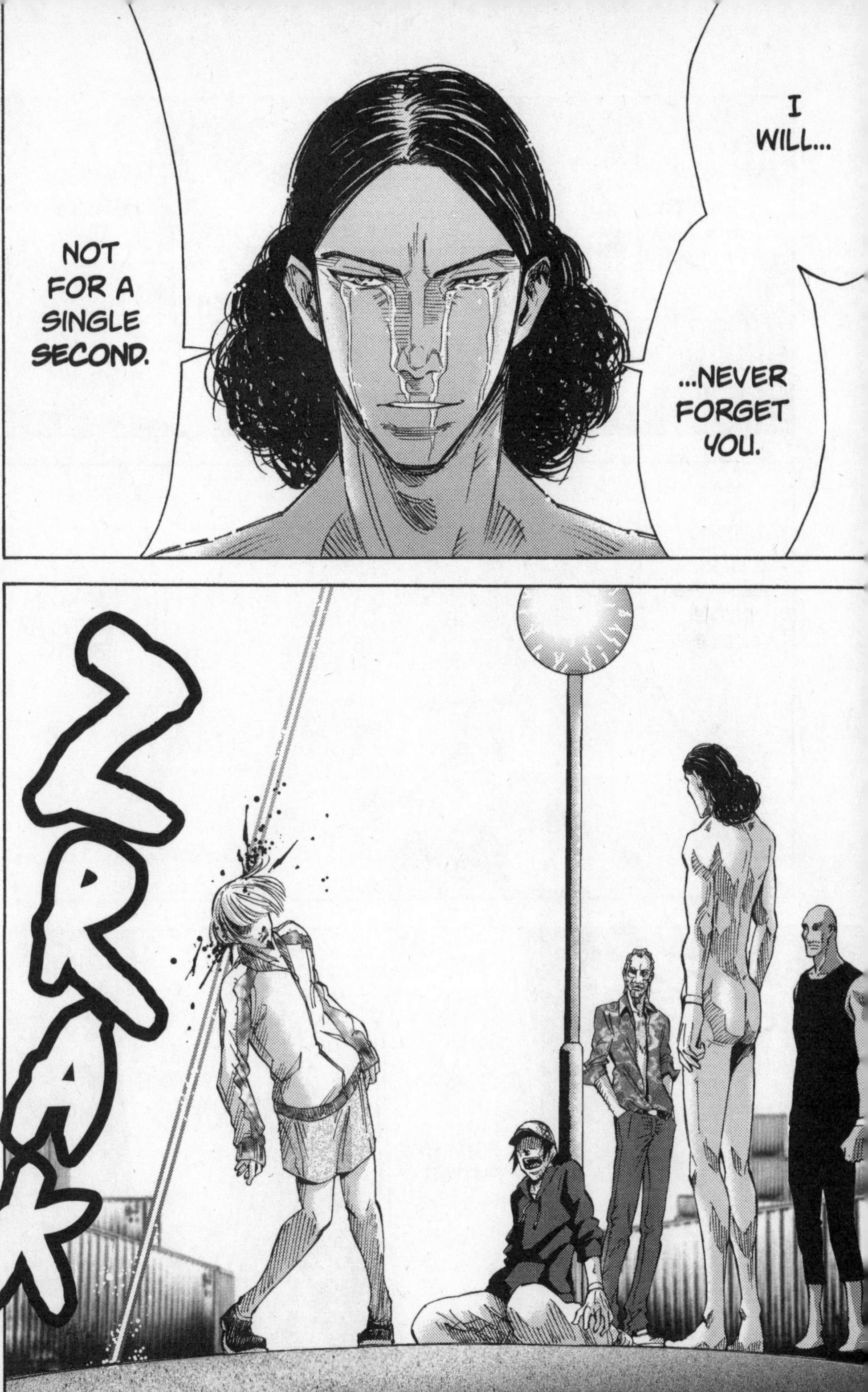
I WILL...
...NEVER FORGET YOU.
NOT FOR A SINGLE SECOND.
ZRAK

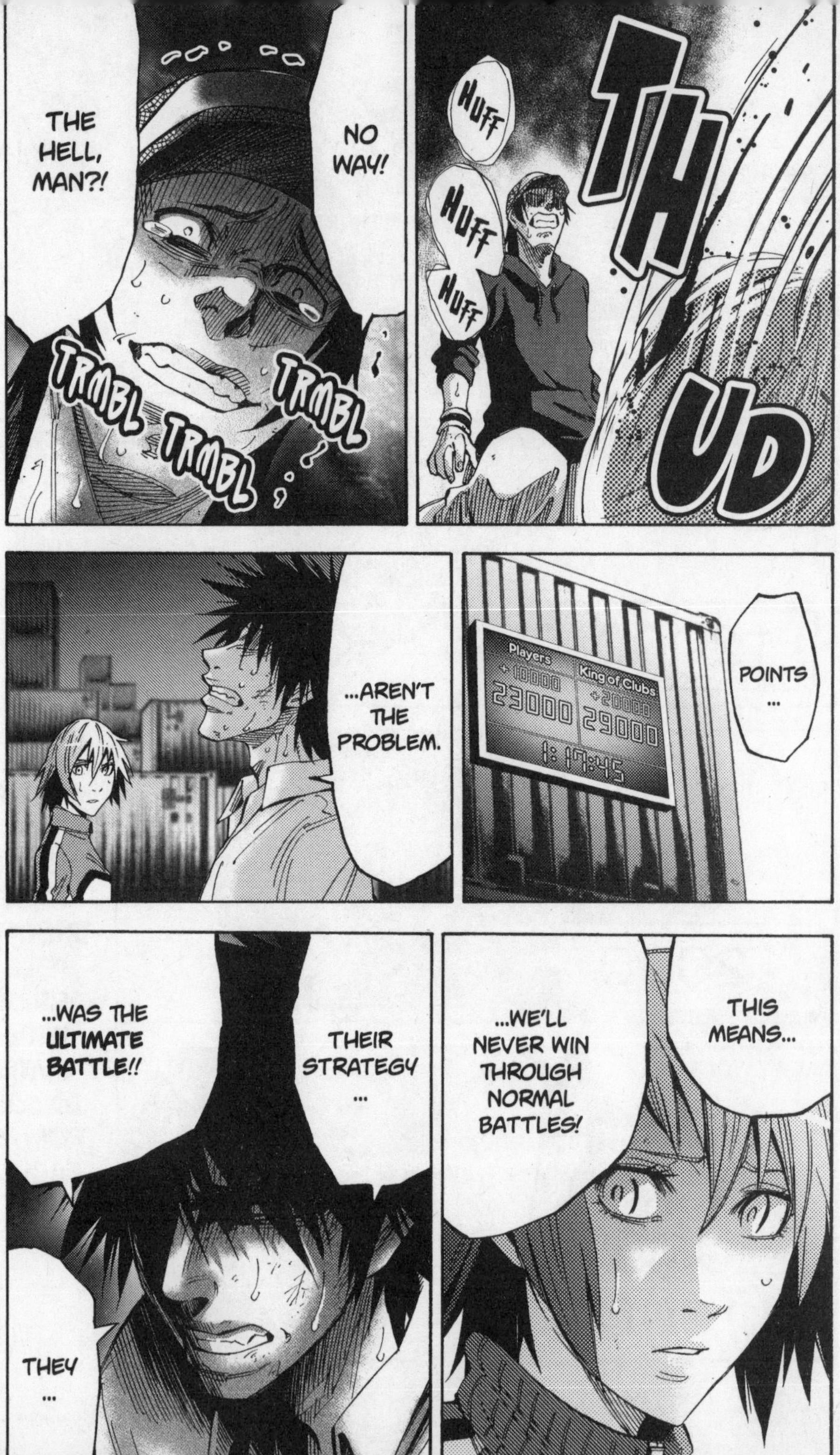
HUFF
HUFF
HUFF
THUD
NO WAY!
THE HELL, MAN?!
TRMBL
TRMBL
TRMBL
Players
+10000
23000
King of Clubs
+20000
29000
1:17:45
POINTS...
...AREN'T THE PROBLEM.
THIS MEANS...
...WE'LL NEVER WIN THROUGH NORMAL BATTLES!
THEIR STRATEGY...
...WAS THE ULTIMATE BATTLE!!
THEY...

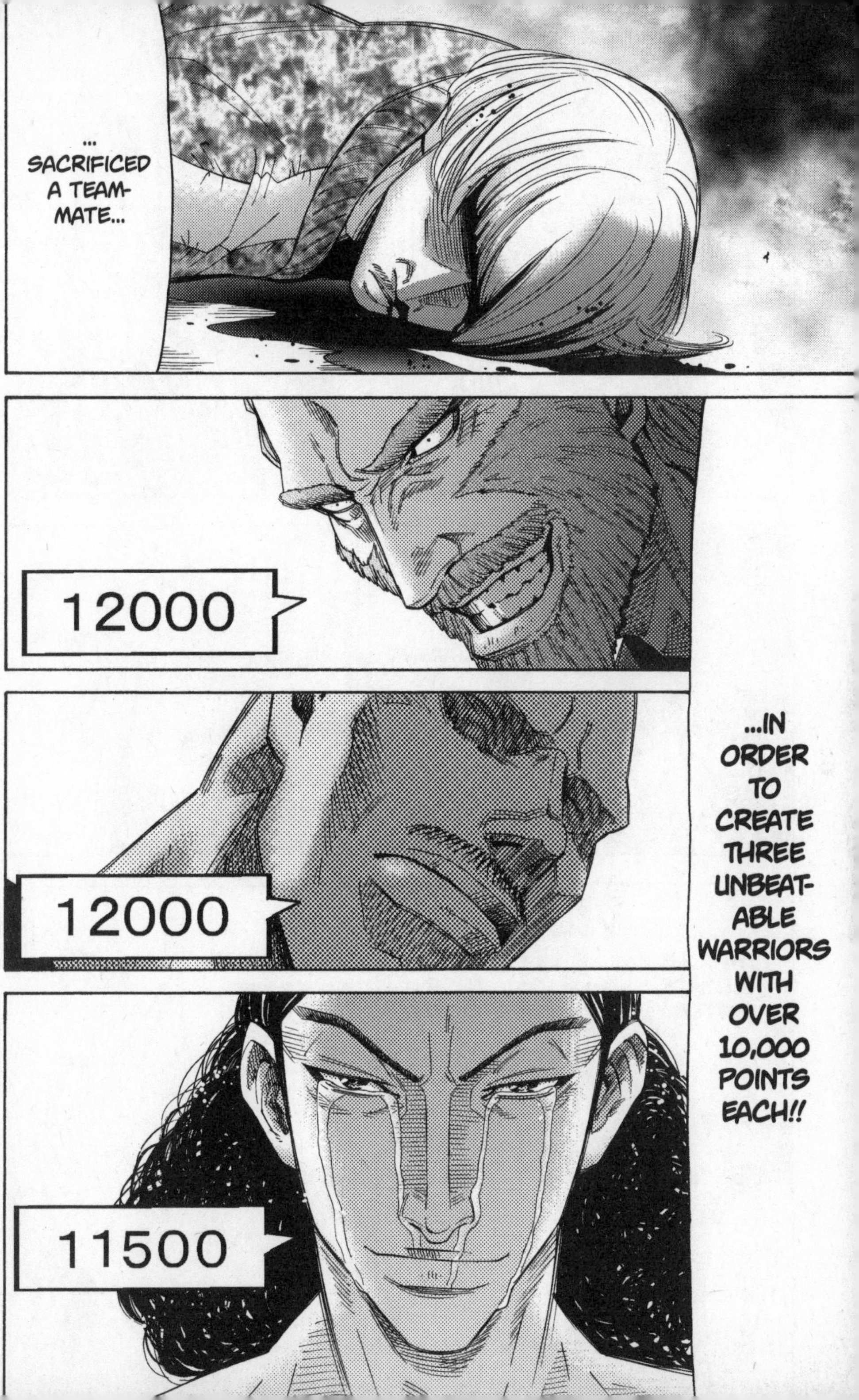

... SACRIFICED A TEAM-MATE...
12000
...IN ORDER TO CREATE THREE UNBEAT-ABLE WARRIORS WITH OVER 10,000 POINTS EACH!!
12000
11500

CHAPTER 36: King of Clubs, Part 4

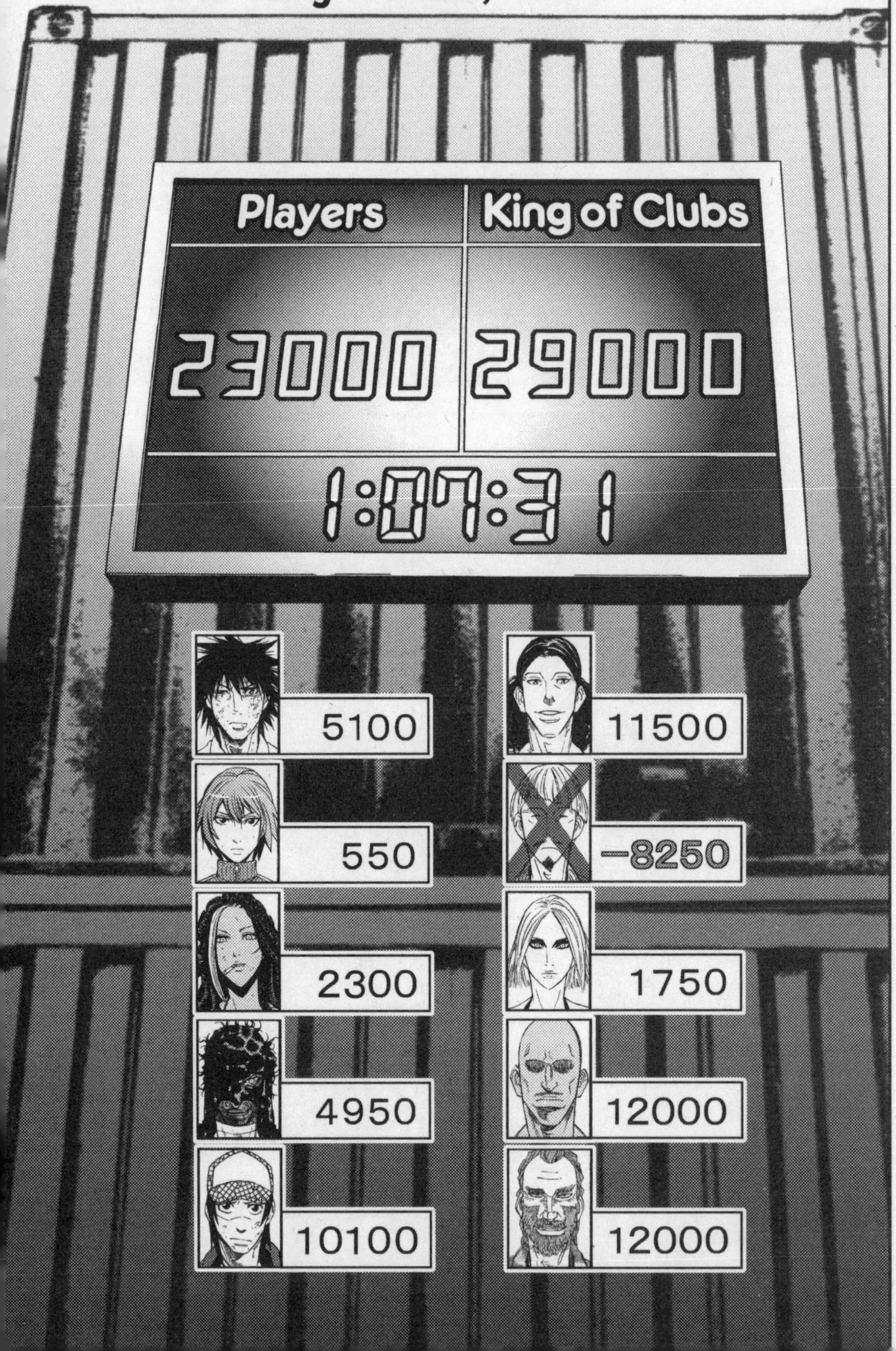
Players
King of Clubs
23000
29000
1:07:31
5100
11500
550
−8250
2300
1750
4950
12000
10100
12000

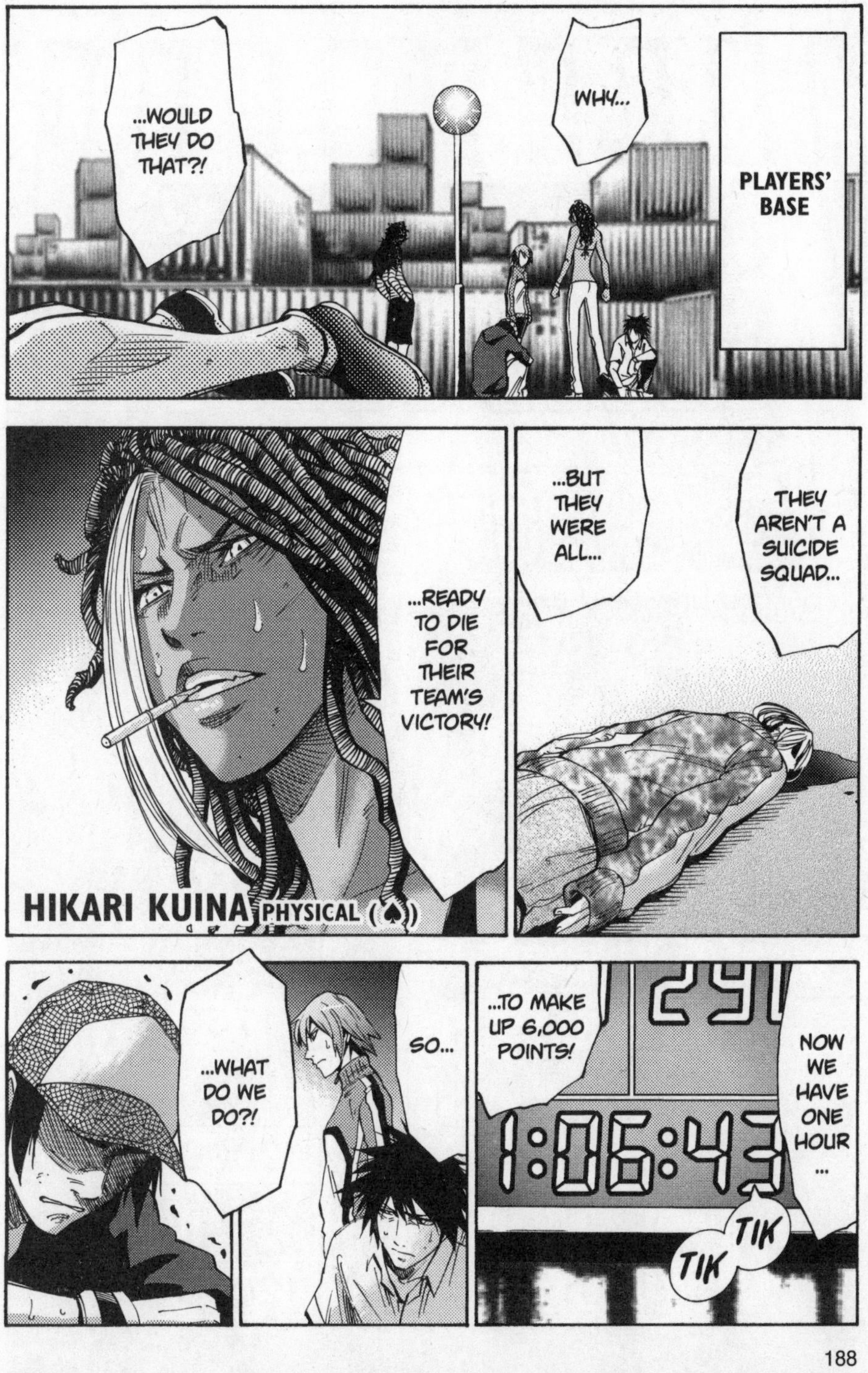
PLAYERS' BASE
WHY...
...WOULD THEY DO THAT?!
THEY AREN'T A SUICIDE SQUAD...
...BUT THEY WERE ALL...
...READY TO DIE FOR THEIR TEAM'S VICTORY!
HIKARI KUINA PHYSICAL (♠)
NOW WE HAVE ONE HOUR...
...TO MAKE UP 6,000 POINTS!
1:06:43
TIK
TIK
SO...
...WHAT DO WE DO?!

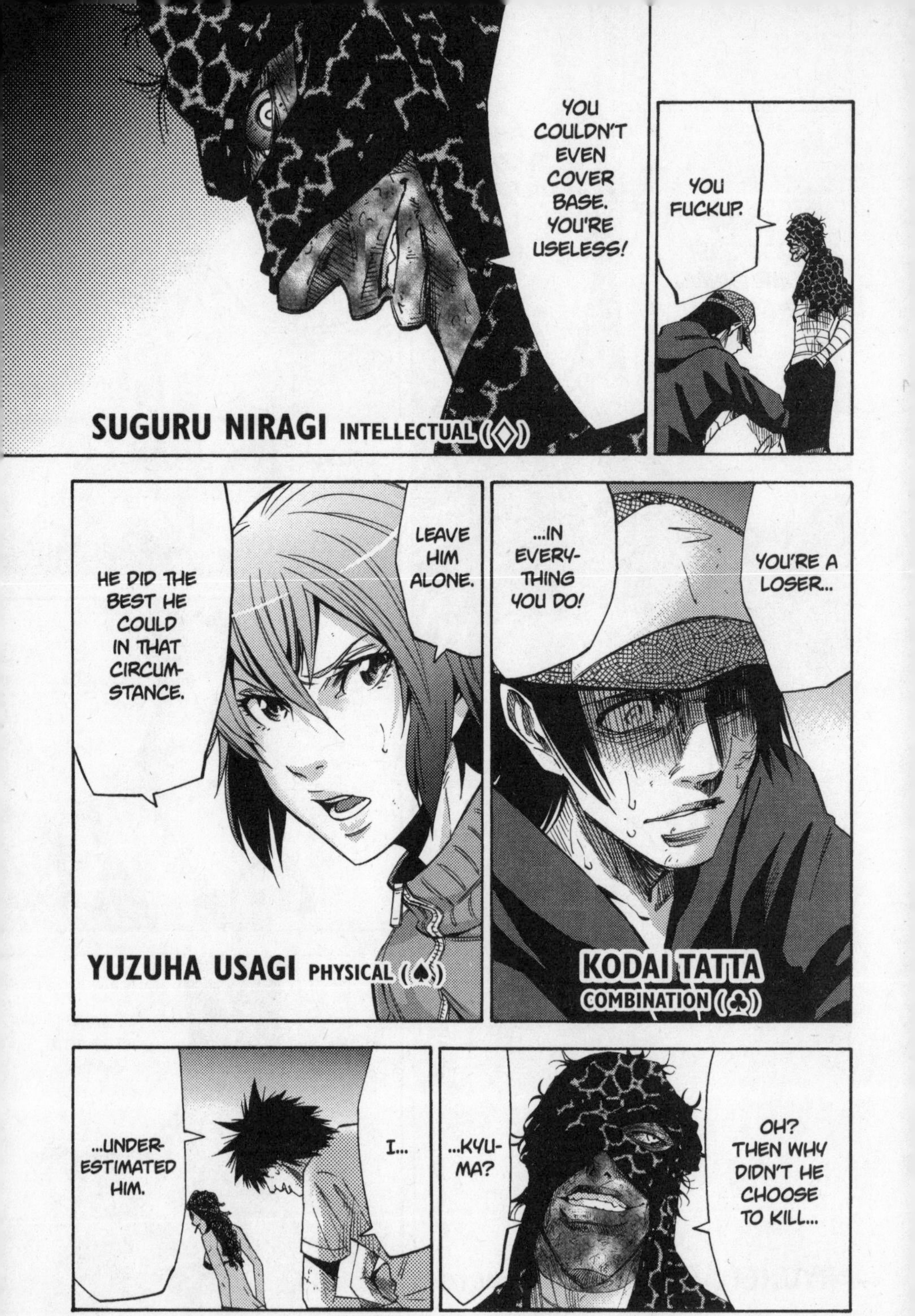
YOU FUCKUP.
YOU COULDN'T EVEN COVER BASE. YOU'RE USELESS!
SUGURU NIRAGI INTELLECTUAL (◇)
YOU'RE A LOSER...
...IN EVERY-THING YOU DO!
KODAI TATTA COMBINATION (♣)
LEAVE HIM ALONE.
HE DID THE BEST HE COULD IN THAT CIRCUM-STANCE.
YUZUHA USAGI PHYSICAL (♠)
OH? THEN WHY DIDN'T HE CHOOSE TO KILL...
...KYU-MA?
I...
...UNDER-ESTIMATED HIM.

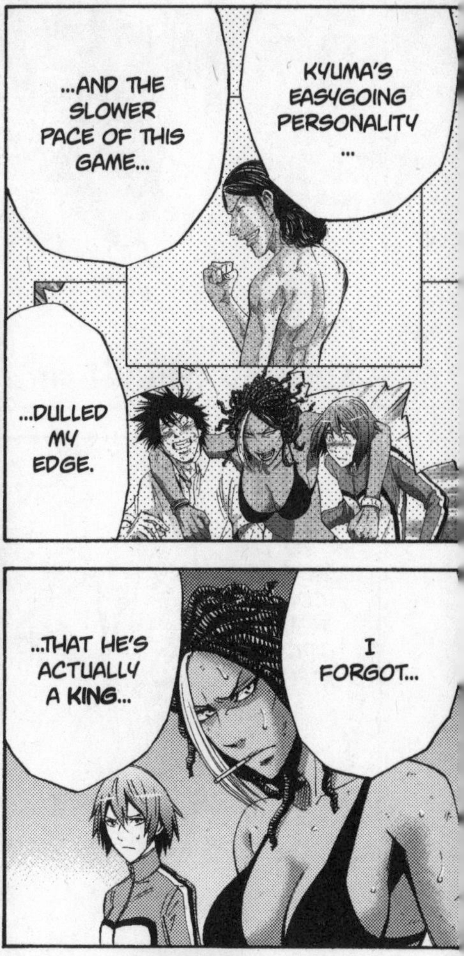
KYUMA'S EASYGOING PERSONALITY...
...AND THE SLOWER PACE OF THIS GAME...
...DULLED MY EDGE.
I FORGOT...
...THAT HE'S ACTUALLY A KING...
...AND THIS IS A GAME...
...OF LIFE AND DEATH.
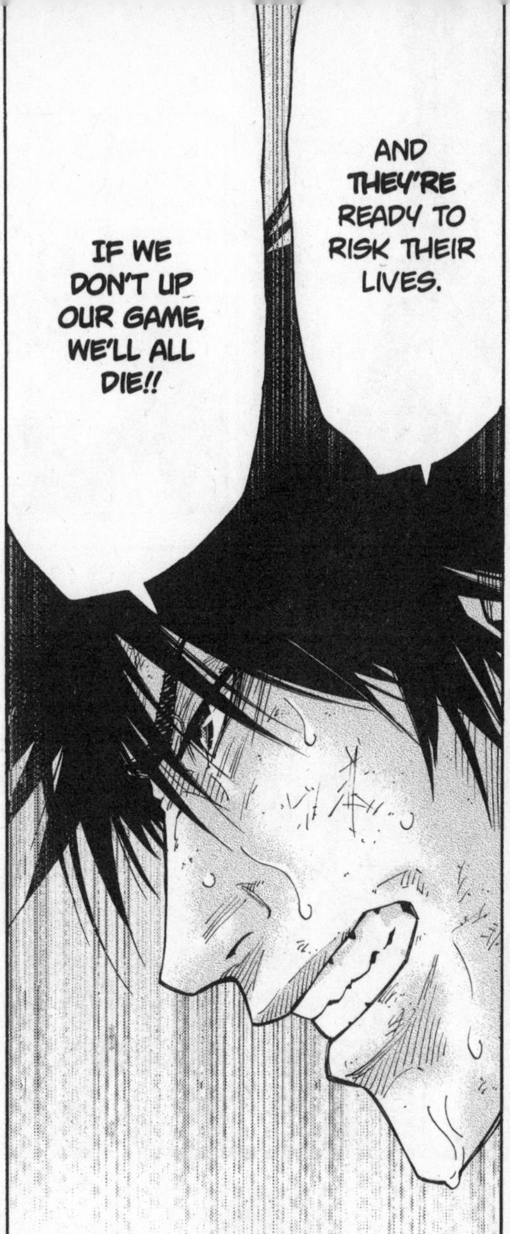
AND THEY'RE READY TO RISK THEIR LIVES.
IF WE DON'T UP OUR GAME, WE'LL ALL DIE!!

RYOHEI ARISU PSYCHOLOGICAL (♡)

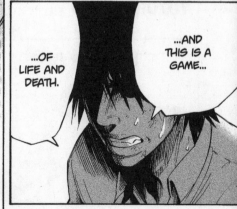

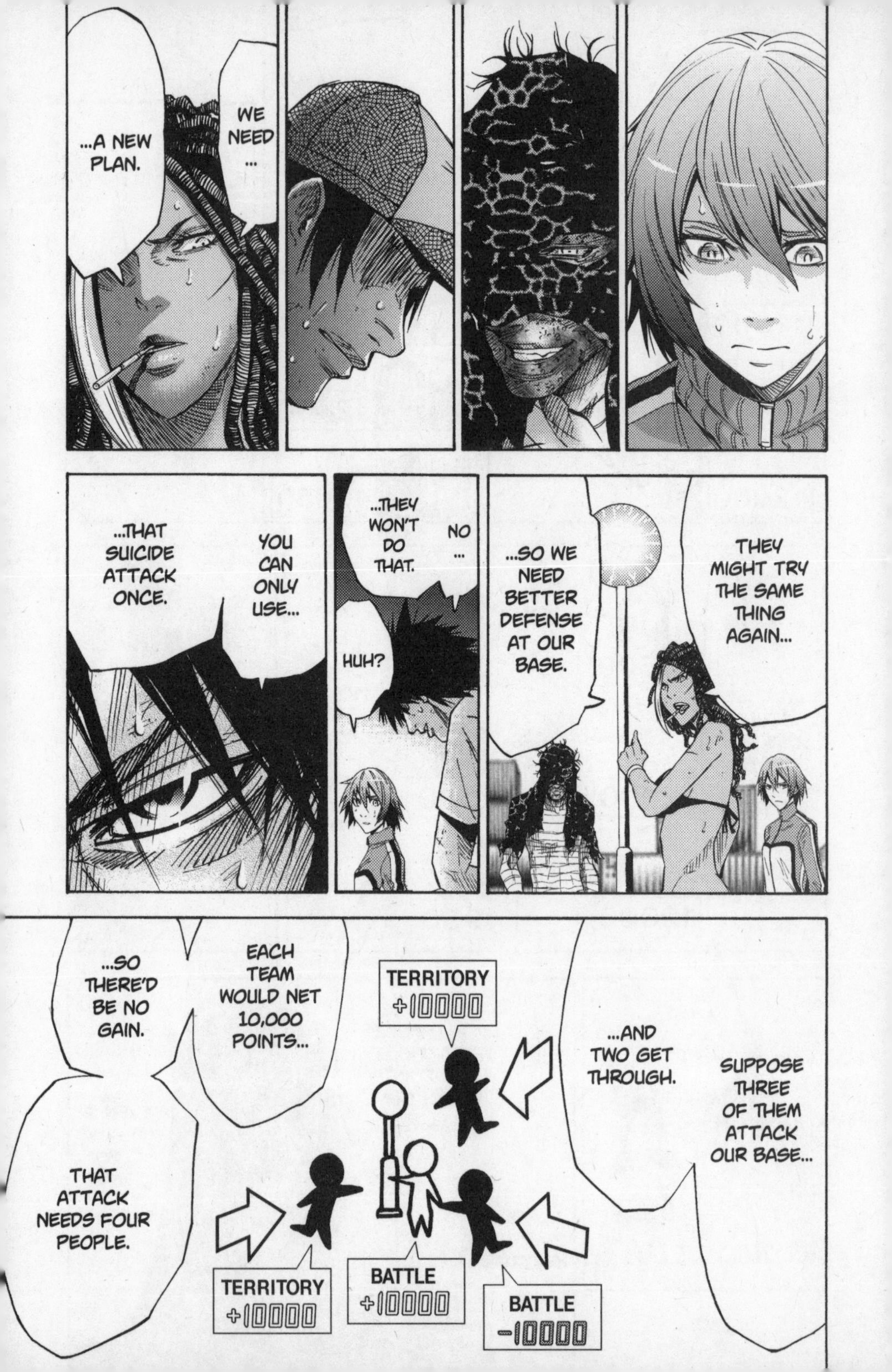
WE NEED ...
...A NEW PLAN.
THEY MIGHT TRY THE SAME THING AGAIN...
...SO WE NEED BETTER DEFENSE AT OUR BASE.
NO ...
...THEY WON'T DO THAT.
HUH?
YOU CAN ONLY USE...
...THAT SUICIDE ATTACK ONCE.
SUPPOSE THREE OF THEM ATTACK OUR BASE...
...AND TWO GET THROUGH.
TERRITORY +10000
BATTLE -10000
BATTLE +10000
TERRITORY +10000
EACH TEAM WOULD NET 10,000 POINTS...
...SO THERE'D BE NO GAIN.
THAT ATTACK NEEDS FOUR PEOPLE.

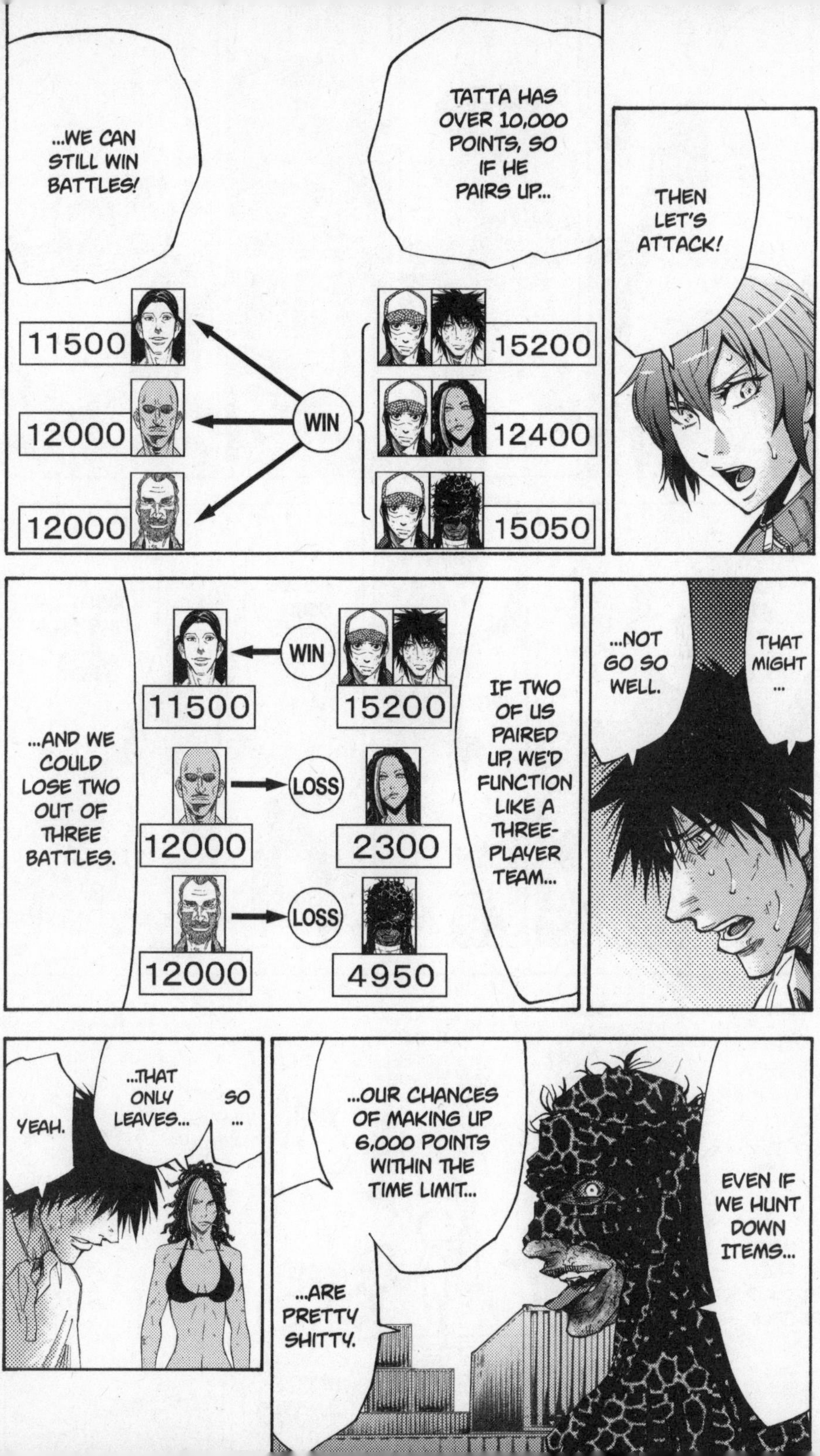
THEN LET'S ATTACK!
TATTA HAS OVER 10,000 POINTS, SO IF HE PAIRS UP...
...WE CAN STILL WIN BATTLES!
15200
12400
15050
WIN
11500
12000
12000
THAT MIGHT ...
...NOT GO SO WELL.
IF TWO OF US PAIRED UP, WE'D FUNCTION LIKE A THREE-PLAYER TEAM...
15200
WIN
11500
2300
LOSS
12000
4950
LOSS
12000
...AND WE COULD LOSE TWO OUT OF THREE BATTLES.
EVEN IF WE HUNT DOWN ITEMS...
...OUR CHANCES OF MAKING UP 6,000 POINTS WITHIN THE TIME LIMIT...
...ARE PRETTY SHITTY.
SO ...
...THAT ONLY LEAVES...
YEAH.

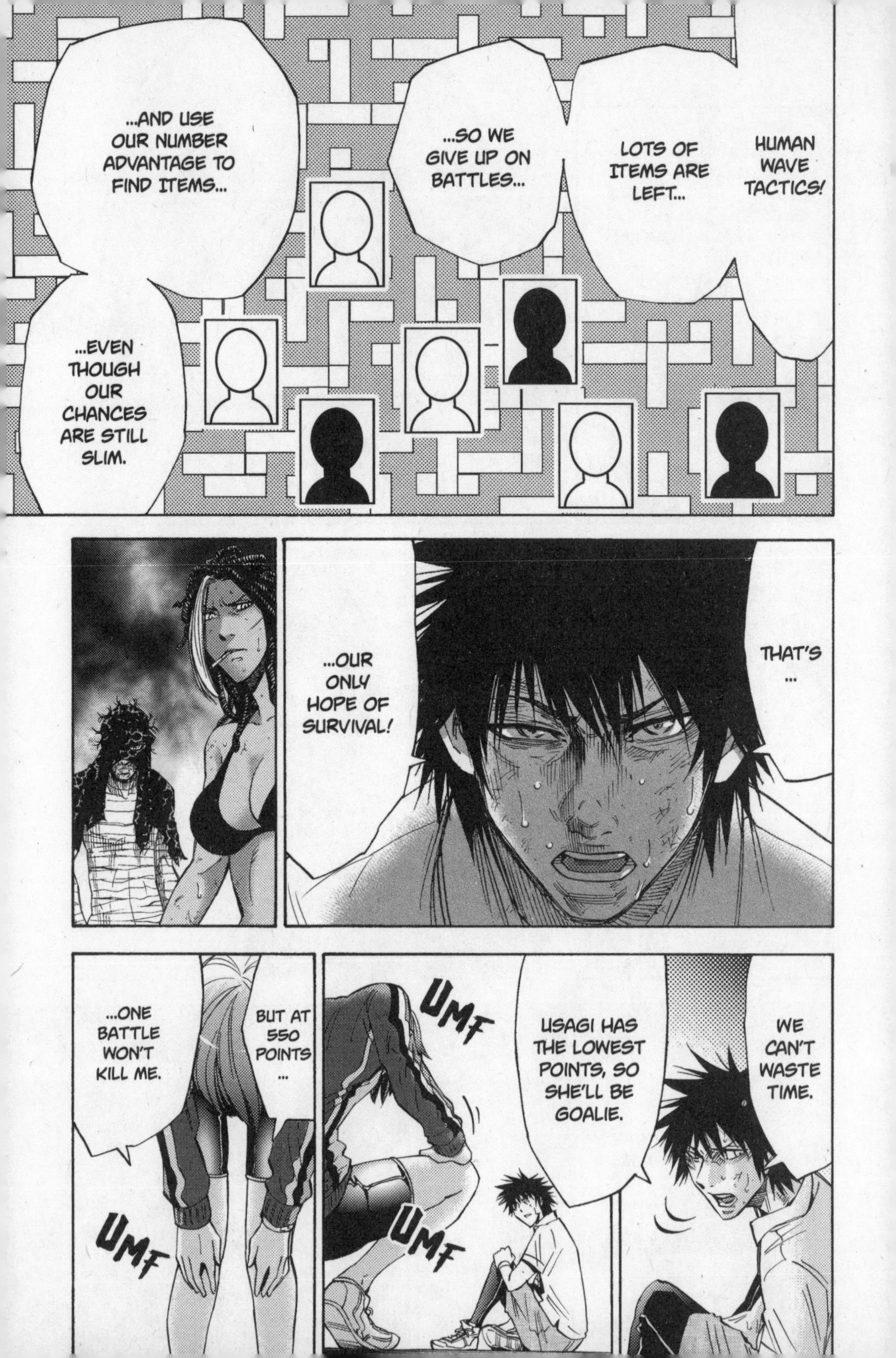
HUMAN WAVE TACTICS!
LOTS OF ITEMS ARE LEFT...
...SO WE GIVE UP ON BATTLES...
...AND USE OUR NUMBER ADVANTAGE TO FIND ITEMS...
...EVEN THOUGH OUR CHANCES ARE STILL SLIM.
THAT'S ...
...OUR ONLY HOPE OF SURVIVAL!
WE CAN'T WASTE TIME.
USAGI HAS THE LOWEST POINTS, SO SHE'LL BE GOALIE.
UMF
UMF
BUT AT 550 POINTS ...
...ONE BATTLE WON'T KILL ME.
UMF

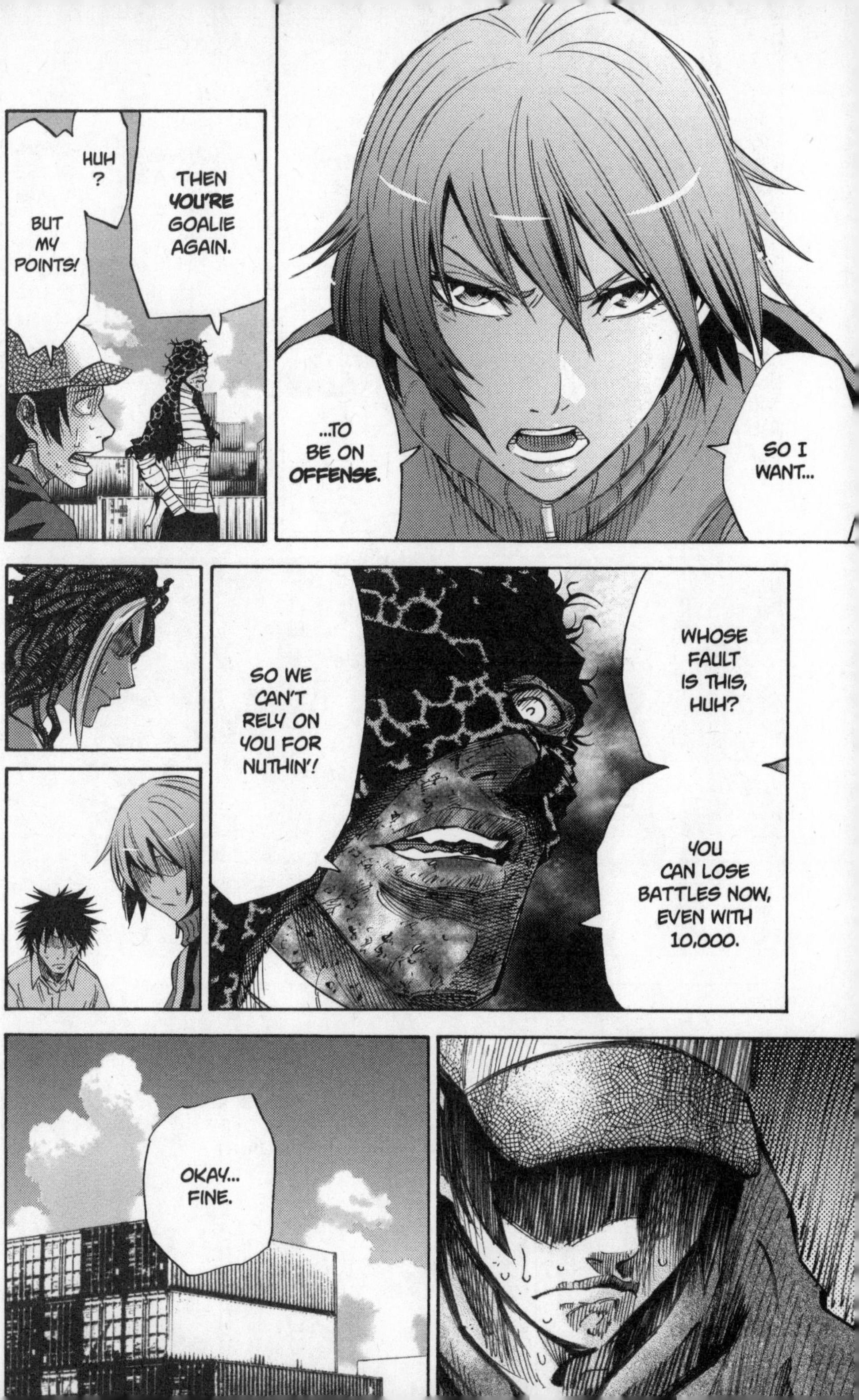
SO I WANT...
...TO BE ON OFFENSE.
THEN YOU'RE GOALIE AGAIN.
HUH?
BUT MY POINTS!
WHOSE FAULT IS THIS, HUH?
YOU CAN LOSE BATTLES NOW, EVEN WITH 10,000.
SO WE CAN'T RELY ON YOU FOR NUTHIN'!
OKAY... FINE.

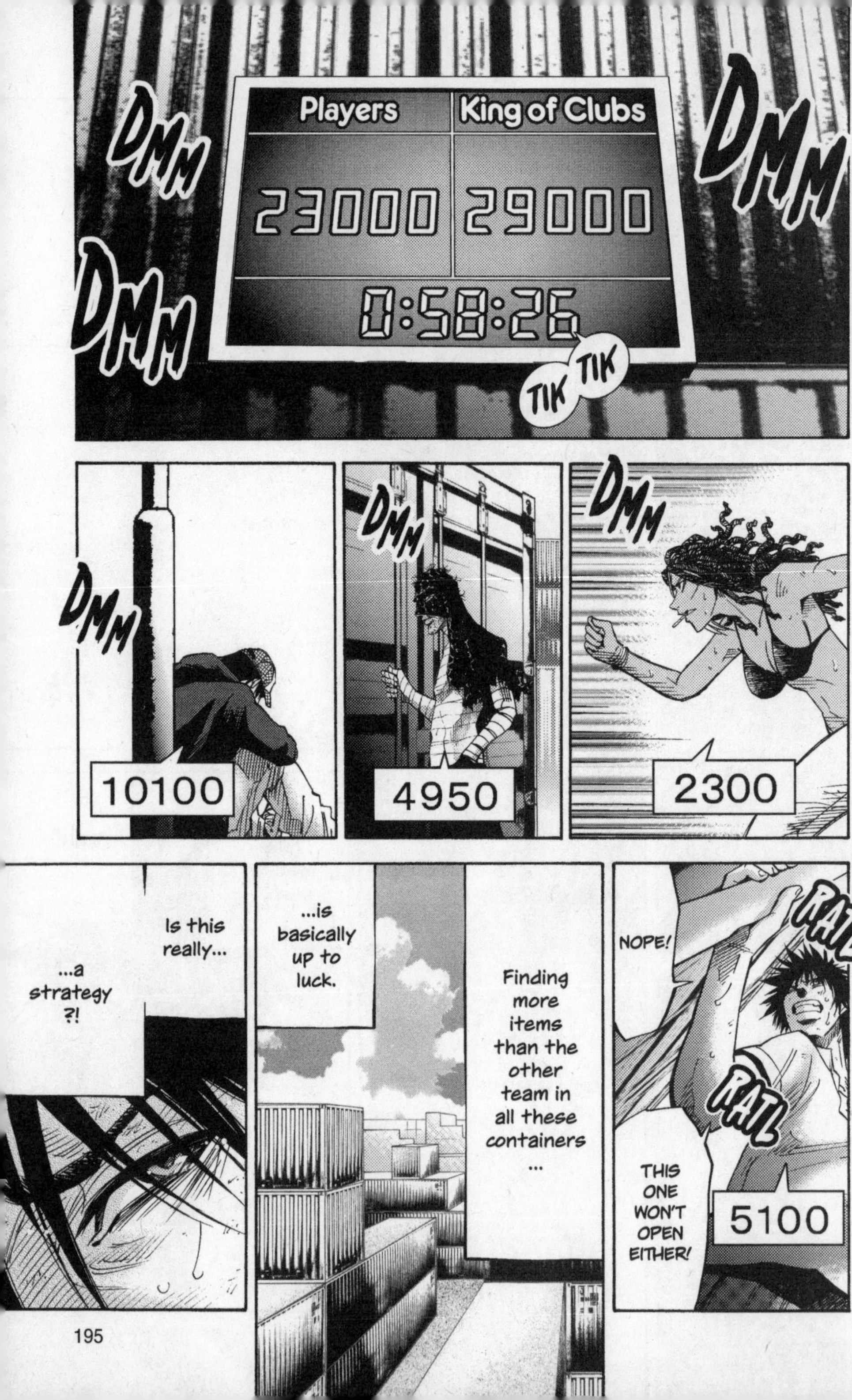
Players
King of Clubs
23000
29000
0:58:26
DMM
DMM
DMM
TIK
TIK
DMM
2300
DMM
4950
DMM
10100
NOPE!
RATL
RATL
THIS ONE WON'T OPEN EITHER!
5100
Finding more items than the other team in all these containers...
...is basically up to luck.
Is this really...
...a strategy?!

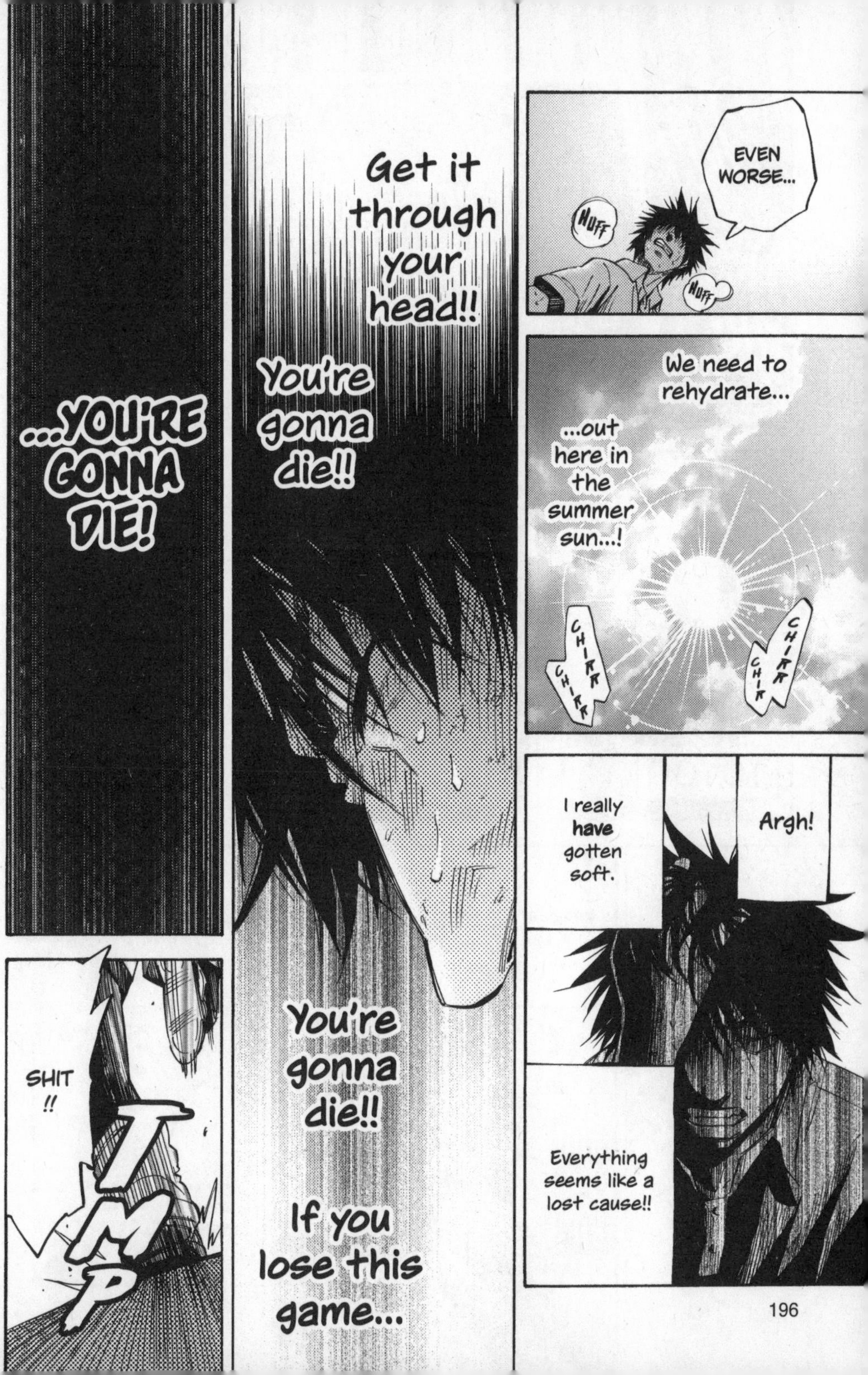
HUFF
EVEN WORSE...
HUFF
We need to rehydrate...
...out here in the summer sun...!
CHIRR CHIRR
CHIRR CHIRR
Argh!
I really have gotten soft.
Everything seems like a lost cause!!
Get it through your head!!
You're gonna die!!
You're gonna die!!
If you lose this game...
...YOU'RE GONNA DIE!
SHIT!!
TMP

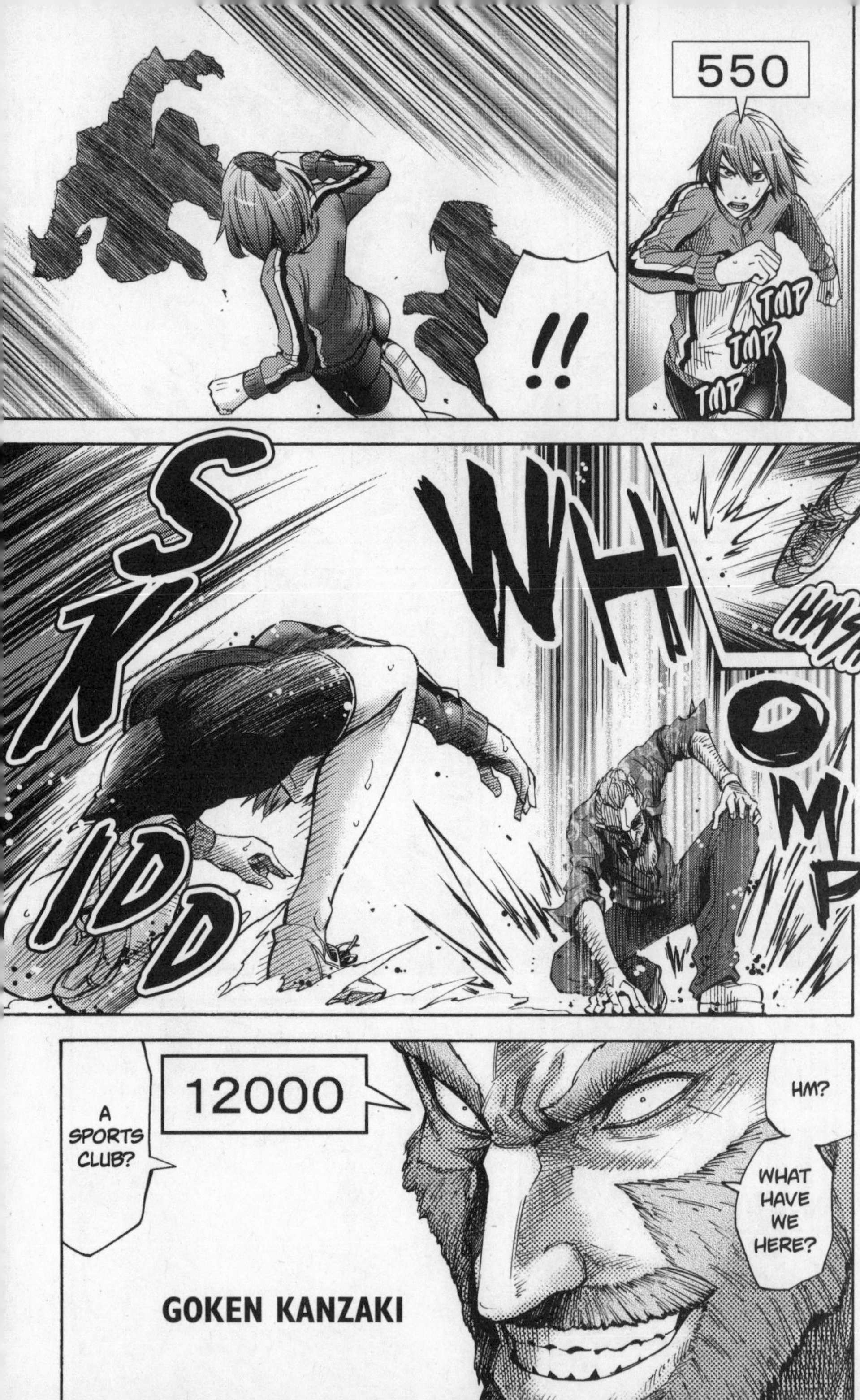

550
TMP
TMP
TMP
!!
HWSH
WHOMP
SKIDD
HM?
12000
WHAT HAVE WE HERE?
A SPORTS CLUB?
GOKEN KANZAKI

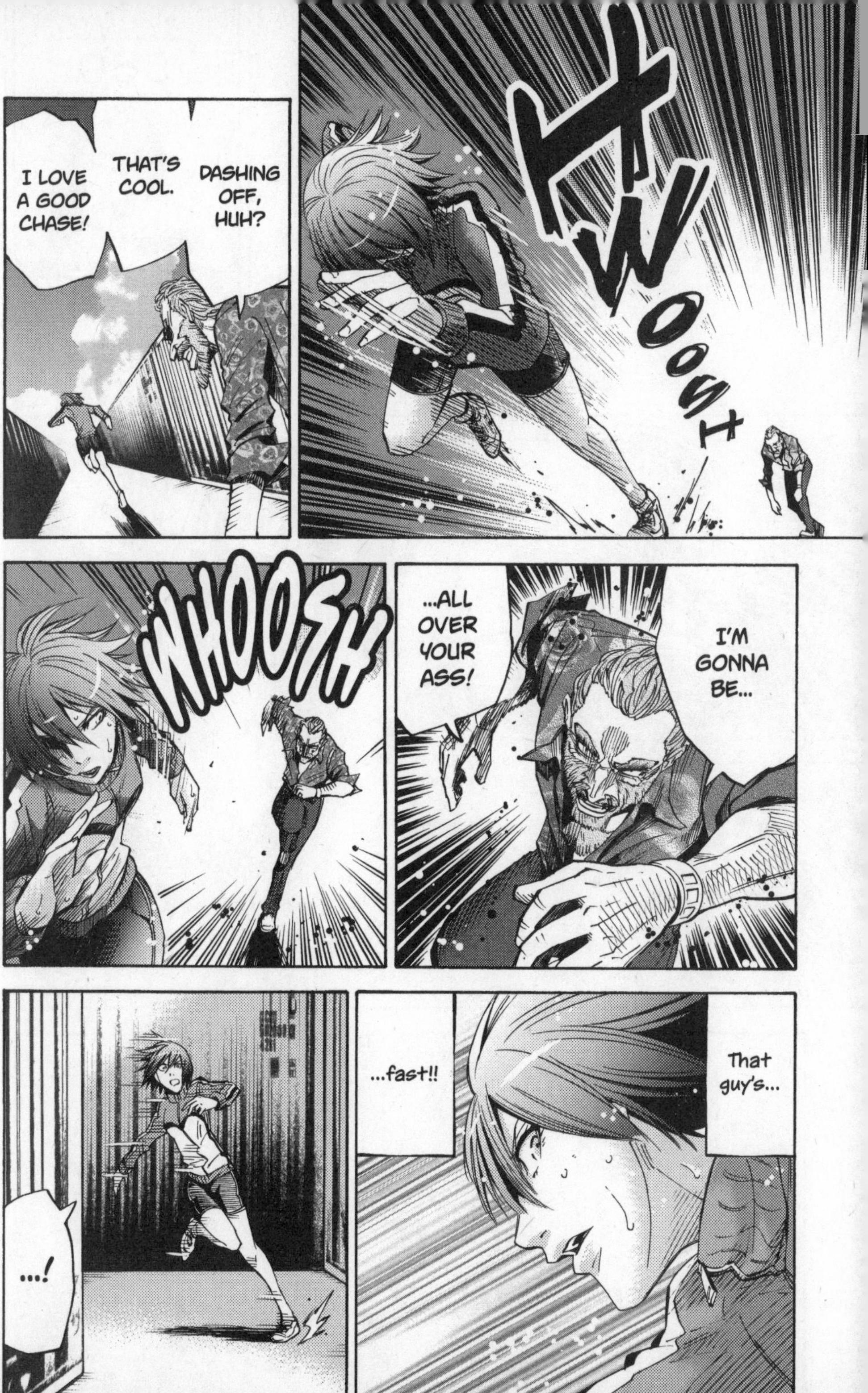
WOOSH
DASHING OFF, HUH?
THAT'S COOL.
I LOVE A GOOD CHASE!
I'M GONNA BE...
...ALL OVER YOUR ASS!
WHOOSH
That guy's...
...fast!!
...!

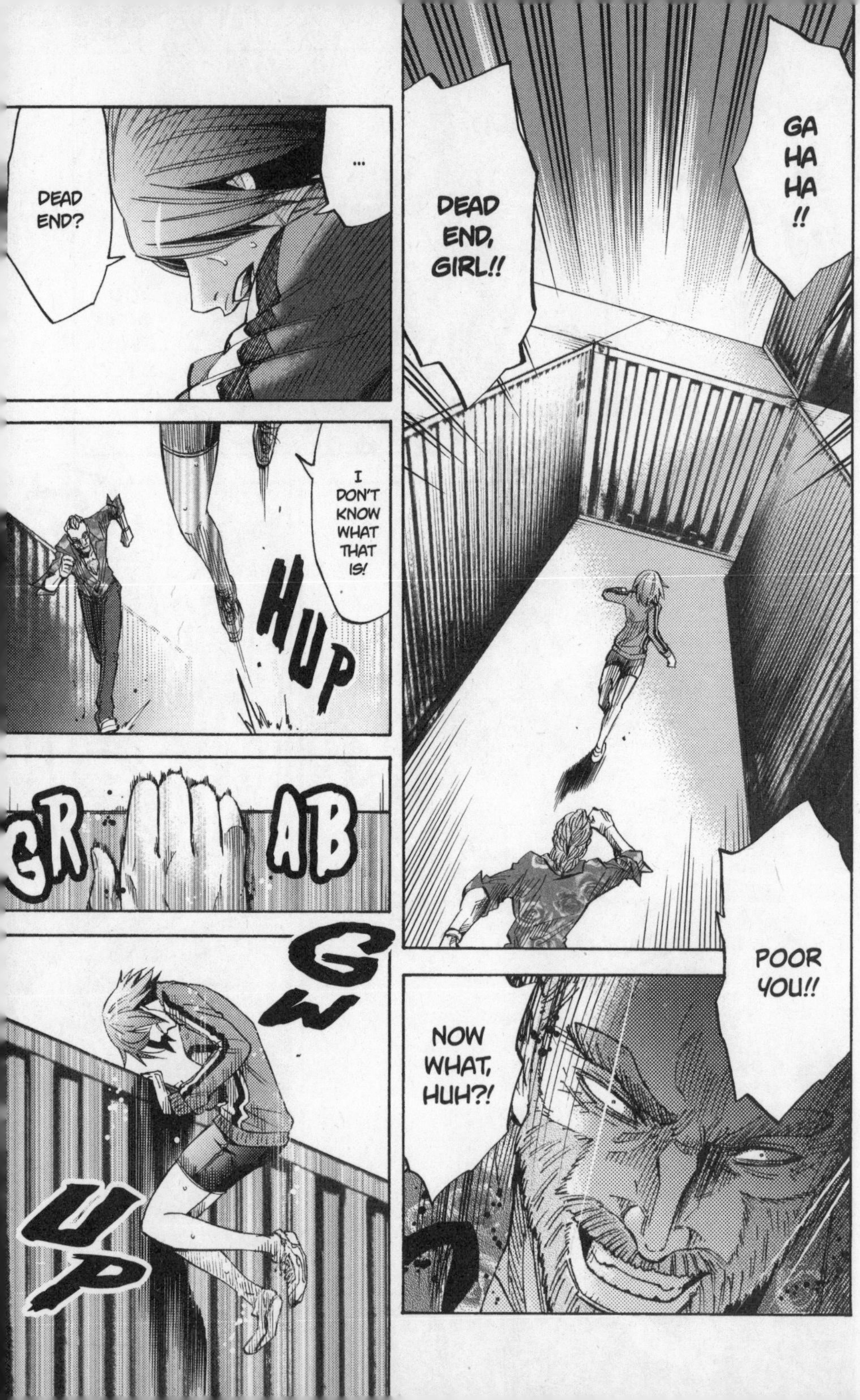
GA HA HA!!
DEAD END, GIRL!!
...
DEAD END?
I DON'T KNOW WHAT THAT IS!
HUP
GR AB
POOR YOU!!
NOW WHAT, HUH?!
GW
UP

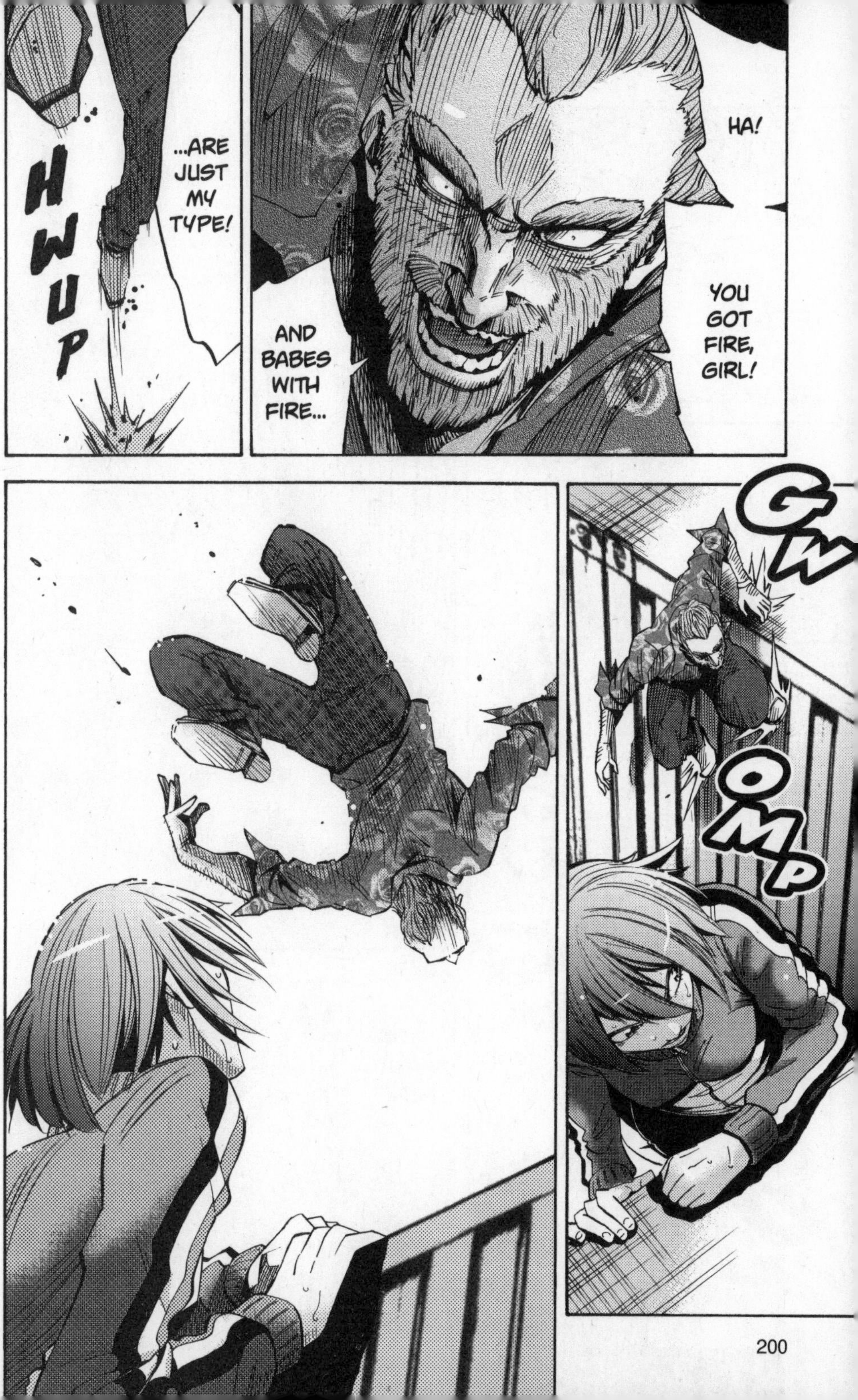
HA!
YOU GOT FIRE, GIRL!
AND BABES WITH FIRE...
...ARE JUST MY TYPE!
HWUP
GWOMP

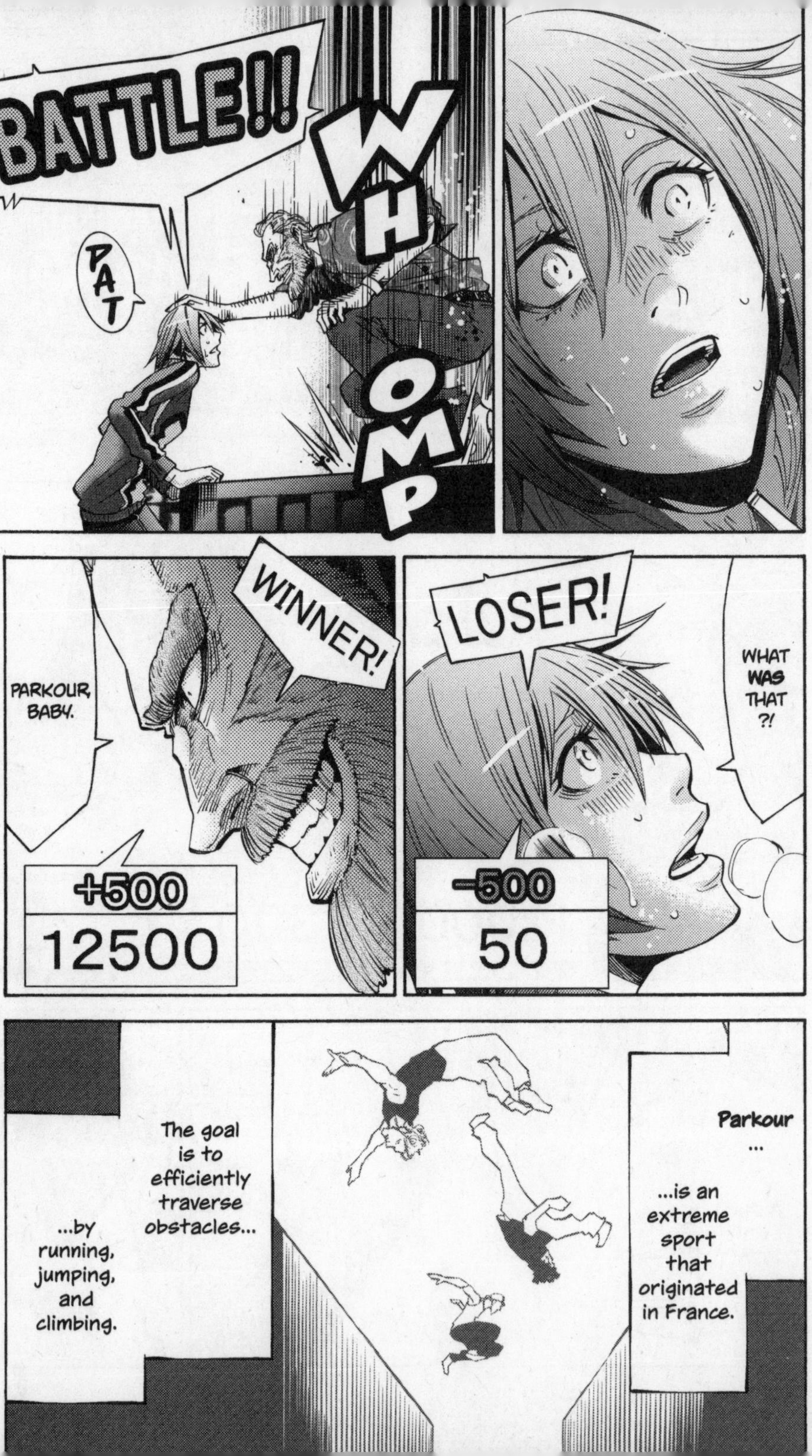
BATTLE!!
WHOMP
PAT
LOSER!
WHAT WAS THAT ?!
-500
50
WINNER!
PARKOUR, BABY.
+500
12500
Parkour...
...is an extreme sport that originated in France.
The goal is to efficiently traverse obstacles...
...by running, jumping, and climbing.

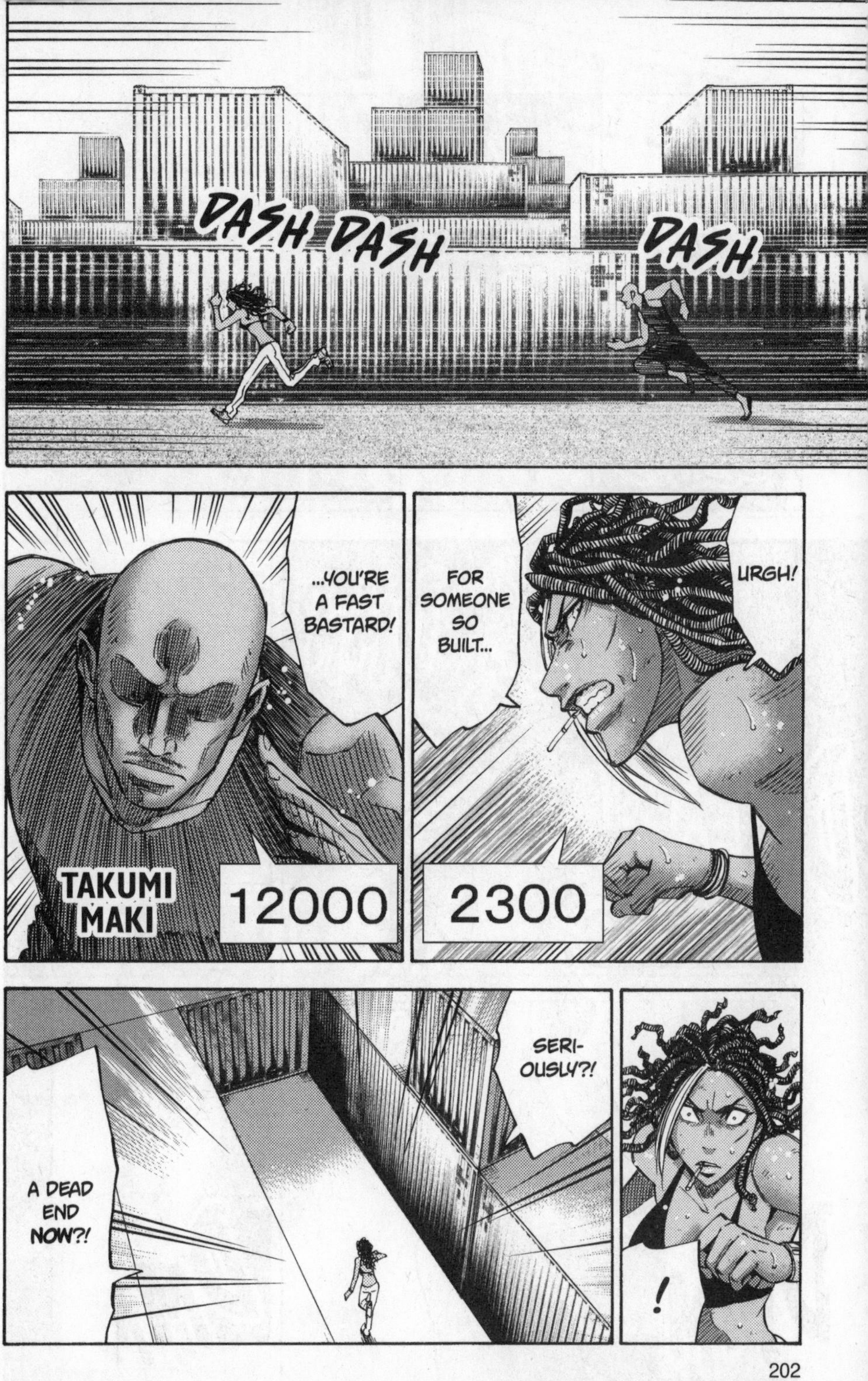
DASH
DASH DASH
URGH!
FOR SOMEONE SO BUILT...
2300
...YOU'RE A FAST BASTARD!
12000
TAKUMI MAKI
!
SERI-OUSLY?!
A DEAD END NOW?!

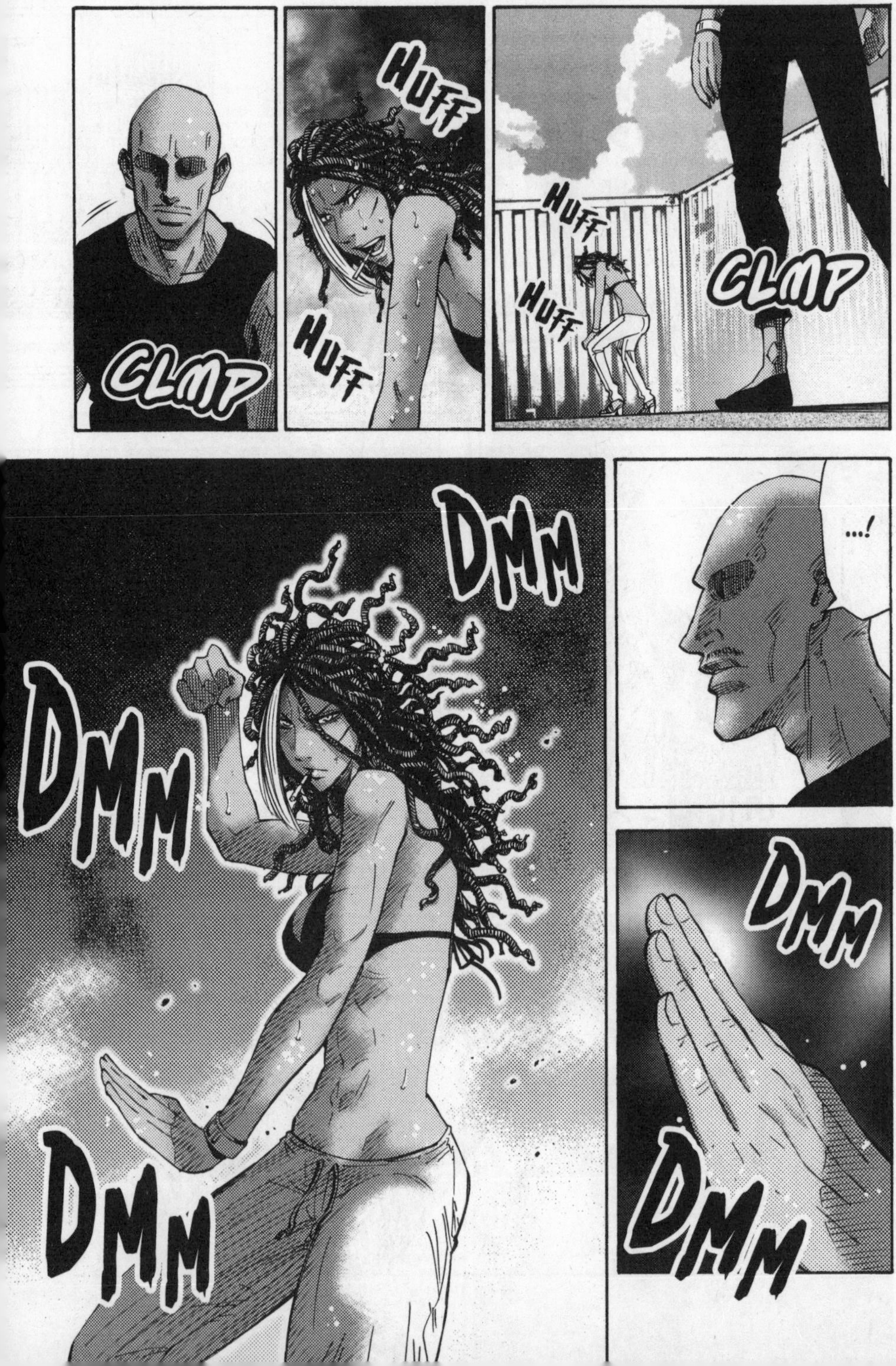
HUFF
HUFF
CLMP
HUFF
HUFF
CLMP
...!
DMM
DMM
DMM
DMM
DMM

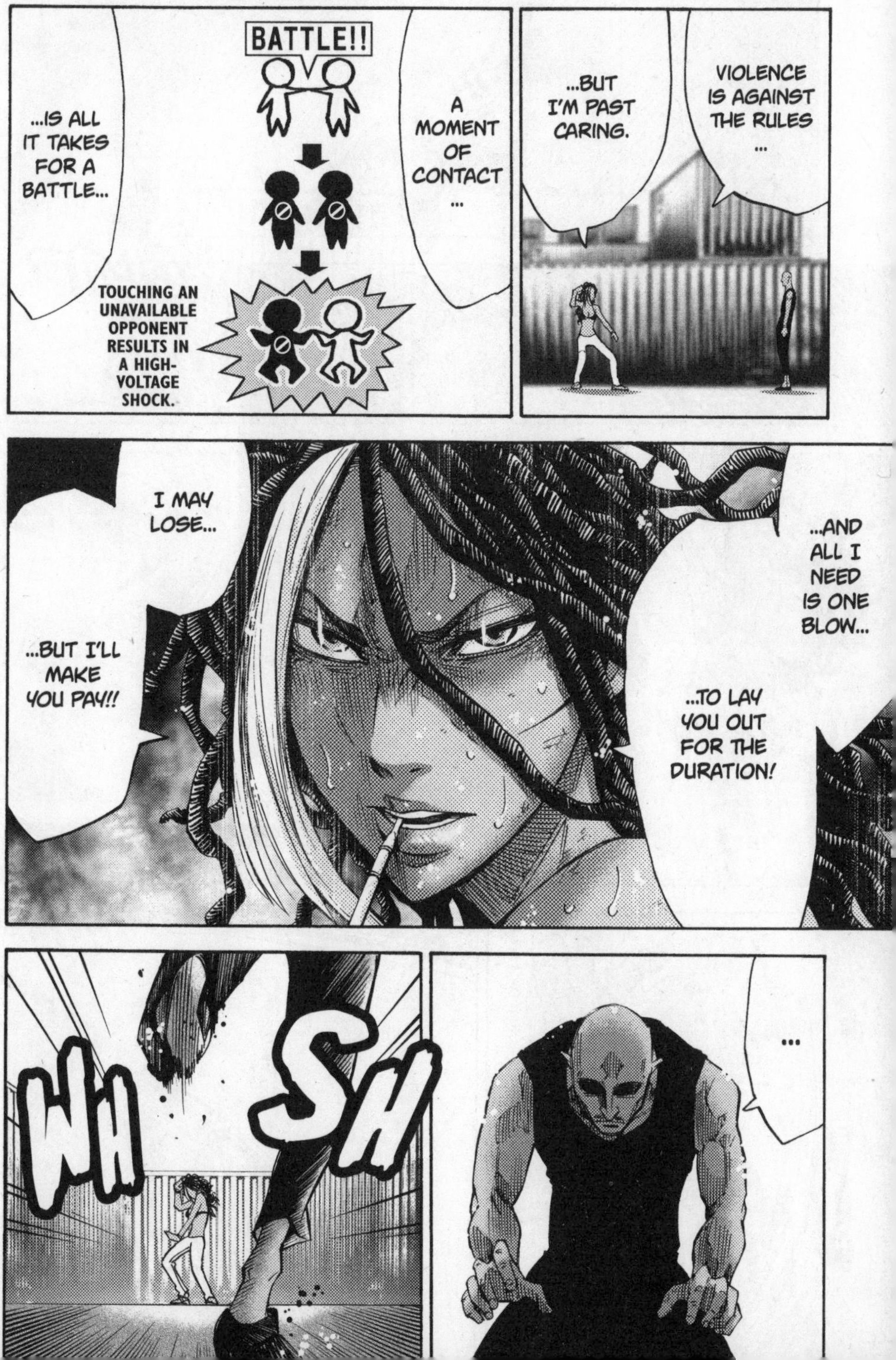
VIOLENCE IS AGAINST THE RULES ...
...BUT I'M PAST CARING.
A MOMENT OF CONTACT ...
BATTLE!!
...IS ALL IT TAKES FOR A BATTLE...
TOUCHING AN UNAVAILABLE OPPONENT RESULTS IN A HIGH-VOLTAGE SHOCK.
...AND ALL I NEED IS ONE BLOW...
...TO LAY YOU OUT FOR THE DURATION!
I MAY LOSE...
...BUT I'LL MAKE YOU PAY!!
...
WHSH

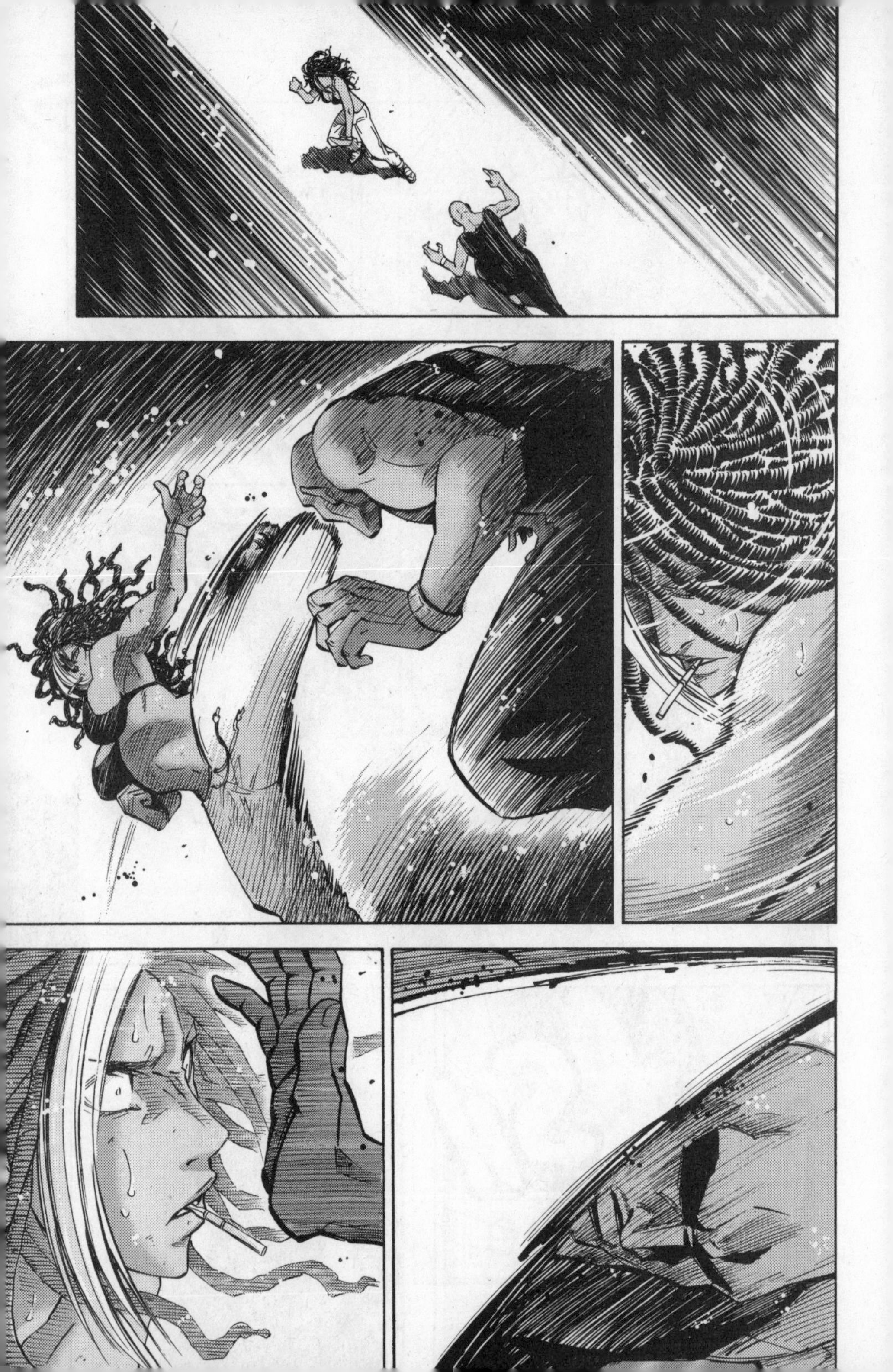

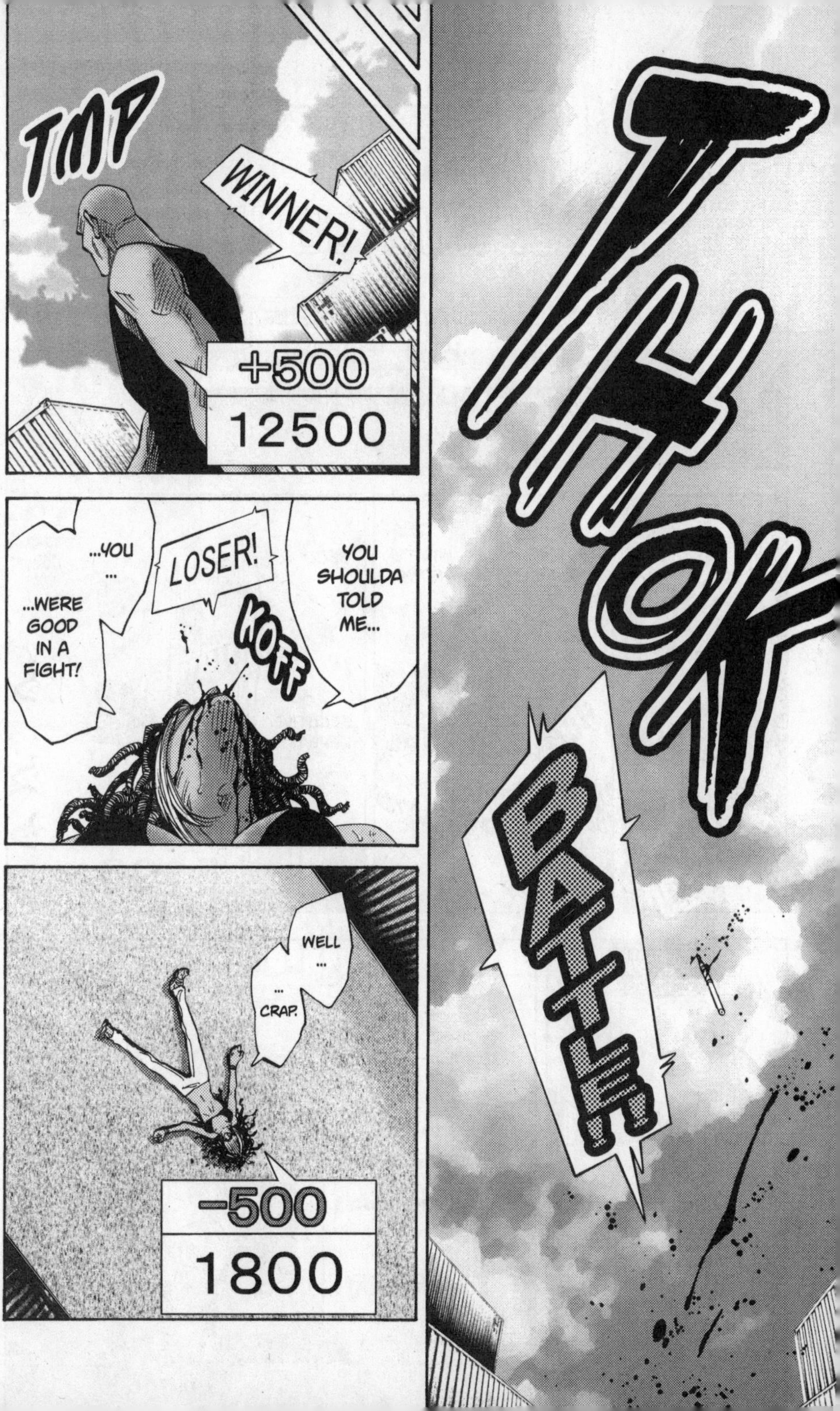
THOK
BATTLE
TMP
WINNER!
+500
12500
YOU SHOULDA TOLD ME...
KOFF
LOSER!
...YOU ...
...WERE GOOD IN A FIGHT!
WELL ...
... CRAP.
-500
1800

...POINTS HAVE CHANGED.

Players	King of Clubs
-500	+500
22000	30000

PING

BOTH TEAMS'...

PING

0:49:07

KCHAK

...!!

CREAK

...WITH EVERYONE?!

WHAT'S WRONG...

HUFF

HUFF

HUFF

A SECOND...

...CONSECUTIVE DEFEAT?!

AGAIN?!

TUMP

TUMP

TUMP

5100

...OUR—

...FOR...

CHALK UP ANOTHER ITEM...

IT OPENED!!

I DID IT!!

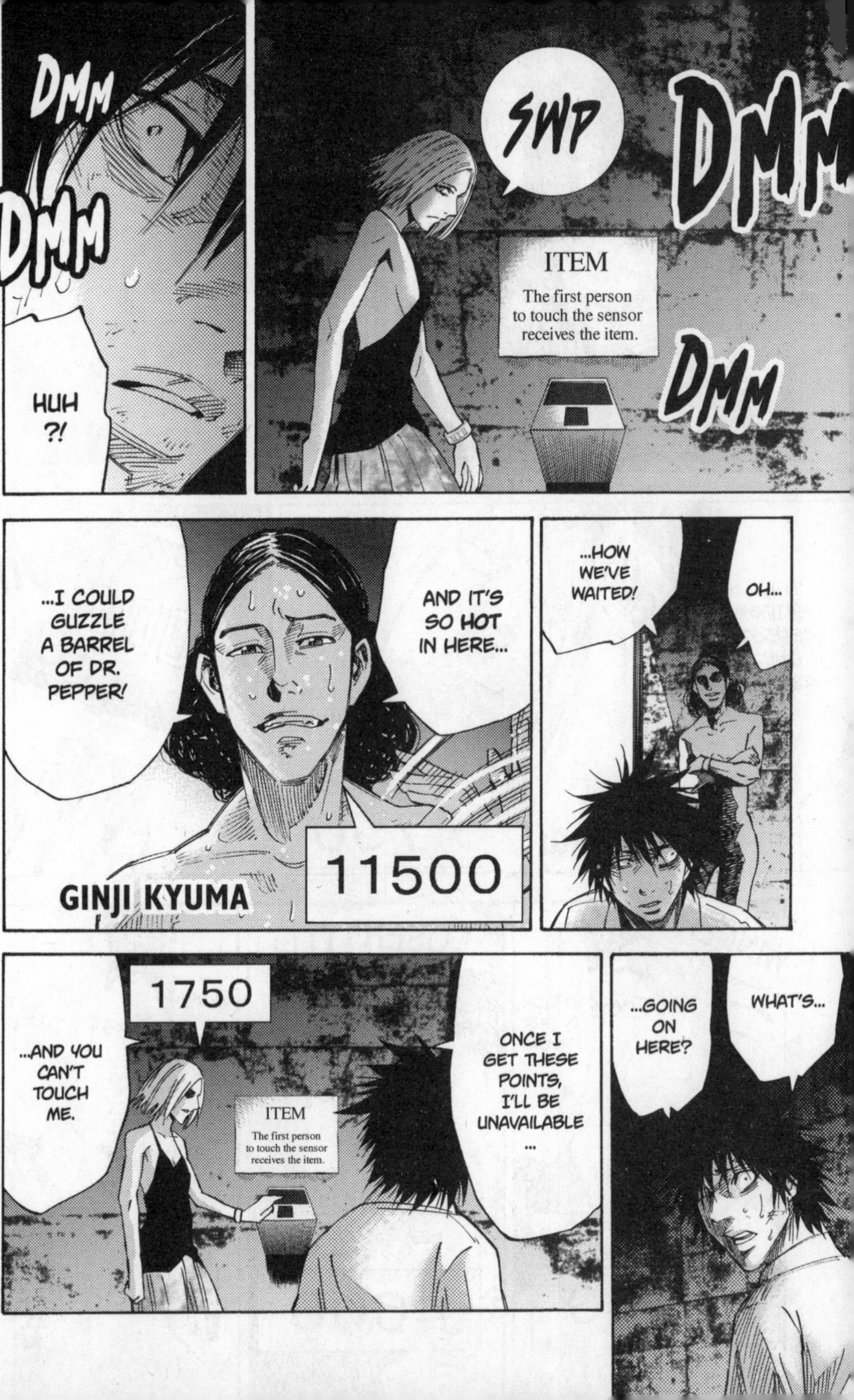
SWP
DMM
ITEM
The first person to touch the sensor receives the item.
DMM
DMM
DMM
HUH ?!
OH...
...HOW WE'VE WAITED!
AND IT'S SO HOT IN HERE...
...I COULD GUZZLE A BARREL OF DR. PEPPER!
GINJI KYUMA
11500
WHAT'S...
...GOING ON HERE?
ONCE I GET THESE POINTS, I'LL BE UNAVAILABLE...
1750
...AND YOU CAN'T TOUCH ME.
ITEM
The first person to touch the sensor receives the item.

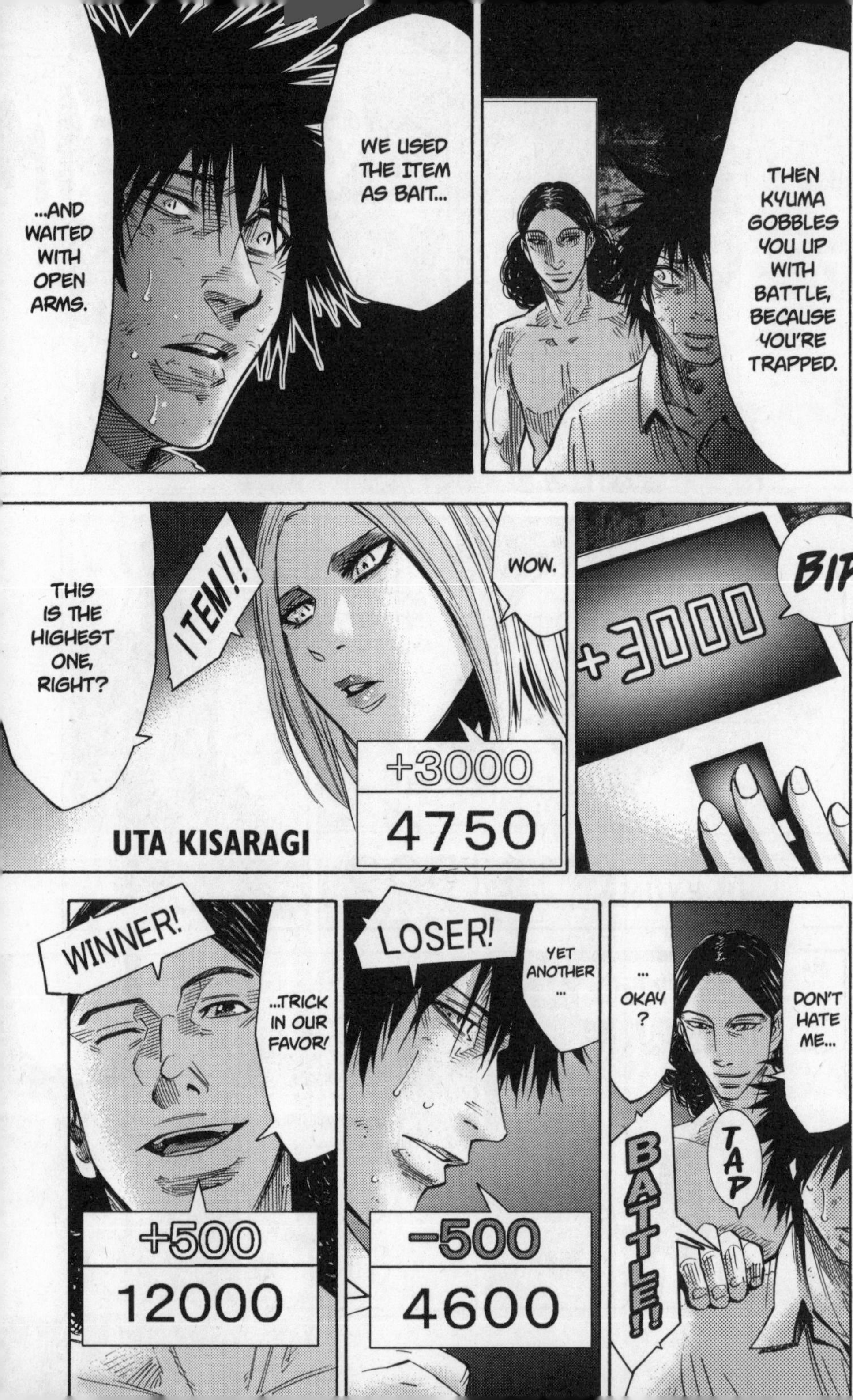
THEN KYUMA GOBBLES YOU UP WITH BATTLE, BECAUSE YOU'RE TRAPPED.
WE USED THE ITEM AS BAIT...
...AND WAITED WITH OPEN ARMS.
BIP
+3000
WOW.
ITEM!!
THIS IS THE HIGHEST ONE, RIGHT?
+3000
4750
UTA KISARAGI
DON'T HATE ME...
...OKAY?
TAP
BATTLE!!
YET ANOTHER...
LOSER!
-500
4600
...TRICK IN OUR FAVOR!
WINNER!
+500
12000

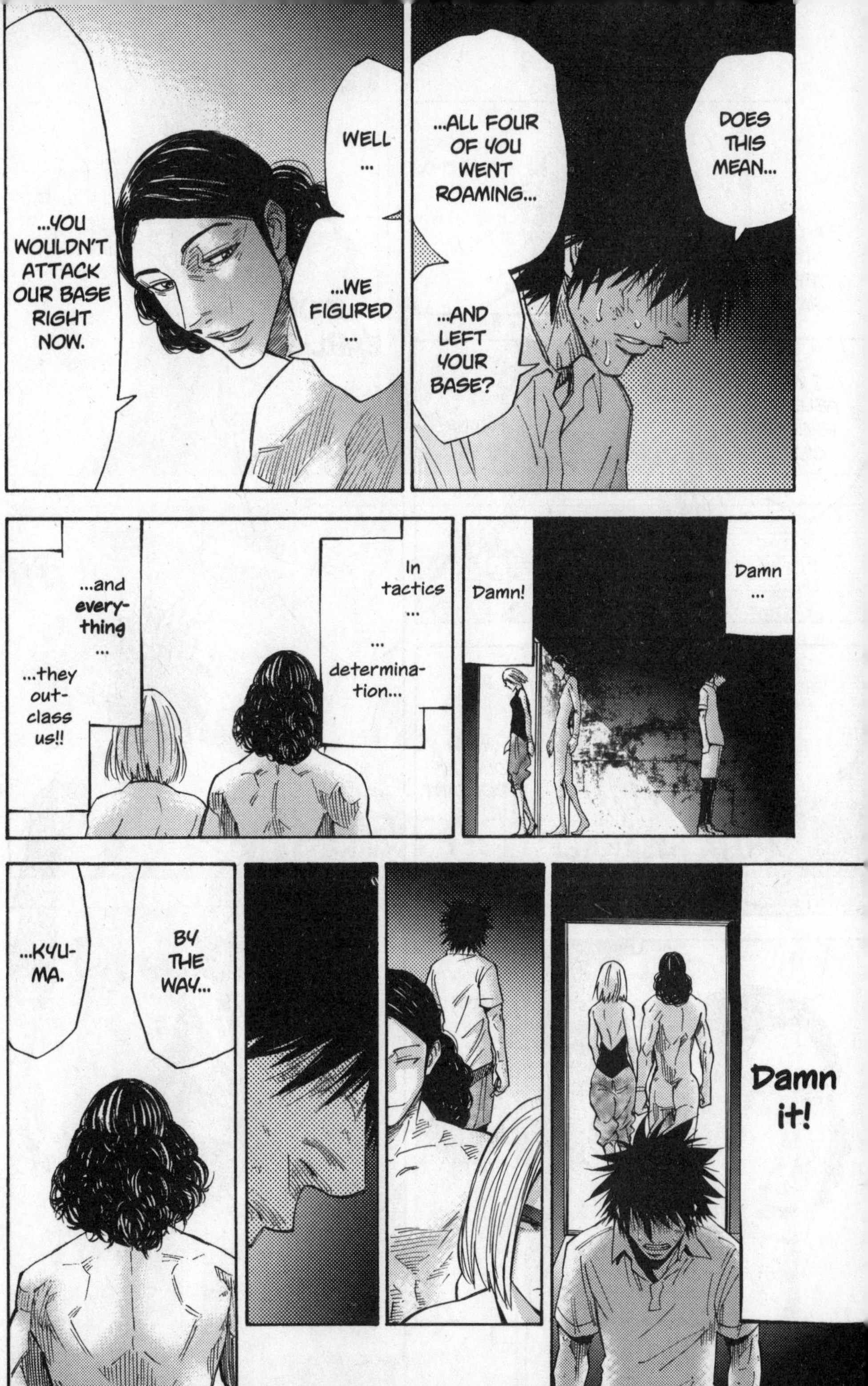
DOES THIS MEAN...
...ALL FOUR OF YOU WENT ROAMING...
...AND LEFT YOUR BASE?
WELL ...
...WE FIGURED ...
...YOU WOULDN'T ATTACK OUR BASE RIGHT NOW.
Damn ...
Damn!
In tactics ...
... determination...
...and every-thing ...
...they out-class us!!
Damn it!
BY THE WAY...
...KYU-MA.

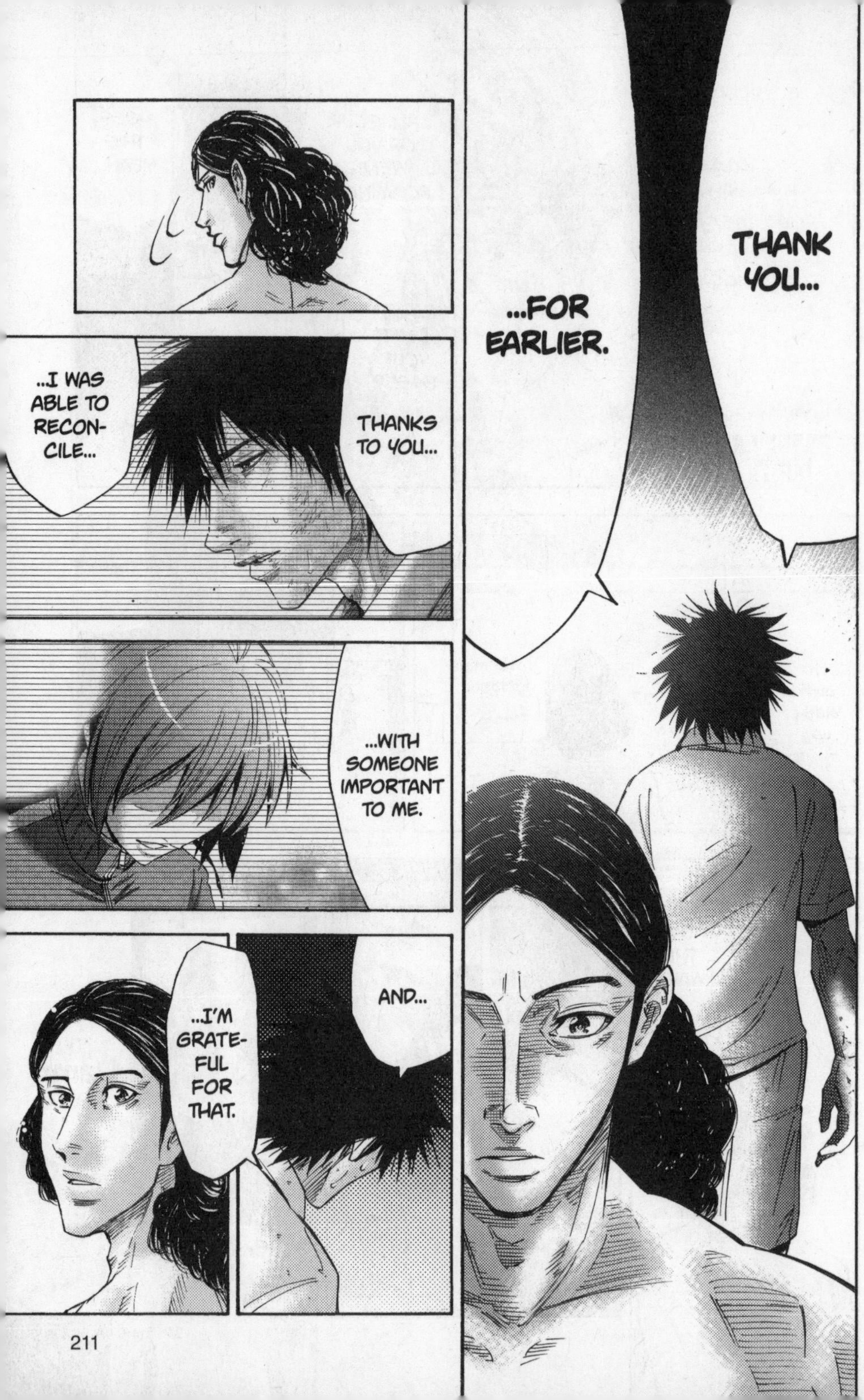
THANK YOU...
...FOR EARLIER.
THANKS TO YOU...
...I WAS ABLE TO RECONCILE...
...WITH SOMEONE IMPORTANT TO ME.
AND...
...I'M GRATEFUL FOR THAT.

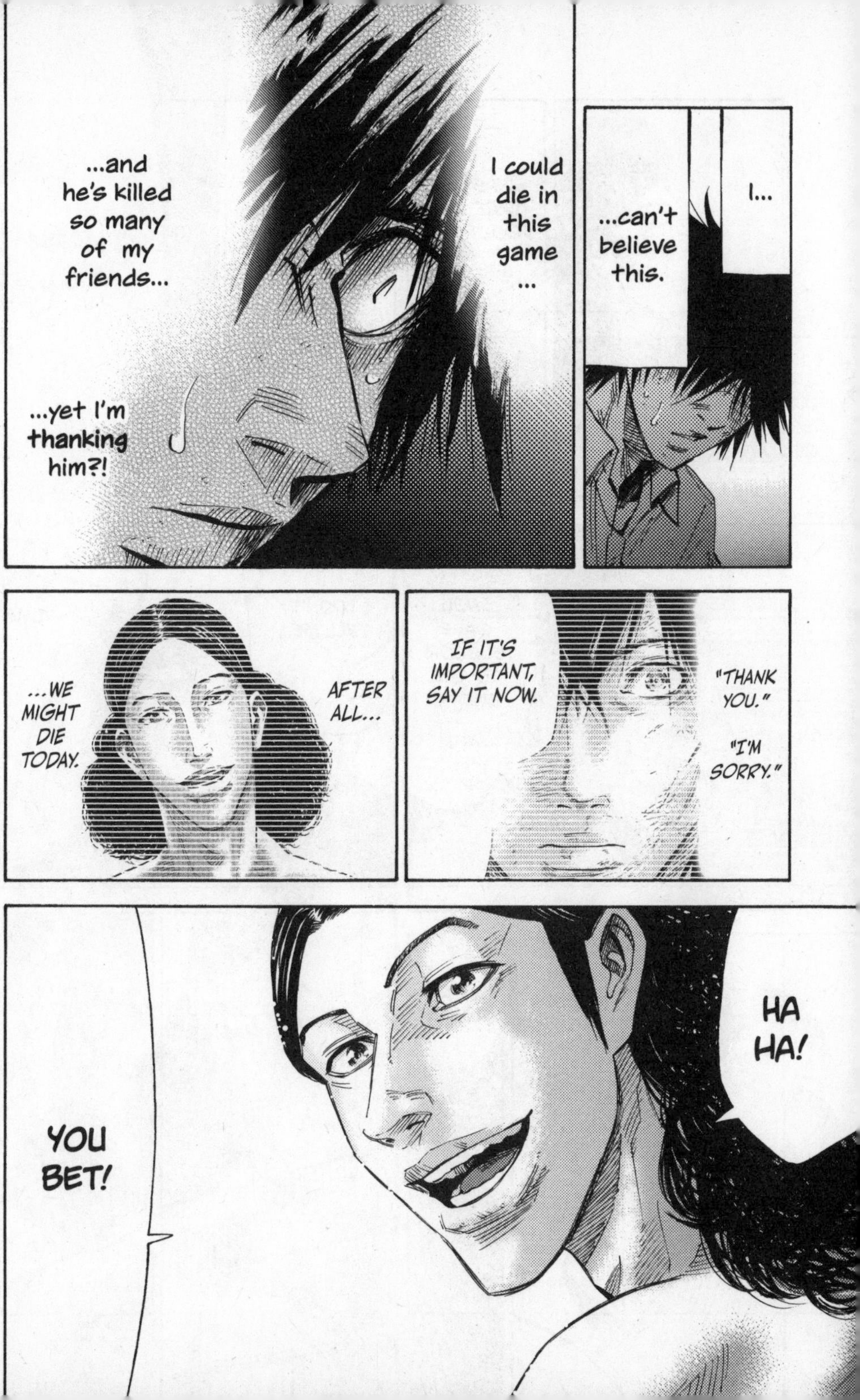

I...
...can't believe this.
I could die in this game...
...and he's killed so many of my friends...
...yet I'm thanking him?!
"THANK YOU."
"I'M SORRY."
IF IT'S IMPORTANT, SAY IT NOW.
AFTER ALL...
...WE MIGHT DIE TODAY.
HA HA!
YOU BET!

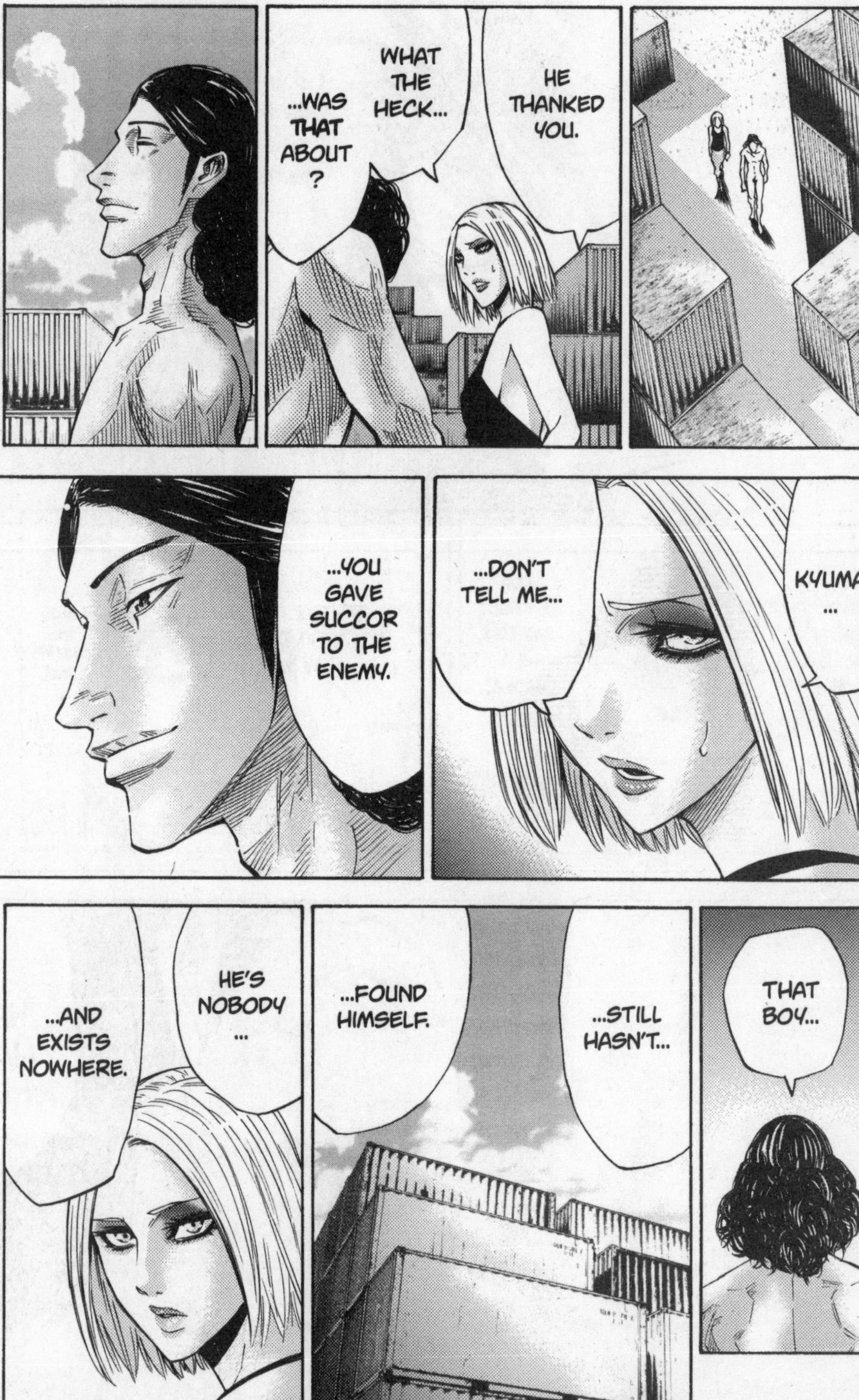
HE THANKED YOU.
WHAT THE HECK...
...WAS THAT ABOUT?
KYUMA...
...DON'T TELL ME...
...YOU GAVE SUCCOR TO THE ENEMY.
THAT BOY...
...STILL HASN'T...
...FOUND HIMSELF.
HE'S NOBODY...
...AND EXISTS NOWHERE.

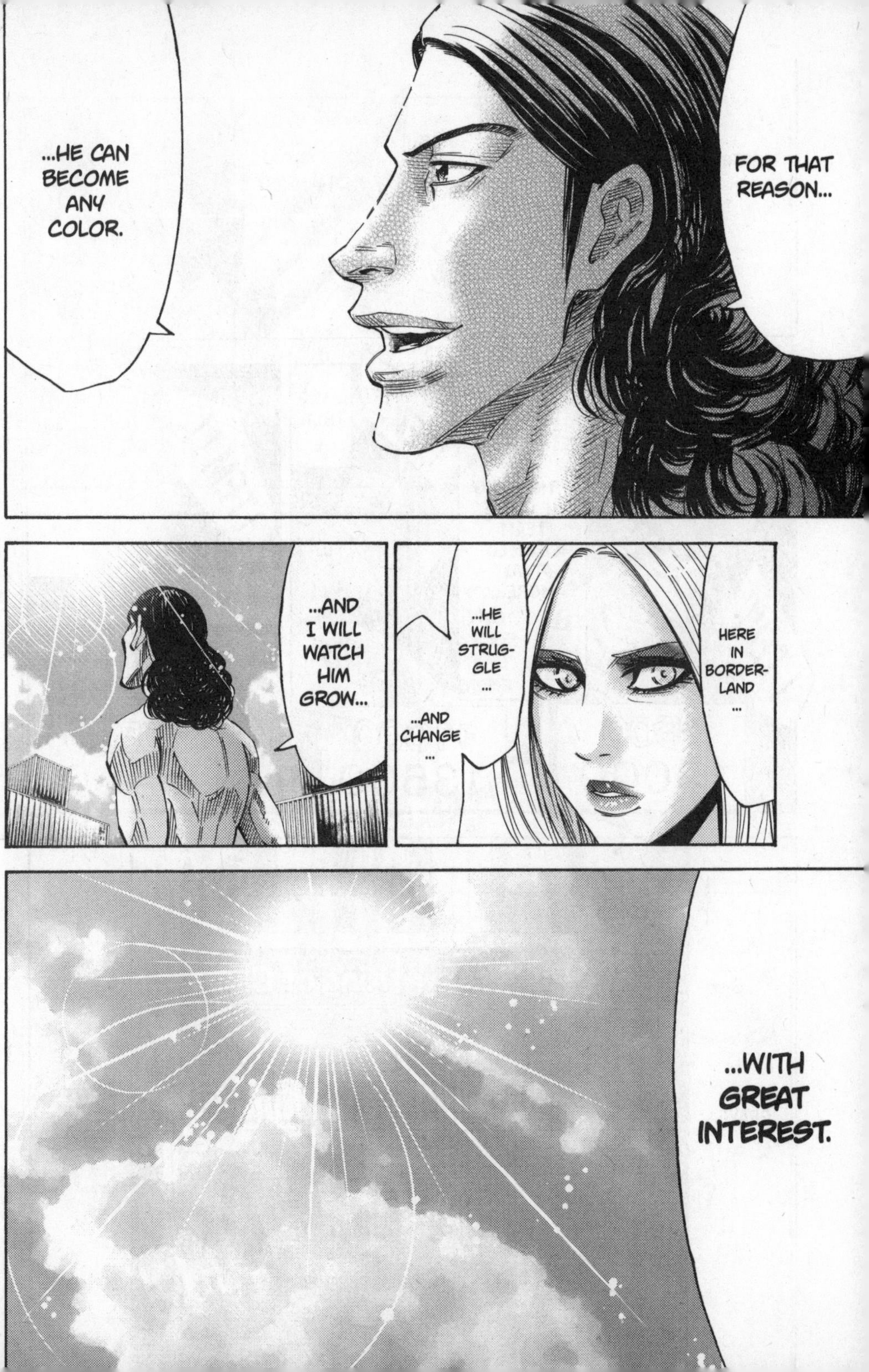

FOR THAT REASON...
...HE CAN BECOME ANY COLOR.
HERE IN BORDERLAND ...
...HE WILL STRUGGLE ...
...AND CHANGE ...
...AND I WILL WATCH HIM GROW...
...WITH GREAT INTEREST.

LATER...

...TO MAINTAIN THEIR LEAD.

...THE KING OF CLUBS TEAM CLAIMED TWO MORE...

ITEM!!

ITEM!!

...AND THEN...

...NIRAGI CLAIMED AN ITEM...

ITEM!!

+500
13000

+1000
13500

+1500
6450

...IS GRAVE.

Players	King of Clubs
23000	35000

0:40:22

DMM

DMM

DMM

THE STATE OF THE GAME FOR ARISU'S TEAM...

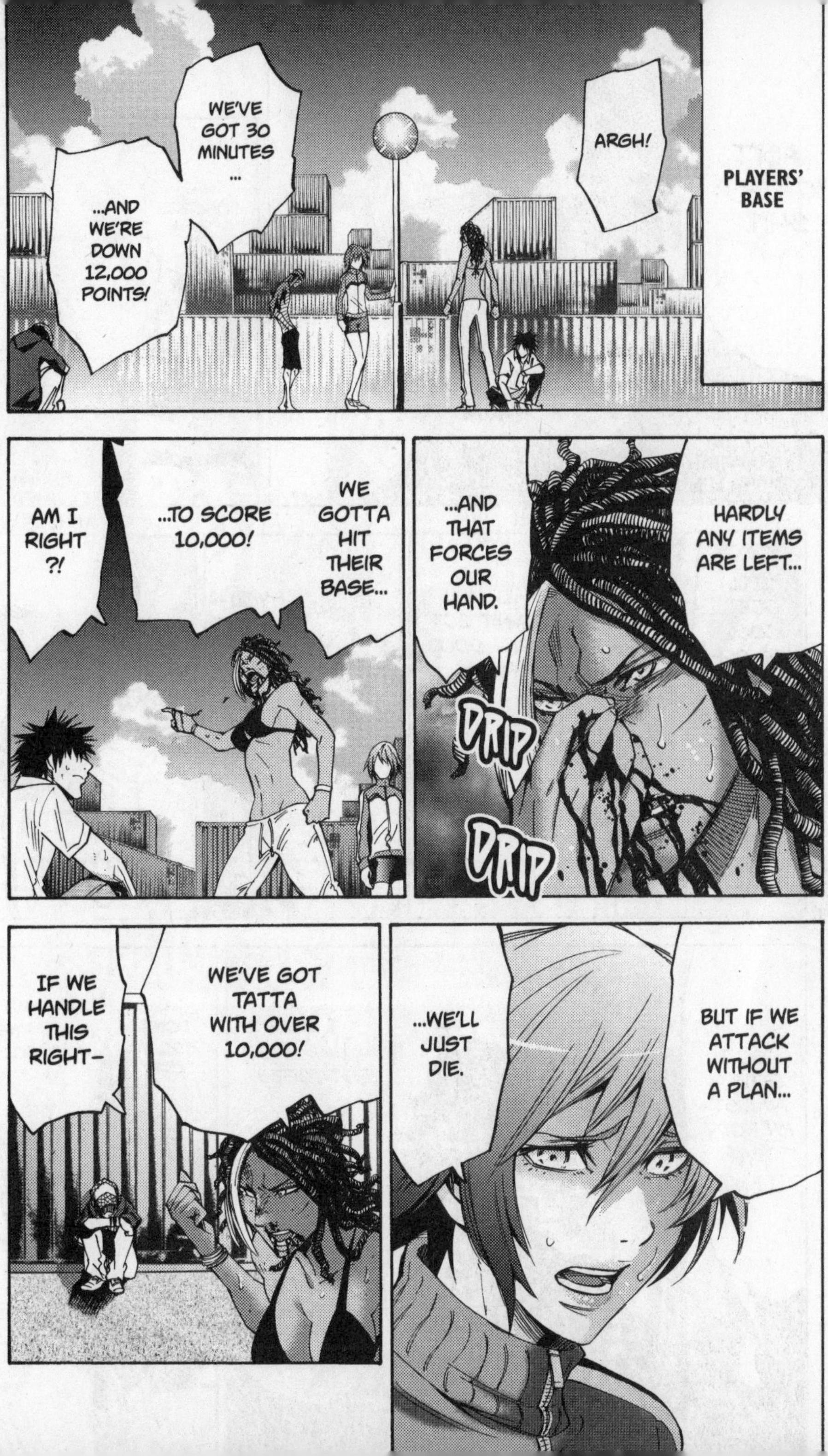
PLAYERS' BASE
ARGH!
WE'VE GOT 30 MINUTES ...
...AND WE'RE DOWN 12,000 POINTS!
HARDLY ANY ITEMS ARE LEFT...
...AND THAT FORCES OUR HAND.
DRIP
DRIP
WE GOTTA HIT THEIR BASE...
...TO SCORE 10,000!
AM I RIGHT ?!
BUT IF WE ATTACK WITHOUT A PLAN...
...WE'LL JUST DIE.
WE'VE GOT TATTA WITH OVER 10,000!
IF WE HANDLE THIS RIGHT—

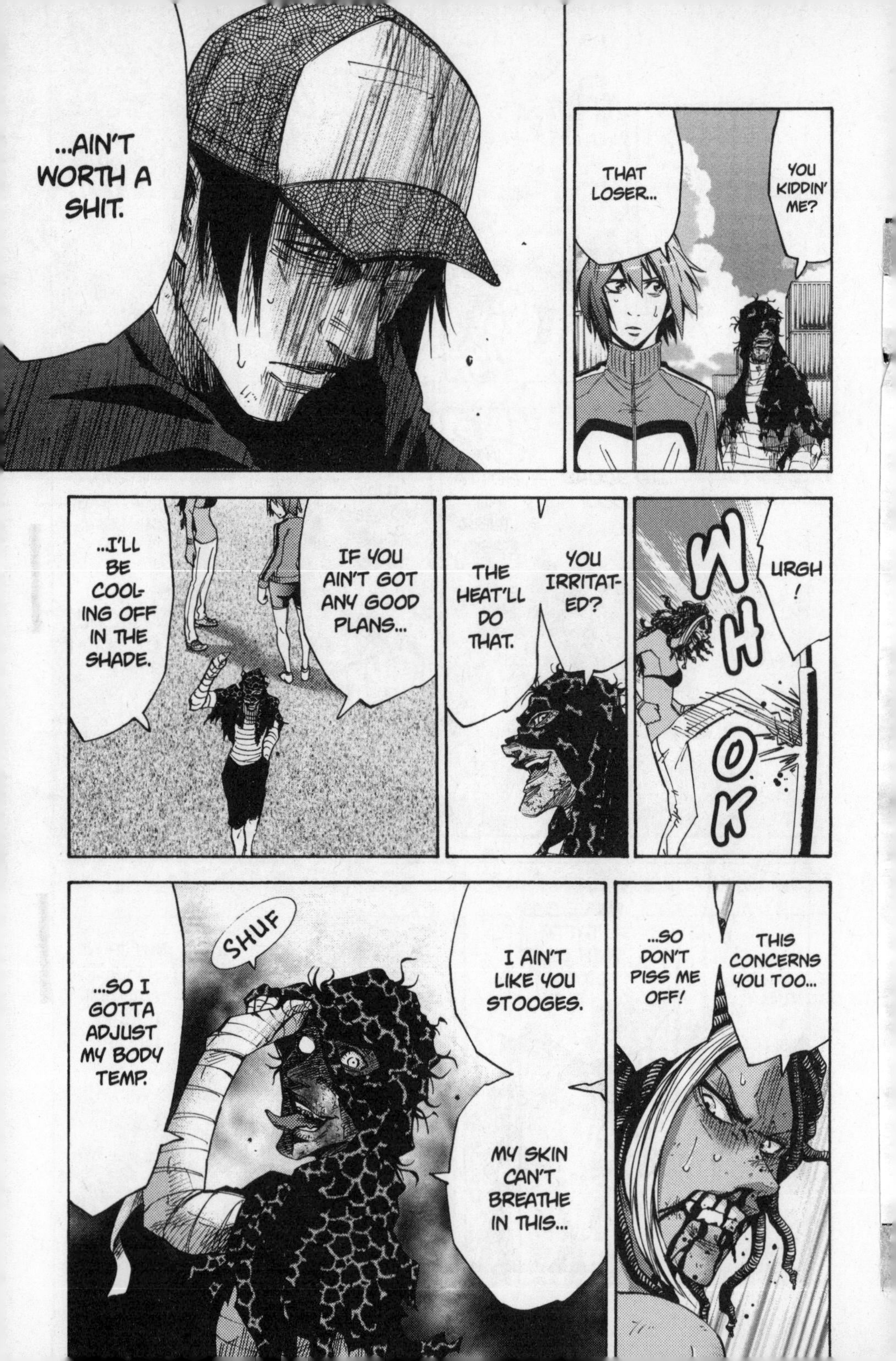
YOU KIDDIN' ME?
THAT LOSER...
...AIN'T WORTH A SHIT.
W H O K
URGH!
YOU IRRITATED?
THE HEAT'LL DO THAT.
IF YOU AIN'T GOT ANY GOOD PLANS...
...I'LL BE COOLING OFF IN THE SHADE.
THIS CONCERNS YOU TOO...
...SO DON'T PISS ME OFF!
I AIN'T LIKE YOU STOOGES.
SHUF
MY SKIN CAN'T BREATHE IN THIS...
...SO I GOTTA ADJUST MY BODY TEMP.

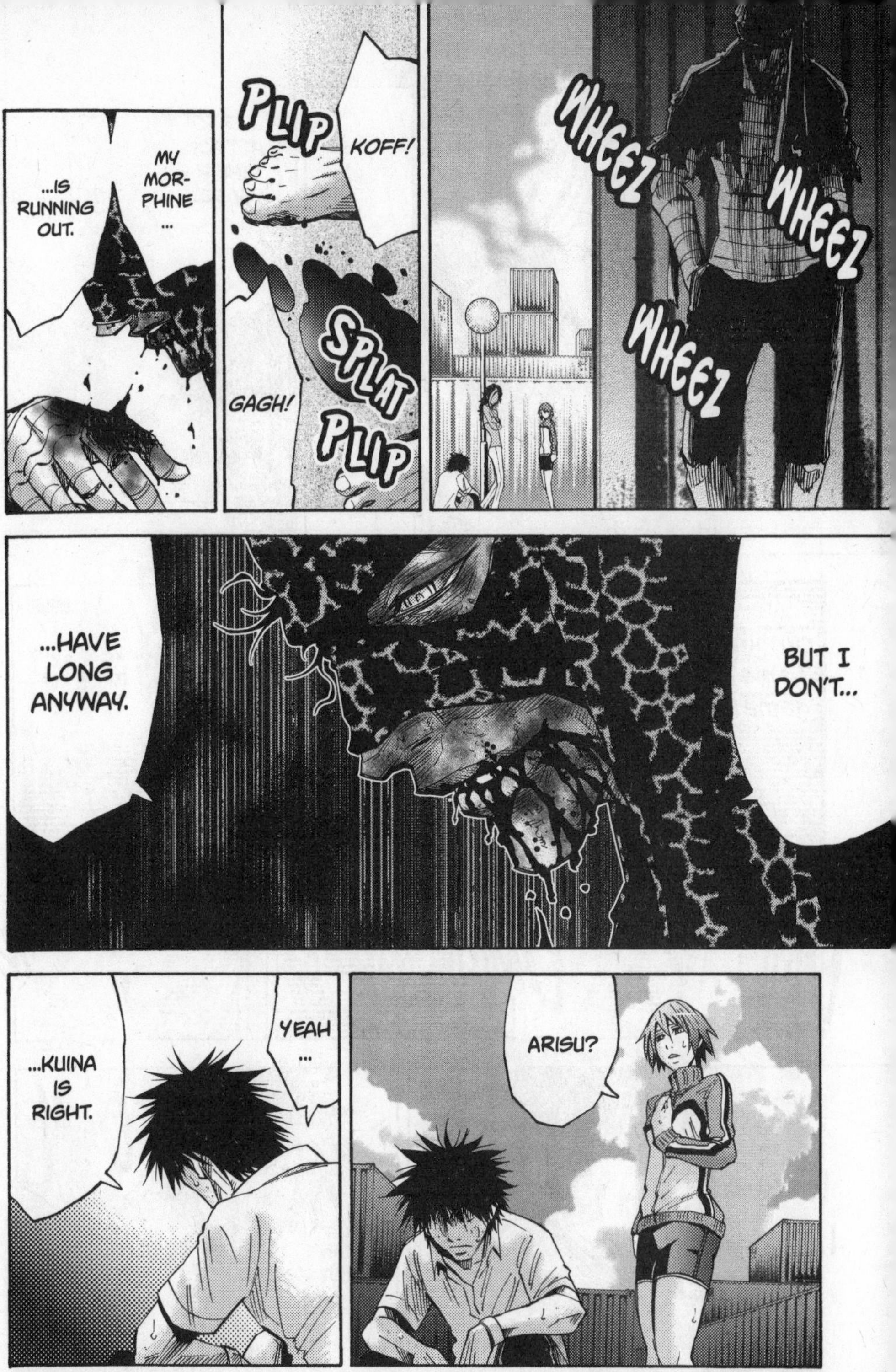
WHEEZ
WHEEZ
WHEEZ
KOFF!
PLIP
SPLAT
GAGH!
PLIP
MY MORPHINE...
...IS RUNNING OUT.
BUT I DON'T...
...HAVE LONG ANYWAY.
ARISU?
YEAH...
...KUINA IS RIGHT.

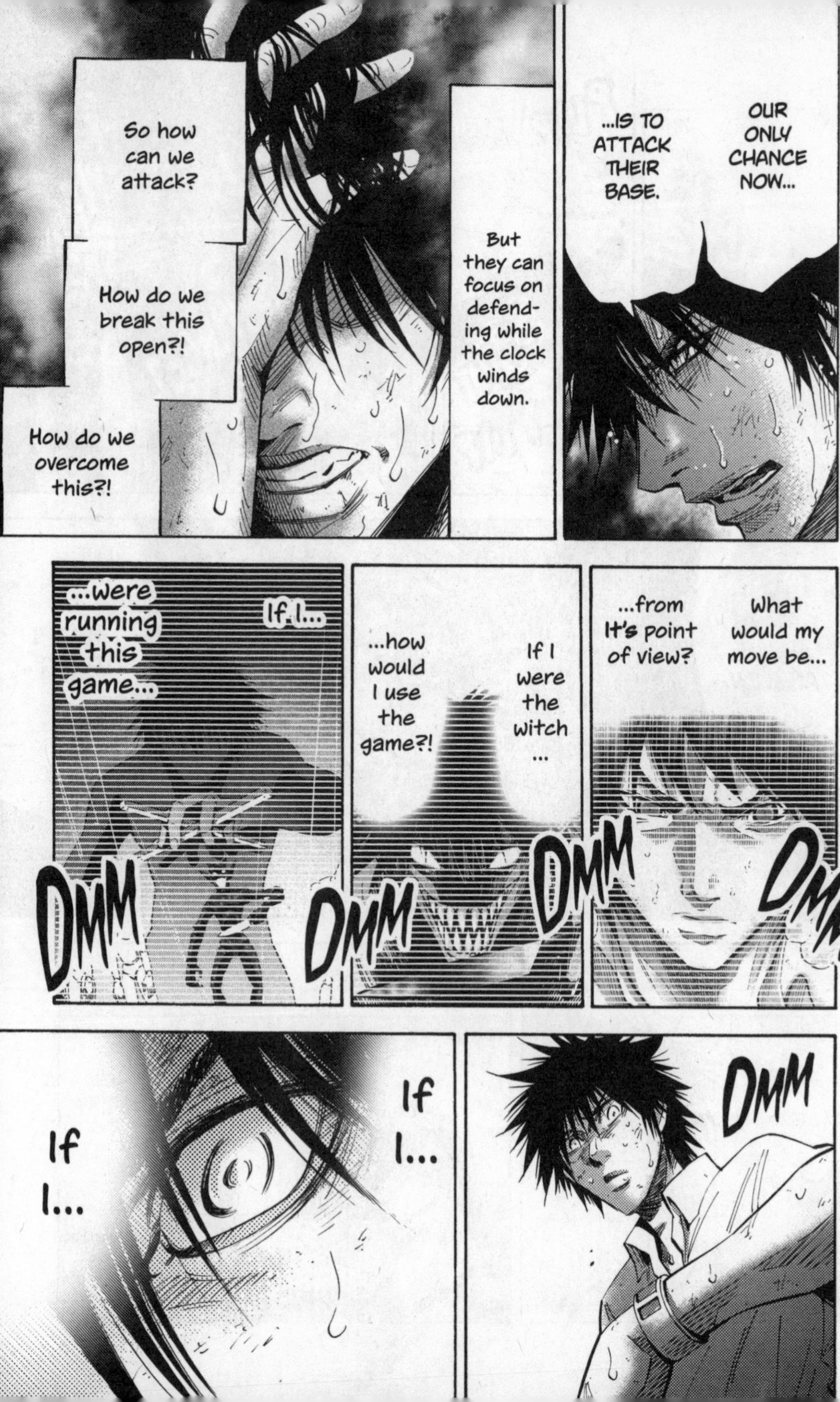

OUR ONLY CHANCE NOW...
...IS TO ATTACK THEIR BASE.
But they can focus on defend-ing while the clock winds down.
So how can we attack?
How do we break this open?!
How do we overcome this?!
What would my move be...
...from It's point of view?
DMM
If I were the witch...
...how would I use the game?!
DMM
DMM
If I...
...were running this game...
DMM
DMM
If I...
If I...

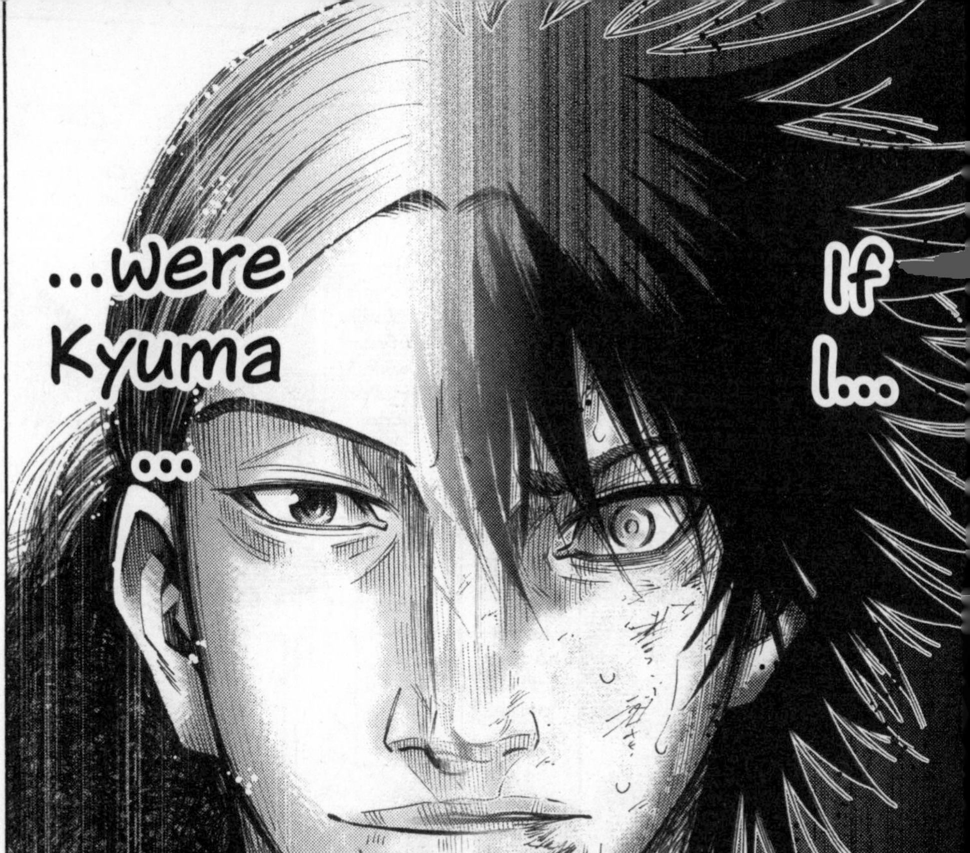
If I...
...were Kyuma...
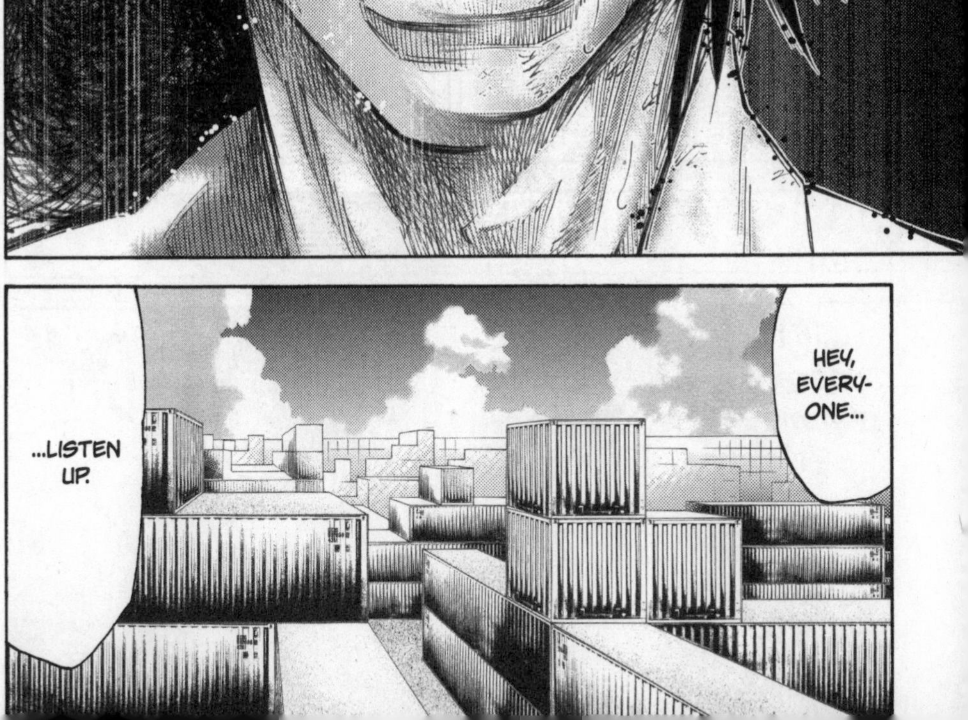
HEY, EVERY-ONE...
...LISTEN UP.

CHAPTER 37: King of Clubs, Part 5

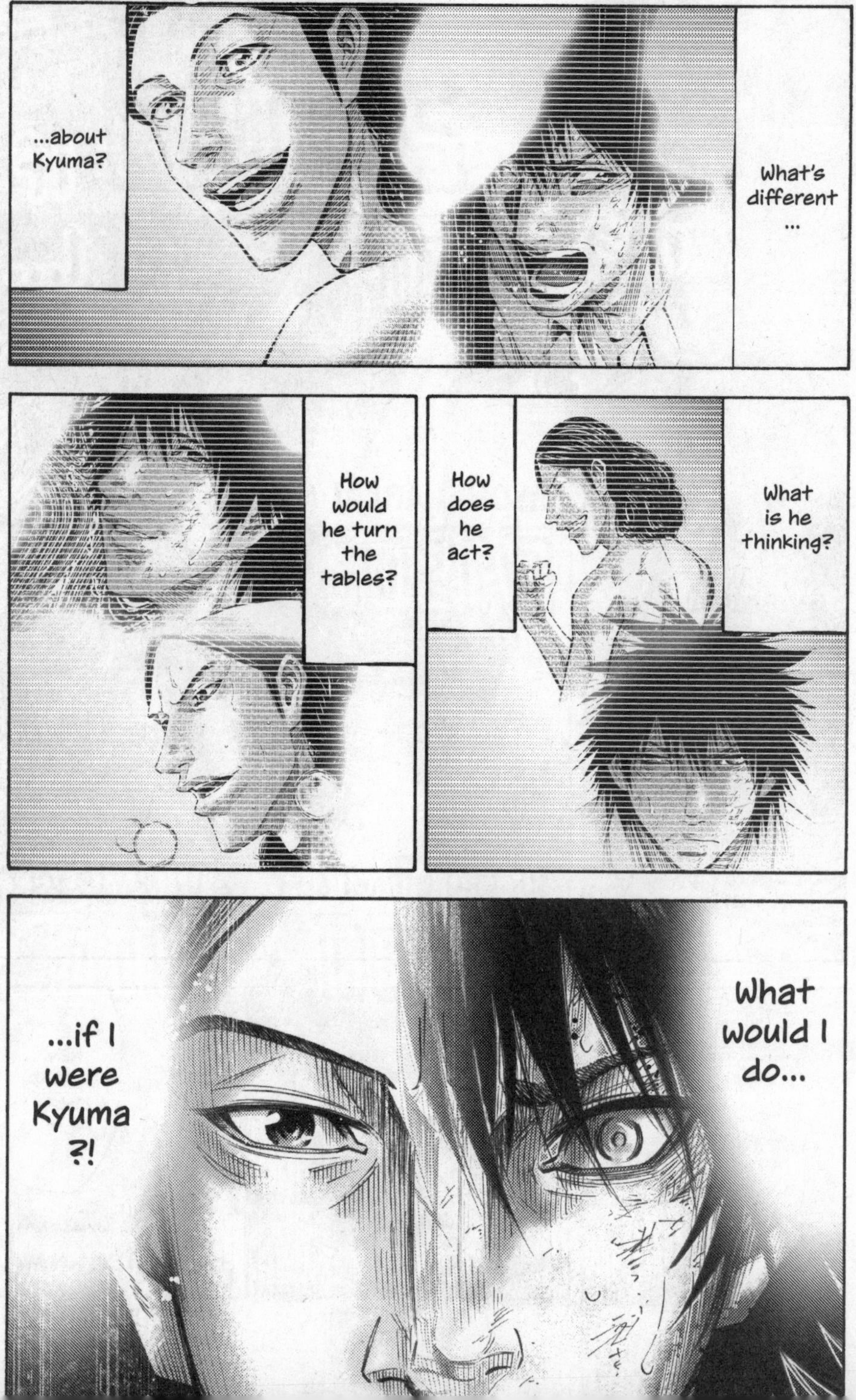
What's different ...
...about Kyuma?
What is he thinking?
How does he act?
How would he turn the tables?
What would I do...
...if I were Kyuma ?!

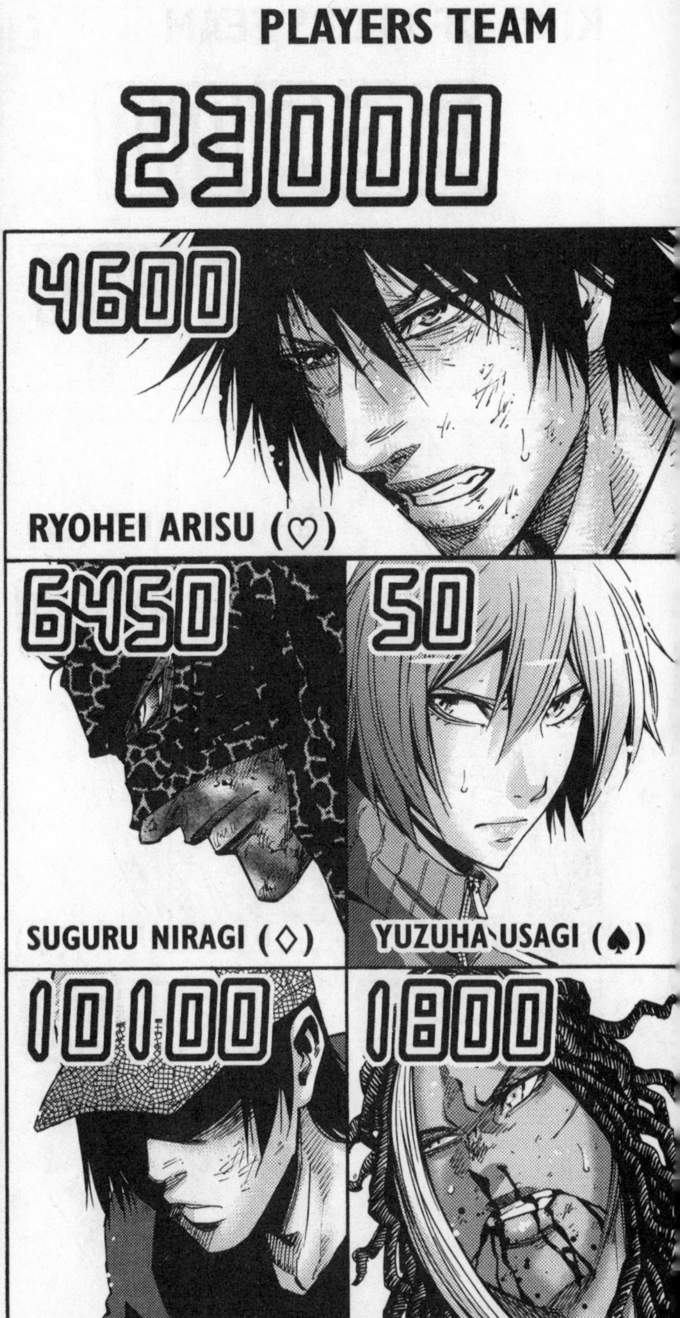
PLAYERS TEAM
23000
4600
RYOHEI ARISU (♡)
50
YUZUHA USAGI (♠)
6450
SUGURU NIRAGI (◇)
1800
HIKARI KUINA (♠)
10100
KODAI TATTA (♣)

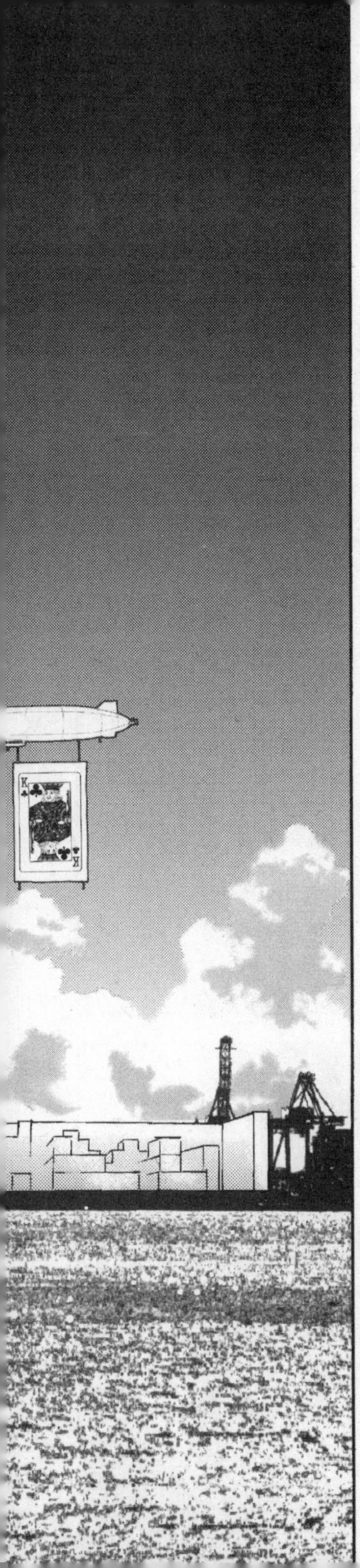

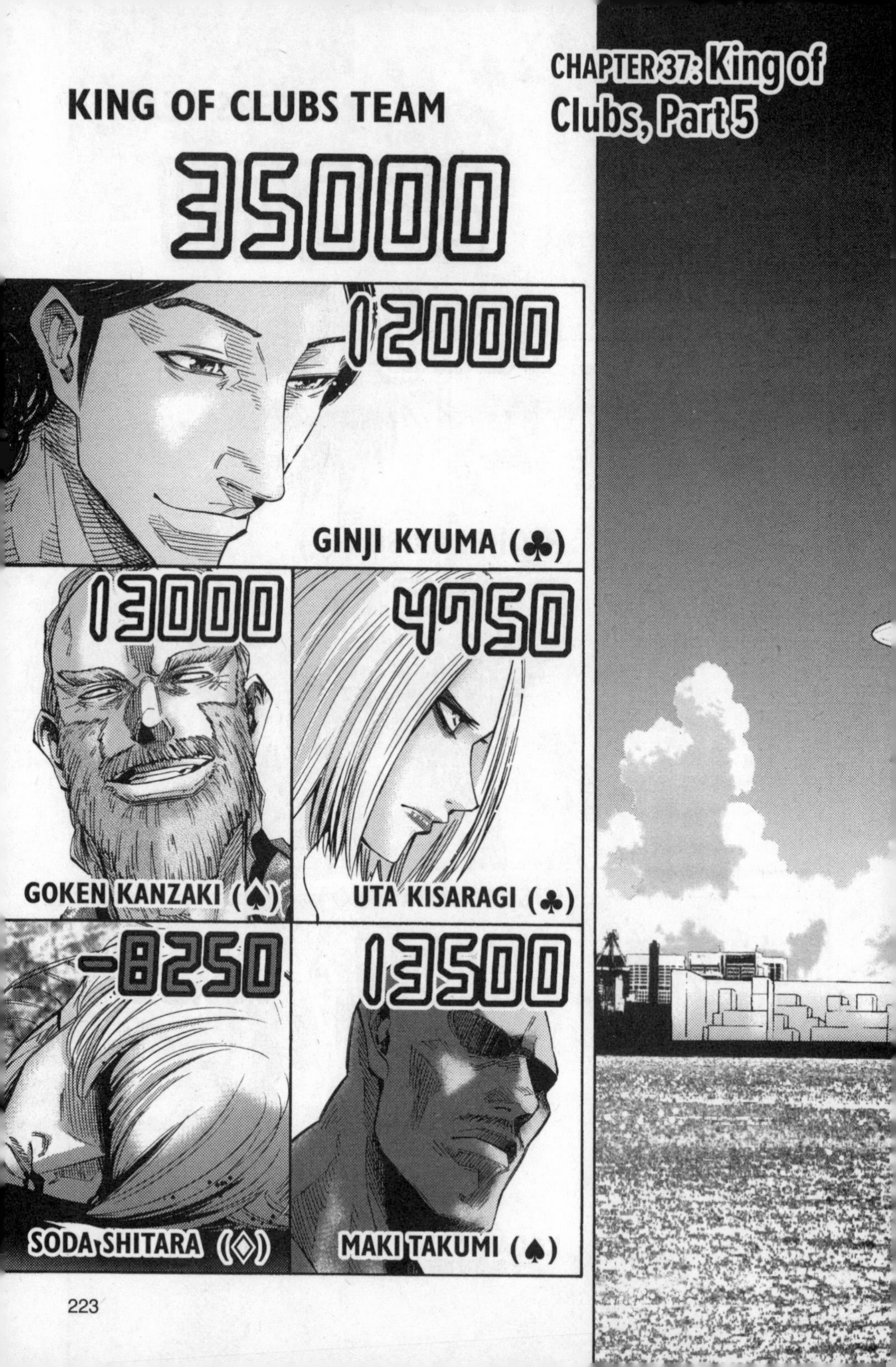
CHAPTER 37: King of Clubs, Part 5
KING OF CLUBS TEAM
35000
12000
GINJI KYUMA (♣)
4750
UTA KISARAGI (♣)
13000
GOKEN KANZAKI (♠)
13500
MAKI TAKUMI (♠)
-8250
SODA SHITARA (◊)

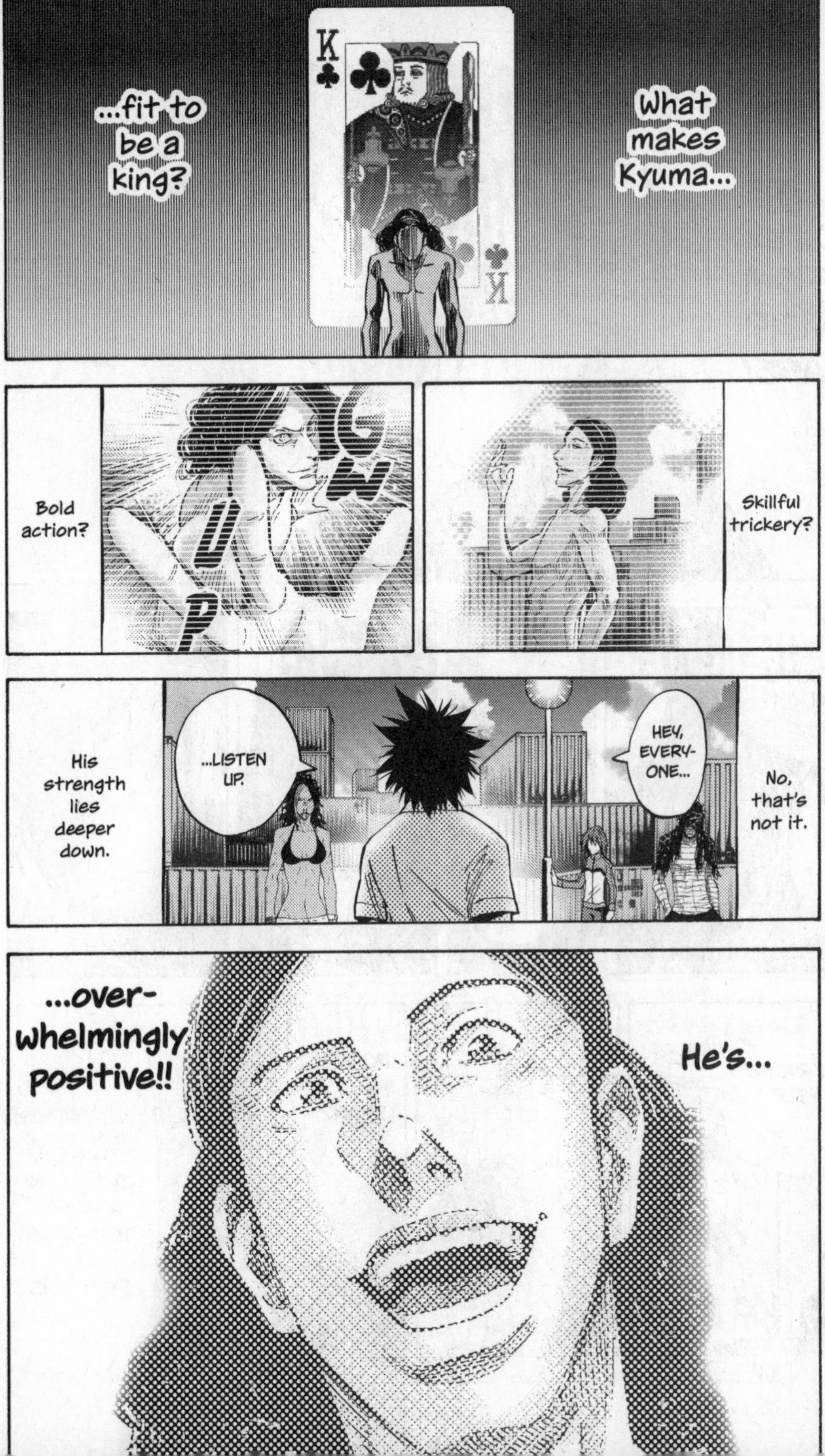
What makes Kyuma...
...fit to be a king?
Skillful trickery?
Bold action?
No, that's not it.
HEY, EVERY-ONE...
...LISTEN UP.
His strength lies deeper down.
He's...
...over-whelmingly positive!!

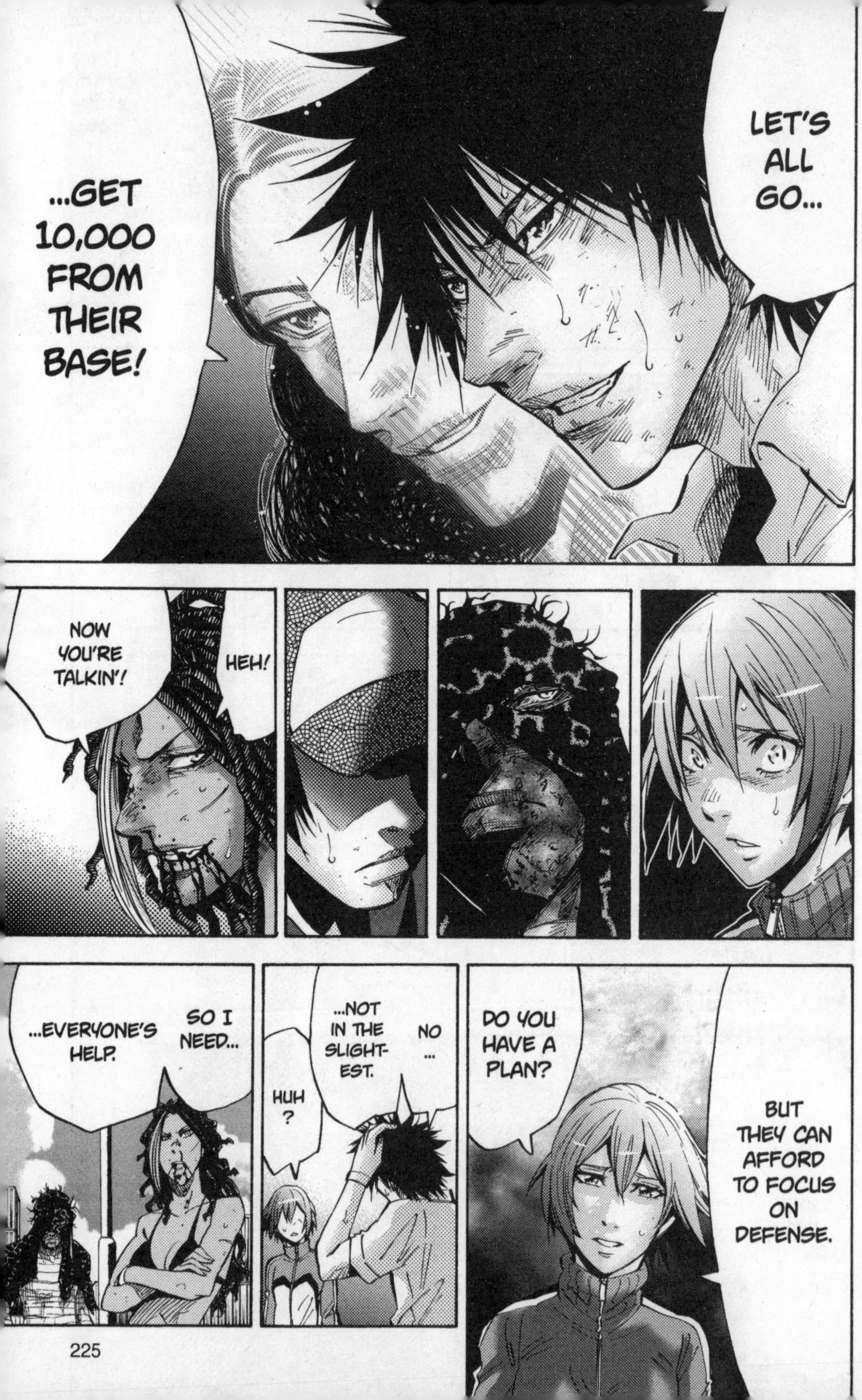
LET'S ALL GO...
...GET 10,000 FROM THEIR BASE!
HEH!
NOW YOU'RE TALKIN'!
BUT THEY CAN AFFORD TO FOCUS ON DEFENSE.
DO YOU HAVE A PLAN?
NO ...
...NOT IN THE SLIGHT-EST.
HUH ?
SO I NEED...
...EVERYONE'S HELP.

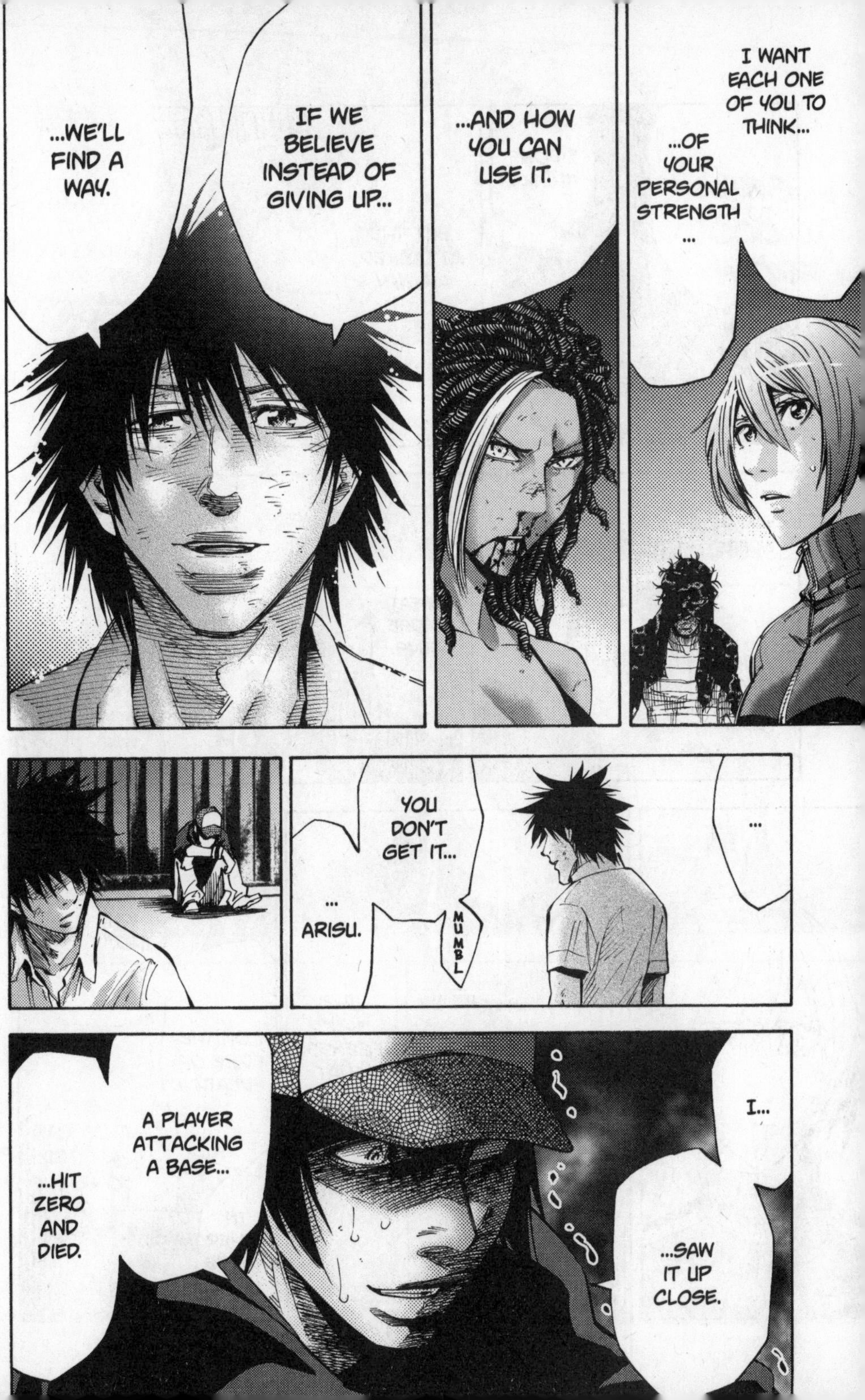
I WANT EACH ONE OF YOU TO THINK...
...OF YOUR PERSONAL STRENGTH...
...AND HOW YOU CAN USE IT.
IF WE BELIEVE INSTEAD OF GIVING UP...
...WE'LL FIND A WAY.
...
YOU DON'T GET IT...
MUMBL
...ARISU.
I...
...SAW IT UP CLOSE.
A PLAYER ATTACKING A BASE...
...HIT ZERO AND DIED.

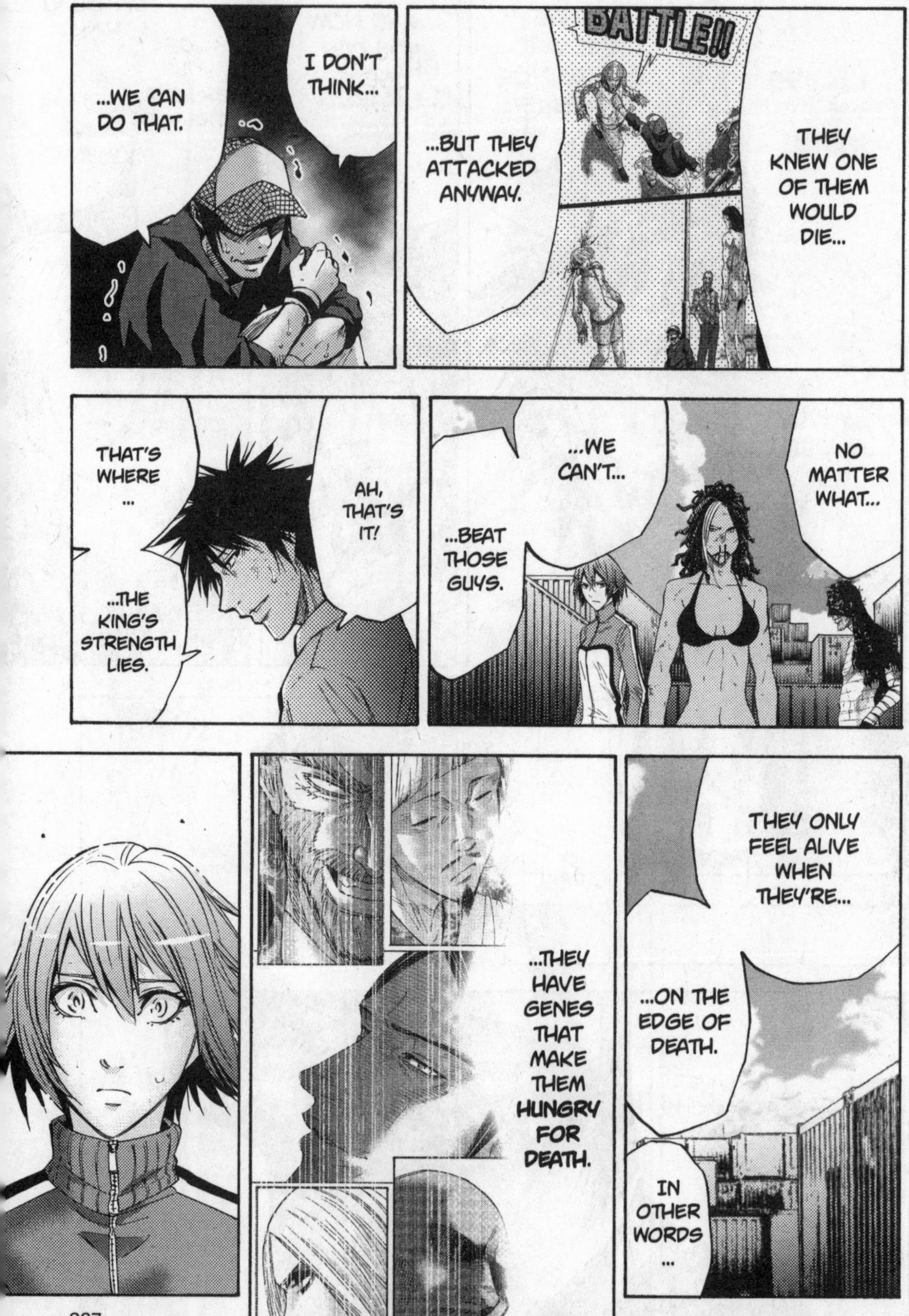
THEY KNEW ONE OF THEM WOULD DIE...
BATTLE!!
...BUT THEY ATTACKED ANYWAY.
I DON'T THINK...
...WE CAN DO THAT.
NO MATTER WHAT...
...WE CAN'T...
...BEAT THOSE GUYS.
AH, THAT'S IT!
THAT'S WHERE ...
...THE KING'S STRENGTH LIES.
THEY ONLY FEEL ALIVE WHEN THEY'RE...
...ON THE EDGE OF DEATH.
IN OTHER WORDS ...
...THEY HAVE GENES THAT MAKE THEM HUNGRY FOR DEATH.

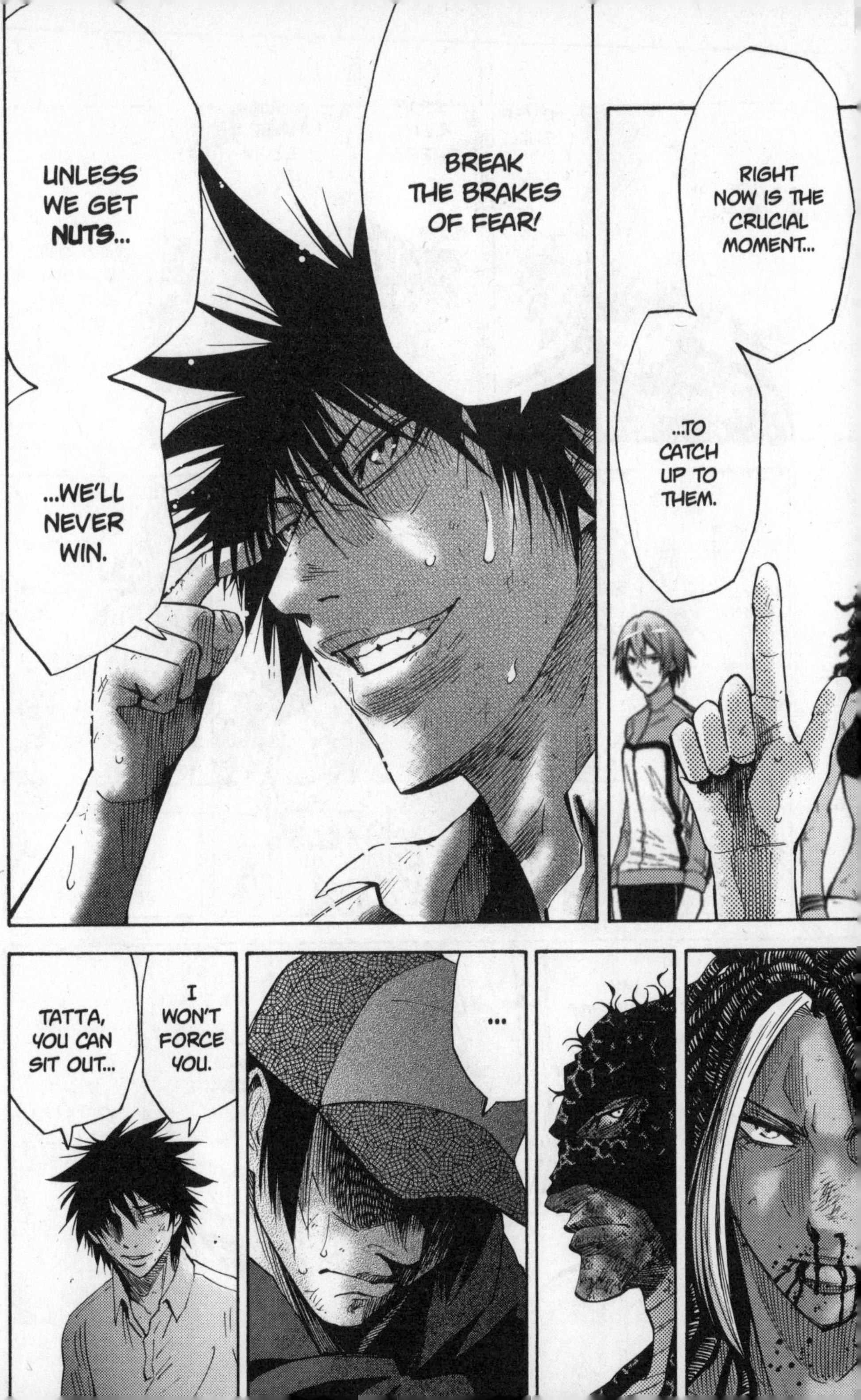
RIGHT NOW IS THE CRUCIAL MOMENT...
...TO CATCH UP TO THEM.
BREAK THE BRAKES OF FEAR!
UNLESS WE GET NUTS...
...WE'LL NEVER WIN.
...
I WON'T FORCE YOU.
TATTA, YOU CAN SIT OUT...

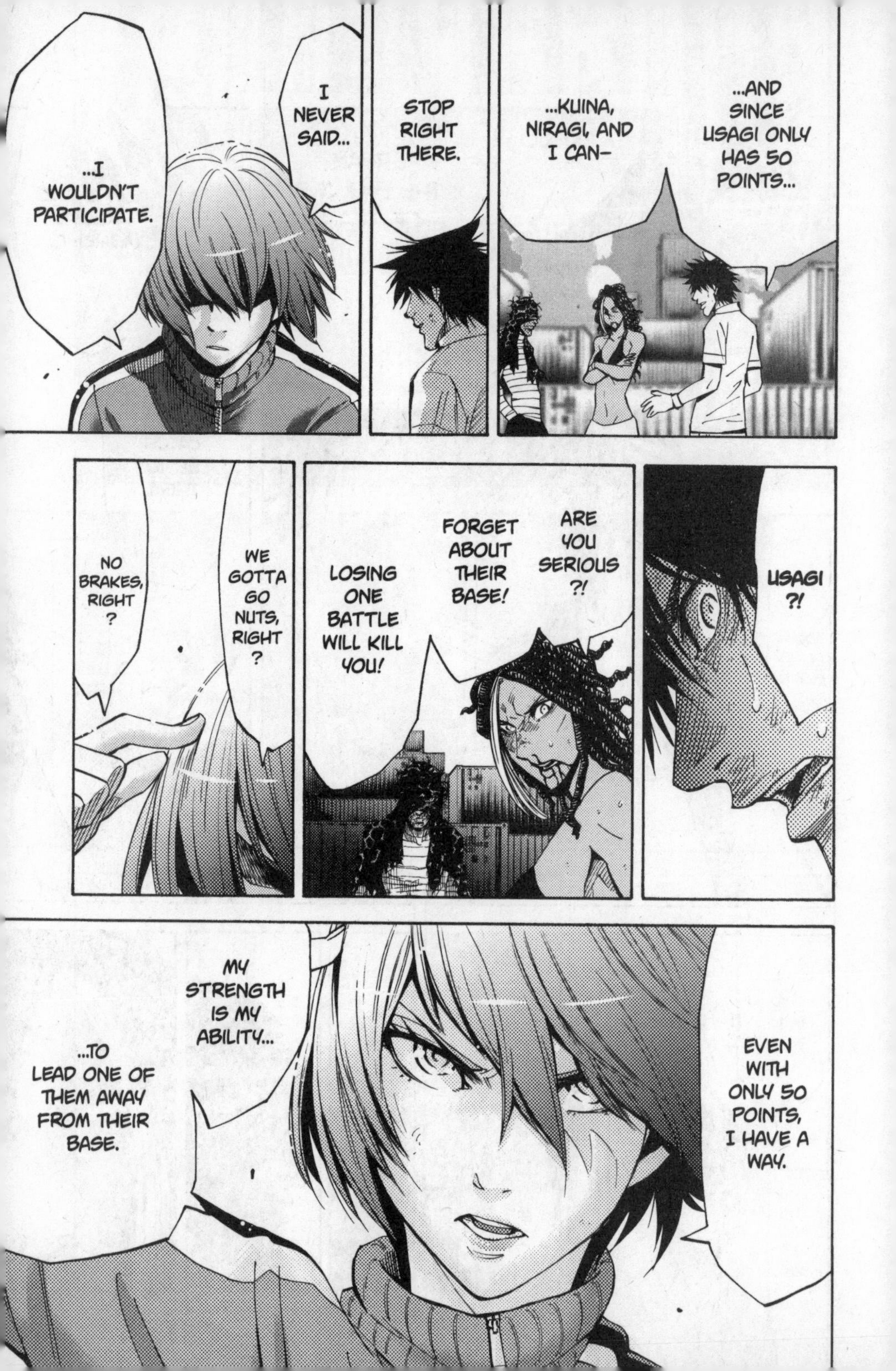
...AND SINCE USAGI ONLY HAS 50 POINTS...
...KUINA, NIRAGI, AND I CAN–
STOP RIGHT THERE.
I NEVER SAID...
...I WOULDN'T PARTICIPATE.
USAGI?!
ARE YOU SERIOUS?!
FORGET ABOUT THEIR BASE!
LOSING ONE BATTLE WILL KILL YOU!
WE GOTTA GO NUTS, RIGHT?
NO BRAKES, RIGHT?
EVEN WITH ONLY 50 POINTS, I HAVE A WAY.
MY STRENGTH IS MY ABILITY...
...TO LEAD ONE OF THEM AWAY FROM THEIR BASE.

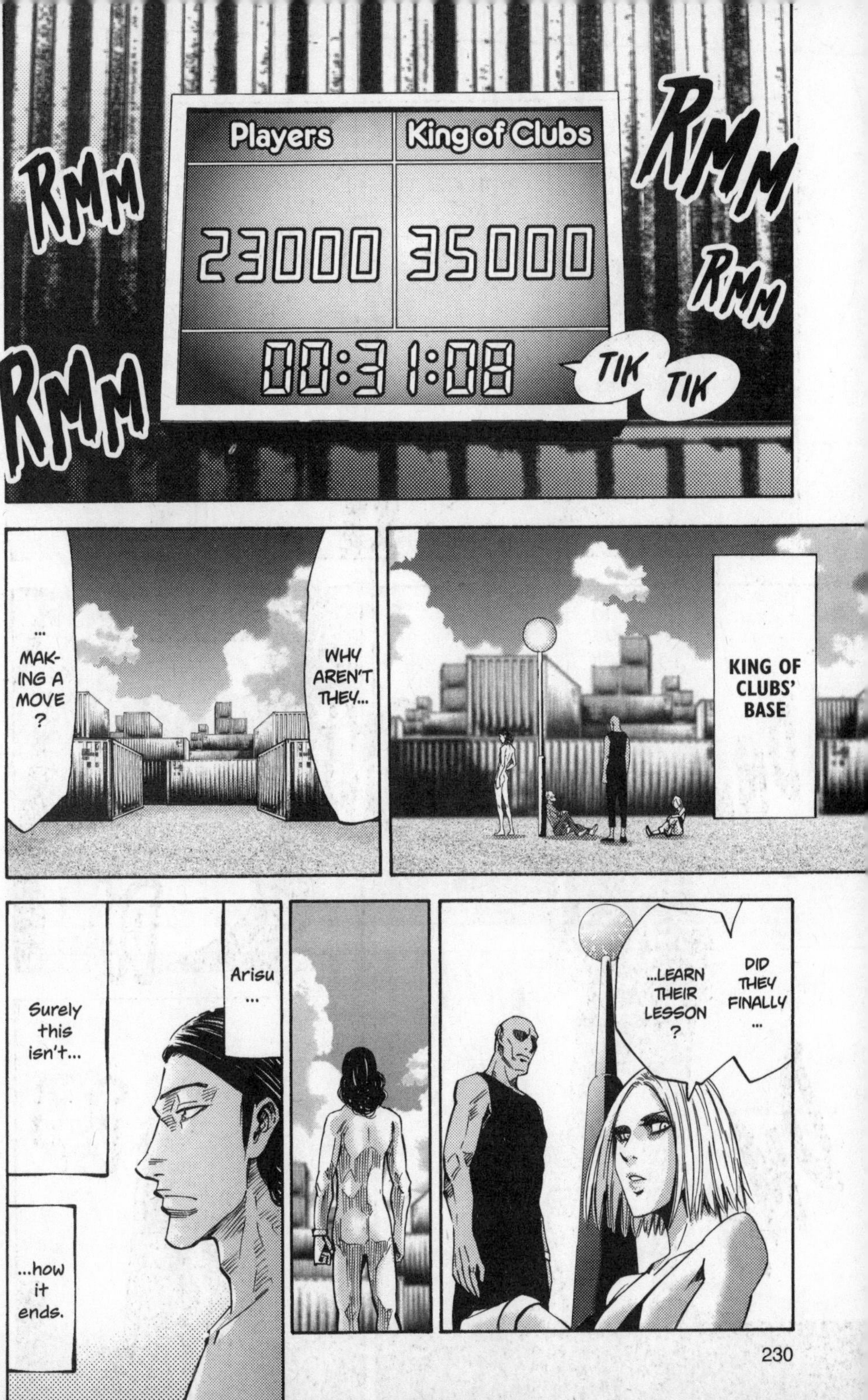
RMM
Players
King of Clubs
23000
35000
RMM
RMM
00:31:08
TIK TIK
RMM
KING OF CLUBS' BASE
WHY AREN'T THEY...
... MAKING A MOVE ?
DID THEY FINALLY ...
...LEARN THEIR LESSON ?
Arisu ...
Surely this isn't...
...how it ends.

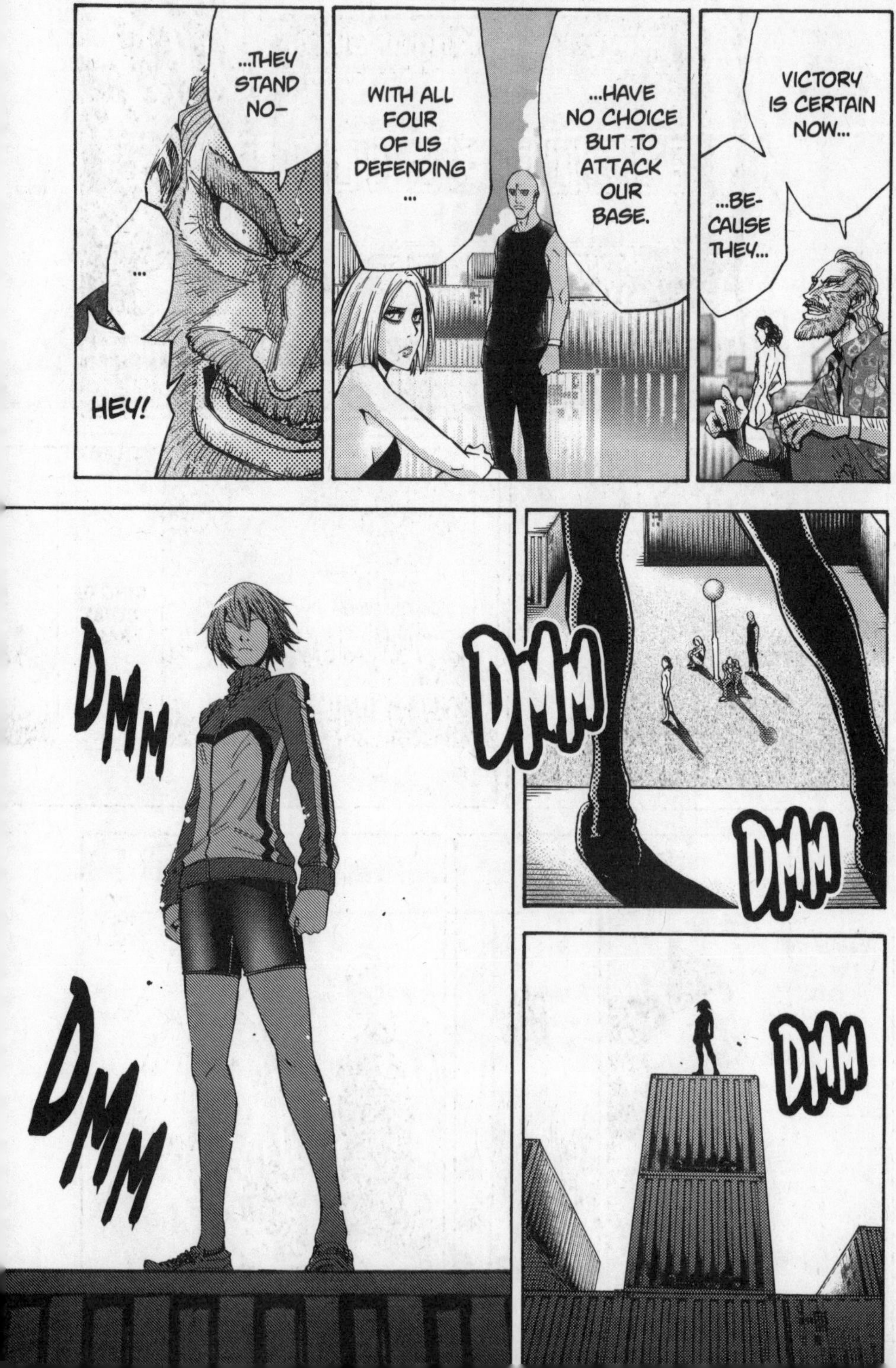
VICTORY IS CERTAIN NOW...
...BE-CAUSE THEY...
...HAVE NO CHOICE BUT TO ATTACK OUR BASE.
WITH ALL FOUR OF US DEFENDING ...
...THEY STAND NO-
...
HEY!
DMM
DMM
DMM
DMM
DMM

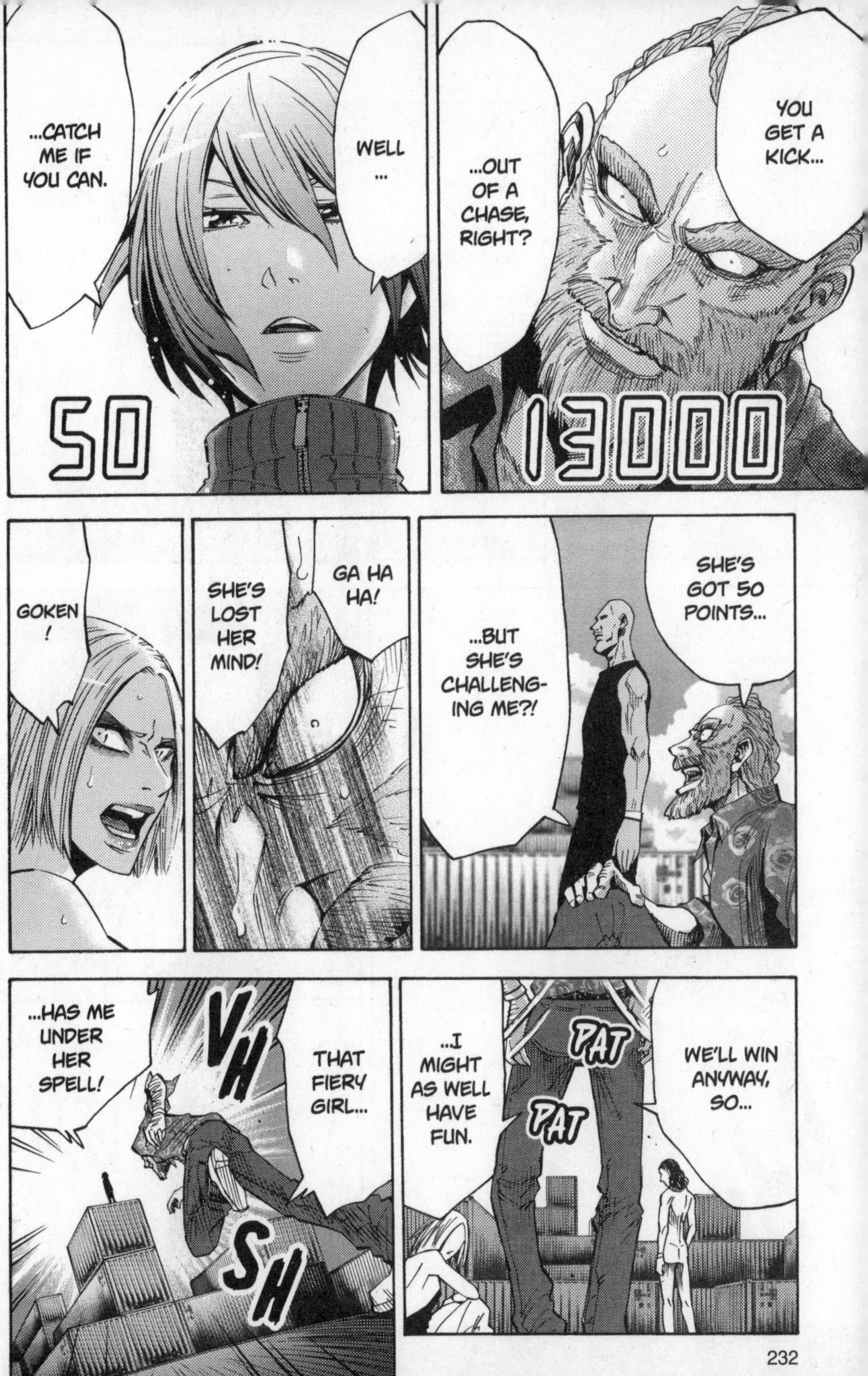
YOU GET A KICK...
...OUT OF A CHASE, RIGHT?
13000
WELL ...
...CATCH ME IF YOU CAN.
50
SHE'S GOT 50 POINTS...
...BUT SHE'S CHALLENG-ING ME?!
GA HA HA!
SHE'S LOST HER MIND!
GOKEN!
WE'LL WIN ANYWAY, SO...
PAT
PAT
...I MIGHT AS WELL HAVE FUN.
THAT FIERY GIRL...
VH
...HAS ME UNDER HER SPELL!
SH

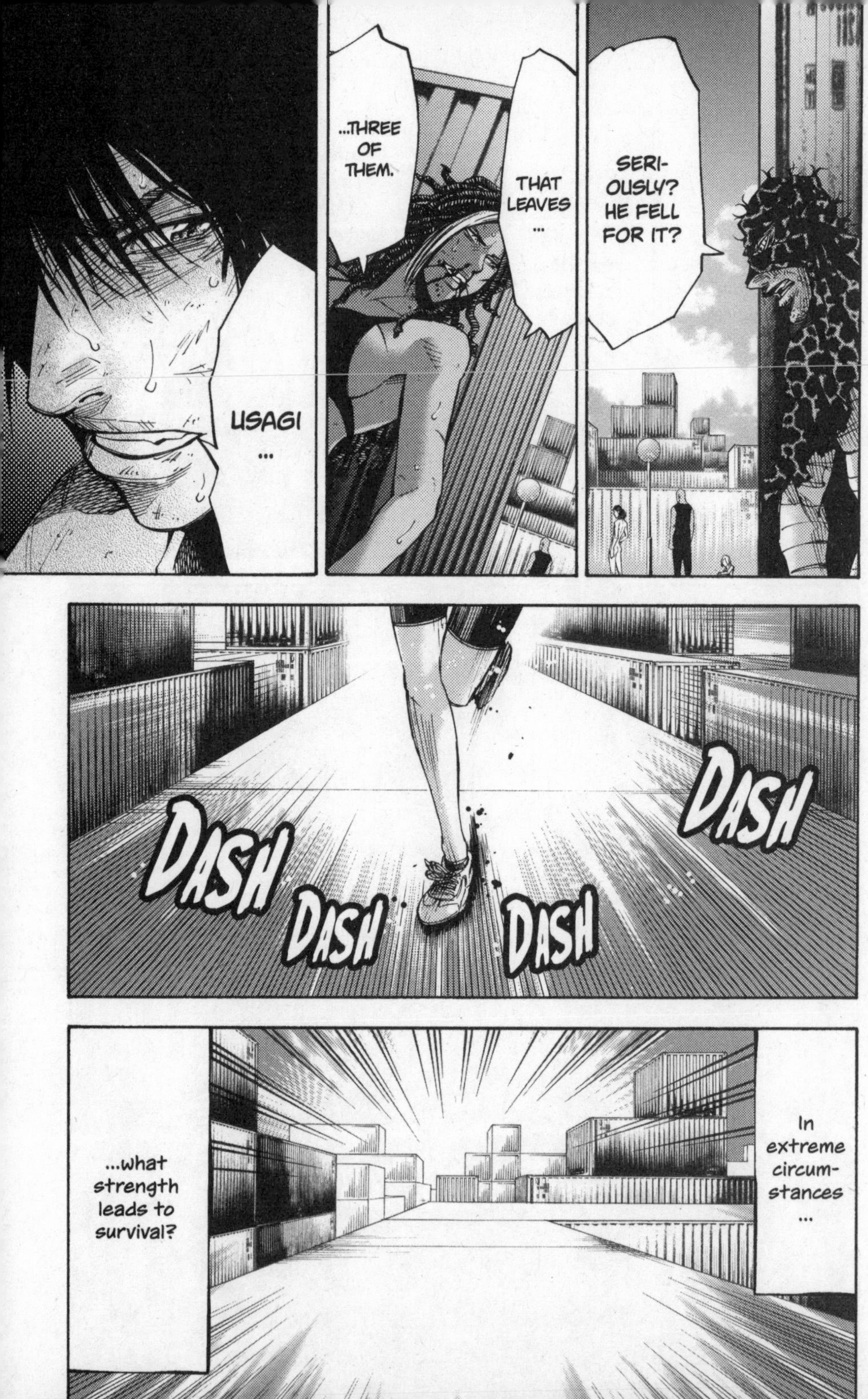
SERI-OUSLY? HE FELL FOR IT?
THAT LEAVES ...
...THREE OF THEM.
USAGI ...
DASH
DASH
DASH
DASH
In extreme circum-stances ...
...what strength leads to survival?

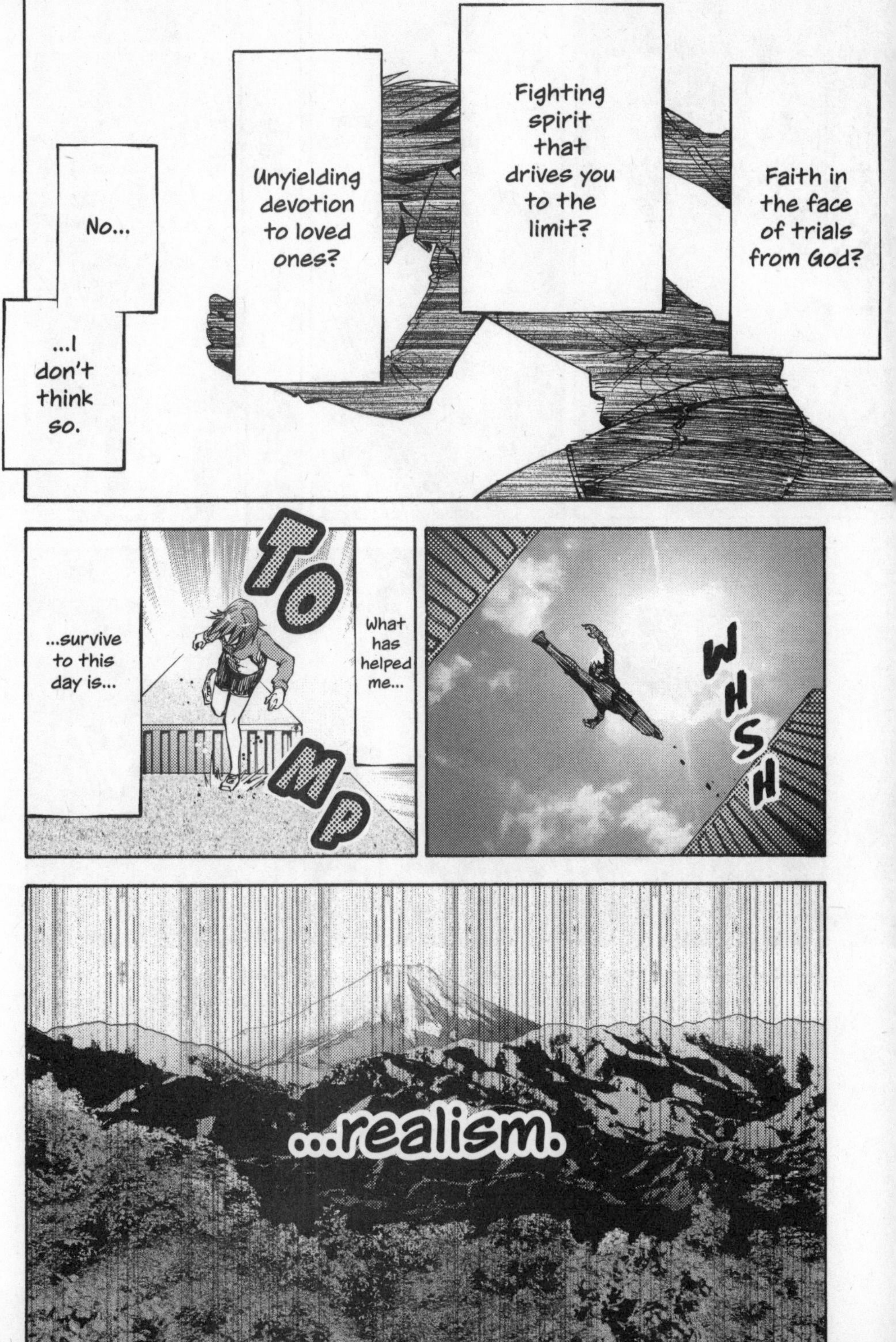
Faith in the face of trials from God?
Fighting spirit that drives you to the limit?
Unyielding devotion to loved ones?
No...
...I don't think so.
WHSH
What has helped me...
TOMP
...survive to this day is...
...realism.

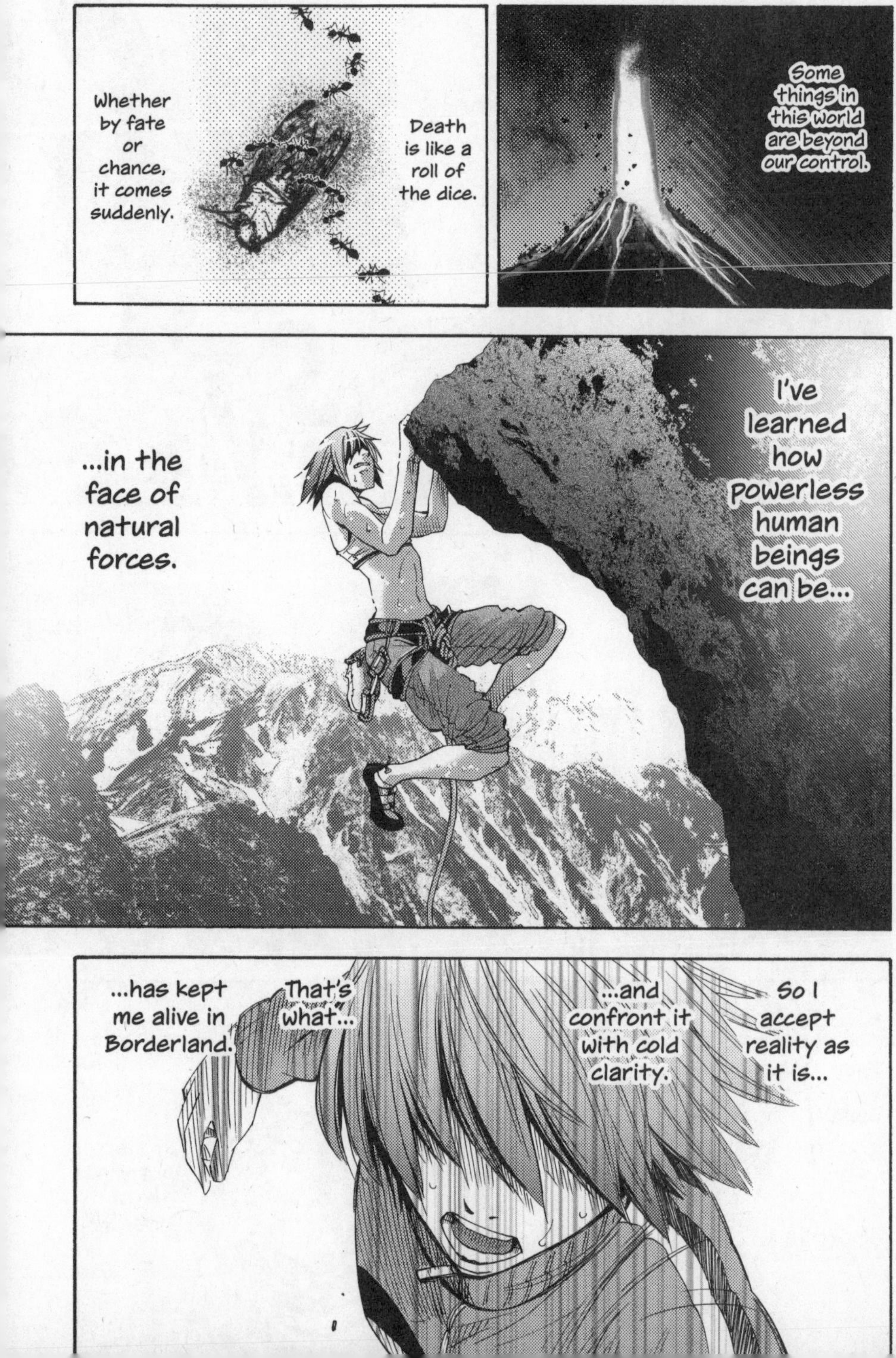
Some things in this world are beyond our control.
Death is like a roll of the dice.
Whether by fate or chance, it comes suddenly.
I've learned how powerless human beings can be...
...in the face of natural forces.
So I accept reality as it is...
...and confront it with cold clarity.
That's what...
...has kept me alive in Borderland.

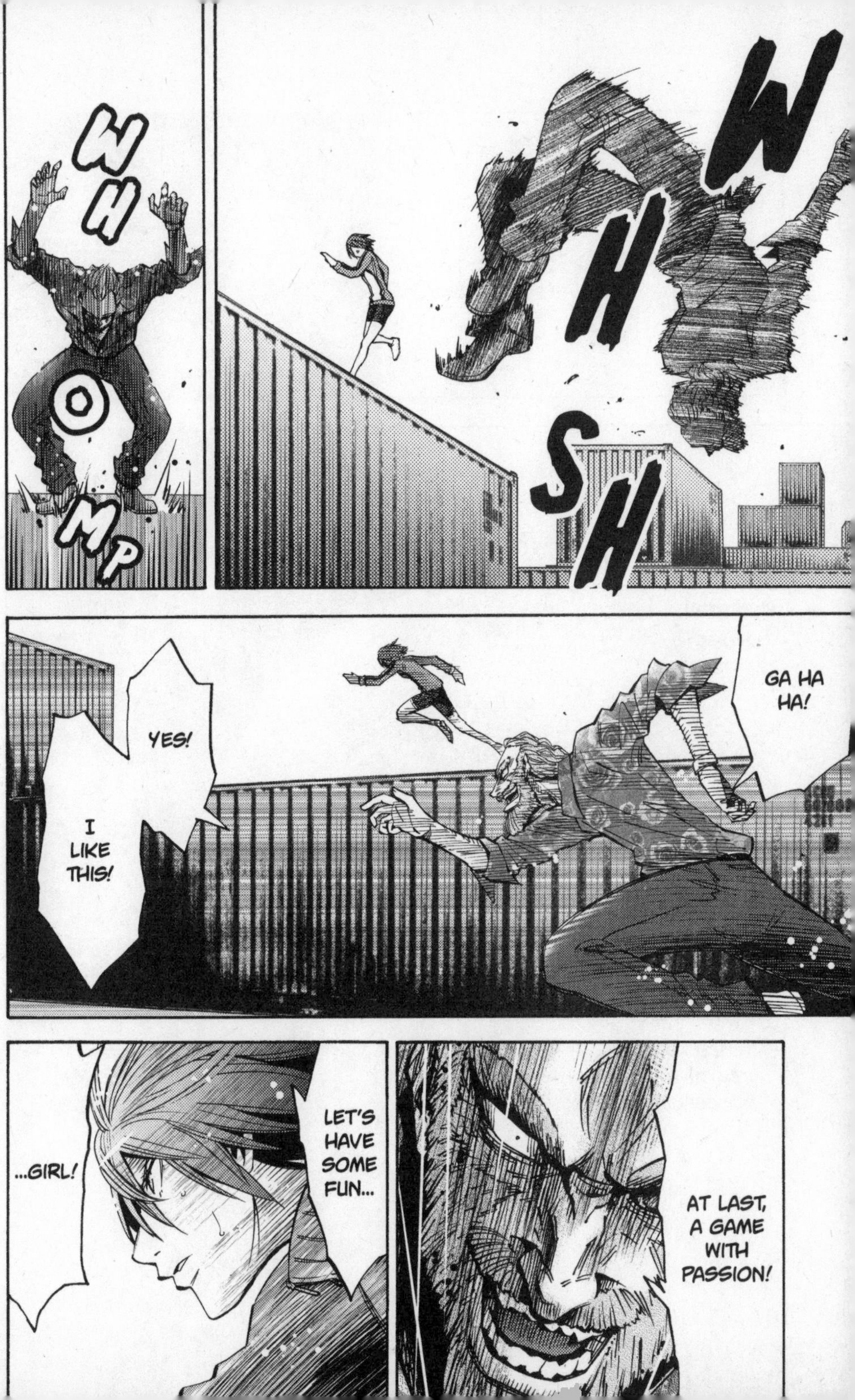
WHSH
WHOMP
GA HA HA!
YES!
I LIKE THIS!
AT LAST, A GAME WITH PASSION!
LET'S HAVE SOME FUN...
...GIRL!

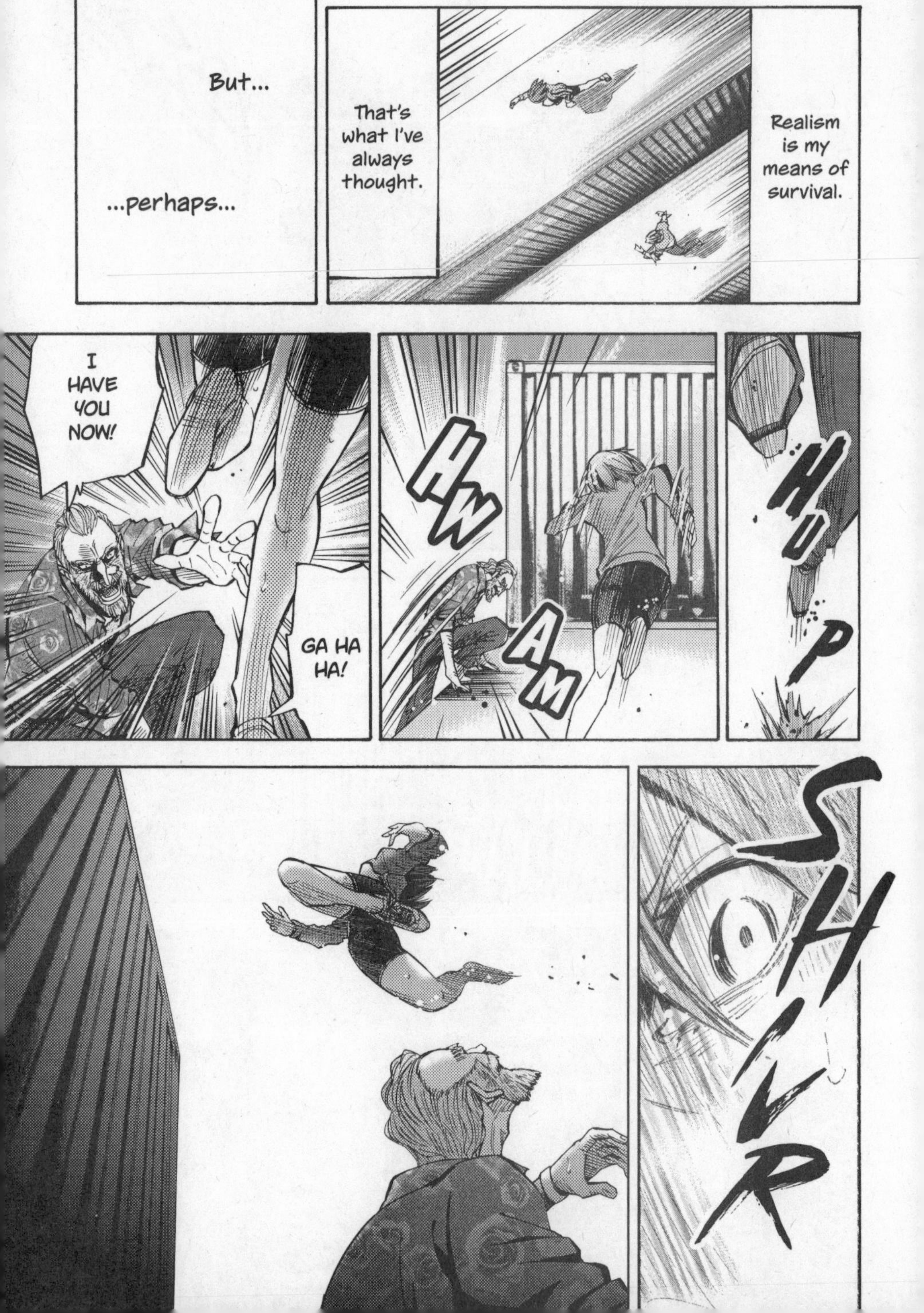
Realism is my means of survival.
That's what I've always thought.
But...
...perhaps...
HUP
WHAM
I HAVE YOU NOW!
GA HA HA!
SHIVR

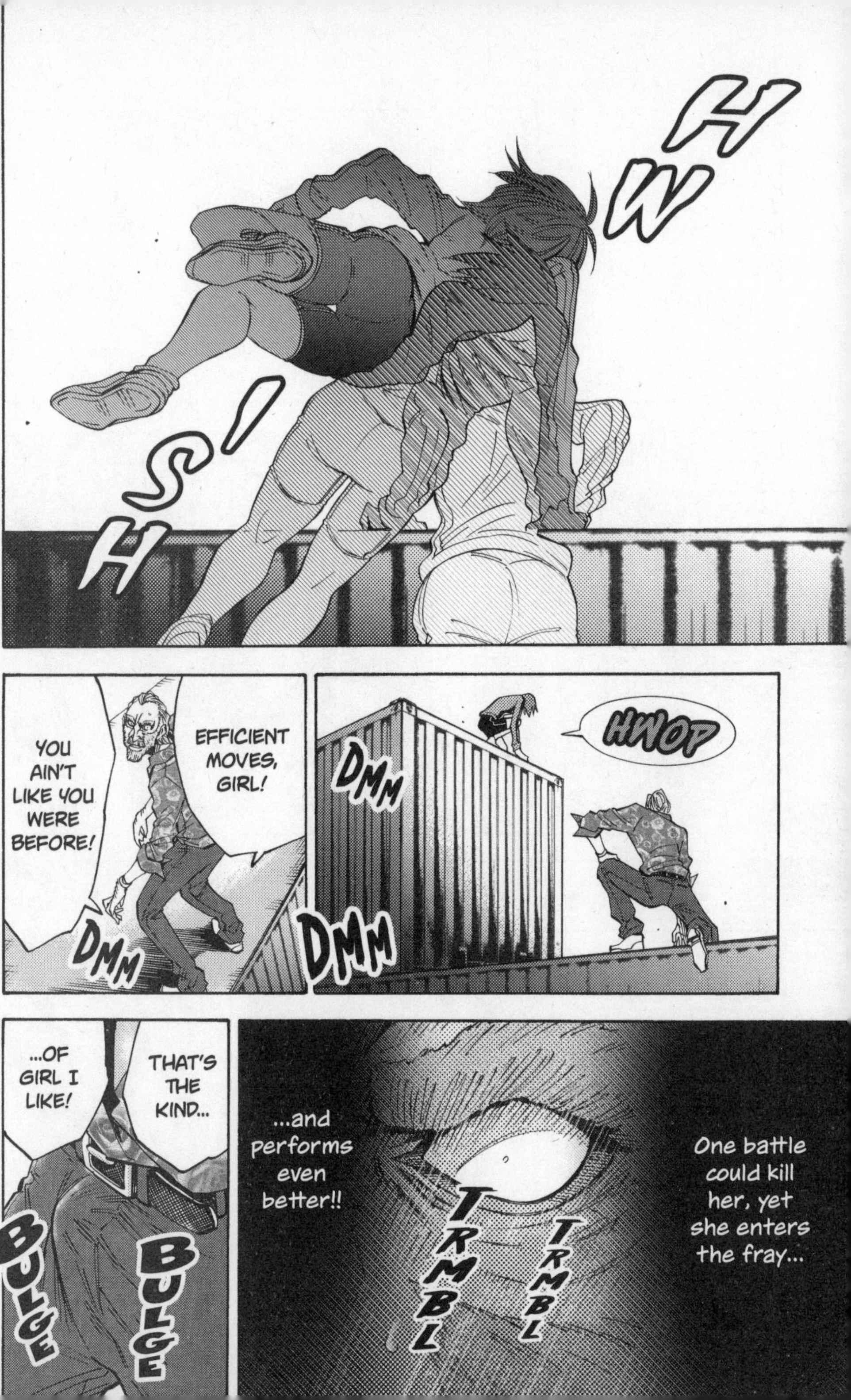
HWISH
HWOP
DMM
DMM
EFFICIENT MOVES, GIRL!
YOU AIN'T LIKE YOU WERE BEFORE!
DMM
One battle could kill her, yet she enters the fray...
...and performs even better!!
TRMBL
TRMBL
THAT'S THE KIND...
...OF GIRL I LIKE!
BULGE
BULGE

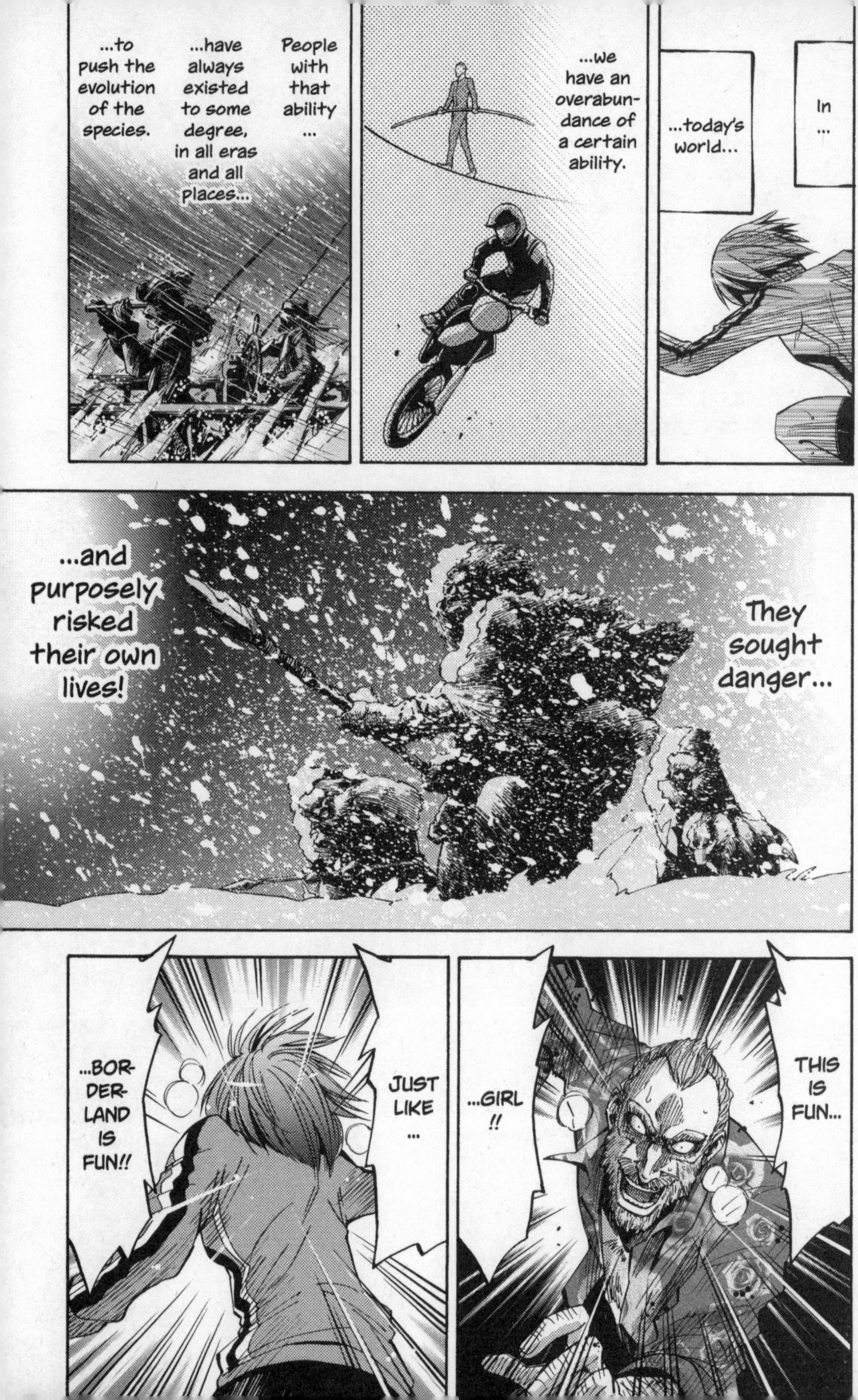
In ...
...today's world...
...we have an overabundance of a certain ability.
People with that ability ...
...have always existed to some degree, in all eras and all places...
...to push the evolution of the species.
They sought danger...
...and purposely risked their own lives!
THIS IS FUN...
...GIRL!!
JUST LIKE ...
...BORDERLAND IS FUN!!

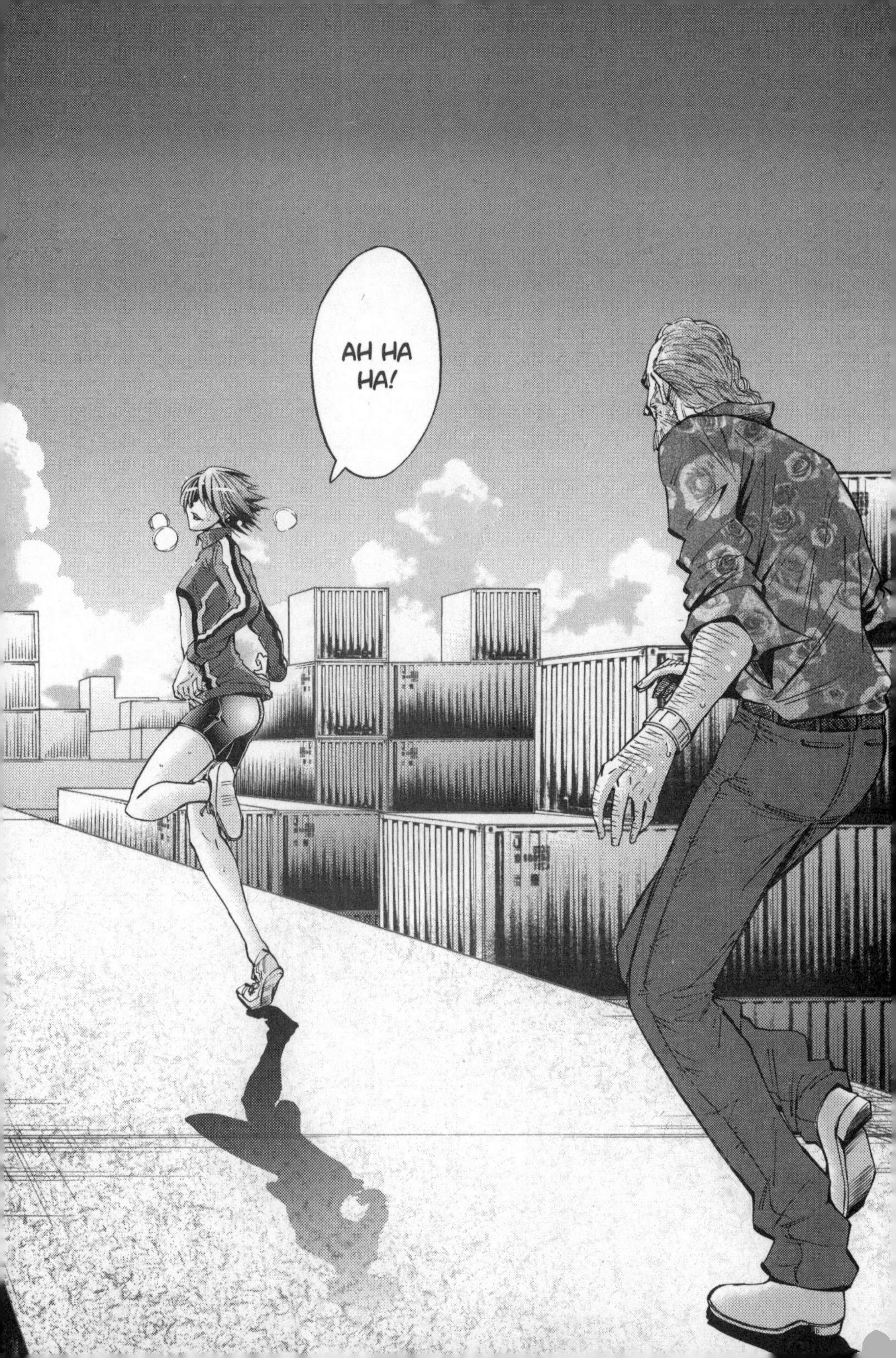
AH HA HA!

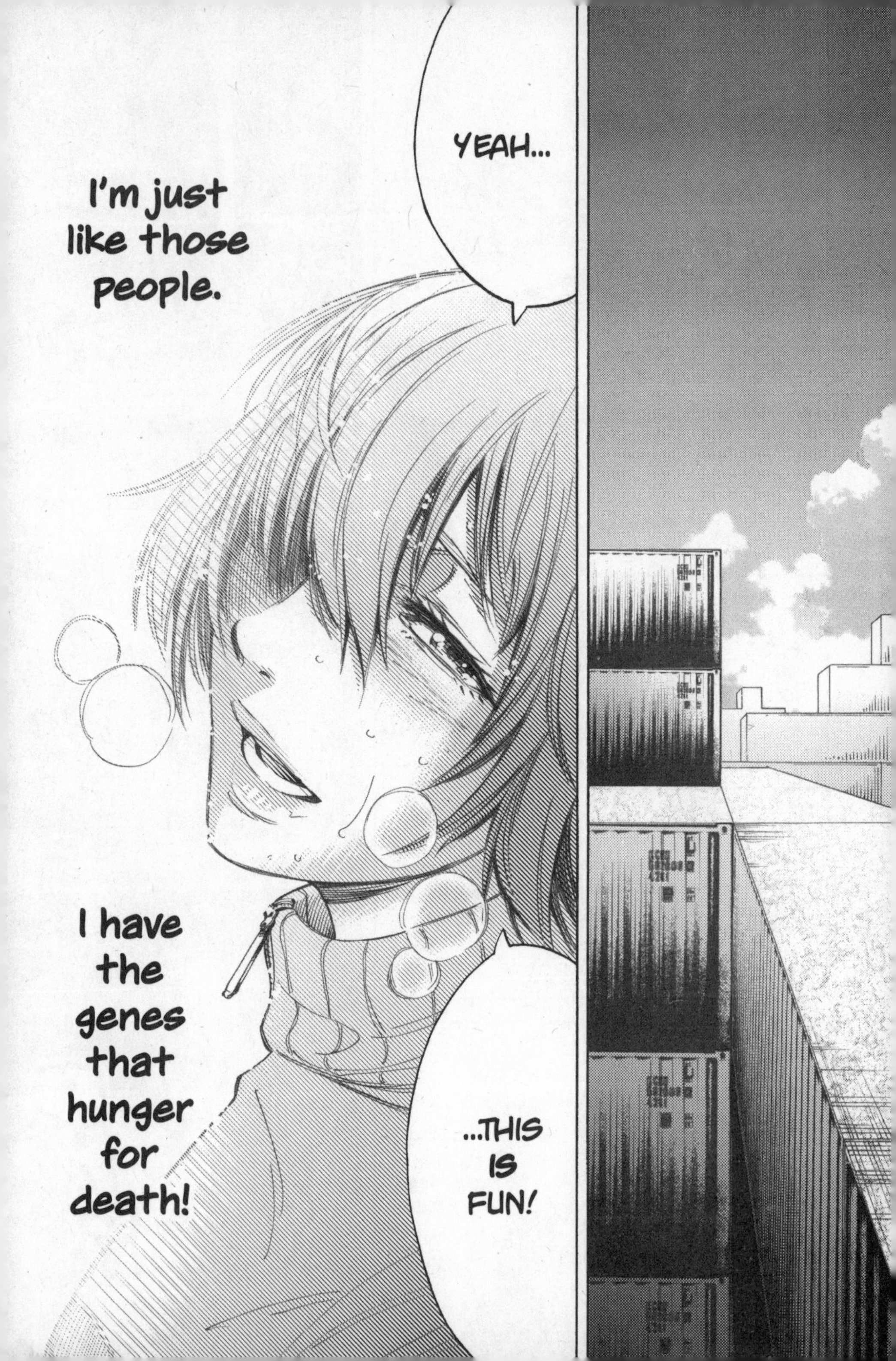
YEAH...
I'm just like those people.
...THIS IS FUN!
I have the genes that hunger for death!

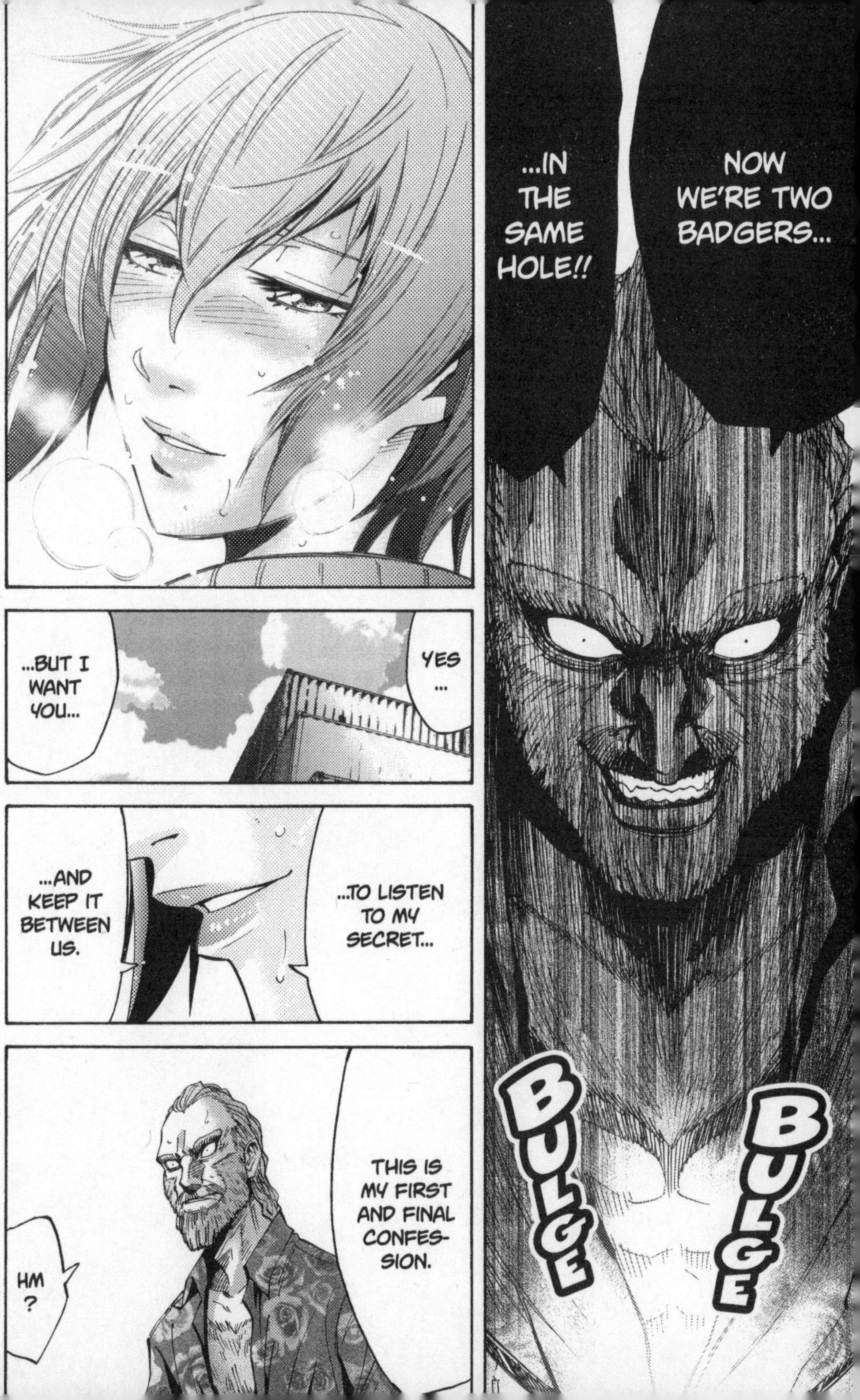
NOW WE'RE TWO BADGERS...
...IN THE SAME HOLE!!
BULGE
BULGE
YES...
...BUT I WANT YOU...
...TO LISTEN TO MY SECRET...
...AND KEEP IT BETWEEN US.
THIS IS MY FIRST AND FINAL CONFESSION.
HM?

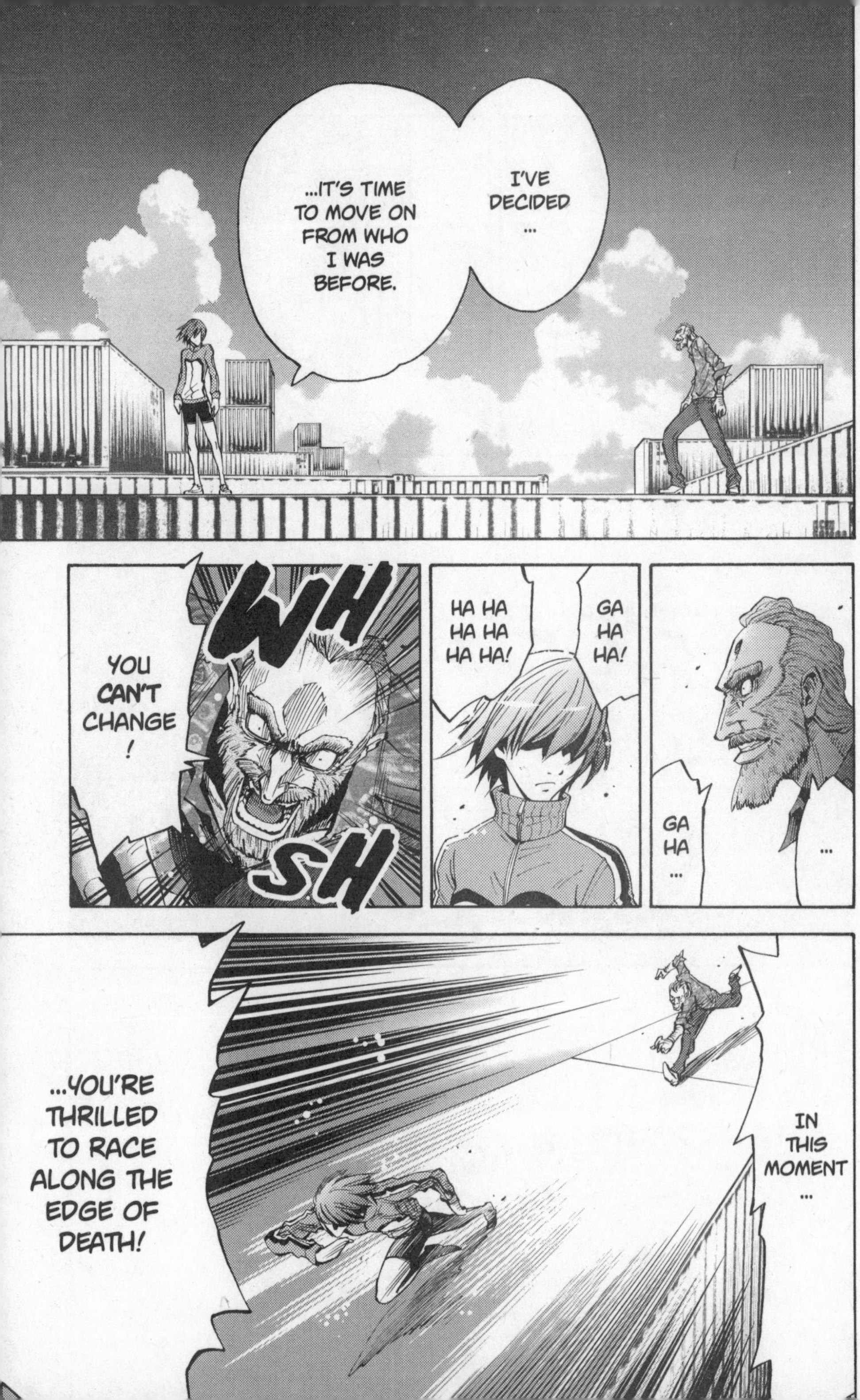
I'VE DECIDED ...
...IT'S TIME TO MOVE ON FROM WHO I WAS BEFORE.
GA HA ...
...
GA HA HA!
HA HA HA HA HA HA!
YOU CAN'T CHANGE!
WHSH
IN THIS MOMENT ...
...YOU'RE THRILLED TO RACE ALONG THE EDGE OF DEATH!

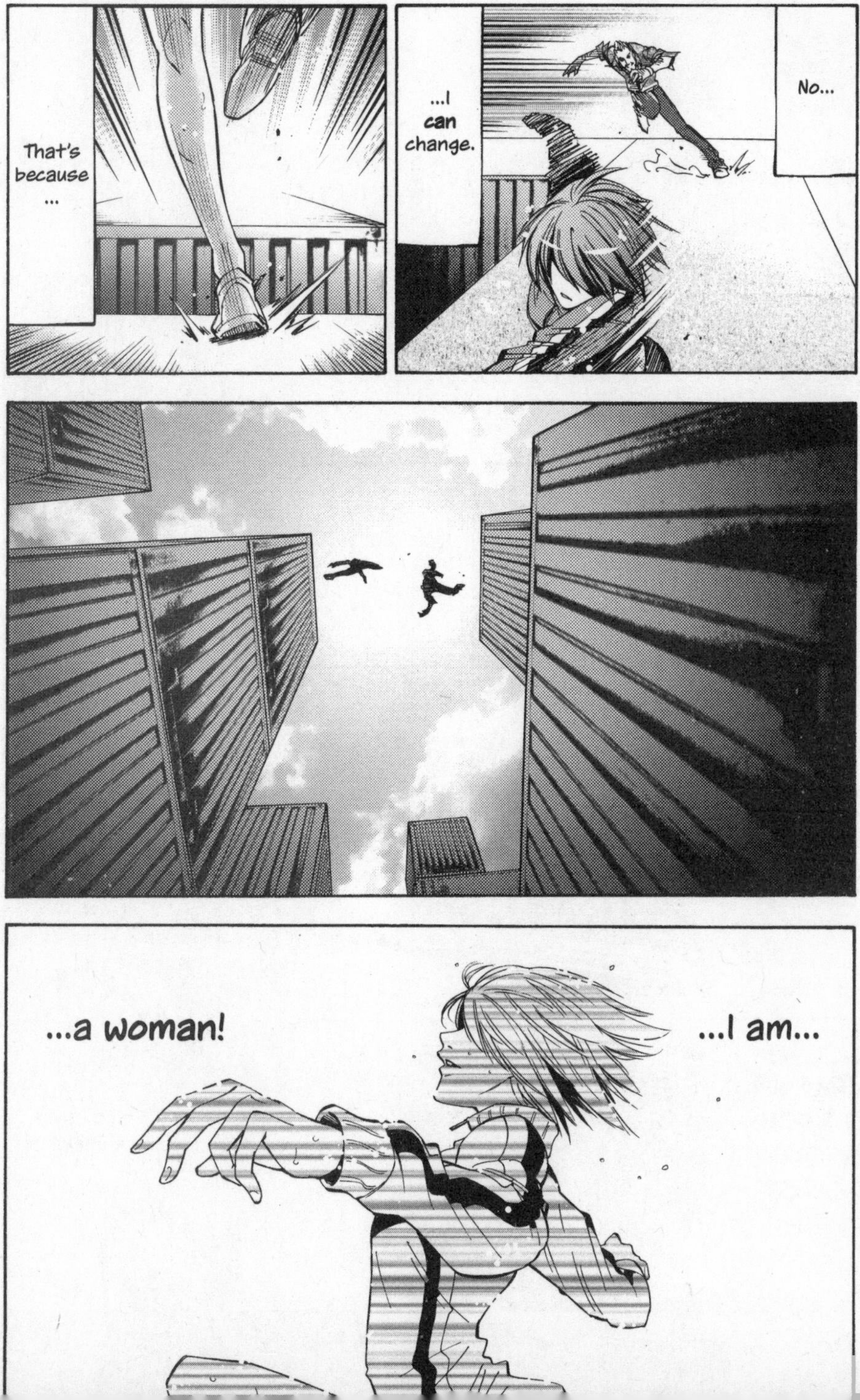
No...
...I can change.
That's because ...
...I am...
...a woman!

...made up my mind.

I've finally...

"...AND DO LIFE OVER."

"I WANT TO GO BACK TO THAT WORLD..."

...because I've forgiven that world.

But that's not...

"...OR LIVE IN FEAR OR RUN."

"THIS TIME, I WON'T BLAME ANYONE ELSE..."

You were walking forward...

I'm sorry.

"...MOVE FORWARD AT YOUR SIDE."

"I'M SORRY. I CAN'T..."

...and I stopped you.

"I... I JUST..."

"WHAT THE HELL?!"

245

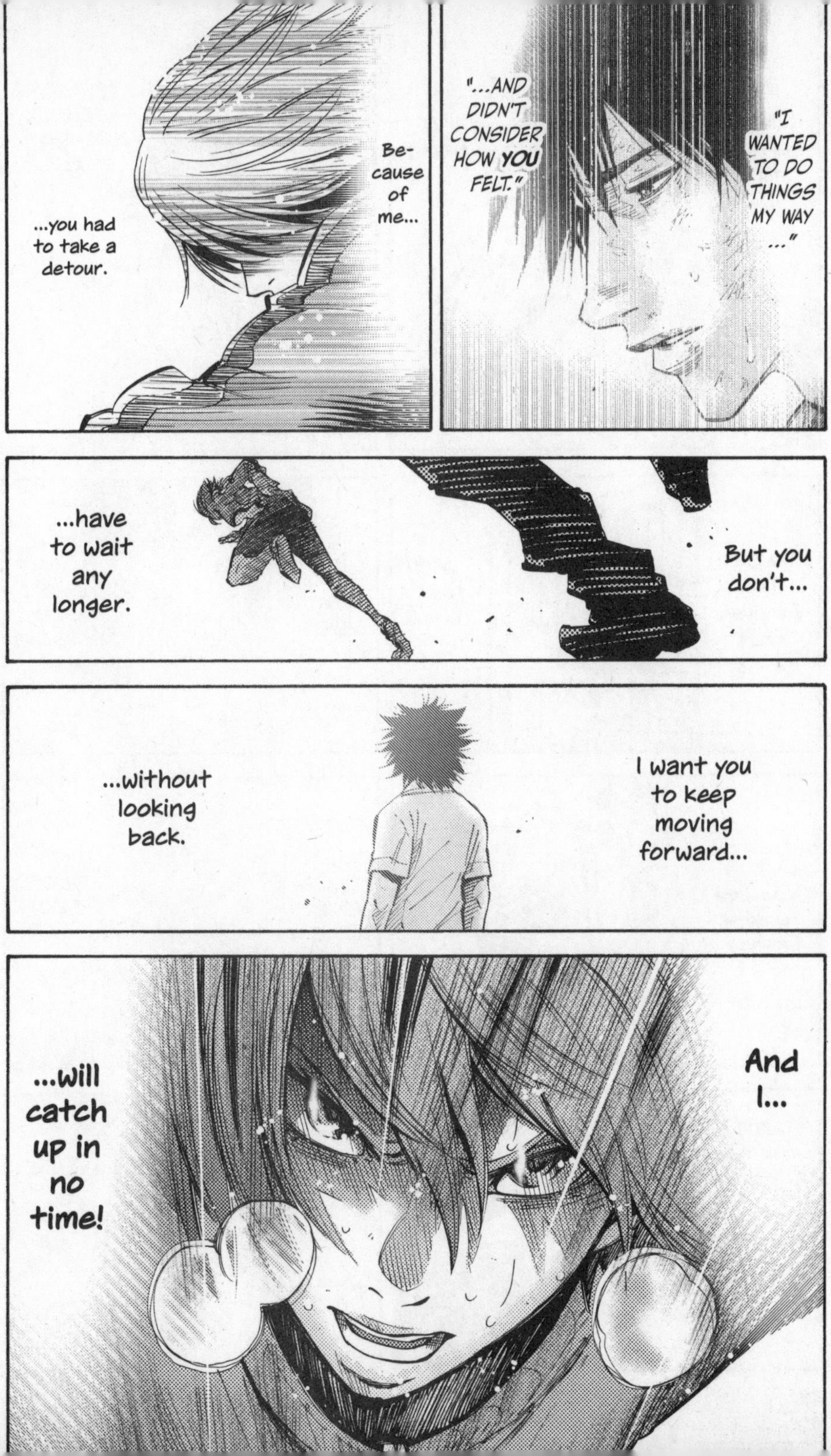
"I WANTED TO DO THINGS MY WAY ..."
"...AND DIDN'T CONSIDER HOW YOU FELT."
Be-cause of me...
...you had to take a detour.
But you don't...
...have to wait any longer.
I want you to keep moving forward...
...without looking back.
And I...
...will catch up in no time!

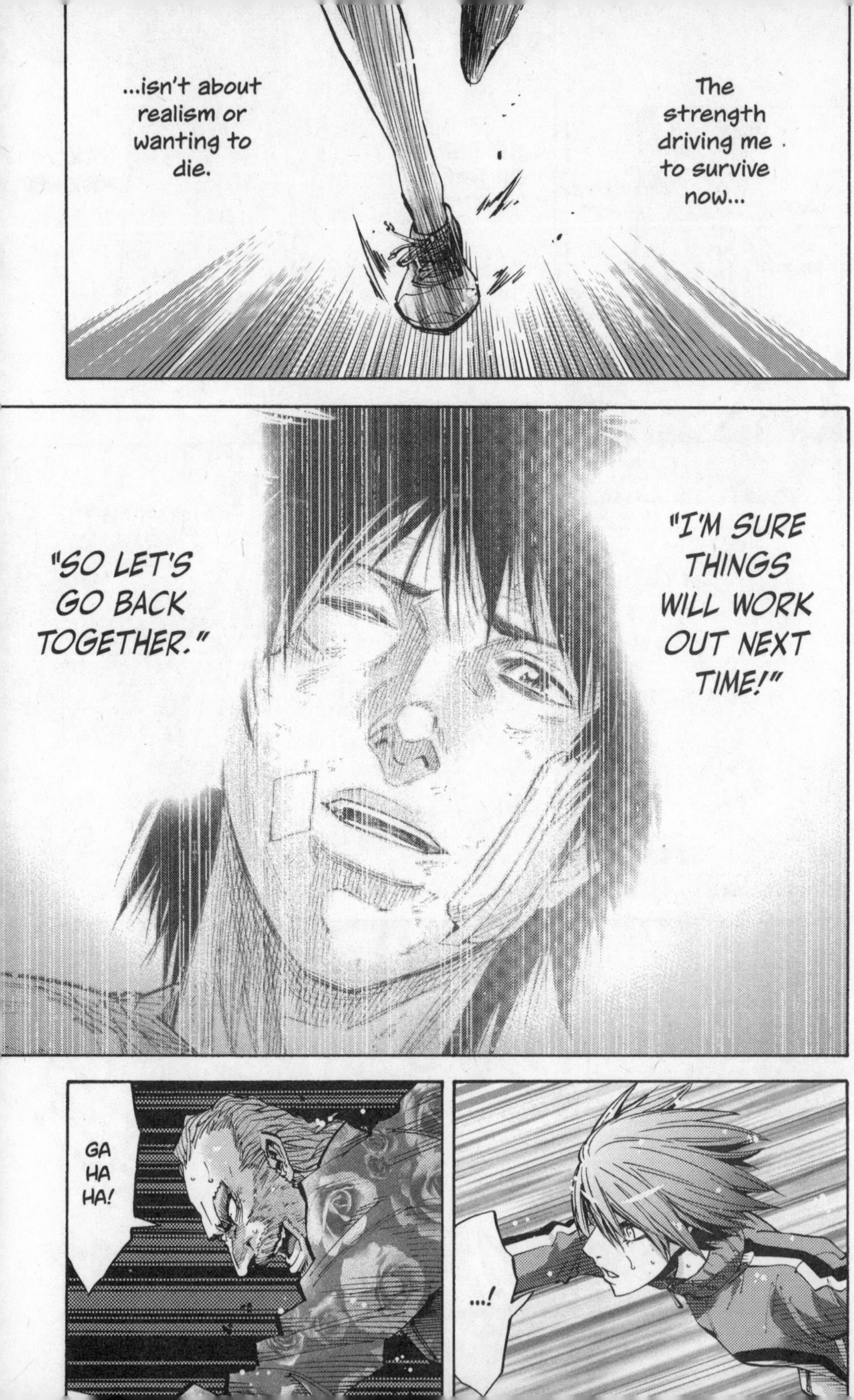
The strength driving me to survive now...
...isn't about realism or wanting to die.
"I'M SURE THINGS WILL WORK OUT NEXT TIME!"
"SO LET'S GO BACK TOGETHER."
...!
GA HA HA!

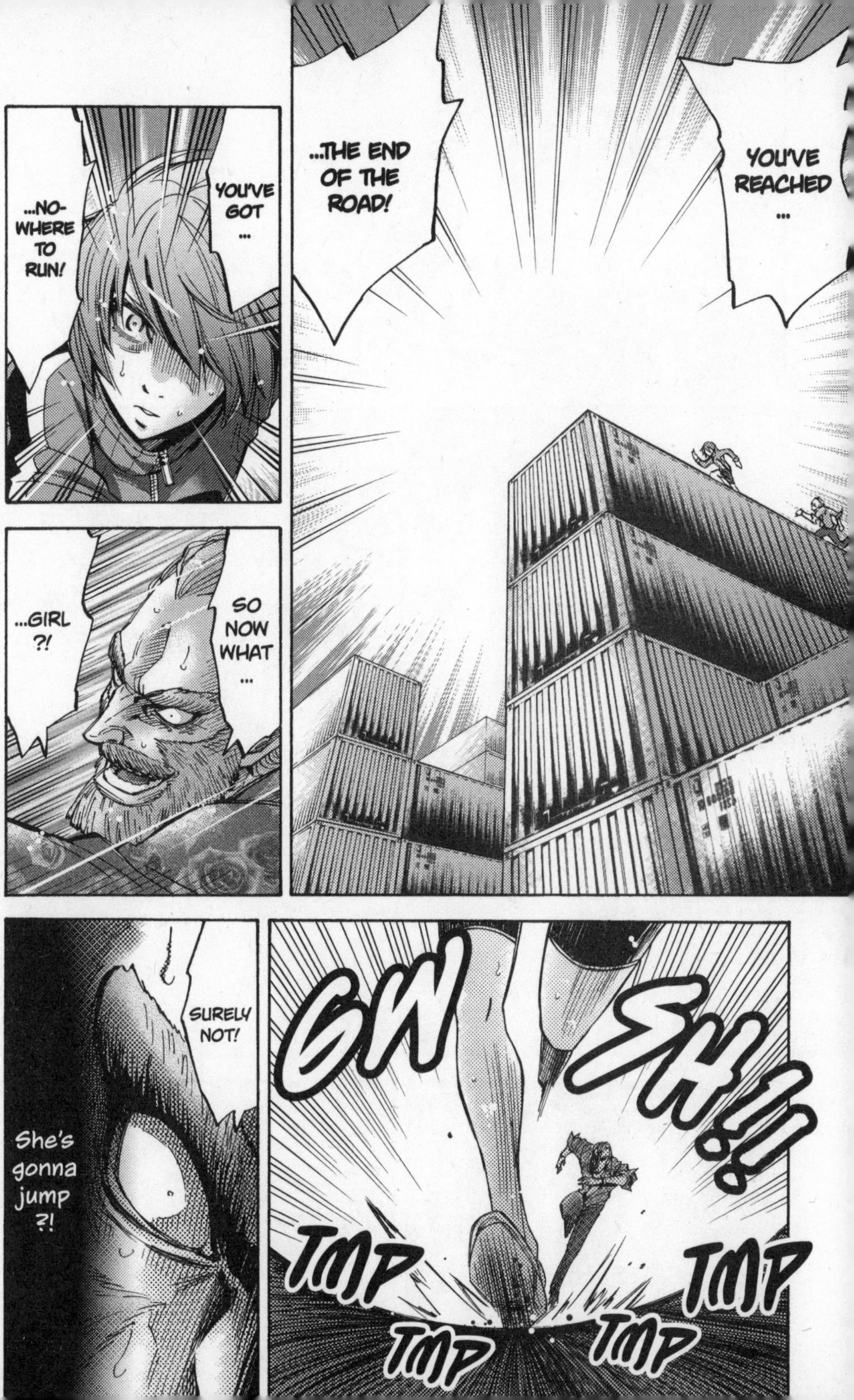
YOU'VE REACHED ...
...THE END OF THE ROAD!
YOU'VE GOT ...
...NO-WHERE TO RUN!
SO NOW WHAT ...
...GIRL ?!
GWSH!!!
TMP
TMP
TMP
TMP
TMP
SURELY NOT!
She's gonna jump ?!

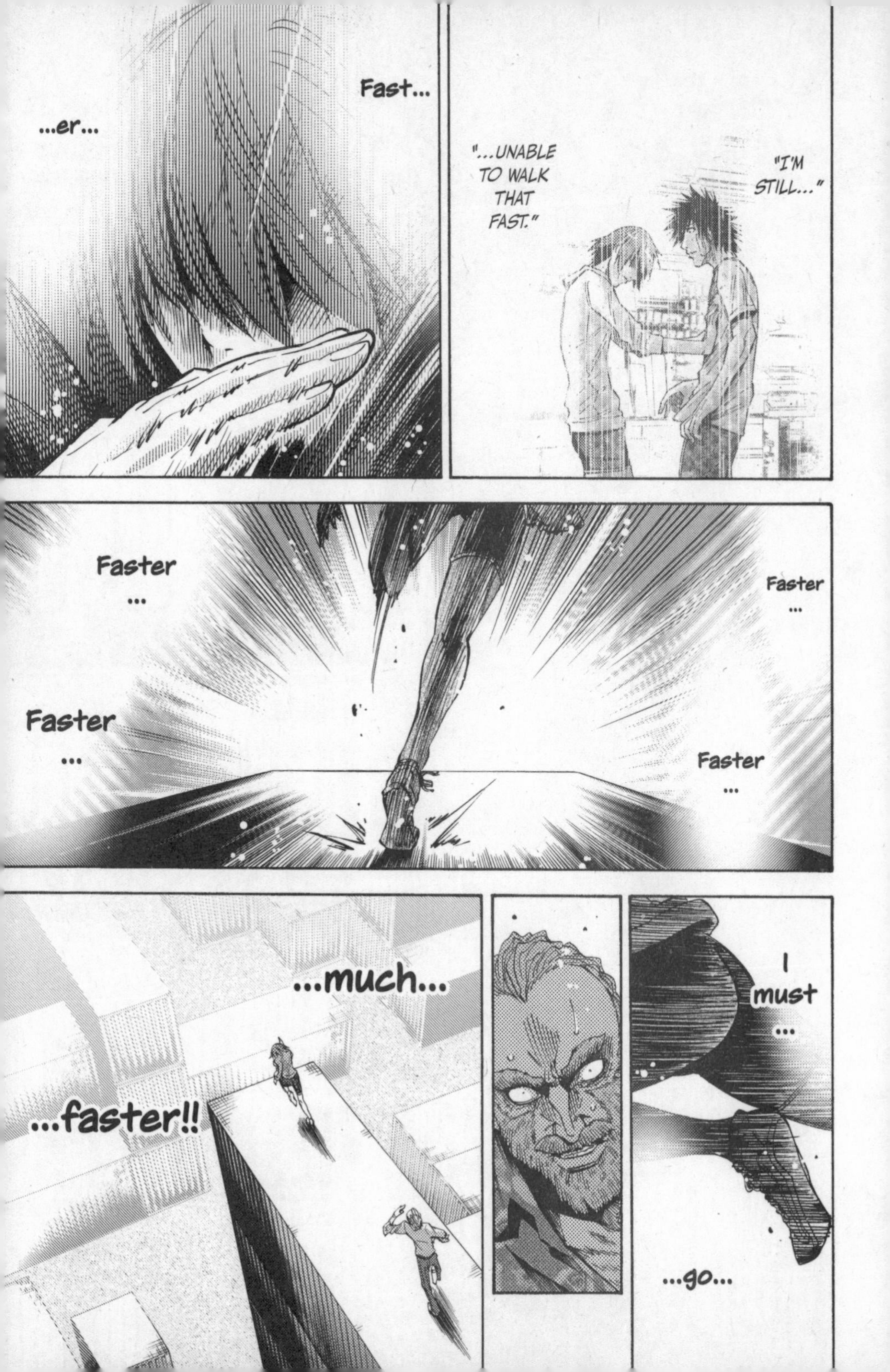
"I'M STILL..."
"...UNABLE TO WALK THAT FAST."
Fast...
...er...
Faster ...
Faster ...
Faster ...
Faster ...
I must ...
...go...
...much...
...faster!!

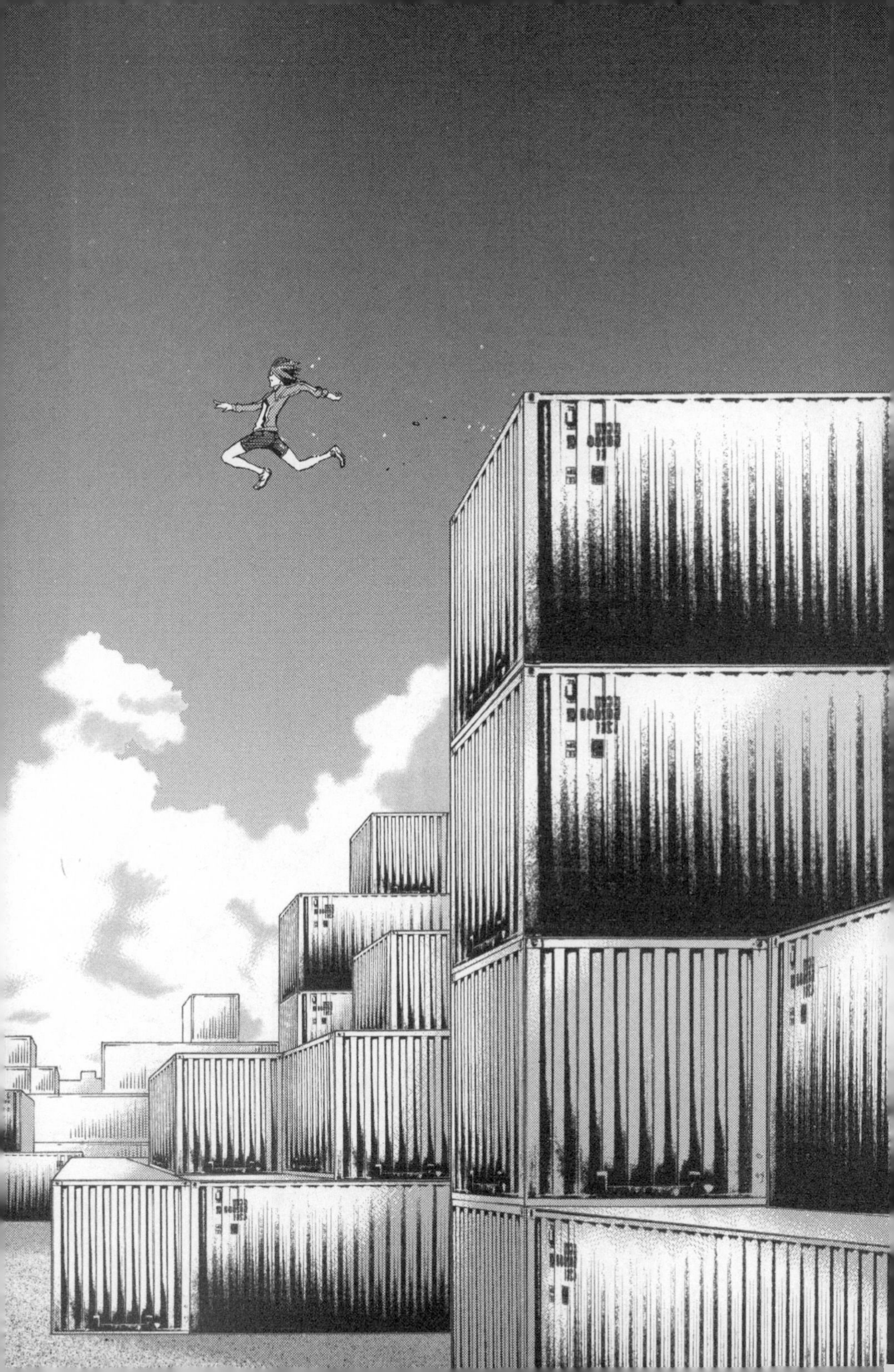

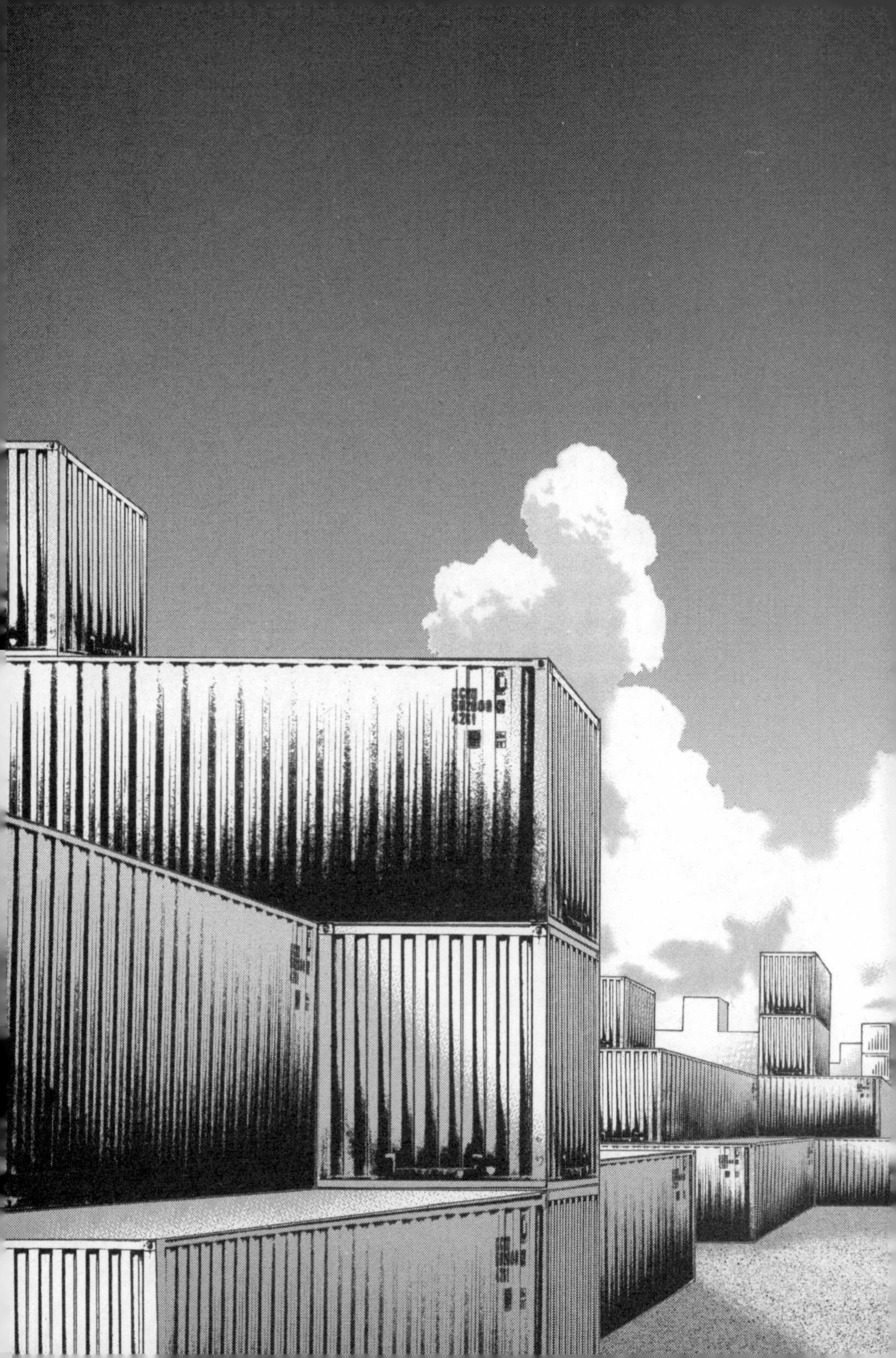

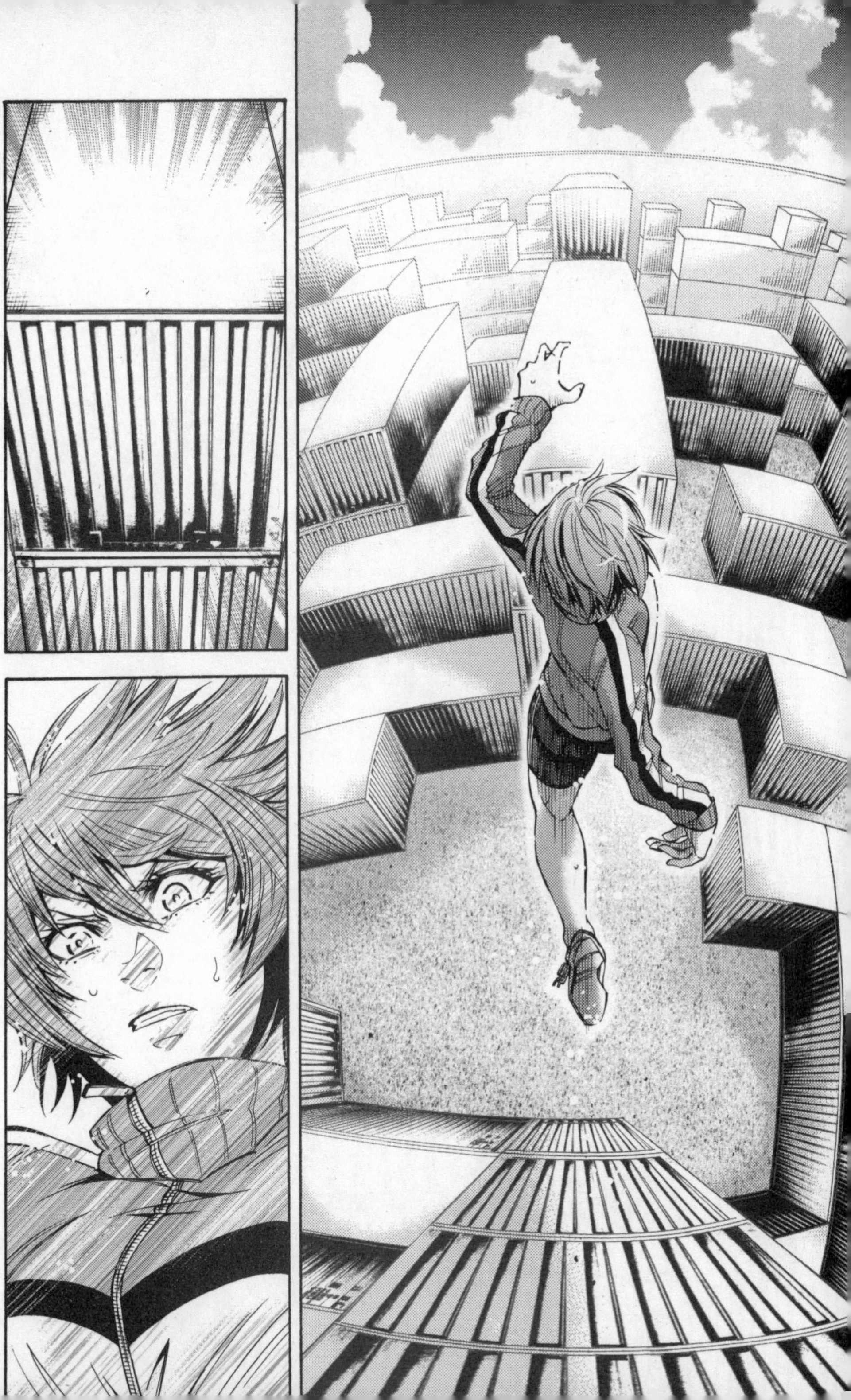

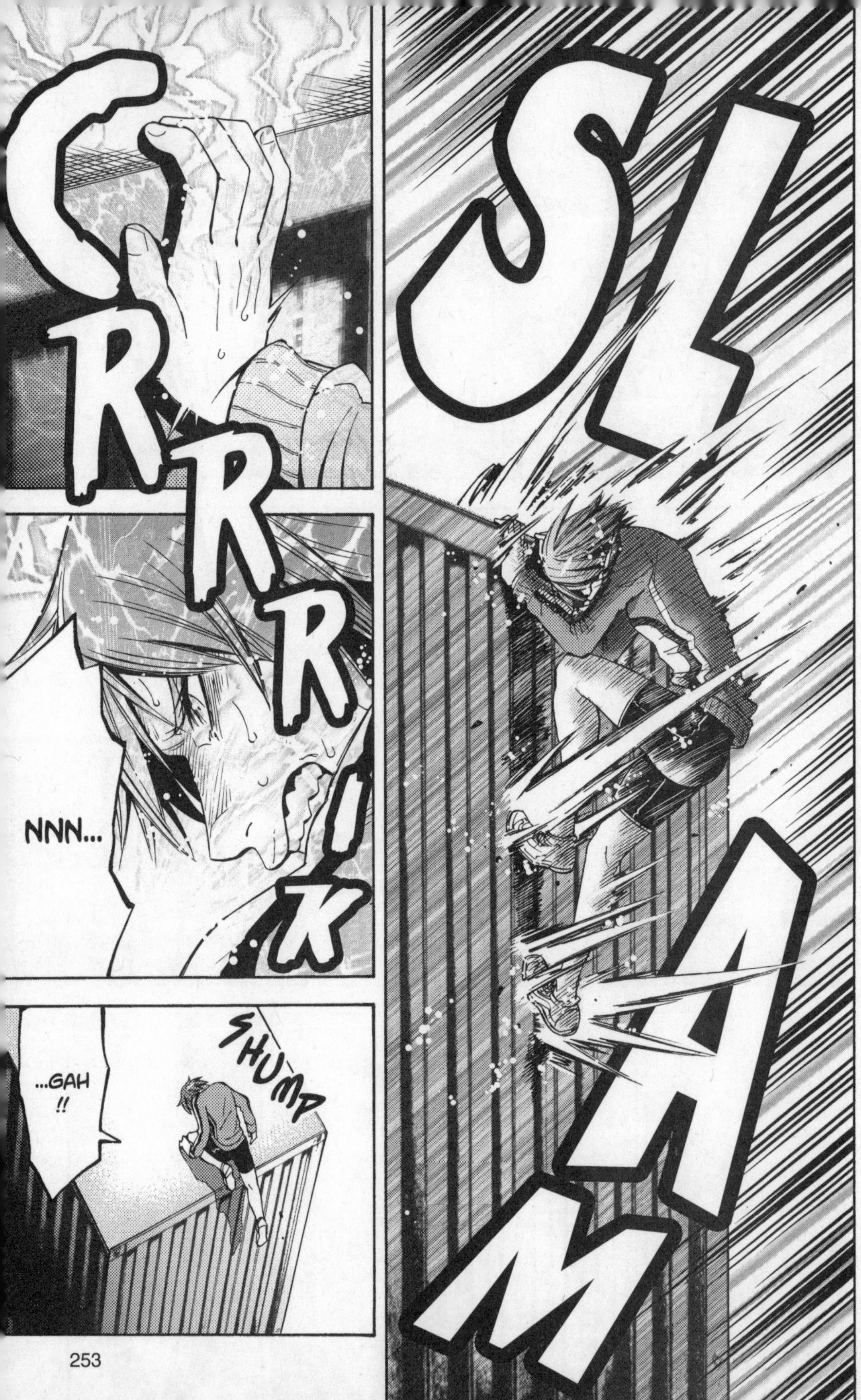
SLAM
CRRRIK
NNN...
SHUMP
...GAH !!

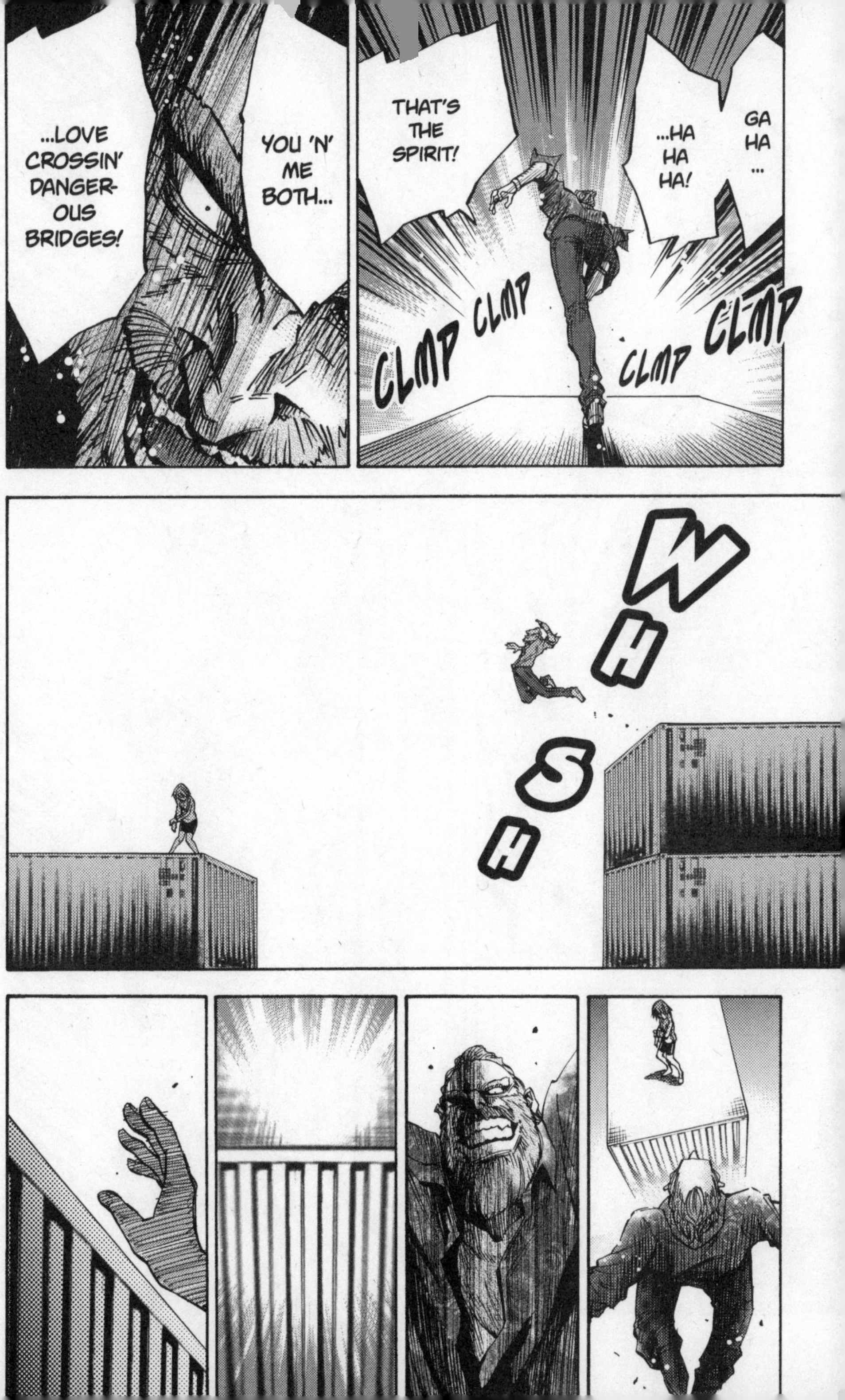
GA HA ...
...HA HA HA!
THAT'S THE SPIRIT!
CLMP CLMP
CLMP CLMP
YOU 'N' ME BOTH...
...LOVE CROSSIN' DANGER-OUS BRIDGES!
WHSH

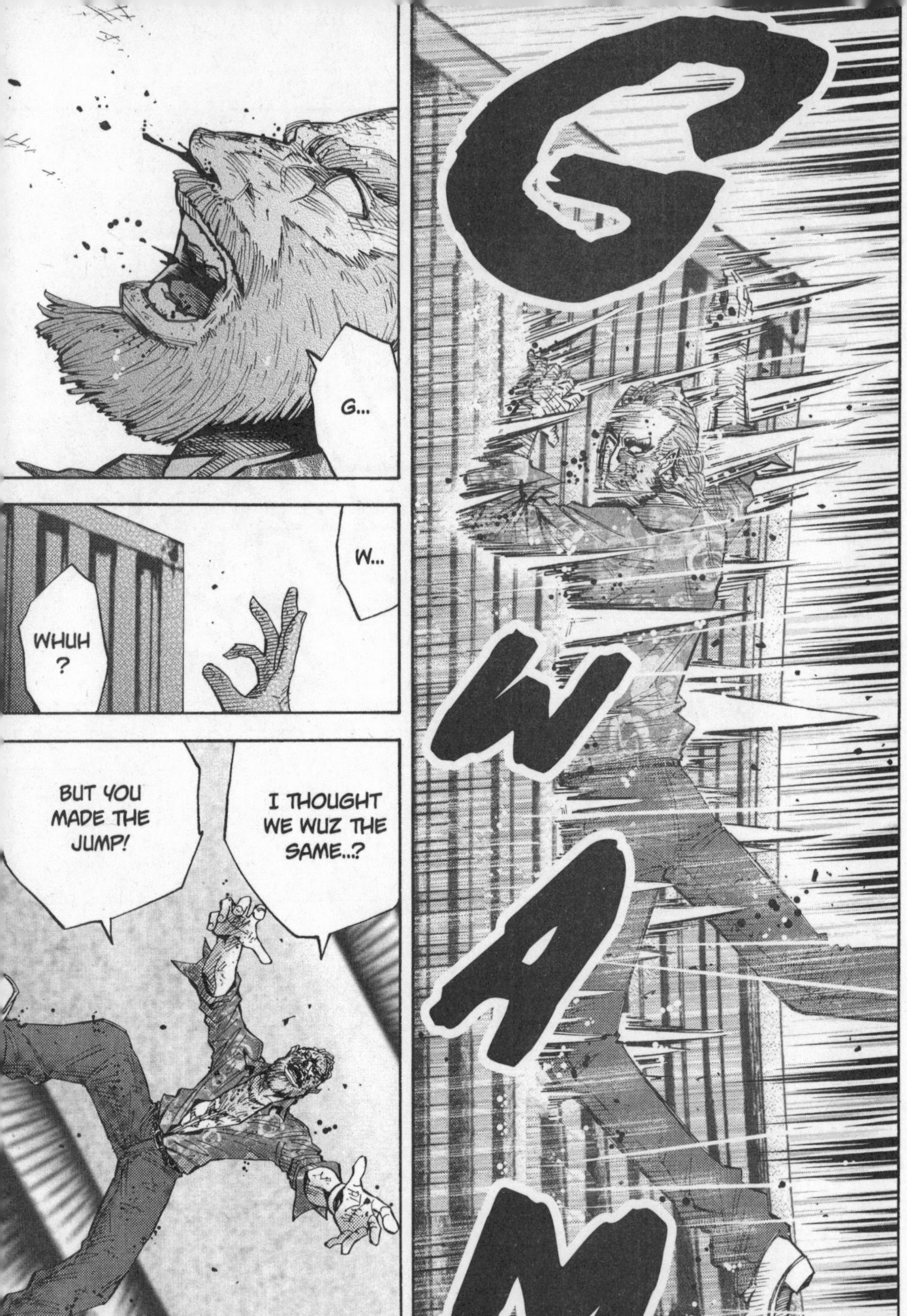
GWAM
G...
W...
WHUH ?
I THOUGHT WE WUZ THE SAME..?
BUT YOU MADE THE JUMP!

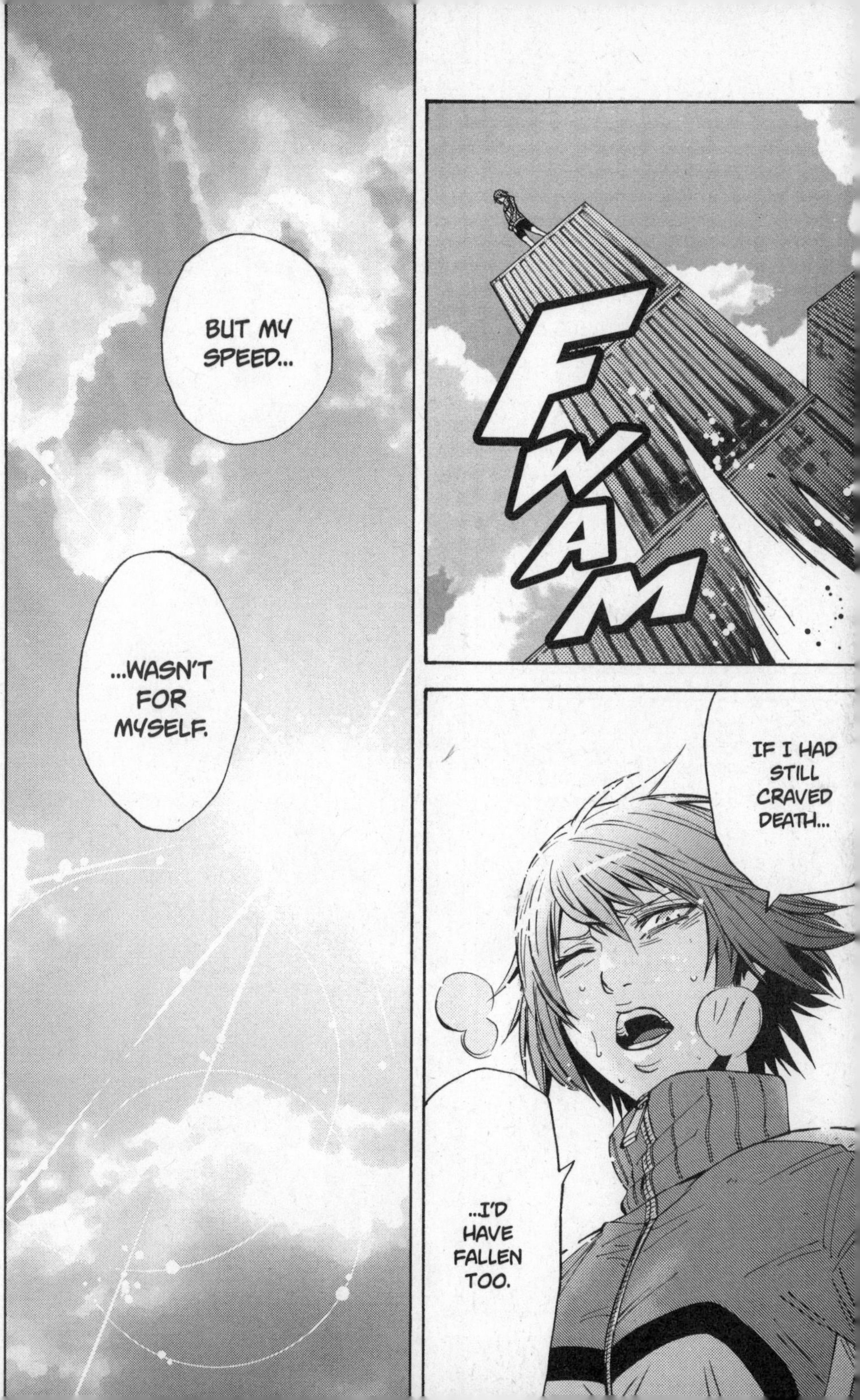
FWAM
IF I HAD STILL CRAVED DEATH...
...I'D HAVE FALLEN TOO.
BUT MY SPEED...
...WASN'T FOR MYSELF.

THE MAIN STORY WILL RESUME IN PART II

THIS IS A SIDE STORY

SIDE STORY 4: Seven of Spades, Part 1

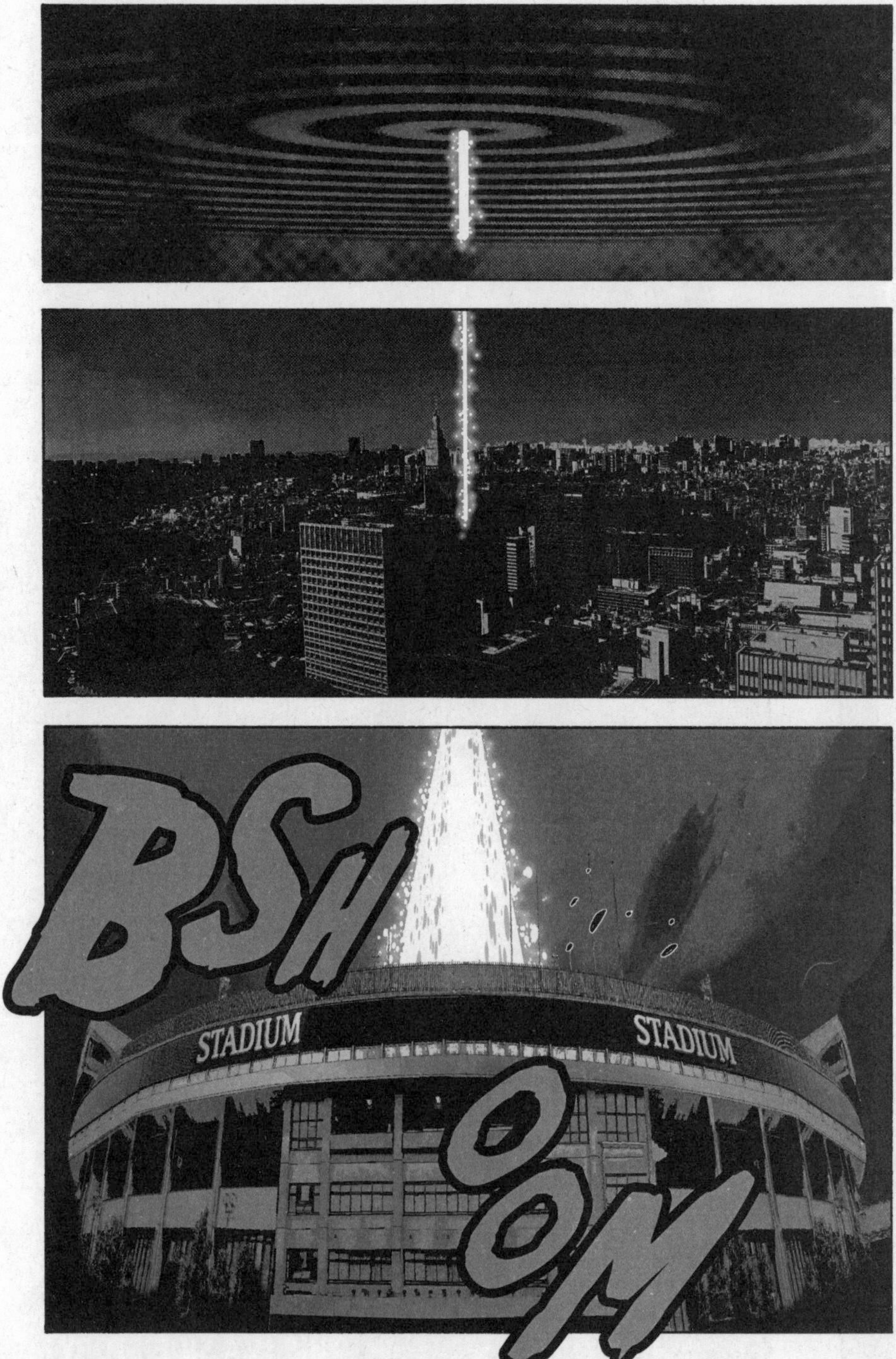
BSHOOM
STADIUM
STADIUM

SIDE STORY 4: Seven of Spades, Part 1

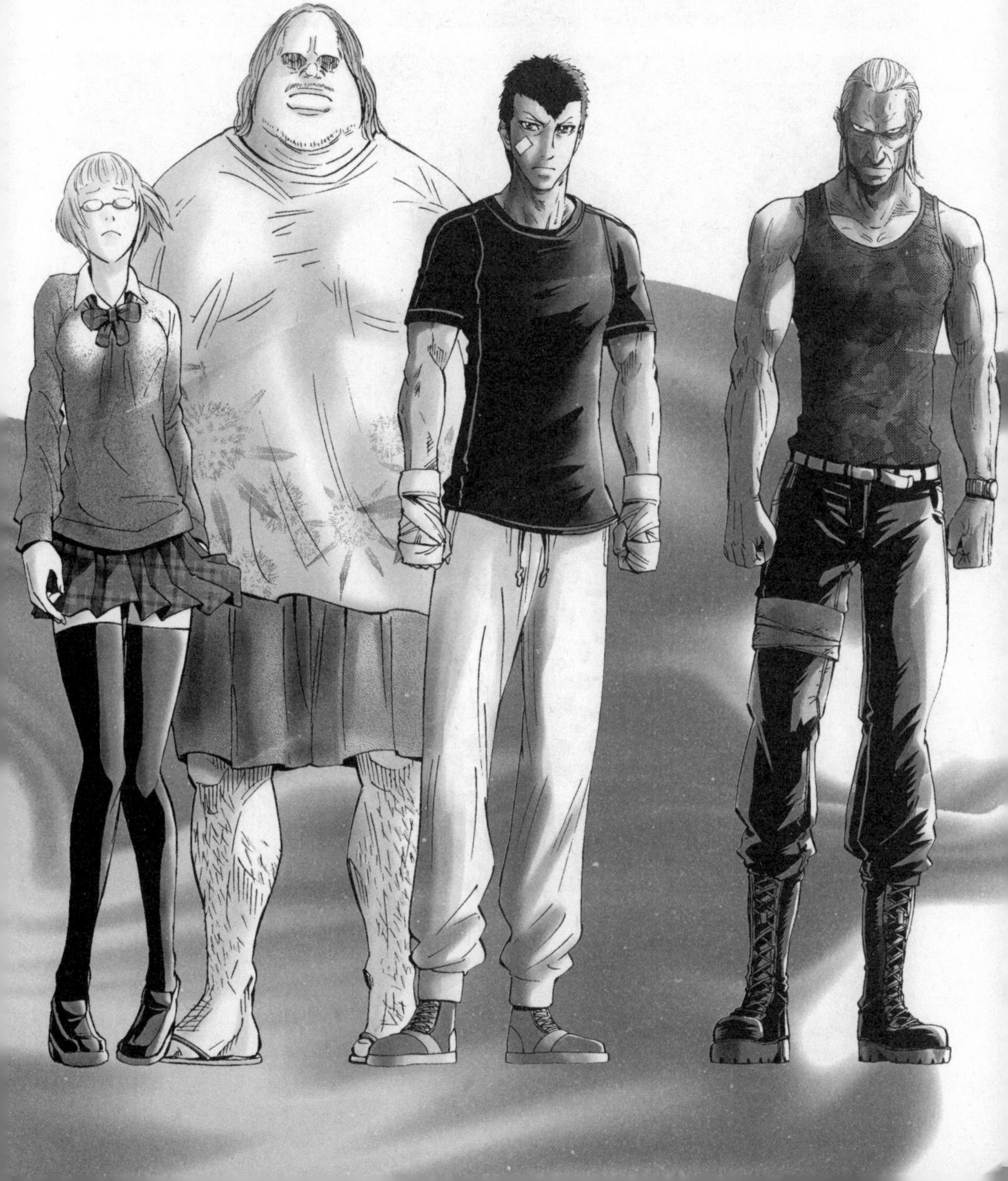

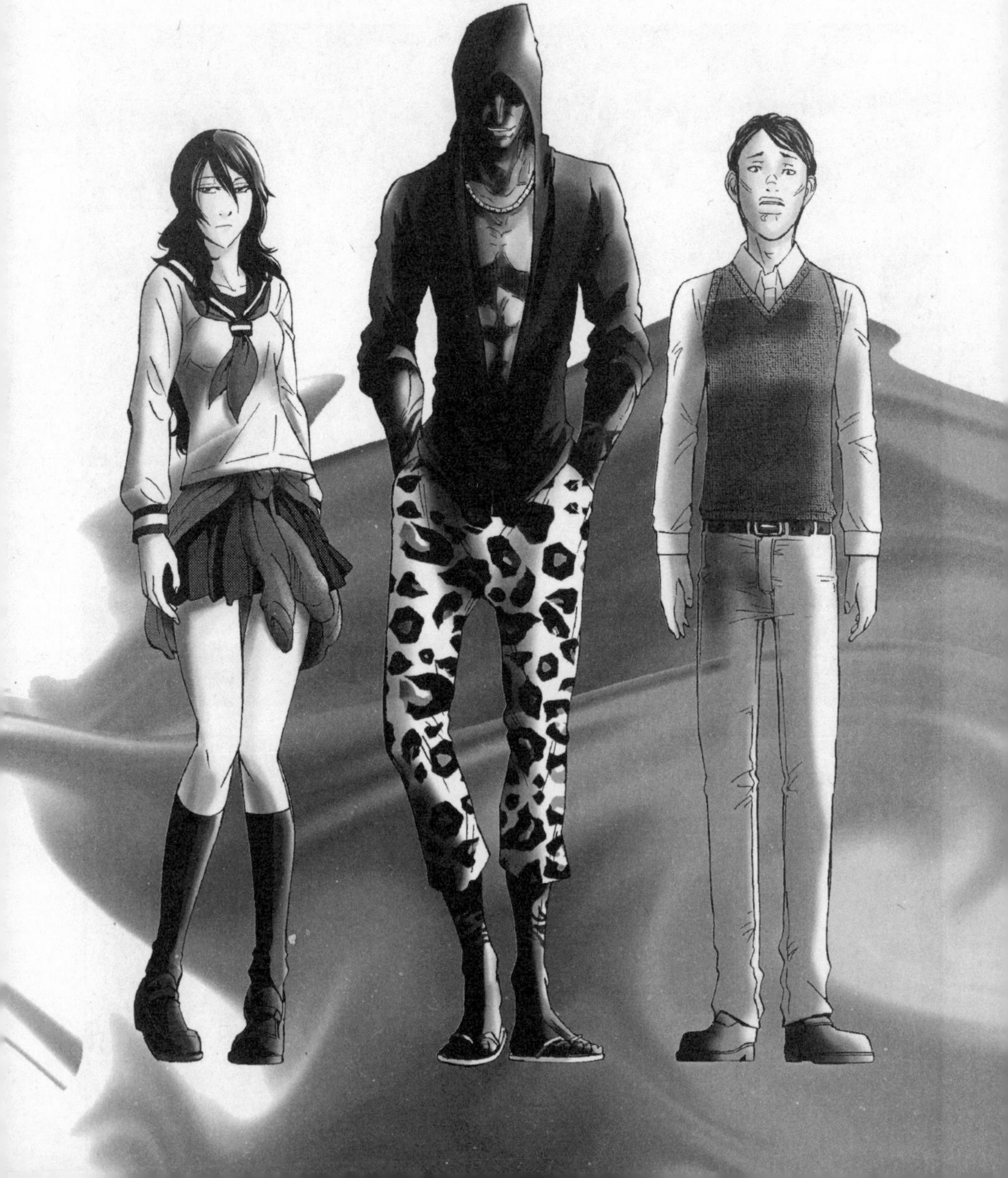

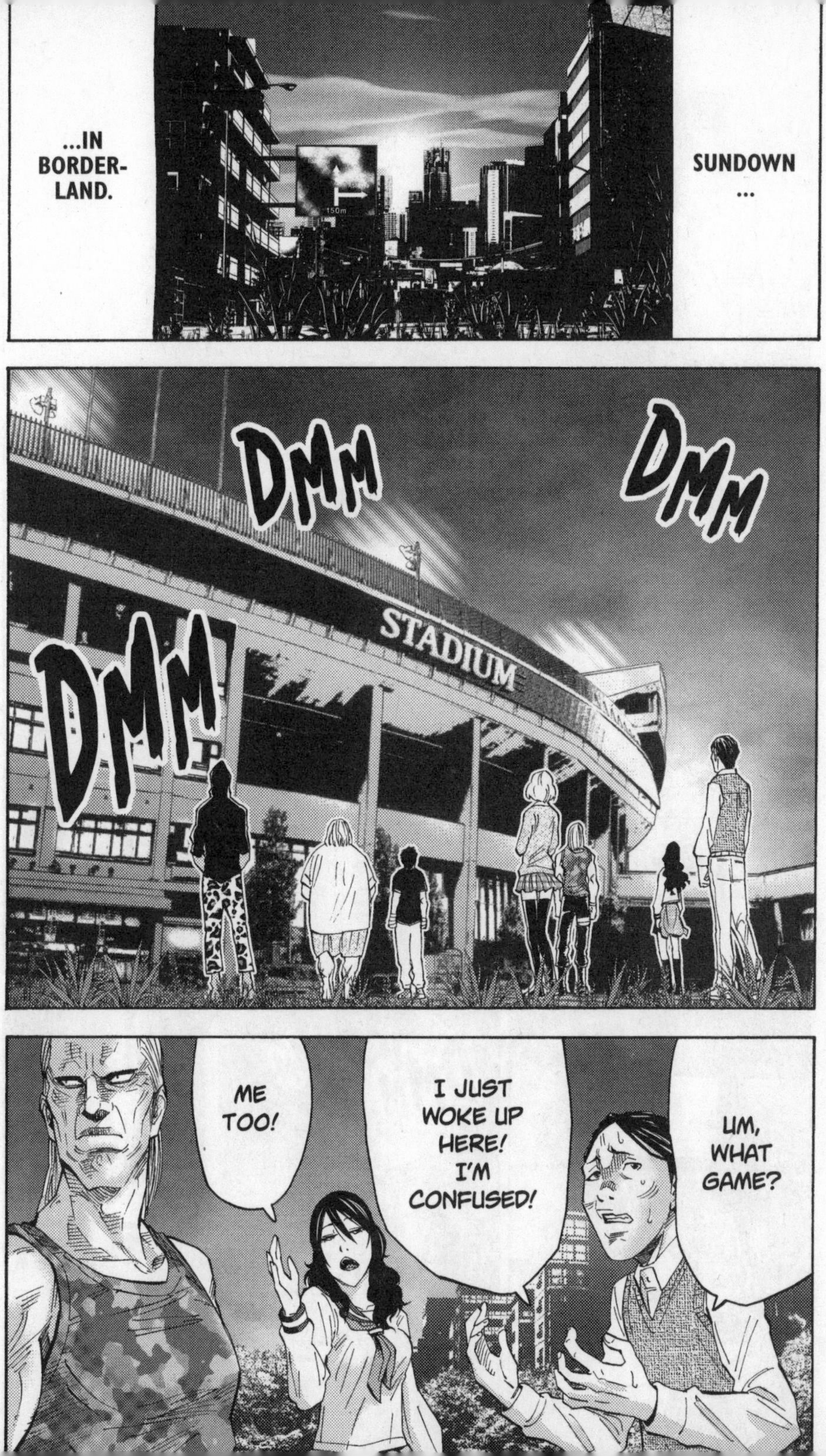
SUNDOWN ...
...IN BORDER-LAND.
DMM
DMM
STADIUM
DMM
UM, WHAT GAME?
I JUST WOKE UP HERE! I'M CONFUSED!
ME TOO!

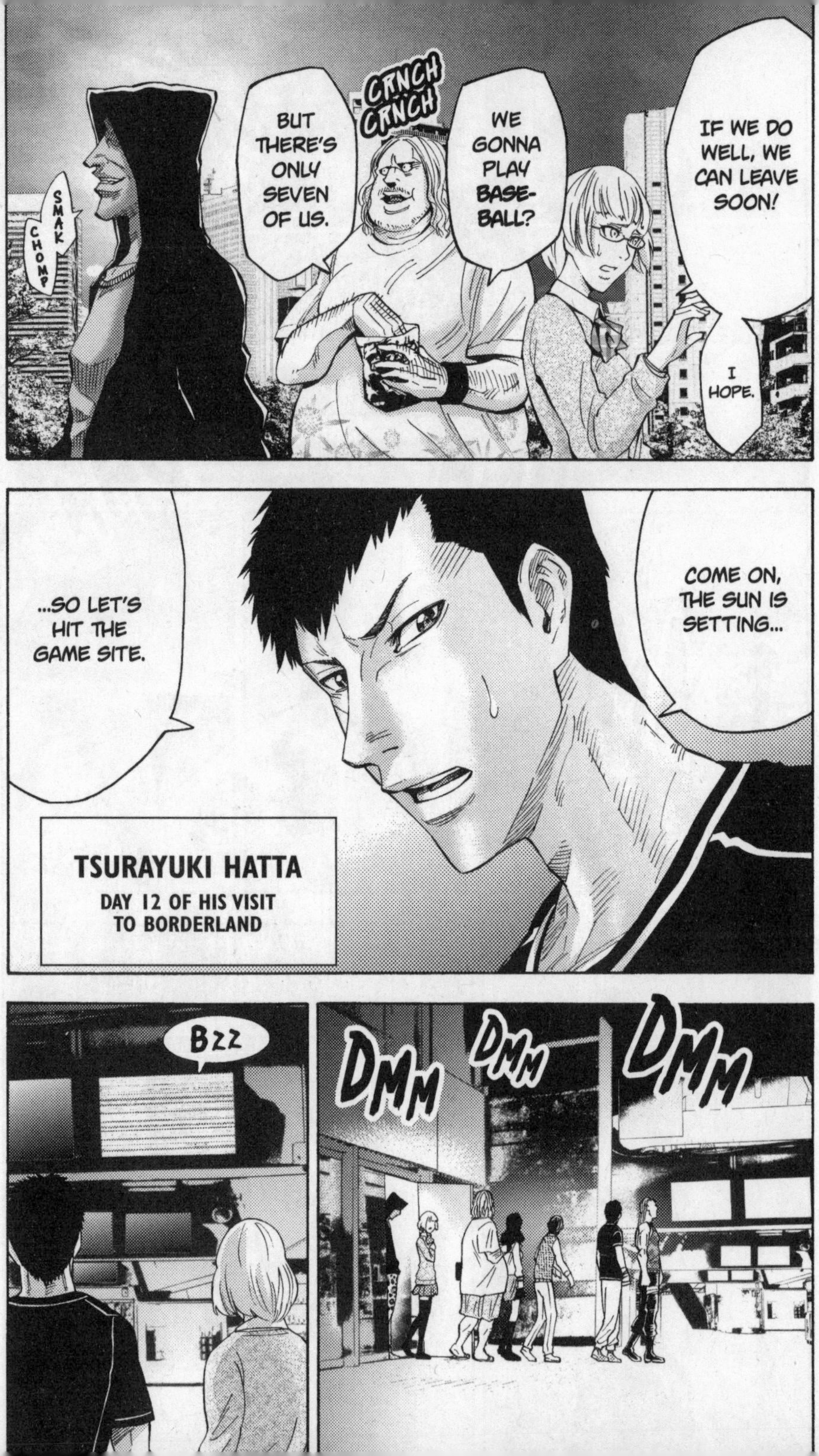
IF WE DO WELL, WE CAN LEAVE SOON!
I HOPE.
WE GONNA PLAY BASE-BALL?
CRNCH CRNCH
BUT THERE'S ONLY SEVEN OF US.
SMAK CHOMP
COME ON, THE SUN IS SETTING...
...SO LET'S HIT THE GAME SITE.
TSURAYUKI HATTA
DAY 12 OF HIS VISIT TO BORDERLAND
DMM DMM DMM
BZZ

SEVEN OF SPADES!!

DMM

DMM

UM, SPADES INDICATES ATHLETIC GAMES AND SEVEN IS THE DIFFICULTY LEVEL.

THAT'S ALL?!

WHAT THE?

HUNH ?!

KLIK

HM ?!

...BUT I'M STILL AN AMATEUR.

YEAH, I BOX...

...A BOXER.

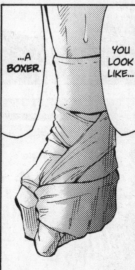

YOU LOOK LIKE...

HEY, YOU.

KLOMP

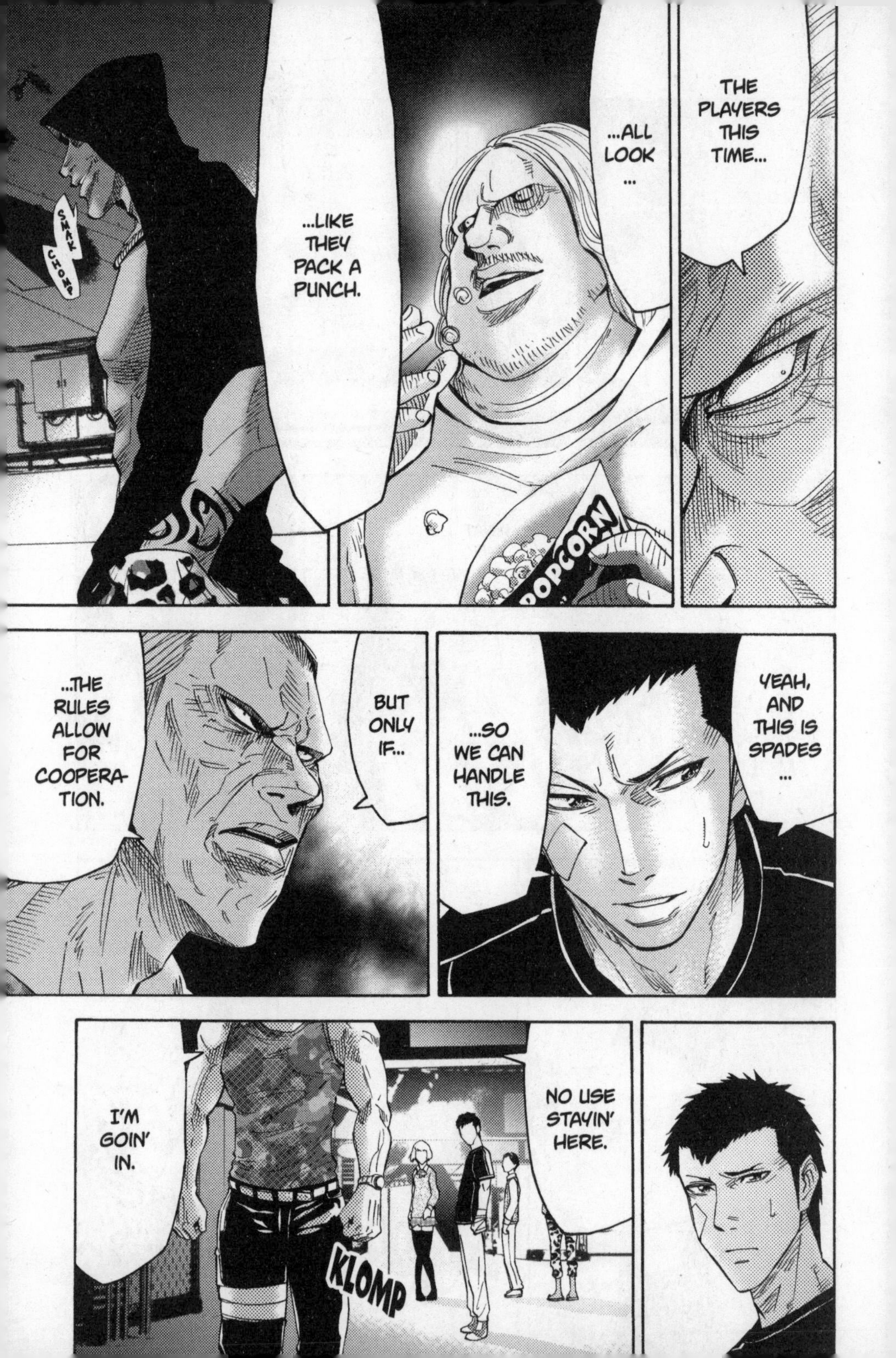
THE PLAYERS THIS TIME...
...ALL LOOK ...
...LIKE THEY PACK A PUNCH.
SMAK
CHOMP
YEAH, AND THIS IS SPADES ...
...SO WE CAN HANDLE THIS.
BUT ONLY IF...
...THE RULES ALLOW FOR COOPERA-TION.
NO USE STAYIN' HERE.
I'M GOIN' IN.
KLOMP

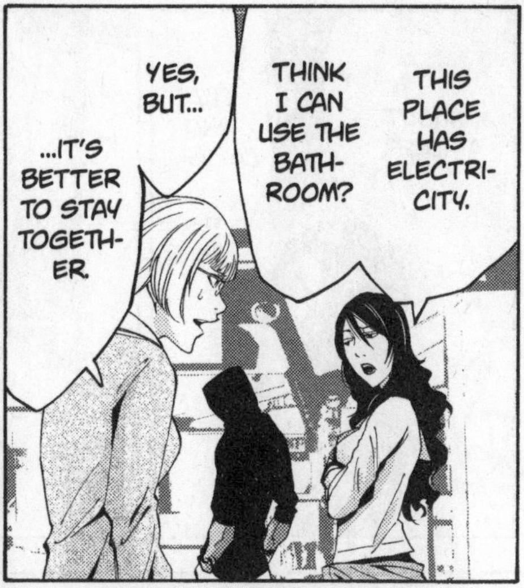
THIS PLACE HAS ELECTRICITY.
THINK I CAN USE THE BATHROOM?
YES, BUT...
...IT'S BETTER TO STAY TOGETHER.
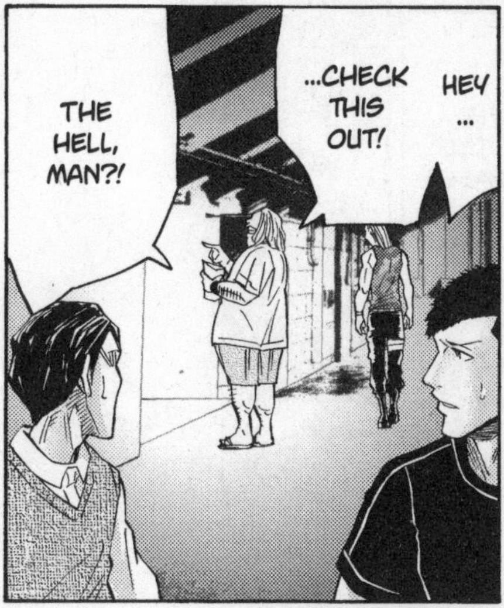
HEY ...
...CHECK THIS OUT!
THE HELL, MAN?!
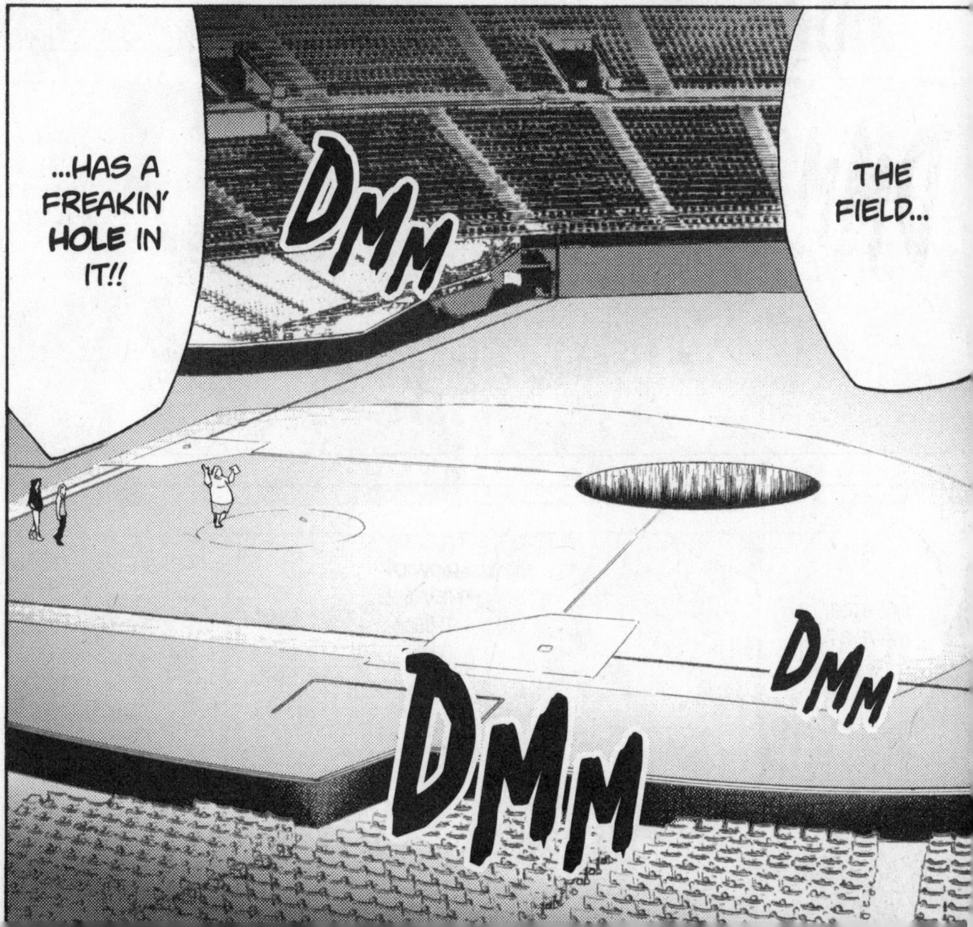
THE FIELD...
...HAS A FREAKIN' **HOLE** IN IT!!
DMM
DMM
DMM

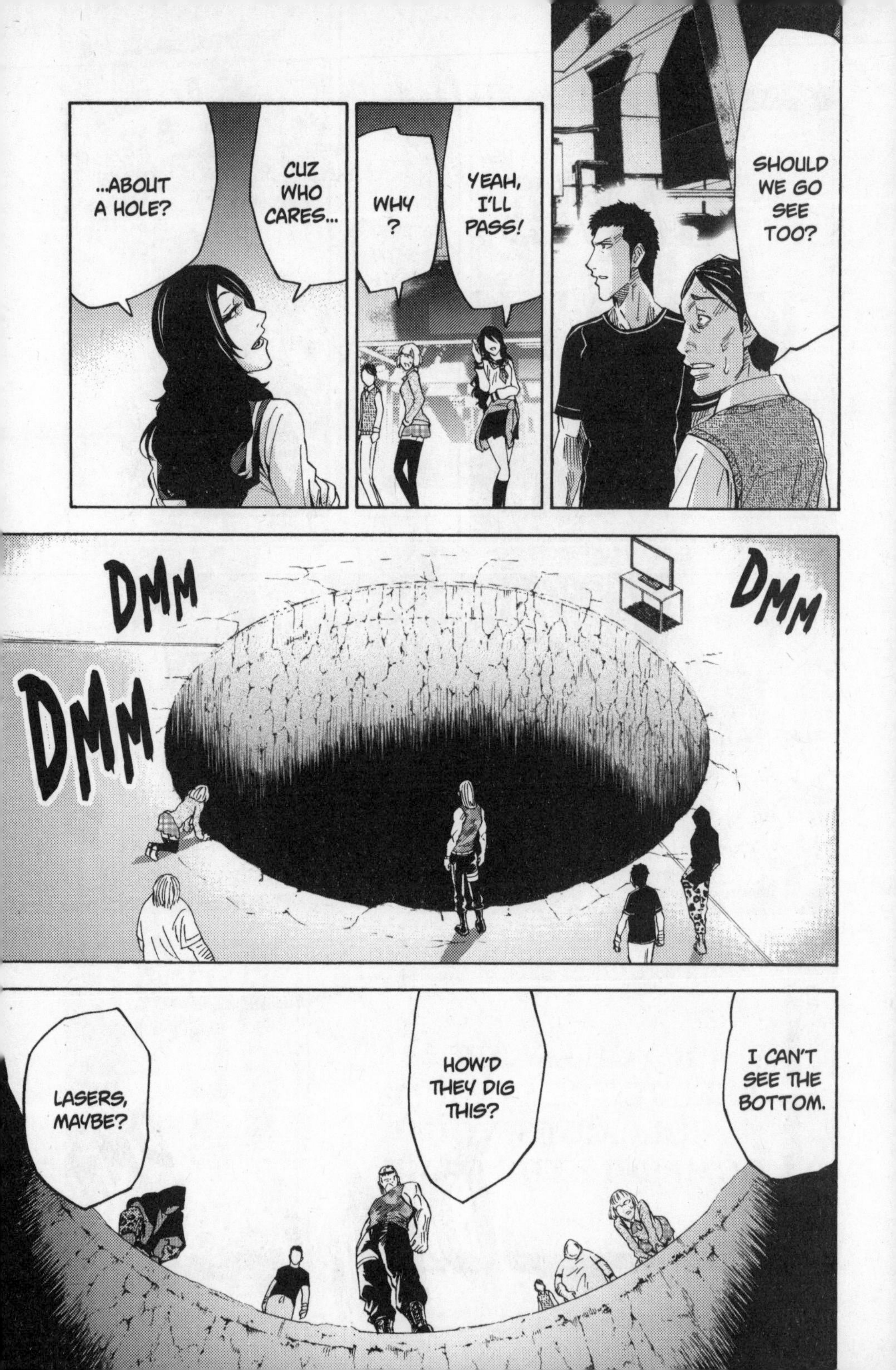
SHOULD WE GO SEE TOO?
YEAH, I'LL PASS!
WHY?
CUZ WHO CARES...
...ABOUT A HOLE?
DMM
DMM
DMM
I CAN'T SEE THE BOTTOM.
HOW'D THEY DIG THIS?
LASERS, MAYBE?

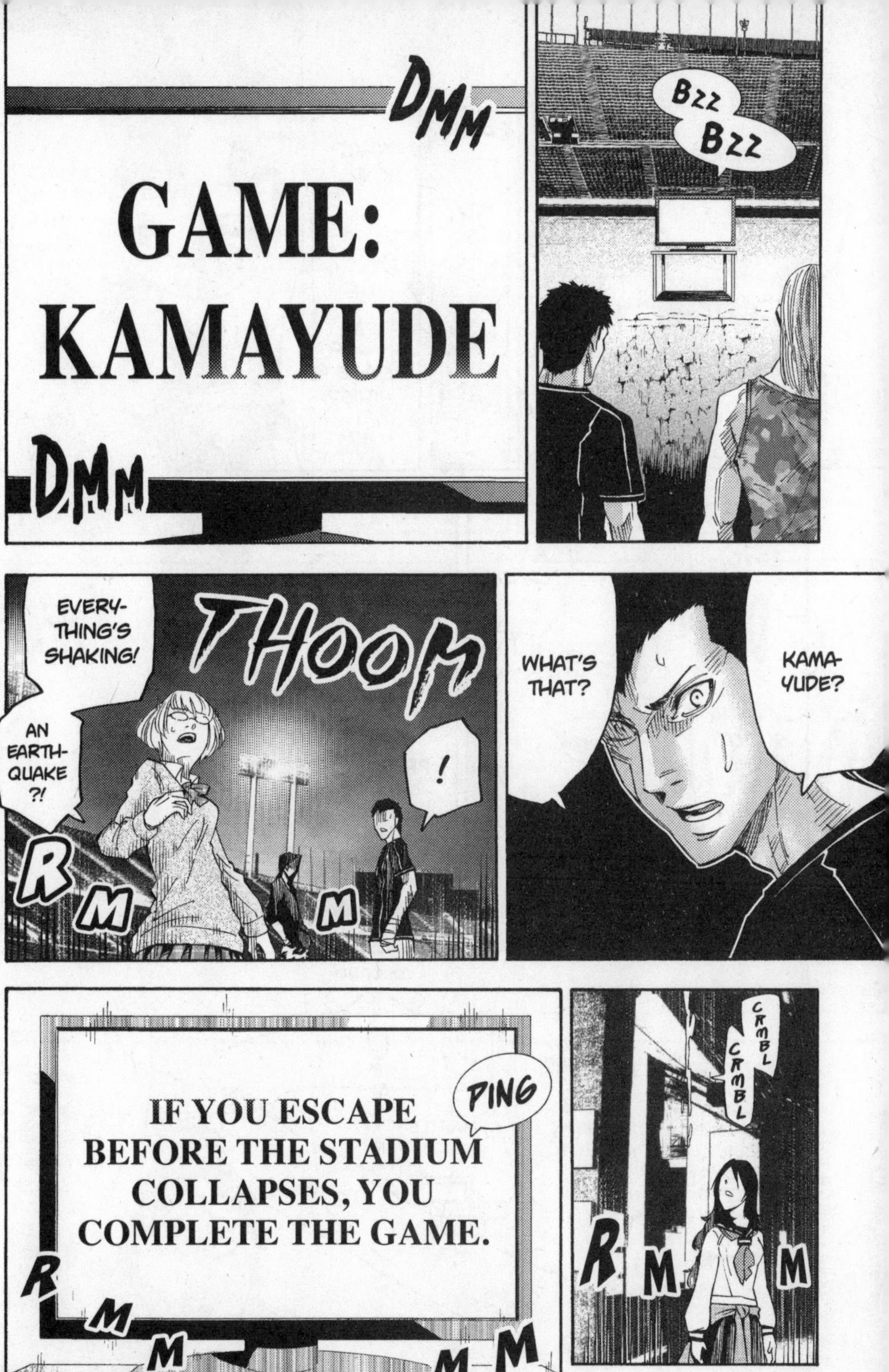
Bzz
Bzz
DMM
GAME:
KAMAYUDE
DMM
KAMA-YUDE?
WHAT'S THAT?
THOOM
EVERY-THING'S SHAKING!
!
AN EARTH-QUAKE ?!
RMM
M
CRMBL
CRMBL
RMM
M
PING
IF YOU ESCAPE BEFORE THE STADIUM COLLAPSES, YOU COMPLETE THE GAME.
RMM
MM

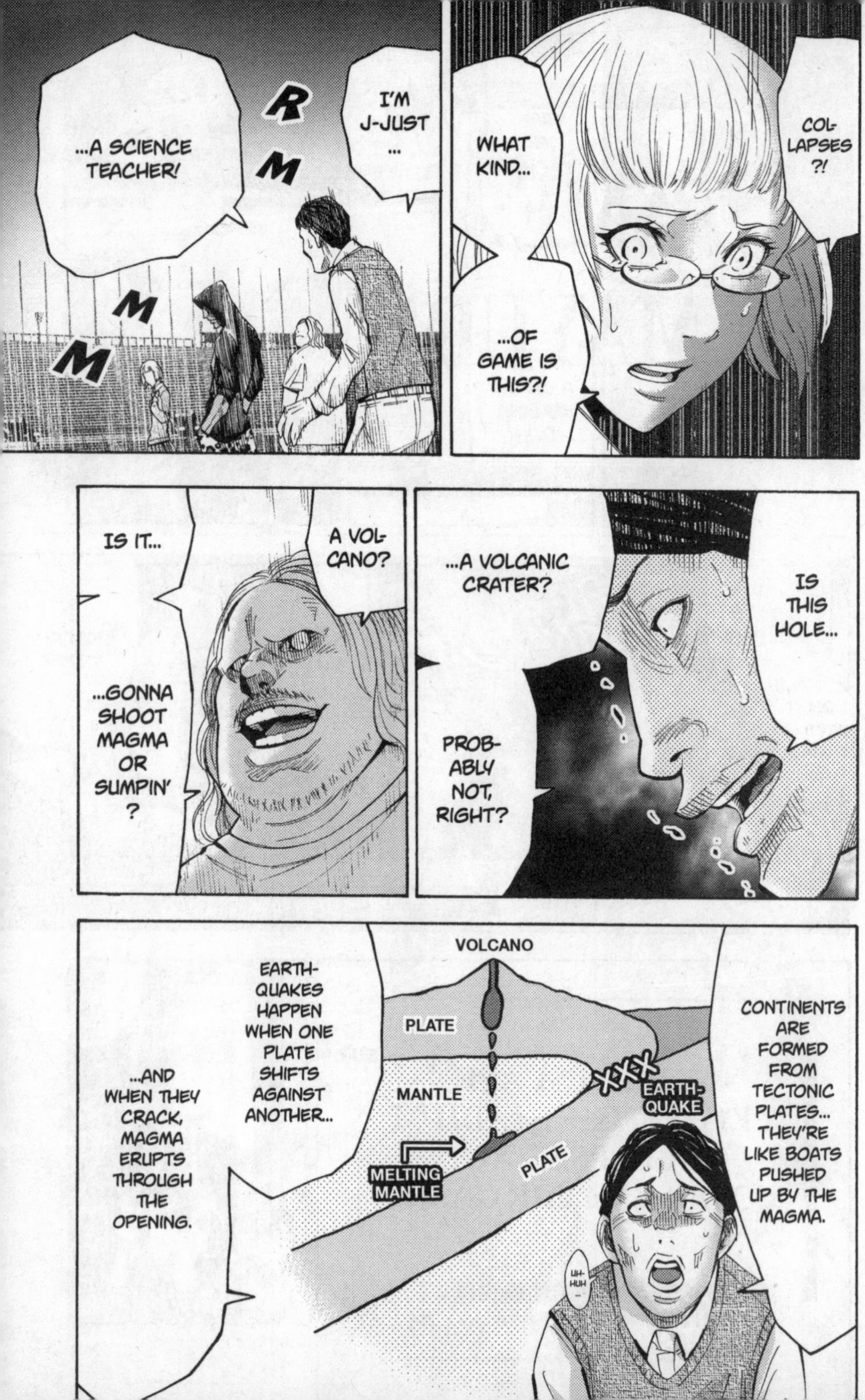
COL-LAPSES?!
WHAT KIND...
...OF GAME IS THIS?!
I'M J-JUST ...
...A SCIENCE TEACHER!
RMMMM
IS THIS HOLE...
...A VOLCANIC CRATER?
PROB-ABLY NOT, RIGHT?
A VOL-CANO?
IS IT...
...GONNA SHOOT MAGMA OR SUMPIN'?
CONTINENTS ARE FORMED FROM TECTONIC PLATES... THEY'RE LIKE BOATS PUSHED UP BY THE MAGMA.
UH-HUH ...
VOLCANO
PLATE
MANTLE
EARTH-QUAKE
PLATE
MELTING MANTLE
EARTH-QUAKES HAPPEN WHEN ONE PLATE SHIFTS AGAINST ANOTHER...
...AND WHEN THEY CRACK, MAGMA ERUPTS THROUGH THE OPENING.

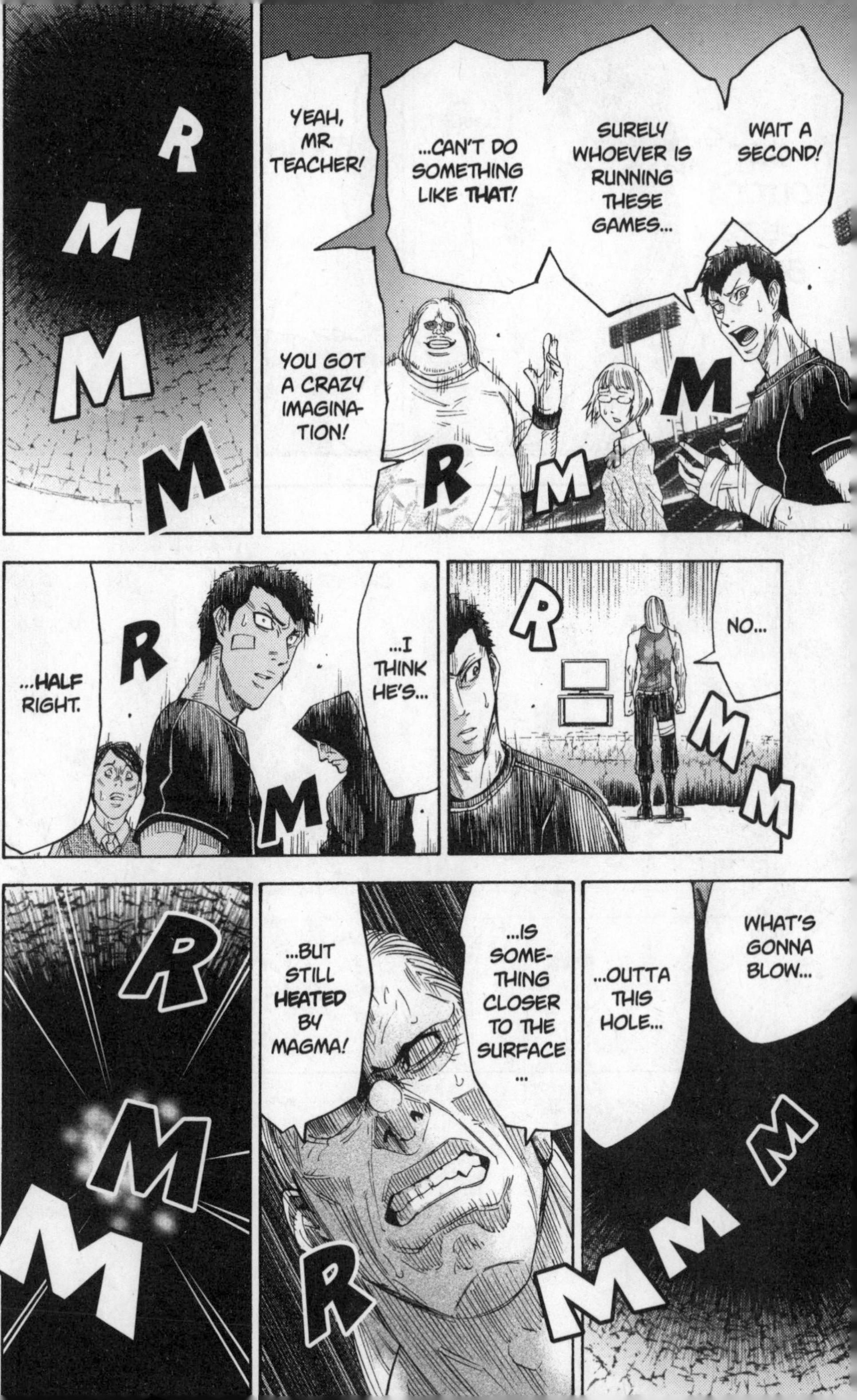

WAIT A SECOND!
SURELY WHOEVER IS RUNNING THESE GAMES...
...CAN'T DO SOMETHING LIKE THAT!
YEAH, MR. TEACHER!
YOU GOT A CRAZY IMAGINA-TION!
MMR
RMMM
NO...
RMMM
...I THINK HE'S...
...HALF RIGHT.
RM
WHAT'S GONNA BLOW...
...OUTTA THIS HOLE...
MMMMM
...IS SOME-THING CLOSER TO THE SURFACE...
...BUT STILL HEATED BY MAGMA!
R
RMMM

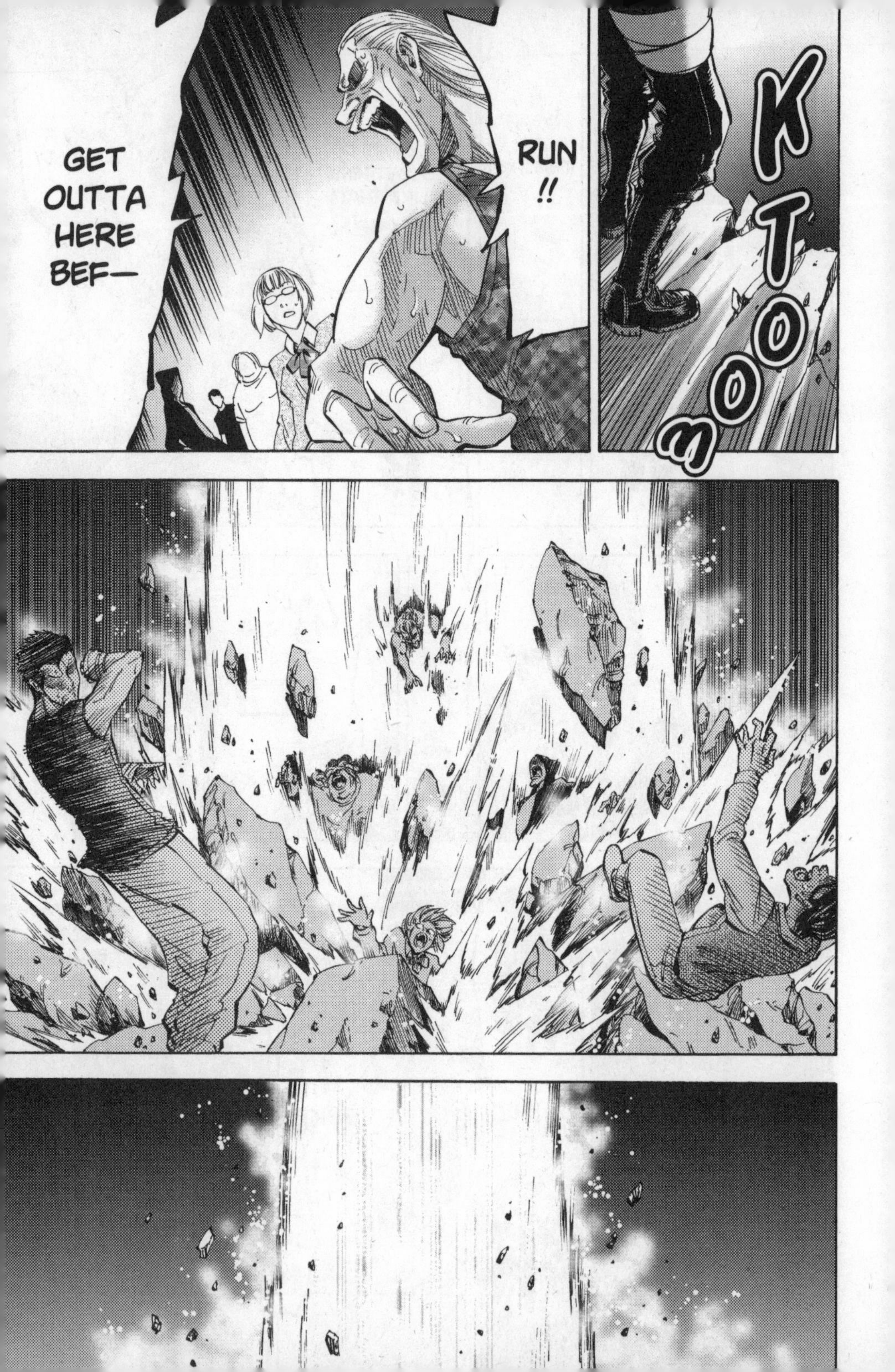
KTOOM
RUN!!
GET OUTTA HERE BEF—

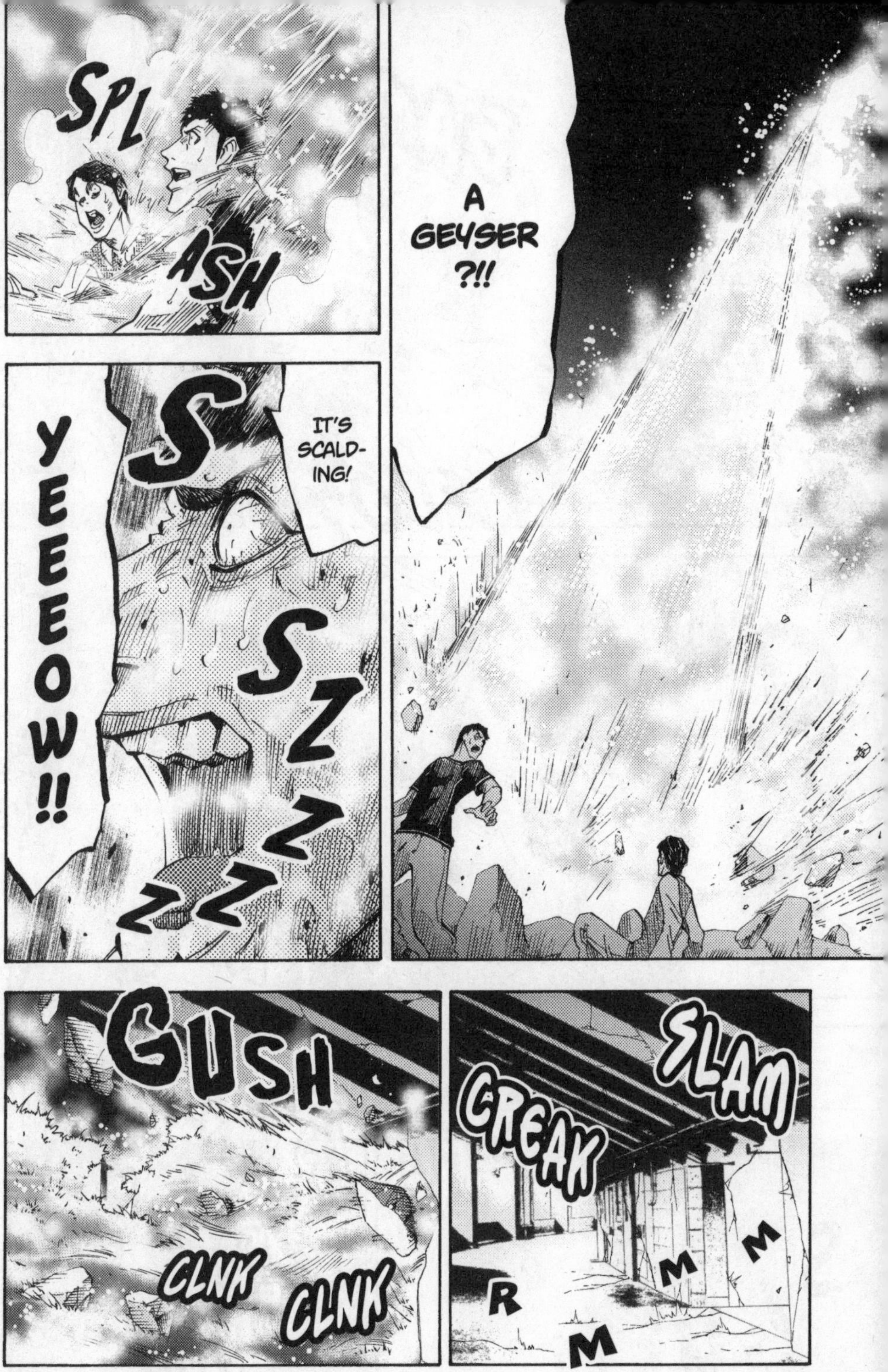
A GEYSER ?!!
SPLASH
IT'S SCALDING!
YEEEEOW!!
SSZZZ
SLAM
CREAK
RMMM
GUSH
CLNK
CLNK

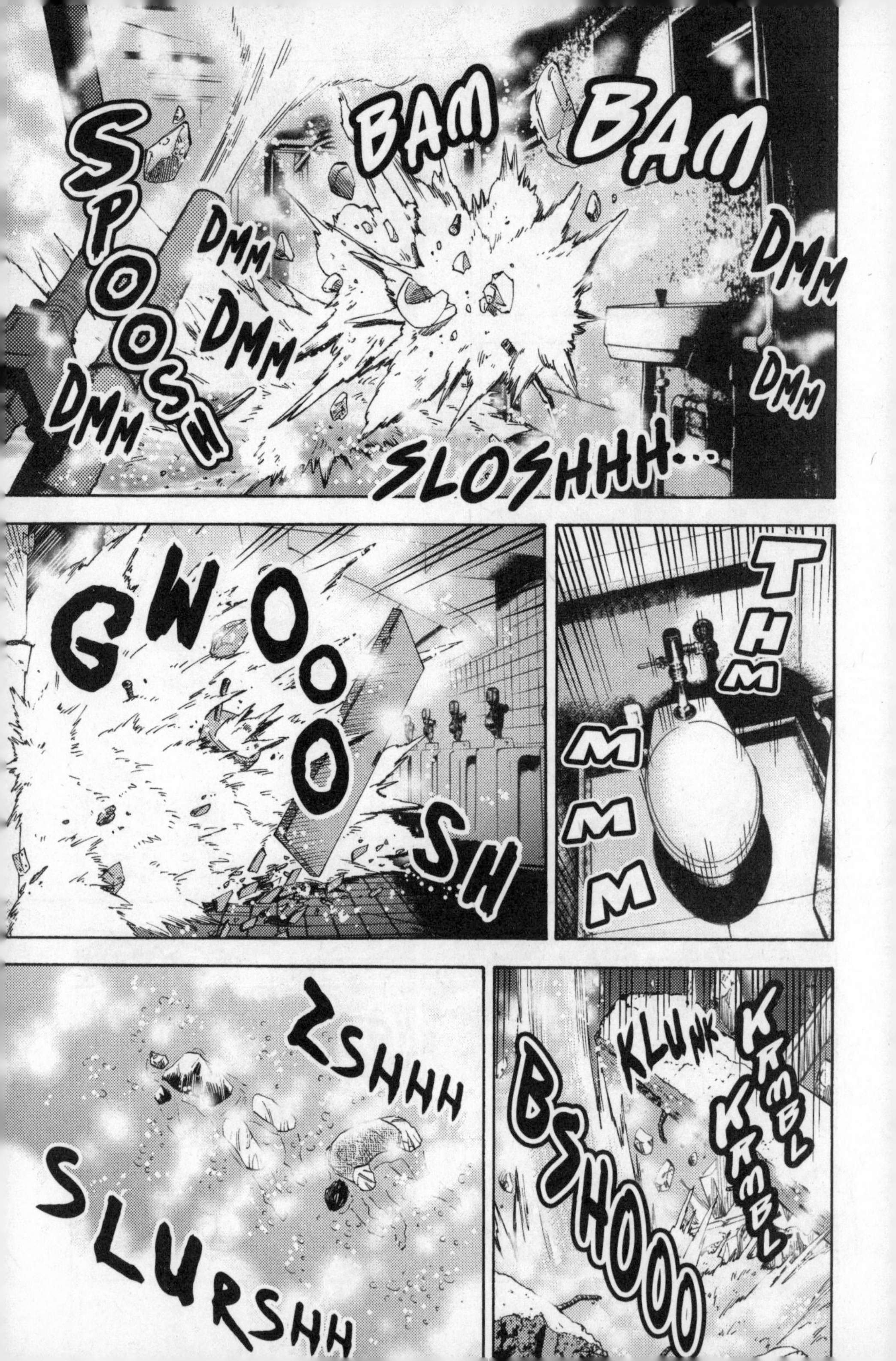
BAM
BAM
DMM
DMM
SLOSHHH...
DMM
DMM
SPOOOSH
DMM
THM
MMMM
GWOOOOSH
KRAMBL
KRAMBL
KLUNK
BSHOOOO
ZSHHH
SLURSHH

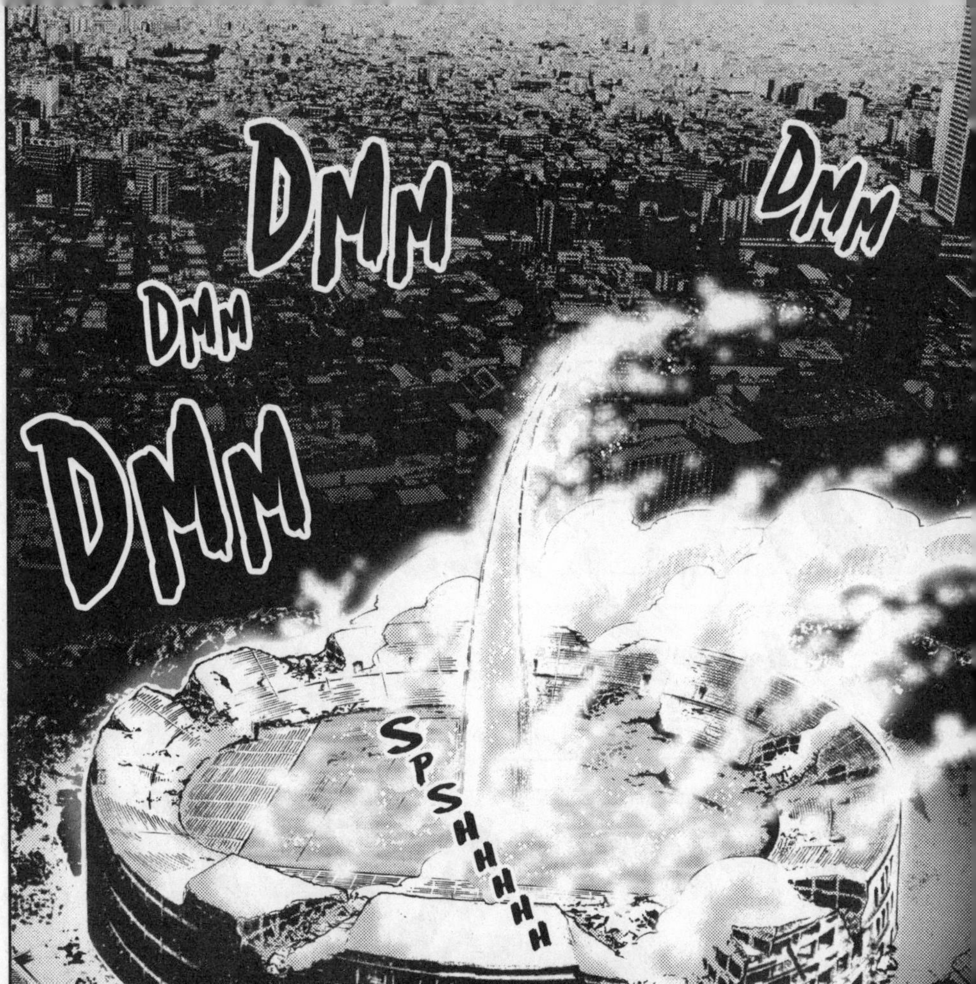
DMM
DMM
DMM
DMM
SPSHHHHH
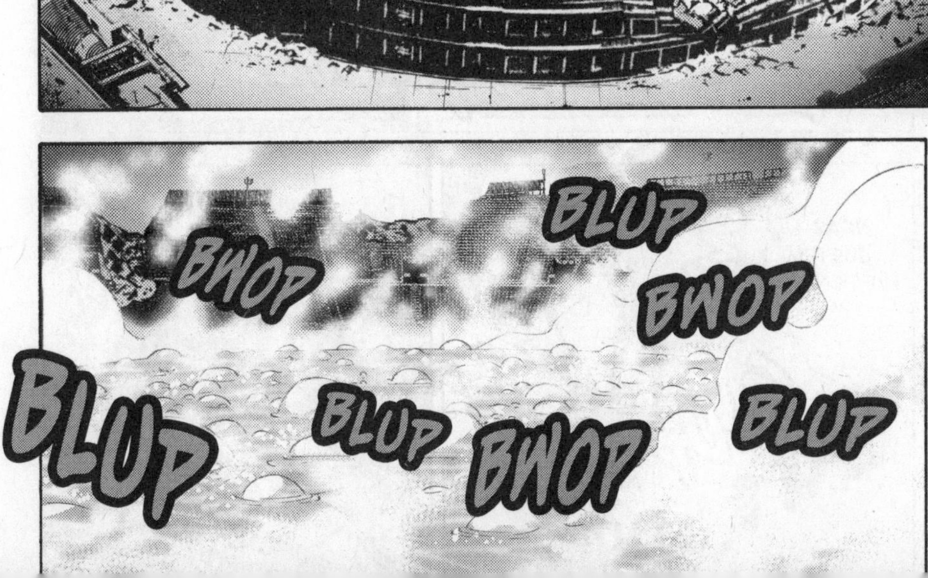
BLUP
BWOP
BWOP
BLUP
BWOP
BLUP
BLUP

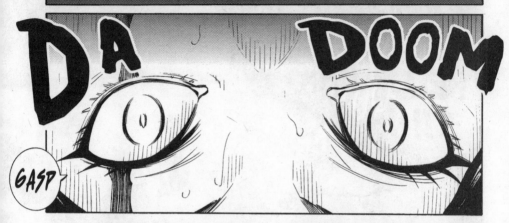

DA DOOM

GASP

WHAH
?!

BLUP

BLUP
BLOP

Rmm

DMM

DMM

DMM

DMM

WHAT
JUST
HAPPENED
?!

GLUP

GLUP

GLUP

GLUP

FSHH

FSHH

SLOSHHH

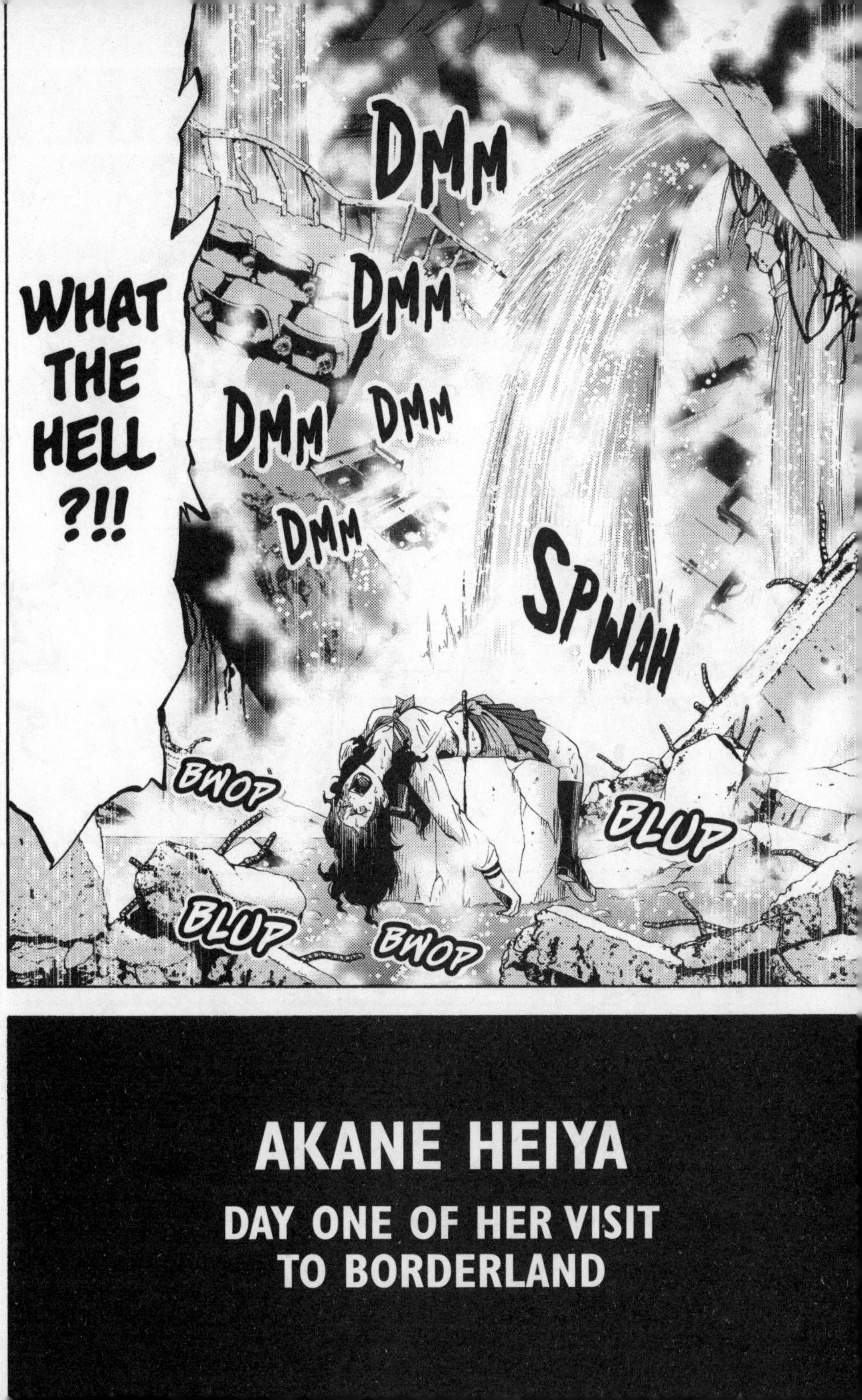
DMM
DMM
DMM
DMM
DMM
SPWAH
WHAT THE HELL ?!!
BLUP
BWOP
BWOP
BLUP

AKANE HEIYA

DAY ONE OF HER VISIT TO BORDERLAND

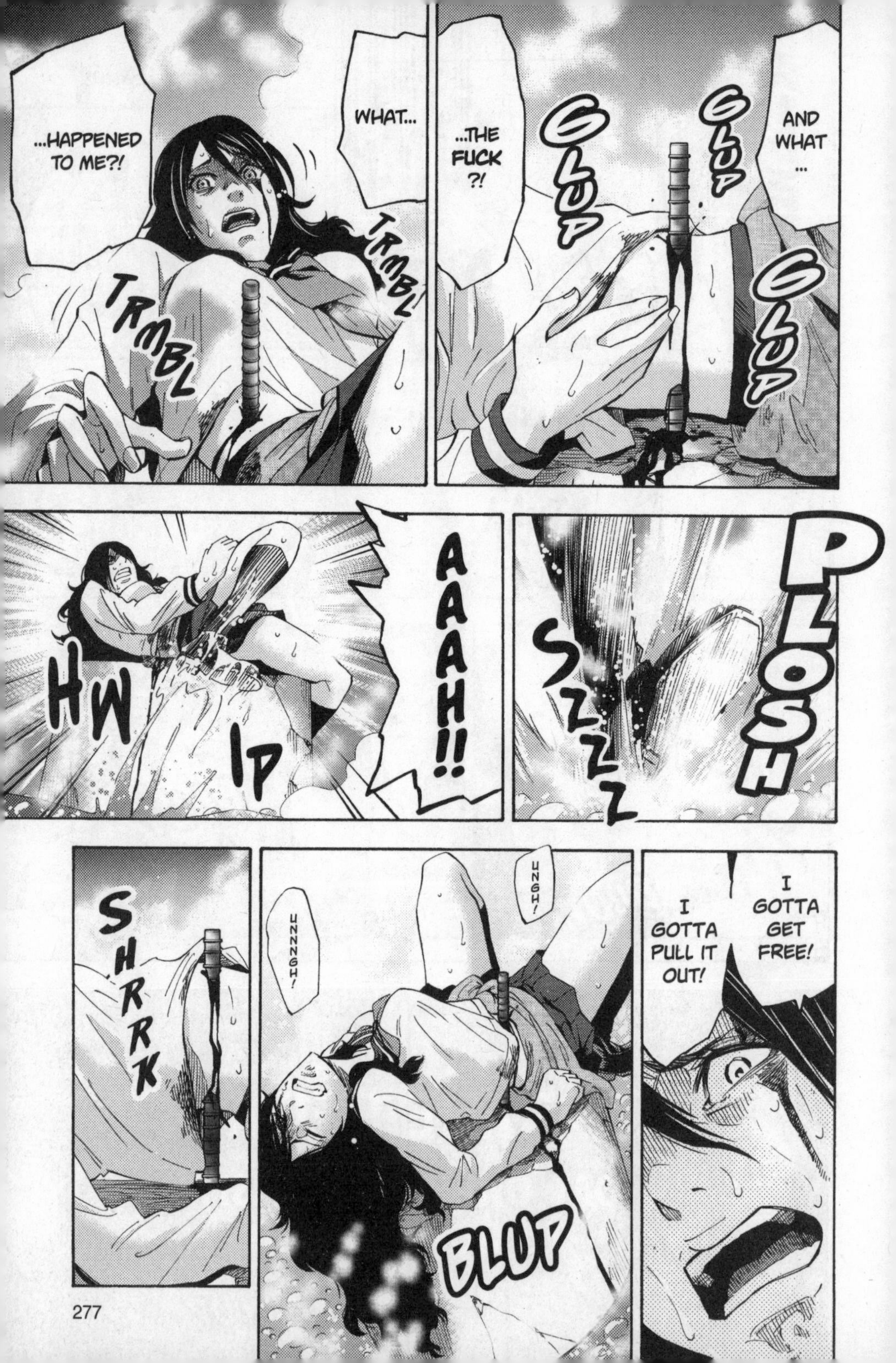
AND WHAT ...
GLUP GLUP
GLUP GLUP
...THE FUCK ?!
GLUP GLUP
WHAT...
...HAPPENED TO ME?!
TRMBL
TRMBL
PLOSH
SZZZZ
AAAAH!!
HWIP
I GOTTA GET FREE!
I GOTTA PULL IT OUT!
UNGH!
UNNNGH!
BLUP
SHRRK

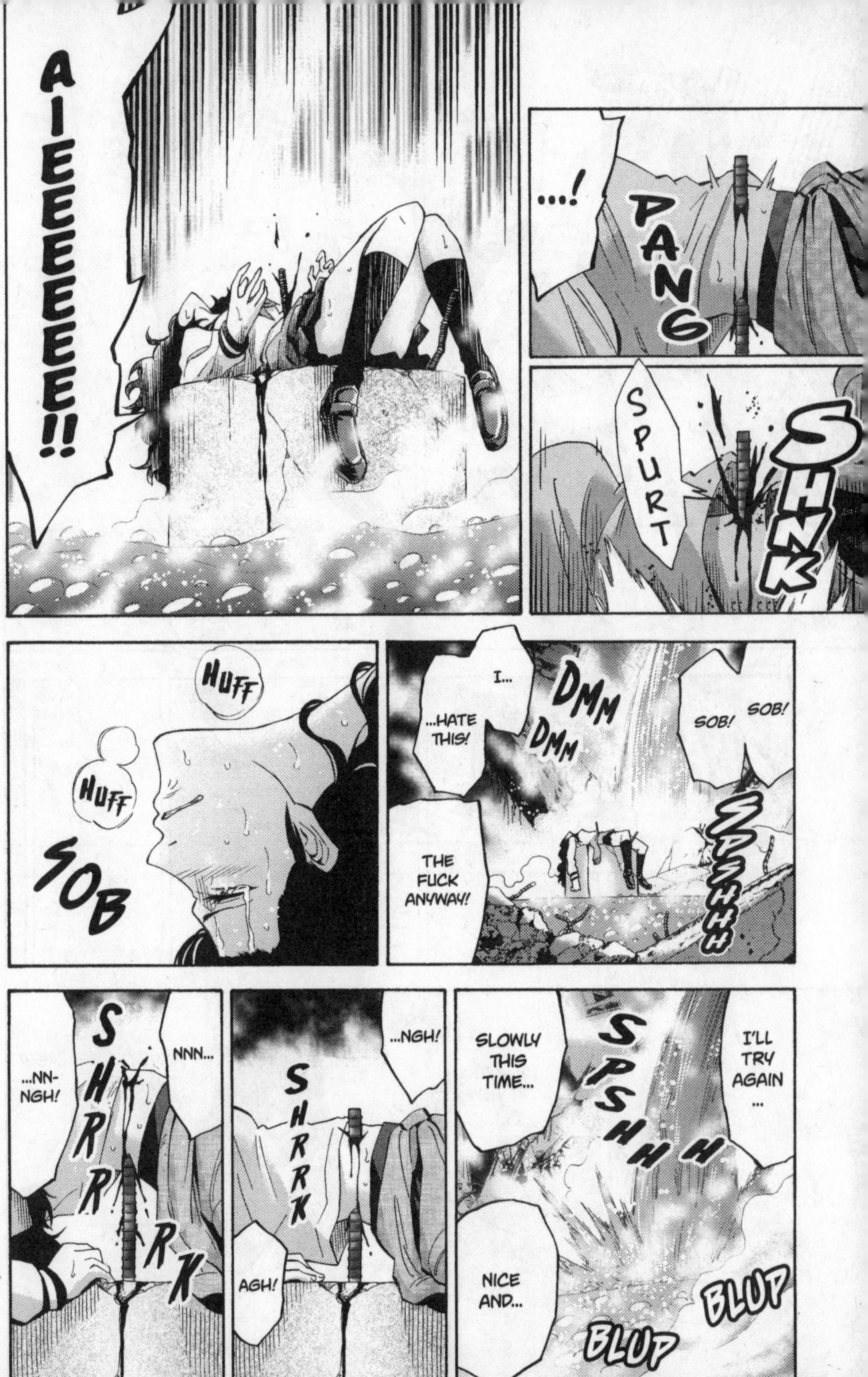
...!
PANG
SHNK
SPURT
AIEEEEEEEE!!
SOB!
SOB!
I...
...HATE THIS!
DMM
DMM
SPSHHHH
THE FUCK ANYWAY!
HUFF
HUFF
SOB
I'LL TRY AGAIN ...
SPSHHH H
SLOWLY THIS TIME...
BLUP
NICE AND...
BLUP
...NGH!
SHRRK
AGH!
NNN...
SHRRRK
...NN-NGH!

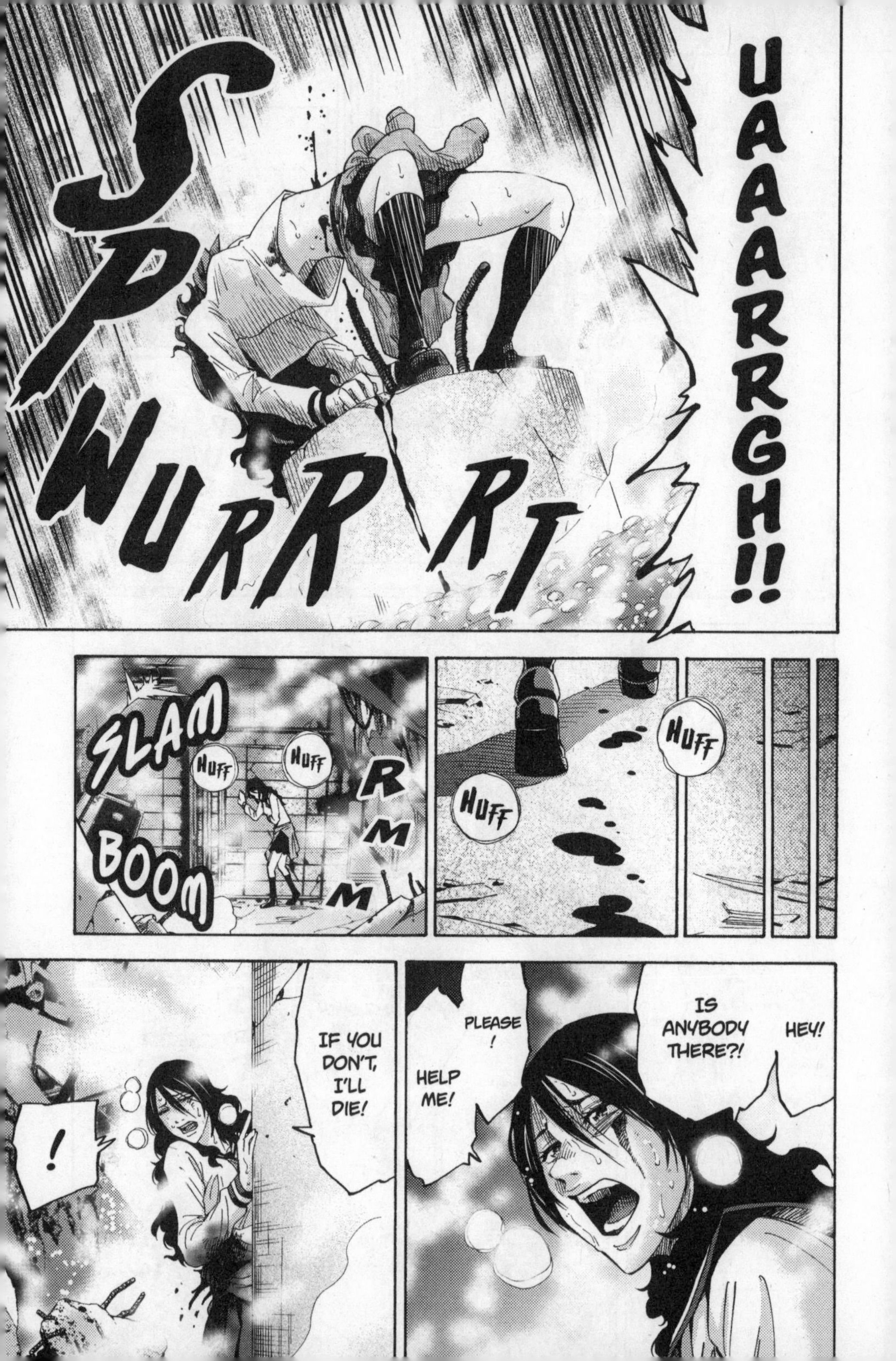
UAAARRGH!!
SPWURRRT
HUFF
HUFF
HUFF
RMM
SLAM
HUFF
BOOM
HEY!
IS ANYBODY THERE?!
PLEASE!
HELP ME!
IF YOU DON'T, I'LL DIE!
!

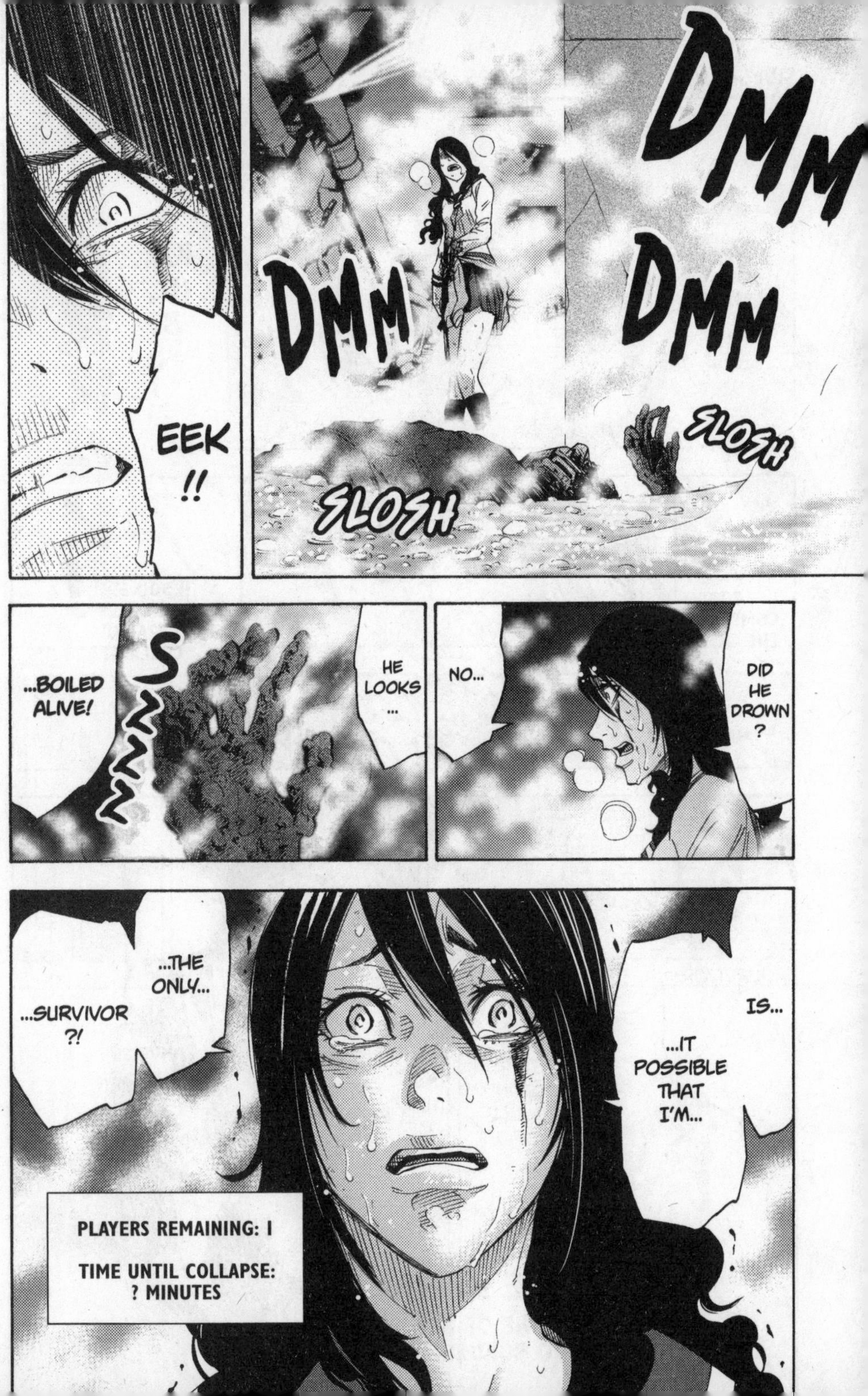
DMM
DMM
DMM
SLOSH
SLOSH
EEK !!
DID HE DROWN?
NO...
HE LOOKS...
...BOILED ALIVE!
IS...
...IT POSSIBLE THAT I'M...
...THE ONLY...
...SURVIVOR?!
PLAYERS REMAINING: 1
TIME UNTIL COLLAPSE: ? MINUTES

SIDE STORY 4: Seven of Spades, Part 2

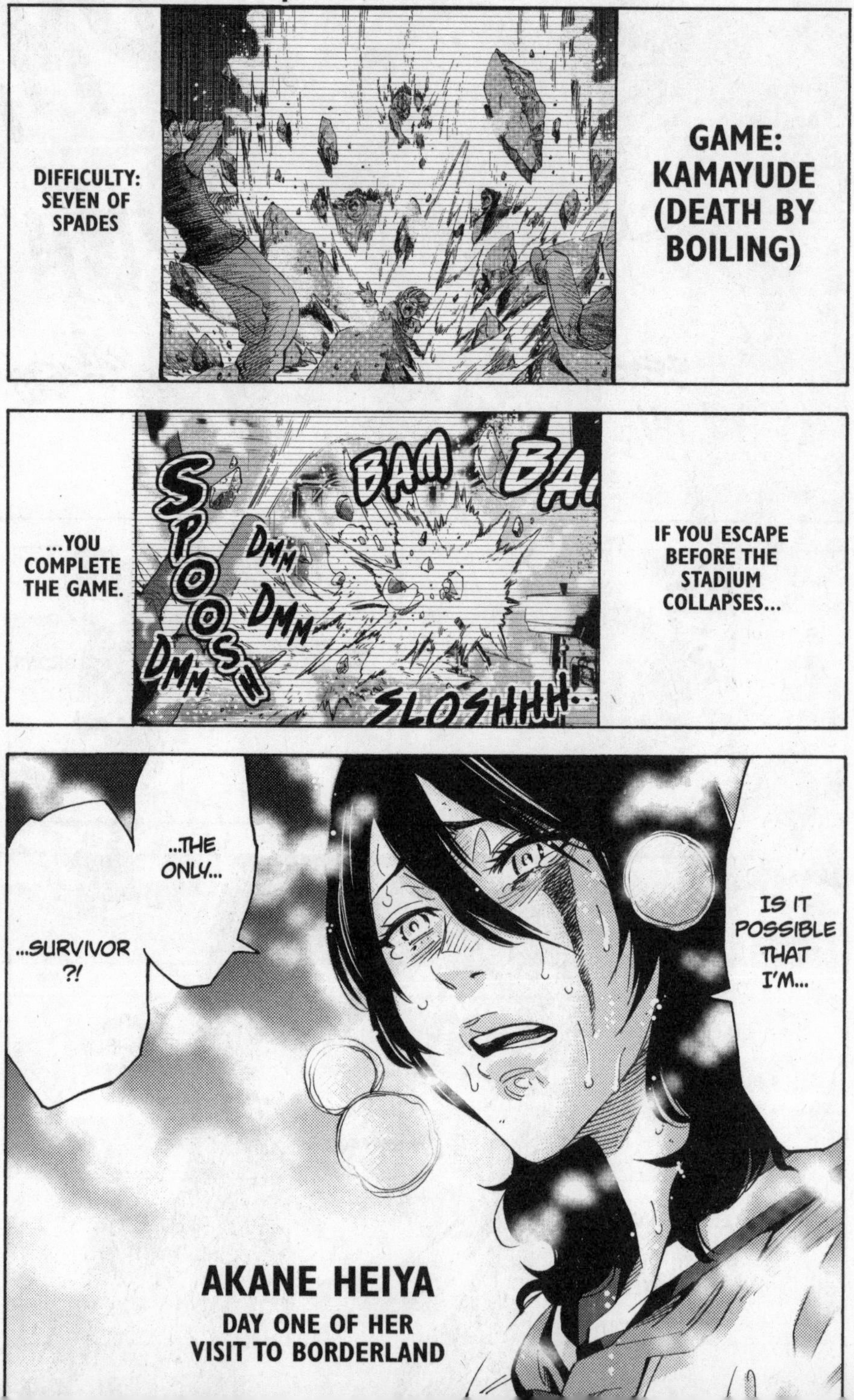
GAME: KAMAYUDE (DEATH BY BOILING)
DIFFICULTY: SEVEN OF SPADES
IF YOU ESCAPE BEFORE THE STADIUM COLLAPSES...
BAM
DMM
DMM
SPOOSH
DMM
SLOSHHH...
...YOU COMPLETE THE GAME.
IS IT POSSIBLE THAT I'M...
...THE ONLY...
...SURVIVOR ?!
AKANE HEIYA
DAY ONE OF HER VISIT TO BORDERLAND

TIME UNTIL COLLAPSE:	PLAYERS REMAINING:
? MINUTES	**1**

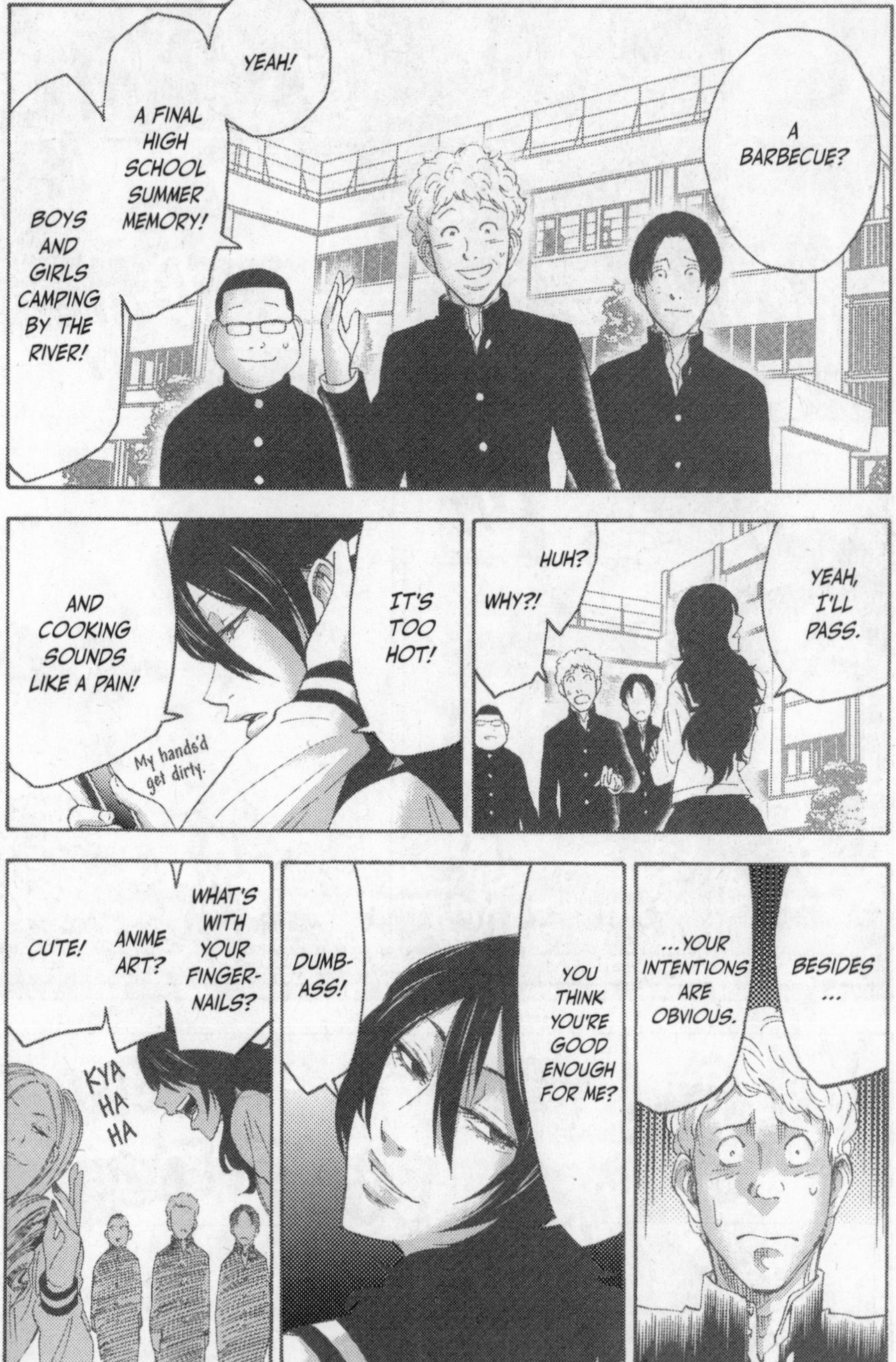
A BARBECUE?
YEAH!
A FINAL HIGH SCHOOL SUMMER MEMORY!
BOYS AND GIRLS CAMPING BY THE RIVER!
YEAH, I'LL PASS.
HUH? WHY?!
IT'S TOO HOT!
AND COOKING SOUNDS LIKE A PAIN!
My hands'd get dirty.
BESIDES...
...YOUR INTENTIONS ARE OBVIOUS.
YOU THINK YOU'RE GOOD ENOUGH FOR ME?
DUMB-ASS!
WHAT'S WITH YOUR FINGER-NAILS?
ANIME ART?
CUTE!
KYA HA HA HA

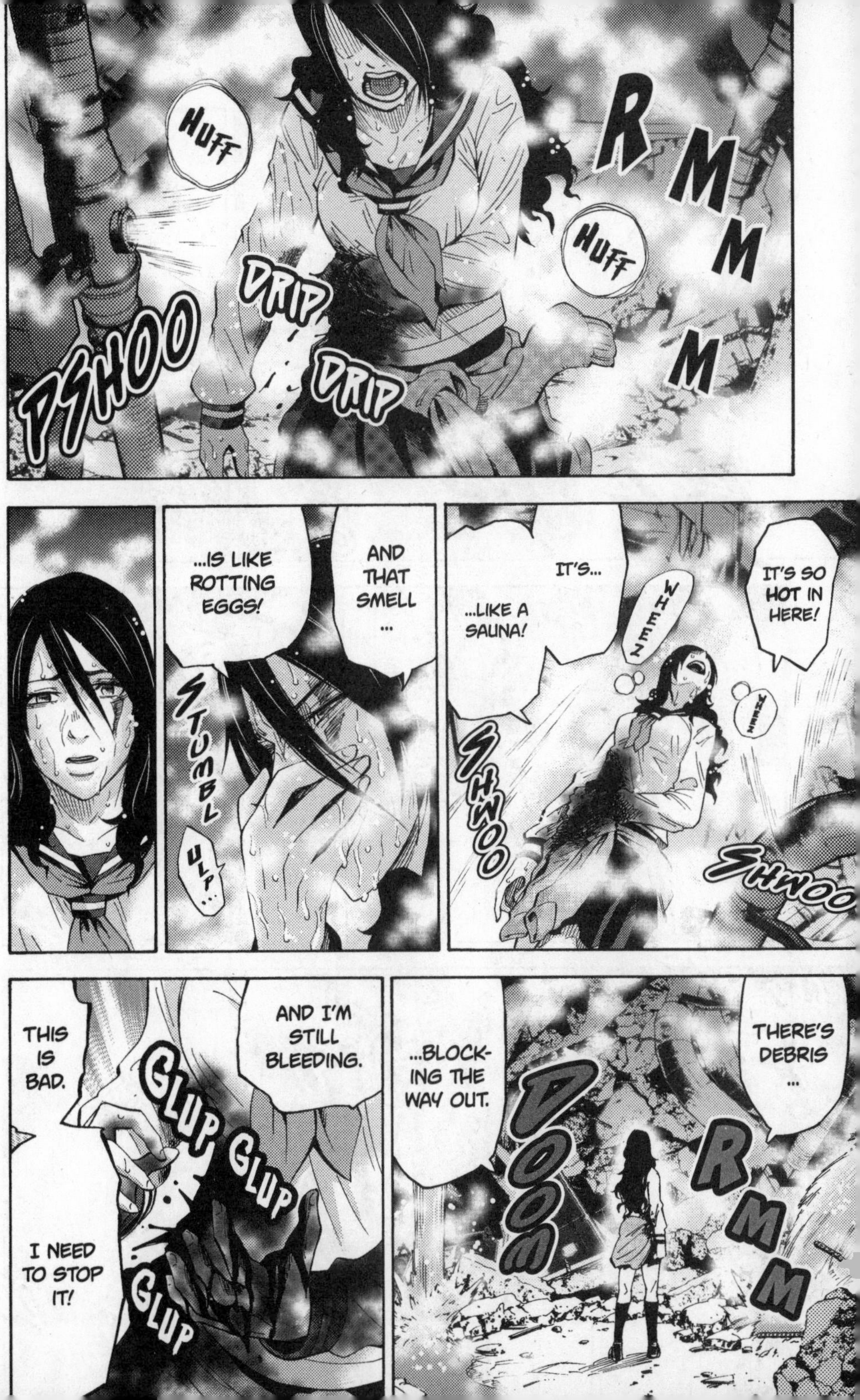
RMMMM
HUFF
HUFF
DRIP
DRIP
DSHOO
IT'S SO HOT IN HERE!
WHEEZ
WHEEZ
IT'S...
...LIKE A SAUNA!
SHWOO
SHWOO
AND THAT SMELL ...
...IS LIKE ROTTING EGGS!
STUMBL
ULP...
THERE'S DEBRIS ...
RMM
...BLOCKING THE WAY OUT.
DOOM
AND I'M STILL BLEEDING.
THIS IS BAD.
GLUP GLUP
I NEED TO STOP IT!
GLUP

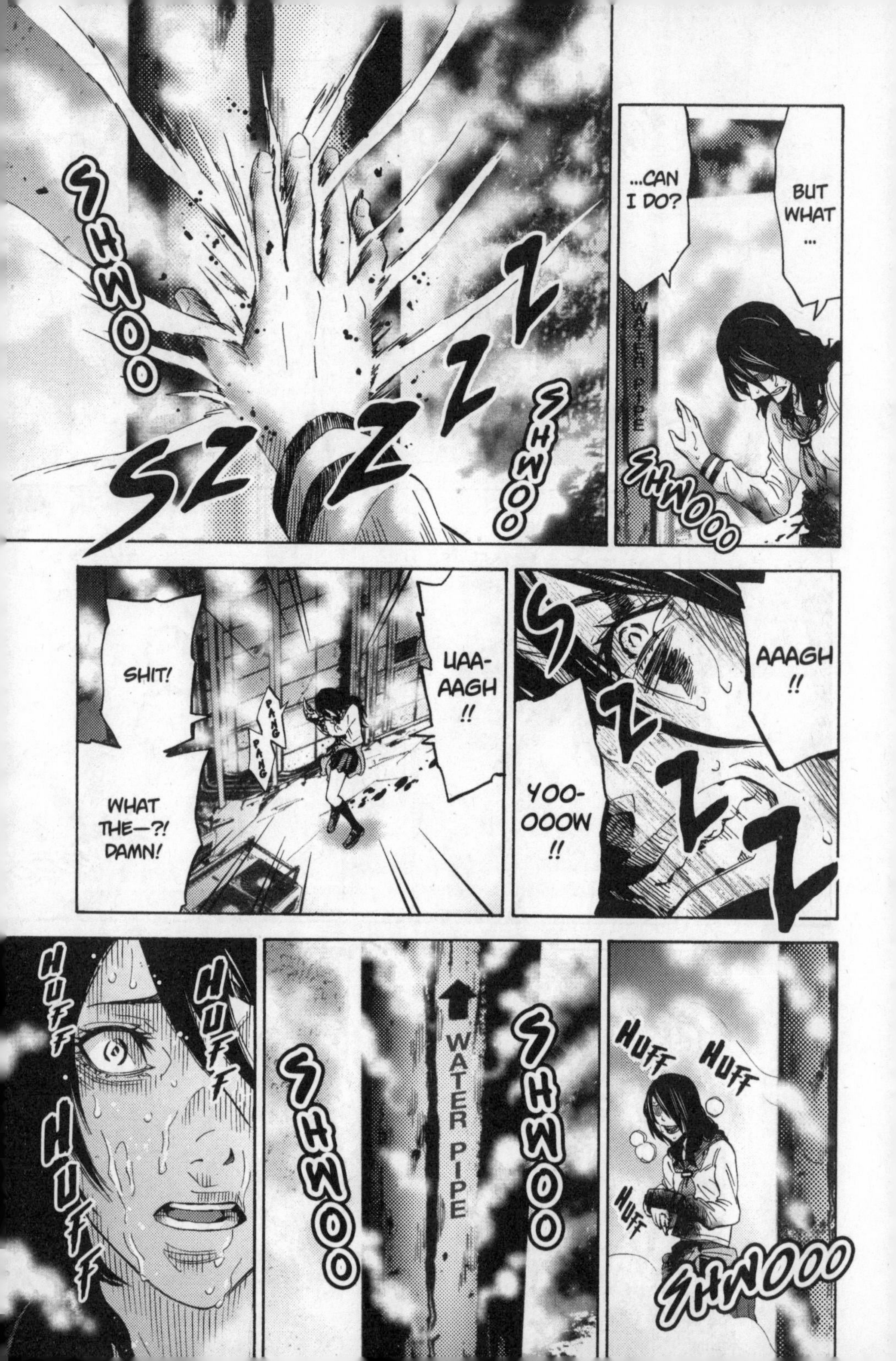
BUT WHAT ...
...CAN I DO?
WATER PIPE
SHWOOO
SHWOO
SZZZZ
SHWOO
AAAGH !!
YOO-OOOW !!
SZZZZ
UAA-AAGH !!
SHIT!
WHAT THE—?! DAMN!
PANG PANG
HUFF
HUFF
HUFF
SHWOOO
SHWOO
WATER PIPE
SHWOO
HUFF
HUFF
HUFF

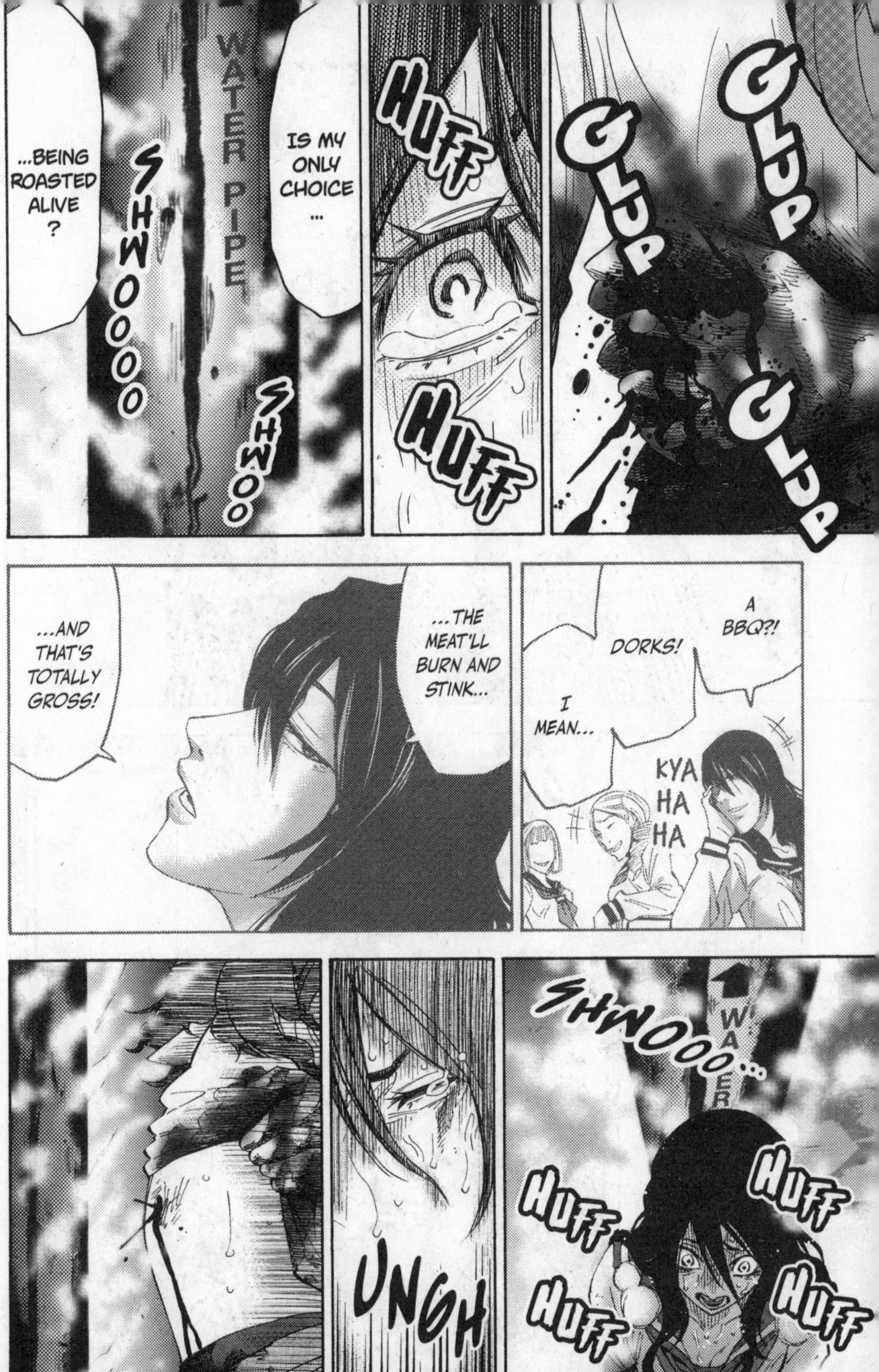
GLUP
GLUP
GLUP
GLUP
HUFF
HUFF
IS MY ONLY CHOICE ...
WATER PIPE
...BEING ROASTED ALIVE ?
SHWOOOOO
SHWOO
A BBQ?!
DORKS!
I MEAN...
KYA HA HA HA
...THE MEAT'LL BURN AND STINK...
...AND THAT'S TOTALLY GROSS!
SHWOOO...
WATER
HUFF
HUFF
HUFF
HUFF
UNGH

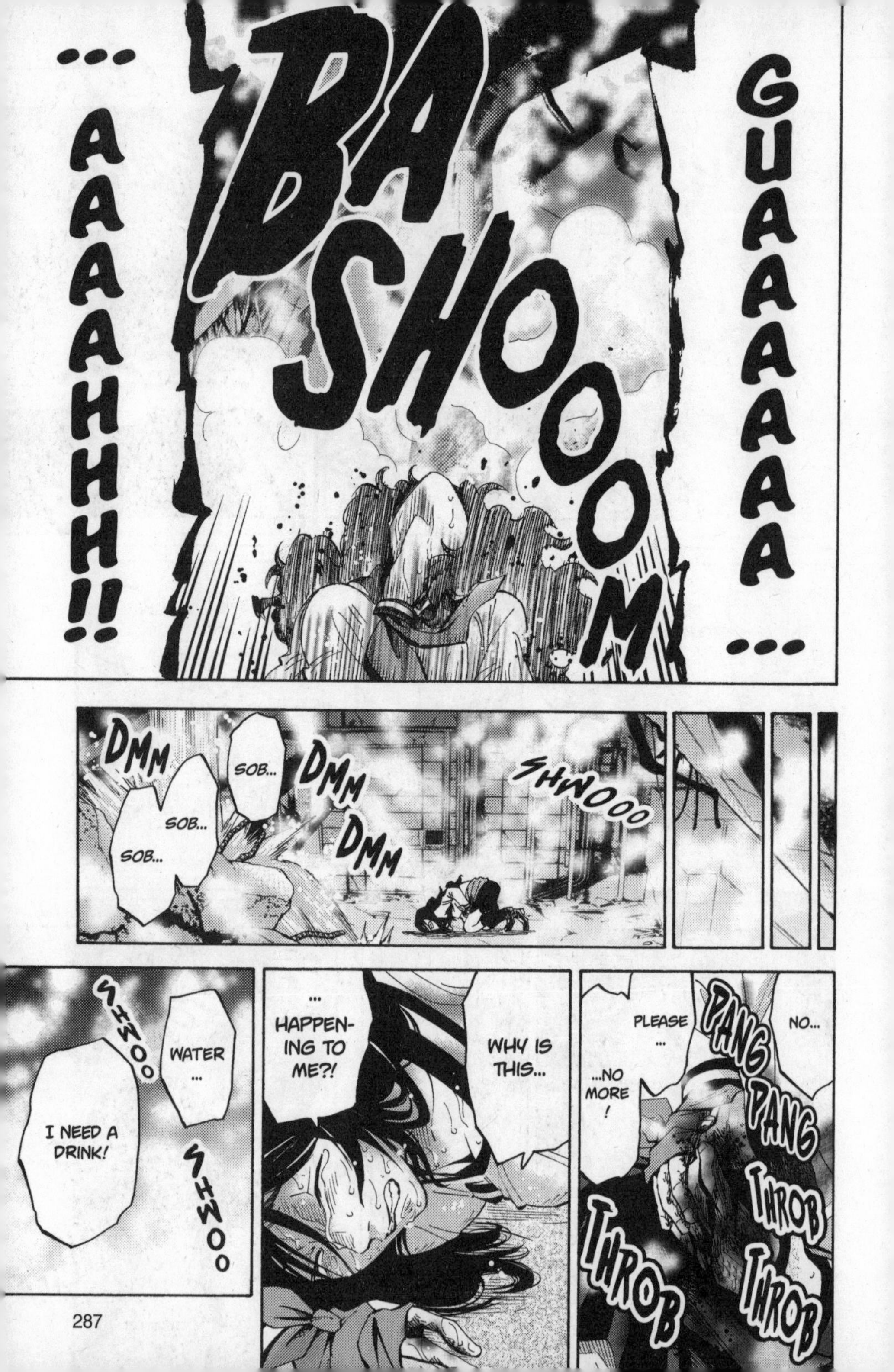
GUAAAAAA...
BASHOOOOM
...AAAAHHHH!!
SHWOOO
DMM
DMM
DMM
SOB...
SOB...
SOB...
NO...
PANG PANG
THROB THROB
PLEASE...
...NO MORE!
THROB
WHY IS THIS...
...HAPPENING TO ME?!
SHWOO
WATER...
I NEED A DRINK!
SHWOO

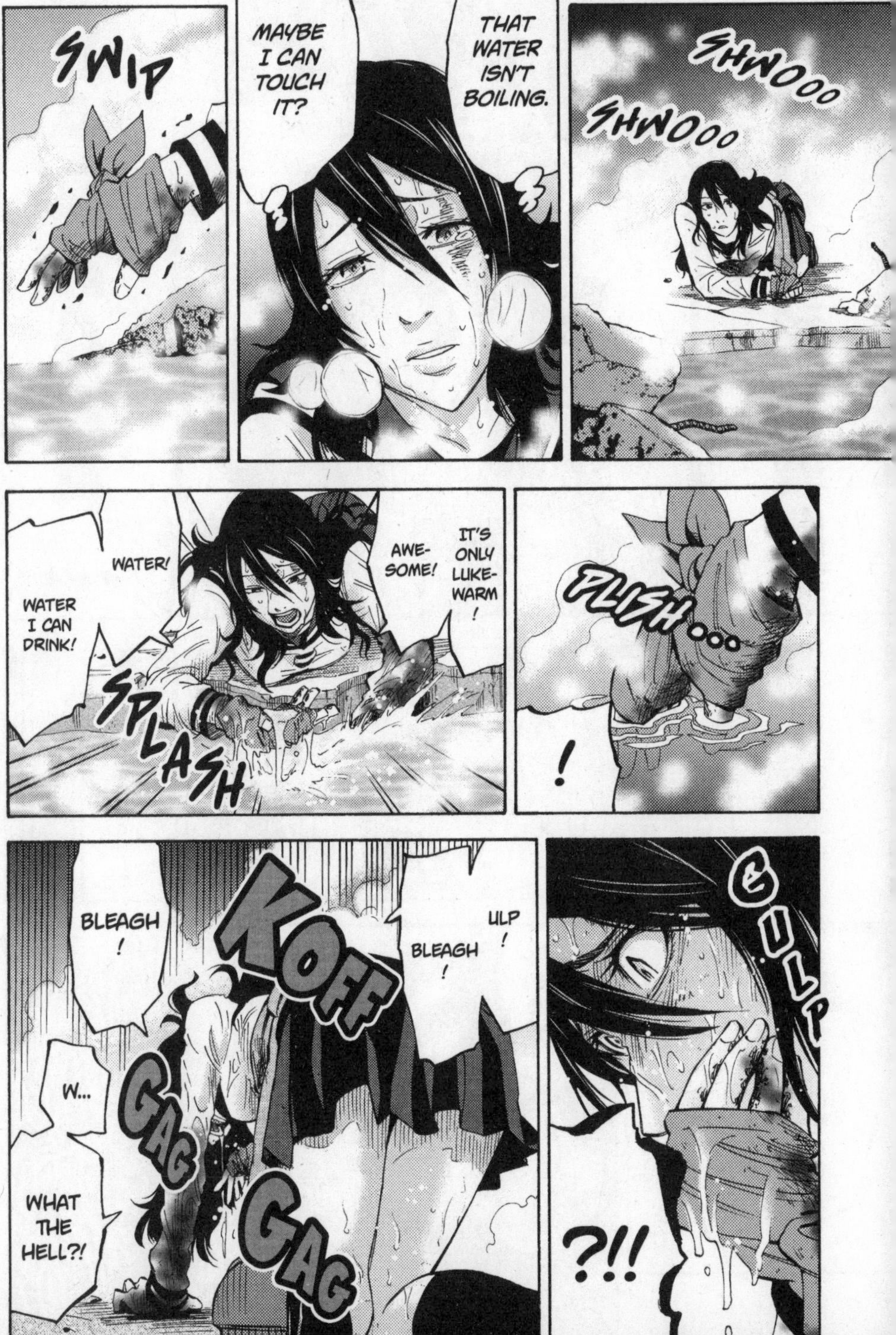
SHWOOO
SHWOOO
THAT WATER ISN'T BOILING.
MAYBE I CAN TOUCH IT?
SWIP
PLISH...
!
IT'S ONLY LUKEWARM!
AWESOME!
WATER!
WATER I CAN DRINK!
SPLASH
GULP
?!!
ULP!
BLEAGH!
KOFF
BLEAGH!
GAG
GAG
GAG
W...
WHAT THE HELL?!

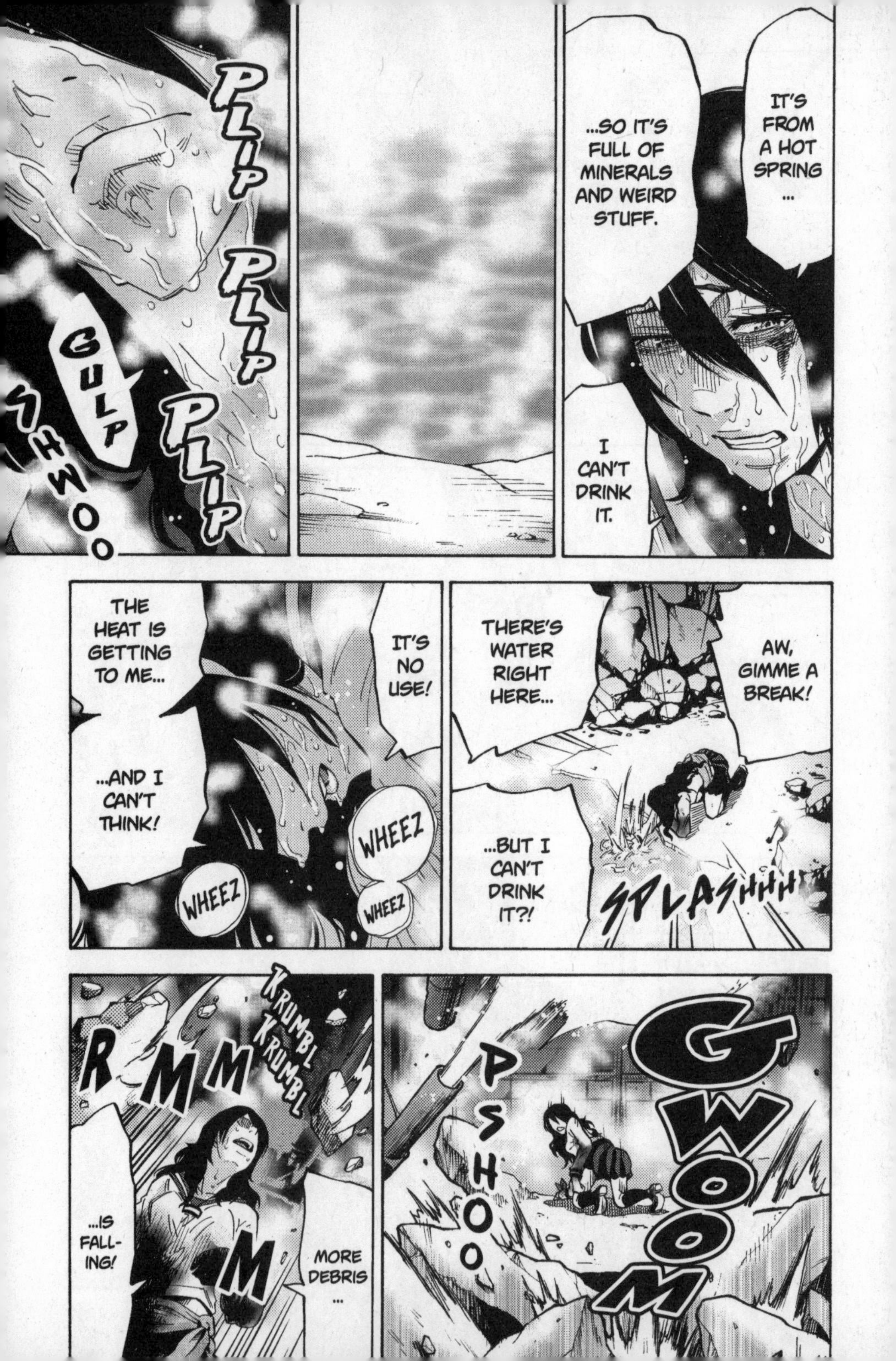
IT'S FROM A HOT SPRING ...
...SO IT'S FULL OF MINERALS AND WEIRD STUFF.
I CAN'T DRINK IT.
PLIP PLIP PLIP
GULP
SHWOOO
AW, GIMME A BREAK!
THERE'S WATER RIGHT HERE...
...BUT I CAN'T DRINK IT?!
SPLASHHH
IT'S NO USE!
THE HEAT IS GETTING TO ME...
...AND I CAN'T THINK!
WHEEZ
WHEEZ
WHEEZ
GWOOOM
PSHOOO
KRUMBL KRUMBL
RMMMM
MORE DEBRIS ...
...IS FALL-ING!

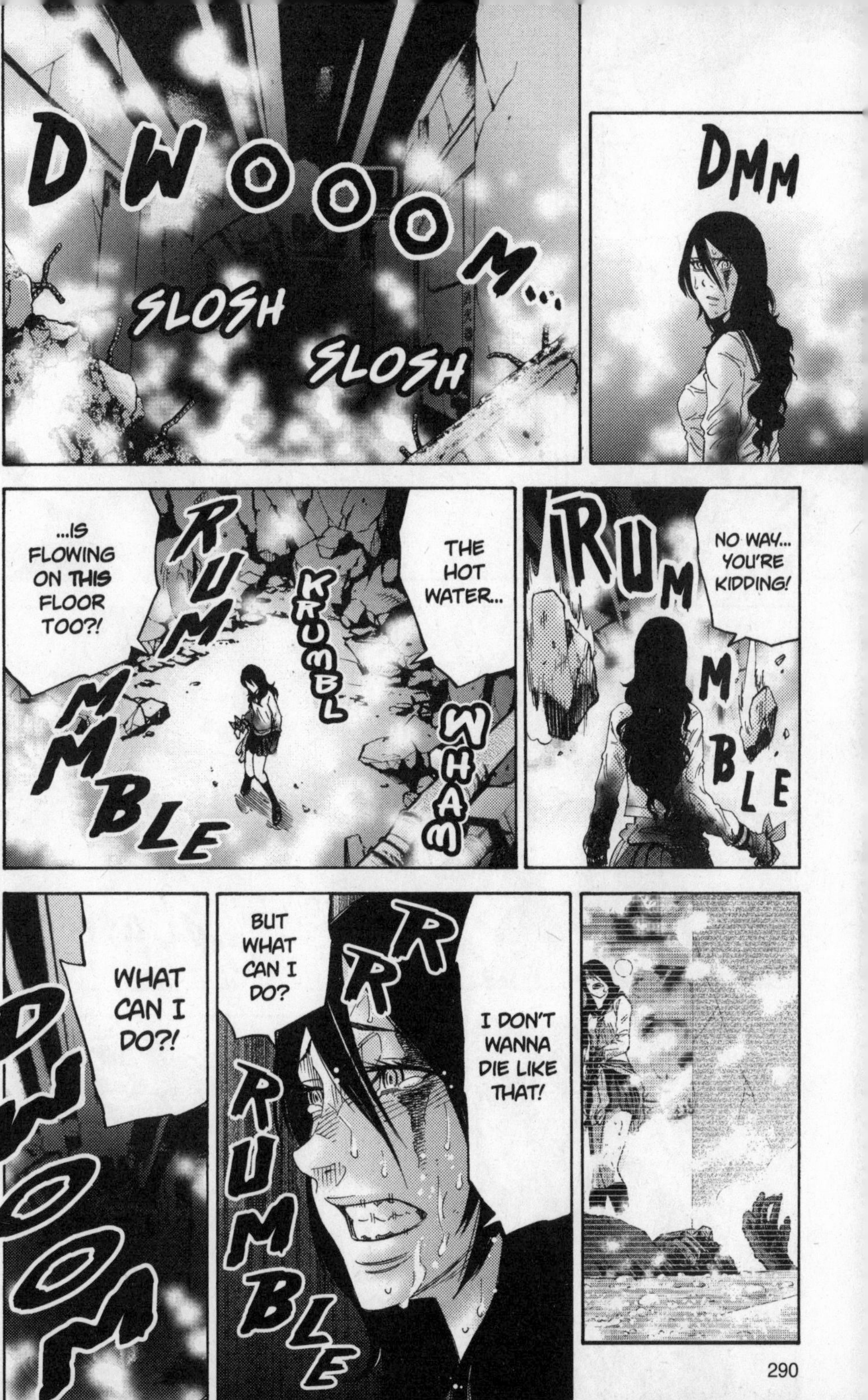
DMM
DWOOOOM...
SLOSH
SLOSH
RUMMBLE
NO WAY... YOU'RE KIDDING!
THE HOT WATER...
...IS FLOWING ON THIS FLOOR TOO?!
RUMMMBLE
KRUMBL
WHAM
BUT WHAT CAN I DO?
I DON'T WANNA DIE LIKE THAT!
RRRUMBLE
WHAT CAN I DO?!
DWOOOM

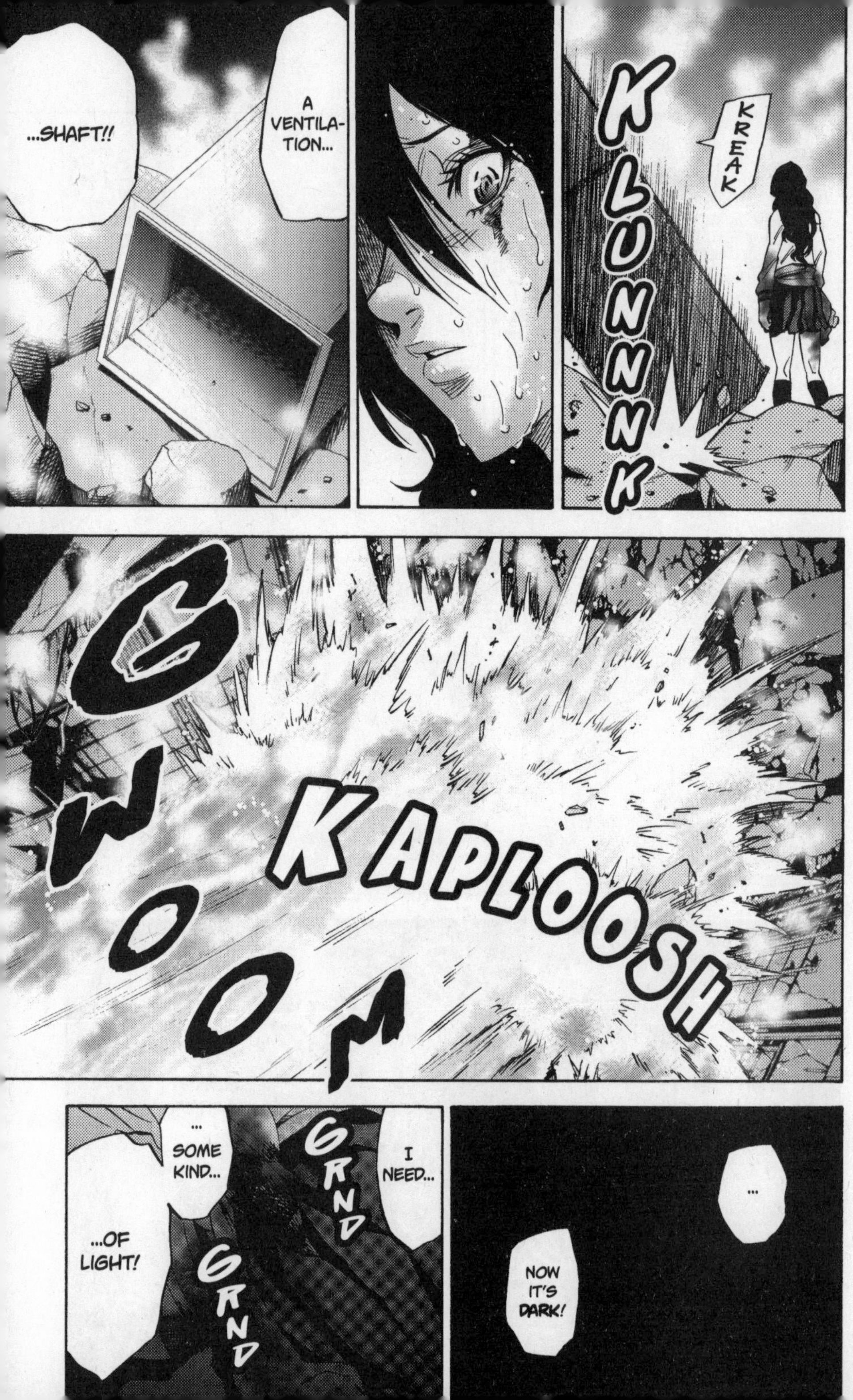
KLUNNNK
KREAK
A VENTILATION...
...SHAFT!!
GWOOM
KAPLOOSH
...
NOW IT'S DARK!
I NEED...
GRND
... SOME KIND...
GRND
...OF LIGHT!

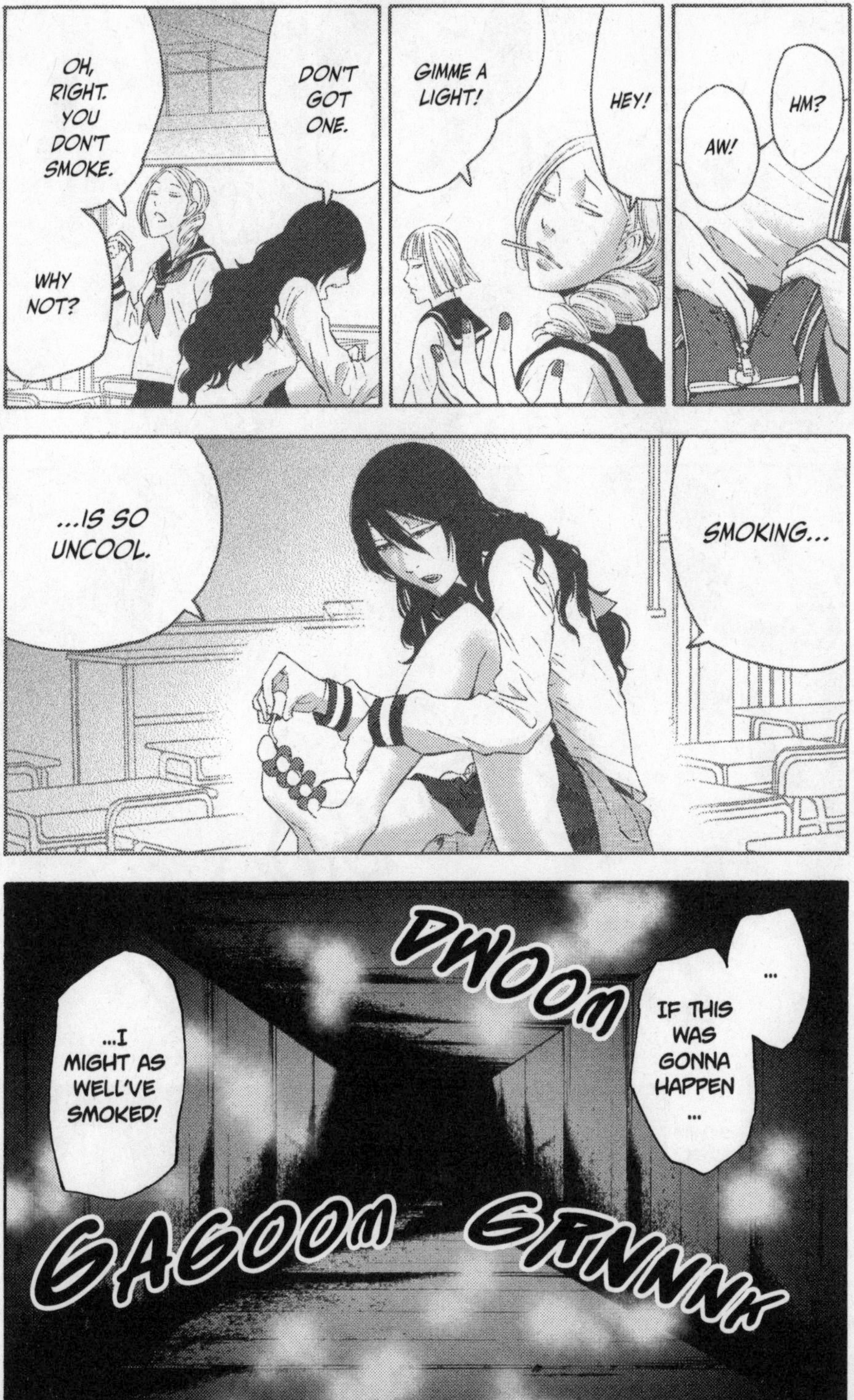
HM?
AW!
HEY!
GIMME A LIGHT!
DON'T GOT ONE.
OH, RIGHT. YOU DON'T SMOKE.
WHY NOT?
SMOKING...
...IS SO UNCOOL.
... IF THIS WAS GONNA HAPPEN ...
DWOOM
...I MIGHT AS WELL'VE SMOKED!
GRNNNK
GAGOOM

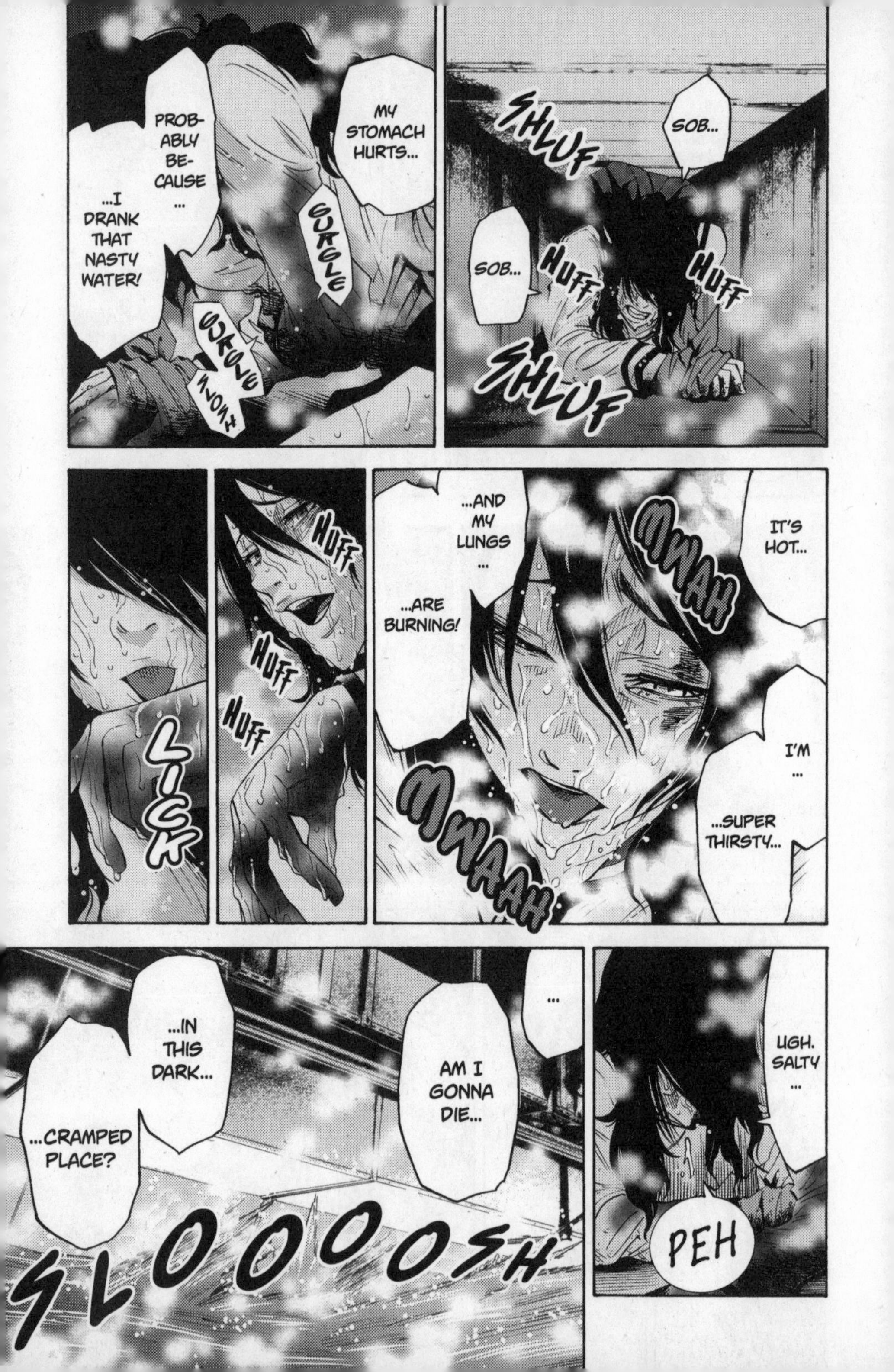
SOB...
SHLUF
HUFF
SOB...
HUFF
SHLUF
MY STOMACH HURTS...
GURGLE
PROB-ABLY BE-CAUSE...
...I DRANK THAT NASTY WATER!
GURGLE
IT'S HOT...
MWAAH
...AND MY LUNGS...
...ARE BURNING!
I'M...
...SUPER THIRSTY...
MWAAAH
HUFF
HUFF
HUFF
LICK
UGH. SALTY...
PEH
...
AM I GONNA DIE...
...IN THIS DARK...
...CRAMPED PLACE?
SLOOOOOSH

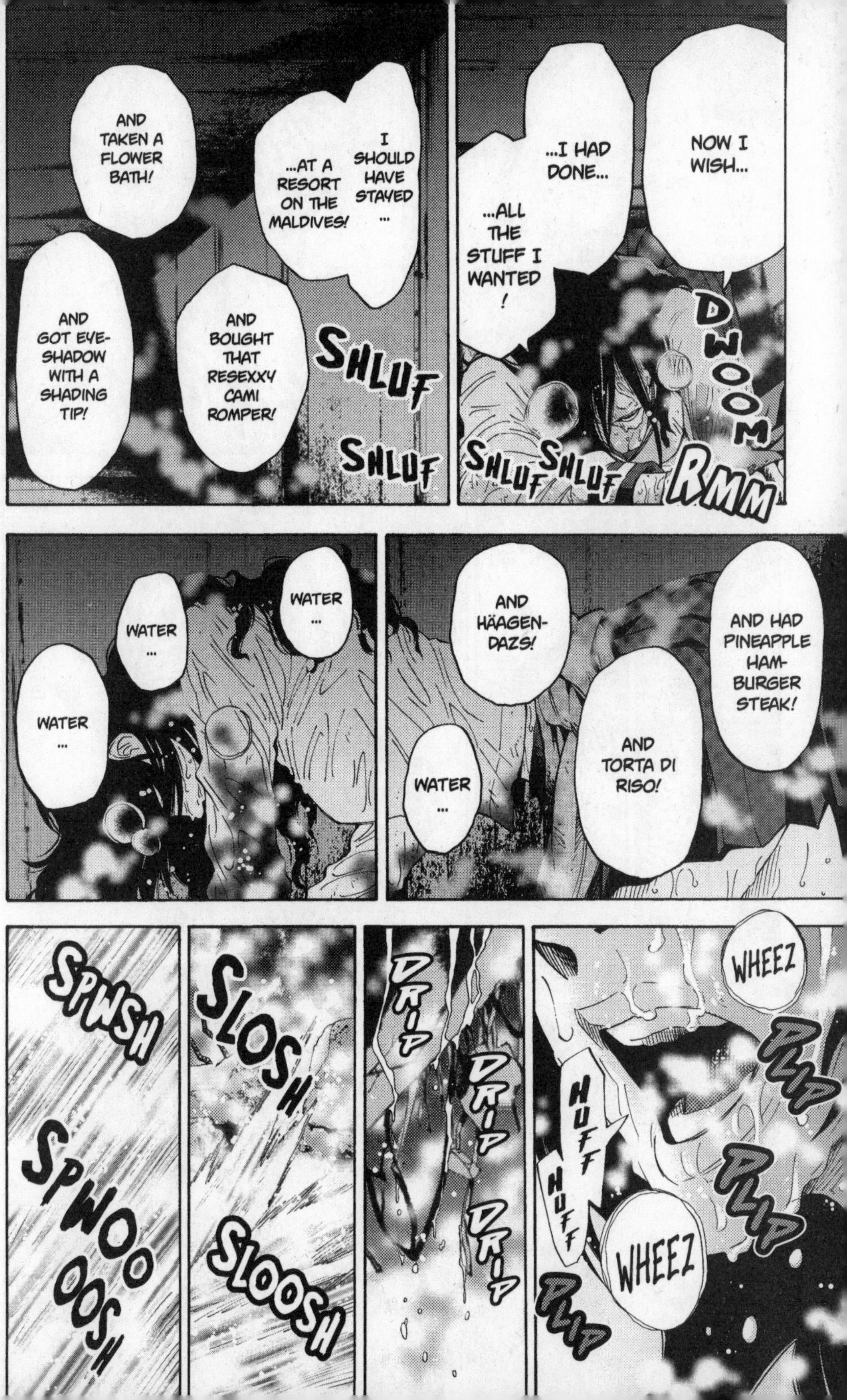
NOW I WISH...
...I HAD DONE...
...ALL THE STUFF I WANTED!
DWOOMRMM
SHLUF SHLUF
I SHOULD HAVE STAYED...
...AT A RESORT ON THE MALDIVES!
AND TAKEN A FLOWER BATH!
AND BOUGHT THAT RESEXXY CAMI ROMPER!
AND GOT EYE-SHADOW WITH A SHADING TIP!
SHLUF
SHLUF
AND HAD PINEAPPLE HAMBURGER STEAK!
AND HÄAGEN-DAZS!
AND TORTA DI RISO!
WATER...
WATER...
WATER...
WATER...
WHEEZ
PLIP
PLIP
HUFF
HUFF
WHEEZ
PLIP
DRIP
DRIP
DRIP
DRIP
SLOSH
SLOOSH
SPWSH
SPWOOOOSH

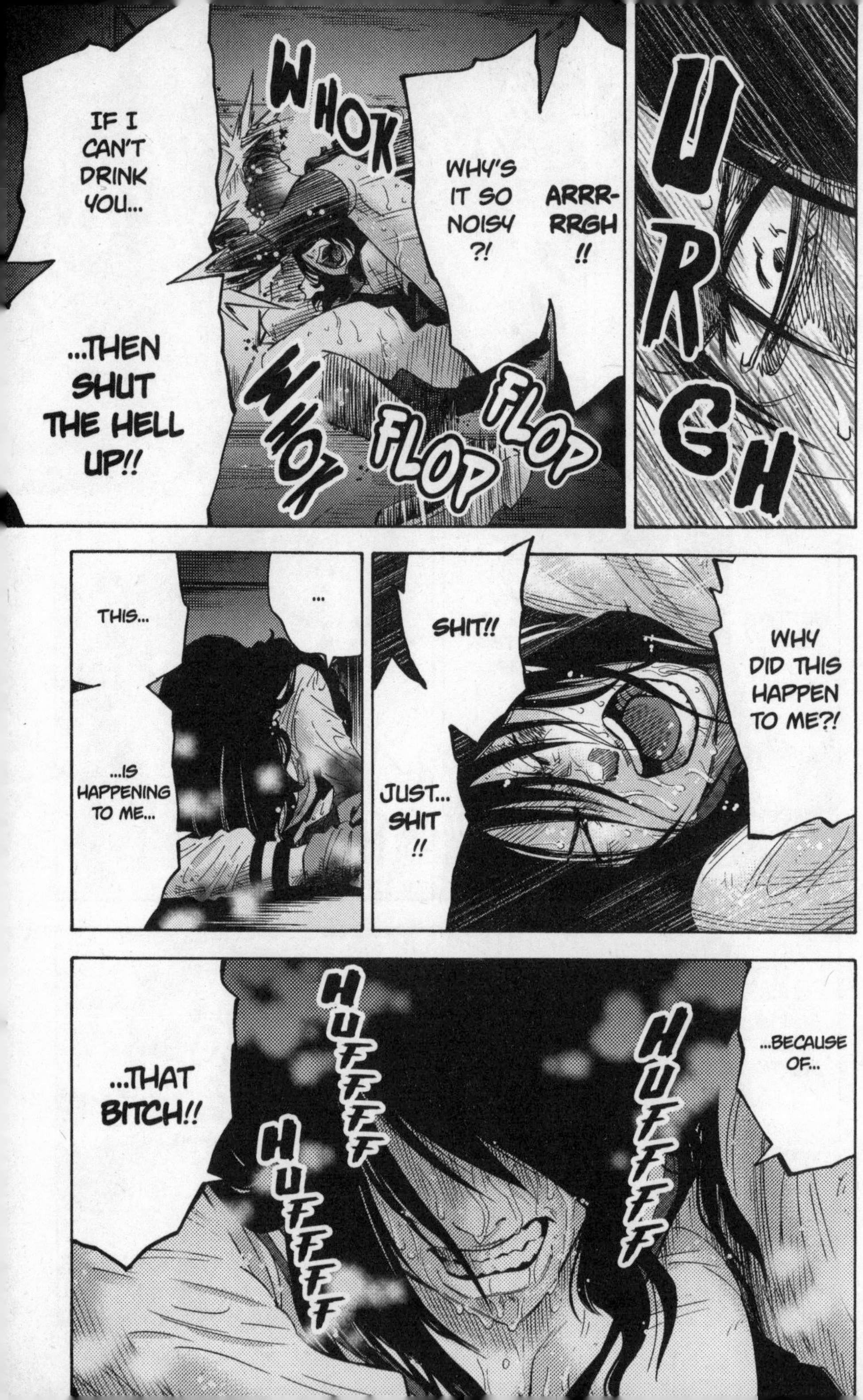
URGH
ARRR-RRGH!!
WHY'S IT SO NOISY?!
WHOK
IF I CAN'T DRINK YOU...
...THEN SHUT THE HELL UP!!
FLOP
FLOP
WHOK
WHY DID THIS HAPPEN TO ME?!
SHIT!!
JUST... SHIT!!
...
THIS...
...IS HAPPENING TO ME...
...BECAUSE OF...
HUFFFFF
HUFFFFF
...THAT BITCH!!
HUFFFFF

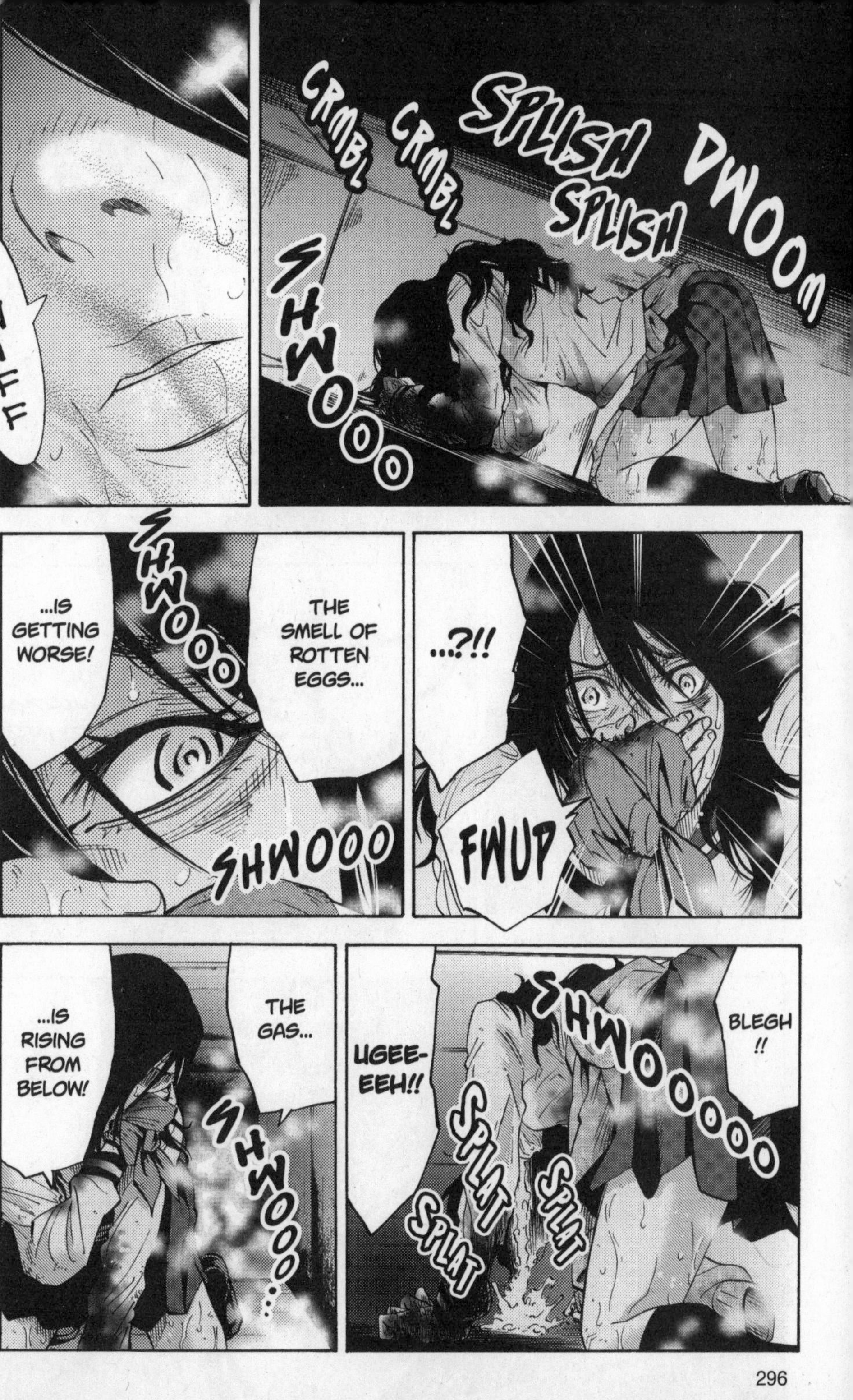
DWOOM
SPLISH
SPLISH
CRMBL
CRMBL
SHWOOO
SNIFF
...?!!
FWUP
THE SMELL OF ROTTEN EGGS...
SHWOOO
...IS GETTING WORSE!
SHWOOO
BLEGH!!
SHWOOOOOO
UGEE-EEH!!
SPLAT
SPLAT
SPLAT
THE GAS...
...IS RISING FROM BELOW!
SHWOOO...

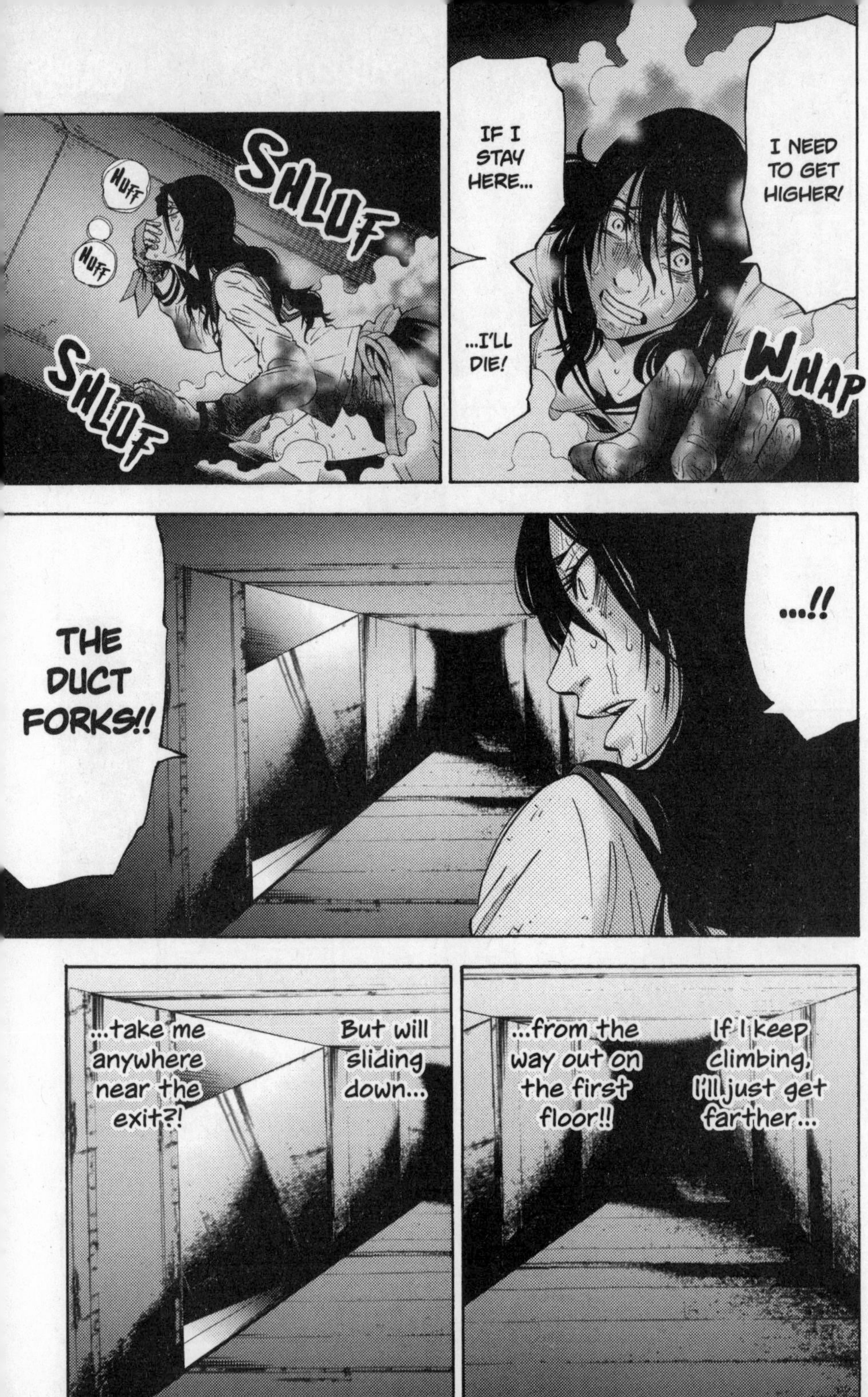
I NEED TO GET HIGHER!
IF I STAY HERE...
...I'LL DIE!
WHAP
SHLUF
HUFF
HUFF
SHLUF
...!!
THE DUCT FORKS!!
If I keep climbing, I'll just get farther...
...from the way out on the first floor!!
But will sliding down...
...take me anywhere near the exit?!

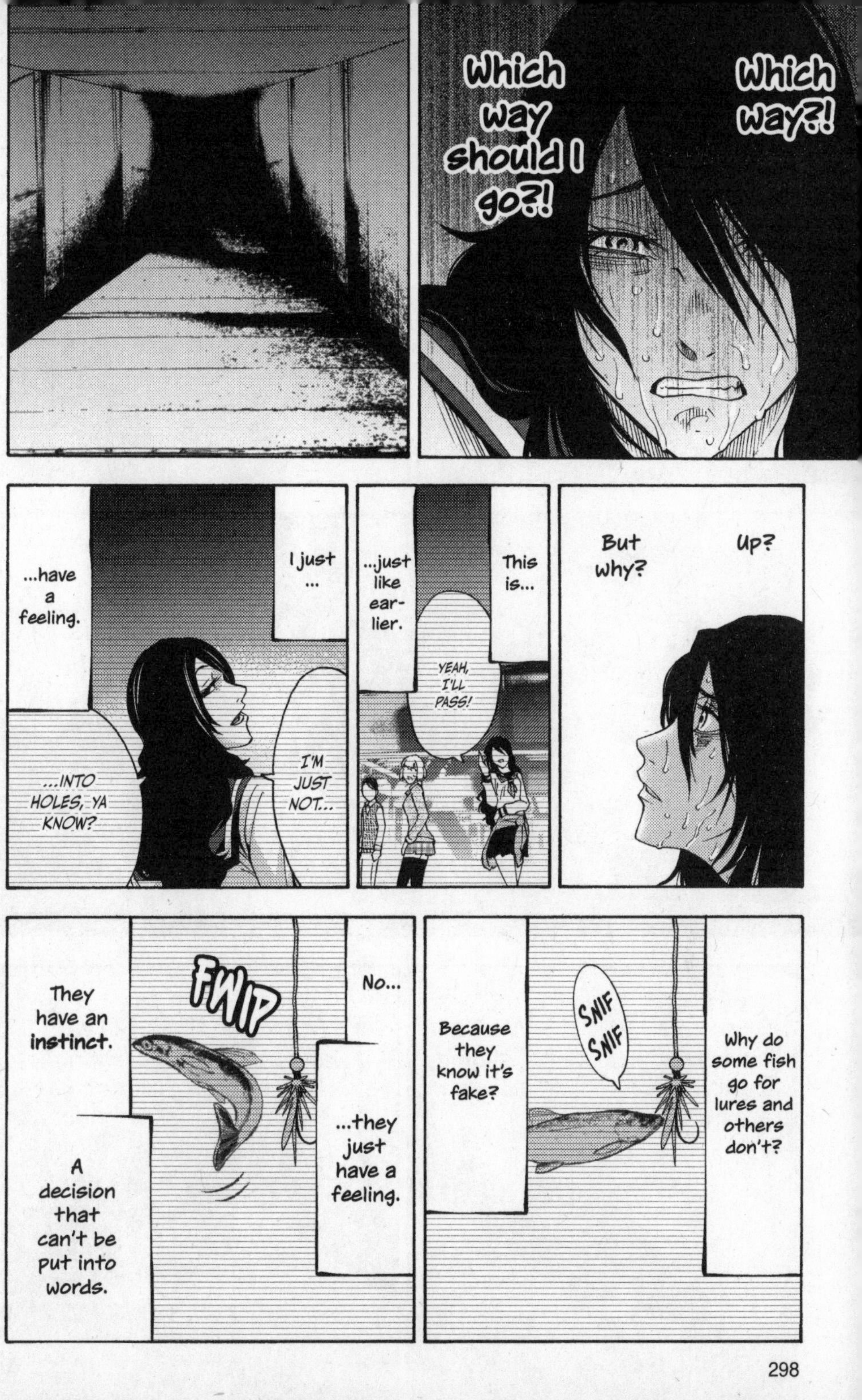
Which way?!
Which way should I go?!
Up?
But why?
This is...
...just like earlier.
YEAH, I'LL PASS!
I just ...
...have a feeling.
I'M JUST NOT...
...INTO HOLES, YA KNOW?
Why do some fish go for lures and others don't?
SNIF SNIF
Because they know it's fake?
No...
...they just have a feeling.
FWIP
They have an **instinct**.
A decision that can't be put into words.

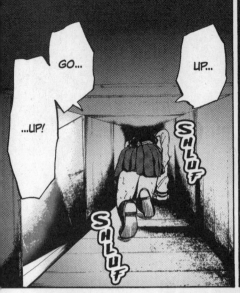

GO...

...UP!

UP...

SHLUF

SHLUF

Trust your instincts!!

UP!!

DMM

DMM

DMM

SHLUF

DMM

DMM

DMM

DMM

BLUP

BLUP

BLUP

DMM

DMM

DMM

DMM

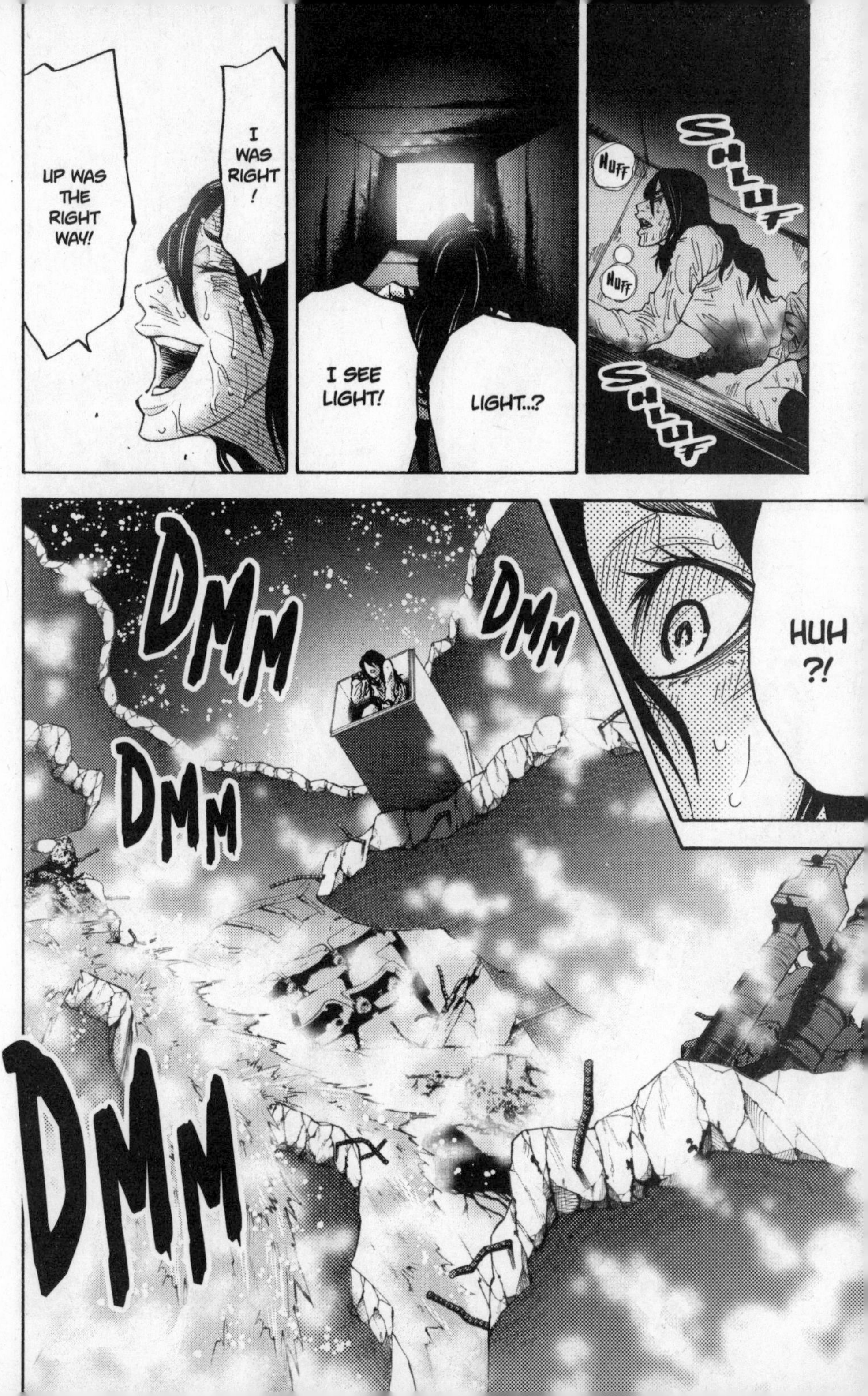
SHLUF
HUFF
HUFF
SHLUF
LIGHT..?
I SEE LIGHT!
I WAS RIGHT!
UP WAS THE RIGHT WAY!
HUH?!
DMM
DMM
DMM
DMM

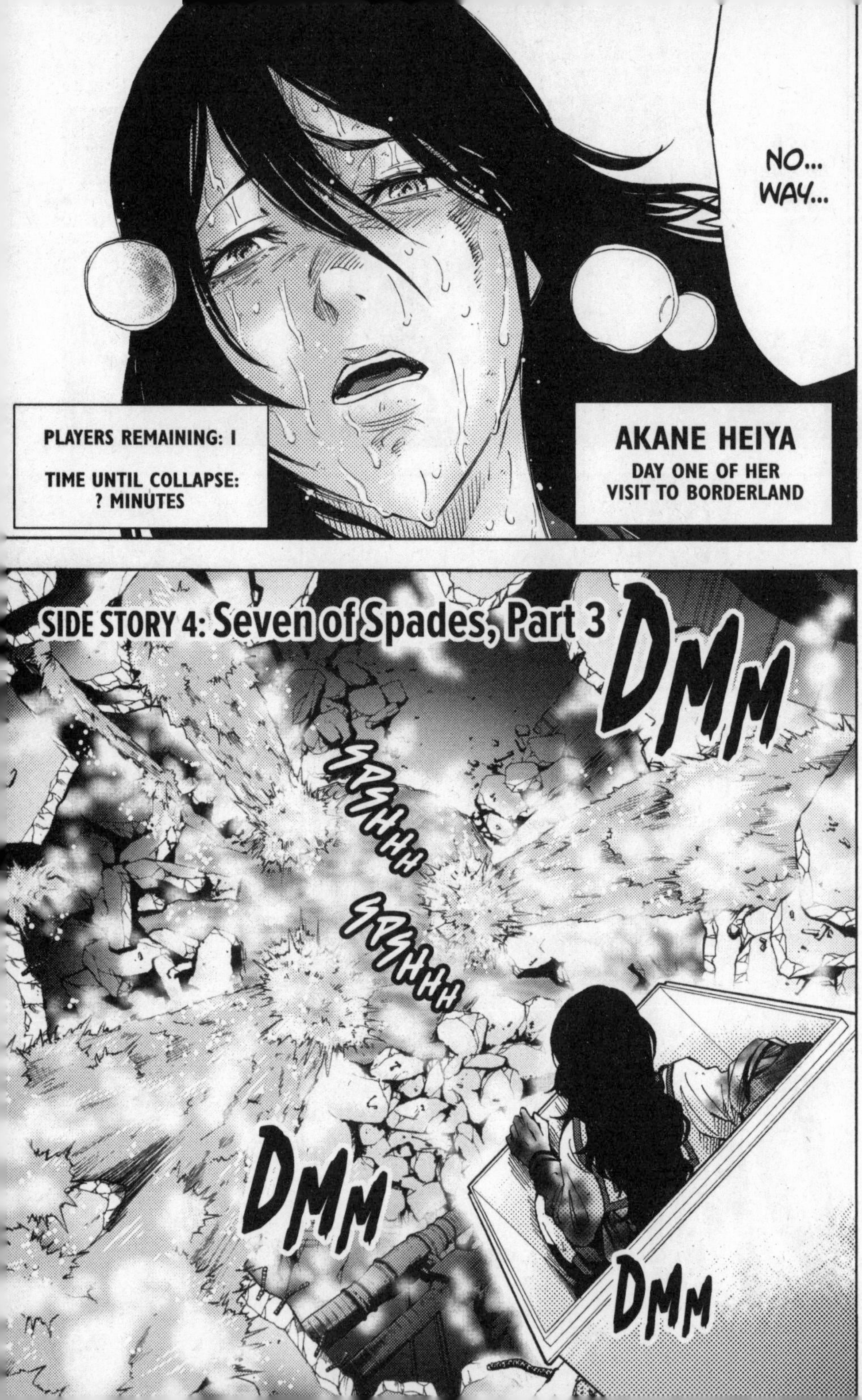
NO... WAY...
AKANE HEIYA
DAY ONE OF HER VISIT TO BORDERLAND
PLAYERS REMAINING: 1
TIME UNTIL COLLAPSE: ? MINUTES
SIDE STORY 4: Seven of Spades, Part 3
DMM
SPSHHH
SPSHHH
DMM
DMM

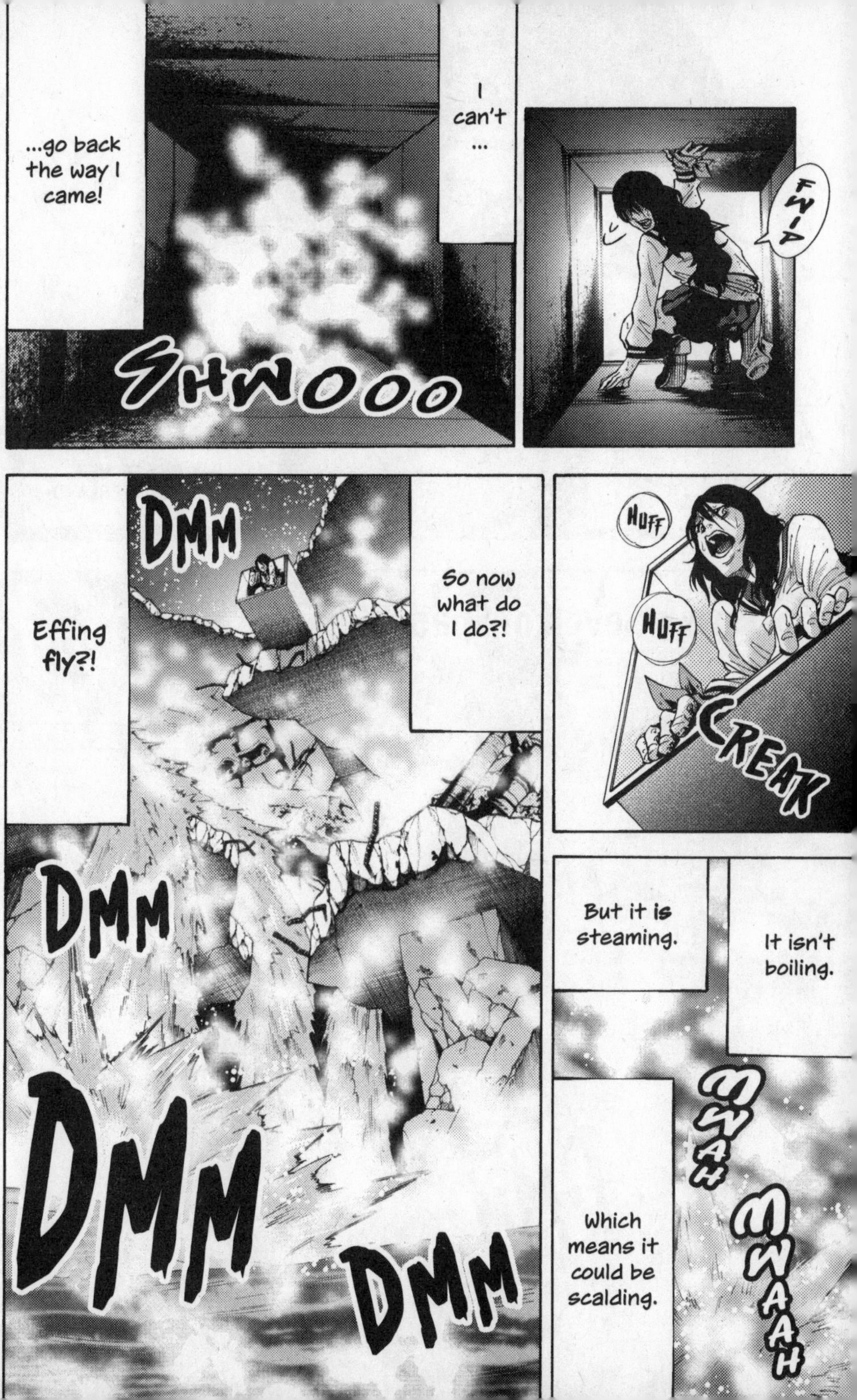
FWIP
I can't ...
...go back the way I came!
SHWOOO
HUFF
HUFF
CREAK
It isn't boiling.
But it is steaming.
MWAH
MWAH
Which means it could be scalding.
So now what do I do?!
Effing fly?!
DMM
DMM
DMM
DMM

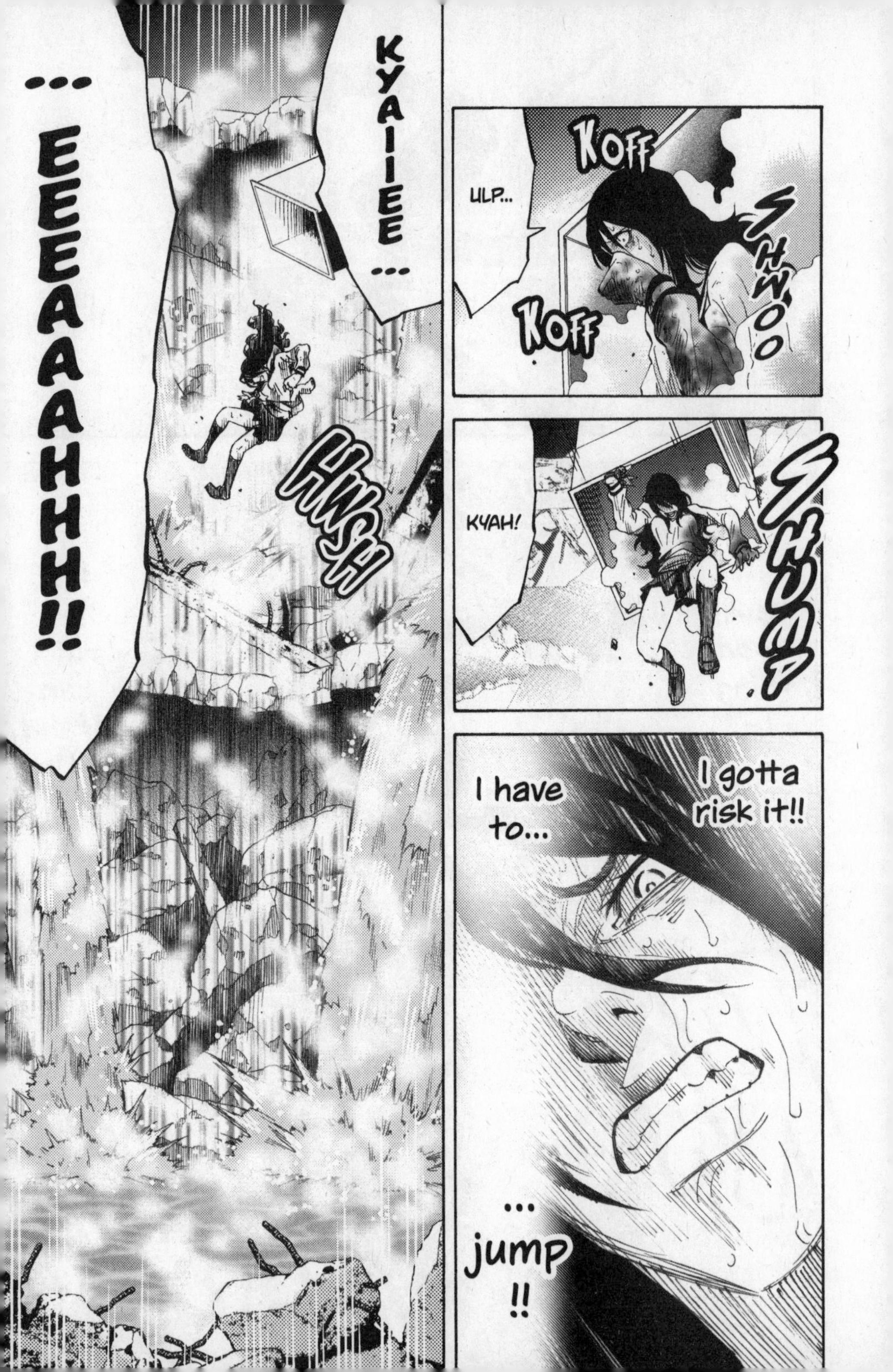
KOFF
ULP...
SHWOOO
KOFF
KYAH!
SHUMP
I gotta risk it!!
I have to...
... jump !!
KYAIIEE ...
... EEEEAAAAHHHH!!
HWSH

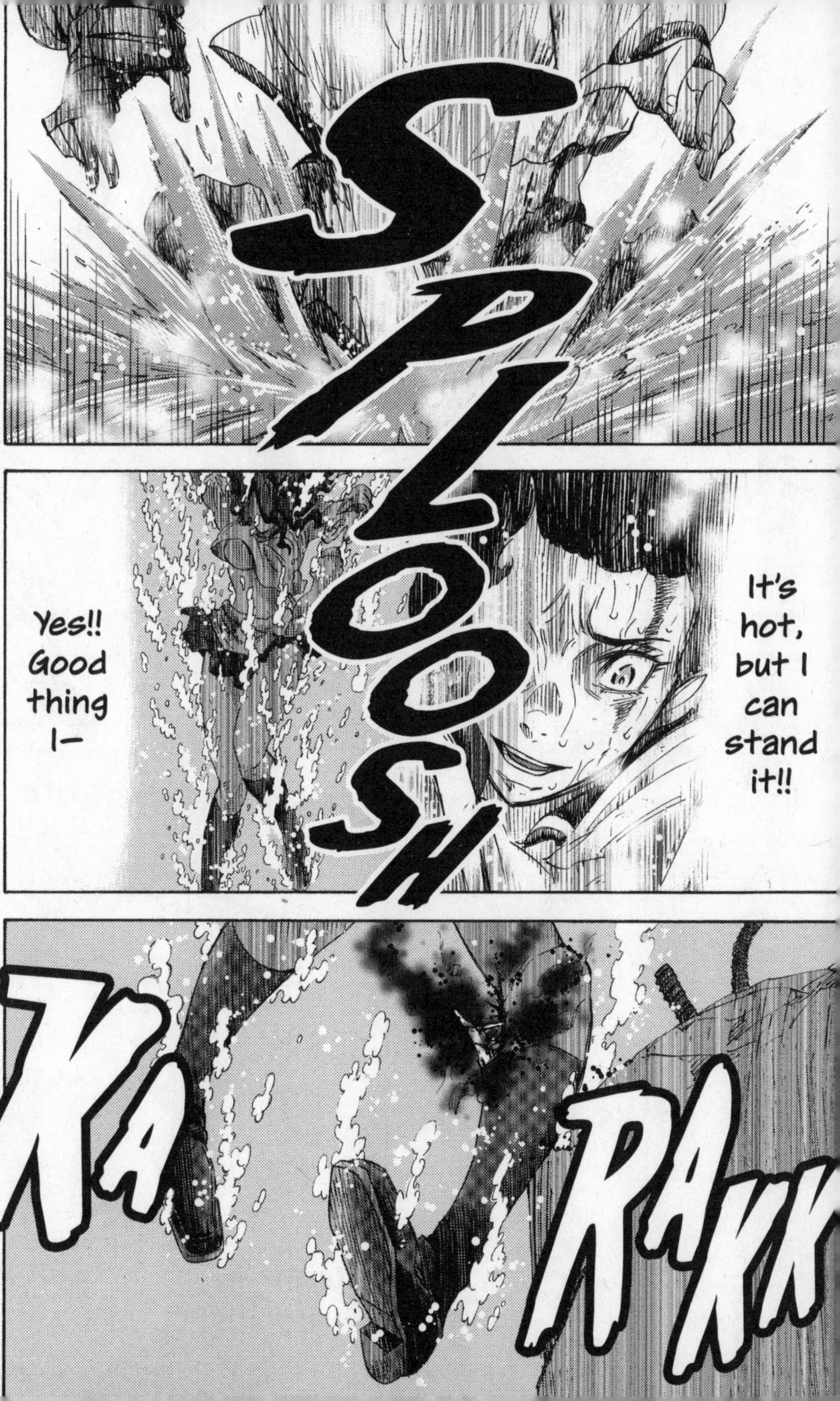
SPLOOSH
It's hot, but I can stand it!!
Yes!! Good thing I—
KA
RAKK

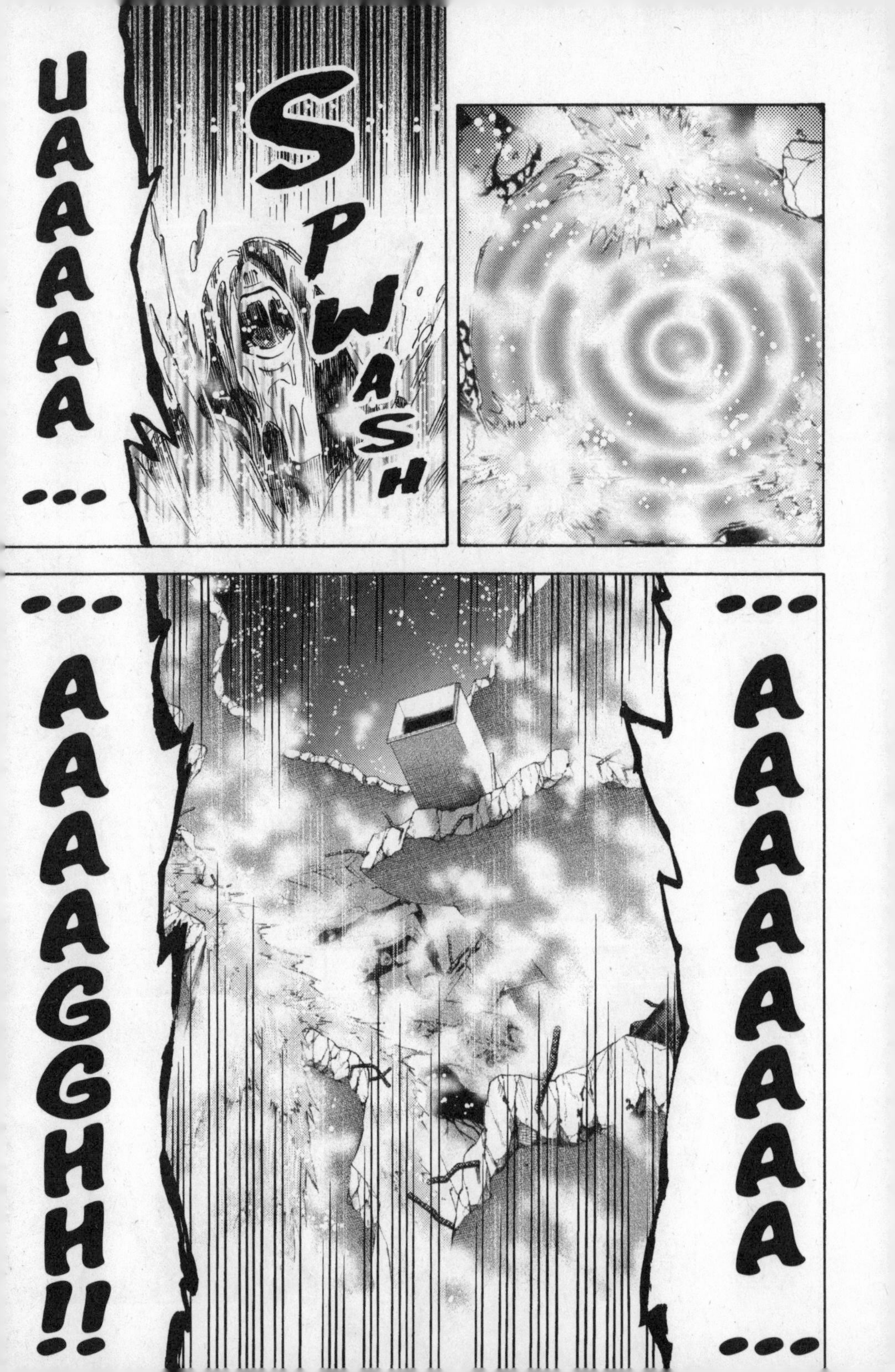
SPWASH
UAAAAA...
...AAAAAAAA...
...AAAAGGHH!!

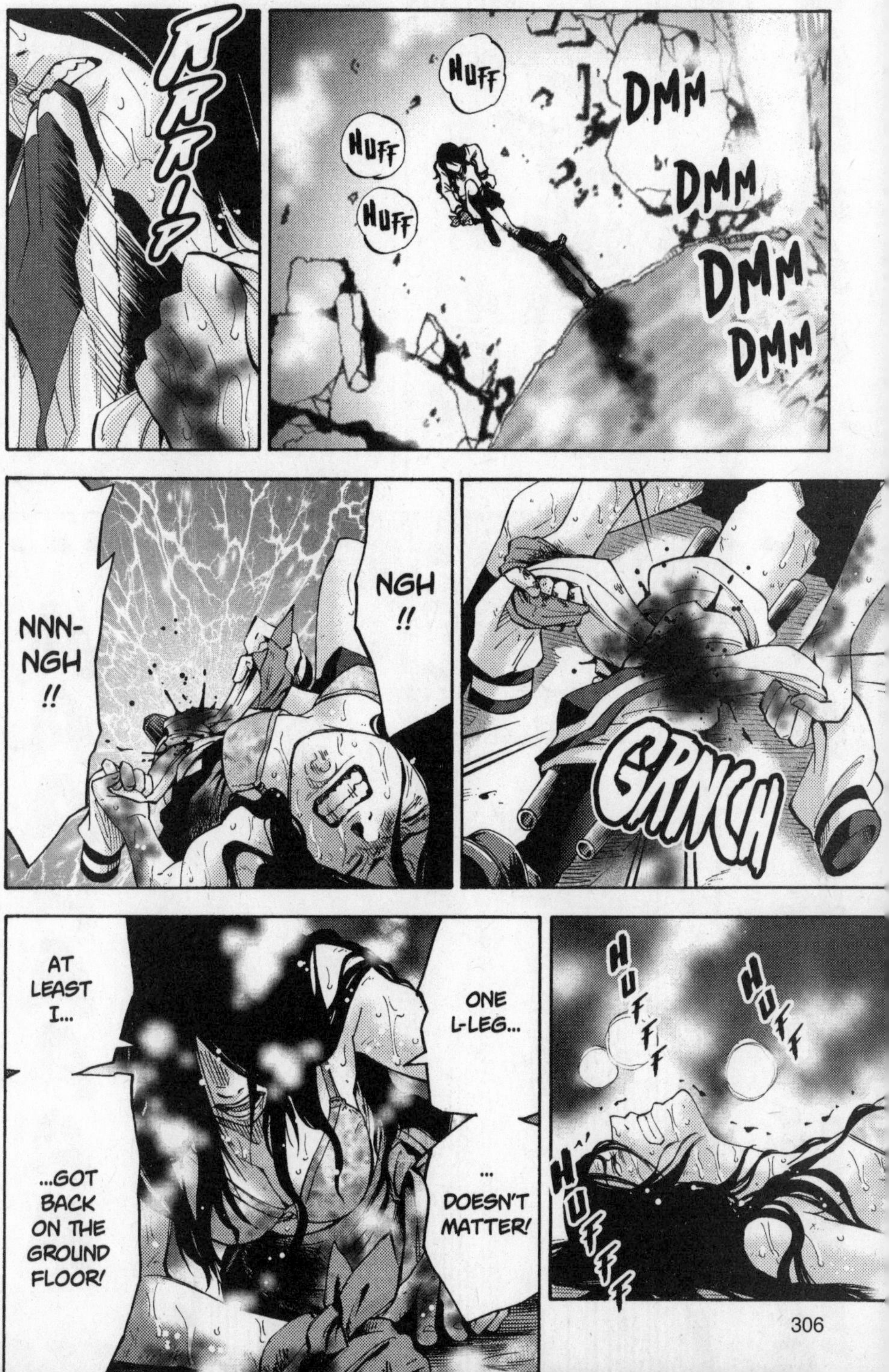
HUFF
HUFF
HUFF
DMM
DMM
DMM
DMM
RRRIP
GRNCH
NGH!!
NNN-NGH!!
HUFFF
HUFFF
HUFFF
ONE L-LEG...
AT LEAST I...
...DOESN'T MATTER!
...GOT BACK ON THE GROUND FLOOR!

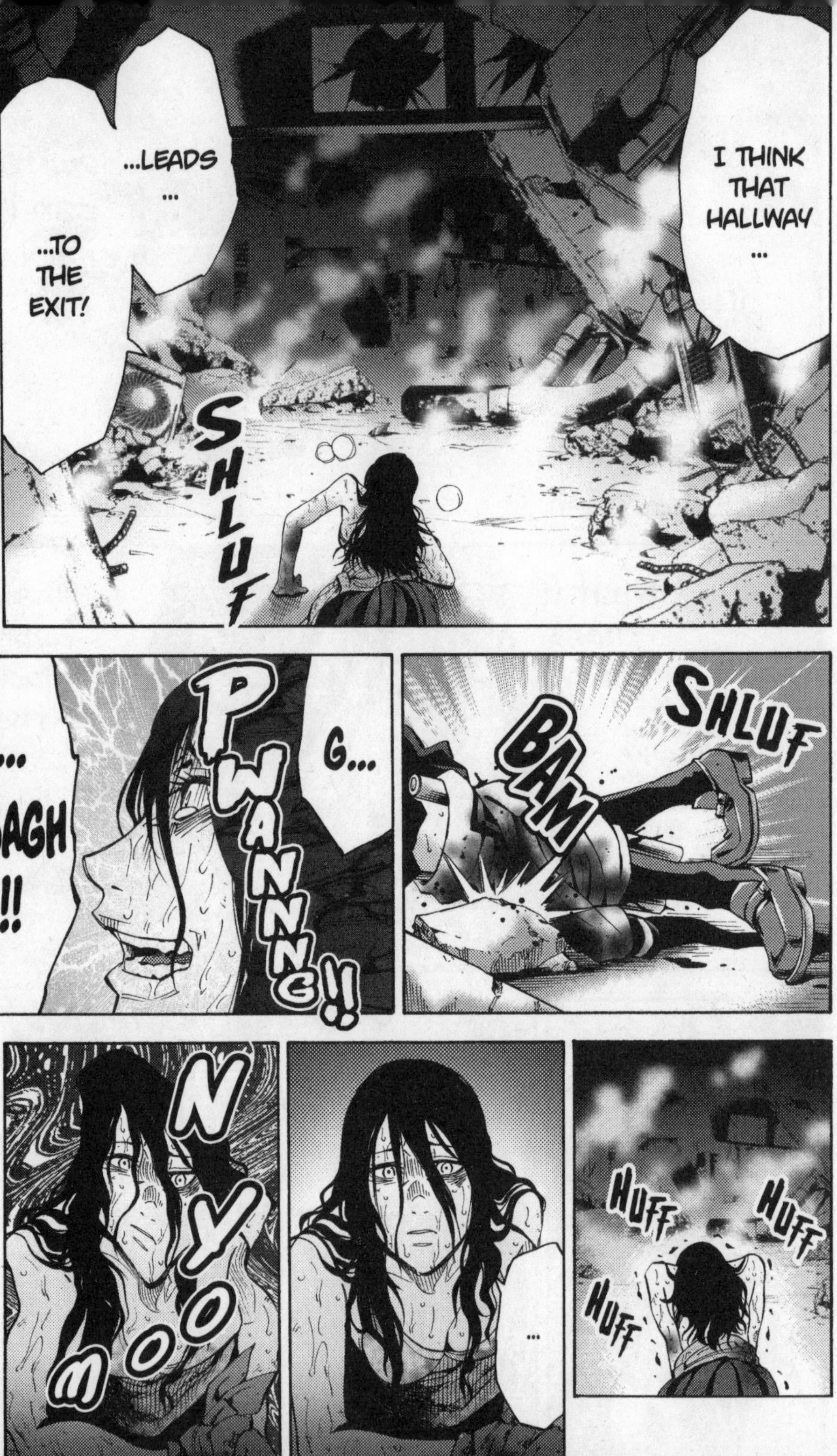
I THINK THAT HALLWAY ...
...LEADS ...
...TO THE EXIT!
SHLUF
SHLUF
BAM
G...
PWANNNG!!
... GGAGH !!
HUFF
HUFF
HUFF
HUFF
...
NYOOOM

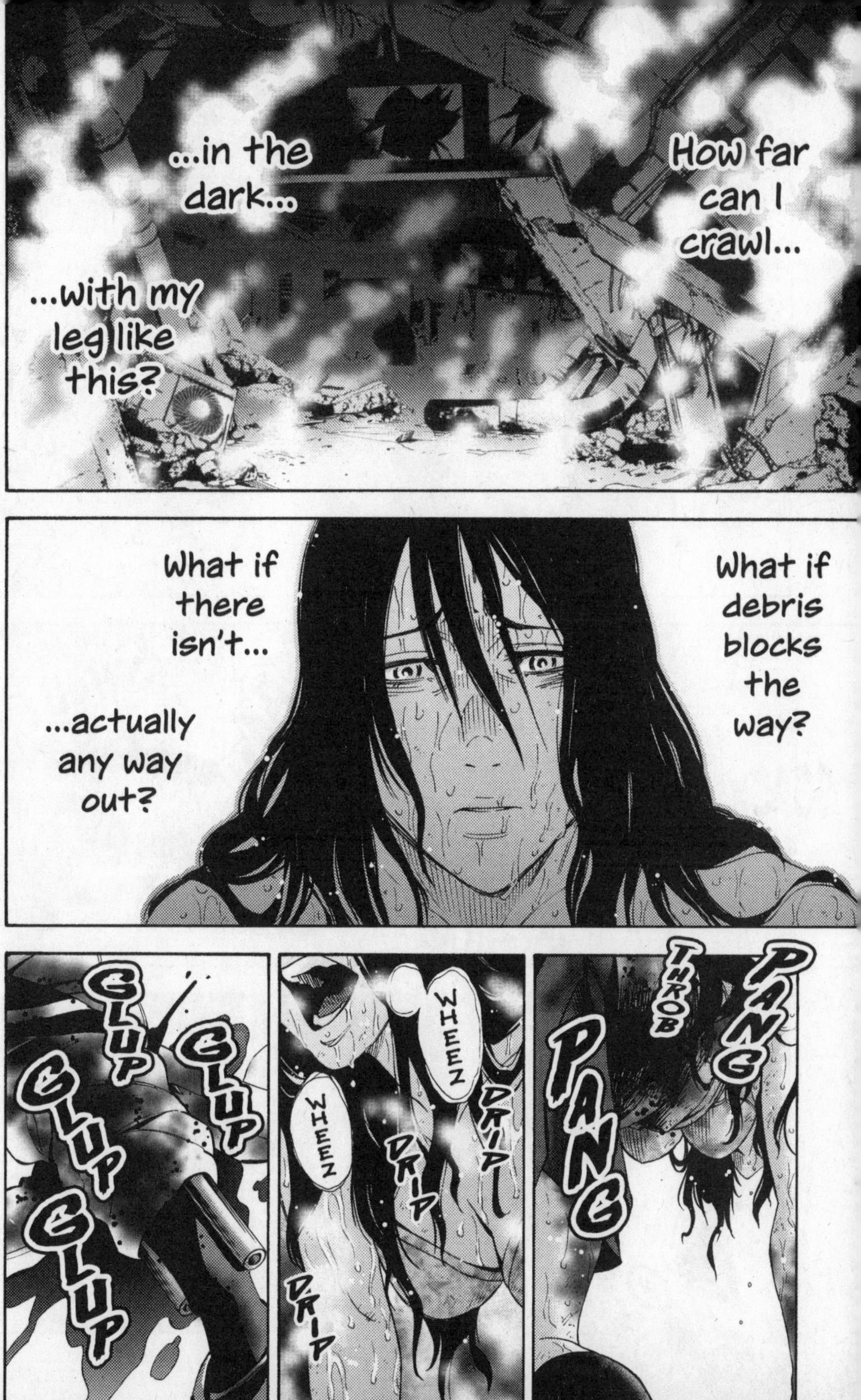
How far can I crawl...
...in the dark...
...with my leg like this?
What if debris blocks the way?
What if there isn't...
...actually any way out?
PANG
THROB
PANG
WHEEZ
WHEEZ
DRIP
DRIP
DRIP
GLUP
GLUP
GLUP
GLUP

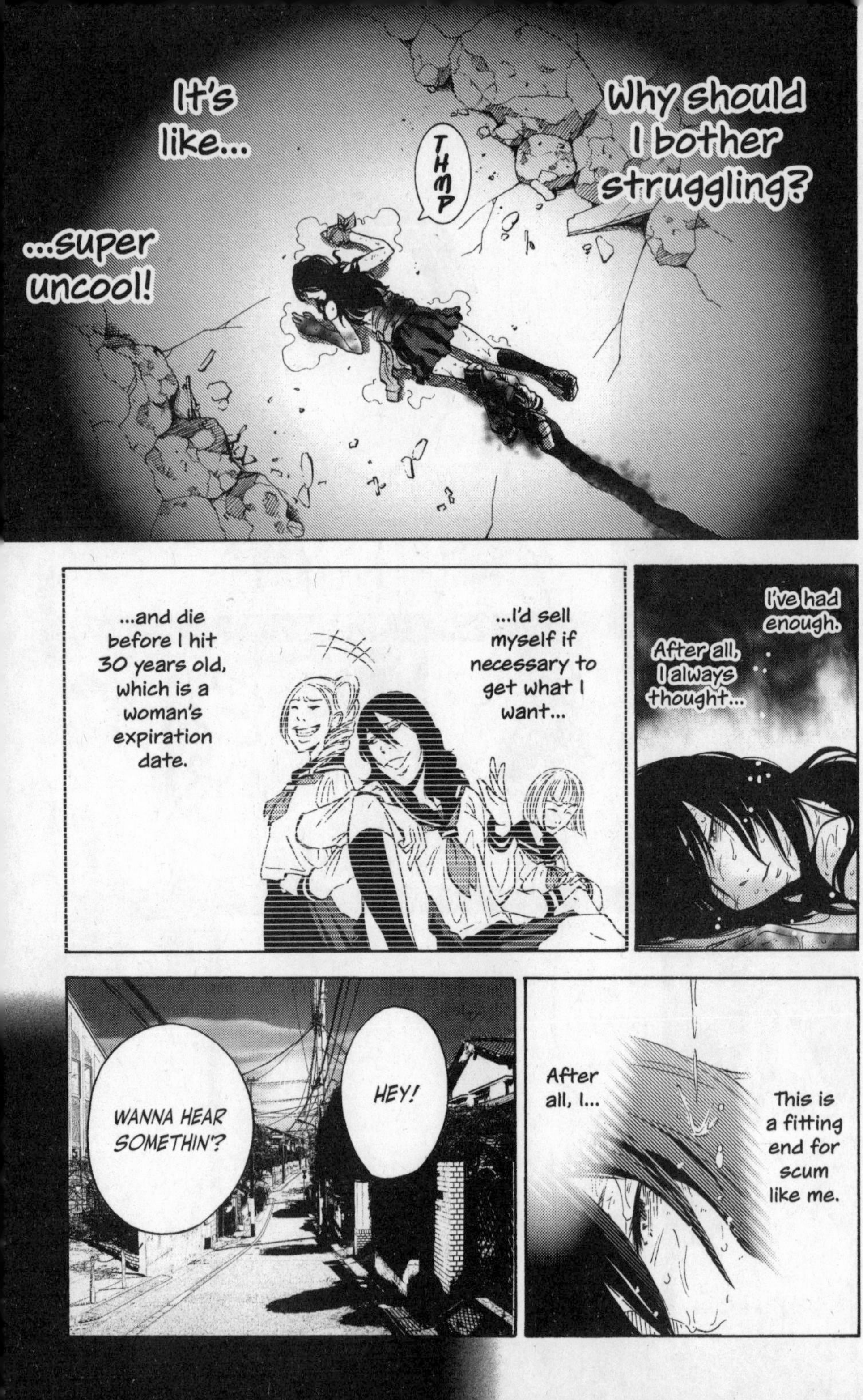
Why should I bother struggling?
THMP
It's like...
...super uncool!
I've had enough.
After all, I always thought...
...I'd sell myself if necessary to get what I want...
...and die before I hit 30 years old, which is a woman's expiration date.
This is a fitting end for scum like me.
After all, I...
HEY!
WANNA HEAR SOMETHIN'?

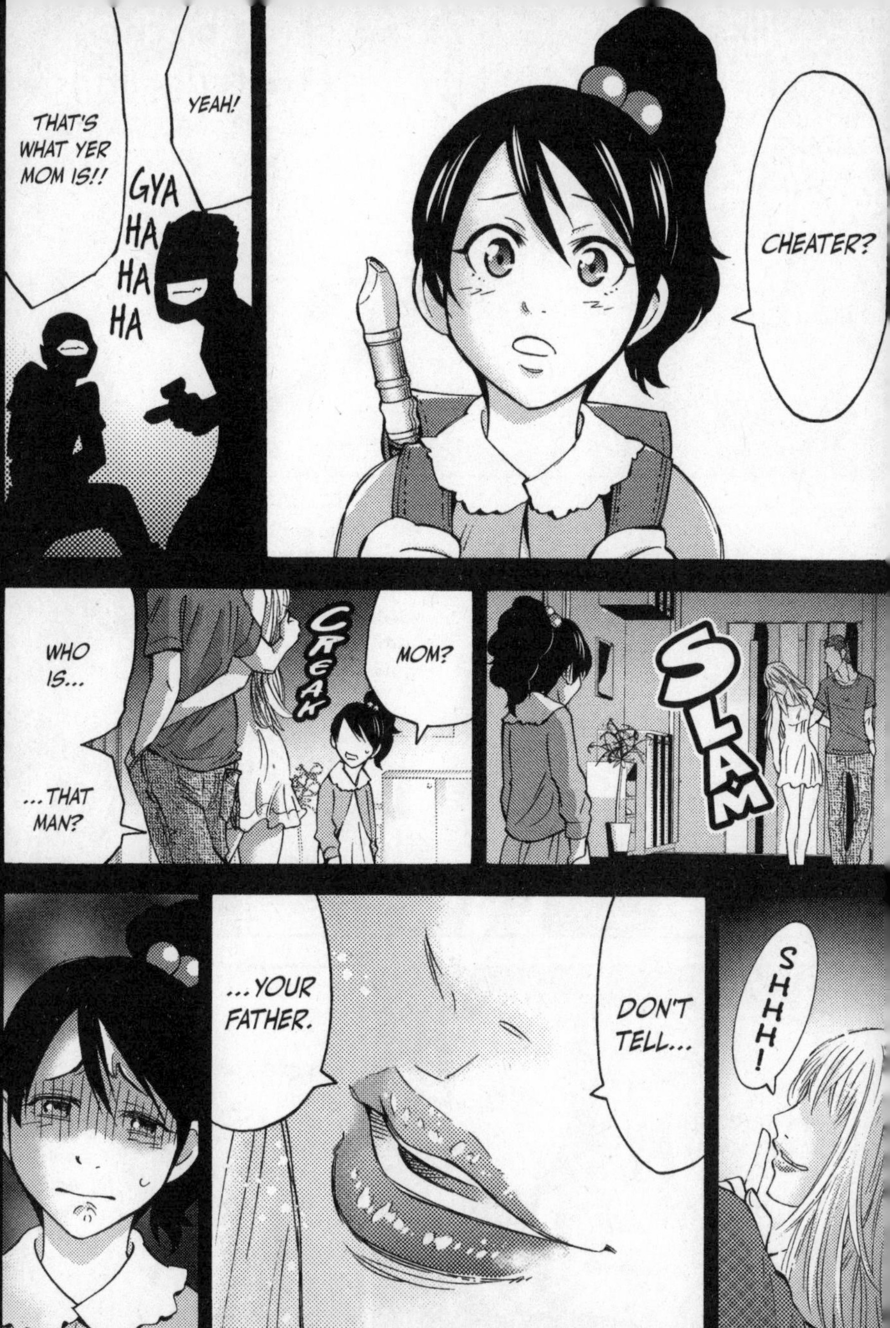
CHEATER?
YEAH!
THAT'S WHAT YER MOM IS!!
GYA HA HA HA
SLAM
MOM?
CREAK
WHO IS...
...THAT MAN?
SHHH!
DON'T TELL...
...YOUR FATHER.

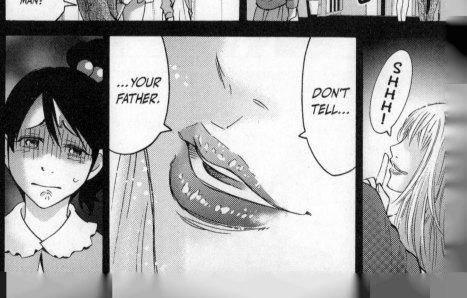

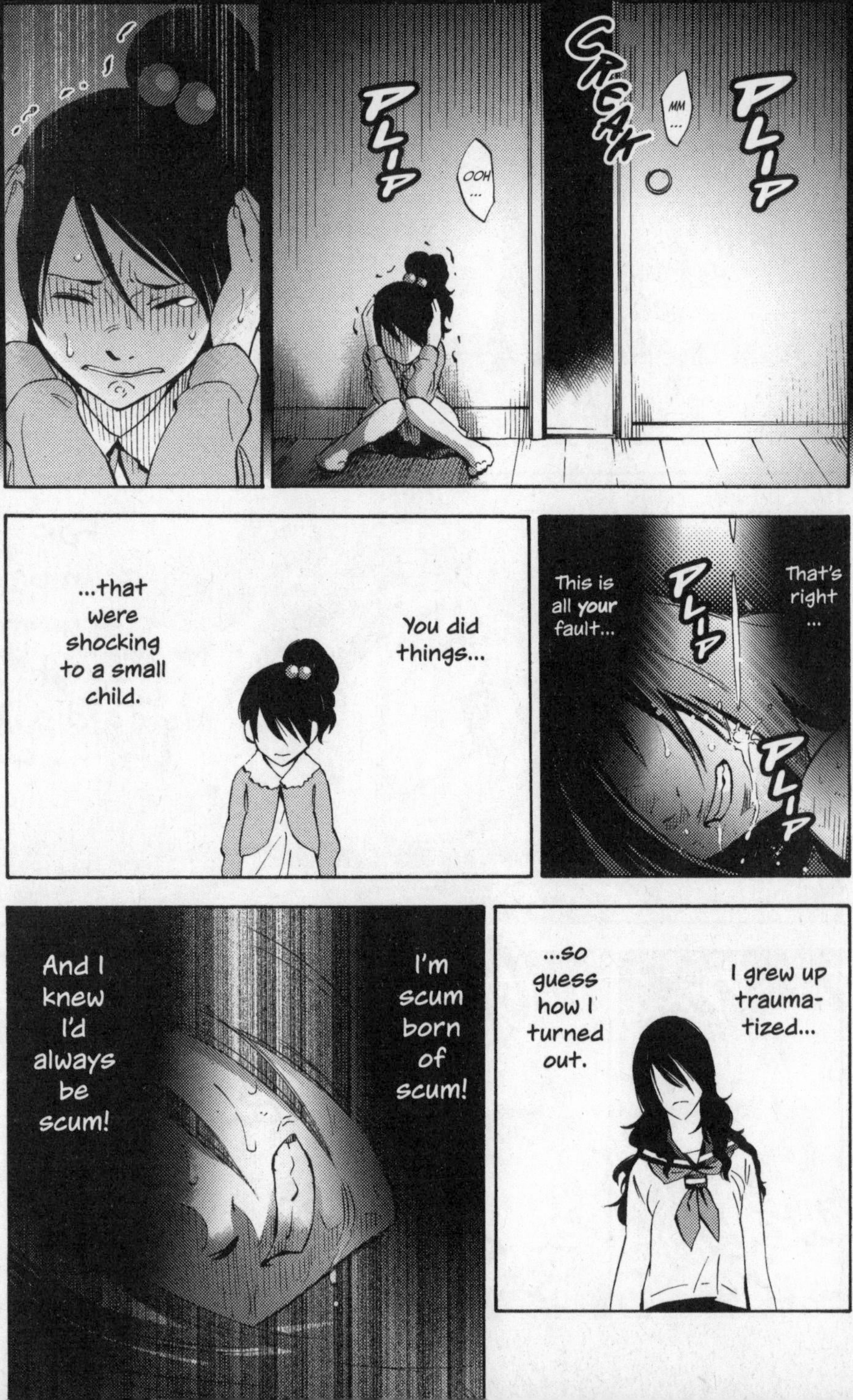
PLIP
MM...
CREAK
PLIP
OOH...
That's right...
PLIP
This is all your fault...
PLIP
You did things...
...that were shocking to a small child.
I grew up trauma-tized...
...so guess how I turned out.
I'm scum born of scum!
And I knew I'd always be scum!

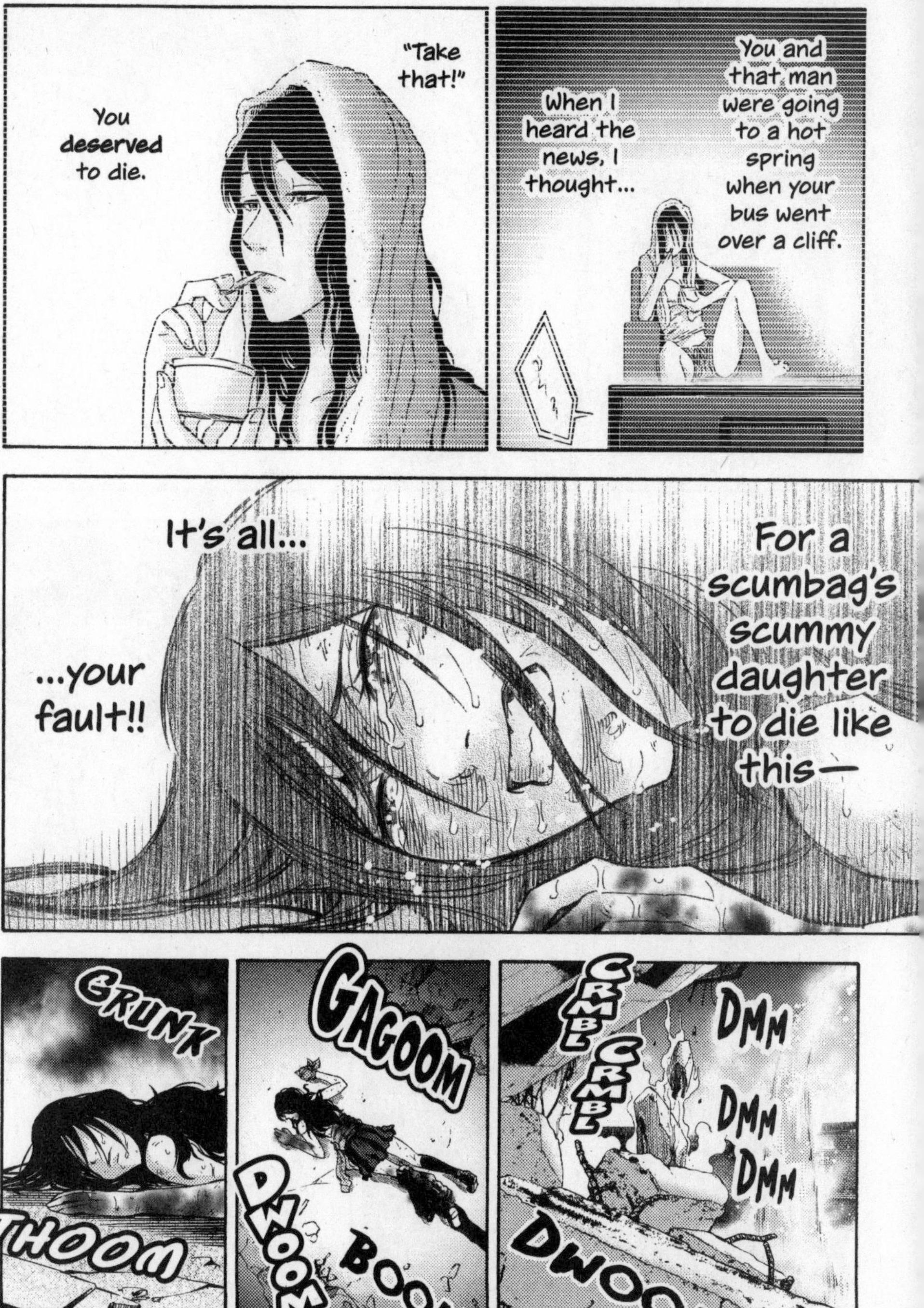

You and that man were going to a hot spring when your bus went over a cliff.
When I heard the news, I thought...
"Take that!"
You deserved to die.
For a scumbag's scummy daughter to die like this—
It's all...
...your fault!!
CRMBL
CRMBL
DMM
DMM
DMM
DWOOM
GAGOOM
BOOM
DWOOM
GRUNK
THOOM

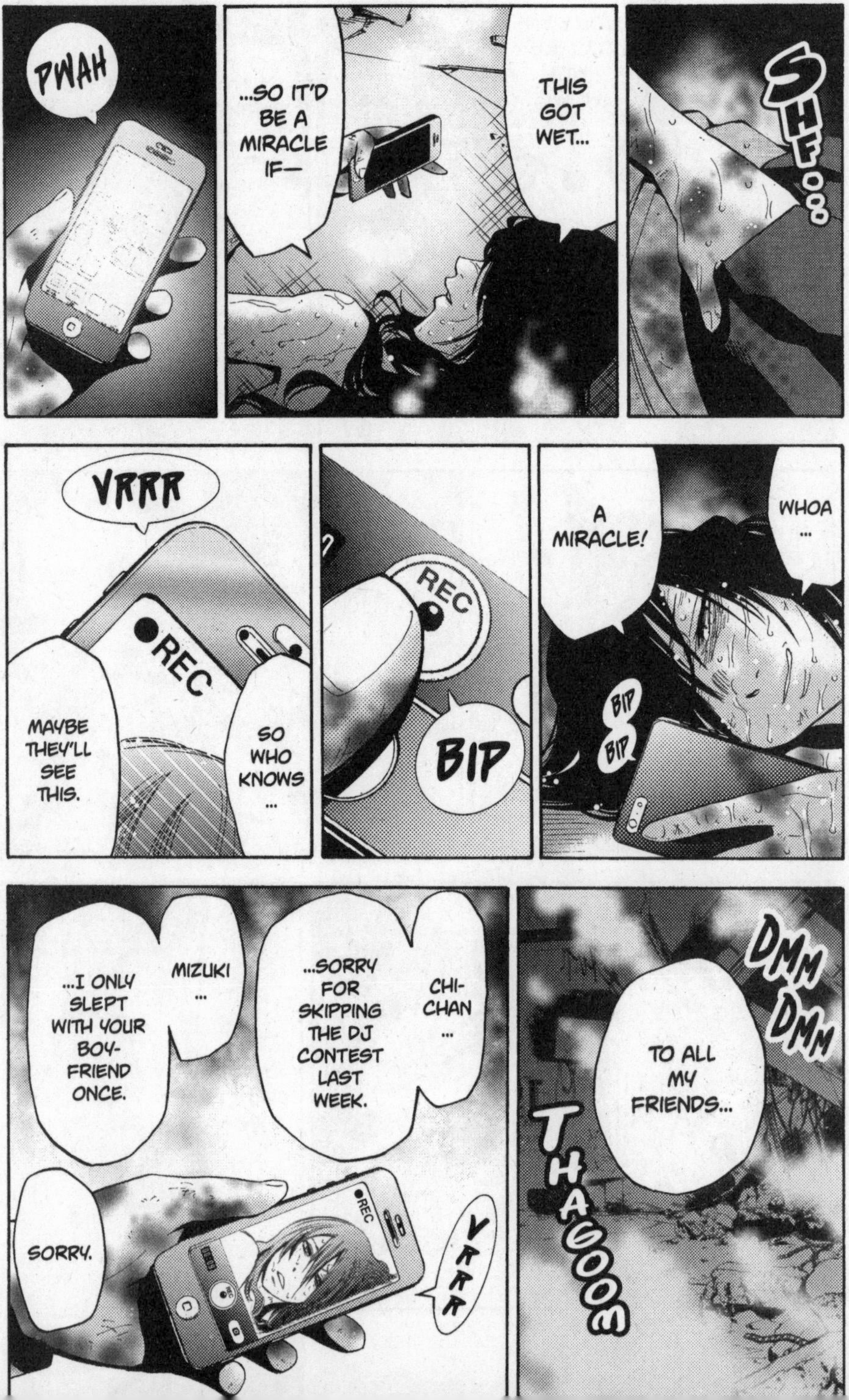
SHFOOO
THIS GOT WET...
...SO IT'D BE A MIRACLE IF—
PWAH
WHOA ...
A MIRACLE!
BIP BIP
BIP
VRRR
SO WHO KNOWS ...
MAYBE THEY'LL SEE THIS.
DMM DMM
TO ALL MY FRIENDS...
THAGOOM
CHI-CHAN ...
...SORRY FOR SKIPPING THE DJ CONTEST LAST WEEK.
MIZUKI ...
...I ONLY SLEPT WITH YOUR BOY-FRIEND ONCE.
●REC
VRRR
SORRY.

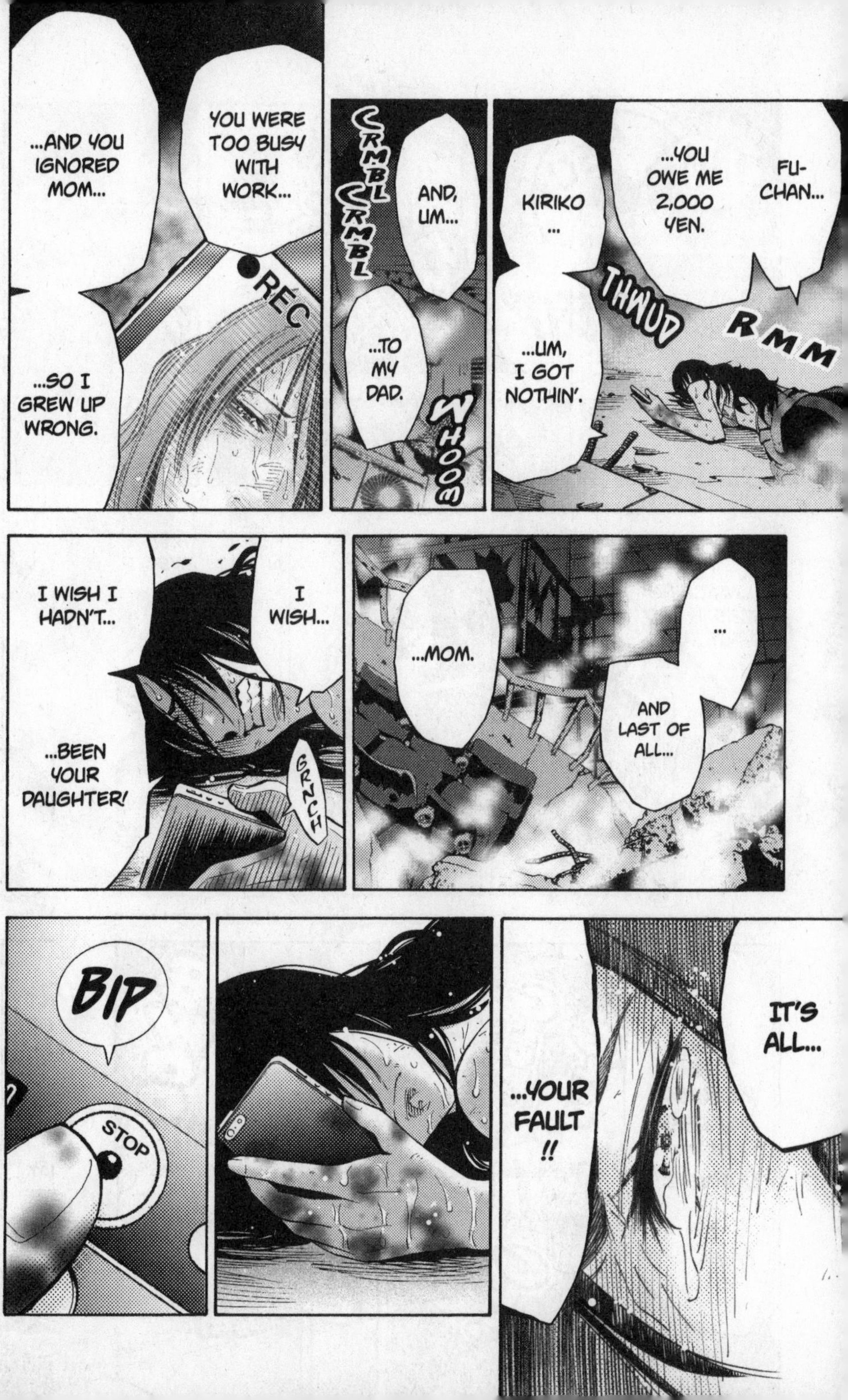
FU-CHAN...
...YOU OWE ME 2,000 YEN.
RMM
THWUD
KIRIKO...
...UM, I GOT NOTHIN'.
CRMBL CRMBL
AND, UM...
...TO MY DAD.
WHOOM
YOU WERE TOO BUSY WITH WORK...
...AND YOU IGNORED MOM...
REC
...SO I GREW UP WRONG.
...
...MOM.
AND LAST OF ALL...
I WISH...
I WISH I HADN'T...
GRNCH
...BEEN YOUR DAUGHTER!
IT'S ALL...
...YOUR FAULT!!
BIP
STOP

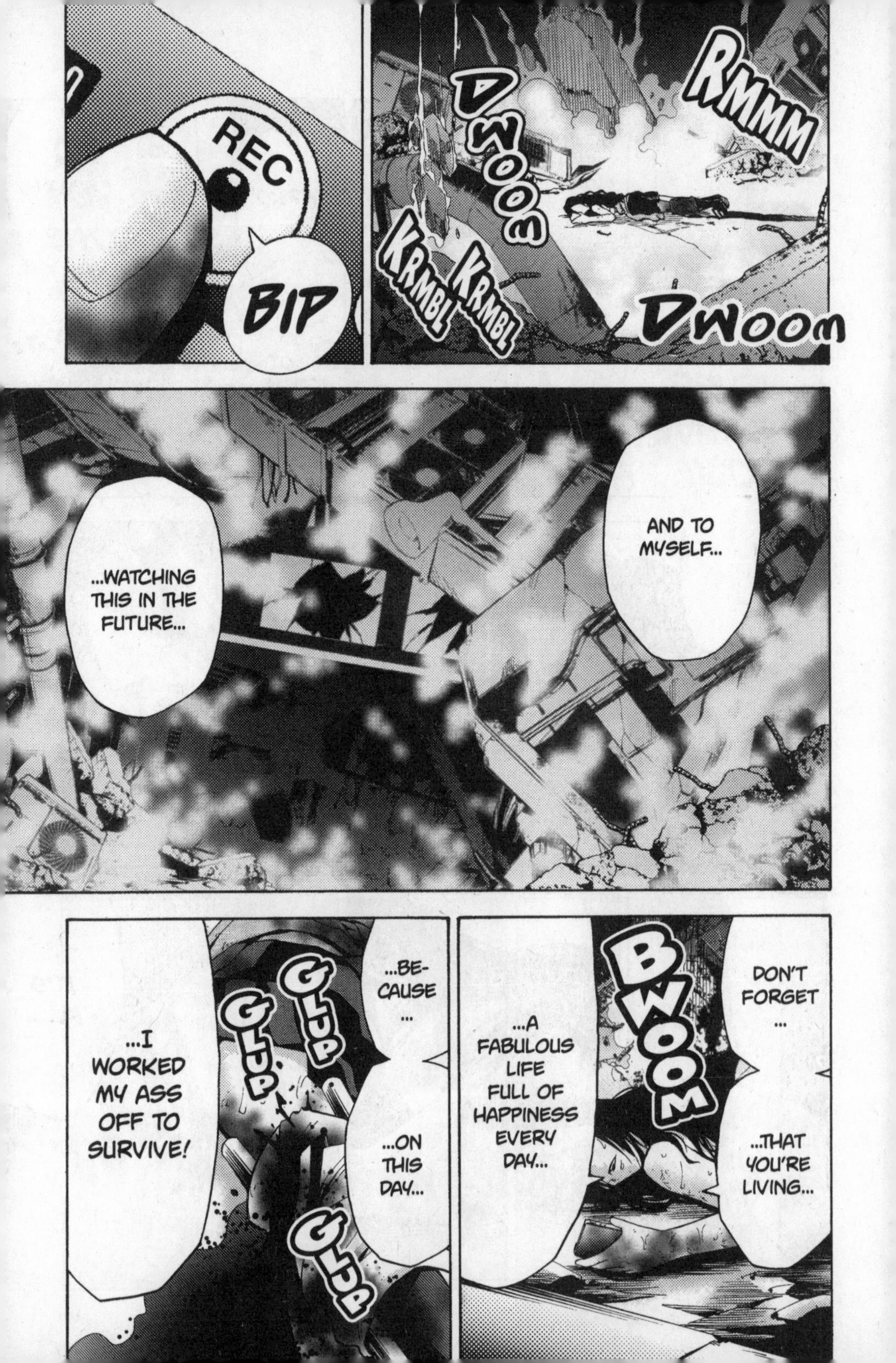
RMMM
DWOOOM
KRMBL
KRMBL
DWOOM
REC
BIP
AND TO MYSELF...
...WATCHING THIS IN THE FUTURE...
DON'T FORGET ...
...THAT YOU'RE LIVING...
BWOOM
...A FABULOUS LIFE FULL OF HAPPINESS EVERY DAY...
...BE-CAUSE ...
...ON THIS DAY...
GLUP
GLUP
...I WORKED MY ASS OFF TO SURVIVE!
GLUP

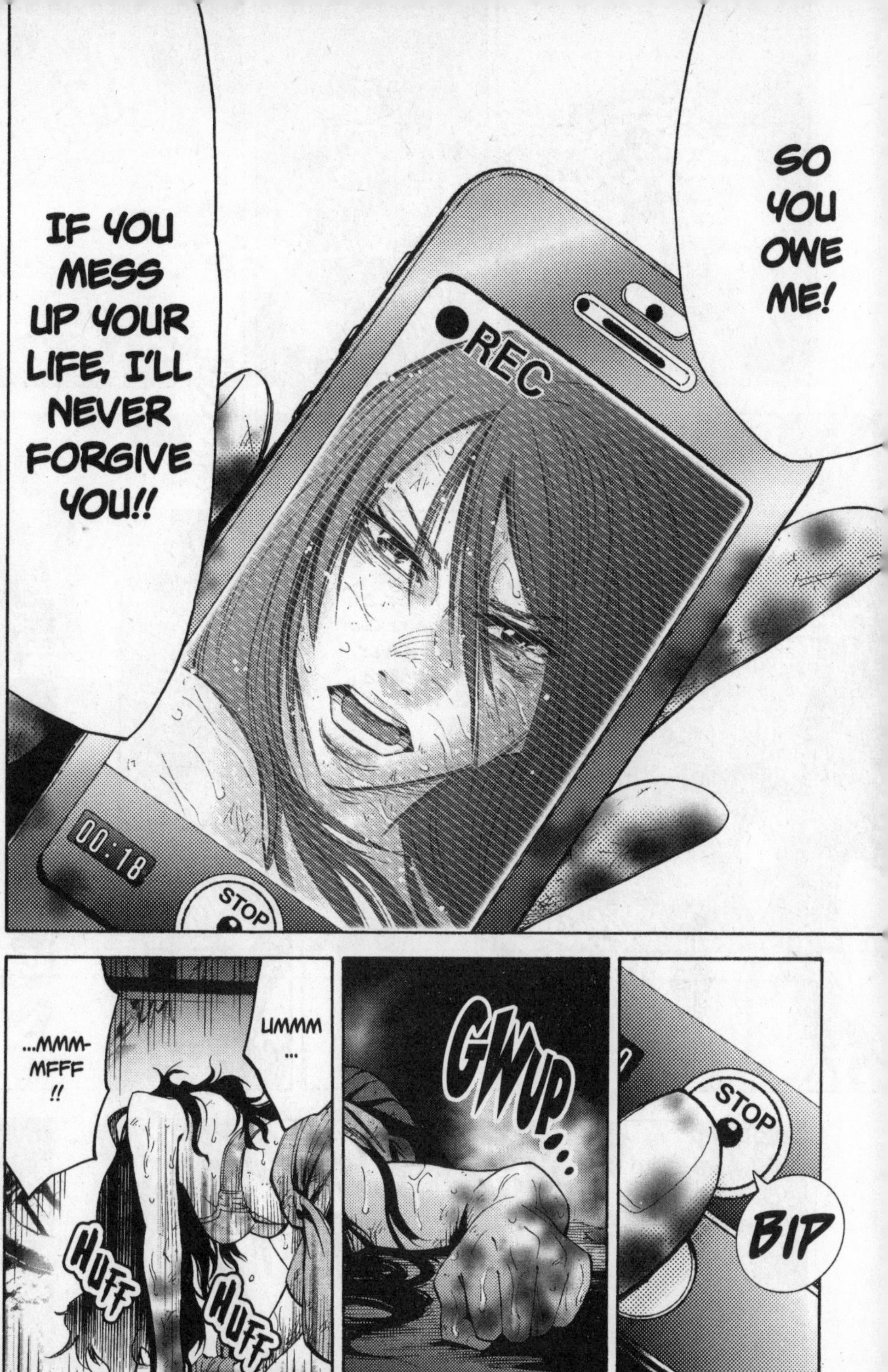
SO YOU OWE ME!
IF YOU MESS UP YOUR LIFE, I'LL NEVER FORGIVE YOU!!
REC
00:18
STOP
STOP
BIP
GWUP...
UMMM ...
...MMM-MFFF !!
HUFF
HUFF

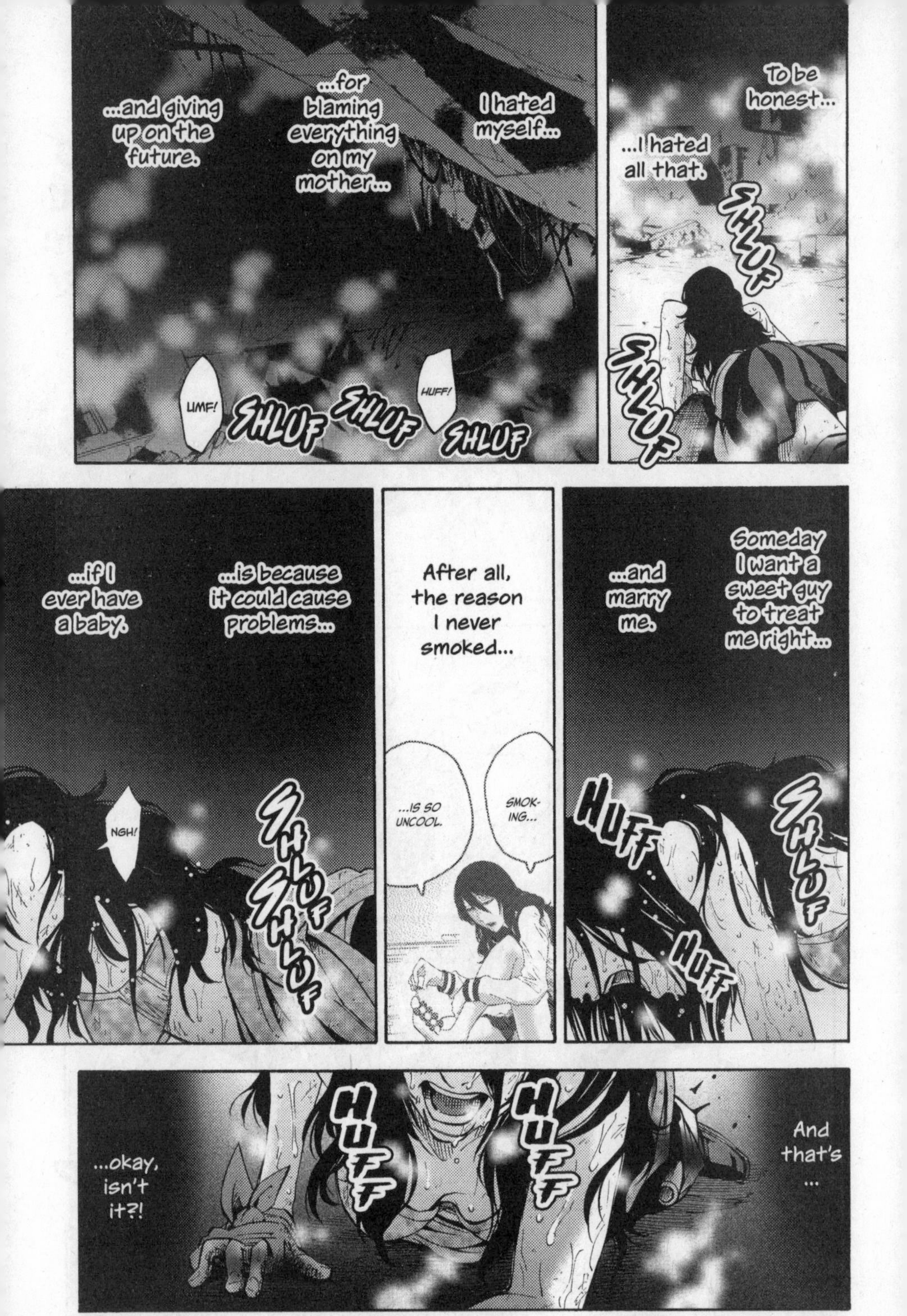
To be honest...
...I hated all that.
SHLUF
SHLUF
I hated myself...
...for blaming everything on my mother...
...and giving up on the future.
HUFF!
SHLUF
SHLUF
SHLUF
UMF!
Someday I want a sweet guy to treat me right...
...and marry me.
SHLUF
HUFF
HUFF
After all, the reason I never smoked...
SMOK-ING...
...IS SO UNCOOL.
...is because it could cause problems...
...if I ever have a baby.
SHLUF
SHLUF
NGH!
And that's ...
HUFF
HUFF
...okay, isn't it?!

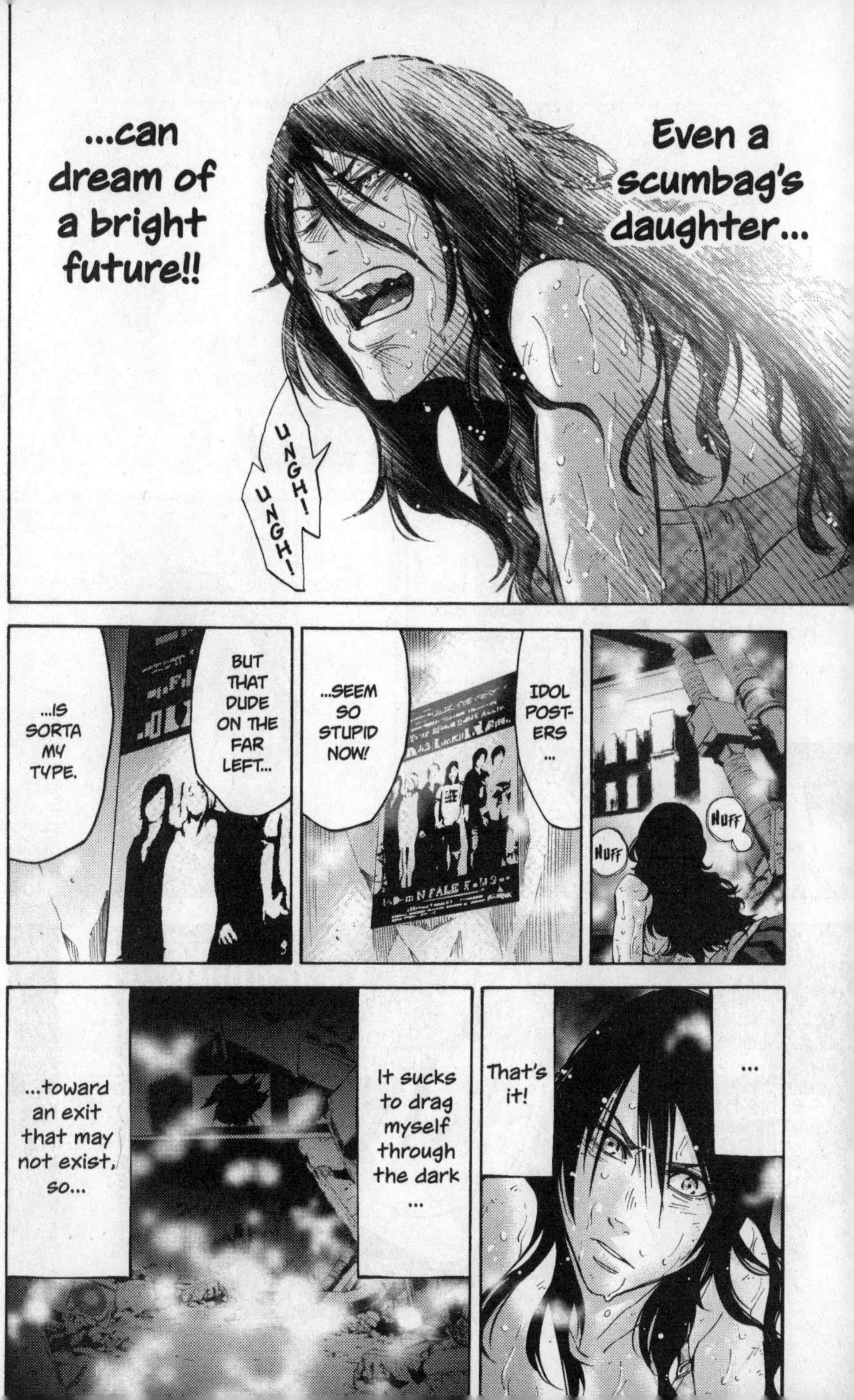
Even a scumbag's daughter...
...can dream of a bright future!!
UNGH! UNGH!
HUFF
HUFF
IDOL POSTERS...
...SEEM SO STUPID NOW!
BUT THAT DUDE ON THE FAR LEFT...
...IS SORTA MY TYPE.
...
That's it!
It sucks to drag myself through the dark...
...toward an exit that may not exist, so...

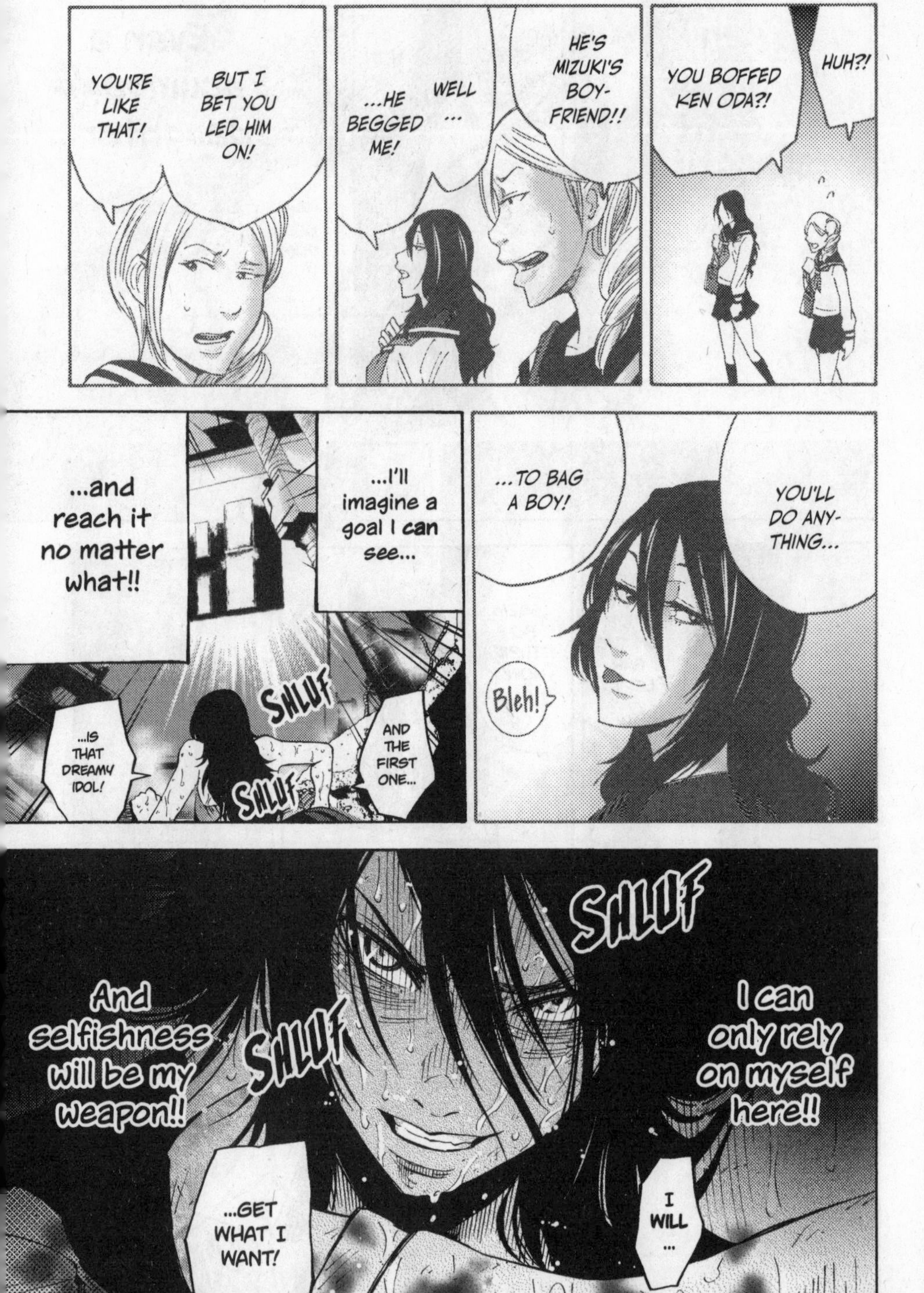
HUH?!
YOU BOFFED KEN ODA?!
HE'S MIZUKI'S BOY-FRIEND!!
WELL ...
...HE BEGGED ME!
BUT I BET YOU LED HIM ON!
YOU'RE LIKE THAT!
YOU'LL DO ANY-THING...
...TO BAG A BOY!
Bleh!
...I'll imagine a goal I can see...
...and reach it no matter what!!
SHLUF
AND THE FIRST ONE...
SHLUF
...IS THAT DREAMY IDOL!
SHLUF
I can only rely on myself here!!
SHLUF
And selfishness will be my weapon!!
I WILL ...
...GET WHAT I WANT!

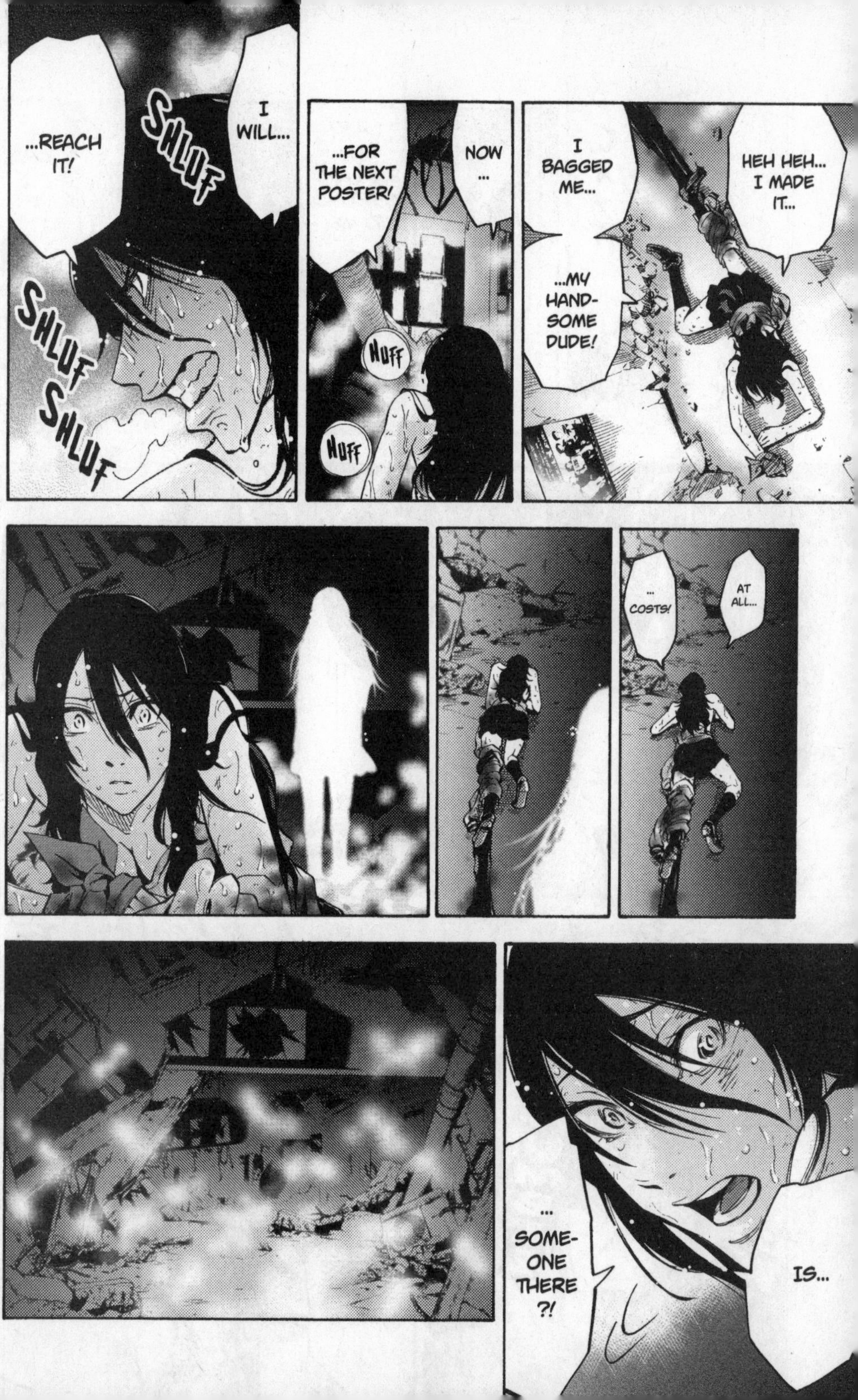
HEH HEH... I MADE IT...
I BAGGED ME...
...MY HAND-SOME DUDE!
NOW ...
...FOR THE NEXT POSTER!
HUFF
HUFF
I WILL...
SHLUF
...REACH IT!
SHLUF
SHLUF
SHLUF
AT ALL...
... COSTS!
IS...
... SOME-ONE THERE ?!

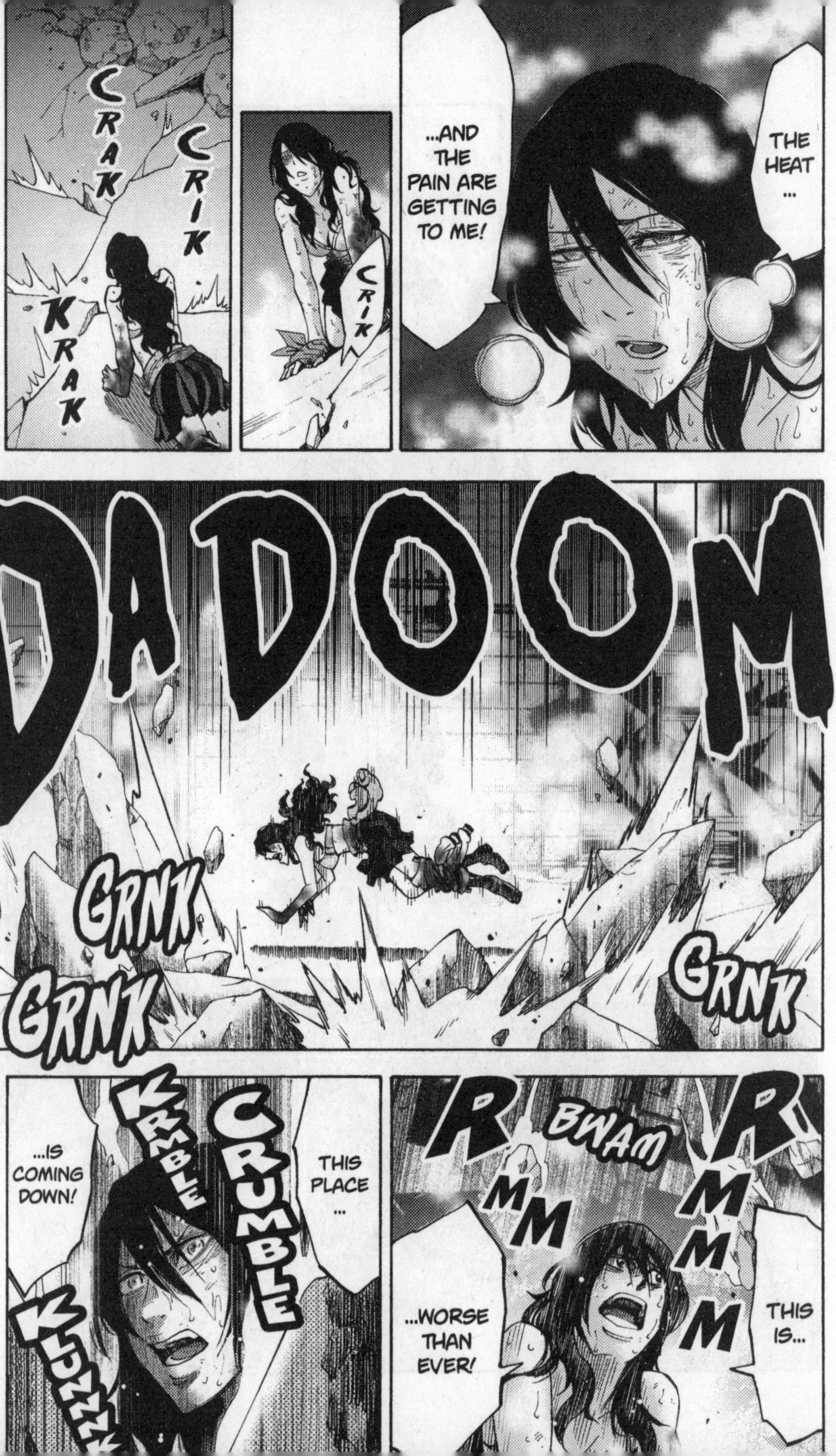
THE HEAT ...
...AND THE PAIN ARE GETTING TO ME!
CRIK
CRIK
CRAK
KRAK
KRAK
DADOOM
GRNK
GRNK
GRNK
RMMMM
BWAM
RMM
THIS IS...
...WORSE THAN EVER!
THIS PLACE ...
CRUMBLE
KRMBLE
...IS COMING DOWN!

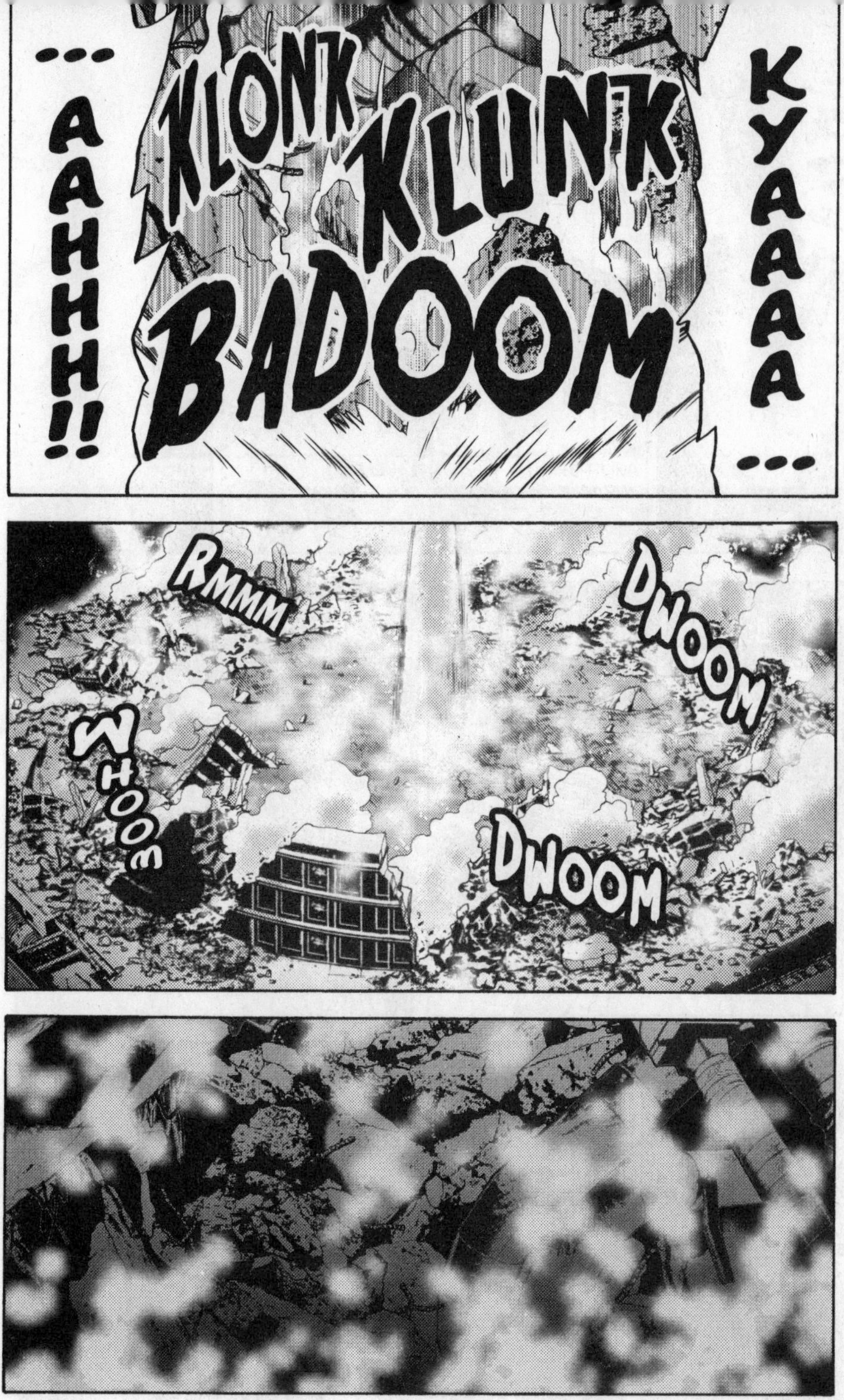
KYAAAA...
KLUNK
KLONK
BADOOM
...AAHHH!!
DWOOM
RMMM
DWOOM
WHOOM

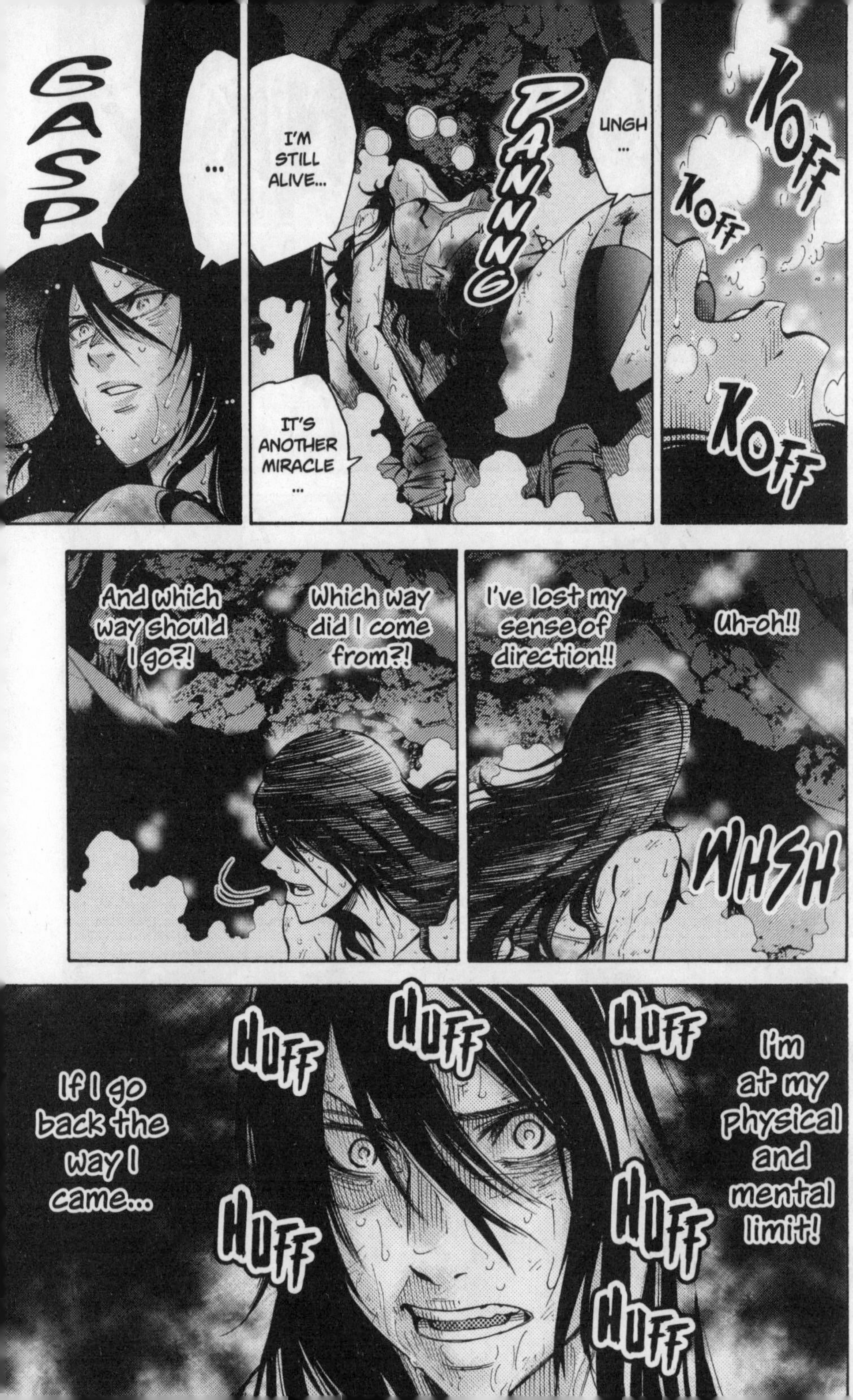

KOFF
KOFF
KOFF
UNGH ...
PANNNG
I'M STILL ALIVE...
IT'S ANOTHER MIRACLE ...
...
GASP
Uh-oh!!
I've lost my sense of direction!!
WHSH
Which way did I come from?!
And which way should I go?!
I'm at my physical and mental limit!
HUFF
HUFF
HUFF
HUFF
HUFF
HUFF
If I go back the way I came...

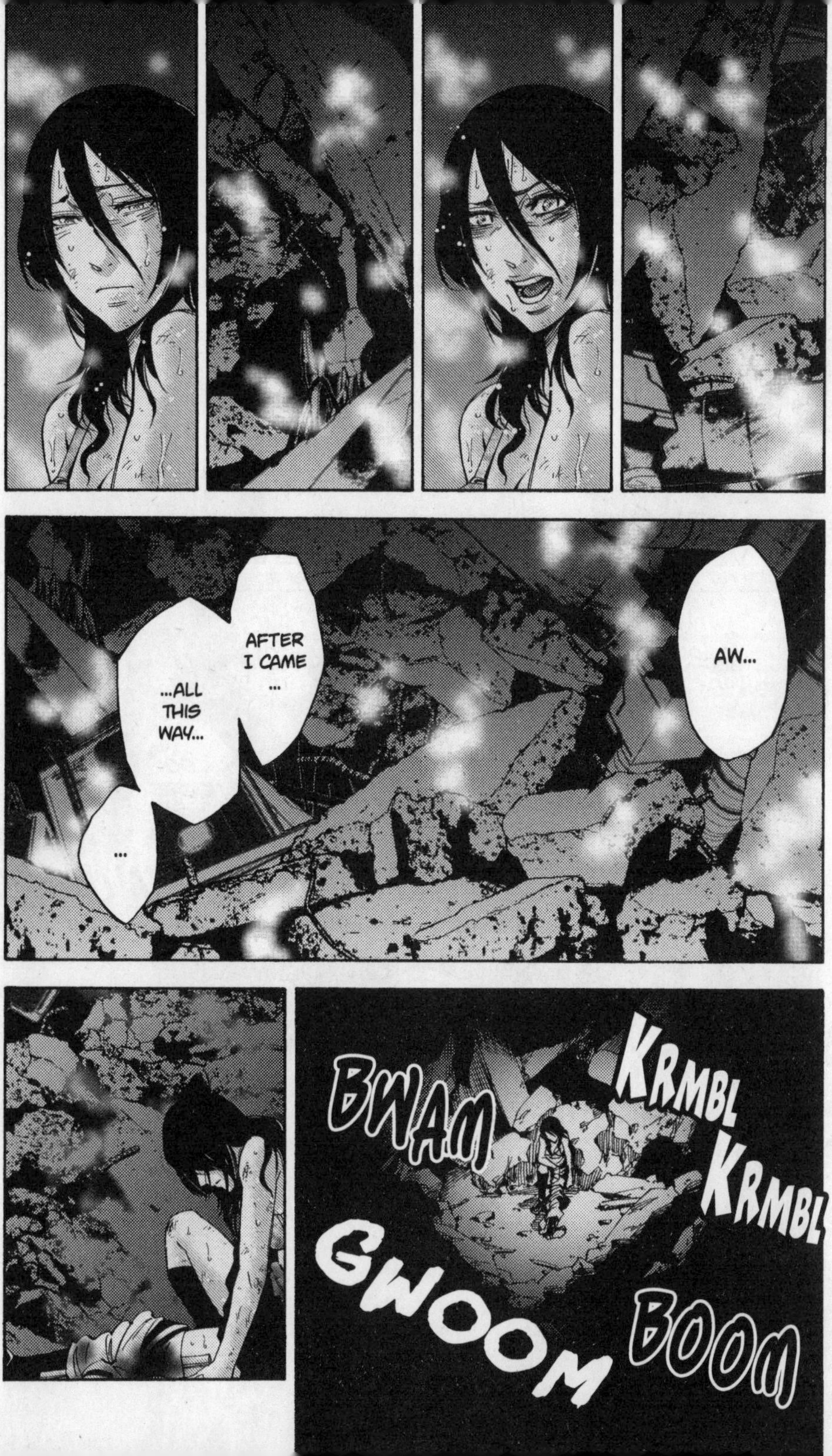
AW...
AFTER I CAME ...
...ALL THIS WAY...
...
KRMBL
KRMBL
BWAM
BOOM
GWOOM

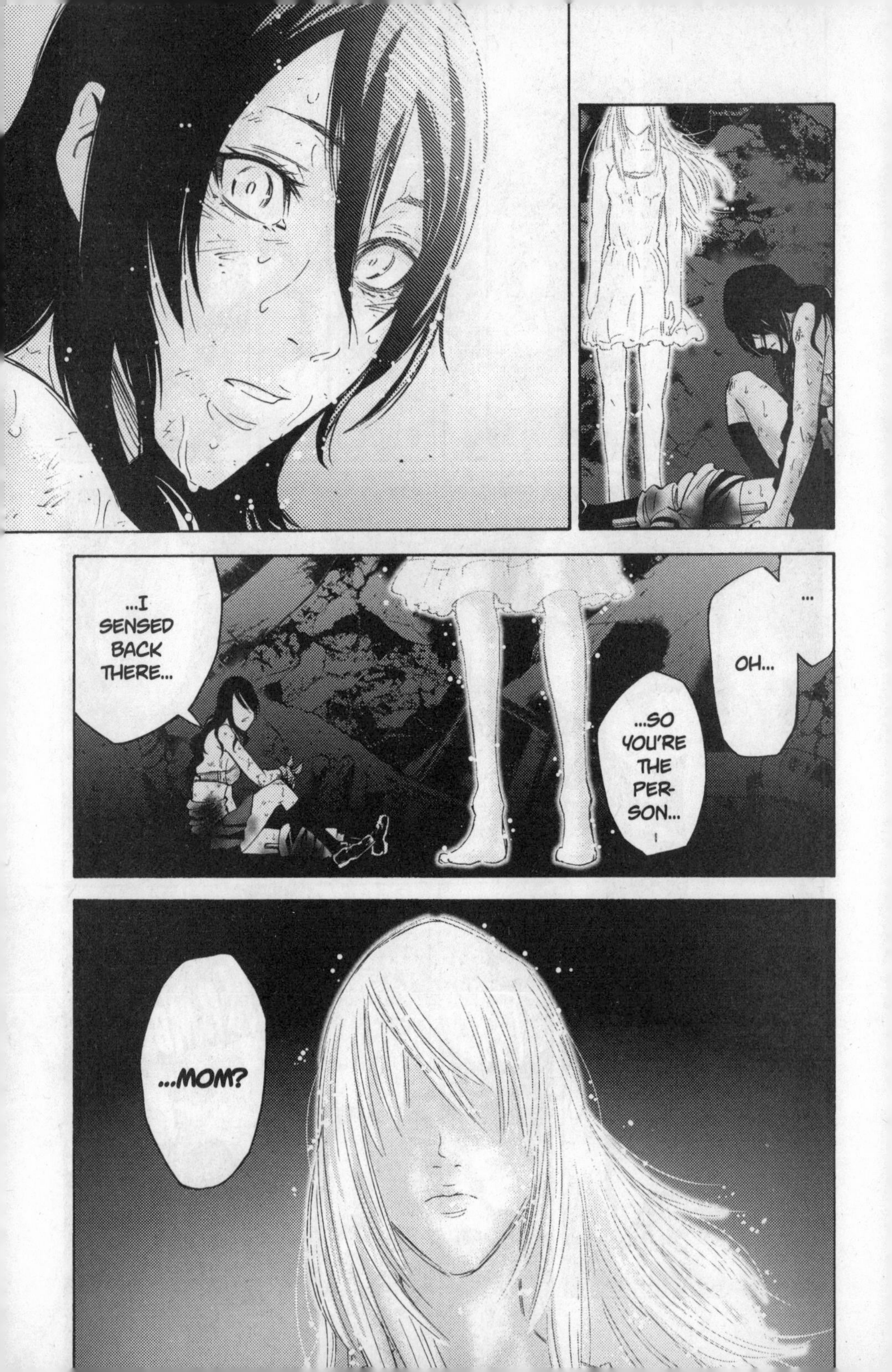
... OH...
...SO YOU'RE THE PER-SON...!
...I SENSED BACK THERE...
...MOM?

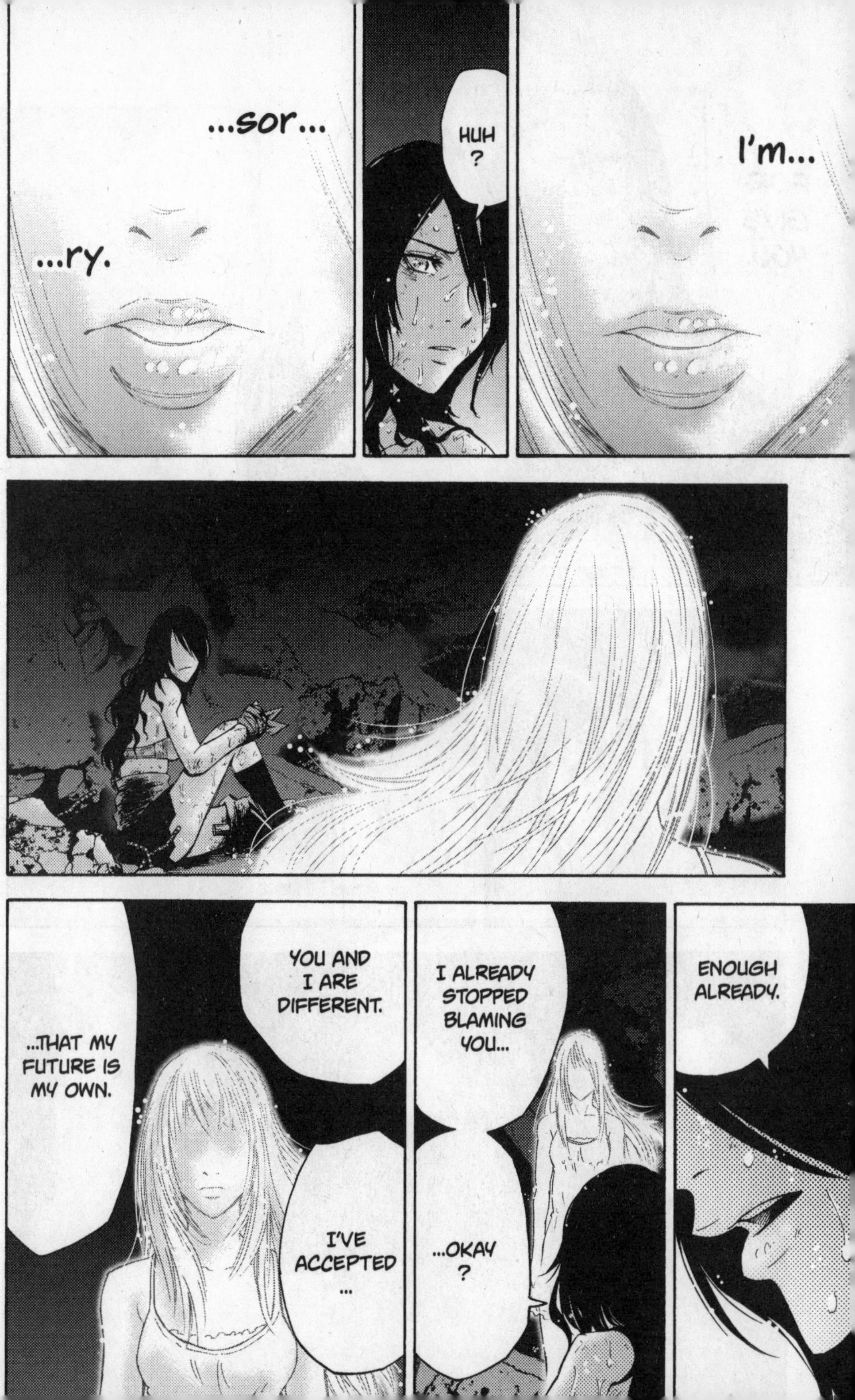
I'm...
HUH ?
...sor...
...ry.
ENOUGH ALREADY.
I ALREADY STOPPED BLAMING YOU...
...OKAY ?
YOU AND I ARE DIFFERENT.
I'VE ACCEPTED ...
...THAT MY FUTURE IS MY OWN.

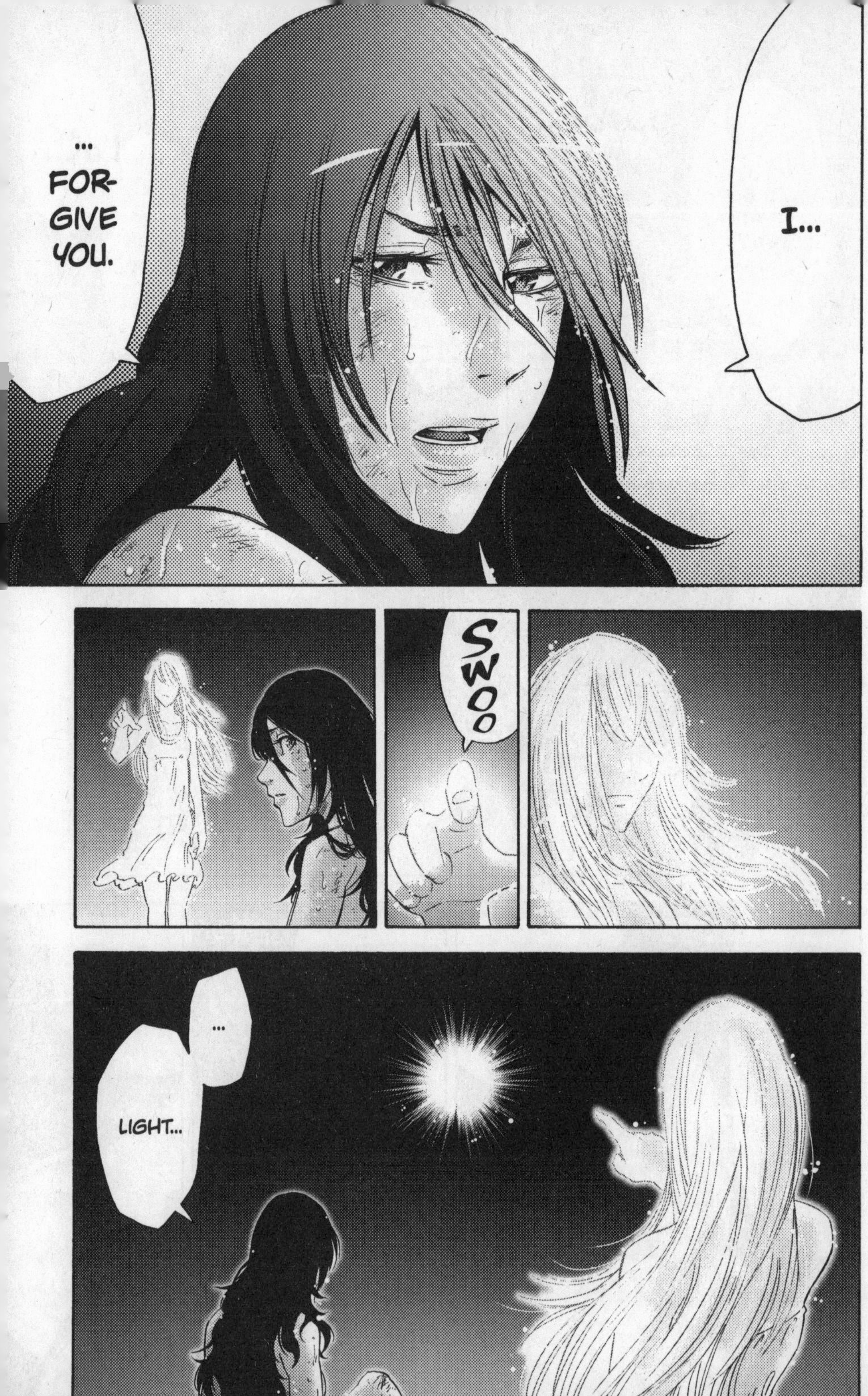
I...
... FOR-GIVE YOU.
SWOO
...
LIGHT...

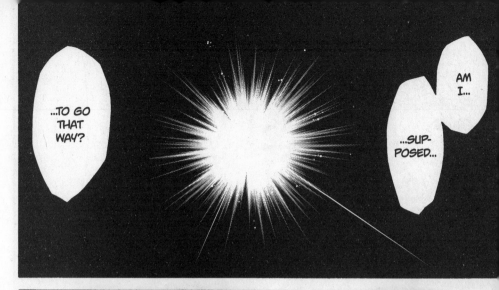

...TO GO THAT WAY?

AM I...

...SUP-POSED...

...MOM.

SEE YA...

...TO SAY THANKS.

DON'T EXPECT ME...

SHLUF

SWOO

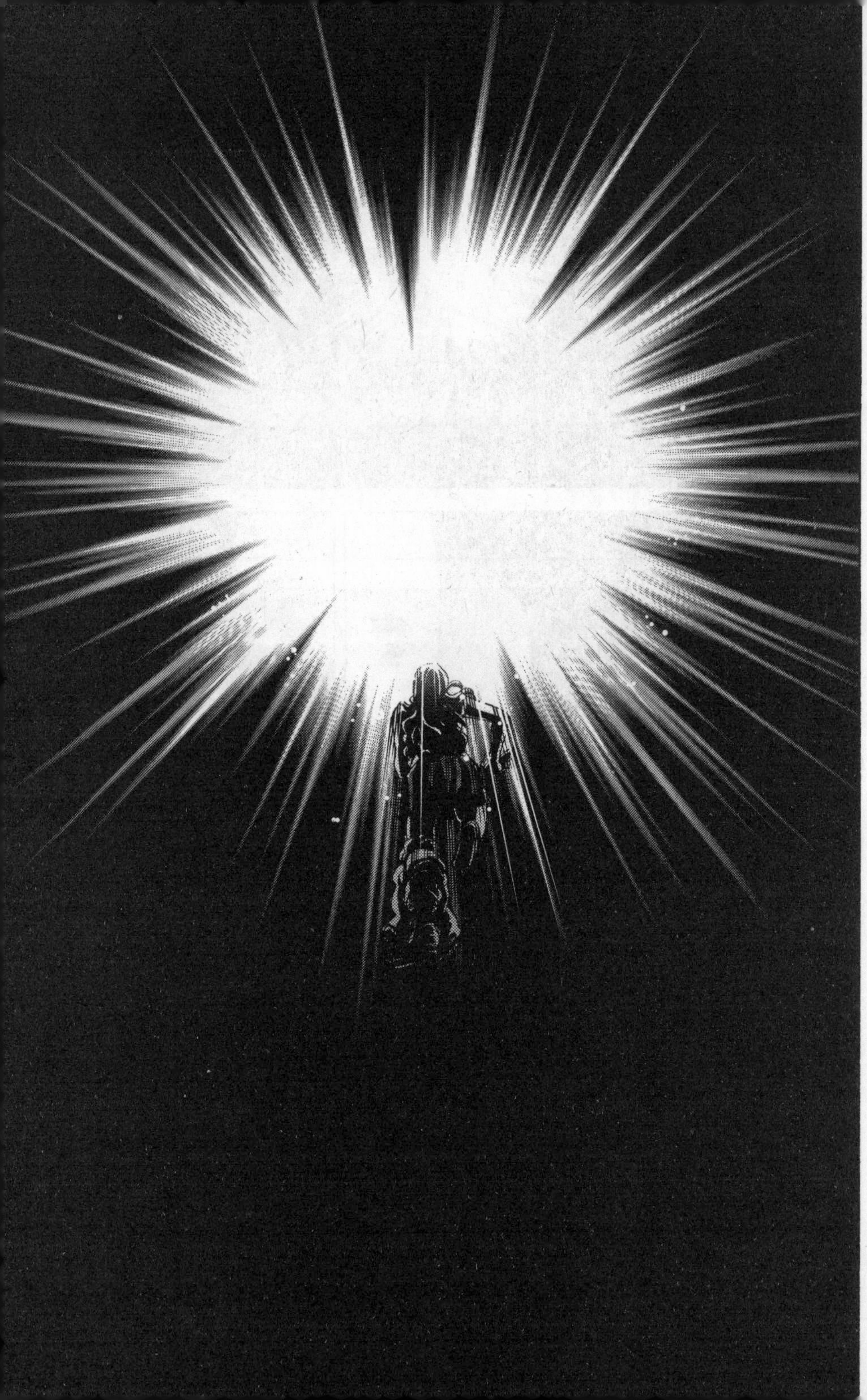

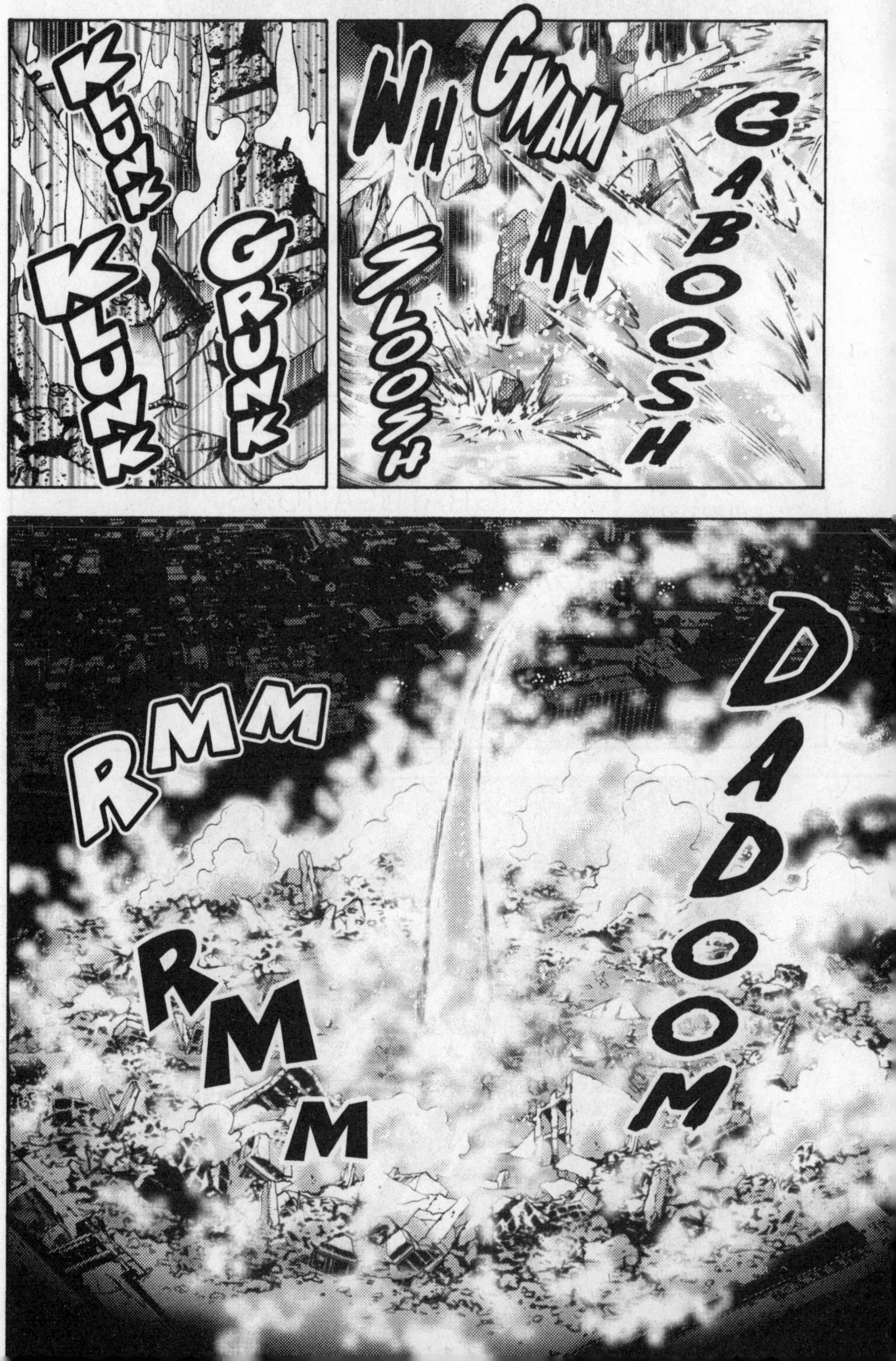
GABOOSH
GWAM
AM
WH
SLOOSH
GRUNK
KLUNK
KLUNK
DADOOM
RMM
RMMM

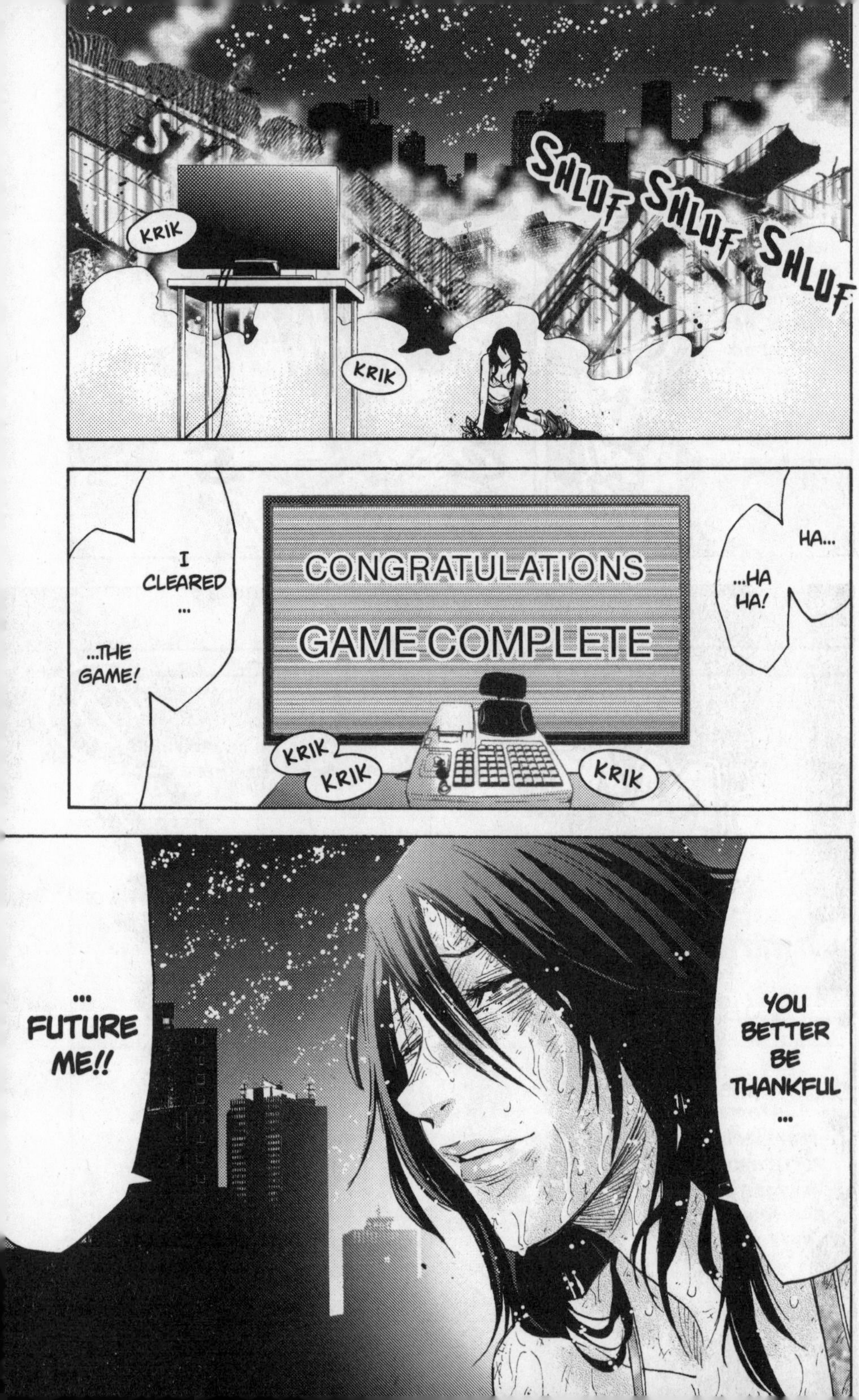
SHLUF SHLUF SHLUF
KRIK
KRIK
HA... ...HA HA!
CONGRATULATIONS
GAME COMPLETE
I CLEARED ... ...THE GAME!
KRIK
KRIK KRIK
KRIK
YOU BETTER BE THANKFUL ...
... FUTURE ME!!

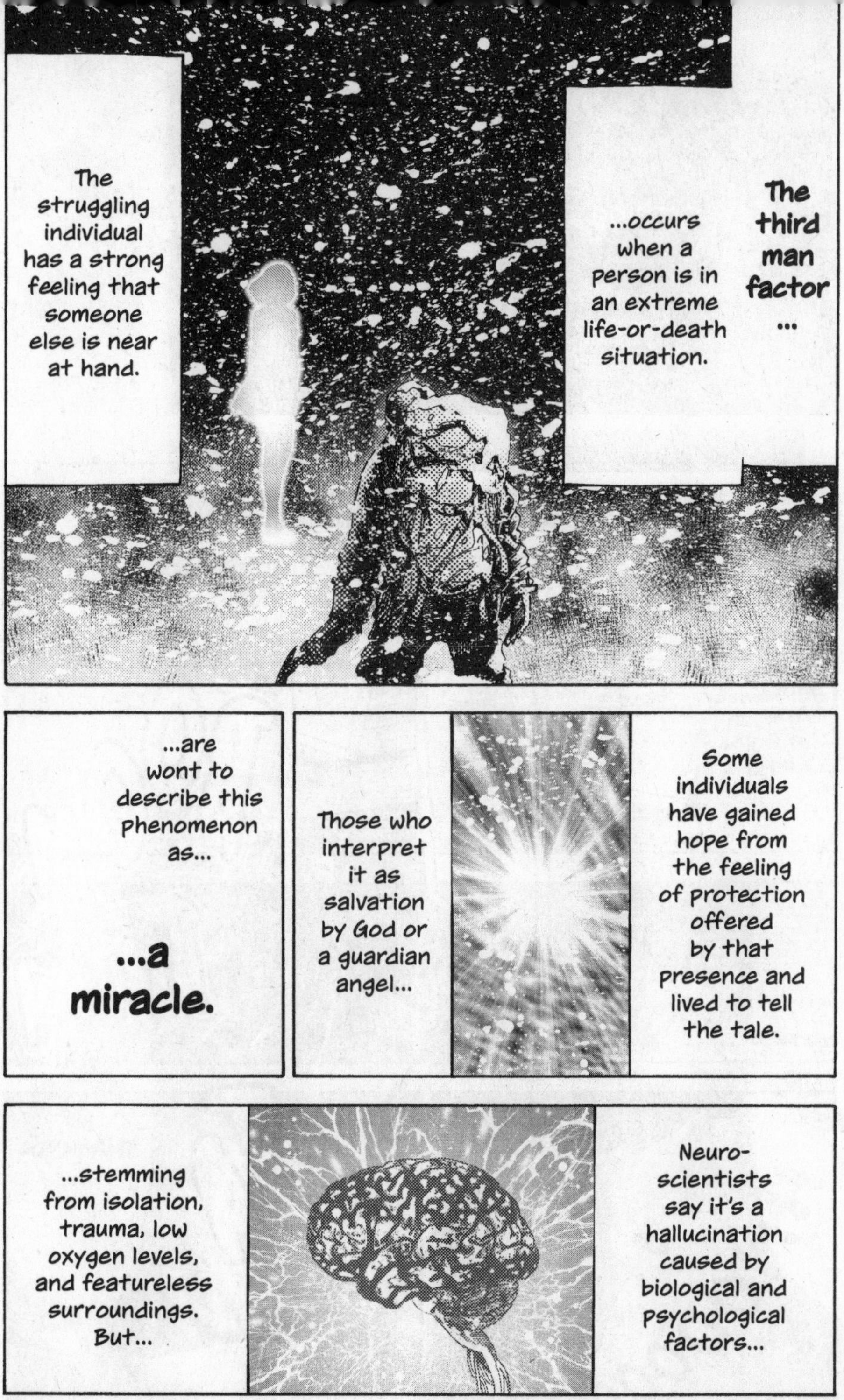
The third man factor...
...occurs when a person is in an extreme life-or-death situation.
The struggling individual has a strong feeling that someone else is near at hand.
Some individuals have gained hope from the feeling of protection offered by that presence and lived to tell the tale.
Those who interpret it as salvation by God or a guardian angel...
...are wont to describe this phenomenon as...
...a miracle.
Neuro-scientists say it's a hallucination caused by biological and psychological factors...
...stemming from isolation, trauma, low oxygen levels, and featureless surroundings. But...

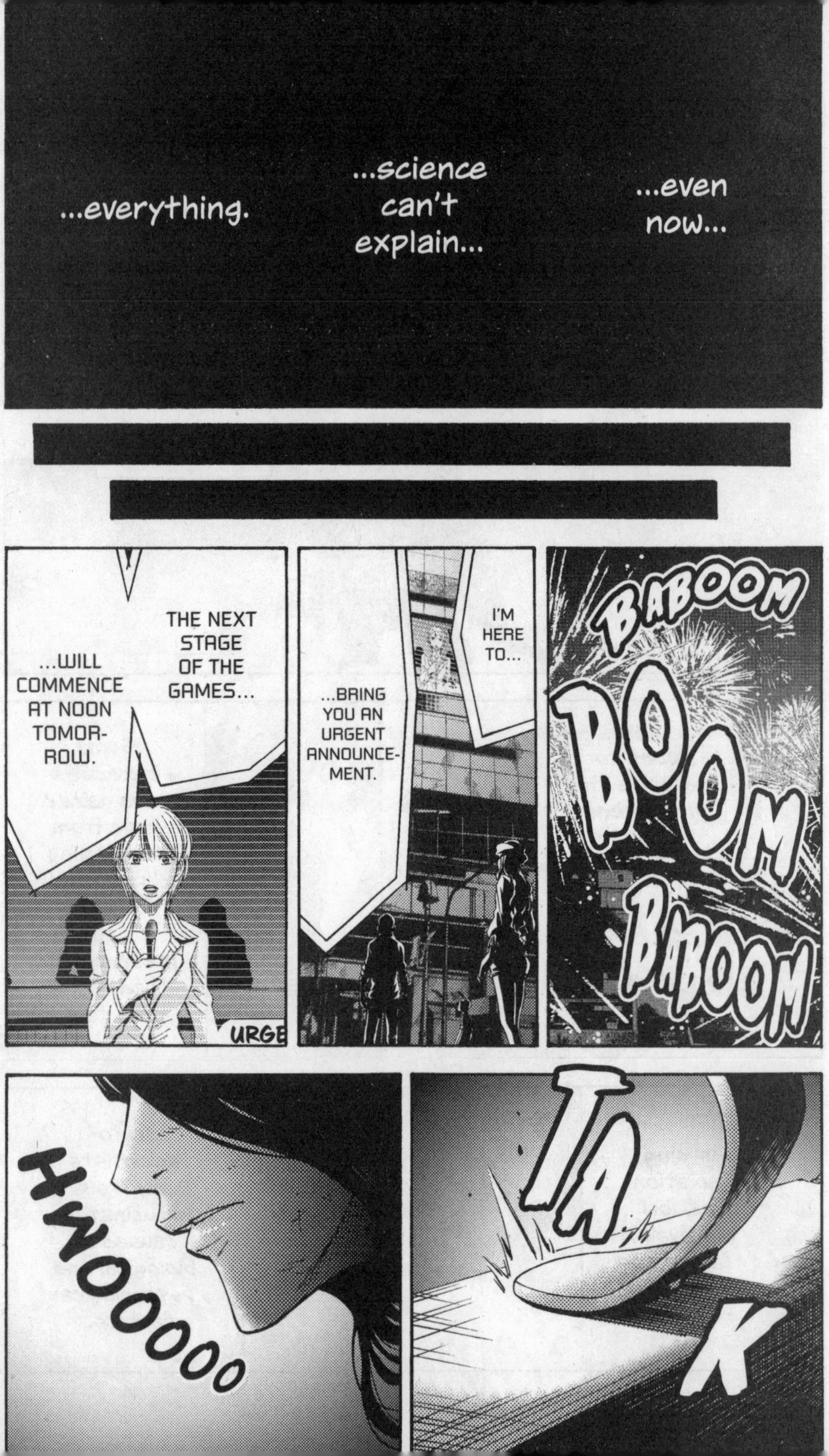

...even now...
...science can't explain...
...everything.
BABOOM
BOOM
BABOOM
I'M HERE TO...
...BRING YOU AN URGENT ANNOUNCEMENT.
THE NEXT STAGE OF THE GAMES...
...WILL COMMENCE AT NOON TOMORROW.
URGE
TAK
HWOOOOOO

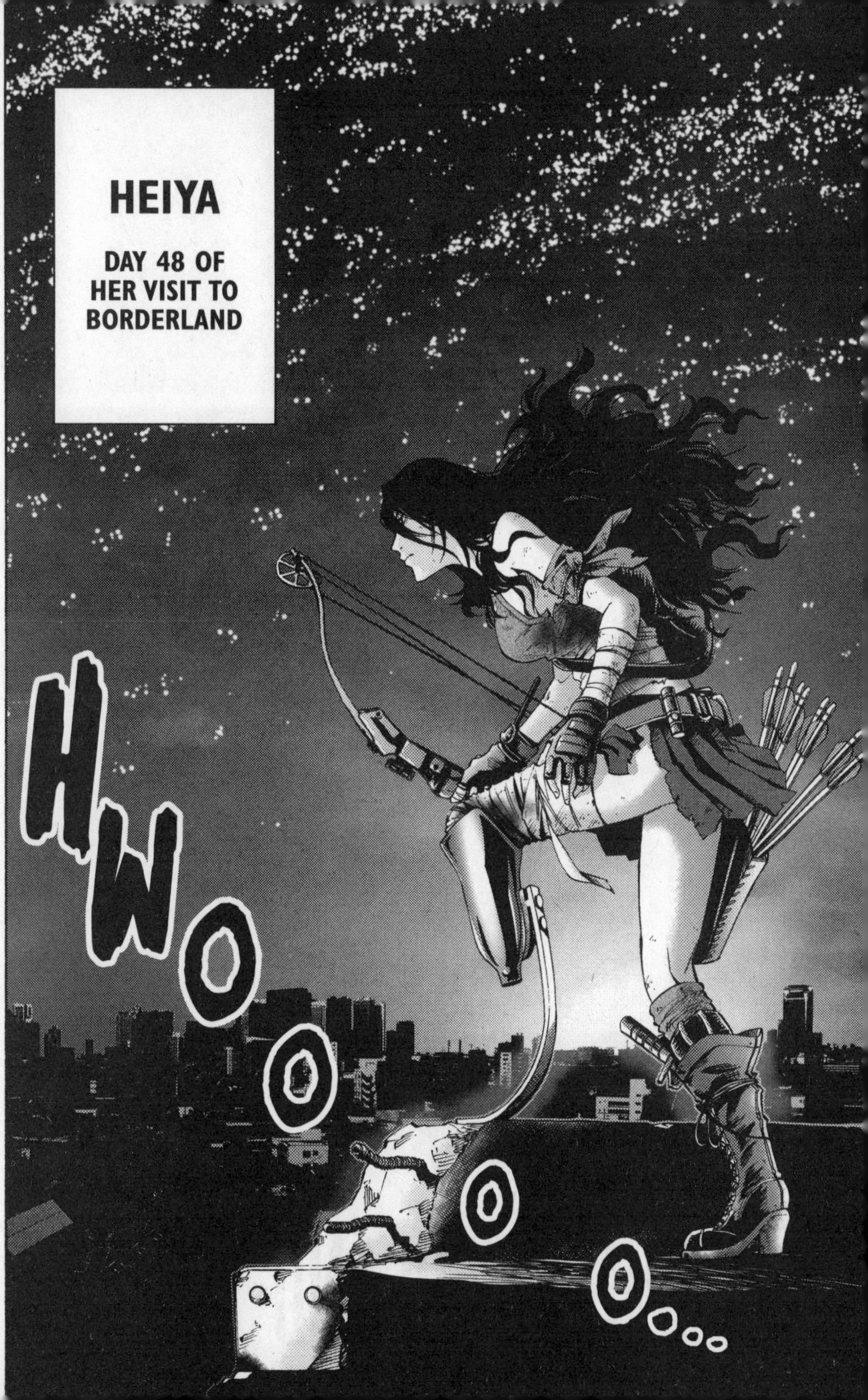
HEIYA
DAY 48 OF
HER VISIT TO
BORDERLAND
HWOOOOOooo

ALICE IN BORDERLAND

UNUSED
ILLUSTRATION

My firstborn came into this world.

The Earth's population just rose by one. It's another life to protect at all costs. And the meaning of life just changed a little.

Thank you. Congratulations. And welcome.

Please, enjoy this wonderful world to the fullest.

— HARO ASO

HARO ASO

In 2004, Haro Aso received *Shonen Sunday's* Manga College Award for his short story "YUNGE!" After the success of his 2007 short story "Onigami Amon," Aso got the chance to start a series of his own— 2008's *Hyde & Closer*. In 2010, his series *Alice in Borderland* began serialization in *Shonen Sunday S* and is now a Netflix live-action drama. *Zom 100: Bucket List of the Dead* is his follow-up series.

ALICE IN BORDERLAND

VOLUME 5

VIZ SIGNATURE EDITION

STORY AND ART BY

HARO ASO

English Translation & Adaptation **JOHN WERRY**
Touch-Up Art & Lettering **JOANNA ESTEP**
Design **ALICE LEWIS**
Editor **PANCHA DIAZ**

IMAWA NO KUNI NO ALICE Vols. 9–10
by Haro ASO

Original Japanese edition published by SHOGAKUKAN.
English translation rights in the United States of America, Canada, the United Kingdom, Ireland, Australia, and New Zealand arranged with SHOGAKUKAN.

Printed in Canada

Published by VIZ Media, LLC.
P.O. Box 77010
San Francisco, CA 94107

10 9 8 7 6 5 4 3 2 1
First printing, March 2023

ratings.viz.com
RATED M MATURE

PARENTAL ADVISORY
ALICE IN BORDERLAND is rated M for Mature and is recommended for ages 18 and up. This volume contains depictions of violence and death.

VIZ MEDIA
viz.com

VIZ SIGNATURE
vizsignature.com

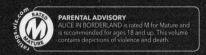

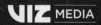

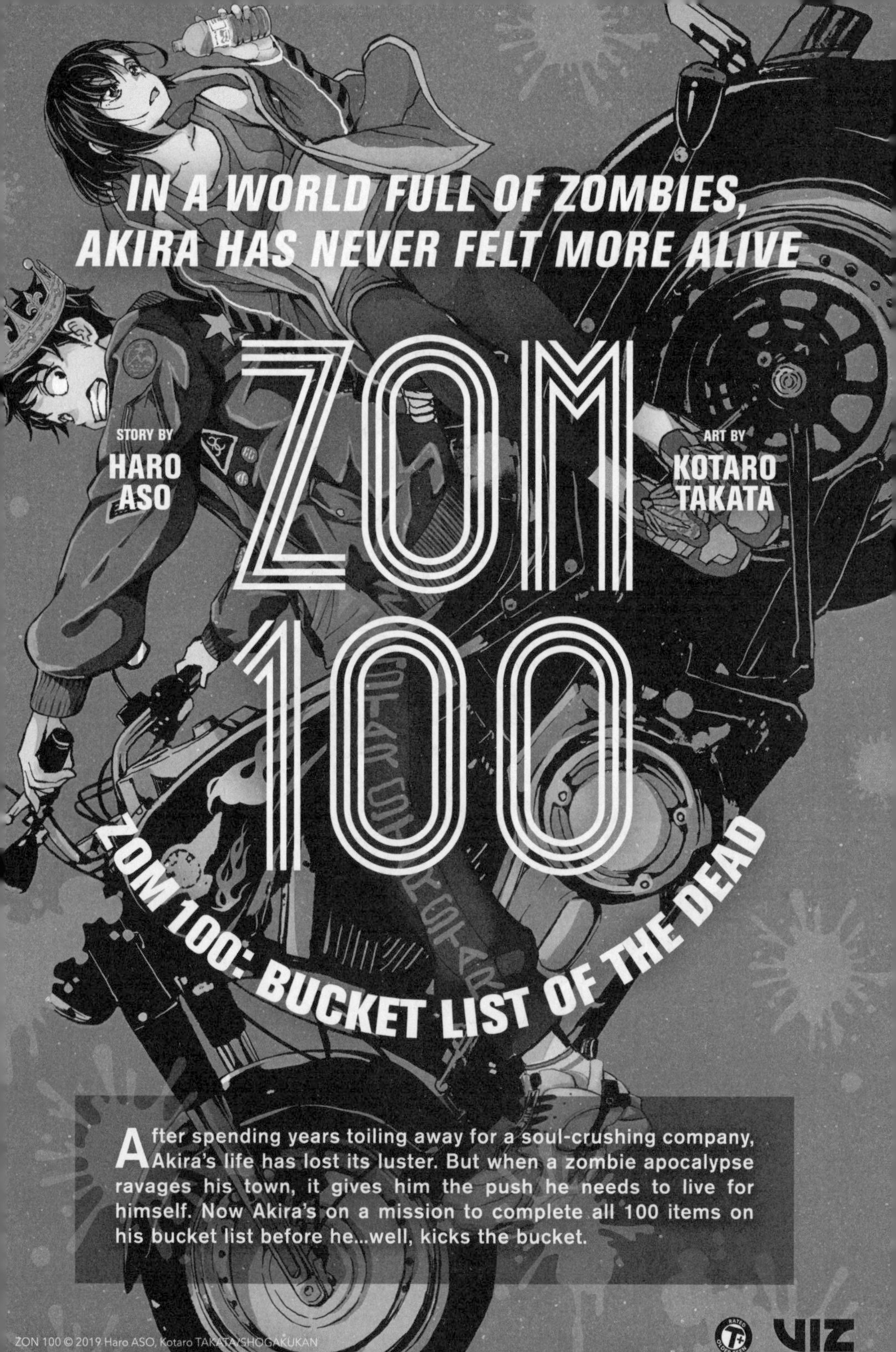

IN A WORLD FULL OF ZOMBIES,
AKIRA HAS NEVER FELT MORE ALIVE
STORY BY
HARO ASO
ZOM 100
ART BY
KOTARO TAKATA
ZOM 100: BUCKET LIST OF THE DEAD
After spending years toiling away for a soul-crushing company, Akira's life has lost its luster. But when a zombie apocalypse ravages his town, it gives him the push he needs to live for himself. Now Akira's on a mission to complete all 100 items on his bucket list before he...well, kicks the bucket.
RATED T+ OLDER TEEN
VIZ

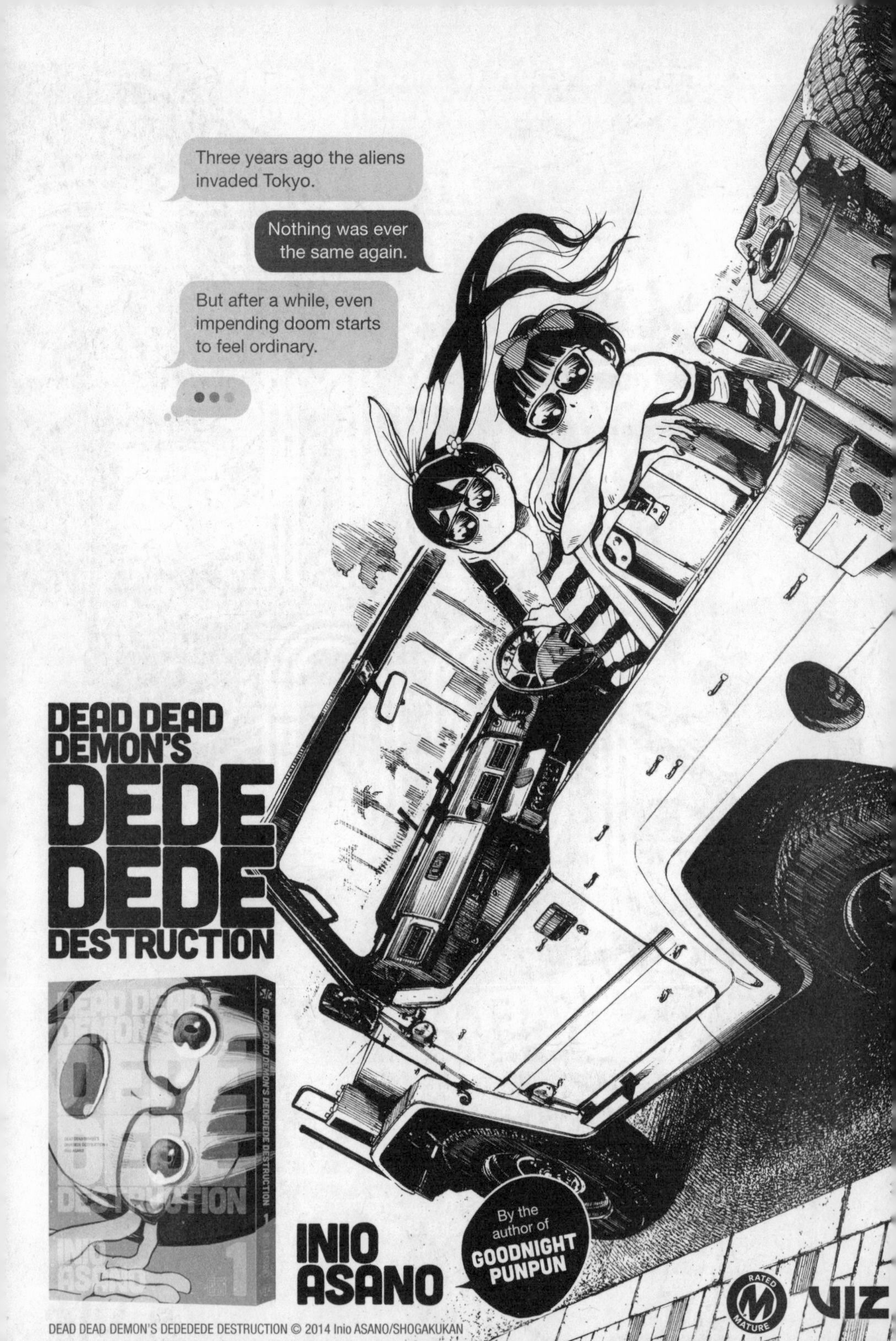
Three years ago the aliens invaded Tokyo.
Nothing was ever the same again.
But after a while, even impending doom starts to feel ordinary.
DEAD DEAD DEMON'S DEDE DEDE DESTRUCTION
INIO ASANO
By the author of GOODNIGHT PUNPUN
RATED M MATURE
VIZ

A deluxe bind-up edition of Naoki Urasawa's award-winning epic of doomsday cults, giant robots and a group of friends trying to save the world from destruction!

20th Century Boys

THE PERFECT EDITION

NAOKI URASAWA

Humanity, having faced extinction at the end of the 20th century, would not have entered the new millennium if it weren't for them. In 1969, during their youth, they created a symbol. In 1997, as the coming disaster slowly starts to unfold, that symbol returns. This is the story of a group of boys who try to save the world.

RATED T+ OLDER TEEN

VIZ

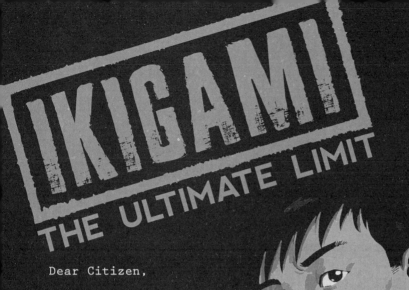

THIS IS THE LAST PAGE

This book reads from right to left.

Turn the book over and start reading from the other side.

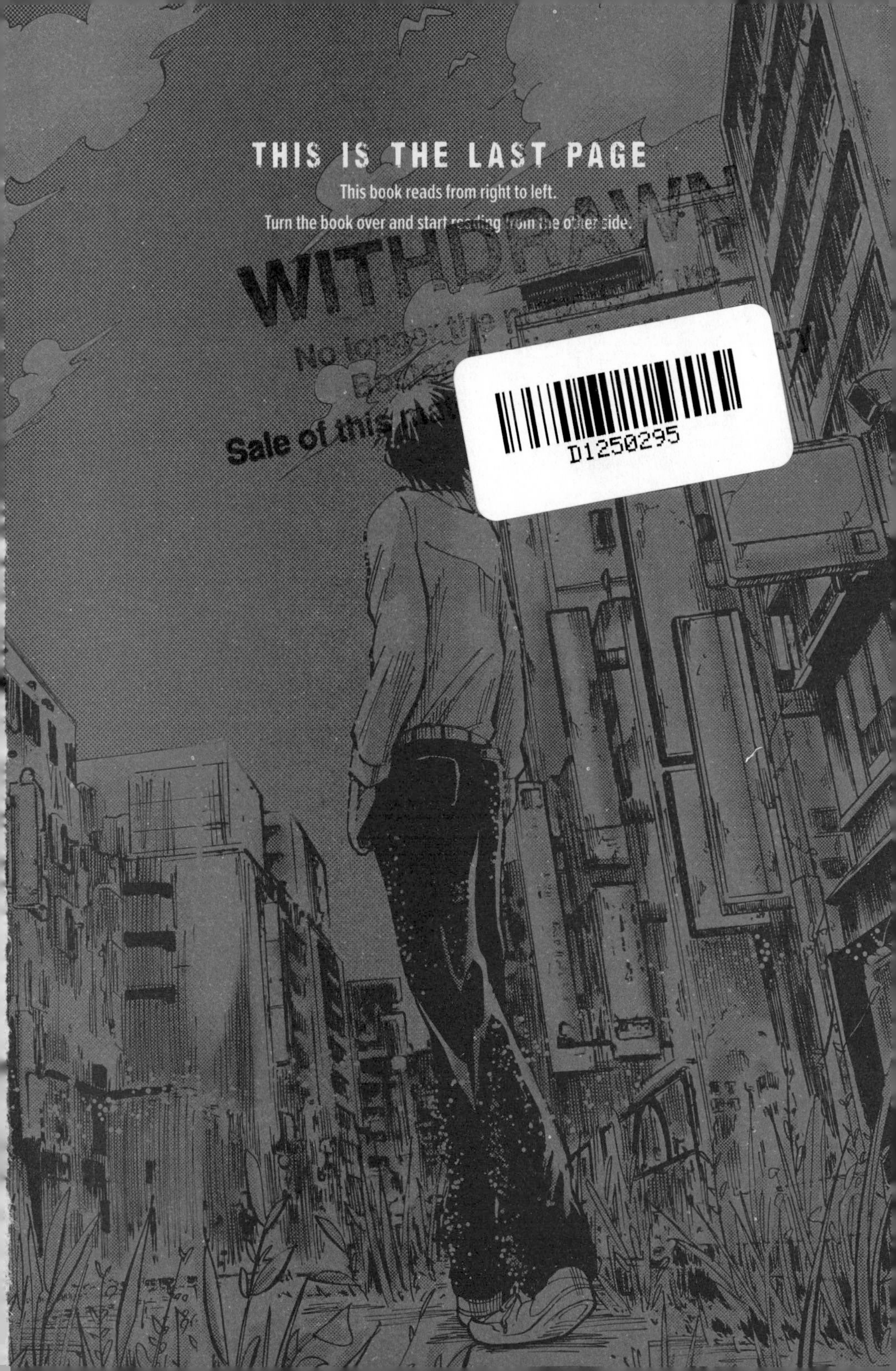